DATE DUE

			PRINTED IN U.S.A.

DICTIONARY OF AMERICAN CHILDREN'S FICTION, 1990–1994

DICTIONARY OF AMERICAN CHILDREN'S FICTION, 1990–1994

Books of Recognized Merit

ALETHEA K. HELBIG

AND

AGNES REGAN PERKINS

GREENWOOD PRESS
Westport, Connecticut • London

Library of Congress Cataloging-in-Publication Data

Helbig, Alethea.
    Dictionary of American children's fiction, 1990–1994 : books of
recognized merit / Alethea K. Helbig, Agnes Regan Perkins.
      p.   cm.
    Includes bibliographical references and index.
    ISBN 0–313–28763–5 (alk. paper)
    1. Children's stories, American—Dictionaries. 2. Libraries,
Children's—Book lists. 3. Best books. I. Perkins, Agnes.
II. Title.
PS490.H45   1996
813'.54099282'03—dc20   96–5813

British Library Cataloguing in Publication Data is available.

Library of Congress Catalog Card Number: 96–5813
ISBN: 0–313–28763–5

First published in 1996

Greenwood Press, 88 Post Road West, Westport, CT 06881
An imprint of Greenwood Publishing Group, Inc.

Printed in the United States of America

The paper used in this book complies with the
Permanent Paper Standard issued by the National
Information Standards Organization (Z39.48–1984).

10 9 8 7 6 5 4 3 2 1

CONTENTS

PREFACE

The *Dictionary of American Children's Fiction, 1990–1994: Books of Recognized Merit* contains critical comments on those books that authorities have singled out for awards or have placed on citation lists during this period. It is the second of a projected series of five-year updates of our two volumes on American children's fiction from 1859 to 1984 and is intended, as are the earlier books, for the use of everyone who is concerned with children's literature in any way: librarians, teachers, literary scholars, researchers in comparative social history, parents, booksellers, publishers, editors—all those to whom literature for children is of vital interest professionally or personally.

This *Dictionary,* which follows *Dictionary of American Children's Fiction, 1985–1989,* contains 567 entries on such elements as titles, authors, characters, and settings based on 189 books by 136 twentieth-century authors. It is a companion to our two volumes of American fiction for children and to *Dictionary of British Children's Fiction* (two volumes) and *Dictionary of Children's Fiction from Australia, Canada, India, New Zealand, and Selected African Countries.*

Although we have dealt with the same awards and citation lists that we used in *Dictionary, 1985–1989,* this book contains almost a third more entries based on fifty-five more books. Most of these books appear on only one or two lists, a factor that seems to indicate that there is less critical agreement about their literary value—perhaps that few are really outstanding. The total number of authors is also greater, with fewer having more than one title represented, and the number of authors who make their first appearance in this book is sizable. This may mean that publishers are reaching out to new writers, a commendable development.

As university teachers of literature for children and young adults for more than twenty-five years and as people trained in the study of literature as literature, we are dedicated to the idea that books for children must be judged by the same criteria as those for adults, keeping in mind, of course, that children are the intended audience. The critical comments found in *Dictionary of American Children's Fiction, 1990–1994* judge each book as imaginative literature, not on other values, regardless of the particular emphasis of the award for which it was chosen.

The entries in this *Dictionary* are of several types, chiefly title, author, and character. A book's title entry gives the plot summary and a critical assessment of its literary value. Other entries about a book provide additional information. Taken together, they form a short essay, complete in itself for classroom or library use, and can serve as a good starting point for further research.

Because our study is of fiction, not of illustration, we have followed the pattern of our earlier *Dictionaries* and have not included stories in picture-book form, since the texts of such books can seldom stand alone and their analysis requires a consideration also of the illustrations. Somewhat arbitrarily, we have set five thousand words as a minimum; most books must be at least that long to develop a story that can function on its own. Books of more than five thousand words are included, even if the illustrations are very prominent. Collections of short stories require a different sort of analysis and plot summary from novels and also are omitted, even if technically they are fiction. Retellings from oral tradition appear if the material has been developed like that in novels, as in *The Winter Prince.* We have not included translations, books with awards given by strictly regional groups, or those issued by organizations to their members only. We have also excluded books chosen by children for awards, since children have limited critical experience.

In the entries about the authors, we have focused on those aspects of the authors' lives most relevant to children's literature and to their particular novels in this *Dictionary.* Although several other published sources give biographical information about writers, none considers all those whose books are in this reference. Having the information in the same volume is not only of convenience for researchers; it is of particular value to libraries on limited budgets.

In presenting our entries we have followed an arrangement convenient for a variety of users.

Title entries. These consist of bibliographical information; the subgenre to which the work belongs; a plot summary incorporating the plot problem (if any), significant episodes, and the conclusion; a discussion of important themes; a brief literary critical evaluation; a note about sequels, if any; and awards and citations in abbreviated form. (A list of the complete names of the awards and citations appears in the front of this book.) Entries vary in length. The number of words in an entry does not indicate the importance or quality of the book, since plots can be summarized more briefly and critical judgments stated more succinctly for some books than for others.

A few books that appeared in one of our earlier *Dictionaries* have received additional awards during this five-year period. The entries for these books are briefer and refer readers to the more complete evaluation in the earlier volume.

Most readers will be acquainted with the terms we have used for subgenres, but a few may need some explanation. By *realistic fiction,* we mean books in which events could have happened some time in the world as we know it, as opposed to an imaginary or fantastic world, and not necessarily that the action is convincing or plausible. *Historical fiction* includes those books in which actual historical events or figures function in the plot, as in *Bull Run* and *Number the Stars,* or in which the specific period is essential to the action and in which the story could not have occurred in any other time, as in *Looking Out, Nightjohn,* and *Steal Away.* Books that are merely set in a past time, like *The Cookcamp* and *Catherine, Called Birdy,* we have called *period fiction.* Although all plots are driven by problems, we have used the term *problem novel* in its more recent sense to refer to those stories in which social, physical, or psychological concerns dominate, as in *Phoenix Rising* and *Grab Hands and Run.*

Author entries. These consist of dates and places of birth and death, when available; education and vocational background; major contribution to children's literature; significant facts of the author's life that might have a bearing on the work; titles that have won awards; frequently titles of other publications, usually with brief information about them; and critical judgments where they can safely be made. Authors whose biographical entries have appeared in earlier volumes are again included, but usually with briefer sketches and references to the original entry.

Character entries. These include physical and personality traits for important, memorable, or particularly unusual characters who are not covered sufficiently by the plot summary. They focus on such aspects as how characters function in the plot, how they relate to the protagonist, and whether the characterization is credible and skillful. Characters are classified by the name by which they are most often referred to or by the name by which the protagonist refers to them, for example, Aunt Effie, O.P., Mr. Hogwood. The name is also cross-referenced in the index under the most likely possibilities. If the character's surname does not often appear in the story, it will usually not appear in the index; when it is included, it is usually as a family name: Logan family, Blossom family, and so on. If the plot summary gives all the significant information about characters, as with many protagonists, they are not discussed in separate character entries. All major characters, however, are listed in the index.

Miscellaneous entries. These include particularly significant settings and elements that need explanation beyond mention in the title entry.

Every book has title and author entries, with entries in alphabetical order for convenience. Asterisks indicate that the item has a separate entry elsewhere in the book. Entries are intended to supplement, not duplicate, one another and when read together provide a unified essay on the book.

A list of awards and their abbreviations appears at the front of the *Dictionary.* A list of books classified by the awards is in the back of the volume. The index includes all the items for which there are entries and such elements as cross references, major characters for whom there are no separate entries, specific place settings, settings by period, and such matters as themes and subjects, books of first-person narration, unusual narrative structures, significant tone, authors' pseudonyms, illustrators, and genres.

From the standpoint of genre, the largest group of books that have won awards continues to be realistic fiction of family life, usually with a problem slant. Few of these deal with simple domestic adventures, once a popular subgenre. Problems of minorities continue to be an important focus. Historical fiction, if one includes period fiction, is somewhat better represented than it was five years ago and includes some of the strongest and most memorable books. More fantasies appear during this period, some of them highly inventive. Few, however, employ the traditional sources of fantasy in children's novels: folklore and hero tale, an approach popularized by Tolkien.

Although many of the novels are highly adventurous, being fast paced and filled with action, few fall into the "good, old-fashioned realistic adventure" or survival story category, a notable exception being *The Voyage of the "Frog."* There are no school stories in the old boarding-school mode (*Lucie Babbidge's House* being fantasy, although set in a girls' school), but more of the books contain school scenes or are built around school situations. Mysteries remain a popular genre, among them some gripping psycho-thrillers. Many of the books are light or even amusing; few, however, are primarily humorous. Even in the hyperbolic *Maniac Magee,* the main intent is an examination of serious contemporary issues rather than just entertainment.

Unconventional families are the focus of a large number of books. Some of these families are solid, supportive units, as in *The Rain Catchers* and *Journey.* Some, pieced together from misfits or outcasts, show promise of stability for the future, like the oddly assorted groups in *Out of Nowhere* and *When the Road Ends.* Even some of the homeless on the streets form family units that are more loving than many biological families, like the street kids in *The Beggars' Ride* and the Central Park dwellers in *Monkey Island.* Traditional families are often fractured or damaging. Mothers, in particular, come off badly, some being flighty and irresponsible, as in *The Brave* and *The One Who Came Back;* some alcoholic, as in *A Share of Freedom, Crazy Lady,* and *No Kidding;* some mentally ill, as in *Stonewords* and *Lyddie.* The mother in *Shizuko's Daughter* commits suicide early in the novel, thereby badly damaging her daughter's life. Alice McKinley's mother, in the series by Phyllis Reynolds Naylor, has been dead for a number of years, but her daughter needs and longs for her as adviser and role model. A number of mothers have second husbands or live-in boyfriends who are abusive to her children, like the sexual predator in *When She Hollers.* Some mothers are so concerned with their own affairs that they are not interested in their children's problems, like those in *Sniper* and *Words of Stone.* Those who fill conventional maternal roles are likely not to be important in the plots.

Stylistically, a number of the books depart from linear narrative. Several are in the form of letters or journals—*Letters from a Slave Girl, Letters from Rifka,* and *Bunkhouse Journal,* among others. Some use a variety of presentations, like the mix of school assignments, sketches, and asides in *Sydney, Herself* and the documents, newspaper reports, and memos in *Nothing But the Truth.* The mix of slang, stream of consciousness, and fragments of action in the novels by

Francesca Lia Block is unusual and initially difficult but, especially in *Witch Baby,* effective in giving a picture of the girl's mental anguish and the hip Los Angeles culture. In Vera Williams's *Scooter,* the illustrations, the typography, and the arrangements of pictures and text contribute to the story in a manner unusual for a novel. In *Make Lemonade* the sentences are arranged on the page in short lines that end in natural thought breaks. Among the most innovative novels are the biographical *The Man Who Was Poe,* in which the historical Edgar Allan Poe participates in the novel as a character and solves the mystery as his fictional detective at the same time, and *Remember Me,* where the murdered girl helps to bring her murderer to justice.

Well over half the novels have female protagonists. About 45 percent have first-person narrators, a development that may be surprising to those who remember the adage of several decades ago that children do not relate well to novels in the ''I'' person. The prevalence of the mode seems to indicate that young readers find first-person narration no more demanding than the also popular very limited third person. Convincing first-person voice, however, is highly difficult to write, and not all authors carry it off well.

Although there are interesting novels in this group, many of them are trivial and will prove ephemeral. In contrast, the Phoenix books, which are selected from those published twenty years earlier, seem undated and still powerful. Taken as a whole, they stand out as models of the best literature for young people.

As with the earlier American books and the companion volumes on British children's fiction and *Dictionary of Children's Fiction from Australia, Canada, India, New Zealand, and Selected African Countries,* we have read every book represented in this *Dictionary* and have done all the research and writing in this volume. We have had some valuable assistance from a variety of sources. We express our appreciation to the Eastern Michigan University Library and the Ann Arbor, Michigan, District Library for the use of their extensive collections. Specifically, we thank the staff of the Ann Arbor District Library Youth Room for their aid and Brian Steimel and Thomas Staicar of the Interlibrary Loan Department of Eastern Michigan University Library for their help in obtaining books not available locally and for their ongoing support and encouragement.

KEY TO AWARDS AND CITATIONS

Addams	Jane Addams Peace Association Children's Book Award
ALA	American Library Association Notable Books for Children
Boston Globe Honor	*Boston Globe–Horn Book* Award Honor Book
Boston Globe Winner	*Boston Globe–Horn Book* Award Winner
Child Study	Child Study Children's Book Committee at Bank Street College Award
Christopher	Christopher Award
C. S. King Winner	Coretta Scott King Award Winner
Fanfare	*The Horn Book Magazine* Fanfare List
IRA	International Reading Association Children's Book Award
Jefferson	Jefferson Cup Award for Historical Fiction
Newbery Honor	John Newbery Medal Honor Book
Newbery Winner	John Newbery Medal Winner
O'Dell	Scott O'Dell Award for Historical Fiction
Phoenix Honor	The Children's Literature Association Phoenix Award Honor Book
Phoenix Winner	The Children's Literature Association Phoenix Award Winner
Poe Nominee	Nominee for the Edgar Allan Poe Award Best Juvenile Mystery
Poe Winner	Winner of the Edgar Allan Poe Award Best Juvenile Mystery
SLJ	*School Library Journal* Best Books for Children
Stone	George G. Stone Center for Children's Books Recognition of Merit Award
Western Heritage	Western Heritage Award

THE DICTIONARY

A

AARON HERKIMER (*Western Wind**), about eight, the son of the only other residents of Pring Island, on which Gran* Benedict has rented a cottage for July and August and where Elizabeth Benedict, her granddaughter, visits. Gran describes Aaron to Elizabeth as a "strange child." She painted his ears excessively large in a portrait of the Herkimer family because, she says, he appears to listen so intently that he seems to be all ears. Although the island is very small and holds no dangers for a boy Aaron's age, his parents seem obsessed with protecting him, an attitude that greatly irks his older sister, Deirdre, 14. Aaron is so inquisitive, bossy, and wildly energetic that he makes Elizabeth tired, but they like each other and share interests, as when they examine gravestones in the tiny cemetery and when she reads and recites stories and poems. Elizabeth senses a vulnerability about Aaron that makes people want to protect him and against which he is in constant rebellion. Aaron takes the sailboat, probably to assert himself against his parents' constant watchfulness. His running off with the sailboat on the foggy evening touches off the fatigue that leads to Gran's stroke and to Elizabeth's learning that Gran's heart disease was the reason that her parents insisted she visit Gran on Pring Island.

ABEL CHANCE (*Rachel Chance**), paternal grandfather to Rachel, who has welcomed to his marginal farm his widowed daughter-in-law, Lara, along with Rachel and eventually little Rider, his cousin Jacob, and Jacob's wife, as well as his mentally disabled nephew, Jonah. Habitually crotchety, he plays the part of an ornery old man but actually is devoted to the family and appalled when Rider is kidnapped. Because he sincerely believes that the law works, he tries to interest people in power in finding the little boy. Since he thinks he will get satisfaction through what he sees as his rights, he is not eager to set off on Rachel's vigilante mission to get her brother back, but he is persuaded by his friend Druid Annie. A free-thinker, he is extremely annoyed by the piety of Pastor Woodie and the followers of Billy Bong, and enjoys taunting them. Abel is also scornful of Annie's fortune-telling and the possibly psychic powers of both Annie and Rachel, which convince both of them that Pearl Sweet has Rider, although their insight may be the result of perceptive observation. During the trip he suffers painful arthritis in his leg and the deprivation that Annie imposes from his usual remedy, whiskey. At the end, he appears to be ready to accept Rider's father to the farm, although he challenges him in his usual crusty manner.

ADA BAUER (*Switching Well**), San Antonio, Texas, girl of the late nineteenth century who finds herself in the twentieth century, the counterpart of Amber* Burak. Ada has many fine qualities; she is polite, loyal, modest, religious, conscientious, and truthful and finds twisting rules for her benefit, as Violet* Little suggests she must do, distasteful. A kind girl who has compassion for the Buraks, she helps search for Amber. Although in her time frame she would not be allowed to associate with Violet, because Violet is African American, Ada is so grateful for Violet's help that she overlooks the girl's race. As does Amber in her time-travel adventure, Ada finds the authorities rushed, judgmental, often rude, and frightening. Since Amber has no siblings, while Ada is living with Mrs. Burak she becomes friends with Grandad Burak, a Holocaust survivor, and at first is queasy about her German heritage. Ada grows up to marry Billy Streicher, the boy next door, who dares Amber to ride the pennyfarthing (bigwheeled) bicycle. His house eventually becomes the Streicher Children's Home in which Violet is housed as a runaway. In a secret hiding place, Ada and Violet find Amber's diary, one of the items that enables Ada to return to her own dimension and also authenticates the fantasy.

ADAM CORREY (*When the Road Ends**), tough foster brother of Mary Jack Jordan and Jane* in the Percy household. Evidently a boy with an alcoholic mother, he has never before been in foster care and has a chip on his shoulder, scorning "the priest," as he calls Father* Matt Percy, delighting in irritating nervous Jill Percy, prone to making disparaging remarks about Jane and Cecile* Bradshaw, and actively insulting Mary Jack. His attitude toward Cecile begins to change when she uses an obscenity to Gerry. After that, he becomes Cecile's supporter in the contest of wills, only rolling his eyes when she occasionally loses her grip on reality. Although he is absent for a portion of their stay at the cabin, he is instrumental in their survival, stealing the car keys from Gerry, driving the car (illegally) to the grocery store, teaching Cecile to write her name again, and helping to fabricate the lies they tell Father Matt to disguise their predicament. His devotion to the stray dog, Goldy, and her one surviving puppy, Silver, shows that under his surface hardness he is as vulnerable as the other three.

AFTERNOON OF THE ELVES (Lisle*, Janet Taylor, Orchard, 1989), novel of an unlikely friendship between two preteen girls, based partly on deception and partly on a deeper understanding of the possibilities of imagination. In an unnamed American town, probably in the 1980s, Hillary Lennox, 9, lives in a well-kept house with a manicured lawn, watched over protectively by her conventional mother. In a ramshackle house surrounded by junk, its yard backing onto Hillary's, lives Sara-Kate Connolly, 11, too thin, dressed in ill-fitting, wrinkled garments and heavy work boots. Apparently her mother lives there, too, although no one ever sees Mrs. Connolly. Hillary knows that there are other occupants of Sara-Kate's yard: elves. Sara-Kate shows her their village: little houses made of sticks with leaf roofs and yards bordered with little stones, even an ingeniously made Ferris wheel, all hidden among old tires, a discarded washing machine, thistles, and poison ivy. At first Hillary is skeptical, wondering if the village might have been made by chipmunks or mice or even, possibly, by Sara-Kate herself, but the older girl is so fierce and convincing that soon Hillary is under the spell of the place and of the elf magic that Sara-Kate explains to her. Before long Hillary abandons her other friends at school, who sneer at Sara-Kate and warn Hillary that she is a bad person. Sara-Kate, moreover, is a difficult friend, sometimes full of fascinating information and ideas, but often brusque, sometimes insulting, frequently ending their play by abruptly telling Hillary to go home now. Occasionally Hillary sees a movement at one of the windows of the Connolly house, where the shades are always tightly drawn. As fall grows into winter, Hillary begins to wonder if Sara-Kate herself might be an elf, with her little, bright eyes, her thin face, her apparent immunity to cold. When Sara-Kate disappears from school for four days in a row, Hillary has the courage to go into her yard and call for her, finally going up to the back door and opening it. She finds a strange room, cold as ice, with the sparse furniture all pulled to the center around a stove that has no oven door, a sort of room within a room. The rest of the downstairs seems to be empty, but Hillary can hear a faint noise from the room above. With uncharacteristic courage, she tiptoes up the stairs, sure that she will see elves if she can surprise them. When she pushes open a door around which light is leaking, she is unable to believe what she sees: Sara-Kate in a big rocking chair, holding a thin, long-legged figure with a sad, white face. At the sight of Hillary, she struggles to her feet, sets her burden in the chair, and charges ferociously at the younger girl, screaming at her to leave and threatening if she tells or even remembers what she has seen. For two weeks Hillary tries to forget. Then her father remarks that he almost ran Sara-Kate down while driving home late at night, and that he saw her run through several yards and into the back of her own. The next time Hillary sees Sara-Kate, their friendship passes into a new stage. Sara-Kate asks if she has money and whether she can get supplies from a store. Hillary takes ten dollars from her mother's wallet, walks alone, as she has never been allowed to do, to the grocery, and, when her money will not cover all her purchases, slips a package of bologna into her pocket. For the first time Sara-Kate asks her inside, and they have a festive lunch in front of the stove, the only heat in the house. The time goes so fast that Hillary's mother comes knocking at the door. Seeing the strange situation in the kitchen and ignoring Sara-Kate's smooth lies and Hillary's protests, she deliberately goes upstairs and discovers Mrs. Connolly. Grownups then take over, with much bustling and good intention and gossip. Mrs. Connolly is sent to a mental institution. Relatives in Kansas are unearthed to take Sara-Kate. The house is repaired and sold. No longer able to fit in with the other girls at school, Hillary wanders around the edges of the yard, trying to keep the workers away from the elf village, trying to come to terms with her guilt at having unintentionally betrayed her friend. Finally she decides to move the elf village to a spot behind her own garage, appropriately full of rocks and briars—a way of preserving what she knows has been of real value in the friendship. The waif-befriended-by-a-privileged-child plot is turned upside down, with independent, strong-willed Sara-Kate not only the leader but also actually bestowing the greater gift—that of imagination and understanding—on protected Hillary. The careful adherence to Hillary's point of view makes the story work on two levels, with her excitement, naive belief, and even her doubts all convincing while at the same time the reader sees more than the little girl can. ALA; Fanfare; Newbery Honor; SLJ.

A. J. MORGAN (*The Beggars' Ride**), the elderly man who owns the hot dog joint known as Atlantic Jack's on the Atlantic City, New Jersey, boardwalk, to which Clare* Caldwell runs, expecting to find her mother's ex-boyfriend and her surrogate father, Joey Morgan, there. A. J. is consistently kind and deferential to Clare, always addressing her as Miss Caldwell, and forgiving or overlooking the problems she causes. He provides her with a place to live and clothes and helps her and the other homeless children in her gang to escape from the authorities. Madame Edna, the boardwalk psychic and long-time friend of A. J., tells Clare that A. J.'s unhappy wife left him, and that Joey, his son, ran away at sixteen, but A. J. kept the silver biplane stored in the basement and the picture of the whole family in it in memory of what he had lost. Apparently his longing for his family motivates him to treat Clare and then the homeless children as family. A. J.'s generosity and forbearance help restore Clare's faith in adults.

ALEXANDER, LLOYD (CHUDLEY) (1924–   ), born in Philadelphia, Pennsylvania; educated at West Chester State Teachers College, Lafayette College, and the University of Paris (Sorbonne); author, freelance writer, and translator. Best known for his novels of fantasy for children—the five frequently honored Chronicles of Prydain, of which *The High King* (Holt, 1968) won the John Newbery Medal—Alexander has also written novels of high adventure and political intrigue set in the fictitious kingdom of Westmark and a group of romantic adventures featuring the intrepid and resourceful heroine, Vesper Holly, among other much-honored books. Another fantasy of adventure, magic, and miracle, *The Remarkable Journey of Prince Jen** (Dutton, 1991) takes place in a mythical Oriental kingdom and was selected as a best book by *School Library Journal*. Like Alexander's Westmark stories, it deals with the relationship between rulers and ruled. For earlier biographical information and title entries, see *Dictionary*,

1960–1984 [*The Black Cauldron; The Book of Three; The Castle of Llyr; The Cat Who Wished to Be a Man; The First Two Lives of Lukas Kasha; The High King; The Kestrel; The Marvelous Misadventures of Sebastian; Tartan Wanderer; Westmark*] and *Dictionary, 1985–1989* [*The Beggar Queen; The Illyrian Adventure*].

ALEX LOCKWOOD (*Libby on Wednesday**), thin, gangly, nervous member of the FFW (Famous Future Writers) workshop at Morrison Middle School. Alex often plays the clown to compensate for the physical problems that come from cerebral palsy, but he does confess that the teasing his disability provokes distresses him sometimes. He has a pleasing sense of humor and is very good at creating parody in his writing. His remake of *Watership Down* about gophers provokes approving comments. Tierney* pays it the highest of compliments when she says that it is "rad." At first Libby thinks Alex is the "strangest person . . . like a robot," but later she concedes that he is the "most quick-witted" of the five members of the group. The children come to refer to him as Alexander the Great and then eventually just as Alex the Great.

ALICE IN RAPTURE, SORT OF (Naylor*, Phyllis Reynolds, Atheneum, 1989), humorous, episodic sequel to *The Agony of Alice,* again starring Alice McKinley of Silver Spring, Maryland, now in what her father calls "The Summer of the First Boyfriend," between sixth grade in elementary school and the beginning of junior high, sometime in the 1980s. The narrator, motherless Alice, lives with her brother, Lester, 19, and her tolerant father, who runs a music store. Patrick*, now ensconced as her steady boyfriend, gives Alice her first, and many subsequent, kisses. Her two best friends, Pamela and Elizabeth*, also acquire boyfriends, and the six of them hang out together, swimming in the afternoons, roaming the neighborhood in the early evenings, going out for ice cream—all harmless activities but all presenting Alice with new concerns. She worries about what to get Patrick for his birthday, why she cannot carry a tune when he tries to teach her, whether they are ready for open-mouth kissing. When her first permanent looks ghastly, she hopes to die until Lester's current girl-friend shows her how to blow-dry her hair. A babysitting job with three-year-old Jimmy Benton almost turns into a real disaster when he chokes on a grape, but Patrick, using the Heimlich maneuver, saves him. During an August week when Alice's father takes her, Pamela, and Elizabeth to Ocean City, Pamela flirts with boys at the beach until the top of her two-piece bikini comes off and she retreats in humiliation behind dark glasses and a man's shirt; Alice's father, suddenly seeing that his daughter has outgrown her old bathing suit, buys her a gorgeous and fashionable new one; and Lester, coming for the weekend, brings Patrick along for a surprise. With long-distance advice, most of it not applicable, from Aunt Sally in Chicago, Alice copes with dinner at the country club to which Patrick's upscale parents belong. Although the main reason for acquiring steady boyfriends, according to Pamela, is to enter seventh grade with a man in tow, Alice decides just before school starts that planning her life around Patrick is too exhausting and not much fun. When she tells him that she no longer wants to go steady and why, she senses his relief. They decide to be just friends again, but special friends. Although the concerns of twelve-year-old girls are often as trying in fiction to the reader as they are to observers in real life, Alice's somewhat skewed point of view makes situations far funnier than in most other books of this age group. She is genuinely baffled by the rules she encounters: Aunt Sally says a girl should never give a boy an article of clothing that might touch the skin; Elizabeth's mother says she may not go steady until high school; Pamela's mother forbids her to kiss until she is sixteen; Lester is in trouble for entertaining his girlfriend in his father's bedroom. Alice's agonies of embarrassment are not as extreme as in the earlier book, and she is more mature. Although it is entertaining, this sequel is not as successful as its predecessor. SLJ. For details about *The Agony of Alice,* see *Dictionary, 1985–1989.*

ALIEN SECRETS (Klause*, Annette Curtis, Delacorte, 1993), science-fiction mystery set in the future on a spaceship on the way from earth to the planet Aurora, also known as Shoon from the name of its indigenous inhabitants, the Shoowa. Expelled from her English boarding school for bad grades and poor behavior, Puck (Robin Goodfellow), almost thirteen and independent minded, embarks for Aurora, where her scientist parents are doing research on the planet recently liberated from conquering Grakk. Just before the *Cat's Cradle,* as the tramp spaceship is called, takes off, Puck observes a fight between two men, in which one pulls a knife on the other and demands some object. When she realizes that the man with the knife has seen her, Puck flees for safety to the lounge of the departing vessel. The small but varied passenger list includes the man with the knife, whose name is Mizzer Cubuk; a married couple, Mizzer and Mz Sigmund; two loud, disagreeable elderly woman traveling companions, Mz Dante and Mz Florette; and an alien humanoid from Aurora named Hush. Hush has a pointed head and distorted facial features, hands, and limbs and speaks in a kind of patois that becomes his most distinguishing aspect as a character. Puck becomes even more tense when she discovers that the captain, Louise Biko, called Captain Cat, and Cubuk are friends and that Mz Sigmund and Cubuk also know each other. Her suspicions increase when Captain Cat asks her to make friends with and keep an eye on Hush. Puck finds she likes Hush, a warm, gentle man. He is sad almost to the point of despair because he has lost the most cherished object of his people, a small, beautifully designed religious statue called the Soo, which he was to bring back to Aurora now that the Shoowa are free. Using a finder that he wears hanging about his neck, he hopes to locate the Soo, which he is certain is somewhere on the *Cat's Cradle.* Complications arise, involving such conventions of the genre as mistaken identity (Cubuk turns out to be a detective, and Mz Sigmund a "news-vid" reporter); horribly spooky wails and howls (made by ghosts of Shoon captives killed by the hundreds aboard the *Cat's Cradle,* when it was a Grakk ship); secret compartments (Puck discovers the Soo secreted in the exoskeleton, or outside layer of the ship, by following the ship's cat, which regularly goes in and out through a tiny, almost invisible aperture); and overheard conversations. Puck's detective work, which involves daring and a good deal of luck, uncovers the thief, Mz Florette, who is really a disguised Grakk, and also helps Cubuk uncover a ring, which is smuggling alien artifacts, although for some time Puck unwittingly hinders his progress. In the suspenseful climax, Mz Florette grabs the Soo, which had been hidden for safekeeping under the navigator's chair on the ship's bridge, and says she will blow up the ship after she ejects herself from a launch pod. She is apprehended with Puck's help, and the Soo is recovered. The ghosts are laid to rest, everyone gets safely to Aurora, Hush's reputation is repaired, and Puck realizes that she has a special aptitude for hyperspace travel and decides that she wants to become a navigator. Unlike most other examples of the science-fiction genre, philosophical ideas are seldom in evidence, although the effect of conquest and imprisonment is evident in Hush's case. The style makes use of much computer and space terminology, the setting features computer and space hardware, and the emphasis is on fast-action adventure, of which the book has an abundance. ALA; SLJ.

ALL BUT ALICE (Naylor*, Phyllis Reynolds, Atheneum, 1992), amusing realistic novel, sequel to *The Agony of Alice, Alice in Rapture, Sort Of**, and *Reluctantly Alice**, all set in contemporary Silver Spring, Maryland. In this fourth book of the series, Alice McKinley, 12, is in seventh grade and is making every effort to fit in, trying to be just like the other girls by having her ears pierced, joining the All-Stars Fan Club, and signing up for the talent show, although she cannot think of a talent to display. Her father, manager of a music store, and her brother, Lester, a college student, are caring and try to be understanding, but Alice feels the lack of a mother or older sister and is much concerned with ''sisterhood'' and ''bonding''—not just with her own best friends, Elizabeth* and Pamela, but with all women, old and young. She is also concerned with sex and romance as explored in her Our Changing Bodies class and in various relationships around her. Lester has three girlfriends: Marilyn, with whom he thinks he may be truly in love; Crystal, with whom he is infatuated; and Loretta, who is pursuing him relentlessly. Alice's father is dating Miss Summers, Alice's language arts teacher, although he does not seem to be moving toward the total commitment Alice expects and rather hopes for. Alice's ''special friend,'' Patrick*, is no longer her boyfriend, as he was in sixth grade, but he still gives her a large box of Whitman's chocolates for Valentine's Day. She also finds herself paired with Brian, one of the trio of good-looking seventh graders she calls the Three Handsome Stooges, elevating her to the status of one of the Beautiful People. Eventually she decides that the teasing and the pretense required to hold on to that social position are too much trouble, and she reverts to her normal self, also dropping out of the fan club and the earring club. The episodic adventures are believable, entertaining, and true to the psyche of the junior high girl. Clever dialogue among Alice, her father, and Lester characterize the family as unusual, intelligent, and supportive. Alice's first-person narration reveals her as unusually honest and frank. ALA. For details about *The Agony of Alice,* see *Dictionary, 1985–1989.*

AMANDA BEALE (*Maniac Magee**), independent, assertive, strong-willed, African-American girl from the East End of Two Mills, who is the first person to talk with Maniac Magee when he arrives in town. She is on her way to school and, suspicious but friendly, shows him the contents of the suitcase she carries: books, many books, including an A encyclopedia volume, put there to keep them safe from her rambunctious younger siblings, Hester and Lester. The conversation with Maniac makes her late to school for the first time in her life. She loans Maniac a book because he so obviously wants one, and she gives him her address so he can return it. He goes to live with her family, at first temporarily. Later, at Mars* Bar's insistence, Amanda searches for Maniac, until she finds him sleeping in the zoo. Then she screeches at him and pesters him until he accompanies her home and agrees to stay.

AMANDA PARISH (*Remember Me**), beautiful daughter of Shari Cooper's mother's housekeeper. Amanda is in love with Jimmy Cooper, Shari's older brother, who has diabetes. When Amanda discovers through overheard conversation that she and Shari were switched in the hospital at birth, she becomes deranged and kills Shari by pushing her off a balcony and then fleeing over the roof. Lieutenant Garrett* finds some dust that implicates Amanda in the murder. Amanda also tries to kill Jimmy by giving him an overdose of insulin and then injects an air bubble into his vein. She knows how to do this because she too has diabetes. After she is apprehended and convicted of murder and attempted murder, she is sentenced to state-supervised psychiatric care. Ironically, her own aunt, a nurse, for reasons of jealousy, switched Amanda and Shari.

AMARIUS AIKENS (*Mama, Let's Dance**), elderly, very kind African-American man who lives in town and takes a special interest in the half-orphaned, abandoned children: Mary Belle, the narrator; Ariel*, her older brother; and Callie*, their little sister. He is unobtrusive about his interest, so that Mary Belle does not know he is watching over them until she sees him walking through the garden one evening. He plants the garden, brings them a chicken dinner, and alerts his niece, Miss Dearly, about them. Later Dearly, a minister and social worker, takes over when Callie falls ill. Amarius harbors a repressed anger about Mama, which comes out when he tells Mary Belle that he always knew that her mother and father would run off and leave their children as though they "were no more 'n wild pups." Amarius is a religious man, and apparently he and Ariel discuss religious topics together. Mary Belle says that Amarius's favorite subject of conversation is God. Amarius is a type figure (the faithful darky), but he serves the plot well.

AMBER BURAK (*Switching Well**), twentieth-century San Antonio, Texas, girl who finds herself back in the nineteenth century. Amber is a more vigorous and spirited child than her counterpart in time travel, Ada* Bauer, and hence is often slapped or switched for "back talk" by the orphanage personnel when she tries to explain her actions. She bravely and cleverly takes the opportunity presented by the program that the children put on for the visiting directors to inform them that Grof is deaf, not feebleminded. Instead of reciting "Crossing the Bar," as expected, she responds with a brief but telling presentation about Grof. Although it is hard to believe that, being a singleton, she can be so capable a caretaker of the Bauer children, she obviously enjoys the pleasures of family interaction. She shows spirit also in riding the pennyfarthing (big-wheeled) bicycle on a dare, thus earning the liking and respect of the Bauer children and Billy Streicher, who hides her diary in his room, where it is found by Violet* Little and Ada and enables Ada to return to her dimension.

AMBER PADGETT (*Forest**), clear-headed twelve year old who eventually figures out that the mink-tailed squirrels of Forest have a language and even begins to understand it. Worried about the terrible things happening in the world and irritated by her father's lack of concern, she occasionally runs away to get a little time to herself when she can think. A very efficient girl, she always plans carefully and organizes her activities competently. She even handles her mother well, calmly explaining that she and her brother, Wendell*, want to talk alone or need to spend the night in the field to watch stars in such a reasonable way that her mother allows it, even thinking that it was her own idea. Most of the time Amber also handles Wendell encouragingly, gaining his great admiration. Although her father is frequently annoyed at her and acts irrationally, Amber explains his conduct to Wendell: he is really feeling guilty and does not want to admit it, so he takes his anger at himself out on the squirrels, insisting that they caused his problem.

AND ONE FOR ALL (Nelson*, Theresa, Orchard, 1989), historical novel of the protests against the Vietnam War covering two years beginning in the fall of 1966. In White Plains, New York, Geraldine* Brennan, 12, from whose vantage events are seen, loves her warm, happy, solidly middle-class family: Daddy, a proud World War II veteran and somewhat authoritarian father, who sells yard lights; Mama, a conscientious homemaker and loving wife and mother; her younger brother, Dub, 5; and her mischievous, rebellious older brother, Wing*, a high school senior poor at his studies, great at basketball, and often in trouble with the nuns at school. Geraldine also admires greatly, and is a little in love with, imaginative, fun-loving Sam* Daily from down the street, a youth Wing's age of seventeen, his best friend and an excellent student who is also good at basketball. Sam is skeptical, however, about the Vietnam War, just the opposite of Wing's pro-war views. The first hint of trouble occurs in December when Geraldine misses her bus home from school and discovers that Wing has been dropped from the basketball team for poor grades. His parents, especially Mama, are upset, because they are afraid he will not graduate and will be drafted. Because he hopes to placate his parents and also sincerely wishes to help his friend, Sam spends much time tutoring Wing, his excuse being that the team desperately needs Wing for the playoffs. Because Wing is working so hard to improve at his studies, his parents plan a big party for his eighteenth birthday in January. Ironically, certain he has blown an English test, Wing enlists in the marines that very day. Sam is furious, Geraldine is heartbroken, and the parents are devastated. Wing leaves for training in South Carolina, and in April, the family, on a shopping trip together for shoes, sees Sam in front of the five and dime passing out leaflets opposing the war. Daddy regards him as a traitor. Sam continues his antiwar activities, is graduated with honors, and enters Georgetown University on a scholarship. The next six months pass quickly, events being summarized in letters between Wing in Vietnam and Geraldine at home. Wing's letters indicate that he has come to have doubts about the value and morality of the war, particularly after his buddy is killed. On Easter Saturday, 1968, marine officers visit the Brennans with the news of Wing's death by mortar shell. In her grief, Geraldine blames Sam, learns from his mother that he is in Washington intending to participate in a march against the war, heads by bus (without informing anyone) to the city, tracks Sam down by the Washington Monument, sobs out her news while protestors chant for peace, and sensing his deep sorrow and shock realizes she does not really wish to hurt him further. Sam takes her home, and afraid she will also lose Sam because of her family's antagonism toward him, she screams out to Daddy that Sam was only trying to help Wing and others like him by his antiwar efforts. After the funeral, Daddy shakes hands with Sam. Later at the Lover's Tree, a place that as children the Brennans and Sam considered sacred, Sam swears that he will always come back but asserts that for now he must continue to work for the peace cause. He agrees with her, as Geraldine repeats their old oath, ''All for one, and one for all.'' The book gives a fine picture of the period. Such judiciously inserted details as mention of specific television shows, the shooting of Martin Luther King, Jr., and excerpts from Lyndon Johnson's State of the Union speech ground the story firmly in its times, while conversations convey the major political issues about the lengthy conflict in Southeast Asia. Daddy epitomizes the point of view of the generation who fought in World War II: loyalty to country and dedication to cause, fight if called but try to avoid being called by doing well in school. Wing and Sam are too carefully foiled but suit the plot, and the underlying idea—that peace was what everyone sought and all needed to work together to achieve it—appears without being expressly stated. Very telling are the intergenerational tensions that threaten to rend apart this ordinary, hard-working, religious, country-loving family, a microcosm of the nation as a whole. The title has an obvious double meaning. ALA; Fanfare; SLJ.

ANGELINA DODD (*Earthshine**), Isaiah Dodd's beautiful, pregnant mother, a friend of Slim McGranahan. Angelina's husband (Isaiah's father) died of AIDS some months before the novel begins, not knowing that Angelina had also contracted AIDS or about the baby. In spite of the worry about the baby's health, Angelina remains positive toward life and motherly toward Slim. Near the end of the novel, Angelina gives birth to a healthy baby girl whom they name Halley. Slim wonders how long Angelina will be around to take care of Isaiah and Halley.

ANNELISE (*Others See Us**), beautiful and much-admired cousin just a little younger than Jared, a girl he has fantasized and written about in his secret journal. Actually a sociopath, Annelise has no feeling for anyone else except to desire their approval, and since she has no real friends, she has written her true thoughts in her journal and so is horrified when it is gone. In it she reveals, with no remorse, that she has tampered with the brakes on Jared's bike, hoping he will have an accident; has given Jared's father extra-strong drinks so that he will become drunk at the family beach party; has no fondness or concern for Amy, the youngest cousin, about whom she makes a public show of devotion; recently drove a girlfriend to attempted suicide; and even drained the gasoline from the motorboat of a local girl, causing her to be caught in a sudden squall and drowned. Although she has only scorn for Jared and their cousin Eric, she flirts with both of them for the fun of seeing them obviously infatuated with her. When Jared is able to read her mind, he finds it boiling and flaming—so hot that he shies away from mental contact. When she engineers the near-drowning and her rescue of Amy, Jared is not surprised, since he has read her thoughts that the child is a bore and would be better off dead.

ARCHIE (*Shadow Boxer**), George and Monty's* uncle, the brother of their deceased boxer father, Tommy. Archie had been their father's trainer and apparently has been approached to open a gym in the neighborhood by Monty, who has aspirations to follow in Tommy's footsteps and who Archie recognizes is talented. Archie has a conscience, however, and knows how much Ma hates boxing because of the way it consumed her husband. Unknown to the boys, Ma visits Archie and persuades him to keep her boys out of boxing. Later, when George asks Archie to keep Monty from boxing, Archie, who has already decided to comply with Ma's request, asks George to let him handle Monty in his own way. After Monty runs from the gym, having seen the video of his dad being horribly mauled by an opponent, Archie ironically tells George that Tommy really won that fight. Neither of them ever informs Monty of that fact, however.

ARIEL (*Mama, Let's Dance**), sixteen-year-old brother of Mary Belle and Callie*, the half-orphaned children abandoned by their mother. Mary Belle says

Ariel is a religious boy who likes to read the Bible, gets straight A's in school, even though he is always tired after working long hours at the gas station after school, is "nice and honest," and has "beautiful gray eyes." He is very serious, loving to the children, and appears in few scenes. His wages buy food and pay the bills, but Mary Belle is always worried about money. Events prove that the children cannot cope alone, as Mama, in the note she leaves when she runs off, suggests they can. Ariel is a realist, a facet of character he shows when he allows the Aikenses to take over and become their guardians and when he comments that their Mama simply did not know how to be a mother. He is too much on the fringes to be a convincing figure in the story.

ARMSTRONG, JENNIFER (1961–   ), born in Waltham, Massachusetts; editor, freelance writer. She is a 1983 graduate of Smith College and worked for two years for Cloverdale Press in New York City before devoting her full professional time to writing. Some of her books have been written for mass-market series, including four for Pets, Inc., for readers three to six years old; the Wild Rose Inn series, for young adults; and, as Julia Winfield, both the Sweet Dreams and Private Eye series for Bantam. Her most ambitious and acclaimed novel is *Steal Away** (Orchard, 1992), a slave-escape story with the main action set shortly before the Civil War and enclosed in a complicated series of frames. It appeared on both the Best Books for Young Adults and the Notable Books lists of the American Library Association and won a Golden Kite award. Armstrong has also written a number of picture books: *Hugh Can Do,* illustrated by Kimberly Root (Crown, 1992); *Chin Yu Min and the Ginger Cat,* illustrated by Mary GrandPre (Crown, 1993); *The Terrible Baby,* illustrated by Susan Meddaugh (Tambourine, 1994); *Little Salt Lick and the Sun King,* illustrated by Jon Goodell (Crown, 1994); and *The Whittler's Tale,* illustrated by Valery Vasilier (Tambourine, 1994).

AUNT EFFIE (*Cousins**), sister of Maylene, Cammy's mother, who is so house proud and self-important that she has driven her teenaged son to feel he can never live up to her expectations and to turn to drink and her daughter, Patty Ann, to become bulimic, although to outward appearances she is the image of a perfect child: beautiful, top of her class at school, and an accomplished pianist, always well-dressed. After Patty Ann is drowned, Aunt Effie insists that her desk be decorated with crepe paper and kept as a sort of shrine, which makes all the children nervous and helps to cause Cammy's terrible nightmares and illness. She refuses to let anyone forget her daughter's death and has led the townspeople to blame L.O.D.,* whom Patty Ann was trying to save, and to drive the unfortunate girl away. When Cammy is ill, Aunt Effie comes to the house and hysterically denounces her for the times when she said mean things to Patty Ann to get back at her cousin for putting on airs and deliberately making her feel inferior.

AUNT LIBBY SCHROEDER (*My Name Is Sus5an Smith. The 5 Is Silent.**), Susan's sophisticated, successful aunt in Boston, who invites her to live with her for the summer. Very good looking and assertive, Libby announces at once that she will not be responsible for Susan, since she resented even the goldfish that took her time and attention, and that her job is demanding so they will see little of each other. Although initially furious at Susan for lending Willy* Gerard her key and thereby giving him the opportunity to rob the apartment and for running up a huge telephone bill, she relents, partly because she realizes she might have prevented both by showing more interest, and she offers Susan a room if she comes to stay through the winter. Her determined effort to leave Utah for college in the East against her conventional parents' wishes parallels Susan's desire to study at the museum school in Boston rather than go to a college near home, as her mother wants her to do.

AUNTY MOSS (*Tehanu**), witch of the village of Re Albi, an ignorant, filthy woman but goodhearted and wise in her own way. She takes great pains to win the trust of the abused child, Therru, and becomes a true friend to Tenar, who had felt some scorn for the old woman when she was a girl newly arrived on Gont. Aunty Moss is crucial to the narrative at several points: she helps nurse Ged when he returns weak and ill; she provides a haven for him when he needs to escape the king's messengers; she explains to Tenar, and therefore to the reader, much about the powers and necessary celibacy of wizards and speculates about where woman's power lies; and in the end she draws Tenar, Ged, and the child back to Re Albi with the news that she is dying. She lives in a dark little house with her chickens, which roost on her bed, and she has a body odor rank as a fox.

AVI (AVI WORTIS) (1937–   ), born in New York City and educated at the University of Wisconsin and Columbia University; librarian, storyteller, teacher of children's literature, and author of more than two dozen highly regarded children's books in several genres and a variety of approaches and tones. His biographical mystery, *The Man Who Was Poe** (Orchard, 1989), was nominated for the Edgar Allan Poe Award. *The True Confessions of Charlotte Doyle** (Orchard, 1990), an action-filled sea adventure featuring an intrepid young woman, won the *Boston Globe–Horn Book* Award, was named to the Fanfare list by the editors of *Horn Book,* and was granted Newbery Honor status and selected by both the American Library Association and *School Library Journal* for their best books lists. *Nothing But the Truth** (Orchard, 1991), a school story told through such devices as diaries, letters, recorded discussions, and telephone conversations, in which a teenaged boy deliberately ruins a veteran teacher's career, was also named to the Fanfare list, chosen by both the American Library Association and *School Library Journal,* and selected as Newbery and *Boston Globe–Horn Book* honor books. *''Who Was That Masked Man, Anyway?''** (Orchard, 1992), a comic novel told entirely in dialogue and examining the nature of heroism, appears on the American Library Association list of best books for middle grades. Also for middle readers is *Tom, Babette, & Simon* (Macmillan, 1995), three humorous stories of magic and transformation. In 1987, Avi and his wife moved from Los Angeles to Providence, Rhode Island, the setting for *The Man Who Was Poe*. For earlier biographical information and title entries, see *Dictionary, 1960–1984* [*Emily Upham's Revenge; Encounter at Easton; No More Magic; Shadrach's Crossing*] and *Dictionary, 1985–1989* [*The Fighting Ground; Something Upstairs*].

B

BABY (MacLachlan*, Patricia, Delacorte, 1993), a realistic novel of family life set in the 1980s on a resort island off the U.S. coast. The plot is quickly summarized: a foundling baby enables a family to confront their grief over the loss of their own baby and start on the road to recovery. Larkin, perhaps ten, tells the story of baby Sophie with restraint and economy of words. As she presents them, her family seems to be happy and productive. Papa*, editor of the island's only paper, tap dances and does the soft shoe for relaxation after work; Mama* paints landscapes; Grandma Byrd* affects unusual combinations of garments to express her lively personality and interacts frequently with family and neighbors. Larkin socializes with Lalo* Baldelli, son of the local innkeeper, but conveys the impression that there is an incompleteness about their lives. The something that is missing gradually becomes evident to the reader, and thus the book works like a mystery. After the last ferry of the year departs for the mainland, carrying the tourists home, Larkin's family find on their driveway a basket containing an almost year-old baby girl. An accompanying note says that her name is Sophie, that she is loved, and that her mother will return for her one day. Papa wants to inform the police, since he knows that abandoning a baby is a criminal act and also because he is afraid for his wife's feelings. Larkin is frightened for Mama, too, but right away Sophie weaves a kind of magic about the family, obviously gratifying a deeply felt need, and they keep her. As the year moves from autumn through winter and into spring, little Sophie grows and blossoms. She walks, talks, and charms family and neighbors, becoming the "island's child." Bit by bit Larkin's parents, Byrd, and Larkin begin to confront the fact of the recent death of Larkin's baby brother, who lived only a day and was buried unnamed. During the year, notes and even money arrive regularly from Sophie's mother, Julia*, who returns when the tourist season begins again in the spring and claims her daughter. Grandma Byrd insists the parents acknowledge the loss of Sophie as they refused to do with the baby boy who died. In talking about the baby, Papa satisfies the longing inside Larkin about the brother she had never even seen and at the same time starts the healing process for himself and Mama. They name the dead baby William and have the name engraved on the headstone. In an epilogue set ten years later, Sophie returns to the island with Julia for Byrd's funeral. It is a time of renewal for them all. The book is a set piece, with the poetic, understated, finely tuned style of folklore from which the plot derives. Underpinning the story also is the ages-old idea of the healing power of words. The main characters have life and dimension, and even those, like neighbors, who appear briefly are deftly sketched, among them old Griffey, who plays the accordion for tourists although he knows only two tunes; Lalo's mother, who capably runs the forty-two-room inn but is so afraid of electricity that she insists that both sides of the toaster be filled so that current will not run out; Portia Pinter, Larkin's romantic schoolmate; the island physician, Dr. Fortunato, who kindly and gently presses Mama about her feelings about Sophie; and Ms.* Minifred, the school librarian who is in love with words. The island setting is clearly realized, and several motifs, like birds, Sophie's ruby necklace, and the game of rock, paper, and scissors, add texture and contribute coherence. Further unifying and strengthening the novel and providing hints of forthcoming events as well are an epigraph of lines from Edna St. Vincent Millay's "Dirge Without Music," passages from other poems and songs, and Sophie's italicized memories of her days with the island family that head the chapters. This book evokes a powerful emotional response and speaks to different ages in different ways. ALA; Fanfare.

BAMBI SUE BORDTZ (*Phoenix Rising Or How to Survive Your Life**), Jessie Castle's "best friend by default." Bambi comes from a family unstable compared to the Castles. Although she seems chiefly occupied with going shopping, her chubbiness, and boys, she influences the plot occasionally, in addition to serving as a foil to both Helen and Jessie. Soon after Helen's death, Bambi seems instinctively to sense Jessie's denial and tells her that she is not crying enough. Jessie regards Bambi as a "birdbrain" and pays little attention to what she says. Bambi also lets slip to Bloomfield* about Helen's cancer, and soon thereafter Bloomfield dumps Helen.

BAUER, MARION DANE (1938–   ), born in Oglesby, Illinois; teacher, writer of novels for children. She attended La Salle-Peru-Oglesby Junior College and the University of Missouri and received her B.A. degree from the University of Oklahoma. She has taught English and creative writing and has published a number of novels with twelve-year-old protagonists, for instance, *A Question of Trust** (Scholastic, 1994), a story of the pain and difficulties for a boy and his younger brother when their parents separate. It was named to the *School Library Journal* list of Best Books for Children. Among her other commended novels are *Rain of Fire* (Clarion, 1983), a Jane Addams Award winner, and *On My Honor* (Clarion, 1986), a Newbery Award Honor Book. For earlier biographical information and title entries, see *Dictionary, 1960–1984* [*Rain of Fire*] and *Dictionary, 1985–1989* [*On My Honor*].

BAYARD MCKNIGHT (*T-Backs, T-Shirts, COAT, and Suit**), the lawyer engaged by Zack, the owner of Zack's Meals-on-Wheels for which Bernadette* Pollack works. Zack wants Bayard to force Bernadette to wear a T-back bikini in order to attract customers and bring in more business. Both men have known Bernadette for many years—from the time Zack was a member of Spinach Hill commune, to which Bernadette also belonged. At that time Bayard was the lawyer for the commune. In 1969, Bernadette was involved in a protest engineered by the commune against the Vietnam War during which they burned draft cards. At that time, she promised Bayard she would never again put him in a position where he would have to rescue her. Ironically, in the T-back controversy, he again comes to her rescue, a kind of knight in shining armor, with whom she seems to be starting a close relationship at the end of the novel.

BECKY PEYTON (*Dixie Storms**), the ex-wife of Flood* Peyton and Dutch Peyton's former sister-in-law. Becky married Flood while still in her teens, and since she came to live with the Peytons while Dutch was very young—only four or five—Becky became a surrogate mother to Dutch. Dutch has missed her very much and clings to the hope that Flood and Becky will reconcile. In the scene Dutch and Bodean overhear, Becky explains to Flood that she simply was too young to cope with his inability to communicate and his tendency to isolate. The reader is left to wonder how she will fare with Bodean, who has been led to believe that Becky is inadequate. Now a real estate agent, she lives in an apartment in Norfolk and seems self-possessed and confident. Ironically, Lucy Cabbot, Flood's current girl, is much like Becky in appearance.

BEETLE (*The Twin in the Tavern**), tough waif, drudge at the Dog's Tail tavern, who at first lords it over Taddy and later becomes his only reliable friend. Son of a sailor and an English girl, he was born in New York. Seeking to escape the beatings from his brutal father after his mother's death, he stows away on a ship he thinks is bound for London, only to land in Alexandria, Virginia. There Neezer finds him, takes him to the Dog's Tail, and keeps him as a slave, threatening to send him back to his father if he tries to run off. Although he pretends he rescues Taddy from the ice house to protect his own self-interest, he actually welcomes the chance to have a friend. Far more streetwise than Taddy, Beetle warns him against confiding in anyone and provides him with essential information for survival in the dismal waterfront dive. He even plans to give Taddy half the diamond he found in the ice. After Neezer discovers the boys eating tea cakes that Taddy has smuggled in, he pulls them from their sleeping place under the kitchen table and shuts Beetle in the ice house. Spared because he is bringing in money by being a pantry boy at the Mainyard mansion, Taddy worries that Beetle may not survive, sneaks into the tavern, finds Neezer and Lucky both sleeping off drink, and steals the ice house keys from Lucky's pocket. When he opens the ice house door, Beetle can barely stand but still thinks clearly enough to realize that he cannot go back to the kitchen. Taddy puts the keys back and, supporting Beetle, takes him through the night to the bakery, where the kind Diggles family takes him in. In the end, Beetle has a choice of living with Taddy in the Mainyard mansion or remaining with the Diggles family, but opts to go with Mrs. Scrat, who has refused to provide an alibi for her husband, Neezer, and while Neezer goes to jail, plans to sell the Dog's Tail and start a small dining room, open to the public.

THE BEGGARS' RIDE (Nelson*, Theresa, Orchard, 1992), contemporary realistic sociological novel set mostly in Atlantic City, New Jersey, involving homeless teenagers. Clare* Frances Caldwell, almost thirteen, of Nashville, Tennessee, runs away from her alcoholic, verbally abusive mother, a two-bit country singer, and her mother's current live-in boyfriend, Sid, who (unknown to Mama) raped Clare and continues to molest her. Clare runs to Atlantic City hoping to live with Mama's ex-boyfriend, Joey Morgan, a saxophonist, whom Clare loves like a father. She discovers that the address Joey gave her is a boardwalk hot dog joint run by his father, A. J.* (Atlantic Jack) Morgan, and that Joey has long since gone to California. Clare flees to a nearby playground, where she is discovered sleeping in the belly of a concrete whale by a group of five street kids—four boys and a girl—who consider the playground their territory, are wary of her at first, but then take her in and call her Fish, after the place where they found her. Each teenager is nicknamed after a token in the game of Monopoly: their cautious, tough, warm-hearted leader, Cowboy*; big, frizzy blond, acerbic Thimble*, who considers Cowboy her boyfriend; patch-eyed (for show), teasing Racer*; skinny, mottled-skinned, giggling, otherwise mute Shoe*, Racer's dear friend; and fat Little* Dog, who is a kind of recording secretary and accountant for the group. The kids consider the boardwalk their territory, where they panhandle, pickpocket, shoplift, scrounge through garbage, perpetrate various scams on tourists and residents, and live after a fashion in such places as abandoned houses and a half-finished parking garage. Among other incidents, Cowboy rescues Clare from a pushy red-haired man whom Cowboy dislikes and addresses as Griffey. Griffey's demeanor repels Clare, since it reminds her of Sid's unwelcome advances. One time the kids accumulate enough money to rent a motel room, where they enjoy such luxuries for them as beds, toilets, and purchased, not garbage, pizza. As part of her initiation into the gang, in which her name is now Hat, Clare is expected to engineer a "hit," which the group decides should be entering A. J.'s basement to find out what the old man reputedly keeps hidden down there. With deep misgivings, Clare slips through the basement door, then tumbles downstairs in the darkness, suffering numerous bruises, a severe head wound, and a badly broken left arm. With amazing generosity, A. J. takes her to the hospital, and the red-haired man, who turns out to be a social worker whom the kids tell her peddles his charges for sex, calls her mother, but Clare chooses to remain with A. J., who treats her like family, buys her clothes, and puts her up in Joey's old room. Although Clare many times feels guilty about accepting his hospitality and gifts, she nevertheless steals from him, smuggling his food to the kids, who have come on hard times because of a police crackdown. Afraid she will be sent home against her will, she takes the gang to the basement for a look at what she has discovered is there—a biplane A. J. and Joey built many years ago—then runs with the gang again. When Racer gets caught stealing watches from a drugstore and is released into Griffey's custody, the gang helps him escape, but Cowboy is knifed by a homeless man during their flight. Clare seeks help from A. J., who flies them all out of the area and away from Griffey to Norristown, Pennsylvania, in his biplane. Since knifing is a criminal offense, the Atlantic City police are informed and, to the children's horror, Griffey is also. Because Cowboy is unable to talk and Thimble, whom Griffey had also molested, refuses to tell about him, Clare goes to the hospital chapel and prays (all A. J. says one can do sometimes). She remembers how the rape had hurt and tells Thimble she has decided to inform her mother about what Sid did. Her decision spurs Thimble to inform on Griffey. When officers are skeptical about Thimble's story, A. J. explodes with indignation. The upshot is that Griffey is put on leave and eventually dismissed but not otherwise punished. Shoe is institutionalized for malnutrition and psychological help to restore his speech; Racer and Little Dog are sent to a group farm; Cowboy and Thimble are placed in foster homes; and several months later, Clare goes home to her mother, who has kicked Sid out and begun treatment for alcoholism. The book's end finds the two trying hard to get along with each other. The plot is judiciously extended for interest with reasonable complications, although the airplane exit seems contrived and too sensational for credibility. Conversation sometimes does not seem accurate either. Since almost all the background of Clare's situation is given through her memories, which are triggered by specific occasions, the details of Clare's home life and the intensity of her emotions about home come out gradually. The gang members are carefully individualized, and if A. J. seems too good for too long, the reasons for his great kindness are eventually revealed and are acceptable. Small details actualize the street setting, as do Clare's thoughts, yearnings, and moral dilemma. These street kids are strongly and sympathetically drawn. They all distrust adults, for good reason, and their efforts to survive as a family when biological ones are denied them seem constantly thwarted by authorities and other adults who pretend concern but really despise them. The pressures and problems of such street people, who also include a homeless nuclear family, are presented without didacticism as an unfortunate modern phenomenon. The title comes from the old saying, "If wishes were horses . . . ," words that occasionally come to Clare's mind. ALA; Fanfare.

BEL-AIR BAMBI AND THE MALL RATS (Peck*, Richard, Delacorte, 1993), lighthearted, facetious, farcical, contemporary realistic novel satirizing family, school, and community life, in which the humor relieves the near-caustic commentary on teen-adult relations. Bill Babcock, noted Hollywood producer of television films, lives in Bel-Air, California, with his family, all of whom are in the entertainment business in some way: his wife, Beth, a smart, good-looking blonde; their daughters, Bambi, 13, who is cool, collected, and intelligent, and Buffie, 11, who also has a cool head and tells the story with a sharp eye for details of character and situation; and Brick, 6, a small lump of a boy, who is aware beyond his years and quick with a quip. When Bill falls on hard times and loses his business for back taxes, he moves his close, comfortable family back to the home town he remembers fondly, Hickory Fork, in an unspecified midwestern state two thousand miles from Los Angeles. Although the family is used to the amenities of an affluent life, like Guccis and Jaguars, they take the move for the most part without grumbling, except for Bambi who is openly determined to get back to Bel-Air as soon as possible. Buffie reports seeing unusual features as soon as they arrive. The town seems to be "all outskirts," interior buildings are boarded up, and the bridge that spans what once was a river and is now a creek is rusty and rundown. There are more peculiarities, too. Grandma Babcock's refrigerator blocks the back door, and, as Brick reports to the girls, "Grandma Babcock packs heat" at night, meaning that she sleeps with her shotgun by her side. The pep rally at school their first day is a pandemonium of ill-bred, raucous, discourteous, even mean young people, a near mob whom the principal barely controls. Food flies across the lunchroom at noon, and grade schoolers rush to finish eating before the dreaded high schoolers arrive. Unplanned fire drills occur often, toilets are blown up regularly, and students board the buses in a rush as soon as they can after school, fearful of being left behind to meet some terrible fate. The teachers speak ungrammatically, are unprepared, and are easily intimidated by their students. Since Bill remembers the town as lively with community involvement and shared activities, he is shocked when he and the girls discover that the once-bustling mall, now rundown, is closed. Gradually the children learn that a gang runs Hickory Fork, "the school . . . the town . . . total," a teenaged mafia of organized crime, as it were. The Mall Rats, bossed by scurrilous Jeeter, and their companion Rattettes, and led by tough-talking Big Tanya, his girlfriend, hold the entire town in thrall. The Rats have slogans and rituals, refer to one another as homeboys and homewomen, and meet regularly in the clubhouse in the closed theater in the mall to plan such activities as blowing up mailboxes and hot-wiring cars. One night Bambi and Buffie sneak out to the mall, where they observe a gang initiation and overhear the members plan to kidnap the star football player of the Hickory Fork archrivals, Pinetree Trace, to ensure victory in the big game. Bambi decides something needs to be done to clean up the town and enlists her parents in the cause. Gradually other outsider youth and townspeople become involved. The family concocts a scheme to use what they know best—their acting abilities—and, later, their talents at filmmaking. Buffie starts out by relating as a class assignment a story that is presented as actual history but is really fiction. She tells the class that since the former owners of the mall property came to horrible ends, the mall is cursed. The Babcocks then sneak into the mall during a Rat meeting and in a hilarious, dramatic scene reenact the sordid tale, thoroughly frightening the gang, who flee in panic. Buffie persuades Little Bob Wire, who is unusually large and strong for his age, the son of the principal, and also an outsider because he is not yet in high school, to impersonate the star player who has been kidnapped. Little Bob plays so well that Pinetree Trace wins the big game. (Although in his teens, Little Bob has deliberately failed classes so that he can stay in grade school and thus avoid the organized crime of high school.) Angry over the loss, the Mall Rats and Rattettes call a skip day on the very day the state examiners arrive. Faced with the real threat of the school's being closed down for lack of students, community members rally around Dad and Mom, who embolden them to reassume authority over their children and take back their town. Dad and Mom produce and direct a family film about a once-great little town that went downhill but was restored by community effort. The film not only has the desired effect in Hickory Fork but also restores the Babcock family fortunes as well. It attracts media attention as prime Babcock family fare, and as a result, the family return to California, where Dad puts the pilot out as a two-part mini-series on contemporary American life. Characters are over-drawn, to good effect; episodes happen thick and fast—sometimes so quickly that one loses track of important details; and the contemporary, witty, brash style gives the book immediacy, although many references and details will date it. The contrasting families provide the central, telling irony. Juxtaposed are a family from what many people consider America's immoral funnyland and the very antithesis of normalcy in family life with those who presumably exemplify rock-bottom, hard-core, salt-of-the-earth America. The latter are shown as far from such because through timidity they have abdicated the age-old roles of parents and authority figures. SLJ.

THE BELLS OF CHRISTMAS (Hamilton*, Virginia, illus. Lambert Davis, Harcourt, 1989), brief period novel of Christmas in an African-American family of southern Ohio, near Springfield, in 1890. The narrator, Jason Bell, 12, de-scribes the preparations for the big day, his excitement, and that of his little sister, Melissy, 7. Among his other wishes is for snow, so that his Uncle Levi Bell will bring his family, including twelve-year-old cousin Tisha, in their cov-ered sleigh, and the young people can take a ride on the National Road, which runs near their house and all across Ohio. With his father, a carpenter, Jason goes down to the road, both of them riding in the wheel-a-chair his father uses when his wooden leg tires him, and wave at the wagon drivers. On Christmas morning Jason finds a wooden train on tracks, carefully crafted by his father and Uncle Levi, and Melissy gets a wooden doll that actually can walk. During the night, snow has begun, and when their older brother Bob takes them down to the road, they see sleighs filled with families. Before long, their cousins arrive from West Liberty, and the children are given a short ride, along with Jason's friend, Matthew Larson, 13, who lives down the road and is sweet on Tisha. More gifts are exchanged, the most surprising being a new wooden leg with a foot carved by Uncle Levi for Jason's father. Jason's older brothers with their families arrive, a sumptuous dinner is served, and the whole group goes to the church celebration where Melissy sings "Up on the Housetop," Tisha recites " 'Twas the Night before Christmas," and Jason sings "We Three Kings." Intended as a picture of prosperous, hard-working African Americans in a warm family setting, the highly illustrated book probably succeeds, but both the pictures and the dialogue seem stiff and artificial. There is no plot, no tension, and no denouement to advance the brief story. Except for the illustrations, nothing indicates that the characters are black. ALA.

BERNADETTE POLLACK (*T-Backs, T-Shirts, COAT, and Suit**), Chloe Pollack's stepaunt, a woman whom Chloe has seen only one time before she goes to spend the summer with her in Florida. Bernadette is a woman of strong will and firmly held convictions. She served as best man when her brother, whom Bernadette raised, married Chloe's mother seven years before the novel begins. Bernadette once lived at Spinach Hill commune, along with Chloe's stepfather and Zack, her employer. There she aroused attention by participating in burning draft cards as a protest against the Vietnam War. At that time, Bayard* McKnight was the commune's lawyer. Ironically, Zack, whom she trusted, is the cause of the controversy that swirls about Bernadette—first, because she will not wear a T-back (thong) bikini (and Zack brings a lawsuit against her to make her do so), and second, because the local church thinks she is a witch. Zack knows that the tattoo that she is reputed to have and that marks her as a witch is really the peace symbol, that it was removed when she had a mastectomy, and that he, Zack, has the same tattoo. Bernadette was a car mechanic before she went to work for Zack. She was unable to continue in that line of work after her operation. Although Chloe matures credibly as a result of her experiences in the story, Bernadette is the more interesting character, both comic and pathetic.

BERNICE (*The Star Fisher**), Joan Lee's classmate, who is also an outcast in the community. Bernice comes from a theatrical family and thus is despised by the other students. Her father, a former tenor, is an alcoholic, her grandmother is disagreeable, and her mother is on the road. Bernice and her sister are determined to have lives that are considered normal and respectable by the general population. Bernice wants to become a secretary and cultivates propriety in speech and behavior. Joan gets the other girls to accept Bernice. Bernice and her family are not entirely convincing, but they serve to show how ingrown and suspicious of strangers the community is.

BETSY (*Lyddie**), friend and roommate of Lyddie Worthen in Lowell, a girl who at first seems abrupt, even rude, given to reading novels and making shocking comments annoying to their very proper roommate, Amelia. When Lyddie starts working in the mill and is confused and exhausted, Betsy reads *Oliver Twist* aloud to her in the evenings, awakening her desire to learn to read better.

Betsy herself is studying, hoping to attend Oberlin College in Ohio after her brother graduates from Harvard, where he has been supported by Betsy's earnings. She develops a cough, however, and eventually must go to the hospital, which costs all her savings. Her lung problems continue, and her uncle from Maine comes to fetch her. Although she declares that she will return and start saving for college again, Lyddie doubts that she will, and the reader is left with the supposition that she will die of tuberculosis.

BETTY-DEAN WEBSTER (*Rachel Chance**), abused wife who finally shoots her brutal husband, uncle of Rachel Chance's friend, Hank*. Betty-Dean has lost her two children to county authorities, who put them in foster homes because their father abused them, and she has suffered the insult of Pastor Woodie's exhorting her to be a faithful and submissive wife. Shortly before Rachel leaves to find her kidnapped brother, she comes upon Betty-Dean in the storeroom of Abel* Chance's barn, where Hank has hidden her after she walked out of the hospital where she was taken from jail. She tells Rachel that she has terminal cancer and has only wanted to die quietly in peace, a privilege her husband denied her. Later Rachel learns from Hank, who says his uncle deserved to be shot, that he and Abel's cousin Jacob have already dug a grave for Betty-Dean on the farm and without telling authorities will quietly bury her when she dies.

BEYOND SAFE BOUNDARIES (Sacks*, Margaret, Dutton, 1989), historical novel set in South Africa from about 1958 to 1963, in which a white girl grows up amid increasingly tense race relations. At fifteen, Elizabeth Levin looks back on the years following her eleventh birthday and compares the problems that she sees in the country to the upheaval in her family when her widower father marries again. At eleven, Elizabeth belongs to a well-off, but not rich, Port Elizabeth family. She is barely aware of any flaw in life except that her dentist father is barred from the golf club because he is Jewish. She is at first uneasy about having a stepmother (fairy tales coming to mind) but soon warms to maternal, sensible Lydia. Her older sister, Evie*, however, almost university age, resents Lydia passionately, revering their mother, as does Mathilda, the African maid. Lydia assumes the role of mother to Evie anyway, preparing her wardrobe for the university as though it were a trousseau, and as wife and homemaker she holds dinner parties and cements relationships with relatives and neighbors, all the time retaining the distance their class dictates with the black servants. Rebellious at home, Evie continues to kick over the traces in Johannesburg, where she becomes romantically and politically involved with a bright, liberal student named Willem* Coetzee, the son, as it happens, of her father's Colored [sic] dental mechanic (denture maker), called Popeye*. In Port Elizabeth, Elizabeth attends school and goes to parties, engages in girl talk and activities with her friends at home and at school, wins a trophy at tennis, and becomes aware of her developing sexuality when she realizes that boys are attracted to her, and she gets pawed and french kissed. She is ignorant of how deeply Evie is involved in the African Movement until she visits her sister at the university, in scenes that launch the book toward its climax. Elizabeth discovers that Evie and Willem have many friends among other races and that the two are leaders in the Movement of the Africans against Prime Minister Verwoerd's repressive government, organizing protests, inciting dissension, and writing and distributing revolutionary leaflets. Elizabeth is present when police raid Evie's apartment; she watches helplessly and fearfully as they throw belongings about and smash the duplicating machine. She hears one of them call Evie a "kaffir-loving bitch." Shortly after, Willem is arrested for the sabotage of the Johannesburg-Pretoria Railway Line, but Evie, on the good word of her father, is put under house arrest at home in Port Elizabeth rather than jailed. One day while Elizabeth is walking home from school, dejected and angry at having been called a "commie Jew" by a schoolmate, Popeye slips her a note from Willem for Evie. Elizabeth withholds the note until after their cousin Ruthie's wedding, and when Evie reads it and learns that Willem is being tortured, she decides to inform on the Movement in return for Willem's release. She calls the police, is told that he has jumped to his death from the window of the interrogation room, and realizes that he has been murdered. Although no other whites go to Willem's funeral, for reasons of safety, Elizabeth slips out with their maid Lena, who attends out of deep respect and gratitude, along with many other similar-minded Africans, Coloreds, and Asians. Soon after, Lydia, concerned for both Evie's safety and the deteriorating health of her increasingly worried husband, arranges with local nuns to smuggle Evie, disguised as a novice, to England. On the day Evie leaves, Elizabeth, now fifteen, gets her first period, an obvious symbol. A couple of days later, she learns that Popeye has committed suicide over his son's death. Her father predicts that Elizabeth will also leave the country, as will, he says, all South Africa's children. She, however, hopes to fight, not as Evie and Willem did, she thinks, but with words. The novel contrasts the comfortable life of this white family with the growing turmoil in the country and, in a limited way, with the home conditions of the blacks and part-blacks. Elizabeth's sexual development and her gradual understanding of political events are credibly handled, but how she will fight "with words" (what Evie has also done) is not clear, except that it may be a reference to what the author and other whites are doing. For the most part, injustices are worked well into the story—the maid Lena's being picked up and jailed by police for not having her passport with her, a clear case of harassment since Lena is just outside the house chatting and not going anywhere; segregated buses and toilets; lack of education; inadequate food and housing; the rape of black girls. Similarly, the awakening of the blacks occurs naturally in the book, both peacefully as at the funeral and angrily, as when, after the Levins' young cook (Lena's daughter) is impregnated by the white boy next door, his sister is raped by a black militant intruder in revenge, and Lena's son is forced by blacks to go out of the country to train as a soldier. White pretensions come through strongly, even among these Jews who are also the objects of discrimination. Also ironic are their close attention to maintaining upper-class appearances, their concern about not drawing undue attention to themselves, and their treatment of blacks as inferior and ignorant servants, although they, like other whites, rely heavily on their labor and know they do. Another strength of the book comes from its depiction of the effect of apartheid on the young of both races—they all suffer, ironically, and perhaps mostly, the bright, young, educated whites, who, like Evie and Willem, are ostracized and vilified and even die, because they have gone "beyond safe boundaries" to stand up for their convictions. SLJ.

BILL (Reaver*, Chap, Delacorte, 1994), contemporary realistic growing-up novel set in the hills of a southern American state, where making moonshine and "shine running" are commonplace. Half-orphaned Jess Gates, the thirteen-year-old narrator, tells how her father, Leonard, a whiskey abuser and moonshine maker, periodically takes off on his raft, floating down the creek with a load of sugar bags and empty jars and leaving her alone on their little farm with her beloved mixed-breed dog, Bill. One day after she waves Dad off on still another "float-away," she returns home to discover Shaft Dudley, the local Alcohol Beverage Control officer, whom the people of the area call Wrong Man and whom her father has warned her against. That day and again later, in a seemingly inept yet clever way, Wrong Man tricks her into leading him to her father, whom on the second occasion he arrests and jails. Sincerely concerned about the girl, who is almost unschooled, burdened with responsibility, and repeatedly placed in morally ambivalent situations with respect to her father and the law, Wrong Man offers her the opportunity to live with him and his "first wife," Nell. Although she finds Nell attractive, Jess refuses. Acting on a note from her jailed father, she goes to his hidden still and empties and cleans the barrels. On the way home, she climbs a big rock, where a chairlike indentation triggers her memory of words supposedly spoken by old Corbin, now reputed to be a ghost who haunts these woods, where he is thought to have buried a treasure. Corbin is believed to have said that treasure seekers sitting "on a throne at sunset" will see his "wedding band," and that will lead to the treasure. While sitting on the thronelike rock, Jess spies a wedding band hanging from a branch, digs beneath it, finds a metal box containing numerous old coins, and hides it in the barn. When she visits her father, whose whiskey breath disgusts her, she mentions the coins, but remembering that Wrong Man had once warned her that Leonard's alcohol problem will only become worse, she refuses to tell him where the coins are. Soon after, she is attacked by Hawkins, a mean and surly ex-jailmate of her father. He demands the coins, kills the family bull, beats Jess, severely injures Bill, who tries to defend her, and takes the box but apparently drowns in the creek. When Bill recovers consciousness after eighty-three days in a coma, through which Jess has solicitously nursed him, and Dad is drinking ever more heavily, Jess decides to accept Wrong Man's invitation and live with him and Nell. Late in the spring, while swimming in the creek, Jess finds intact the box of coins, which she now knows are valuable. The various segments of this posthumously published story are ineptly knit, the climax fight with Hawkins is sensationalized and confusing, and the conclusion is abrupt. The main problem with which Jess struggles—how much loyalty she owes to her father—is set in relief by her deep affection for her dog, in whom she confides and with whom she discusses problems; her gradual understanding of Wrong Man's character and motives; and her awakening sexuality and increasing attraction to Drury, a teenaged neighbor. Some humor of language and situation—Wrong Man's problem with "hair flies," for example, and Bill's swiping all the napkins during dinner at Wrong Man's—lighten the book's inherent seriousness. The author catches the hill-country ambience in speech and attitude and has created in Jess a smart, kind, and thoroughly sympathetic protagonist but fails to achieve the emotional impact and sturdiness of his other novels. SLJ.

BILL RAMSEY (*Unlived Affections**), Willie Ramsey's homosexual father, whom Willie's mother, Kate* Davenport, divorces before Willie is born and who never knows that he has a son. Willie knows almost nothing about him until he discovers the letters that his father wrote to Kate before Kate was killed in an auto accident. From his letters, Bill seems to be a sweet, caring man, who always felt different from other boys; found marriage to Kate difficult sexually; falls in love with Larry, an aspiring teacher; has a brief time of happiness with Larry before being dumped by Larry; and later becomes the lover of a local pharmacist. An artisan in wood, he went to Berea, Kentucky, to study woodworking under Mr. Whitehead*, a noted woodworker, whose business partner he eventually becomes. His discovery that the Shoaltner brothers, neighbors of the Whiteheads, are not related but are a gay couple seems convenient for the plot. Bill "comes out" to Kate because he is uneasy making love to her and also because he believes she deserves a better marriage sexually than he can give her.

BINGO BROWN AND THE LANGUAGE OF LOVE (Byars*, Betsy, illus. Cathy Bobak, Viking, 1989), amusing, often funny boy's growing-up novel, one of a series, set in the American city of Townsville at the time of publication, stronger for its humorous insights into human nature than for its characters or plot. The summer after *The Burning Questions of Bingo Brown,* Bingo (Harrison) Brown copes with his crush on Melissa, his sixth-grade classmate the previous school year at Roosevelt Middle School, whose ambition has been to become a scientist and rock star and who has moved to Oklahoma; learns to handle big, blond, buxom Cici Boles, whose speech is liberally sprinkled with "like" and "you know" and who has a crush on him; deals with Billy Wentworth, the snide and pestering bully who lives next door, always calls him Worm Brain, and is infatuated with Cici, whose favor he pressures Bingo to help him secure; and learns to get along with his increasingly irritable mother, Nance.

Even though he agrees to pay off the $54.29 telephone bill he ran up calling Melissa by cooking supper for thirty-six nights ("But no Hamburger Helper, Bingo.") and to take care of Billy's dog, Misty, while the Wentworths are on vacation because Nance insists, his mother still seems distant and cantankerous. While Bingo is preparing tuna lasagna one afternoon, she bursts through the door, stomps through the house, leaves a hasty note for his father, jumps in her car, and drives off to her mother's. Later his father, Sam, tells Bingo that Nance is unhappy over her unexpected pregnancy, and Bingo is not pleased with the idea of becoming a big brother at this stage in life either. Later he and his father go to Mrs. Harrison's with yellow roses for Nance from Sam and with a casserole called Hot Dog Surprise from Bingo. Although she is not there, they leave both items on the doorstep for her, along with a note saying they love her and want her, Bingo adding that she should bake the casserole at 350 degrees. When his activist grandmother joins the CUT (Clean Up Townsville) protest picket line, Bingo walks, too, and seeing a baby there completely changes his mind about impending sibling-hood. His mother comes home, ironically while Cici is visiting, and happily informs him that it has been decided that she will continue to sell real estate (she was upset at having to give up her job), and Mr. Brown, who has disliked the insurance field, will become a house husband and work on the novel he has long wanted to write. By the end of the book, Bingo has also stood up to Billy, informing him that he needs to present his own case to Cici. When Bingo receives a letter from Melissa, he promptly falls in love with her all over again, and as he writes back to her, he realizes that he has "learned to dog-paddle in the mainstream of life." He has grown up a lot, sees his parents in a new light, and realizes that love can be expressed in a myriad of ways. Although Bingo may have a few too many problems for one book, they are handled sympathetically with just the right amount of melodrama or naiveté ("I am preparing, er, chicken chests.") to fit his stage in life. Characterization is on the surface, except for Bingo, whose dynamism occurs inside and takes him appropriately into early adolescence. The humor stems from situations; Bingo's uninformed reactions (Bingo continues to record his feelings and observations in his notebook); the ironies that home and neighborhood life often present; and the witty, vigorous, contemporary style. Another book in the series is *Bingo Brown, Gypsy Lover**. For details about *The Burning Questions of Bingo Brown*, see *Dictionary, 1985–1989.* Fanfare; SLJ.

BINGO BROWN, GYPSY LOVER (Byars*, Betsy, Viking, 1990), lighthearted realistic contemporary novel of family life and a boy's growing up in the American city of Townsville. Earnest, likable Bingo (Harrison) Brown, previously met in *The Burning Questions of Bingo Brown,* when he is in sixth grade, and in *Bingo Brown and the Language of Love**, the summer after sixth grade, is the only child in a closely knit, middle-class family. The problems Bingo faces in this book are much like his previous ones and to some extent are a continuation of them. As before, they arise from happenstance and the peculiarities of his personality and stage in life. He struggles to find a Christmas present for his girlfriend, Melissa, who has moved to Bixby, Oklahoma; must adjust to his mother's pregnancy and the idea of a baby brother; must come to terms with his own physical and emotional maturation; tries to help Billy Wentworth, the bully next door who continues to deride him as Worm Brain, with his love life; and handles the advances of a girl classmate named Boots. A letter from Melissa in mid-December informing him that she has made him a Christmas gift and that she is reminded of him by the character Romondo in the popular romance *Gypsy Lover* sends him on a fruitless search for a gift for her that costs no more than $3.59, all the money he has, and for a copy of *Gypsy Lover,* to try to find out what she means about Romondo. In the bookstore, he runs into Boots, who later calls him and reads over the telephone what they both feel is a torrid passage about Romondo and his love, Marianna. When Melissa's package arrives, Bingo opens it early and discovers she has sent him a piece of cloth with two handles, which an accompanying note explains is a notebook holder to hold the notebooks Bingo keeps for recording his "burning questions" and observations about life. He shops for her again, this time settling on fifty-nine-cent golden earrings from the sale counter at K-Mart. This problem apparently solved, his relationship with Boots continues through telephone calls, "mixed-sex conversations," which make him uncomfortable but conclude when Boots's mother, having heard about the Romondo-Marianna reading, forbids Boots to call anyone. When Billy tries unsuccessfully to enlist Bingo's help in finding out whether or not Cici Boles is going to give Billy a present, Billy decides to give her one anyway, and by mistake wraps up Brut After Shave instead of perfume. Cici comes to Bingo's house in a huff and demands that he return the unopened gift to the "nerd" next door. To complicate things further, Bingo becomes aware that he has been growing, a matter first evident to his intense chagrin when he encounters Boots in the bookstore, and he is sure that he is all bony arms and wrists, awkward and ugly in his too-small clothes. His main concern, however, and the one about which all these other matters revolve, is the coming baby and his mother's health and often erratic behavior. All goes well until, a little over seven months into the pregnancy, pains send Mrs. Brown to the hospital, where a few days later, she gives birth to Jamie, who, though tiny, is otherwise a "perfect ten," as Bingo's father describes him. Although both she and his father had made light of Bingo's growth problem, his mother shows understanding and sympathy when she tells Bingo that as his Christmas gift from her, he should buy himself a new jacket, wrap it, and put it under the tree. She also shows that she understands his new maturity about time and money (she had forbidden him to call Melissa until he worked off the huge telephone bill he had run up) when she also gives him a five-minute call to Melissa. He calls Melissa, is delighted with the naturalness of the conversation, and realizes that he has indeed been maturing, emotionally and socially, as well as physically. The humor, both hyperbolic and understated, is always gentle and kind, so that readers laugh along with Bingo in his mishaps. The warm family relationships, real-sounding dialogue, natural reactions, and moments of true poignancy produce a credibility that lifts this book miles above the awkward, tasteless, shock-appeal family sit-coms of television. Bingo is highly introspective, ruminative, argumentative, easily worried, independent but still dependent, bright but not smart-alecky, often naive but not innocent, moral but not "goody"—a typical twelve-year-old being brought up by sensible but not perfect parents, close to them and also to his grandmother, whom he still calls Grammy, a late-twentieth-century Henry Huggins. Although knowing the other books about Bingo contributes dimensions of pleasure, this book is substantial enough to stand by itself. For details about *The Burning Questions of Bingo Brown,* see *Dictionary, 1985–1989.* ALA; SLJ.

BLAZE WERLA (*Words of Stone**), ironically named fearful youth, ten years old. Shortest in his class where he has no friends, Blaze is withdrawn, imaginative, and artistic. The son of a high school art teacher and a deceased aspiring writer, he suffers from the loss of his mother, whom he had loved dearly, and recurring nightmares that derive from a fairgrounds fire in which he was severely burned. The summer he meets and forms a friendship of sorts with Joselle* Stark marks a turning point in his life. The words she fashions with stones as a joke on the hillside between their houses eventually cause him to open up to his father, start to paint, and look with greater favor on the woman his father considers marrying. Blaze wins the reader's liking although he sometimes seems exaggerated for effect.

BLOCK, FRANCESCA LIA (1962–   ), born in Los Angeles; author of highly innovative, slangy, punk-culture-inspired novels for older children and young adults and also adult novels that make use of Greek myth and posit art and love as healing forces. Daughter of an artist and a poet, Block attended North Hollywood High and the University of California at Berkeley. Her first novel for young people, *Weetzie Bat* (HarperCollins, 1989), was cited by the American Library Association as a Best Book for Young Adults and a Recommended Book for Reluctant Young Adult Readers, but it also aroused criticism for its difficult and unusual style and its easy acceptance of casual sex. It concerns the daughter of an arty, substance-abusing couple who cruises Los Angeles with her gay friend, both looking for, and finding, the loves of their lives. Her subsequent novels have suffered similar critical treatment. *Witch Baby** (HarperCollins, 1991), cited as a *School Library Journal* Best Book and also a book for reluctant readers, is about the daughter of Weetzie's lover and her attempts to find out who she is and to fit into the aging-hippy-style household. In *Cherokee Bat and the Goat Boys* (HarperCollins, 1992), Witch Baby, Weetzie's daughter, and their boyfriends are in a band that becomes involved in the drug culture of the city. In *Missing Angel Juan** (HarperCollins, 1993), Witch Baby follows her lover to New York and hunts for him through a seamy and surrealistic city with the help of the ghost of Weetzie's father. These novels also have been cited for prestigious lists, but some public and school librarians have refused to have them on their shelves. Critics and admirers alike, however, have agreed that the novels have some highly amusing episodes and paint a picture of the Los Angeles new wave culture that rings true. Block's later novel, *The Hanged Man* (HarperCollins, 1994), explores a darker side of Los Angeles. Her novels for adults are *Ecstasia* (New American Library, 1993) and *Primavera* (New American Library, 1994).

BLOOMFIELD (*Phoenix Rising Or How to Survive Your Life**), Richard Bloomfield, boyfriend of Helen Castle and friend of Jessie Castle. Although she thinks he is not good-looking, chiefly because he is always sneering, and is a "jerk," Helen believes she is in love with Bloomfield. When he wants to have sex with her, she refuses, however, telling him that she is simply not ready. She is hurt when he dumps her after Bambi* Sue Bordtz tells him that she has cancer. Later she forgives him, realizing that he is just afraid, and longs to go to the school graduation party with him, getting a new dress for the occasion, and is almost ready to invite him when he invites her. When, after Helen's death, Jessie accuses him of betraying her sister, he replies that he was scared and an idiot and weeps. His tears point up Jessie's inability to cry over her loss.

BODEAN PEYTON (*Dixie Storms**), Robert Dean Peyton, Dutch Peyton's nephew, 9, son of Flood* Peyton and his ex-wife, Becky*. A thin, lively, mischievous, willful child, Bodean resents Dutch's referring to him as her nephew, often teases her verbally and physically, and, after Norma* Peyton arrives, tries deliberately to hurt Dutch by openly preferring Norma, although Dutch goes out of her way to defend and protect him against bigger boys who bully him. He adores his father and tries to please him in every way. Bodean is just beginning to ask questions about why his mother left and why she never sees him. His favorite expressions are, "Do me a favor" and "Make me an offer," phrases he uses to extreme. He appears to be a younger replica of his father.

THE BOGGART (*The Boggart**), the mischievous, magical, shape-changing little man who inhabits Castle Keep, the old place in western Scotland that the Volnik family inherits. The Boggart lives in a small space between two blocks of stone high up on the wall of the castle library. He has gotten on variously with the MacDevon clan, who have mostly accommodated him, and grew very fond of the last clan chief, the MacDevon. When the MacDevon dies, along with his ancient dog, Fergus, the Boggart is so lonely and forlorn that his wails resound through the hills, disturbing the sleep of the people in the area. Although the Boggart causes much trouble for the Volniks, both deliberately and otherwise, the reader sympathizes with the bereft, displaced "mannie" and finds funny his attraction to and problems with modern technology. A particularly poignant scene occurs at the Chervil Theater, when, during the song of mourning over Imogen's body in *Cymbeline,* the Boggart reacts to the words that recall his grief over the MacDevon and an earlier chief he had loved, takes over the lighting board, and submerges the theater in a glow that fills everyone with awe.

THE BOGGART (Cooper*, Susan, Macmillan, 1993), fantasy of the supernatural set mostly in Toronto in a recent year. When Robert Volnik, the artistic director of the Chervil Theater, inherits Castle Keep in the western Highlands of Scotland, he and the rest of his family—Emily*, about twelve; her brother, Jessup*, 10; and his wife, Maggie, co-owner of an antique shop—are unaware that they have also acquired the Boggart*. "For more centuries than he can count," the tiny, mischievous creature, invisible to human eyes and indigenous to Scotland, has inhabited the old house, becoming especially fond of the last chief of the resident clan, the MacDevon, and his ancient dog, Fergus, who die of old age together. The Volniks visit their castle, which they decide they must sell, first selecting items to take back to Canada for Maggie's shop. Each child is allowed one choice, and Emily picks an old desk, inside of which the Boggart inadvertently falls asleep and thus is carried to Toronto. He perpetrates a series of tricks and misdeeds both comic and disturbing, among them swiping pizza and a jar of fudge sauce; hiding inside Jessup's school lunch and eating his peanut butter-and-jelly sandwich; swiping personal items like Robert's razor; and turning himself into the puck while Jessup is playing hockey. He is entranced by such modern inventions as electricity and television. Arguments flare among family members, who blame one another for the disturbing incidents. A serious misadventure occurs on Halloween, for which the Boggart is filled with apprehension deriving from age-old beliefs about the Celtic Eve of Samhain. The Boggart sets out to protect his new family in the old way and unwittingly destroys Robert's prize holly bush by tearing off branches and attaching them over doors and windows to keep the Samhain hag away. He douses Maggie, who is dressed as a witch, with ice-cold water, because he is certain she is the ancient hag. Two members of the theater company from the British Isles tell Emily that it sounds as though a Boggart is at work. To Emily's consternation, Dr. Stigmore, a psychiatrist and one of Maggie's customers, observes the Boggart's antics in the shop one day and becomes convinced that Emily is causing them. She is entering adolescence, and he thinks she is probably emitting large amounts of psychic energy and suggests that she enter psychoanalysis. Two very disrupting events occur through the Boggart's action. He tampers with the lighting during a rehearsal of *Cymbeline,* attracting the attention of the media who assume the theater is haunted. When he tinkers with traffic signals, Emily is struck by a car, suffering a broken ankle and rib and many bruises. Jessup recalls an obscure remark of Tommy Cameron, the boy Jessup's age in Scotland, who was a good friend of the MacDevon and had discovered his body. Jessup phones Tommy, who confirms the existence of the Boggart and also sends a batch of pictures of the Castle Keep area hoping to entice the Boggart to come home. The Boggart, however, does not know how to get home, and the children do not know how to communicate with him. The Boggart solves one part of the problem by speaking through Jessup's computer, in phrases that at first Jessup thinks are computer "garbage," but a Scottish theater member identifies them as Gaelic and translates them to say that the Boggart wants to return to his own country. Finally, to the children's horror, the Boggart interjects himself into Jessup's Black Hole game and as a flittery blue flame is actually drawn into a black hole. The children are terrified for his safety and consult a pal of Jessup who suggests they reverse the "info loop" and go into the black hole, too. They do, with great fear, and contact the Boggart there, giving Jessup the idea of sending the Boggart home by computer. He mails the disc containing the Boggart to Tommy Cameron, who inserts it into his computer and brings the Boggart out and home again. The Boggart seems none the worse for his transatlantic excursion and immediately resumes his old ways by playing tricks on the Maconochie, the Volniks' lawyer, who has bought Castle Keep and retired there. In this story of respect for even the smallest of creatures, family relationships are authentic, the children are pleasingly and distinctively depicted, adults are earnest and likable but mostly on the fringes, and such scenes as the Halloween fracas and the lighting phenomenon at the theater are particularly well done. On the whole, the style is polished and moves right along, and the extensive use of detail gives the scenes and characters substance. For example, Jessup observes that Castle Keep is in the part of Scotland where *Kidnapped* takes place. The point of view alternates between the Boggart and the children, although most scenes are drawn from their perspective, but the Boggart is the main character, a charming combination of whimsey, mischief, and poignancy. He and the sense of old beliefs holding fast stand out. How the children, who lack magic in the usual sense, get in and out of the computer game is unclear, and that part of the story jars, but having the Boggart enter the game and be gobbled up by it seems acceptable, because the Boggart is an Old Thing and has repeatedly shown his vast capability with magic. The computer scenes inventively combine old and new magic, depending on whether the point of view is the Boggart's or the children's. ALA.

BOOTS GRANT (*The One Who Came Back**), young mother of Alex, a dancer and cocktail waitress who has let her parents raise her son while she pursued her career and many boyfriends. Since her mother's illness, Alex has come to live with Boots in the run-down trailer, but she has no real idea of how to act as a parent and is more interested in whether the policeman bringing her son home is married than in what caused him to be picked up. Alex blames himself for her inability to get a dancing job and the poor place they have to live. In the end, Alex accepts her flighty behavior and realizes that he has to be more mature than she acts.

THE BORNING ROOM (Fleischman*, Paul, HarperCollins, 1991), historical novel of family life set from 1851 to 1918 in Ohio on the Stillwater River, near Lanesville. Georgina Caroline Lott recounts the major events of her family as they occur in or involve the ''borning room,'' a small room set aside for illness and childbirth. She is born there, and eight and a half years later, when her mother unexpectedly starts in labor, she helps Cora, a runaway slave she has hidden in the barn, deliver her brother, Zebulon. Grandfather* Lott dies there, and in 1865, so does Mother, probably because an inexperienced doctor gives her an overdose of chloroform in delivering her twins, only one of whom lives. In 1857 eight-year-old Zeb lies in the room near death with diphtheria, choking for breath, when Clement Bock, the new teacher, saves him by blowing crushed eggshell down his throat to break the membrane created by the illness. Three years later, having married Clement, Georgina gives birth to her daughter, Emmaline Bellflower Bock, named after her mother and the type of apple that Grandfather brought from New Hampshire and planted in Ohio. The last chapter is a conversation between Georgina and an unnamed artist painting her death portrait, as one had painted Grandfather's so many years before. Through these major events a picture emerges of the musical, loving family, respectful of each other's beliefs and concerned for nature, books, and others in the community. Georgina is an endearing character—bright and assertive for a girl of her era and devoted to her home and her little brother, Zeb. Her annoyance with Aunt Erna, who takes over after Mother's death, never erupts into open rebellion but makes her seem more human. Many of the other characters, even minor ones, are memorable. Quietly written, the book presents each episode, however sad or dramatic, as part of the continuity of life. ALA; Fanfare; SLJ.

BOUTIS, VICTORIA, author of novels for children and young people. She grew up in a mill town similar to the Fairmore Hills, Pennsylvania, of her Jane Addams Award–winning *Looking Out** (Four Winds, 1988), which revolves around a girl whose parents are communists during the anti-communist hysteria of 1953. Boutis also published *Katy Did It* (Greenwillow, 1982), about a girl and her father who take a three-day hike in the Adirondacks. Boutis attended the University of Wisconsin and City College of New York, receiving her B.A. in Southeast Asian studies. She has made her home in Ossining, New York, and has two children.

THE BRAVE (Lipsyte*, Robert, HarperCollins, 1991), novel of the prize-fighting world, set in New York City and State at about the time of its publication. Native American Sonny Bear (George Harrison Bayer), 17, has grown up mostly on the Moscondaga Reservation, where his jewelry-making mother drops him with her Uncle Jake whenever her erratic life takes a turn for the worse. Ignoring the white blood of his father, a Vietnam victim, Jake has tried to instill in Sonny a pride in his Indian heritage, particularly in the Running Brave cult of his grandfather, and he has taught him to box in an effort to control his rare but sudden bursts of violence. Cheated in a small-town match, Sonny and Jake barely escape with their skins, and Jake lets the boy take off, as he has wanted to, for New York City to join the army. As he gets off the bus, he is intercepted by a young black hood and drug dealer called Stick, who sees him as an easy mark, and his accomplice, a blonde called Doll*. Naive Sonny is soon robbed and coerced into their operation, sent as an unwitting decoy with a drug delivery about which the police are tipped off, then arrested while Stick gets away with a much bigger deal. The arresting officer, Sergeant Alfred Brooks, who has been doggedly attempting to bust Stick, tries to persuade Sonny to give evidence, but the boy's experience with whites and the law has filled him with distrust, so he is sent to a correctional facility. There he gets into immediate trouble and is almost killed by an in-house gang. He wakes up after ten days in the hospital, where Brooks, an ex-fighter, has agreed with Jake to release Sonny into his custody to train until he can return to the city to work in Donatelli's Gym. Although his mother appears with a rich boyfriend from Phoenix and tries to claim him, Jake sends him off to the city where he becomes a janitor in the gym, now run by Henry Johnson, and works out with fat black Martin* Witherspoon as his training partner. Gradually he improves and begins to control what Jake calls the "hawk" that lives inside him and occasionally bursts out—what Brooks calls his "fire"—until he is the hope of the local fight group to win the Gotham Gloves Title, the top amateur bout. Although Doll shows up at one of the fights, Brooks keeps Sonny away from her. Just before the big fight, Stick shoots Brooks in the back and leaves him paralyzed. Because someone—maybe his mother, maybe Stick—tipped off the commission that he had once fought professionally, Sonny is barred from the title match. With Martin, Sonny goes to face Stick and forces him to the hospital where Brooks can make the arrest. In the end Sonny, now able to control his emotions, starts the long, hard climb toward the title through poorly paid fights in small towns with Martin, his manager, publicity agent, and friend. Brooks, Henry Johnson, and Martin's father are all characters in an earlier book, *The Contender,* set also mostly in Donatelli's Gym. Scenes of the training and of the fights are vivid and compelling, and those around "The Deuce" (Forty-second Street) where Stick operates are ominous and ugly. Sonny is a believable character with his suppressed rage and reluctance to accept help from either Jake or Brooks, but his ability to draw, mentioned several times, seems extraneous. Fanfare. For details about *The Contender,* see *Dictionary, 1960–1984.*

BREAKING THE FALL (Cadnum*, Michael, Viking, 1992), psycho-thriller set in recent years in a middle-class neighborhood in Oakland, California. The narrator, Stanley North, 16, feels inadequate and unsure of himself. He knows his parents are not getting along. His mother is often away on business trips, and his father, an accountant, is an inarticulate, unhappy man. Stanley sometimes thinks that he may be at least partly to blame for their failing marriage. In addition, he is confused about his relationship with beautiful Sky Tagaloa, a classmate; feels inferior about cars around her older brother, Tu, who would like Stanley to join him in tinkering with his old white Chevy; and regrets the torn ligament that keeps him from baseball, which he enjoys. He yearns for the "alive" feeling that Jared Trent, a boy much like himself in circumstances, assures him he will feel when Stanley joins in the dangerous "game" of breaking into houses, while the inhabitants are in bed asleep, and stealing from their bedrooms some small, tangible evidence of entry. The novel opens in the midst of Stanley's first such attempt, one in which he gets the feeling of exhilaration but fails to steal, because the man of the house awakens and grabs his gun. Later Stanley returns with Jared to the same house for another attempt. Their discovery that the people have installed a silent alarm heightens their sense of excitement but also shortens their visit. They both get away without being caught, but Stanley feels guilty at fleeing before Jared does, a sense of shame that Jared plays on in order to keep Stanley involved. After his parents split up, Stanley comes up with an idea for breaking away from Jared and almost pulls it off. He enters the same house, in great fear and trembling, but also with great determination to succeed this time on his own. He comes away with a lumpy object, which turns out to be the wife's wallet. As Stanley was certain he would, Jared enters Stanley's house during the night. He taunts Stanley that the occupants of the broken-into house are drunks and leaves before Stanley can give him the wallet with the command that Jared should prove himself by taking it back. The next morning, Stanley learns from his father that Jared was found dead from a fall "onto the freeway" and tells his father about the game. His father, who had been almost distraught when he discovered Stanley gone because he thought Stanley had run away to be with his mother, returns the wallet, and Tu enlists Stanley's help in improving his pitching. The breaking and entering scenes are masterpieces of high, on-the-edge-of-the-seat tension and make up for such plot lapses as the abrupt conclusion, the unexplained circumstances of Jared's fall, and the failure of the people to press charges. Short, rapid-fire sentences and fragments of sentences project the sense of Stanley's fear and the conflict he feels that comes from his desire to be at least as good as Jared at the game, while at the same time also knowing that what he is doing is wrong. The short chapters often end with cliff-hanging situations or statements. Stanley and Jared are effective contrasts in character. Jared is immoral; he knows wrong from right but delights in the power that comes from manipulating people into doing wrong. Unlike Jared, Stanley discovers reasons for not tempting fate: he has a caring father; a new friend, Tu, who has more wholesome interests, although he is no more adept at them than Stanley; an attractive sister; and Mr. Milliken, a perceptive teacher, all of whom can catch Stanley before he falls. If social commentary concerning the effects of disintegrating families on teenagers is intended, it is not explicit. Poe Nominee.

BRENDA TUNA (*Buffalo Brenda**), star of the book, boisterously overweening, opinionated, and open to the charge of being exceedingly conceited if she were not so obviously intelligent, civic minded, and thoroughly likable. Her curious last name derives from her paternal grandfather, Vladimir Tunitsky, called Grandpa Tuna in the book, who emigrated to the United States from

Rumania. He changed his name to George Washington Tuna, because, as he informed the judge, "It's an all-American name . . . [that] will speed up our melting better." Brenda's father makes and sells costumes, and her mother, an unusually large, heavy woman, is a potter. The Tunas occupy an extra-large city lot enclosed with a white board fence and containing an unmowed meadow with three sheep, a goat, and two geese. The family favor natural foods and fibers. Brenda's parents' unusual patience and understanding frustrate her. She wishes they were more like the parents of other adolescents and less flexible about her iconoclastic inclinations.

THE BROCCOLI TAPES (Slepian*, Jan, Philomel, 1988), animal novel set in Hawaii, told as if recited into a tape recorder. Usually outgoing, gregarious Sara Davidson, 11, is lonely and unhappy with her parents and her brother, Sam*, 13, during their stay in Hawaii for five months, feeling unpopular in her new school, worried about her grandmother who is ill, and neglected by her mother, whose concern for the grandmother occupies her attention. Their rented house is on a finger of land that ends in a field of lava rocks. There Sara and Sam find a black cat trapped by one leg caught between two rocks that have shifted from the pounding of the surf. When they rescue it, they find that it is starving and too wild to touch. Although they know they cannot keep it because their father is allergic and they cannot take it back to Boston with them, they secretly feed it and gradually get it to trust them. At the lava field they also meet hostile, wary Eddie* Nutt from Sam's class, whose surly father owns a pet store and whose Hawaiian mother, they eventually learn, left three years earlier with an old boyfriend. All the story is recorded by Sara and most of it sent to her sixth-grade class and former teacher, Miss Hasselbauer, in Boston as part of an oral history project. Because the cat has a strong preference for the broccoli that Sam hates, they name it Broccoli. They watch it fill out and become less scruffy as day after day they leave food for it, although it remains independent and somewhat aloof. They also join Eddie in building a wall to form a pool of water that the surf splashes onto the rocks, and he, like Broccoli, gradually begins to trust them. Events reach a climax when the grandmother dies and Eddie's mother, now living with a lover in Arizona, sends for her son. Believing his father does not want him and unwilling to join his mother, Eddie runs away, intending to live in the lava field. Although he hates roughing it, Sam goes with him. When his absence is discovered, Sara confesses all about Broccoli. Their mother engineers a reconciliation between Eddie and his father, but their father insists that they find a home for Broccoli, a complicated job because she is about to have kittens. Sara is devastated when they find Broccoli drowned in their pool, but she and Sam rescue the kittens and, when they are old enough, give away most of them. The last two, black like the mother, they and Eddie secretly put with the white kittens of the beautiful, prize, long-haired pet shop cat, then organize their classmates and a feature writer for the local newspaper to arrive at opening time and make a big thing of the white cat adopting the two black orphans, so that Mr. Nutt allows them to stay. Interspersed among the tapes sent to Boston are some that Sara plans to erase, telling her more private feelings of loneliness, sadness at her grandmother's death, and first-love attraction to Eddie. Her voice is convincing, since she is a very vocal child, and her attitude toward Sam, both irritated and protective, is believable. Although Broccoli is focus and trigger for most of the action, the real story is in the various personal relationships in both the Davidson and Nutt families. ALA; SLJ.

BRO DAVID (*The Mozart Season**), David Shapiro, 16, Allegra's older brother. He is a talented cartoonist but is not as openly devoted to his art as she is to her music. He helps her to keep the competition in its proper perspective. He also helps her to see that, although she is all right and he loves her, she is not "normal," as girls of 12 go and as she thinks she is. For example, he points out that if she were really "normal" she would be a Mall Baby, devoted to seeking out and thoroughly taking in every shopping mall around. David is a foil for his sister, a pleasant, astute young man.

BROOKS, BRUCE (1950–   ), born in Virginia; teacher, author of novels for young people. Now a freelance writer, he lives in Silver Spring, Maryland. His best-known novel is his first, *The Moves Make the Man* (Harper, 1984), which was named a Newbery Honor Book and to the American Library Association Notable Book and Best Books for Young Adult lists and the *Horn Book* Fanfare list. It is echoed in situations and characterization by *What Hearts** (Harper-Collins, 1992). Also on the Notable Book list is *Everywhere** (Harper and Row, 1990), a novel of a boy whose love keeps his dying grandfather alive. Both it and *No Kidding** (Harper, 1989), a strange, futuristic fantasy, are on the *School Library Journal* list of Best Books for Children. Typically his novels leave ethical questions unresolved but contain memorable scenes and characters. For earlier biographical information and title entries, see *Dictionary, 1985–1989* [*The Moves Make the Man; Midnight Hour Encores*].

BRYCE STEVENS (*The Secret Keeper**), father of Matt Stevens, the boy for whom Anne Lewis acts as keeper (companion-sitter) during her summer at the Beaches, the exclusive club on Lake Michigan. Bryce is a handsome, deeply tanned, blue-eyed, blond man, and Anne is immediately attracted to him, in spite of having been warned about him by Mrs. Larimer. Later Anne learns that his charm and affability mask the deep anger and hatred he feels for the residents of the Beaches, especially the Larimers. He married Jess Larimer, the Larimers' only child, and they lived in a modest house in nearby Laketown. The Larimers opposed the marriage but gave Jess money so that she could continue to have some of the luxuries to which she had been accustomed. Bryce resented their actions, became abusive, and when Jess decided to leave him, he assaulted her, killing her accidentally. In exchange for Bryce's agreeing never to contact Matt, the Larimers and Bradfords fixed things to look as though Jess died in an auto accident. Bryce's return to the area provokes the disturbances at the Beaches the summer that Anne works there and probably leads to his murder.

BUDDY MEADOWSWEET (*Monkey Island**), kind, cheerful, take-charge young African-American man, who with Calvin* Bosker befriends Clay Garrity in the park where he lives with other homeless persons. Buddy left his home in South Carolina at seventeen; he worked in a New York City zoo until employees were cut back and then as a janitor until laid off. Unemployed, without income, he could no longer maintain an apartment and took to the streets, where he met Calvin Bosker, whom he continues to help, even though lifting the old man when he is drunk is giving Buddy a bad back. He makes a little money gathering and redeeming cans. Buddy takes good care of Clay, all things considered, managing to secure some nourishing food and warm clothes for him, and although his common sense tells him the boy needs a proper place, he never forces Clay but remains respectful of the boy's feelings and wishes. He and Clay become very fond of each other. At the end, Buddy has a job again, is living in a shelter for the homeless, has enrolled in high school at night, is saving money to get a place of his own, and says he has plans. Although the ending for Buddy is upbeat, the reader can see that his situation is precarious. Buddy represents the high-minded street person, one who is on the streets through no fault of his own and who never loses his ideals and self-respect.

BUFFALO BRENDA (Pinkwater*, Jill, Macmillan, 1989), exuberant, zany school novel set in the 1980s in the upper-middle-class community of Florence, Long Island, and featuring a strongly delineated central character. India* Ink Tiedelbaum, 14, the narrator, describes the escapades of her best friend, Brenda* Tuna, as Brenda sets out to make the two girls ''the outstanding stars in high school that they should have been in junior high.'' India begins by flashing back to seventh grade, where Brenda was inclined, among other iconoclastic and exhibitionist behavior, to wear to school such proscribed garb as a hula skirt and a halter top. India also reports Brenda's assertion that her great problem in life as she enters her teens is her inability to ''express her independence . . . and rebel'' as teenagers are supposed to, because her parents are too agreeable and understanding. When the two girls embark on their freshman year, Brenda decides that they will make their mark in Florence High by taking over the school paper, the *Florence Weekly Crier.* She spearheads two exposés, the nature of which is revealed by their headlines: ''Popularity Breeds Contempt—for You'' and ''Rating the Faculty.'' The first arouses the ire of both insiders and outsiders among the student body, and the second angers the faculty to such an extent that the paper is administratively disbanded. The news staff then relocates to Brenda's home, reorganizes as the underground *Florence Free Press,* and continues investigative reporting, most notably with another exposé that rocks the community as well as the school—a story that horse meat is served in the school cafeteria as hamburger. When they are sophomores, Brenda decides to establish a Boosters Club for the Florence Buffalos, a wimpy football team, and to provide the school with a live bison as a mascot. By the time of the big game with their archrivals, the Glen Harbor Devils, she has enlisted the student body and many of the parents in fund-raising efforts to buy western costumes and a bison, Flo, and antagonized the administration by building a pen for Flo at one end of the football field. The administration in turn has antagonized the students and community by attempting to have Flo and her brand-new baby, Tuna Surprise, taken to the slaughterhouse. Brenda helps the Florence Buffalos win the big football game by using Flo to demoralize the opposition but afterward agrees that it is for the best when her Grandpa Tuna and the adviser-teacher, Ms.* Samansky, arrange to take the bison to an animal farm in Maine. At the very end, Brenda feels validated as a teenager because her parents have intervened to head off some of her ill-advised antics and, irrepressible as ever, is considering an un-specified project that India fears may get them tarred and feathered and run out of town. This book contains a full assortment of interesting and outlandish char-acters, including Grandpa Tuna, who gets the idea of pacifying the frightened Flo with oatmeal-raisin cookies; staunch cohorts Slick and the Boys, who are ace students and competent musicians but who act and dress like gang members for effect; and disagreeable, snide English teacher Osgood. Home and school scenes have the flavor of lived, or perhaps carefully observed, experience; humor ranges from subtle to extreme slapstick; and the extensive dialogue is filled with psychobabble, quick quips, and nimble repartee, which give the book speed and immediacy and tie it to the contemporary teenaged scene. All these make for lightweight but consistently entertaining reading. Parents are refreshingly por-trayed as helpful and sensible, while numerous jabs at inept, crude, and self-interested administrators and teachers unfortunately have considerable relevance. ALA.

BULL RUN (Fleischman*, Paul, illus. David Frampton, HarperCollins, 1993), historical novel in sixteen voices telling of the first great battle of the Civil War in July, 1861, at Bull Run near Manassas Junction, Virginia. Each character speaks in several brief chapters—some as few as three, one as many as six. Except for General Irvin McDowell, commander of the Union forces, all are fictional but based on actual memoirs, diaries, and other records. Among them are Gideon Adams, an African American from Ohio, who, being very light skinned, clips his hair close, changes his name to Able, and enlists as a white man after Negro (*sic*) volunteers are rejected. Although he lives in fear of dis-covery, he is a genuine patriot and at the end determines to reenlist and continue fighting. Others on the Union side include Dietrich Herz, German immigrant, who loses both his legs; A. B. Tilbury, cannoneer from Maine; and James Dacy, illustrator for the *New York Illustrated News,* essentially a bystander who tries to rally the fleeing Yankees. Other noncombatant observers are Nathaniel Epp, a photographer who does a brisk business making portraits of soldiers who are afraid they will die leaving no record of their existence, and Edmund Upwing, a cabman who drives a group of wealthy people from Washington to picnic and enjoy the spectacle of the battle. On the Confederate side, among others, are little Toby Boyce, 11, who joins the army band but, itching to be in the conflict rather than in the rear, sneaks off toward the fighting until, horrified and repelled by the mayhem and suffering, starts walking back to Georgia; Shem Suggs, a simple lover of horses who enlists in the cavalry to be near them and is most affected by their deaths and suffering in the battle; Dr. William Rye, healer by profession and personal philosophy, who nonetheless becomes part of the southern forces and works to exhaustion amputating shattered limbs, sewing up wounds, trying to save the men he can with few supplies under terrible conditions; and Carlotta King, a slave brought along by her master, who wades across Bull Run and heads north. A couple never see the battle but are nevertheless deeply affected: Flora Wheelworth, a Virginia woman, takes wounded into her home and nurses them, both Southerners and Northerners, and Lily Malloy, 12, of Minnesota, loses her brother Patrick, who enlists mostly to get away from their abusive father and is killed at Bull Run. The kaleidoscopic picture is made somewhat easier to follow by small woodcuts introducing the brief chapters, each containing the initials of the speaker and a motif identifying his or her role, and fine maps of the battle area on the end papers. Though on a much smaller scale, the book is similar to the PBS Civil War series, giving a picture of the conflict through individuals who played a part. While the novel demands a fairly sophisticated reader, it may not be difficult for young people used to following television programs with several concurrent story lines. It is designed also to be performed as readers' theater. ALA; Fanfare; O'Dell; SLS.

BUNKHOUSE JOURNAL (Hamm*, Diane Johnston, Scribner's, 1990), period novel in the form of a diary written by a young worker on a sheep and cattle ranch in southwestern Wyoming in 1910. Hurt and furious after his father, once a lawyer and now an alcoholic and derelict whom he has been supporting, attacks and humiliates him in front of all the people in the boarding house where they were living, Sandy Mannix, 16, has run off from Denver. He has made his way to the isolated ranch near Rock Springs of his cousin, Karen* Hamilton and her husband, John, where he has worked for the summer. His journal starts at the end of the season. John is upset because Ed, the only ranch hand who usually stays through the winter, has left, saying Sandy needs a home more than he does. Through the fall Sandy is worried about John's hostility and haunted by a mental picture of his father's freezing to death in an alley. Through Karen's sister in Denver, he sends a letter to his father and learns that his older brother, Doug, who has previously refused to take any responsibility for their father, is paying for a bed in a disreputable, fleabag hotel for him. With some of his summer earnings, Sandy has a mail-order quilt sent to his father. He also orders winter clothes for himself and new violin strings for Joanna* Lockridge, a twelve-year-old orphan who runs an even more isolated sheep ranch with her aging, half-blind great-aunt Bea, a pair whom Karen and John try to help. When the Donnevilles, nearby ranchers, have a dance for everyone in the surrounding area, Karen makes a dress for Joanna, and they all go together, but the occasion is marred when Mrs. Donneville's sister, Christine, flirts with Sandy and hurts Joanna's feelings. Shortly before Christmas, a letter from Karen's sister reports that Sandy's father died after a drunken fall. Gradually through the bitter, lonely winter, with the help of sympathy from Karen and Joanna, Sandy comes to terms with his father's death and his earlier rejection, even learning something of the unhappy marriage of his parents and the influence of his grandmother, who spoiled her son and destroyed her daughter-in-law's chance of happiness. He also comes to understand John better and to see that the relationship between John and his father paralleled that of his own. By mid-April, Karen is about to have a baby, after previous miscarriages. Sandy has decided to go back to Denver in the fall, to a year in college for which his grandmother set up a trust fund before her death. He leaves open the possibility that he may return to file a homestead claim on land and eventually team up with Joanna. Unlike journal entries in many other novels that use this form, these are convincing; they are neither too long nor too literary for a boy turning seventeen, nor do they explain to the reader things one would expect the writer to take for granted. Sandy's vacillating between anger at his father and worry about him, and, after the death, his deep depression, ring true, as does his confusion about the problem of Christine and Joanna. A picture emerges of a sensitive boy, forced to care for an irresponsible parent after his grandmother's death when he was twelve, craving love and appreciation but always unsure of it. The cold, the loneliness, and the hard work of a ranch winter before good roads, automobiles, radio, or electricity are made graphically clear. Western Heritage.

BUNTING, (ANNE) EVE(LYN BOLTON) (1928–   ), born in Maghera, Northern Ireland; prolific writer of picture books and novels for middle school readers and young adults. In her first fifteen years as a professional writer, she published more than one hundred books and has continued her amazing output— some novels of suspense, many problem novels on contemporary themes, a number set in Ireland, some lightweight fare for younger readers. Among the last is *Coffin on a Case** (HarperCollins, 1992), a detective novel for middle-school readers that won an Edgar Allan Poe Award. Somewhat more serious but for the same age group is *Our Sixth-Grade Sugar Babies** (HarperCollins, 1990), about a class project to teach children that parenthood requires responsibility. Bunting is a graduate of Methodist College and attended Queen's University, both in Belfast, before emigrating to the United States and becoming a citizen. She and her husband live in Pasadena, California. For earlier biographical information and a title entry, see *Dictionary, 1985–1989* [*Is Anybody There?*].

BUSS, FRAN LEEPER, minister, teacher, oral historian. She grew up in a small midwestern city, married young, had three children, and was divorced while living in the West. Her struggle to survive and support her family, which included a period on welfare, gave her strong empathy for women in similar plights, and although she later remarried and completed her formal education, she has dedicated much of her professional energy to recording the stories of such women and aiding them. She has been a campus minister in the United Church of Christ, has taught women's studies at the University of Wisconsin at Whitewater, and has been founder and director of a women's crisis and information center. She has traveled widely in the United States, taping the life histories of poor and working-class women of various ethnic and racial backgrounds, a collection now placed with the Schlesinger Library on the History of American Women at Radcliffe College. These recordings form the basis for her books for adults, among which are *Dignity: Lower Income Women Tell of Their Lives and Struggles* (University of Michigan Press, 1985) and *La Partera: Story of a Midwife* (University of Michigan Press, 1980). Her experiences aiding Salvadoran refugees led to her novel, *Journey of the Sparrows** (with Daisy Cubias, Lodestar, 1991), a story of a young girl who arrives in Chicago nailed into a crate with her pregnant sister and her little brother, of their desperate efforts to survive as undocumented immigrants, and of her return to Mexico to retrieve her baby sister who was abandoned there when their mother was arrested and returned to El Salvador. It received the Jane Addams Award. Buss lives with her husband in Tucson, Arizona.

BYARS, BETSY (CROMER) (1928–   ), born and raised in Charlotte, North Carolina; graduate of Queens College; for twenty-five years a popular writer of realistic novels of contemporary family life for early adolescents. Although most of her books are individual, some appear in series, including the lighthearted set about the unusual Blossom family. Also for middle graders are the series about the misadventures in growing up of twelve-year-old Bingo Brown. Named to the *School Library Journal* list of best books for children were *Bingo Brown and the Language of Love** (Viking, 1989), which was also selected by Fanfare; *Bingo Brown, Gypsy Lover** (Viking, 1990), which was also an American Library Association Notable Book; and *Wanted . . . Mud Blossom** (Delacorte, 1991), an engaging dog story, which also won the Edgar Allan Poe Award, was named to Fanfare, and was selected as a best book by the American Library Association. Previously she received the John Newbery Medal for *The Summer of the Swans* (Viking, 1970). For earlier biographical information and title entries, see *Dictionary, 1960–1984* [*The Cartoonist; The House of Wings; The Midnight Fox; The Night Swimmers; The Pinballs; The Summer of the Swans*] and *Dictionary, 1985–1989* [*The Burning Questions of Bingo Brown; The Blossoms and the Green Phantom; Cracker Jackson*].

BYRD (*Baby**), Larkin's grandmother, described as an elegant, regal woman of seventy, with white hair piled high and "rows of neck wrinkles like necklaces." She affects eccentric clothes, like lacy, black long underwear decorated with tiny jewels. Byrd is practical and realistic, however, and she knows the danger to the family in taking in Sophie, a year-old baby left in the driveway. She hopes the child's presence will prove to be healing (a baby boy had died shortly after birth) as it does, and informs Larkin and Lalo* of the importance of giving Sophie something of them to take away with her when her mother, Julia*, comes for her. Although in speaking to the children in this way, Byrd refers to such intangibles as love and memories, she also gives Sophie her ruby necklace, which becomes an item the child cherishes and always carries. Sophie wears the ruby when she returns ten years later for Byrd's funeral.

C

CADNUM, MICHAEL, author of short stories, poetry, and several novels, including two nominees for the Edgar Allan Poe Award: *Calling Home** (Viking, 1991), a psycho-thriller about a teenaged alcoholic whose addiction drives him to murder a friend; and *Breaking the Fall** (Viking, 1992), about a teenaged boy caught up in a dangerous game of breaking and entering for thrills. Both books are skillfully constructed for maximum suspense. Cadnum has also published books of poems, among them *The Cities We Will Never See* (Singular Speech, 1993); several short story collections, including *Ghostwright* (Carroll and Graf, 1992) and *The Horses of the Night* (Carroll and Graf, 1993); and *Nightlight: A Novel* (St. Martin's, 1989), for adults. He has made his home in Albany, California.

CALIFORNIA BLUE (Klass*, David, Scholastic, 1994), environmental novel with father-son relationship problems, set in the early 1990s in the small northern California lumber town of Kiowa. When John Rodgers, 17, a high school distance runner, discovers a butterfly not listed in any of his field guides, he does not tell his father, who has never been sympathetic to John's interest in "bugs," or his mother, who is upset by her husband's recently discovered leukemia. Instead, he takes his specimen in his terrarium to his biology teacher, Miss Anne Merrill, upon whom he has a secret crush. Miss Merrill gets in touch with her professor at the University of California, Hammond Eggleson, a world-class entomologist, who hurries to Kiowa. John leads them by a back way to the place he found the chrysalis on land belonging to the lumber company for which his father and most of the men in town work. After his parents go to the hospital in San Francisco, John, alone for the first time in his life, learns two things, both indirectly: that his father's cancer is much further advanced than first suspected and that Dr. Eggleson is going to address a town meeting about the possibility of stopping the cutting of old-growth trees to protect the butterfly's habitat. With a premonition that his life is about to change drastically, John attends the meeting, where Dr. Eggleson suggests a reasonable compromise that is rejected by the angry crowd. Although he has tried to keep John's role a secret, at a critical moment the boy stands up and takes responsibility for the find. The next morning he has half a dozen angry and threatening messages on the answering machine and eggs spattered all over the front of the house. At school he is at first shunned, then beaten up. When he gets away, he boards a bus to San Francisco. There he wanders around and takes a room at a small hotel, where the kindly manager tries to talk him into going home. Moved by the man's genuine concern, John tries to contact his parents, only to learn that they have returned to Kiowa. Impulsively he crosses the Bay Bridge to Berkeley and looks up Dr. Eggleson, who takes him to a meeting of environmental activists about to start for Kiowa to stop the accelerated cutting of old-growth timber, the lumber company's response to the threat of a restraining order. John rides to Kiowa with a young activist named Mark and joins the others in a march to the mill, where a group of angry workers awaits them. In the ensuing fracas, he meets his father, who raises his hand to strike John. To his own horror, John swings at his father, connects with his jaw, and knocks him down. Appalled, John runs and is overtaken by Miss Merrill in her car. She takes him to her apartment and lets him spend the night there but gently rebuffs his sexual advances. In the morning his mother, frantic with worry, comes to Miss Merrill's apartment, finds him there, and persuades him to come home. When they meet again, his father is still hostile, but he does come to watch John run in the last meet of the year, the first he has ever seen, since he and John's older brother were football players and considered track a sissy sport. John comes in, as usual, second. On the way home he takes his father, both certain he is dying, to see the blue butterflies, now officially named Rodgers California Blue, in the company forest, and they talk for the first time. Although there is no mutual understanding, John does learn something of his father's childhood struggle under a brutal alcoholic father, and his father sees what means so much to John. The book's strength lies in its avoidance of easy answers or a happy ending. In spite of its clear preference for the environmental point of view, it shows the legitimate concerns of the townspeople fairly and the extremism of some of the activists. John's misery at being caught between the two groups is well depicted. The romance developing between Miss Merrill and Dr. Eggleson is predictable and contrived, but not important enough to harm the novel. SLJ.

CALLIE (*Mama, Let's Dance**), seven-year-old little sister of Mary Belle and Ariel*. A sweet, pretty child with fragile health, she is very close to her Mama, with whom she loved to dance and who abandoned her and her siblings. She is a gentle, fun-loving girl, well liked in school and chosen to be May queen. She knows that Mary Belle is under great pressure and tries to behave for her but sometimes rebels anyway. Callie enjoys making lists, and after Callie dies, Mary Belle finds a list in which Callie says warm and loving things about Mary Belle, ending with the comment that Mary Belle is her ''best friend.'' Although the list hurts, it is also a consolation to the girl to read the words that she had longed to hear spoken and to know that Callie understood, in part at least, Mary Belle's problems.

CALLIE THOMPSON (*Learning by Heart**), Rachel's African-American classmate and eventually her closest friend. At the beginning of fifth grade, Rachel notices that Callie is the only black child in school and for the first time actually understands why. The African-American children all go to a different school in the de facto segregated community. Callie is a fine student and at least overtly does not suffer from racism. She is the leading Girl Scout, with the most badges in the troop. Rachel is proud to be her camp buddy and responds when Callie keeps her from settling for less than her best.

CALLING HOME (Cadnum*, Michael, Viking, 1991), psycho-thriller set in recent years in Oakland, California. Although he will not admit to having the disease, narrator Peter Evers, 16, shows the classic signs of alcoholism. He cannot sleep without a substantial nightcap, needs a drink to function in the morning, plans his drinking carefully, fondles bottles lovingly, and often drinks alone. His grades have dropped drastically, he has few friends, and he gets on poorly with his divorced mother. Once a promising art student, he cares little any more about that pursuit and less and less about his classes. He has three chums he hangs out with: fun-loving, teasing, happy-go-lucky Mead Litton; pretty, unhappy, spoiled Angela, who steals bottles for him from her father's liquor supply; and serious African-American Lani, who is talented on the piano and at softball. While on a midnight drinking spree in the basement of the empty house next door, Peter blasts Mead in the head with his fist, a terrible blow that strikes the other youth dead instantly. Mead had jokingly picked up a bottle of cognac prized by Peter and dropped it to the floor where it shattered, spraying liquor in all directions, infuriating Peter, and provoking the fatal blow. Although Peter leaves Mead's body lying there, he is sincerely concerned about the Littons, especially Mr. Litton, who is in poor health, and during the next eight weeks he phones them regularly, pretending to be Mead, assuring them he is all right, and giving them the impression that he has run away. Peter lies cleverly also to their mutual friends and Inspector Ng. His life outwardly goes on in much the same way as before. He cruises around and has sex with Angela, whose older brother Jack unsuccessfully warns him to stay away from; is hauled into the school office a couple of times for poor grades; socializes a little with elderly Ted, a neighbor whose hobby is toy trains; has spats with his mother; visits his father in southern California, with whom he considers living, but learns that his father is marrying again; and is encouraged by Lani to resume his art. During these weeks he becomes gradually more and more obsessed with death, however, and sometimes even feels he has become Mead. He continues to drink and once almost steals his mother's jewelry to buy liquor. The Littons, increasingly puzzled and hurt by what they believe is their son's odd behavior, tape a phone call, conclude that Peter is impersonating Mead, and confront him with their suspicions. On his way home from this encounter, Peter confesses to Lani, whose lawyer father gets him to the district attorney and eventually into treatment. Peter is remanded to Camp Modoc in northeastern California, evidently a work and treatment center, and book's end finds him home again. He must continue therapy but seems unable to differentiate himself from Mead. The book opens dramatically with one of Peter's laconic, evasive telephone calls to the Littons, a scene that teases the reader about who is calling whom and why, gives a good sense of Peter's slippery hold on reality, and some idea of the deviousness of the alcoholic mind. The meandering pattern of the rest of the book accentuates the tension, supports Peter's psychological disintegration, and gives the feel of the hazy world of the alcoholic. The last pages of the novel, which deal with Camp Modoc and the aftermath, are too sparing in details to be completely clear. Poe Nominee.

CALVIN BOSKER (*Monkey Island**), "an old [street] man with a thick, tangled white beard, muddy, sunken eyes, and hanks of gray hair hanging on either side of his long, shrunken cheeks," who befriends Clay Garrity, allows him to share his sleeping quarters in a broken wooden crate, and gives him advice and encouragement. Educated and articulate, Calvin once taught tenth-grade mathematics but lost everything in a fire after he retired. He then took to the streets. Often cross, cynical, and inebriated, he was saved from death by Buddy* Meadowsweet when he lay drunk under a laundry truck and has been living with Buddy ever since. When Buddy visits Clay in the hospital, Buddy reports that Calvin is very ill ("all the drinking, all the years. Losing everything. Being lonely"), and when Buddy and Clay talk later, after Clay has found his mother, Buddy informs Clay that Calvin is dead. Like Clay, Calvin has family elsewhere, but they have disregarded him. Calvin represents aged unfortunates in society.

THE CANADA GEESE QUILT (Kinsey-Warnock*, Natalie, illus. Leslie W. Bowman, Cobblehill, 1989), realistic novelette set in the hills of northeastern Vermont just after World War II, in which a young girl discovers that life brings change and nothing remains the same. Ten-year-old Ariel lives happily on the family farm with her father, mother, and maternal grandmother. Soon after she sees the Canada geese returning in March, she learns that her mother will have a baby in the fall and starts to worry about how it will feel to be a big sister and about what present to give the new baby. Grandmother comforts her by sharing some of her experiences as the eldest of eight children and also helps her plan a special quilt for the baby. A gifted artist, Ariel draws a picture of three Canada geese flying over cattails, which Grandmother, a talented quilter, starts to make into a coverlet. When Grandmother suffers a stroke and must be hospitalized for some weeks, Ariel worries about her and also about the unfinished quilt. After Grandmother comes home, somewhat disabled, withdrawn, and often abstracted, and lies silently in her bed, Ariel feels alienated from her and the family. One day, however, Ariel decides to share what happened in school that day with Grandmother, and although the old woman does not respond, Ariel continues to tell her about her experiences anyway. Gradually the old woman opens up, and by the time the baby comes, she is able to walk and speak, though with difficulty, and even to cook and bake. Without Ariel's knowing it, she finishes the baby's quilt and makes another almost like it for Ariel. Although she knows her Grandmother will die before many years pass, Ariel appreciates the love the two share. This quiet story of family life promotes the traditional values of family closeness and affection. Everything goes as expected (Ariel even acquires a baby brother), and the book leaves the reader feeling upbeat and reassured about the essential goodness of life. The mostly full-page, black-and-white illustrations (perhaps charcoal) have a pleasing smudginess that accentuates the text's respect for nature and create the sense of memoir. ALA.

CANDY ARELLANO (*The One Who Came Back**), Candelario, classmate of Alex Grant and Eddie Chavez, who suffers from a disease that makes his bones brittle so that they break easily and heal poorly. He pulls himself through the halls on short crutches, always waiting until the other students are in classrooms to avoid the risk of being bumped. An irrepressible showman, he makes a production of his late entrances and lists ''stand-up comedian'' on his questionnaire about career preferences. Since their classmate, Gwen Martens, worked as a volunteer in Children's Hospital where he was a patient, she and Candy are old friends. When Alex has a fight in the cafeteria, Candy joins in by striking Alex's opponent with his crutch and is knocked down but miraculously is not injured. It is mainly the thought of Candy, who left blank the portion of the questionnaire asking what he expected to be doing in ten years, and the crippled boy's love of life that keeps Alex from shooting himself.

CAPTAIN ANDREW JAGGERY (*The True Confessions of Charlotte Doyle**), master of the *Seahawk* on which Charlotte Doyle makes her transatlantic voyage from Liverpool to Providence in 1832 and where Zachariah* is cook, carpenter, and surgeon. The captain has such a reputation for cruelty toward his men that no one will sign on his ships. On this voyage, the crew consists of men previously brutalized by him. Having attempted unsuccessfully to get redress in the admiralty courts, they decide to take justice into their own hands, sign on again, and mutiny while at sea. After the hurricane, Charlotte sees the captain differently; he is not elegant in appearance as she had previously thought, being the worse for the storm's wear, and she notes that the furnishings in his cabin are tawdry and cheap. Thus his appearance is symbolic of her newly gained knowledge of his character and an important stage in her growing up. Although the stereotyped sea captain villain, his character is drawn with some subtlety.

CARL (*The Cookcamp**), a truck driver at the Minnesota construction camp seemingly as large as the vehicle he drives. A snoose-spitting (snuff-using), ham-handed man of few words, and those with a northern European dialect, Carl is ironically motherly in the way he carries and treats the unnamed boy protagonist. At the store in Salvang, Carl buys the boy a pocketknife with two blades and a black handle with an eagle on it. The boy is very proud of the knife, although having it increases his longing for his mother. Like his partner, Gustaf*, Carl exhibits the kindness and warmth of the work-hardened, rough-talking construction men.

CARVER MIDDLETON (*Staying Fat for Sarah Byrnes**), the boyfriend of Eric Calhoune's beautiful writer mother. Throughout most of the book, Eric considers Carver a wimp, but the man eventually earns his deep respect, and at the end Eric decides to call him Dad, whether or not Carver and his mother ever get married. Eric has learned that Carver served two tours of duty in Vietnam, although he was dubious about American objectives, because he felt it was the right thing to do under the law. Afraid that Mr. Byrnes, even if caught, will get off with only a token punishment of perhaps seven years in prison for assaulting Eric, Carver hunts the man down and beats Mr. Byrnes until his face is almost unrecognizable. Later Carver admits freely that what he did was wrong under the law but feels his action was morally justified. Eric comments: "Boy, ain't it a trip where heroes come from."

CASSANDRA (*The Harmony Arms**), middle-aged psychic who lives at the Harmony Arms Apartments and becomes friends with Sumner* and Gabriel* McKay. A very large, much overweight woman, she wears a Dodgers baseball cap and garishly patterned muumuus with huge pockets, in which she carries cans of beer that she pulls out and drinks with a flourish. She gets around on black roller blades with green neon laces, when she is not tearing about in her old, decrepit Nash. Her psychic abilities were recognized when she was very young, and once she was highly regarded for her predictions by famous movie stars. She still makes predictions, which sometimes come true in an offbeat way. Cassandra is easy to be around because she looks for people's good points and makes comments that boost people's egos. She says that in her next incarnation she wants to be a catcher for the Astros. She values her friends highly. Cassandra is the stereotype of the faded, goodhearted, likable alcoholic.

CASSEDY, SYLVIA (1930–1989), born in Brooklyn, New York; graduate of Brooklyn College; teacher of creative writing, translator, and writer for children and young people of fiction and poetry. After publishing stories for picture books, she turned to novels, which are notable for how sensitively they depict the innermost thoughts and feelings of early adolescents. Among these is *Lucie Babbidge's House** (Crowell, 1989), a fantasy about an orphan girl who creates an existence for dolls she discovers. Published posthumously, the book was named to the Fanfare list. For earlier biographical information and a title entry, see *Dictionary, 1985–1989* [*M. E. and Morton*].

CAT (*Journey**), Journey's older sister, no age given, who seems so accepting of her mother's departure that she either has been expecting it or has not been particularly close to the woman. Cat exhibits a wry, sardonic sense of humor, for example, when she notes that Grandfather* and Journey are "two of a kind," a remark that somewhat prepares the reader for the conclusion. Cat says that Grandfather takes pictures because he "wants to give you [Journey] back everything that Mama took away," a statement that, since little of the family past life is described, has minimal meaning for a thinking reader. Cat is realistic enough to get Journey out of bed when he retreats there and to state, also sardonically, that Mama cares about them "the only way she can," which is from a distance and with money. Cat overshadows her brother in interest as a character.

CAT RUNNING (Snyder*, Zilpha Keatley, Delacorte, 1994), period novel of a girl's growing up during the Great Depression in the northern California town of Brownwood, in which a major element is a community of Okies, displaced persons from the dustbowl of the Midwest. The third-person account is tightly focused from the point of view of Cat (Catherine) Kinsey, 11, called Fast Cat, because she is the fastest runner in school and expected to win the top money prize for her school in the footrace at the annual Play Day (field day) for the schoolchildren of the region. Cat has begged her father, Charles*, a storekeeper, to allow her to wear slacks like the other girls when she runs, but he refuses, ostensibly on religious grounds. In retaliation, she stubbornly refuses to race. Furious at him and at her mother, Lydia*, for not supporting her request, Cat runs deep into the canyon down past a cascade to a remote area, where she discovers a small, secluded grotto. She fixes the place up as a kind of clubhouse and furnishes it with a few cherished items, among them her doll Marianne. The grotto becomes her refuge from what she sees as her father's abrupt, authoritarian, penny-pinching ways; her mother's spineless attitude and frequent illnesses; the chiding of her much older half-brother, Cliff; the snide remarks of her much older half-sister, Ellen, who dislikes Lydia; and her classmates' teasing, because an Okie boy, Zane* Perkins, whom everyone despises, handily wins the footrace on Play Day. After she discovers a filthy ragamuffin of four or five in the grotto one day, events occur that lead her to see both Zane and her father differently. The child turns out to be Sammy (Samantha) Perkins, Zane's little sister. Although Cat yells at the child to stay away from the grotto, she also feels guilty about keeping the pitiful little girl from playing with Marianne, whom Sammy calls Lillybelle. Although most people look down on the Okies as thieving ne'er-do-wells, Cat becomes interested in the Perkins children, who also include Spence and Roddy, both younger than Zane but older than Sammy, and in their story, how they once had a home and farm in Texas, which they lost to a bank. Since then they have been migrants, following the crops. When she learns from Zane that Sammy is ill with "dust-lung," a respiratory infection, Cat visits the child in the Perkinses' dilapidated shack in Okietown, taking with her an old sweater that she knows Sammy can use. She learns that the Perkinses plan to leave for Bakersfield because there is no more work in the Brownwood area, and she asks her father to hire Mr. Perkins to help at the store. After he refuses, she learns from Cliff that the store is almost bankrupt, and she begins to see her father differently. When heavy rains close the school, Cat checks on the grotto and finds it flooded. She retrieves Marianne-Lillybelle and takes the doll to Sammy. The Perkinses are upset because the little girl has worsened, probably with pneumonia. Since Mr. Perkins cannot get the old Studebaker to work and everyone else has left Okietown, Cat offers to run for help, and Zane joins her. They race to Cat's house, a terribly hard run barefoot in the drenching rains. Cat blurts out their story, admits Zane outran her, and then faints. The Kinsey family doctor hospitalizes Sammy, and he and his wife take in Mrs. Perkins, while the rest of the Perkinses prepare to move to Bakersfield, where the government is constructing a camp for the Okies. Before they leave, Zane appears at Cat's door with a handkerchief his mother has embroidered for her and a letter from Sammy inviting Cat to visit her in the hospital. Zane and Cat shake hands and part friends, each respecting the other's ability to run. Although there are some exciting moments, this is a quiet story for the most part. Sammy's speeches are unconvincing, and the Okies' unschooled speech seems forced, but Zane, Sammy, and Cat are well-drawn figures. The area around the grotto, Cat's discovery of the grotto and furnishing it, and her feelings about her father, Zane, and the Okies are depicted in credible detail. Best is the convincing way that Cat grows in her understanding of her father and of the plight of the Okies, as exemplified by Zane and Sammy. SLJ.

CATHERINE, CALLED BIRDY (Cushman*, Karen, Clarion, 1994), period novel set in 1290 in Stonebridge, Lincolnshire, detailing the growing up of an English girl of country nobility and her efforts to assert that she is more than a piece of property, to be sold in marriage to the highest bidder. At thirteen, Catherine, who is known in her family as Birdy, begins a journal, inspired by Edward, her brother who taught her to read before entering an abbey and who thinks it may help her learn to control her volatile emotions. In the year her writing covers, she faces a number of serious problems, the most plaguing being her father's effort to find her a husband willing to forgo a dowry and pay handsomely for the privilege. She manages to discourage the first few suitors who turn up at their manor house by blacking out her front tooth, acting crude or wild, or even setting fire to the privy when one is inside, but the middle-aged man she refers to as Shaggy Beard is not put off by her behavior. She is continually at odds with her father, Sir Rollo, from whom she has inherited her stubborn and assertive character and who responds by smacking her across the head or seat. She is frequently in conflict with her eldest brother, Robert, who teases, pinches, and belittles her, and with her nurse, Morwenna, who corrals her to do needlework and other ladylike tasks and slaps her soundly for impertinence or efforts to escape. Even her gentle mother, Aislinn, tries to shame her into more conventional behavior and direct her to act in a more approved manner. Her true love and admiration go to the goat boy, Perkin, whom she has known all her life and who aspires to be a scholar, but she also has a brief crush on her mother's brother, her uncle George, who returns from the Crusades and falls in love with Birdy's friend, Aelis. Jealous and feeling left out, Birdy tries to work a curse to destroy their love, then suffers guilt when they have a falling out and Aelis is married to a very wealthy boy of seven and George marries a well-to-do widow with a cheerful disposition but a mind a bit off. Birdy also worries about her mother, who has suffered five miscarriages, is pregnant again, and almost dies giving birth to little Eleanor. As a prospective lady of a manor, Birdy is more and more in charge of what nursing and doctoring is done at Stonebridge, especially as her mother is indisposed. Much of the book's interest is in the picture of medieval life, in both the manor and the village, where Birdy joins the activities, and in the abbey, the town of Lincoln, and the castle of Aelis's child husband. The odors, fleas, and discomforts among both the common people and the highborn are fully reported. Each entry is introduced by a quotation from a book of saints' days, many of them with bizarre details and a convincingly medieval tone. While Birdy is clearly an atypical girl of the late thirteenth century, her education and her struggles to control her own life are explained in a believable way, and her feeling of being trapped is well evoked. Her eventual escape from marriage to Shaggy Beard, after she has finally agreed, is predictable but satisfying. Newbery Honor; SLJ.

CECILE BRADSHAW (*When the Road Ends**), schoolteacher sister of Father* Matt Percy, who suffers a concussion in the automobile accident that kills her husband. Afflicted with aphasia, memory lapses, and an injured arm, she nevertheless copes at her isolated cabin and is relieved when mean, fat Gerry leaves, even though she absconds with the grocery money. Before long, Cecile asks the children to call her Aunt Cecile, and she plots with them to keep anyone from knowing their true circumstances. Guided by Mary Jack Jordan and Adam* Correy, she learns to write her name again so that she can sign checks at the grocery store and holds herself together, with difficulty, when her old friend, Al Stewart, comes to dinner. Even before she starts to improve, she shows occasional flashes of her old spunk and dignity and has a more realistic understanding of people than her brother does. In the end, she seems destined to recover and somehow, perhaps through marriage to Al, to keep the children with her.

CELINE (Cole*, Brock, Farrar, 1989), realistic girl's growing-up novel that starts on a Thursday and ends on Saturday a week later, contemporary in period, tone, and structure. While her French professor father is on an extended lecture tour in Europe, Celine Morienval, about sixteen, lives in a tiny Chicago apartment with her stepmother, Catherine, who is only six years her senior and with whom she gets on poorly. Her life during this week, as witty, frank, artistic Celine describes it, is full of stressful situations. It is three weeks before school ends, and Celine's main ambition is to spend the summer with an adult woman friend in Florence, where she can roam the Tuscany hills and paint. Her father has agreed, provided Celine "shows a little maturity," a statement Celine interprets to mean she must pass all her classes, stay out of trouble, and not get pregnant. Problems crop up—some having to do with school, others with her home life. Since she must do a portrait for art class, she decides to paint her friend Lucile Higgenbottom, whom she considers beautiful enough to be in television, but when this does not work out, she elects to do a self-portrait of herself as a beast, a picture she works on throughout much of the book. Her English teacher orders her to redo her composition on *Catcher in the Rye,* an effort that comes to nothing, because she either puts it off or gets interrupted by having to babysit little Jake Barker, about six, who lives across the hall. Since she already has all the academic credits she needs to graduate, Celine's most serious school problem concerns swimming class, which she hates and cuts regularly but which her counselor tells her is an absolute requirement. She must cope with Jake's emotional problems, because his parents are getting a divorce, and she develops a crush on Jake's father, who is also an artist, when she accompanies Jake and Mr. Barker on a visit to Jake's senile grandmother. Also during the week, she has dinner with Lucile and afterward is dragged off to a party by Lucile, Lucile's boyfriend, and Dermot Forbisher, who fancies himself Celine's boyfriend. The party turns wild, and Lucile drinks too much and vomits down the inside of her sweater. The last Saturday is filled with disasters. To help out Mrs. Barker, Celine agrees to deposit Jake with his father, who is to take him to his psychotherapist. She does so, arriving at Mr. Barker's apartment just as Mr. Barker turns up with his current flame, Miss Denver, Celine's lovelorn art teacher. Celine leaves hastily and takes Jake to his appointment. Inadvertently she is ushered into another doctor's office, where she unburdens herself of her problems to the astonished man, who ends up writing her an excuse from swimming, thus solving her graduation problem. In spite of her seemingly scatterbrained ways and apparent reputation at school and home for irresponsibility, Celine shows more levelheadedness and common sense than the adults around her. Her father neglects to keep in touch with the family, her stepmother goes off for the weekend with a professor who takes his mother along, and Mr. Barker seems unable to handle adult male commitments. Celine, on the other hand, realizes that leaving Jake with Mr. Barker would be disastrous for both, has the presence of mind to stick Lucile in the shower to wash away the vomit, and also knows that the truth needs to be told about the wild party. Her conversations with Jake, however, and her reflections and flashbacks show that her self-esteem is none too strong, that she misses her real mother very much, and that her brashness and occasionally idiosyncratic behavior mask a tender ego, perhaps damaged by her unstable family life. Emphasis is on the revelation of Celine's character and feelings and on the psychosocial consequences of divorced, divorcing, and blended families. Although the book's structure seems unfocused, as is the case with many recently published novels, retrospect shows this one to be tightly organized, with the pieces fitted carefully together for effect. The humor both plays down the social commentary and strengthens Celine's characterization, although sometimes it seems too generous and even strained. Celine's discourse is sharp and apt and at times like a stand-up comic's dialogue, filled with one-liners and topical references, which may eventually date the book. As it stands, this is both a funny and a poignant look at a girl whose situation is typical of many young people today. Fanfare; SLJ.

CHARLES KINSEY (*Cat Running**), father of Cat Kinsey and of her half-siblings Ellen and Cliff. He is a graying man of about fifty, some twenty years older than Lydia*, his second wife. Because he refuses to allow her to wear slacks, saying that "women in men's clothing are an abomination," Cat regards him as rigid, crude, and unfeeling. Since their house seems run-down, at least compared to what it once was, and he refuses to fix it up, she thinks he is a miserly skinflint. Charles dominates the family, talking only when he feels like it and most of the time not paying much attention to what anyone else wants. He is the respected owner of Kinsey's Hardware, where both Ellen and Cliff work. After he refuses to hire Mr. Perkins to replace a worker who has retired, Cliff informs Cat that their father is not replacing the worker not because he is too stingy to do so but because the store is facing bankruptcy, as are many other stores in the Great Depression.

CHARLIE WORTHEN (*Lyddie**), younger brother of Lyddie, ten years old when the story starts. Together with Lyddie, he keeps the farm going through the winter after their mother has left with the two younger girls. His mother sells his labor to the miller, where he is well treated and eventually allowed to become an apprentice. A lively, bright boy, he has shared the work with Lyddie and tried to lighten her responsibility, quoting their mother's misspelled letter, "We can still hop." When he comes to fetch Rachel* from Lowell, he has not grown much but seems bigger and strange to Lyddie. Although he originally shared her fervent desire to return to their farm, he sensibly sees that becoming part of the miller's family will be best for him and for Rachel and does not understand the depth of Lyddie's commitment to keeping them together.

CHAZ (*Shadow Boxer**), the young man from the Big Brothers Association assigned to George and Monty*. Ma contacts the association because she feels that her sons need a man in their lives and because she knows that George is becoming too serious about his role as the man of the family. Chaz is pleasant and accommodating and takes his task seriously. Monty likes him right away, but George resists, although he agrees to give Chaz a chance. On their first outing together, Chaz takes them and Fred* the Head to the Basketball Hall of Fame in Springfield, Massachusetts. Chaz tries hard to show the boys a good time, in spite of the obstacles George puts in his way, but on their return home, George tells Chaz that, although he is a nice guy, he should never come back.

CHECKING ON THE MOON (Davis*, Jenny, Orchard, 1991), girl's growing-up novel set in Washco, a run-down section of Pittsburgh, Pennsylvania, at about the time of publication. Cab Jones, 13, the narrator, used to living in Texas with her mother and her brother, Bill, 18, feels abandoned and apprehensive when her mother takes off for Europe with her new husband, a world-famous pianist, leaving Cab with Maddie Doyle, a grandmother she has never met before. Although even-tempered Bill, who is taking summer classes at Pitt, is some help, Cab's whole life is strange to her: working in her grandmother's neighborhood restaurant, EATS; living in the apartment upstairs; missing her friends in Texas. Gradually she gets to know most of the regulars at EATS: Mr. Johansson, the shoe repairman; Hannah, who runs the junk shop; Cranston Oliver, the librarian, known as Shakespeare; Mac, the local policeman; Lucy, who runs the Salvation Army center; Virginia, one of the residents at the center; and her toddler daughter, Marvel. Her life picks up interest when she meets Tracy Sibowski, apparently the only girl in Washco her age, the lively, self-confident eldest in a big family who is convinced that she is destined for greatness, although she is not sure at what. Tracy persuades Cab to enter a summer class in reading and writing taught by Shakespeare, in which she meets Mr. Bernstein, who writes poems to his wife, killed fifty years earlier by Nazis; Mr. Tson from Cambodia, who wants to learn to read the Declaration of Independence; Virginia, who just wants to learn to read to Marvel; and others. Although Washco soon seems like a friendly neighborhood, crime in the area creates problems. Mr. Johansson is mugged and hospitalized. Worse, Jessica, the beautiful girl Bill has been seeing, is raped as she goes from her cashier job at the movie to her car across the street. Bill is so traumatized by the attack on Jessica that he ignores Cab most of the time, leaving her lonely and worried about what will happen to her at the end of the summer. At first stunned, the community is galvanized into action by Tracy's mother, Sally, and Mr. Johansson, and at a meeting at EATS they decide to form patrols to walk the streets and escort late workers home. Mostly Tracy and Cab are relegated to afternoons, but once they walk the midnight-to-three beat with Bill and Tracy's father. Although the streets become safer, the people realize that they need more support from the city, and they organize a vigil, which is so successful that the mayor appears and promises more street lights and police protection. In the middle of the speeches, a taxi pulls up, and Cab's mother and stepfather emerge, just returned from Europe. When they announce that they have enrolled Cab in a school in Belgium, she has mixed feelings—not wanting to uproot her life again, but also glad they have not forgotten her, and surprised that she is now confident she can cope with the change. Since Bill has decided to forgo his scholarship to Wisconsin and stay in Washco to live with Grandmother and give Jessica emotional support, and Cab's stepfather has provided money to hire Virginia and other help at EATS, only Tracy mourns. Cab gives her the advice Bill gave her when they were leaving Texas: look at the moon and think that it is the same no matter where you are, shining on friends everywhere. What happens in the story is less important than the characters, strongly drawn without stereotyping, and particularly Cab, who grows from a hurt, antagonistic child to a self-assured young person able to look forward without fear. Even Cab's mother, who appears only at the opening and briefly at the end, is a well-drawn, believable person. Cab's voice, telling it all, is a skillful mixture of skeptical, vulnerable, and amused. Seedy Washco becomes almost a character itself, with a history and charm behind its faded exteriors, dilapidated buildings, and cobblestone streets. SLJ.

CHILDREN OF THE RIVER (Crew*, Linda, Delacorte, 1989), realistic sociological problem novel about refugees from Cambodia (Kampuchea) set in Willamette Grove, Oregon, in 1979. When in 1975 the Khmer Rouge attack their village on the Mekong River, Sundara Suvann, 13, flees to America with her Uncle Tep Naro's* family, leaving behind in Phnom Penh her father (a teacher), mother, little sister, and childhood sweetheart. Four years later, the Teps live in a new American tract house and drive a new car, both of which they have earned by strict saving and hard work. The adults find their new life difficult and worrisome. Sensible, hard-working Uncle Naro now has a good job as an accountant; irascible, overly concerned Aunt Kem Soka* is a food service worker at the local university; and Grandmother (Naro's mother) grumps and complains, longing for the old days; but the boys, Pon, 6, and Ravy, 10, seem to be quite happy with life in America and have found friends, especially Ravy who likes the technology and football. Bright, pretty, earnest, and responsible, Sundara earns all A's at the local high school, plans to become a doctor, helps about the house, and works in the fields picking fruits and vegetables in season to earn extra money. But she has no friends her age and misses her own family. She wonders what became of them, but she loves and respects her uncle and aunt and has confidence in them when they assure her they will choose a good man for her to marry. Tension arises when she consents to be interviewed for a research paper on Cambodia by handsome, blond football star Jonathan* McKinnon. Although she knows that a good Khmer girl does not speak to boys, especially white ones, she is flattered by his attention and soon is attracted to him. She shares her story with him and discusses Khmer customs and the differences between Khmer and American ways with him. She spends a very pleasant afternoon sailing with him and his father (a pediatrician) and mother and is impressed with their beautiful house, the parents' warmth, and the family's closeness. Trouble comes when Soka arrives home one day while Jonathan is stopping to invite Sundara to go for a ride. When Soka finds out that Sundara has not only been in Jonathan's company at school but also went sailing with him, she is furious and forbids Sundara to have anything more to do with him. Sundara's spirits reach their lowest ebb when a letter brings news of her sweetheart's death. For a time she longs to die, sure that she is being punished in this life for past misdeeds. When Ravy reports that Jonathan has been hurt in a game, however, Sundara visits him in the hospital anyway, glowing in his attention and love. When Soka finds out that the friendship has continued, she threatens to throw Sundara out, but Naro intervenes and calms her. Then Dr. McKinnon, who has volunteered to care for the Khmer who are in a camp in Thailand, asks that Sundara help him with Khmer language and customs. Naro is flattered that a wealthy, high-class American would ask and persuades Soka to allow it. She agrees but with the proviso that Sundara not speak to Jonathan. When they learn that Valinn, Soka's younger sister, has been found and is coming to the United States, aunt and niece reach an understanding. Sundara learns that Soka's extreme protectiveness is not because she is rigidly traditional and wants to impress other refugees, particularly higher-class ones, but because she had promised Sundara's mother always to take good care of her. When Valinn arrives, Sundara learns that her little sister has been found and will also soon be coming to America. Delighted, Sundara shares this good news with Jonathan and tells him she loves him. Since life is both precious and precarious, she concludes that she must share such thoughts and emotions with those she loves while she can. Adding texture to the story are the Teps' refugee counterparts, the Poks, a haughty Cambodian high-class military family who are always ready to criticize and whose son gambles, and the Lams, Vietnamese who also work in the fields for extra money and whose son with his very light skin Soka thinks might be a good match for Sundara. Since the Teps' house is the largest among their group of refugees, the others gather there frequently. Their conversations vividly reveal their disappointments, fears, hopes, and values. The plight of Moni, Sundara's young widow friend, contrasts with Sundara's situation, as does the freedom of the American girls she observes at school. The characters are types and only a few have dimension, and the plot is obvious and predictable and provides the means for conveying information about the refugees. The first chapter describes the dramatic flight and puts the reader squarely on Sundara's side. It points up her reactions to American ways and her desire to fit in yet stay close to her family and Khmer heritage. The river of the title refers both to the Mekong and to the river of life. IRA.

CHIP CLEWT (*The Weirdo**), Charles Clewt, 17, a very bright young man who graduated at fifteen from high school and has been employed for a year and a half helping Tom Telford, a graduate student from North Carolina State, track, tag, and document bears in the Powhatan Swamp. Badly burned in the plane crash that killed his mother and his sister, Chip has undergone numerous surgeries in the past ten years to repair his damaged face and arm, but he still has a bizarre appearance, with half his head normal looking and the other half slick, hairless, and almond colored, and one hand virtually useless. For eight years after the accident, he lived with his grandparents in Columbus, Ohio. His guilt-ridden artist father, John, had tried to drink himself to death, but after a friend from his service days found John, took him to Alcoholics Anonymous, started him painting again, and found him a job as the spillwayman for the Lake Nasemond feeder ditch to the George Washington Canal, Chip has come to live with him in the isolated house, where they see few people. It is an awkward relationship, since Chip hardly knows his father and worries that the drinking may start again. His work with Tom has given him confidence and a great love for the bears they count, but Tom disappears and later is shown to have been murdered. After it becomes known that Chip is working to have the hunting ban extended, someone shoots out the window where he and his father are eating and slashes their car tires. John wants to leave the area, but Chip stubbornly insists on staying to continue documenting bears and to try to discover Tom's murderer. Sam Sanders is the first girl Chip has ever dated or even really talked with, and when she defies her hunter father to stand by him, his spirits soar.

CHOI, SOOK NYUL, born in Pyongyang, Korea; teacher, author, notably of two autobiographical novels set in Korea in 1945. Choi received her B.A. degree from Manhattanville College. She has taught elementary school in New York City and, more recently, creative writing to high school students and has served as an author for a Boston Public Library creative writing workshop. Her *Year of Impossible Goodbyes** (Houghton Mifflin, 1991), the story of her escape with her little brother from North to South Korea after first the cruel Japanese occupation and then the takeover by doctrinaire Russians, received high critical commendation, including citations by the *Bulletin of the Center for Children's Books,* the New York Public Library Best Book for Teenagers list, and the ALA Notable Books list. Its sequel, *Echoes of the White Giraffe* (Houghton Mifflin, 1993), is set in a refugee village in Pusan. Among her other publications is a picture book, *Halmoni and the Picnic,* illustrated by Karen Milone-Dugan (Houghton Mifflin, 1993). Choi has two daughters and lives in Cambridge, Massachusetts.

THE CHRISTMAS KILLER (Windsor*, Patricia, Scholastic, 1991), tense suspense novel set in the 1990s about a serial murderer who is killing teenaged girls during each holiday season in the small Connecticut town of Bethboro. Central to the plot are elements of communication with the dead that are presented as realism but may be considered fantasy. Although she hardly knew Nancy Emerson, Rose (Rosecleer) Potter begins having vivid dreams and waking visions after the slightly younger girl disappears. In the first vision, Nancy appears at her window, and the two fly to a woodsy area, where Nancy points to a grove of pines. Rose's twin, Jerram*, with whom she used to be exceptionally close but who recently seems more distant, advises her to tell someone, but when she and her friend, Grace, report the dreams to the police, she is treated as an overimaginative child. Her dance teacher, Muriel* Westa, thinks she has been working too hard. The town bum, Wallace Romola, a brain-damaged young man rejected by his wealthy family, tries to tell her something but cannot communicate clearly. When Nancy's body is found in pine woods near Cape Cod, the police question Rose again but remain skeptical. Another night Nancy appears again, and Rose flies with her to the Danville dump, where she indicates a pile of old tires. After a second girl, Cynthia, a friend of Nancy, disappears, Jerram suggests she consult old Mackey, the retired police chief, who seems more inclined to think her dreams have significance. As she rides her bike home in the snowstorm, she is trailed by a car but gets back safely, though chilled and coming down with flu. A few days later, when the Danville dump tire pile is investigated, a girl's skeleton is found, having possibly been there for five years. In the case of Cynthia and later, Carla Fentesso, a girl from a nearby town, Rose gets directions from Nancy to their bodies, and although the police promise to keep that information confidential, soon everyone in town knows. On each body is a red plastic flower. The newspaper begins getting enigmatic letters from the killer, and Rose receives anonymous telephone calls in the same vein. Walking home from dance practice, Rose is asked directions from a man who says he knows her father and suggests she get in the car and show him the way. She refuses and later she realizes that if he really knew her father he would know the way to their house. At church, Nancy's mother loudly accuses Rose of being a witch. Together Rose and Jerram visit old Mackey's sister, Martha, who is expert in psychic phenomena, and she helps Rose regress into a state between life and death, where she talks to Nancy and some of the other girls, getting some information about the killer but no clear details. Trying to live as normally as possible, Rose goes to rehearse her dance with Muriel, who has promised to get a "big name in dance" from New York to attend the recital. She finds Muriel, her throat slit, in the bathroom, and a look-alike, obviously Muriel's twin brother, stalking her with a knife. She fends him off verbally for a few minutes, then is saved by Wallace Romola, who beats him viciously with the dancer's baton. The narrative is interrupted frequently by brief passages in the killer's mind, letting the reader know that he has marked Rose for his next victim. In the last passage, when he is in prison, he is already planning to come looking for her when he gets out. The intensity of the novel is increased by false leads, some pointing to Wallace as the murderer, some to Jerram, since the killer mentions his sister and seems to be referring to a twin. The tone of increasing terror is well sustained. Rose is as much afraid of her gift of second sight as of the murderer and is baffled by why Nancy chooses to communicate with her. Her mother's explanation, extracted from her painfully, that Rose died briefly in her womb and then returned to life, is ingenious if not entirely convincing. Full of suspense, this is a genuine thriller. Poe Nominee.

CLARE FRANCES CALDWELL (*The Beggars' Ride**), thirteen-year-old girl who runs away to Atlantic City, New Jersey, to get away from her abusive, alcoholic mother and her mother's boyfriend, Sid, who is molesting her. In Atlantic City, she joins a gang of homeless street kids. A pretty, caramel blond, Clare hacks off her hair and dyes it orange before running; she wears cut-off jeans, a mottoed t-shirt, and her mother's old green spiked shoes, and she helps herself to forty-four dollars from her mother's purse for bus money. Over and over, Clare struggles with her distaste for the way of life she lived with Mama and her conscience over having run away, leaving no word, taking the money, and the stealing she does with the gang. Repeatedly Mama's assertion that she is worthless like her thieving father comes to mind. Finally Clare realizes that the only way she can help herself, the kids, and others like them against the deviant social worker Griffey and his sort is to tell Mama about what Sid did to her. Her telling Mama is an act of true courage.

CLARENCE HOPKINS (*The Road to Memphis**), African-American youth, friend and neighbor of Stacey*, Cassie, Christopher-John, and Little Man Logan. He is the father of the baby whom unmarried Sissy Mitchum is carrying. He joins the army and returns to the Strawberry region for the Reverend Mr. Gabson's funeral, at the time when his friend Moe* Turner assaults the redneck Aames boys. Clarence also is baited by the Aameses but accepts the humiliation. Later, he accompanies Stacey on the drive to take Moe to Memphis, out of the reach of the Aameses although Moe has already begun to suffer headaches. These intensify on the journey, causing him to be of no practical help and eventually to become a hindrance to them. He dies of an unexplained massive attack while being cared for by an old black woman when the others are in Memphis. Sissy cares less for his loss than she does about the possibility of Harris (her twin) being blamed for Moe's escape. Clarence's character, his headaches, and his relationship with Sissy are not as believable as other aspects of the novel.

CLASS TRIP (Rice*, Bebe Faas, HarperCollins, 1993), novel of mystery and suspense set mostly on an island in the western corner of Vermont, presumably in the 1990s. Seven high school students, their instructor, Mr. Holmberg, and his wife spend the first night of their science field trip during spring break at a hostel before embarking on a canoe trip to Shadow Island in Storm Lake, where they will study flora and fauna for extra credit. Angie, the narrator, was formerly a science nerd, overweight and wearing horn-rimmed glasses, but has recently transformed herself and found her way into the crowd that forms the highest social stratum at Oakbridge High School. Still, she cannot forget Michael Giddings, the fellow nerd she really loved, who was killed the previous year in an automobile accident after some of this same crowd tricked him into overdrinking, just for the fun of seeing such a serious boy drunk. Angie has joined the trip at the urging of Christabel Collins, queen of the ''in'' crowd, and Tracy Fisher, swimming champion, both of whom need her help with science. Also in the group are Melanie Downes, Christabel's catty and mean-spirited sidekick; Ron Johnson, Christabel's boyfriend; Chip Marshall, Melanie's boyfriend; and James Sherwood, whom Angie likes best in the crowd but about whom there is some mystery concerning his emotional breakdown and long absence from school the preceding year. When both the Holmbergs are stricken with a severe intestinal affliction, the young people, insisting that they can manage by themselves, take off in two of the rented canoes, but not before they hear reports of an escaped mental patient named Amos Fletcher in the area and learn that the third canoe has been stolen. Shadow Island, when they finally reach it, lives up to its name; it is a gloomy place in the middle of a lake surrounded by high bluffs, and the sun seldom reaches it. The cabin they have been looking forward to is primitive, dirty, and decrepit. With much grousing they start to clean the cabin and outhouse, then separate to collect wood before a threatened rain storm. Six of them return to the cabin, but not Chip. They find him dead near the beach, his head bloody. Horrified, they put his body in a shed and, since it is too late to start back that night, plan to leave early in the morning and meet the Holmbergs, who should be following them by this time. In the morning, however, the canoes are gone. Reasoning that someone else must be on the island, they set off in twos to search, and Angie and James catch a glimpse of a man in a red flannel shirt scrambling down to the lake and reappearing in a canoe headed back toward the river. His departure relieves them, but soon Tracy dies, evidently poisoned by something in her nasal spray. One by one they become victims, until only Angie and James, who have grown very fond of each other, are left. The solution of the mystery is a trick ending, cleverly enough handled but not particularly convincing. The characters are all stereotypes, and the premise that Angie has lost weight, become beautiful, and been invited into the exclusive crowd is hard to believe. Amos Fletcher is a predictable red herring, and even the geography seems designed for the convenience of the plot: the young people travel down a large river and turn into a smaller one, also running downhill, which empties into Storm Lake. Their developing suspicions of each other and the tensions these produce are the strongest elements of the story. Poe Nominee.

CLEARY, BEVERLY (BUNN) (1916–   ), born in McMinnville, Oregon; librarian, long-time author of popular books, mostly episodic novels for eight- to ten-year-olds. Her best-known writings are in four series: the Henry Huggins books, including those about Ellen Tibbetts and the dog, Ribsy; the Ramona books, including those about her sister, Beezus; the fantasies about Ralph, the mouse; and for slightly older children, *Dear Mr. Henshaw* (Morrow, 1983), an epistolary novel of a boy's difficult adjustment to his parents' divorce, and its sequel, *Strider** (Morrow, 1991), in which Leigh Botts acquires a dog, a Queensland heeler, and becomes happier with his life. It was named to the *Horn Book* Fanfare list. Cleary has been the recipient of many other honors, including the 1975 Laura Ingalls Wilder Award from the American Library Association for total contribution to children's literature. For earlier biographical information and title entries, see *Dictionary, 1859–1959* [*Beezus and Ramona; Henry and Ribsy; Henry Huggins*]; *Dictionary, 1960–1984* [*Dear Mr. Henshaw; The Mouse and the Motorcycle; Ramona and Her Father; Ramona Quimby, Age 8; Ramona the Pest; Ribsy; Runaway Ralph*]; *Dictionary, 1985–1989* [*Ramona Forever*].

CLETUS UNDERWOOD (*Missing May**), neighbor boy Summer's* age, whom Summer dislikes. She thinks he is ''insane'' and a ''lunatic,'' because he collects things that she feels are strange, like potato chip bags, and because he so obviously enjoys life. She is also jealous of him because her Uncle Ob* enjoys his company. Cletus likes unusual photographs and clippings and carries his collections around in a suitcase. He urges Summer to use her imagination, which he says is evident in her school writing. His afterlife experience at the age of seven leads to the lightening of Summer's and Ob's grief at losing May*, their aunt and wife respectively. Ironically, he is a colorful foil to the somber Summer.

COFFIN ON A CASE (Bunting*, Eve, HarperCollins, 1992), mystery for middle school readers starring the narrator, Henry Coffin, 12, son of a private investigator in the Los Angeles area, presumably in the early 1990s. While his father is out of town on business, motherless Henry takes on the case brought by sixteen-year-old Lily Larson, whose mother has disappeared. Because she has twice before appealed to the police with false alarms, Lily is reluctant to go to the authorities, but she has various clues: her mother's car is at their isolated house in one of the canyons, with the groceries, some of the frozen goods now melted, not put away; one of the plywood storks she sells to new parents is missing, but the tags that announce ''It's a Boy'' or ''It's a Girl'' are in the car trunk; the careful mileage record, checked with the odometer, shows that Lily's mother came back directly from her last scheduled stop; a blue jacaranda blossom is crushed on the driver's-side floor; the car radio is tuned to a rock station, although Lily's mother listens only to classical music. With Lily's great dane, Maximillian, locked in the house, the mileage record and map in hand, and Lily driving the big red Chevrolet Impala, the two retrace her mother's trail and realize that she might have stopped at one of the newly renovated houses on Chaparral Road. At the first house, Henry, pretending to take orders for his school's chocolate drive, sees a jacaranda tree, and, accosted by a woman as he is peering into the garage, spots one of the wooden storks. By his surprise, he gives himself away and is manhandled into the house and thrown into the basement. There, in the dark, he finds Lily's mother, who tells him that she saw a man carrying what looked like a Snugli, a baby sling worn in the front. She dashed after him, sensing a sale prospect and carrying a stork, only to see that the baby was really a jade statue. She was grabbed and dragged to the basement. Henry remembers his father's reading that a Ming Dynasty statue was stolen from a museum. Realizing that they must get the woman to open the door before her partner arrives and possibly kills them, Henry piles their shoes, his belt, the contents of her purse, and everything else he can find in the clothes dryer, stations himself just beside the door, and gives Mrs. Larson the word to start the machine. At the terrible clatter, the woman opens the door, Henry seizes her wrist and pulls her down the steps, then dashes out and bolts the door behind him. He discovers that the telephone wires have been cut, but he grabs the baby sling containing the jade statue and straps it on just as a man comes in the door. In a wild chase, Henry throws a full dustpan in the man's face, temporarily blinding him, escapes, and jumps into the swimming pool filled with foul water and decaying leaves. Hidden in the muck, he slips off the baby sling, lets the statue sink to the bottom, and stays concealed until police cars, summoned by Lily, arrive. Although the plot is simple, action scenes are gripping. Henry's early adolescent crush on beautiful Lily, who is described as looking like the cartoon goldfish, Cleo, adds humor, and his fantasies about his own mother, who walked out when he was six weeks old, make his strong interest in finding Mrs. Larson plausible. With just over 100 well-leaded pages of fairly large type, the book is undemanding. Poe Winner.

COLE, BROCK (1938–   ), author and illustrator of picture books and novels. *Celine** (Farrar, 1989), about a precocious, artistic, sixteen-year-old girl forced to spend the summer with her stepmother, was named to the Fanfare list by the editors of *Horn Book* and selected as a best book by *School Library Journal.* For earlier biographical information and a title entry, see *Dictionary, 1985–1989* [*The Goats*].

COLLIER, CHRISTOPHER (1930–   ), educator, historian, and writer. A professor of history, he has collaborated with his brother, James Lincoln Collier*, on several highly regarded books of American historical fiction for young readers. The first of these, *My Brother Sam Is Dead** (Four Winds, 1974), is their most critically acclaimed novel. A story of a family's troubles during the American Revolution as told by the younger son, it was a finalist for the National Book Award, a Newbery Honor Book, a Fanfare book, a *Choice* selection, and a Phoenix Award Honor Book of The Children's Literature Association. For earlier biographical information and a title entry, see *Dictionary, 1960–1984* [*My Brother Sam Is Dead*].

COLLIER, JAMES LINCOLN (1928–   ), born in New York City; musican and freelance writer. He has contributed many articles and stories to magazines and journals on various subjects; written books of fiction and nonfiction; and with his brother, Christopher Collier*, a historian and professor of history, published several critically acclaimed novels of American historical fiction, for which Christopher does the basic research and James does the writing. Of their novels drawn from American history, the most honored has been *My Brother Sam Is Dead** (Four Winds, 1974), an accurate, terse, dramatic story of a Connecticut family's involvement in the American Revolution. Told from the standpoint of the younger son, this novel, their first collaboration, was a Newbery Honor book, a *Choice* selection, a Fanfare book, a finalist for the National Book Award, and a Phoenix Award Honor Book of the Children's Literature Association. For earlier biographical information and title entries, see *Dictionary, 1960–1984* [*My Brother Sam Is Dead*; *Rock Star*].

COMAN, CAROLYN, author of *Tell Me Everything** (Farrar, 1993), a novel for middle grade and early teenaged readers, which was named to both the American Library Association and the *School Library Journal* lists of best books. Her first novel, it is the emotionally engaging story of a twelve-year-old girl's coming to terms with the loss of her single-parent mother, who died while rescuing a boy lost on a mountain. Coman also wrote the story for a picture book, *Losing Things at Mr. Mudd's* (Farrar, 1992), and published a book of biographies, *Body and Soul: Ten American Women* (Hill, 1988). She lives in Newburyport, Massachusetts.

COMMANDER COATRACK RETURNS (McNair*, Joseph, Houghton Mifflin, 1989), humorous, often funny, contemporary realistic novel of family and school life in an Ohio city, involving a too-conscientious girl and an overly directed, repressed boy. The best part of life for Lisa Archer, 13, the aspiring astronaut who tells the story, is taking care of her mentally disabled brother, Cody, 5, especially when they play spaceship in the hall coatrack and Cody is Commander Coatrack. Life changes for the worse after Mom and Dad start seeing psychiatrist Dr. Barnes, who urges them to let go of their feelings of guilt at having produced a child with disabilities, relieve Lisa of the responsibilities of taking care of him after school, and spend more time with him themselves. Soon after, Cody is also enrolled in a special school. Another disappointment follows: Lisa has an argument with her best (actually, her only) friend, Van (Vandelle) Barnsdorf, a bright, opinionated, fat, punk-dressing, outspoken feminist, over methods of advancing the cause of women's rights. At just about the same time, Lisa strikes up an acquaintance with another odds-out early teenager: newly arrived Robert Wormer, witty, intellectually active son of an air force colonel. Robert easily assumes different personas at school and elsewhere, apparently on whim. Lisa later learns that these different personalities, especially of those people who succeeded and became famous, like Columbus, Sir Walter Raleigh, and Elvis Presley, help him compensate for feelings of inferiority brought on by put-downs from his authoritarian parents. Caught up in his exotic and exciting behavior, Lisa tries impersonating celebrities, too, like Scarlett O'Hara and Annie Oakley, at school and elsewhere, but at home she becomes even more angry and jealous when she learns that Cody is being encouraged to talk and that Mom is home-coaching him to reinforce what he is getting at school both verbally and substantively. The story's climax comes when Lisa wool-gathers in history class, is jolted from her reverie by her teacher, pretends to be Eleanor Roosevelt in defense, and produces magnificent answers to a series of questions posed by the teacher about Mrs. Roosevelt and her period but also incurs the teacher's wrath and is sent to the principal. Afraid of being expelled and ruining her fine scholastic record, Lisa drops the pretending, an action that puts off Robert. Then Robert is attacked by school bully Jimmy Pinto, who insists that Robert give his own name when asked and stop the acting. When Robert keeps repeating celebrity names anyway, Jimmy beats him up badly. Lisa flees from the schoolyard to Cody's school at the hospital, grabs her brother, and races home to play the coatrack game, attempting to get her life back to what she thinks is normal; to her dismay, Cody does not respond as he once did, having progressed beyond that sort of Lisa-directed play. The upshot is that Dr. Barnes helps the Archers to work together as a family, Mom and Dad sharing responsibility for Cody with Lisa; and Robert, who has become a terrible discipline problem at school after the beating, decides to be just Wormer the Wondrous and with his family sees Dr. Barnes. Van is still ardently feminist but has toned down both her verbal advocacy and her punk appearance, and she and Lisa become friends again. The plot is unevenly sustained and sometimes not well motivated, the children's voices and wisecracks get tiresome, the pitch remains at the top of the register for too long without relief, the ending is predictable, and the meaning of the title is unclear. The adults are mostly ridiculed, with school teachers in particular having few redeeming features; on the whole, they are an inept bunch. Slapstick, hijinks, and punny, flip, smart-aleck chatter keep the book light and fast paced but do not obscure such serious and important issues as parenting, interpersonal relationships within families, and the need for everyone to establish a satisfying sense of self. SLJ.

CONLY, JANE LESLIE (1948–   ), born in Virginia; daughter of Newbery Award–winning author Robert Leslie Conly (Robert C. O'Brien), who has become a highly commended novelist in her own right. After the death of her father, she completed his unfinished novel, *Z for Zachariah* (Atheneum, 1974), and has more recently written two sequels to his fantasy, *Mrs. Frisby and the Rats of NIMH* (Atheneum, 1971): *Rasco and the Rats of NIMH* (Harper, 1986) and *R-T, Margaret, and the Rats of NIMH* (Harper, 1990). Both are illustrated by Leonard Lubin and both received Children's Choice citations from the International Reading Association. A departure from her father's work is *Crazy Lady** (HarperCollins, 1993), a novel of neighborhood relationships in which a boy, at first one of a group that harasses an alcoholic woman and her son with mental disabilities, becomes a defender of both. A Newbery Honor book, it was chosen by the American Library Association as a Notable Book for Children and as a Best Book for Young Adults. Conly is a graduate of Smith College and attended the Johns Hopkins University Writing Seminars program. She and her husband, Peter Dwyer, a public interest lawyer and musician, have two children and live in Baltimore, Maryland. For biographical information about Robert O'Brien and title entries, see *Dictionary, 1960–1984* [*Mrs. Frisby and the Rats of NIMH; Z for Zachariah*].

CONRAD, PAM (1947–   ), born in New York City; teacher of creative writing; poet and writer of fiction for children and young people. She has written stories for picture books, books for just-readers, and several well-received novels for early adolescents and young adults. An Edgar Allan Poe Award Winner and a *Boston Globe–Horn Book* Honor Book, *Stonewords** (Harper, 1990) is a time-travel fantasy about a friendship between a contemporary girl and a ghost girl from 1870. For earlier biographical information and a title entry, see *Dictionary, 1985–1989* [*Prairie Songs*].

THE COOKCAMP (Paulsen*, Gary, Orchard, 1991), period novel with socio-logical problem story aspects set for a few weeks during World War II in the forests of northern Minnesota. His father away fighting in Europe and "Uncle Casey" now living with his mother, an unnamed five-year-old Chicago boy is sent to stay with his grandmother* who cooks for a camp of men building a road through the Minnesota forest toward Canada. After a weary and lonely day-and-a-half train ride, where kindly porters look after him, he arrives about midday at the Pine, Minnesota, depot, to find that his grandmother is not there and the agent knows no Anita Halvorson. The agent is persuaded to keep the boy until the train's return run, and late in the day "an enormous dump truck suddenly exploded out of the forest . . . and screeched to a halt barely a foot from the wall of the depot." The small, thin grandmother and the huge, rough, kind driver, Carl*, alight, scoop the boy up, and whisk him over eighty miles of road through the woods to the cookcamp. There the boy does odd jobs and helps his grandmother prepare and serve meals for the nine rough, joking, snoose-spitting (snuff-using) road builders. He thrills to the stories she tells for her "little thimble," as she calls him, about the old days in her native Norway, and in the evenings Gustaf*, the caterpillar driver, holds him on his lap while the men play rousing games of whist. During the day, Gustaf sometimes takes him on the big Cat to load gravel onto the trucks, and Carl often lets him sit on his lap while he drives the big truck to transport and dump the gravel. The summer days pass quickly. On the surface, the boy is happy, but he misses his mother very much, a sadness that steadily increases. Not long after the boy arrives, he lets slip to his grandmother about Uncle Casey. That night he is awakened by the sound of his grandmother's writing, and for several nights after, she pens letters to his mother. During the day she often cries, swears, and swats flies with angry determination. On Friday, the once-a-week trip to town for supplies, Carl takes her and the boy in the big truck to Salvang, where she sends the letters to Chicago, telling the store owner to "mail them good and hard." There are two major excitements at the camp: moving the cook trailer to another site and rescuing Harvey when a tree falls on him, mangling his arm. While the grandmother and Carl take Harvey to town and put him on the train to the doctor, the boy sleeps with the men in their trailer, helps Gustaf make "slum stew," and rides on Pete's truck, where he runs out of spit trying to imitate Pete's snoose-spitting. When he misses his mother so much he bursts into tears, all the men try to cheer him by making faces and tickling him. The grandmother returns with a wire from his mother instructing her "Dear Pump-kin" to take the train home. Before he departs, the grandmother tells him stories about his dead grandfather, Clarence, and their small farm on the northern prai-ries and snuggles him close. When he leaves the cookcamp, the boy does not know he will never again see his grandmother as a boy. The last brief chapter, entitled "Portrait," is the story of the grandmother's life from her girlhood in Norway through the deaths of her nine children to the arrival of the boy with his own son, to whom she gives apple pie flavored "with sugar and simmanon on top" and a glass of milk, as she did years ago to comfort his father. The short, fast-moving story is set up with brief chapters, which are mostly summarized narrative or description. The first one grips the emotions immediately as it sets the domestic situation of a boy not wanted. The episode in which Harvey is injured is also memorable, not only because of the danger involved in the construction work, which is only partially exploited, but also because of the picture it gives of the limited medical assistance of the time. The grandmother is a pleasing character inadequately developed, and the men, mostly presented as hard, tough, ironically polite and tender choral characters, are extremely likable. The descriptions of the woods reveal a keen appreciation for the out-of-doors, and the author's sensory, concrete style makes the descriptive passages vivid. The tone, however, projects an adult's perceptions of what the child must be feeling and thinking rather than presenting the sense of the child's lived experience from his perspective. The reader must intuit much of the lean plot, and the last chapter about the grandmother seems tacked on. SLJ.

COOPER, SUSAN (MARY) (1935–   ), born in Burnham, Buckinghamshire, England; journalist and author of books for adults and children, who has made her home near Boston. She is best known in children's literature for her series of fantasies based on English and Welsh folklore known as *The Dark Is Rising,* of which the last, *The Grey King,* received the Newbery Award. Also based on Celtic lore is *The Boggart** (Macmillan, 1993), an American Library Association selection, about a Canadian family who acquire a mischievous little man while on a trip to Scotland. For earlier biographical information and title entries, see *Dictionary, 1960–1984* [*The Dark Is Rising; Dawn of Fear; The Grey King; Over Sea, Under Stone*].

CORMIER, ROBERT (EDMUND) (1925–   ), born in Leominster, Massachusetts; author best known for *The Chocolate War* (Pantheon, 1974) and other popular and highly controversial novels for young adults. Cormier attended Fitchburg State College and has been a scriptwriter and newspaperman. *We All Fall Down** (Delacorte, 1991), a novel of the random trashing of a suburban home and the aftermath for both the family members and the vandals, shares the use of sociopathic characters and the downbeat ending of his major books, including *I Am the Cheese* (Pantheon, 1977) and *After the First Death* (Pantheon, 1979). It was a nominee for the Edgar Allan Poe Award. In a departure from his usual practice, Cormier wrote *Other Bells for Us to Ring** (Delacorte, 1990) for a younger audience with a girl as protagonist. It was cited by *The Horn Book Magazine* on its Fanfare list. For earlier biographical information and title entries, see *Dictionary, 1960–1984* [*The Chocolate War; I Am the Cheese*] and *Dictionary, 1985–1989* [*Beyond the Chocolate War*].

COUSINS (Hamilton*, Virginia, Philomel, 1990), novel of family life in a small town in the American South, presumably in the late twentieth century. Cammy, 11, is very attached to Gram Tut, 94, and although children are not allowed in the Care Home without an adult, she often sneaks into the nursing home to see her grandmother after day camp, which she attends because her parents are divorced and her mother, Maylene, is working. Her sixteen-year-old brother, Andrew, supposedly keeps track of Cammy but is more concerned with helping their cousin, Richie, who drinks heavily and cannot get or keep a job. Andrew blames Richie's mother, Aunt* Effie, for her son's problems, since she is a perfectionist and sets standards he cannot live up to. Her attitude clearly is affecting her daughter, Patty Ann, who is Cammy's age and strives to be perfect in grades and appearance and is bulimic. Patty Ann also attends day camp, as does another, more distant cousin, Elodie Odie, or L.O.D.* as the children call her, an orphan who lives in the summers in the Christian Shelter while her adoptive mother does migrant labor. Cammy's social status is somewhere between the two—below that of Patty Ann, of whom she is jealous, but higher than that of L.O.D., whom she alternately scorns and sympathizes with. On a group walk at the day camp, the children slide down a steep bank to the Little River, which is in flood from recent rains. L.O.D. loses a sneaker in the mud and, while trying to retrieve it, is swept out into the river toward the deep hole the children call Old Bluety. As the director and the other children watch helplessly, Patty Ann wades in, swims behind L.O.D., and gives her a strong push toward the bank but is herself dragged toward Old Bluety and disappears. In the weeks that follow, Cammy, unable to cope with the horror of her memory and her feelings of guilt, begins to have nightmares and hallucinations, seeing Patty Ann sitting on her bed or walking in her room. She becomes ill and, waking once, is surprised to recognize that the man sitting beside the bed is her father, whom she scarcely knows though he lives in a nearby town and employs Andrew in the summers. He takes her to see L.O.D. who, shunned by the people in town, now lives and works in the migrant camp with her mother. That helps some, but Cammy does not recover until her father and Andrew bring Gram Tut, in her wheelchair, to the house. The old woman directs Maylene in cooking the dinner, but mostly she talks to Cammy, frankly saying that she knows she will die soon, but that they all will die, and that you just "have to put a focus on each little thing that comes before you. Just one thing at a time." When they return Gram Tut to the Care Home, Cammy has begun to "put a focus" on the whole situation and regain control of her emotions. There is some indication that the father may return to the family, or at least become more involved with his daughter. The relationship of the three girl cousins is the center of the story, but Andrew's efforts to help Richie, even though he is blamed by both his mother and Aunt Effie for many of Richie's faults, are also important. The most believable and interesting aspect, however, is the love between the old woman and the little girl. The dialect is rural southern, but otherwise there is nothing except the dust jacket illustration to indicate that the characters are African American. ALA; Fanfare.

COWBOY (*The Beggars' Ride**), Warren, runaway youth of fifteen or sixteen who heads the gang of homeless children with whom Clare* Caldwell exists for several months. In Racer's* words, Cowboy thinks ''he got to watch out for the whole world, take care of every hard case [of runaways] he runs across.'' After the death of his mother, who had been abused by his father, Cowboy ran away from home. ''Bonehead moves'' brought him into contact with Griffey, the social worker whom Cowboy liked and trusted until he discovered that Griffey was peddling his charges for sex. The kids in the gang like, respect, and for the most part obey Cowboy, because they realize that he is sincerely concerned about them.

CRAZY LADY (Conly*, Jane Leslie, HarperCollins, 1993), boy's growing-up novel set in Tenley Heights, a neighborhood of Baltimore, Maryland, at the time of its publication. Motherless Vernon Dibbs is having trouble in junior high, especially in English since he reads poorly and cannot spell. When, by chance, he does a favor for Maxine Flooter, the crazy alcoholic woman who lives in the next block with her mentally disabled son, Ronald, she offers to find him a tutor. Although he has often joined his friends in teasing and taunting Maxine and is leery of getting involved with her, he is worried enough about his grades to go with her to meet Miss Annie, an old black retired teacher living in the other half of Maxine's duplex. Miss Annie sets up a strict schedule for Vernon and asks that he pay her not in money but in such work as cleaning up Maxine's trash-filled yard and digging her a garden. When Maxine is arrested for being drunk and disorderly, he even takes her welfare checks to the jail for her to sign so that Miss Annie can arrange to have the rent paid. He begins to see that when she does not drink, Maxine is a sensible, concerned mother and that Ronald, although he is older than Vernon and does not talk, understands well and has a sweet nature. Vernon is present when Ronald's beautiful special-education teacher makes a home call, and he is so smitten that when she suggests that Ronald could enter the Special Olympics if he had a sponsor and some gym shoes, he volunteers to go with Ronald. Then he organizes a neighborhood carnival to get money for the shoes. To his surprise, even the boys who have yelled at Maxine take part, and many people on the street who have shunned the drunken woman contribute time and talent. Vernon and his friends take Ronald shopping and buy him new clothes and a pair of red-and-white checked Converse high tops with red laces. At the Special Olympics Ronald is greeted by friends from school and has a wonderful time, but on the way home his teacher, who has given them a ride, casually mentions that Ronald will be leaving to live with his aunt and uncle in North Carolina. Vernon is furious and even Miss Annie is surprised, but they learn that Maxine has made the arrangements, knowing that the social services people will take Ronald away from her and exerting what little control she has to send him to relatives. Despite the title, the focus of the book is on Vernon and his development of understanding. Scenes with his siblings show that he has suffered from low self-esteem and that his father is too busy to provide the attention his children need. In the end his father, who cannot really read, asks Vernon to teach him, figuring that he will be more patient than his more academically talented brothers and sisters, an element that seems added to nail down a point but is not well integrated into the rest of the story. Many of the other elements seem contrived for effect. Whether Ronald will thrive in the more stable environment or pine for his mother and familiar neighborhood is not clear, and what will happen to Maxine is not even explored. ALA; Newbery Honor.

CREW, LINDA (1951–), born in Corvallis, Oregon; writer of novels for children and adults. She was graduated from the University of Oregon in 1973 and the next year married Herb Crew. They settled on Wake Robin, a small fruit and vegetable farm near Corvallis. Their experiences with a family of Cambodian refugee farmworkers led her to write her critically acclaimed first novel, *Children of the River** (Delacorte, 1989). This International Reading Association Award winner describes a young refugee girl's difficulties in reconciling her family's traditional ways with the customs of her new country. Crew's family experiences also form the basis for her next novels, *Someday I'll Laugh about This* (Delacorte, 1990), a girl's growing-up story built around the setting of Crew's grandfather's beach cabin in Yachats, Oregon, and *Nekomah Creek** (Delacorte, 1991), an American Library Association Notable Book of nontraditional family life, in which the father keeps house and pandemonium often reigns. Its sequel is *Nekomah Creek Christmas* (Delacorte, 1994). Crew has also contributed to periodicals and written a novel for adults, *Ordinary Miracles* (Morrow, 1992), revolving around the problem of infertility.

CRUTCHER, CHRIS(TOPHER C.) (1946–), born in Cascade, Idaho; high school teacher, child and family therapist, and critically acclaimed author of novels and short stories that address the issues confronting and the attitudes of young adults, often combining teenaged boys, growing up, and sports. His books have been praised for their sympathetic understanding of their subjects and sensitive portrayals of their protagonists. A graduate of Eastern Washington State University, he lives in Spokane, Washington, where he works in the area of mental health. His first four novels—*Running Loose* (Greenwillow, 1983), *Stotan!* (Greenwillow, 1986), *The Crazy Horse Electric Game* (Greenwillow, 1987), and *Chinese Handcuffs* (Greenwillow, 1989)—were all named to the American Library Association List of Best Books for Young Adults, and *The Crazy Horse Electric Game* was also a *School Library Journal* Best Book. Also selected by *School Library Journal* is *Staying Fat for Sarah Byrnes** (Greenwillow, 1993), about the enduring friendship between two young people marginalized by society, he by his girth and she by her disfiguring facial scars. Crutcher has also published *Athletic Shorts: Six Short Stories* (Greenwillow, 1991) and has contributed to *Spokane* magazine.

CUBIAS, DAISY, Salvadoran poet, activist. Coauthor with Fran Leeper Buss* of *Journey of the Sparrows* (Lodestar, 1991), Cubias has suffered many of the hardships detailed in the novel. In the 1980s her sister, brother, and brother-in-law were murdered in El Salvador, leaving behind orphaned children. Cubias lives with her son and her remaining relatives in Milwaukee, Wisconsin.

CURTIS (*The Treasure Bird**), African-American youth, friend of Matt. Curtis and his family live in the apartments not far from the house that Matt's mother, Marly*, has inherited and were built on land once held by Marly's ancestors. Curtis is interested in hunting for treasure and hopes some day to become a professional treasure hunter. He has already done some investigating into Marly's family's treasure and persuades Marly to sign a paper giving him a share of the treasure if they should find it. He buys a house for his family with his share. After Marly pays the taxes and fixes up her house, the rest of the money is invested for the children's college educations.

CUSHMAN, KAREN, born in Chicago; museum director, author of historical period novels for young people. She has two M.A. degrees, one in museum studies and one in human behavior, and is the assistant director of the Museum Studies Department at the John F. Kennedy University in the San Francisco Bay area, where she lives with her husband and daughter. Her first novel, *Catherine, Called Birdy** (Clarion, 1994), narrated as the diary of a medieval girl, daughter of a minor country noble, was named a Newbery Honor book by the American Library Association and a Best Book for Children by the *School Library Journal.* Her second novel, *A Midwife's Apprentice* (Clarion, 1994), is also set in the medieval period.

CUSICK, RICHIE TANKERSLEY (1952–), born in New Orleans; writer of popular horror novels for early adolescents and teenagers. Nominated for the Edgar Allan Poe Award, *Help Wanted** (Archway, 1993) is an action-filled, lighthearted, yet suspenseful gothic novel of a girl who answers a help-wanted ad posted on her school bulletin board and becomes involved in spooky and terrifying experiences revolving around the inhabitants of a large, secluded, old mansion. Among Cusick's other thrillers are *Evil on the Bayou* (Dell, 1984), her first novel; *The Lifeguard* (Scholastic, 1988), winner of an International Reading Association Award; *Trick or Treat* (Scholastic, 1989), named a Book for the Teen Age by the New York Public Library; *Vampire* (Pocket Books,

1991; *Fatal Secrets* (Pocket Books, 1992); and *The Locker* (Pocket Books, 1994). A graduate of the University of Southwestern Louisiana, she lives near Kansas City, Kansas, with her husband, Rick, a book designer, calligrapher, and graphic artist.

D

DADI (*Shabanu**), Dalil Abassi, father of Phulan* and Shabanu and husband of Mama. He represents the ideal desert tribesman and camel raiser. Dadi is clearly the practical strength of the family, and he takes seriously his responsibility to provide materially for and guarantee the safety of those dependent on him. He is kind, gentle, and warm, and Shabanu enjoys his company and loves and respects him. He discusses problems with Mama but makes final decisions and carries them out. He appears mostly in domestic scenes but also in a few rare instances among the men, as when Shabanu observes him wrestling, at which he is good enough that the other men wager on his winning. As does Mama, Dadi knows that strong-willed Shabanu may have a hard time in their culture, and, at the end, after he beats her for running away, he cradles her in his arms and sobs out his sorrow.

DALE THORNTON (*Staying Fat for Sarah Byrnes**), school bully, whom his father insists remain in eighth grade ''until he got it right,'' becomes very antisocial, terrorizes his classmates in various ways, beats them up for their lunch money, and finally drops out of school at age sixteen, still in eighth grade. Because Vice Principal Mautz is their common enemy, Dale joins Sarah Byrnes and Eric Calhoune in publishing the scurrilous underground paper, *Crispy Pork Rinds,* in which they deride Mautz. After Eric joins the swimming team, Sarah and Dale become good friends. Sarah confides in Dale some of the information—that Sarah's mother's ambition was to go to Las Vegas and become a dancer or dealer, and that Sarah's father had deliberately burned her—that enables Eric and Lemry* to help her. Dale also helps Eric get medical attention after Mr. Byrnes knifes him. Dale seems oafish and stupid but is mechanically knowledgeable and has practical good sense.

DAVIS, JENNY (SCHNEIDER) (1953–), born in Louisville, Kentucky; educator, novelist for young adults. Davis received her associate degree from Allegheny Community College and, before earning her B.A. and M.A. degrees from the University of Kentucky, worked as a child advocate for Appalachian region hospitals in Hazard, Kentucky. Later she taught sex education for the Fayette County Health Department in Lexington. Her novel, *Checking on the Moon** (Orchard, 1991), is set in a run-down section of Pittsburgh, a community that rallies its members to patrol their dangerous streets and demand better protection from the city. It was named to the *School Library Journal* Best Books for Children list. Davis's novels are noted for their sensitive and convincing characterization. For earlier biographical information and title entries, see *Dictionary, 1985–1989* [*Good-bye and Keep Cool; Sex Education*].

DAWN MITCHELL (*Owl in Love**), science lab partner of Owl Tycho and the only friend her age Owl has ever had. Dawn's first overture to Owl is in sharing her drop of blood to analyze when Owl tells her that she is afraid she will faint if she draws her own, although actually Owl does not want to reveal that she has black fairy blood rather than the human variety. At Dawn's typical suburban house, she lies cheerfully to her mother, gorges herself on sweets even when she wishes she could lose weight, and views her parents with rather fond cynicism. After she is convinced that Owl has a crush on Mr. Lindstrom, the science teacher, she takes it upon herself to promote the affair, even getting what she thinks is a love potion from Owl's father, mixing it into candy, and leaving it in Mr. Lindstrom's mailbox. Since it is a glove potion, for softening kid leather, it causes only severe hiccups. An undeterred Dawn continues to help Owl, even hiding the boy she thinks is Owl's brother and fears is a convict in her family garage. At the end she complains that she has done all the work of the friendship and that Owl has not even tried to find out about her crush on a schoolmate, and she asks, "You're not used to being friends with anybody, are you, Owl?" Although outspoken and tactless, Dawn is the most perceptive character in the novel, and she figures out before anyone else that Owl and Houle, the boy hiding in the garage, can transform themselves into birds and that Houle is actually Mr. Lindstrom's son, David.

THE DAY THAT ELVIS CAME TO TOWN (Marino*, Jan, Little, Brown, 1991), realistic novel of family life set in the small town of Harmony, Georgia, about forty minutes' driving time from Savannah in the summer of 1964. Problems trouble the narrator, Wanda Sue Dohr, 13, the weeks before her idol, Elvis Presley, arrives in Savannah for a concert. Momma is often irritable, tense, and overworked, particularly since Poppa drinks up the profits from his plumbing business and she must take in boarders to make ends meet. She even rents the little attic room that is supposed to be Wanda's to tart-tongued, bossy, fat April May Dohr, Poppa's younger sister. Wanda dislikes hearing her parents argue, Momma's expecting her to keep tabs on Poppa, and having to help so much around the house, but she does enjoy looking at Elvis's picture, playing his records, and pretending that she is dancing with his arms about her. Things pick up for Wanda and for Momma when a new tenant, beautiful Mercedes* (pronounced Mer-SAY-dez, she insists) Washington, takes the attic room. A pop singer who has been all over, to judge by the stickers on her bags, she has stylish clothes, gorgeous hairdos, and a warm and outgoing manner. Wanda is thrilled when Mercedes mentions that she went to the same high school that Elvis did, though Mercedes hastens to assure Wanda that forty-two others were in the same class. After Poppa returns from a plumber's convention in New York that he simply took off for, he swears off the bottle again, but bickering and frayed nerves continue, although Mercedes is an ameliorating influence because she makes Momma and Wanda feel good about themselves. When Mr. Gingrich, another boarder, offers to drive Mercedes to her Savannah gig one night, Mercedes invites Wanda and Momma to go along as her guests for the performance and dinner. They leave, dressed in their best, after Momma sees Poppa to bed; but he is drunk, so they do not tell him where they are going. They have a splendid time, and on the way home Wanda spots a sign advertising an Elvis concert in September. She hopes that Mercedes can get tickets, since she is sure Elvis will remember Mercedes and want to treat her to a free concert for old times' sake. She even writes to Elvis, signing Mercedes's name. While they are in Savannah, Poppa awakens sober to an empty house and is so worried he decides to join Alcoholics Anonymous. Momma's spirits soon improve, and she feels better about life in general and also about the baby on the way. Poppa decides it is time to get rid of abrasive April May and deliberately sets about getting her long-time boyfriend, Mr. Murphy, jealous. Mr. Murphy proposes, and soon preparations are under way for the wedding. The ceremony over and the party almost done, excitement, stress, and the fear that Poppa may have sampled the punch that one of the Murphys spiked with vodka bring on Momma's labor pains, and the baby, a boy, is born so prematurely they fear for his life. In an acid moment earlier, April May had told Wanda that Mercedes is "a nigger girl," whom Momma should not allow to live in her house. Having received a form letter back from the Presley ticket service, Wanda thinks that Mercedes is simply a liar. She confronts Mercedes about both matters. Mercedes explains that her father was black, her mother white, and her stepfather white, emphasizes that she never said she was a friend of Elvis's, and promises that she will buy tickets for Wanda. All turns out well: the baby survives, Wanda attends the concert with her best friend, and Wanda learns that she needs to be careful about jumping to unfounded conclusions. The book moves fast with superficially developed, stock characters and incidents and tackles too many problems in the manner of the new realism books of the sixties and seventies. Wanda's warm relationship with her father is a good feature; he is never shown as ugly or abusive, just as a nice man whom the other characters say drinks too much. AA immediately changes his life, a turn for the better that seems too pat, and April May is too nasty and mean for credibility. The other boarders are one-dimensional. Mr. Collins is always ready with an apt quotation from literature, and Mr. Gingrich is the understanding plumber's helper at work, a solid support at the boarding house, and hopelessly in love with Mercedes. Mercedes is the most interesting figure, far overshadowing Wanda, who is a generic sort, with whom almost any adolescent can identify. The style is mundane and almost all dialogue. SLJ.

DEFELICE, CYNTHIA, storyteller and author of stories for picture books and of critically acclaimed novels for later elementary and early high school–aged readers. Her most highly regarded book is *Weasel** (Macmillan, 1990), which was named to both the American Library Association and *School Library Journal* lists of best books. A tense and dramatic historical novel set in 1839 in southern Ohio in what was once Shawnee Indian territory, it focuses on the moral dilemma of a boy who gets involved with a renegade Indian fighter. DeFelice's other books include novels of mystery and suspense, *The Strange Night Writing of Jessamine Colter* (Macmillan, 1988), *Devil's Bridge* (Macmillan, 1992), and *The Light on Hogback Hill* (Macmillan, 1993). *Lostman's River* (Macmillan, 1994) concerns threats to the Everglades ecosystem. *When Grandpa Kissed His Elbow* (Macmillan, 1992) and *Mule Eggs* (Orchard, 1994) are realistic picture books, and *The Dancing Skeleton* (Macmillan, 1989) is a folktale retold. A professional storyteller, part of the Wild Washerwomen team of storytellers, she lives with her husband in Geneva, New York.

DEIRDRE MOREAU (*The Mozart Season**), flamboyant, eccentric friend of Allegra Shapiro's mother. Deirdre is a brilliant concert soprano who travels widely and stays with the Shapiros while singing in the Portland, Oregon, area. Allegra thinks her exotic in appearance and behavior but likes her very much and admires her talent. Both attracted to and a little afraid of Deirdre's mood swings, she is astonished and yet comforted when she learns that Deirdre is so nervous about performing that she routinely throws up before concerts and always wears a raincoat to keep from soiling her beautiful dresses. Deirdre gives Allegra needed moral support and encouragement and is the first person who is uninhibited enough to dance with the dancing man ("Why on earth doesn't somebody dance with that man?") whom she calls Mr.* Trouble, and thus Allegra is able to bring some comfort into the old man's life. Deirdre has a tragic past. She lost her young daughter to a hit-and-run driver, her husband could not handle the resulting stress and bereavement and left her, and a new male interest dropped her to pursue a Ph.D. In spite of her sorrows, Deirdre exudes a vibrancy and love of life that are also attractive to Allegra. In one of the book's most memorable scenes, Deirdre spontaneously initiates and leads a timpani concert consisting of interested bystanders on the metal columns in the Portland Rose Garden, a happy, thoroughly involved group of pickup musicians who have a glorious time making their noisy music among the flowers and fountains. Deirdre represents the thoroughly dedicated, typical artist, one whose music has become almost her entire life.

DELIVER US FROM EVIE (Kerr*, M. E., HarperCollins, 1994), realistic problem novel set during the recent devastating floods in eastern Missouri, mostly
on a farm in the bottomlands of the Mississippi River, beginning in September
and lasting one year. Parr Burrman, the sixteen-year-old narrator, is glad that
his older brother, Douglas, is studying agriculture at the university in Columbia,
and that his older sister, Evie, 18, enjoys working their farm and gets along well
with their father, because he, Parr, wants to do almost anything but farm. He
knows, however, that Evie would like to go to college. He knows, too, that
although Dad often supports Evie against their mother, their mother keeps trying
to get Evie to dress and act more feminine, forgo her usual jeans, boots, man's
jacket, slicked-back haircut, and chain smoking, and pay attention to the advances of their young farmhand, Cord Whittle. Parr drops comments here and
there that prepare readers for the revelation later that Evie is a lesbian. The
matter of her sexual orientation takes on importance in the family and attracts
attention in the claustrophobic farming community when she and beautiful,
blond, private school–educated Patsy Duff, indulged and willful daughter of the
wealthy local banker and community "boss," become friends, and rumor makes
them a homosexual item. Mr. Duff blames Evie for leading Patsy astray, the
Burrmans think Patsy is the aggressor, and Dad, who has a note at Mr. Duff's
bank, gets nervous. As the year passes, the family struggles to sort out their
feelings about Evie's homosexuality and to remain loyal, which ironically Mom
does better than Dad, who eventually no longer speaks to his daughter. Counterpointing the girls' romance, which is surreptitious and long distance, since
Patsy is away at school, is that of Parr and pretty Angela Kidder, who sensibly,
despite her fundamentalist father, concludes that she can understand how Evie
and Patsy must feel. Since she loves Parr, she says she would not like anything
or anyone's attempting to force her and Parr apart. When Cord Whittle and Parr
get drunk on beer, Cord decides to hang a sign compromising the two girls on
the town war memorial in an attempt to put the onus for the relationship on
Patsy and thus get rid of her, but the stunt backfires. Evie takes off for St. Louis
and Patsy and then for France, and shortly after heavy rains produce immense
floods, which almost wipe out the farms in the area, including the Burrman
place. Although Doug decides he will go to veterinary school and not farm and
Evie decides to remain in New York City with Patsy, Parr still hopes for some
vocation other than farming once he is graduated from high school. Dad chooses
to remain on the farm. Angel dumps Parr, however, saying the flood is God's
judgment. Parr replies that it is the result of geography, not morality, and that
the Mississippi was never intended to be a canal. In the fall, Evie visits, and
before she returns to the city, Dad is speaking to her again, albeit grudgingly.
The family love Evie and accept her as theirs, even if they do not approve of
her way of life. Parr is an engaging narrator, a likable if not always honest or
sensible boy. Evie is stereotypically pictured as the "butch" member of the
"dyke" pair. Although she is not an easy person to warm to, one can hardly
help but feel sympathy for her in her isolation; she is intelligent, hard working,

clever, and witty. Various attitudes about homosexuality, and lesbians in particular, are voiced by different segments of the family and community, but the Burrmans' discomfort never seems tangible. The plot is overforeshadowed, and the conclusion is predictable. The several references to the power of nature—for example, the motto Parr's teacher has on her blackboard, which reads, NEVER CAN CUSTOM CONQUER NATURE, FOR SHE IS EVER UNCONQUERED, and the flood that literalizes that sentiment—emphasize the legitimacy of Evie's sexual orientation as being natural and something she cannot help. A strength of the book is its keen sense of small town and farming community life. The title comes from a statement that Cord makes while the congregation recites the Lord's Prayer in church. SLJ.

DENNIE HALLIDAY (*Grams, Her Boyfriend, My Family, and Me**), oldest child in the large, close Halliday family, a senior in high school, and a take-charge sort of girl. She comes up with most of the ideas and shakes her younger brother, Andy, out of his self-professed ''policy of noninvolvement.'' Dennie, who is somewhat of a feminist, encourages her mother, Liz, when Liz decides for financial reasons to go back to working outside the home, but Dennie also announces that she has certain after-school obligations that she will not give up. She is also very perceptive about what is going on in the house and between her parents and informs her sister, Molly*, and Andy about her observations. She is pleased when Grams moves in, because Grams can help with babysitting the twins and also because Grams has a car that Dennie will be allowed to drive. In the episode involving dinner at the house of their friends, the Carlsons, Dennie is mortified at having to sit with the children. She does most of the planning of Grams's wedding and elopement. Dennie is a convincing, well-drawn character.

DERBY, PAT (1942–   ), born in Sussex, England; educated at Columbia University; writer of contemporary realistic novels of family life and growing up for middle grade and teenaged readers. *Grams, her Boyfriend, my Family, and Me** (Farrar, 1994), a *School Library Journal* selection, is a fifteen-year-old boy's account of how his family life changes when his father's mother, widowed Grams, moves in and meets a man with whom she falls in love and decides to marry. Derby's other books include *Visiting Miss Pierce* (Farrar, 1986), in which a teenager visits a convalescent home as a school project and becomes interested in the stories an old woman tells about her brother. *Goodbye, Emily, Hello* (Farrar, 1989) is a story of friendship and self-discovery. Derby's books deal with matters important to families of today with insight and humor. She lives in San Leandro, California.

DIANA GOSS (*Lyddie**), mill girl in Lowell, Massachusetts in the 1840s, who is kind to Lyddie Worthen when she starts in the weaving room, teaching her how to run the machines, giving her paper and ink to write to her mother and brother, Charlie*, and helping her to decipher the corporation regulations. Although her roommates warn her that Diana is an agitator, trying to get signatures on a petition to reduce the workday from thirteen to ten hours, Lyddie continues to be friendly to her. When Lyddie is injured by a flying shuttle, Diana gets her medical aid from a new young doctor, with whom Lyddie later sees her. Before Diana leaves Lowell, she confesses to Lyddie that she is pregnant, cannot be married since the man already has a wife whose father is a mill owner, and is leaving so as not to put the labor movement into disrepute. After Lyddie departs from Lowell, she hunts up Diana in Boston, hoping to help her out with the baby, but Diana has found a position in a seamstress shop whose proprietor is ill and who is willing to help with the baby, offering family support to Diana, who has never had a family. One of the best-educated and self-assured girls in the mill, Diana sees the injustices in the system that masquerade as benevolent concern for the workers.

DIXIE STORMS (Hall*, Barbara, Harcourt, 1990), realistic novel of family life and a girl's growing up; takes place over a few weeks one hot midsummer near the contemporary corn- and tobacco-raising town of Marston, Virginia. Although her nephew, Bodean* (Robert Dean), 9, often back-talks and teases her; her schoolmates Ethan and Kenny deride her lack of a figure; she misses her former sister-in-law, Becky*, Bodean's mother; and, motherless, she has gradually assumed the homemaker's role, the narrator, Dutch (Margaret) Peyton, 14, feels generally happy and comfortable with her warm, close, farm family. She loves and respects her strong, resilient Papa*; shares confidences with her father's sister, widowed Aunt Macy, although Macy frequently shirks her responsibilities, pleading headaches; and is proud of her handsome, much older brother, Flood*, although he is stubborn and distant. Only two things would make life perfect: a reconciliation between Flood and his former wife, from whom no one ever hears and whom Flood has taught Bodean to despise; and a good rain to save the tobacco crop and maybe the farm, though Dutch does not dwell on these concerns. Suddenly more troubling is Papa's news that Dutch's Richmond cousin, whom Dutch has never met, Norma* Peyton, 15, is coming to visit. The only child of Papa's estranged brother, Eugene, a bank employee, Norma will stay while her parents attempt to resolve their marital problems. Norma is so pretty, sophisticated, well built, and self-assured that she makes Dutch feel awkward, naive, and plain. Everyone else is infatuated with Norma and tries hard to please her, especially Bodean. Norma shares Dutch's room, and they do some things together—for example, go to Blue Hole to swim and to church—and Norma expands Dutch's horizons, but the relationship is uneasy. Norma does not help about the house, she chases and easily catches Kenny, and then even pursues Flood. A greater problem emerges for Dutch when she cleans Flood's room and discovers a horde of letters from Becky to Bodean, hidden away under the mattress, unopened. Troubled by the moral dilemma, now that she has an address, she writes to Becky in Norfolk, telling of her discovery and inviting her to telephone. Then Papa tells Dutch that Norma's parents are getting a divorce, a confidence that in a moment of anger Dutch hurls at Norma. When she confesses to Papa, he says she must apologize, and she does, but the distance between the cousins widens. Then Dutch discovers that Flood has been coming home drunk late at night, that the tractor has been repossessed, and that the prolonged drought has forced them to dip into next winter's food supply. When they see Norma off on the bus, however, her obvious apprehension about what lies ahead makes Dutch like and feel sorry for her. Later that day, Becky arrives unannounced, responding to Dutch's letter. That night Dutch and Bodean overhear an emotional conversation between Becky and Flood that explains the breakup and in which Flood finally agrees that Bodean may visit Becky in Norfolk. Dutch still hopes the two will reconcile, even when Flood dates pretty, dark Lucy Cabbot from church, a music teacher who looks much like Becky. Flood, however, is happy, and although he has long hoped for a cattle ranch out West, he gives the $15,000 he has saved to Papa to pay off debts on the farm and equipment. He also tells Dutch to let go, just as Norma once did, saying Dutch is possessive and controlling and wants people her way. Dutch is resentful but concedes there may be truth in what he says. Then Ethan asks her to go steady, and she realizes that the road ahead may be rocky, but like the weather, just then coming up with what looks to be a thorough rain, life holds beautiful moments, too. The author makes skillful use of familiar conventions from the southern regional novel: the proud, closely knit family shaken by a visitor who evokes new perspectives; the carefully delineated characters; the individualized dialogue; the hot, stifling, suddenly breaking weather that serves as a backdrop for the restrained but tense emotion. The reason for Becky's departure and the divorce provides the book's main suspense, a situation that seems reasonable since Dutch was only eight when Becky left. Not so believable are the several instances in which Dutch gains information by just happening to be on the spot or eavesdropping, especially since she has a well-developed moral sense. Traditional values of family togetherness and forbearance, forgiveness, neighborliness, hard work, religion, and the like undergird the story and set in relief the fractures in Flood's and Norma's lives. ALA; SLJ.

DOLL (*The Brave**), young, blond street girl, probably a prostitute, who hangs out with a drug dealer, Stick. She helps waylay the Native American boxer, Sonny Bear, when he gets off the bus, steals his wallet and his backpack, and lies repeatedly, but she seems to have some redeeming qualities, including a genuine love for her baby, Jessie. She phones for Sonny at Jake's, giving her name as Heather, and at least twice she shows up at his fights, but whether it is at Stick's instigation or because she really is interested in Sonny is not clear. She seems to be one of a stable of girls belonging to a pimp named Mo. It may be that Stick also pimps for her. Sonny is greatly attracted to her, much more than to pretty, respectable Denise, Martin* Witherspoon's sister.

DONAY (*Taste of Salt**), big, tired, old Haitian black man, who like Djo is a slave laborer cutting cane on a *central,* or sugar plantation, in the Dominican Republic. Donay warns Djo against falling into debt, saying, "For then they do own you." Dreaming of buying shoes for his mother or light bulbs for Titid (Aristide), Djo does not understand at first how company stores work to the detriment of the laborer. Ironically, he falls into great debt to buy a coffin for Donay, because he does not want his dear friend's body to be dumped into the ground. Also ironically, he does not learn until much later that that is exactly what did happen to Donay's body. Donay is a calm and gentle man who never complains or becomes angry, even when, for example, they must sleep on concrete without bedding and rations are extremely short. Donay has worked for so many years as an impressed laborer that when he was able to return to Haiti, he no longer knew anyone there and decided to go back to the plantation. Djo tells Donay about Titid and urges him to help the priest in the struggle for justice. They lay plans for escape, but Donay dies before they can leave. Djo realizes that Donay is a great man; he takes pride in doing his work well and closes his mind to insults and degradation, and hence rises above his unfortunate condition and proves himself superior to his tormentors. Donay is a surrogate father to the homeless boy.

DORRIS, MICHAEL (ANTHONY) (1945–   ), born in Louisville, Kentucky; professor of anthropology and chair of the Native American Studies Department at Dartmouth College in New Hampshire, and writer of scholarly works, nonfiction, and novels for adults and children. A graduate of Georgetown University with a B.A. and of Yale University with a M.Phil., he has had a distinguished career in academe, teaching at various universities in the United States and abroad and serving as a consultant to the National Endowment for the Humanities and television and on such boards as Save the Children Foundation and the United States Advisory Committee on Infant Mortality. Part Modoc, he has worked to advance the interests of Native Americans in various capacities as well as by his writings. The adoptive father of a child with fetal alcohol syndrome, he has been active in alcohol research. With his wife, Louise Erdrich, a part-Chippewa novelist and poet, he has published, among others, the acclaimed novel *The Crown of Columbus* (HarperCollins, 1991), for adults. Individually he has written *A Yellow Raft in Blue Water* (Holt, 1987), a novel for adults, and the nonfiction *The Broken Cord: A Family's Ongoing Struggle with Fetal Alcohol Syndrome* (Harper, 1989), also published as *The Broken Cord: A Father's Story* (Collins, 1990), as well as other books of nonfiction about Native Americans, short stories, and essays. For young readers, he published *Morning Girl** (Hyperion, 1992), a short novel of family life set among Native Americans on a Caribbean island at the time of Columbus's arrival. This book was chosen by the editors of *The Horn Book Magazine* for the Fanfare list and received the Scott O'Dell Award for Historical Fiction. *Guests* (Hyperion, 1994), also for young readers, concerns an Algonquin boy and girl living in Massachusetts at the time of the Pilgrims' Thanksgiving.

DOUBLE TROUBLE SQUARED (Lasky*, Kathryn, Harcourt, 1991), mystery-detective fantasy novel set in contemporary Washington, D.C., and London, England. Fraternal twins almost identical in appearance and gifted with mental telepathy, Liberty Bell Starbuck and her brother, July Burton Starbuck, 11, (so named because they were born on the Fourth of July) are delighted when their father, Putnam Starbuck, takes a job as undersecretary to the U.S. ambassador to the Court of St. James. In London, they will be able to pursue their strong interest in Sherlock Holmes. Moving to London also are their five-year-old twin sisters, Charly and Molly (identical redheads, who are also telepathic and who were named for Charlotte Amalie in the Virgin Islands, where they were born). These four children together often cause double trouble squared. Staying home in Washington is their mother, Madeline, because she must attend to her business of manufacturing dance costumes. Zanny Duggan, an ex–elementary teacher, acts as nanny and also home-schools the children, particularly in British life and history. Strange shadows, which the two older children have occasionally glimpsed near the bronze bust of Sherlock Holmes in their Washington house, and eerie echoes that interrupt their telecommunications at home also haunt them in London. One foggy night, when Liberty and July are mysteriously awakened, they take a walk through Holmes's area to Pinchin Lane. There they are accosted by a huge, snarling doberman pinscher and its mean-spirited male owner, who threatens them in words identical to those uttered by the kennel keeper in the Holmes novel *The Sign of the Four*. Other unusual occurrences include being seemingly guided to a house for rent off Devonshire Place, which turns out to be attached to the dwelling in which Sir Arthur Conan Doyle once lived; encountering the same mean-spirited man working as a warder, or beefeater, in the Tower of London and also later while they are on a picnic in the country to celebrate their twelfth birthday; and spotting a small, strange, sooty waif skulking about the streets. One night during a severe thunderstorm, July detects what appears to be a tiny crack at the corner of the ceiling in their attic room. When the two inspect it, Liberty discovers a sealed compartment containing a manuscript. Partially materializing then is Shadrach Holmes, a garrulous almost-ghost, who tells them the long and intriguing story of how Doyle had written a story combining elements of "The Adventure of the Speckled Band" and *The Sign of the Four* and including the character of Shadrach as Sherlock's twin brother. Later, when Doyle divided the manuscript into the two accounts, he abandoned the figure of Shadrach, as he also eliminated the surly beefeater figure, who would have been another villain like Moriarity, and the waif, who was to be a Baker Street Irregular. Shadrach entreats the children to "get these drafts [of manuscript] to the public and fully appreciated . . . [so that he is not forced to] spend my eternity in a terrible kind of limbo." With Zanny's help and that of a young lawyer with whom Zanny falls in love, the children get the manuscript approved by the local Sherlock Holmes society and announced to the public in a special ceremony. During the proceedings, to which Liberty wears boy's clothes because women are not allowed, she tears off the garments, thus living up to the Starbuck family motto, *Sui Veritas Primo,* Truth to Self First. She and July are widely feted for their discovery of another peculiarly British treasure and have an audience with the queen at Buckingham Palace. All the family appear in the newspapers. Shadows and echoes recede from Devonshire Place, and Shadrach is liberated at last by being revealed as an actual Holmes character. A fast-moving, well-paced, carefully constructed plot; a lively and gently eccentric family; and a light and peppy style contemporary in tone and allusions make up for the shallow characterizations. Information about Doyle, Holmes, and twinning is subtly worked in. Humor is controlled and often arises from inventive situations; for example, the opportunity to cruise around Greater London in a luxury stretch limousine as a birthday treat is among the book's clever touches. The Starbucks seem as engagingly typical of the nineties as were the Moffats of the twenties and the Austins of the sixties. Poe Nominee.

DRAGON'S GATE (Yep*, Laurence, HarperCollins, 1993), third in a series of historical novels, following *The Serpent's Children* and *Mountain Light,* all about the uprising against the Manchu rulers in China and the Chinese immigrants to California in the 1860s. Starting in Three Willows Village in Kwangtung Province, China, this novel centers on the narrator, Otter, the baby adopted by Cassia and Squeaky who is now a fourteen-year-old student. When his adoptive father and uncle, Foxfire, return for a visit to the village, where they are treated like royalty, Otter begs to be allowed to go back with them to the Land of the Golden Mountain, where they have sought their fortunes in the goldfields, but Cassia insists that she needs him to become manager of her investments, which have become extensive, although much of the local culture and many villagers are being destroyed by the British-imported opium. A disagreement that results in the accidental death of a Manchu soldier puts Otter in danger, however, and Cassia arranges that he travel to the United States to join his father and uncle. The gold having nearly run out, they have joined the railroad builders trying to push the Central Pacific through the Sierras, despite the bitter winter weather and the iron-like stone that is almost defeating the tunnelers. The terrible living and working conditions and the humble positions of his father and even his uncle are great shocks to Otter, who has led a favored life in China. Foxfire is a crew chief, with a crew made up of misfits: mentally damaged Shaky, quarrelsome Dandy, pessimistic Bright Star, Honker the hypochondriac, Doggy the thief, and Curly the gambler. Otter learns that the westerners do not honor their labor agreement signed with the Chinese, or Tang men; they enforce their orders with whips, and, worst of all, they allow no one to leave the mountain. Their Irish overseer, Kilroy, is especially brutal, even to his own son, Sean, who becomes a secret friend of Otter. Although Otter gradually accustoms himself to the grueling work, he suffers from Kilroy's whip, from the extreme cold, and most of all from disillusionment with Foxfire, who seems too conciliatory to the westerners and unrealistically idealistic about prospects for the continuing fight against the Manchus in China. After Squeaky is blinded by an explosion caused by a risky technique, used in an effort to speed the tunnel work, and a snow slide wipes away a whole hut and its Tang occupants, Otter bargains with Kilroy: he will try to get to the top of the peak and set off a dynamite charge to create an avalanche away from the tunnel mouth, to keep the overload of snow from crashing over the work camp and burying them all; in return Kilroy will look the other way when Otter escorts his blind father down the mountain and escapes to San Francisco. Foxfire, trying to redeem himself in the boy's eyes and his own self-esteem, volunteers to accompany him, and Sean, who understands the use of a compass, insists on going, too. During the terrible climb, Sean falls into a ravine, injuring his ankle, and has to turn back. Foxfire crashes down a frozen waterfall, breaking his leg and cutting himself up badly. At his urging, Otter struggles on and sets off the charge, but on returning he cannot find Foxfire, who has crawled off to die and give Otter a chance to make it back to camp. After his recovery from exertion and injuries, Otter decides to stay on the mountain, hoping to find his uncle's bones in the spring and to send them home for burial. With the help of Sean, who has been sent to headquarters until his ankle heals, Otter discovers how much difference in pay lies between the westerners and the Tang people, and with the help of the crew, now welded into a cohesive force, he organizes a strike that begins to decrease the disparity. The novel ends at Promontory Point, Utah, in May, 1869, where the east-bound and the west-bound railroads meet, and the westerners have a big celebration that does not acknowledge the Tang men, who are largely responsible for its completion. Besides the historical facts, documented in an afterword, the novel gives a vivid picture of the little-known suffering and sacrifice of the Tang workers, the near slavery in which they were kept, the danger and difficulty of their work, and the extreme cold of winter in the mountains. Some incidents, like Doggy's losing his fingers to frostbite just after his crew has chipped in to replace his stolen guitar, seem contrived, though ironically memorable. No effort is made to use language in narration or dialogue different from that of the late twentieth century. ALA; Newbery Honor.

E

EARTHSHINE (Nelson*, Theresa, Orchard, 1994), realistic contemporary problem novel set in Los Angeles, from January to June, concerning a family whose father is dying of AIDS. Events are related by the only child, Slim (Margery Grace) McGranahan, 12, by her own admission, a "hard-angle, sharp-elbow type—sort of spiky looking," who lives by preference with her divorced father, Mack (Hugh Alan McGranahan the Third); Mack's live-in companion, Larry Casey, a commercial artist, who is "like a big bear with a beard"; and Sister, their gentle golden retriever. Slim dearly loves Mack, a once handsome, now emaciated, hairless, but still very personable, lighthearted, and often funny actor, who has developed the brownish-red splotches of AIDS-related Karposi's sarcoma, coughs a great deal, and has been growing steadily weaker. Slim's best friend is Isaiah Dodd, 11, a "funny-looking kid with glasses," whose father died of AIDS, whose mother, Angelina*, now has AIDS, and whom Slim met at the All Saints Episcopal Church support group for "kids who are living with PWAs" (Persons With AIDS). Slim, who knows of but has not really accepted her father's inevitable death, is often irritable, argumentative, and inclined to look on the dark side of things. Isaiah, however, is always sunny, insists that there is no such thing as death, and believes that some miracle will occur to save their loved ones. The story shifts from scenes in the support group to scenes at the McGranahan home and back, with just a few scenes elsewhere. At the support group, the leader, sweet, little, curly-haired Ms. Crofford, has the children write their innermost feelings in a notebook. At first Slim has little to say except swear words, but later she becomes more articulate and pours out her feelings cathartically, although she contributes little to the group otherwise. After Ms. Crofford's friend dies, Isaiah suggests that the group write to the President about the need for more AIDS research. Isaiah is delighted when he receives a response, but Slim knows it is just a form letter. The group then decides to raise money by sponsoring a booth at the local carnival, called Potpourri because all sorts of small things are sold there. During the festivities, two big black trucks smash through the fence, and skinheads yell "perverts" and "sicko queer diseases'' at them. Mack's illness worsens, he is hospitalized a couple of times, and Larry gives up his job to stay at home to care for him. Both think that Slim should begin to plan to live with her mother, but Slim resists the idea, and once even takes her mother's telephone number out of Larry's Rolodex. The story rises to a climax after Isaiah finds a newspaper article about a place of miracle healings in Hungry Valley north of Los Angeles. Supposedly a Miracle Man, a kind of healer, lives there; after an earthquake created what appears to be the Face of God on the side of the mountain, healings were said to have occurred. Isaiah's excitement spreads, and one Sunday a busload of people from the church leaves for Hungry Valley, Larry driving. After some mishaps, they arrive, only to discover to their disappointment that the healings were pure media hyperbole. At afternoon's end, a golden light suffuses the area, and they leave feeling peaceful anyway. Mack declines rapidly after the outing, which tired him out, and Slim reluctantly telephones her mother with the news, since she now realizes that her mother deserves to know. Mack dies peacefully, with Larry, Slim, and Sister present. After the memorial service, Larry, Isaiah, Angelina, Sister, and Slim return to Hungry Valley to scatter Mack's ashes, which the wind catches and blows back on them. They return home feeling that, because of the wind's action, they will always have something of Mack with them. Characters are individualized but still stereotypes, obviously foiled; scenes are conventional and occasionally extravagant; the pace is uneven; style is detailed, contemporary, and conversational; and although the author avoids didacticism and sentimentality, the story seems to be more about AIDS than about people coping with the disease. Isaiah's speeches in particular sound off-key, but he is a more interesting figure than Slim. Aftershocks from earthquakes and plentiful rain from El Niño provide atmospheric background. Both poignancy and hilarity are used to advantage, and the tone is upbeat and hopeful. A subplot revolves around Isaiah's family situation. The title refers to a natural phenomenon of sunlight reflecting from earth to the moon. SLJ.

EDDIE NUTT (*The Broccoli Tapes**), little, wiry classmate of Sam* Davidson, whom he and Sara meet in the lava field where they rescue a cat. Son of a mixed-race Hawaiian mother, he is darker than his Scotch-Irish father from Canada, who runs a pet shop in the mall and lavishes affection on his white pedigreed cat, Princess Di. Surly and suspicious at first, Eddie gradually comes to trust the Davidsons, and they learn that his mother left with a lover three years before and that he thinks his father hates him because he is like his mother. Although he pretends he does not care, he is deeply hurt by his father's rejection. In the end he has made peace with his father and opted to stay in Hawaii but plans to visit his mother the next summer and probably fly to Boston to see Sara and Sam again. His touchy relationship with the Davidsons parallels their problems with Broccoli, the cat they have found.

ED LINDNER (*The Secret Keeper**), teenaged son of the owner of the local hardware store and naturalist for the children at the Beaches, the exclusive Lake

Michigan club at which Anne Lewis is a keeper (companion-sitter). Ed is a keeper for Robin, a boy at the club, who is accused of destroying the wild flowers that Bryce* Stevens actually ruined in a fit of anger. Ed is attracted to Anne and tells her much about the Larimer family and the area around the Beaches. He says that the Larimers gave Jess Larimer Stevens money to maintain her wealthy lifestyle after she married Bryce, a matter that was a source of irritation in their marriage. When Anne tries to consult Ed about what to do after she realizes that Bryce was probably murdered, Ed puts her off right away, apparently jealous that she is still thinking about Bryce.

EDMUND (*The Man Who Was Poe**), Edmund Albert George Brimmer, the English boy of eleven whom Edgar Allan Poe* befriends in Providence, Rhode Island. Edmund is presented as brave and very determined to find his sister. He is puzzled when the body of the woman who is thought to be Aunty Pru (and finally is identified as Aunty Pru) is found, because he does not recognize the dress on the body as belonging to her. Later the dress is discovered to belong to Edmund's mother. Because Dupin-Poe sends Edmund on errands and because the boy does not always trust Dupin-Poe and thus follows the man to keep tabs on him and also does some investigating of his own, Edmund is the means by which most of the information Dupin-Poe needs to solve the mystery is found. In his jaunts, Edmund gets into a number of tight spots, occasions that increase the story's tension considerably. The psychological connotations of the contrast between the characters of the boy and the man add to the pleasure of the novel for adult readers.

ELIZABETH (*Alice in Rapture, Sort Of**; *Reluctantly Alice**; *All But Alice**), Alice McKinley's friend from elementary school, the only girl in seventh grade who refuses to get her ears pierced. From a traditional Catholic family, Elizabeth is very proper and finds discussion of sex in Our Changing Bodies class embarrassing and painful. When she confesses to Alice that her mother is going to have a baby, she is humiliated because it means her parents, after more than a dozen years of marriage, must still be having intercourse. After Alice becomes one of the Beautiful People of seventh grade (also known as the Famous Eight), she ignores Elizabeth, who inevitably is left out of many of the junior high activities, but eventually they become close friends again.

ELIZABETH CRAWFORD (*Stepping on the Cracks**), eleven-year-old daughter of a policeman and best friend of Margaret* Baker. Elizabeth is pretty, forward, audacious, and clever, the opposite of Margaret, who is comparatively indecisive and shy. The leader in most of their activities, Elizabeth often bullies or shames Margaret into doing what she wants. Her impulsiveness and quick tongue often land the two in trouble. Whereas Margaret helps the army deserter Stuart* Smith out of true compassion, Elizabeth sees him as a means of controlling Stuart's brother, school bully Gordy* Smith. The two girls are obvious foils. The book's title comes from her version of an old game: "Step on a crack, Break Hitler's back!"

ELLERBY (*Staying Fat for Sarah Byrnes**), Steve Ellerby, Eric Calhoune's classmate, swim-team partner, and best male friend, the never-serious son of an Episcopal priest known to support such controversial issues as rights for homosexuals. Ellerby drives a pale blue 1973 Pontiac, which is flamboyantly decorated with slogans and paintings and whose horns blare out a tuba version of "The Old Rugged Cross" and Mahalia Jackson's "The Lord's Prayer," the vehicle being an obvious satire on overly zealous Christian philosophy and behavior. Ellerby has deep respect and liking for his father, who modified his religious thinking and activity after the death of his elder son, a brilliant boy about to enter the seminary; henceforth, among other changes, he devoted more time to his wife and remaining son. Ellerby says he now respects his father so much he would trash his beloved Christian Cruiser if his dad asked him to. He admires his father for admitting that there are no easy answers to the existential problems of life. Ellerby appears frequently in the novel, at swim-team practice, during which he and Eric deride Mark* Brittain; in Contemporary American Thought class, where he honestly admits to feeling shame over the way he has treated Sarah Byrnes because of her scars; at Eric's home; and on the street in the Cruiser. Ellerby is instrumental in helping Eric in many ways and is his trusted confidant. Ellerby is a very likable character, if overdrawn for effect.

ELLIE JACOBY (*Tell Me Everything**), Roz Jacoby's mother. Ellie is considered a hero because she died trying to rescue a teenaged boy lost on a mountain. She was hurt and impregnated with Roz in a brutal rape, about which Roz knows and from which Ellie has obviously never recovered psychologically. She has become somewhat of a recluse and is regarded as crazy by some people. She bakes bread for a living, refuses to send Roz to public school, teaching her at home instead, and takes refuge from her hurts and finds strength in her religion. According to Roz, she prays and talks to God and about God a lot. The circumstances of her death are not clear. Apparently she and Roz had been camping out in back of their big, old farmhouse; Ellie left the tent early one morning without waking Roz and was later found dead on the nearby mountain. Roz had no information about her mother until late in the day, having spent the time from morning until night waiting in the house for Ellie.

ELMORE, (CAROLYN) PATRICIA (1933–   ), born in Miami, Florida; elementary school teacher, freelance editor, and writer of training and informational materials for adults and mysteries for elementary and middle grade readers. Her popular series about Susannah, the eleven-year-old super-sleuth, includes *Susannah and the Blue House Mystery* (Dutton, 1980), in which Susannah and her friends search for a treasure; *Susannah and the Poison Green Halloween* (Dutton, 1982), in which Susannah and her friends discover who put poison in their trick-or-treat candy; and *Susannah and the Purple Mongoose Mystery** (Dutton, 1992), a nominee for the Edgar Allan Poe Award, in which Susannah directs the effort to bring a neighborhood arsonist to justice. Plenty of action, extensive dialogue, and a clever and engaging protagonist make these books entertaining introductions to the genre for the intended audience. With Cynthia Chase, Elmore published *Ginny, the Office Assistant* (McGraw-Hill, 1967), a vocational book. She received her A.B. from the University of South Carolina–Columbia and studied further at the University of Miami–Coral Gables, New School for Social Research, and San Francisco State University. She lives in Albany, California.

EMILY VOLNIK (*The Boggart**), sister of Jessup* Volnik and one of the family that acquire the magical little man whom they call the Boggart*. Emily is the more sensitive of the two Volnik siblings, feeling a deep affinity to nature and animals and being interested in conservation and ecology. She tells some of the theater people about the mishaps in the Volnik household and thus learns that a boggart may be at work. She and her brother particularly dislike Dr. Stigmore, whom they call the "creep." He is a psychiatrist who is interested in antiques and is a customer at their mother's antique shop. Emily is both angry and frightened when her parents think that, as Dr. Stigmore suggests, the strange occurrences are poltergeist phenomena, arising from Emily's disturbed, early adolescent emotions. Her mother wants her to enter psychoanalysis with Dr. Stigmore until he gives an interview to the newspapers and agrees to go on television about the Volniks' situation. Then she sees him for the warped opportunist that he is.

EMMETT BABBIDGE (*Lucie Babbidge's House**), Lucie Babbidge's five-year-old brother in the fantasy part of the novel. Lively and witty, Emmett provides what little humor there is in the story. He is fond of taking remarks literally and ruminating on ideas to their logical, or illogical, conclusions. Some member of the household is always urging him not to be silly. After Emmett is kidnapped, Mr. Broome assumes his function as verbal comic. Emmett serves to demonstrate Lucie's acumen, since everything he thinks and says she really makes up.

ENCHANTRESS FROM THE STARS (Engdahl*, Sylvia Louise, Atheneum, 1970), science fantasy set in the future on the planet Andrecia. Elana, about twenty, an agent of the Anthropological Service of the Federation, a highly advanced civilization, employs bravery and wit to save the feudal Youngling society from being conquered by invading Imperialists. Three distinct narrative modes, an engaging heroine, and a judicious combination of philosophy and action produce a thought-provoking story about cultures in different stages of development coming into conflict with one another. The sequel is *The Far Side of Evil*. Phoenix Winner. Previously the novel received the following citations:

Choice; Fanfare; Newbery Honor. For a longer entry, see *Dictionary, 1960–1984.*

ENGDAHL, SYLVIA LOUISE (1933–   ), born and raised in Los Angeles; computer specialist and freelance writer best known for her science fiction of space travel and exploration for young adults. Her books are more concerned with ethical matters than with technological advance. Her first novel, *Enchantress from the Stars** (Atheneum, 1970), has won for her continuing critical attention. Involving the confluence of three cultures in three different stages of development, it was a Newbery Honor Book, a Fanfare book, and a *Choice* selection and received the Phoenix Award of The Children's Literature Association. For earlier biographical information and title entries, see *Dictionary, 1960–1984* [*Enchantress from the Stars; This Star Shall Abide*].

ERNIE SMITH (*Rosemary's Witch**), Rosemary Morgenthau's friend and partner in obviating the power of the witch who lives in the woods near their houses. Ernie is fat, extremely talkative, and comfortable to be around, yet, like Rosemary, he has few friends. He has an outgoing, almost overwhelming personality and sounds like a television host, the vocation he aspires to. Although he sometimes seems silly, he is also a thinker and cares about people. He feels that really important things are not taught in school and cites as examples such matters as why people stay married and why dogs howl. He provides comedy for the story and also ballast for the character of the more serious and diffident Rosemary. Ernie comes up with the idea that the untoward events going on in the area are the work of a witch and thus launches Rosemary on the path to success.

EVERYWHERE (Brooks*, Bruce, Harper and Row, 1990), brief novel of a boy's love and concern for his grandfather and his effort to save the old man after he suffers a heart attack. The narrator, Peanuts, 10, who spends his summer holidays in Richmond, Virginia, with his grandparents, has been directed to play with Dooley, a local black boy, while Dooley's aunt, Lucy Pettibone, nurses the grandfather. At eleven, Dooley is much more confident and knowledgeable than Peanuts, and he organizes a way to cure the old man by a soul switch, which he learned from a comic book about Indians. First he climbs to the bedroom window to peek in and see which animal the grandfather most resembles and decides on a turtle. He gets Peanuts to take him to a nearby stream, where they find a black box turtle. When Peanuts realizes that Dooley intends to kill the turtle by beheading it with the jigsaw in the garage, he is troubled and cannot make himself go into the garage, where he and his grandfather have spent many happy hours making things. Instead Dooley sends him into the house to bring down one of his grandfather's bow ties and some nail polish, with which he will paint the grandfather's initials on the turtle's back. Dooley directs Peanuts to climb up on the roof to watch for the exact moment to make the switch and signal him as he waits at the garage door. As Peanuts peeks in the window he sees his grandfather having some sort of spasm and Lucy pounding on his chest. Peanuts waves his arms frantically for help and then hears the jigsaw, realizing that he has inadvertently given the signal. He shouts, "No! Don't do it," until his grandmother opens the window and pulls him into the room; his grandfather, suddenly relaxing, whispers, "Okay. Sure. I won't." Dooley meets Peanuts in the yard, elated that the switch has worked, but seems a little ashamed when reminded of the death of the turtle. As the grandfather recovers, he keeps saying that he was all ready to go when someone had to go and call him back. When he and Peanuts go out to the garage, they find the turtle, still alive with the initials on his back and the remains of an old chicken neck on the floor. Peanuts, feeling he owes Dooley something, follows him to the Negro church, climbs a tree where he can look in the window, and sees Dooley wearing the grandfather's bow tie. The story leaves some puzzles. Whether Dooley is a trickster, deliberately making Peanuts think the turtle is saving his grandfather when it is actually his own love and willpower operating, or whether Dooley has lost his nerve to kill the turtle and is relieved that the man is living despite his failure, is not clear. The title comes from an experience that the grandfather and Peanuts share one evening—a feeling of floating off in another world, of being "everywhere," and the boy's plea at his grandfather's bedside for him not to go "everywhere." Just when the action occurred is also not clear; the sidewalks in that older section of Richmond are newly laid, but the grandfather is a World War I veteran. ALA; SLJ.

EVIE BERG (*Life's a Funny Proposition, Horatio**), a dentist, mother of Horatio Tuckerman, daughter-in-law of O.P.* After the death from smoking-induced lung cancer of her husband, Joshua Tuckerman (a university professor of literature and playwright called Y.P., from Young Professor, to distinguish him from his father, O.P. or Old Professor), she moved her family to Spring Creek, Wisconsin, to join a dental practice there. She bought a lakefront house large enough to provide a studio for her hobby of pottery. Evie has begun to date, but Horatio resents her boyfriends, her dressing up for them, and her not being able to take him places because she is out on dates. She tries to explain to him her loneliness and her need for male company. Ironically, her latest boyfriend, Paul Miller, whom Horatio privately refers to as Pink Gums Paul, dumps her for an old girlfriend on the night Horatio's team loses the big local chess tournament. Evie says that they were both "creamed."

EVIE LEVIN (*Beyond Safe Boundaries**), Evelyn Levin, older sister of Elizabeth Levin, the narrator. About age sixteen when the novel begins, Evie seems a terribly spoiled brat for her spiteful and lengthy antagonism to their father's new wife. She is redeemed in the reader's eyes by her later complete devotion to the anti-apartheid cause. While she is at the university, she rooms with a young woman from India and distributes her considerable wardrobe to the poor.

Later, however, she is willing to compromise her principles and even give her life in order to save the life of fellow political activist Willem* Coetzee. Her departure for England is intended to represent the exodus of justice-seeking, fair-minded, young white South Africans, the future of the country being sacrificed for the cause of white supremacy.

EZRA KETCHAM (*Weasel**), the sometime Indian fighter and companion of Weasel* who befriends Nathan Fowler and his family. Since Ezra cannot speak, Nathan learns his sad history from Weasel. Both Weasel and Ezra were among the forces dispatched by the U.S. government fifteen years before the story begins with orders to clear the Ohio River area of Shawnee Indians to make way for white settlers. Ezra changed in attitude toward the Indians, however. He became convinced that they were being treated unjustly, and when he took an Indian wife, he incurred the suspicion and dislike of the settlers and the hatred of Weasel, who cut out Ezra's tongue and then forced the man to watch while he murdered Ezra's wife and unborn child. According to Nathan's father, the Ketchams and the Fowlers were friends before the murder, Mrs. Fowler having helped the pregnant Mrs. Ketcham when the Ketchams were driven from town. Ezra has become shy of people and lives as a recluse in a remote cabin. He wears tattered animal skins and a tall stovepipe hat atop his long, tangled hair. He is especially fond of Nathan's sister, Molly, whom he treats with deep tenderness. At the end, Ezra leaves to join his slain wife's people in Kansas, where they were taken by removal.

F

THE FACE IN THE BESSLEDORF FUNERAL PARLOR (Naylor*, Phyllis Reynolds, Atheneum, 1993), lighthearted mystery for middle readers, one of a series that includes *The Mad Gasser of Bessledorf Street, The Bodies in the Bessledorf Hotel,* and *Bernie and the Bessledorf Ghost.* In the small Indiana town of Middleburg in the 1990s, the Magruder family live in and manage the thirty-room Bessledorf Hotel, between the bus depot and the funeral home. Mr. Magruder wants only to keep his guests happy and not to fail at this enterprise, as he has at many others; Mrs. Magruder wants to feed everyone well and get her romance novels published; Delores, 20, who works in a parachute factory, wants romance; Joseph, 19, who is studying to be a veterinarian, wants more pets, besides Mixed Blessing, a Great Dane, Salt Water, a parrot, and Lewis and Clark, their two cats; Lester, 9, wants more, and more unusual, things to eat; Bernie, 11, wants fame, specifically, to be in the *Guinness Book of World Records.* With his two friends, Georgene Riley and Weasel, Bernie thinks he may have the opportunity if they solve the crime at the Higgins Roofing Company, where pension funds are missing from the safe and the vice president has disappeared, leaving signs of a struggle and a blood-stained room. After Mixed Blessing follows the scent of the blood to the basement, where they find a chuck roast stuffed behind the water heater, suspicions shift from kidnapping or murder of the vice president to the possibility that he stole the funds after laying a false trail. Because the vice president's car is still in town and police have watched the bus depot closely, Bernie believes the man must be hiding until the furor dies down. Two incidents are especially suspicious: a man checks into room 54 of the hotel wearing a hairpiece, strange glasses, and possibly a false nose, and carefully avoids Officer Feeney, the cop on the beat; and from his bedroom window Bernie more than once sees a man, possibly Moe or Joe, the sons of the funeral director Woe, climb the fire escape to the roof of the building at night. After a series of humorous situations based on misassumptions, the man in room 54 turns out to be Mr. Fairchild, owner of the Bessledorf, who has come from Indianapolis incognito to check up on the Magruders. In the meantime, the funeral home with much fanfare has opened its drive-in window, at which people can drive up, view the corpse, and sign a guest book, all without leaving their cars. Bernie and his friends think that Moe and Joe, who need money to pay for the drive-in window, might be in league with the Higgins Roofing vice president, are hiding him on the funeral parlor roof, and probably have buried the stolen money in a recent grave, to be dug up again at their leisure. Several schemes to get to the roof, to dig up a recent grave, and to try mysticism involving chanting and a candle all are thwarted or backfire on Bernie and his friends. In a final effort, the three sneak out at night and through the drive-in window see the corpse standing upright in its coffin. They appeal to Officer Feeney, who arouses Woe, insists on looking around, and discovers two bodies in the mourning room. Bernie spots that the hair color has changed on the corpse in the window, and indeed, it is the vice president who has moved the corpse, hoping to dress it in his clothes, fake an accident, and then disappear with the money he has been hiding, to everyone's astonishment, in the attic of the hotel, traversing the space between the two buildings on a ladder he keeps on the roof. The children do not get into the book of records, and Officer Feeney, who has hoped to be switched from a street beat to homicide, is also disappointed. The plot is mostly a comedy of errors, with farcical situations and deliberately overdrawn characters, never serious or threatening. The idea of the drive-in window, with the lighting, opening curtains, and soft music triggered by a car or walker in the driveway, is exploited for its inherently amusing qualities. Poe Nominee.

FATHER MATT PERCY (*When the Road Ends**), Episcopal priest who takes in Mary Jack Jordan, Jane*, and Adam* Correy as foster children and his disabled sister, Cecile* Bradshaw, as a matter of conscience, and causes his disagreeable wife, Jill, to explode in fury and threaten to leave. A good man but weak, he usually takes the path of least resistance, agreeing in order to placate Jill to let the three children spend the summer with Cecile at her remote cabin, although it is obvious that she is not well enough to handle the responsibility. On his weekly visits to check on them, he believes their stories of the whereabouts of Gerry, the young woman who is ostensibly caring for them but actually left with the grocery money, because it is easier than investigating. Although he is genuinely fond of Mary Jack and Jane, his simplicity seems at least partly assumed so that he will not have to take action.

FELIPE RAMIREZ (*Grab Hands and Run**), twelve-year-old son of Paloma* and the political activist Jacinto. Felipe, Paloma, and Romy*, Felipe's younger sister, flee from El Salvador for Canada after Jacinto disappears and his motorcycle is found abandoned. Felipe is a bright boy and good in school, but he realizes that his book learning and intelligence will be of little use if he gets impressed into the army as his uncles were. He and Romy stay with their maternal grandparents in the hills during the summer, because it is safer for them there than in San Salvador and the grandparents can use his labor, but when the soldiers come, Felipe must hide in the lagoon under the maguey fiber one night in order to avoid impressment. The experience is frightening. His knowledge gained from books is sometimes important to them on the flight to Canada. For example, he can read maps. At the detention center, he works shelving supplies and at learning English.

FELL BACK (Kerr*, M. E., Harper, 1989), suspenseful, fast-moving, mystery-detective novel involving drug use among teenagers set in the late 1980s during the winter semester in Gardner School, an exclusive boy's prep school in Cottersville, Pennsylvania, sequel to *Fell.* John Fell*, the seventeen year old who tells the story, is now a senior and an envied member of the socially elite secret society known as The Sevens. When in January he sees the body of another Seven, universally disliked Paul Lasher, lying lifeless on the icy pavement at the foot of the Tower, Fell instinctively knows the death was not suicide. Lasher's beautiful sister, Lauren, insists it was, because Lasher had for some time been giving away valuable possessions to Rinaldo Velez, a "townie" who waits tables for The Sevens—items like his VCR, his word processor, and his Gstaad watch. Lasher's mother, a psychiatrist, who speaks in a strong German accent, says at his memorial service that he suffered from a hormone problem, but Lasher's father, also a prominent psychiatrist, has doubts that the death was a suicide. It is well known too that bad blood existed between Lasher and Creery (Cyril Creery), another Seven, resident cynic, marijuana user, and general rule breaker. Moreover, Dib (Sydney Dibble), Fell's former roommate and best friend, once overheard a quarrel in which Lasher threatened to kill Creery. Then, curiously, Fell is asked to help David Deem, a former Seven who is now a prosperous local businessman and Gardner benefactor, keep tabs on his beautiful, high school–aged daughter, Nina, who has become involved with a drug dealer named Eddie Dragon. Fell finds Nina very attractive, if strong-willed and self-engrossed, and they date frequently. He discovers later that she never broke off her relationship with Dragon. Fell also keeps watch on Playwicky Arms, a local apartment house where Lasher had an apartment and conducted card games. There Fell observes Creery's stepbrother, Lowell Hunter, a young man from Miami with a Mark Twain–like white haircut and mustache, and later, Lauren and Creery, being very chummy, to his surprise. Lauren informs Fell that she is very much in love with Creery, who, she says, is not mean as people think; that Lasher opposed their romance; and that Creery is afraid of what The Sevens might do to him. To add credence to what Lauren says, Dib has found on Lasher's word processor a letter from him to The Sevens' captain saying that an enclosed letter indicates that Creery needs to be disciplined with some secret club procedure known as The Sevens Revenge. Then Creery's body is found at the base of the Tower, also apparently a suicide, to judge from a letter of his posted on a bulletin board. The smashing climax occurs at the annual Charles Dance in March, to which every Seven must come dressed as a historical

Charles. At intermission, Fell, who has invited Nina, sees her leaving the dance with a "Charles" whose wrist bears a dragonfly tattoo identical to the one she wears on her chest. He realizes she has dumped him for Dragon, pursues them, and is taken captive by Dragon, who reveals that he is an FBI undercover drug agent named Ted Draggart and says Deem is a local drug facilitator. At Deem's place, they are all captured by Hunter, who turns out to be a drug dealer. He killed Creery (who had killed Lasher) because he wanted to continue to use Creery's family's legitimate businesses in Miami as a front for his illegal activities. As Fell and Draggart are about to be hustled away to their deaths, The Sevens appear, having suspected trouble when Fell left the dance and called the police, who soon arrive. Fell also learns that Lasher had given Rinaldo his things to buy his silence, because Rinaldo knew that Lasher had been intercepting Creery's mail. Characters and events are stock for the genre but strongly drawn, and the convoluted plot grabs early and holds steadily throughout. What keeps this book from being just another teenaged detective story are its well-delineated school setting and its bright, sensitive, sensible, likable hero. There is just enough romance, and the tension that develops between Fell and Dib, who is a junk food addict and near the end begins to indulge in alcohol, seems natural and a good lead-in for further adventures. The style is vigorous, contemporary, and often witty, although current expressions and allusions may soon date the book. Poe Nominee.

FELL, JOHN (*Fell Back**), student at exclusive Gardner School, who becomes involved in solving a murder. Fell is the son of a deceased Brooklyn, New York, policeman turned private detective, and the comments Fell remembers his father made occasionally about law enforcement procedures and detecting sometimes help Fell out. Fell is close to his mother and little sister, Jazzy, a good student and a gourmet cook. He is at Gardner through the generosity of a millionaire and a member of The Sevens quite by chance. When he planted a tree, a school entrance ritual, he named it Good-bye, a word with seven letters. Naming the entrance tree with a seven-letter word is the only way to enter the society. Among other Sevens' secrets he learns is that the punishment called the Sevens Revenge does not exist.

FERGUSON, ALANE, author of picture books and novels for middle grade readers and young adults. Her initial interest in writing came from her mother, Gloria Skurzynski, whose best-known book is *What Happened in Hamelin* (Four Winds, 1978) and who has written adventure stories set in the West. Ferguson's first book was *That New Pet!* (Lothrup, 1986), a picture book illustrated by Catherine Stock. Her second was a mystery, *Show Me the Evidence** (Bradbury, 1989), which won an Edgar Allan Poe Award in the Young Adult Novel category. Both that book and a more recent mystery, *Overkill* (Bradbury, 1992), concern teenaged girls who are wrongly accused of murder. Among her titles for younger children are *Cricket and the Crackerbox Kid* (Bradbury, 1990), a story of prejudice in a small town, and *The Practical Joke War* (Bradbury, 1991), about sibling rivalry and high jinks. Ferguson lives in Sandy, Utah, with her husband and three children. For biographical information about Gloria Skurzynsky and title entries, see *Dictionary, 1960–1984* [*What Happened in Hamelin*] and *Dictionary, 1985–1989* [*Trapped in Slickrock Canyon*].

FINDING BUCK MCHENRY (Slote*, Alfred, HarperCollins, 1991), sports novel of a Little League baseball team that learns about the old Negro leagues and about true team spirit. When Jason Ross, 11, is cut from the Baer Machines in Arborville, Michigan, he is crushed until the African-American school custodian, Mr. Mack Henry, gives him a lesson in base running and quizzes him about the Pittsburgh Crawfords, the Homestead Grays, the Kansas City Monarchs, and other teams he has never heard of, although he can recite statistics for all the prominent players on major league teams, past and present. Determined to see whether the old man is lying, Jason bikes to The Grandstand baseball card store run by Jim Davis and learns that a new set of cards has just been issued for the Negro leagues, operating from about 1900 to 1946 but never formally recognized by white baseball. Among cards of the new set he finds Buck McHenry, who ''after several scrapes with the law'' retired early and worked as a school janitor in Michigan. Putting this together with Mr. Henry's obvious knowledge of the game, Jason decides that he is really McHenry, aged from the blurry picture and using his name now divided in half. Since rejects from the regular Little League teams are scheduled to start an expansion team, Davis agrees to sponsor it if they can line up a coach. Jason pedals to Mr. Henry's modest home and finds that both he and his wife are worried about their eleven-year-old grandson, Aaron, who has come to live with them and is badly depressed by the death of his parents and his brother in a car accident while he was playing baseball. Although Mr. Henry denies that he is Buck McHenry, he orders his grandson to pitch to Jason in the backyard, where he has hung an old mattress on the side of a shed, and Jason is astonished by Aaron's skill and speed. At the prodding of Mrs. Henry, who knows her grandson needs friends and interests, Mr. Henry allows that he might have been Buck McHenry and agrees to coach the team if Aaron will pitch. Fired by this knowledge, Jason and Aaron bike to the lavish home of Chuck Axelrod, a Detroit television sportscaster who recently moved to town, to help his son call the other rejects to come to a team meeting. Although Jason is disgusted to discover that Kim* Axelrod is a girl, he soon learns that she is assertive and a good, competitive ball player. In spite of having promised not to tell, Jason lets Chuck Axelrod know that Mr. Henry is really Buck McHenry, and the sportscaster seizes on this as a theme for his evening program. When the three youngsters cannot recruit any of the rejectees, they go to the park, where Mr. Henry is waiting, to call off the team meeting. Chuck Axelrod drives up in his white Lincoln, overpowers Mr. Henry's objections to being revealed as Buck McHenry, and lines up the Baer Machine team, who have shown up, to play a three-inning practice game against three-player Grandstand. His camera crew, summoned earlier, arrives from Detroit and, despite Mr. Henry's obvious discomfort, Chuck Axelrod interviews him about the hardships and prejudice suffered by the Negro teams, then films the practice game, in which Aaron's superb pitching and Kim's feisty fielding win for the Grandstand, two to zero. Later Jason and Kim decide that Aaron should watch the sportscast with them. They bike to his house and overhear Mr. Henry actually weeping because the falsehood he has perpetuated (he is not actually Buck McHenry) will soon be broadcast. Without making their presence known, Jason and Kim ride back and part, each going home. Jason is so overcome by remorse that he can hardly stop crying to watch the show and is astonished that Axelrod, warned at the last minute by a call from Kim, has revised the segment, describing how they all tried to make Mack Henry become Buck McHenry and how the old man, who did play semiprofessional ball in his youth, coached three players who were able to beat a nine-member team, and is willing to coach the Grandstand the rest of the year if enough eleven year olds will volunteer. Soon Jason's telephone is ringing off the hook, and he lines up fifteen potential members for the next day's practice. Like other sports novels by Slote set in Arborville, a slightly disguised Ann Arbor, this story is unpretentious, clearly written, and has detailed and exciting game descriptions and believable characters. The strongest element is the information about the old Negro leagues and the semiprofessional black players before baseball integration, all presented without any sense of didacticism. Poe Nominee.

FISH & BONES (Prather*, Ray, HarperCollins, 1992), unusual mystery that ultimately involves racial tensions in the small town called Sun City in northwest Florida, in 1971. The narrator, African-American Bones (Bonapart) Russ, 13, whose father is a trash collector, has been a good friend of Fish Baker since before the boy was injured and brain damaged by a fast-pitched baseball. Now a sweet, docile adolescent, Fish is used by many in the community, black and white alike, for any job they want done free, since he never refuses or complains. He is often the butt of tricks, especially by Duck Tanner and his bunch, tough black kids a few years older, and white Skip Goodweather, 18, whose father owns the Bar & Grill and is reputed to be the local Ku Klux Klan leader. Fish will even steal if told to, but he is not a suspect when the bank is robbed in broad daylight by someone wearing a Halloween pig mask and identified by the teller, Betsy Gisendeiner, as a black man, though she admits he was almost completely covered up by the mask, long sleeves, and gloves. Toad Man, a filthy old trickster who helps Bones's father on the garbage route, enlists Bones to find the robber and share the thousand dollar reward. Suspicion shifts from one person to another in Sun City. Three members of Duck Tanner's gang are found to have new ten-dollar bills with serial numbers of the stolen money on them, but they all have iron-clad alibis. The Reverend Black, the Methodist minister who has had free lawn service from Fish for years and whose daughter,

Doris, is sweet on Bones, finds bills from the robbery pinned to his clothesline, and some are found tucked into the coffin of an old lady. The engagement and plans for an immediate wedding of Skip and Betsy are announced, making Bones suspect that Betsy recognized Skip as the robber and is blackmailing him; he has motive, since the Bar & Grill, which he has been managing, is losing money, and suspicion is general when a packet of the stolen bills is found in his car during the wedding. Later, however, Betsy admits that she is pregnant, explaining the hasty marriage. Because he lives at the edge of Abernathy Swamp, Bones has become an expert snake catcher and was last year's champion at the Annual Sun City Rattlesnake Rodeo for catching the longest rattler, an honor that Skip covets. This year Bones is sure his snake will take the prize again and is shaken when Skip's is a half an inch longer. Both are astonished when Long Mose* Baker, Fish's older brother who is on leave from the Marine Corps, comes up with one almost a foot longer. Then Mose lets the snake's head slip out of the noose, and the crowd scatters in panic. Mose seems to notice that Bones is suspicious and afterward seeks him out, inviting him to play pool and even asking him to a meal at the home in the swamp Fish shares with their mother. One day he takes both boys fishing and tells Bones the story that no one mentions any more: when he was just a little boy, his father was lynched by a Klan group from a tree right in the swamp. Bones is dismayed that even his own father has never told him this local history. Putting the pieces of the puzzle together, he realizes that everyone who has fallen under suspicion or been embarrassed by the robbery money is connected with the lynching or has abused Fish in some way. He even suspects that the bare spot on the Baker garden, which Mose seems to be tending solicitously, has something buried other than seeds. The mystery culminates when one of the local toughs lures Fish across a shaky old bridge, long condemned, and it collapses. The whole town joins in a rescue effort. Bones, riding with Mose, spots Fish and is thrown out as the boat hits rocks and Mose is swept over the falls. Bones grabs Fish's body, discovering that a plank from the bridge has been driven right through it. Skip, coming dangerously near in his motorboat, throws Bones a rope and he, gripping Fish's body, is pulled out. Mose's body is never found, and Mrs. Baker leaves town immediately after the funeral. Later Bones finds a freshly turned mound of earth in the bare patch in the garden. The open-ended plot works well. Although almost certain that Mose committed the robbery, Bones never knows whether he survived and was joined by his mother, and although knowledge of the lynching changes his view of the town, the way white and black join without question to try to rescue Fish shows him that the relationship is more complicated than it seems. The well-evoked setting on the river and in the swamp, where Bones poles and rows his leaky boat, is one of the strengths of the book, and the rattlesnake hunt is a memorable scene. Poe Nominee.

FITZSIMMONS (*A Little Bit Dead**), the elderly storekeeper who takes a fatherly interest in Reece*. Fitzsimmons helps outfit the young man, makes possible his escape from the posse, advises him not to marry Kathryn* Forrest, and even tries to bribe the jury at Reece's trial. His wife, Cora, suffers from "arthuritis." Shanti*, the young Indian man Reece rescues, alleviates her pain by diet and massage.

FLEISCHMAN, PAUL (1952–   ), born in Monterey, California; author of many different kinds of books for young people. The son of Sid Fleischman*, well-known author for children, he attended the University of California at Berkeley and received his B.A. degree from the University of New Mexico at Albuquerque. In 1989 his *Joyful Noise: Poems for Two Voices* (Harper, 1988) won the Newbery Medal. Two books of short stories, *Graven Images: Three Stories* (Harper, 1982) and *Coming-and-Going Men: Four Tales of Itinerants* (Harper, 1985), received critical acclaim for their haunting irony. Also set in New England of an earlier period and sharing much the same tone as these is *Saturnalia** (Harper, 1990), a novel of early Boston with a wide cast of characters held together by the story of a Narraganset Indian boy slave, apprenticed to a printer. In addition to other recognition it was named a *Boston Globe–Horn Book* Honor Book. History in other parts of the country serves as background for *The Borning Room** (HarperCollins, 1991), a story of a pioneer family in Ohio, and *Bull Run** (HarperCollins, 1993), a novel of the Civil War composed of vignettes of a number of people involved on both the Union and Confederate sides, which won the Scott O'Dell Award for Historical Fiction. All three of these books have also been named to the American Library Association Notable Books list, the *School Library Journal* list of Best Books for Children, and the *Horn Book* Fanfare list. For earlier biographical information and a title entry, see *Dictionary, 1985–1989* [*Rear-View Mirrors*].

FLEISCHMAN, SID (ALBERT SIDNEY) (1920–   ), born in Brooklyn, New York; reporter and writer of screen plays; for thirty years popular in children's literature for his tall-tale, fast-action novels for elementary-aged children, especially the outrageous fantasies featuring Josh McBroom; his Newbery Award–winning *The Whipping Boy* (Greenwillow, 1986); and the novels with an American historical background. Among his other comic, convoluted, melodramatic adventures are *The Midnight Horse** (Greenwillow, 1990), which was selected by both the American Library Association and *School Library Journal,* was nominated for the Edgar Allan Poe Award, and tells of a late nineteenth-century orphan's problems with an avaricious relative; and *Jim Ugly** (Greenwillow, 1992), also on the American Library Association list, about a boy's search for his missing father in the old Wild West, in which he is assisted by his dog, Jim Ugly. Fleischman's son, Paul Fleischman*, also a novelist, received the Newbery Award for his book of poems, *Joyful Noise* (Harper, 1988). For earlier biographical information and title entries, see *Dictionary, 1960–1984* [*By the Great Horn Spoon!; Chancy and the Grand Rascal; The Ghost in the Noon-*

day Sun; Humbug Mountain; McBroom Tells the Truth; Mr. Mysterious and Co.] and *Dictionary, 1985–1989* [*The Whipping Boy*].

FLIP-FLOP GIRL (Paterson*, Katherine, Lodestar Dutton, 1994), novel of friendship and a troubled sibling relationship, set in Brownsville, Virginia, in the early 1990s. Torn from her familiar Washington, D.C., environment after the death of her father, Vinnie (Lavinia) Matthews, 9, is lonely and angry; she is resentful toward her family's reduced financial circumstances, toward her eccentric stepgrandmother who has taken the family in, and especially toward her brother, Mason, 5, who is getting all the attention because he abruptly stopped talking. Starting at Gertrude B. Spitzer School is misery. Vinnie is wearing the wrong kind of clothes, the other girls are unfriendly, the building is old-fashioned, and Mason's kindergarten teacher seems to blame her for his refusal to talk or cooperate, but Mr. Clayton, her teacher, almost makes up for everything else. Innovative and patient, he seems to like Vinnie, praises her imagination, gives her barrettes to hold her overgrown hair out of her eyes, and once even drives her around in his sporty red car to find Mason, who has run away from her. The only girl to pay any attention to Vinnie is Lupe (Maria Guadalupe) Mahoney, a tall, lanky girl who wears a long dress and flip-flops and whose father is in prison for killing her mother. Vinnie plays hopscotch with her but is jealous that Mr. Clayton gives Lupe a pair of his old high-topped black sneakers and stands up for her to the bullying assistant principal. After a less than joyous Christmas, Vinnie does not want to return to school, especially because Mr. Clayton has been married during the vacation. Already tardy, feeling abandoned, she stalls in the schoolyard and, filled with sudden fury, makes deep scratches in Mr. Clayton's car with her barrette, even signing her initials, L. M. Since she expects to be discovered, probably arrested, and sent to prison, she is at first relieved when Lupe is accused of the vandalism and expelled from school. Filled with guilt, Vinnie takes her frustration out on Mason, shouting at him, ''I don't ever want to see your stupid face again.'' Later, when her grandmother tells her he has disappeared, she rushes off to the convenience store, learns that he might have been there and left with Lupe, then trudges the long way to the shack in the center of a pumpkin patch where the girl lives with her grandmother. Lupe knows nothing of Mason's whereabouts but willingly joins Vinnie's hunt for him. They hear a faint call, and they spot him in the center of the railroad trestle that crosses almost over the shack. Directing Vinnie to talk calmly to him, Lupe climbs to the trestle, inches out to Mason, and carries him back to the house, where he gets warm and talks normally. Although Vinnie has always thought he was just pretending to be unable to speak, she is deeply grateful and admits to herself for the first time that his silence probably resulted from her deliberately scaring him at the funeral home where they viewed their father's body. The next day, Vinnie confesses to Mr. Clayton that she is the vandal and, with Lupe's help, gets a lawn-care and errand-girl job to help pay his insurance deductible. The story is seen through the eyes of Vinnie, who feels convincingly neglected and miserable, and whose anger at Mason, whom she recognizes as manipulative, is understandable, yet the characters of the little boy, the mother, and the grandmother are also well developed and their difficulties are not belittled. Lupe, however who knows Vinnie scratched the car and says nothing, is almost too forbearing to be believable. SLJ.

FLOOD PEYTON (*Dixie Storms**), Dutch Peyton's much older brother of about thirty-three, Becky's* ex-husband, and Bodean's* father. Flood is handsome enough to be considered a good catch by the women of the area. He is stubborn enough to defy Papa* occasionally: over money matters, among them, the brand of tractor, which he thinks should be a John Deere; by coming home drunk, although he knows Papa will not tolerate such behavior in the house; and even by uncouth table manners. Flood longs to have a ranch in the West, but after he sees the emotional toll of his hard-headedness on Becky and Bodean, gets interested in Lucy Cabbot, and realizes the farm may be lost, he gives Papa the cash he has saved. He usually ignores Dutch, as he does most other people unless there is some compelling reason to do otherwise, but occasionally he comes out strongly in her defense. Flood is an interesting combination of character facets.

FOREST (Lisle*, Janet Taylor, Orchard, 1993), animal fantasy about a conflict between squirrels and humans in the small town of Forest somewhere in the United States about the time of its publication. The narrative is on two levels, just as is the town: Lower Forest occupied by humans in typical boxframe houses with square lawns, and Upper Forest, flourishing in the high tops of an ancient hardwood forest, connected by a complicated spiral of branchways through which a great number of mink-tailed squirrels scamper, seldom seen by the humans below. Among the residents of Upper Forest are Woodbine, a dreamy young mink-tail; Brown Nut, his practical older sister; Laurel, Brown Nut's friend; and Barker, a bully who delights in baiting Woodbine. The two levels make contact when Amber* Padgett, 12, runs away from home, angered at her father's obtuse ignorance of nature and threats to the environment. Competent Amber climbs a white oak, nails her sleeping bag securely to form a hammock, and settles down for the night, watched by a number of the squirrels who consider her an alien invader. Feeling guilty because he yelled at his daughter and smacked her but unwilling to admit it, Mr. Padgett takes out his anger by insisting that his son, Wendell*, 8, go squirrel hunting with him, blasts into a tree with his shotgun, and almost shoots Amber. His daughter, disgusted but not hurt, picks up a squirrel lying stunned on the ground and carefully carries it home. Above, Woodbine and Laurel see her taking Brown Nut away and worry, although Woodbine, who has made eye contact with Amber, is inclined to think she has good intentions. Hot heads and the power hungry prevail on both sides. In Upper Forest, Barker sees his chance and persuades the Elders, the group of old gray squirrels, who make policy for the others, that they must form an army and declare war. When Amber and Wendell climb back at night to the sleeping-bag hammock with Brown Nut, who seems to have recovered, they are attacked. Amber, who suffers a concussion, a broken wrist, and cracked teeth in the subsequent fall, refuses to explain the little bites all over her shoulders, but Wendell is pressured into implicating the squirrels. Mr. Padgett, who has already suggested a town hunt, now organizes a search-and-destroy mission. After their fall, Wendell and Amber retrieve Brown Nut, and when Woodbine and Laurel come to get her, Amber is convinced that the mink-tails have real language and an intelligent civilization. She and Wendell take a bus to Randomville to consult the author of a book on woodland animals, A. B. Sparks, who turns out to be a tiny professor with a vicious-looking half-hyena dog named India. Alerted to the danger, Professor Sparks cancels her classes and quickly drives with the children to Forest. In the meantime, Woodbine and Laurel, who have been captured by Barker's lieutenants and imprisoned, are rescued by Brown Nut and persuade the Elders of their terrible mistake in trusting Barker and of the need to stop the disastrous conflict. When Amber, Wendell, and Professor Sparks reach the townsmen, who are about to blast away at the surrounding squirrels, the Elders arrive simultaneously. Amber is able to interpret their orders to the squirrels to retreat, and Professor Sparks persuades the men, who have been very frightened despite their firepower, to put down their guns in a show of good faith. The strange conflict has many exciting moments, but the strongest element in the novel is the characterization of the children and their parents, with numerous sly digs at fathers and mothers who do not bother to listen to their children. Professor Sparks is a fortuitous element to bring about the happy, if not entirely convincing, denouement. SLJ.

FOX, PAULA (1923–   ), born in New York City; graduate of Columbia University; writer for thirty years best known for her contemporary realistic problem novels for later elementary readers and early adolescents. Among her many honors was the John Newbery Medal for the American historical novel, *The Slave Dancer* (Bradbury, 1973), a book about the slave trade, which deviates from the bulk of her work. In her customary vein are *Monkey Island** (Ochard, 1991), a serious problem novel of homeless persons in New York City, which appears on both the American Library Association and Fanfare lists; and *Western Wind** (Orchard, 1993), a quiet story of a girl growing up on her grandmother's rocky island off Maine, which was nominated for the *Boston Globe–Horn Book* Award and was selected by *School Library Journal*. In 1978, she received the Hans Christian Andersen Medal for her total work for young readers. For earlier biographical information and title entries, see *Dictionary, 1960–1984* [*Blowfish Live in the Sea; How Many Miles to Babylon; The King's Falcon; Maurice's Room; The Portrait of Ivan; The Slave Dancer; The Stone-Faced Boy*] and *Dictionary, 1985–1989* [*The Moonlight Man; One-Eyed Cat; The Village by the Sea*].

FRANK (*Shadow Boxer**), the "elephant man," to whom Nat* the super introduces George and Monty*. Frank plans to hold a yard sale, needs help setting it up, and will pay the boys for their work. Monty is appalled by the man's appearance—deformed body, huge head, and warty skin—and soon runs out. George, however, stays to the end of the sale and returns home with his pay in returnable bottles and cans. He finds Monty sitting on the doorstep and scolds him, asserting that he (Monty) thinks he is tough, but Frank is an example of what real toughness is.

FRED THE HEAD (*Shadow Boxer**), Fred Rafkin, friend of Monty*, brother of Mary B., or Herbie, as George, the narrator, calls her. Fred goes everywhere with Monty, and Herbie attaches herself to George, accompanying him on his paper route, although never invited. Because Fred's head is eggplant shaped, the kids call him Fred the Head, but Monty does not tease Fred as the others do. George tells of Monty's friendship with Fred to show how goodhearted Monty is. The Rafkins occupy an upstairs apartment for about six months in the neighborhood in which George and Monty live. Herbie is expected to take care of the house, and although her father derides her at every turn, she remains remarkably faithful to her tasks. The boys notice that Fred stays out of the house as much as possible. Mr. Rafkin is an unpleasant sort, and since George and Monty's Ma says the man gives her the willies, the boys start referring to the whole family as the Willies. After it becomes obvious that Mr. Rafkin is a drunken abuser of his children, Ma, who works for the State Rehabilitation Commission, tries to get Social Services to intervene but fails because she has not personally witnessed incidents of abuse. After Mr. Rafkin is reported, the Willies suddenly move away. Monty is furious because he knows, as do George and Ma, that the abuse will continue and the children will continue to be ostracized.

G

GABRIEL MCKAY (*The Harmony Arms**), fourteen-year-old son of Sumner* McKay. Gabriel has been living with his mother, but since she is going on an extended bicycle trip, he must accompany his father to California. He is embarrassed to be around his puppeteer father and resents having to spend the summer with him. By book's end, he has come to see that the residents of the Harmony Arms apartment house like Sumner for what he is, inside, and that Sumner often expresses his feelings through his Timmy the Otter puppet rather than directly. The "sex talk" that Gabriel and his father have helps the boy see that his feelings toward Tess* Miller are normal, and at the end he has a healthier attitude toward his sexuality as well as toward his father and other people in general.

GARRETT (*Remember Me**), Lieutenant Garrett, police detective who investigates Shari Cooper's death. From the beginning, Garrett suspects murder and doggedly remains on the case, even when other officers openly disparage him about it. He is portrayed as an excessive drinker, and at first Shari feels that he will not accomplish much. She changes her opinion of him after she observes the care he gives to even the smallest of details and she learns that his daughter is a drug addict. After Shari is cleared of suicide, she and her friend Peter put on an act in which they pretend to be an angel and a devil contending for Garrett's daughter and frighten her into seeking help for her addiction. She stops taking drugs, and as a result Garrett stops drinking. Garrett is the typical seemingly bumbling cop, who triumphs because of persistence and wit. The drug reformation is overly speedy and seems contrived for effect.

GERALD (*Monkey Island**), the socially aware man who comes to the park at six o'clock in the morning to pass out coffee, doughnuts, milk, and cheese sandwiches that he and his cook rise early to prepare for the homeless people. He is always pleasant and kind. Financially secure, even well off, he has a house in the city and one in the country. His work among the street people has become his mission. In his desk at home he has a pile of police summonses to remove from the park the old van he uses as a food stand. After the van is hauled away, he continues to serve the park people and later finds a new place down by the river where he feeds more homeless. He represents direct people-to-people assistance to the unfortunate.

GERALDINE BRENNAN (*And One for All**), twelve-year-old younger sister of Wing* Brennan. Her acceptance of Sam* Daily's need to lobby openly against the Vietnam War demonstrates the importance of considering people's motives rather than just their actions. Unlike Wing, Geraldine is a good student, a tomboy who resists growing up, but, as she learns she must accept bras, for example, she also realizes she must accept such other realities as a dear brother's going off to war and an almost equally dear friend's opposing the very war that eventually claims her brother's life. Geraldine is not a strongly delineated character—she is quite ordinary, except for being such a fine student—but her typicalness adds considerably to the book's irony.

G.G. (*Libby on Wednesday**), Gary Greene, the most arresting of the five members of the FFW (Famous Future Writers) workshop at Morrison Middle School, the least liked by the others, and a general terror in school. G.G. claims attention by his antisocial, threatening behavior. Wherever he goes, he appears to be "looking for prey." Libby writes in her notebook that he seems to be "the reincarnation of someone horrible—like Hitler, maybe." His stories for the workshop are gruesome, science-fiction pieces about robots, violence, and killing. Later the group learns that they reflect the atmosphere of his life with his divorced, alcoholic father, once a famous football player, who is mean and violent when he drinks.

GHOST CAVE (Steiner*, Barbara, Harcourt, 1990), mystery-adventure novel set during the summer of 1954 in Pine Creek, a small town in the hills and bluffs of northern Arkansas in what was once Osage Indian territory. Marc Schaller, 11, seeking a reward for Native American Indian artifacts, explores a cave that Bluedog, his beloved Australian blue sheepdog, falls into, and discovers an Indian grave mound. Later he and two pals, Eddie and Hermie, carefully excavate it and uncover the skeleton of an Indian boy, along with the skeleton of a dog and some items like arrowheads, a bow and arrow, a clay pot, a tomahawk, and a medallion. Marc, the only active spelunker of the three, keeps mum about the cave, although he knows that he should always let his father know when and where he is exploring underground. In the days since his mother has been hospitalized for tuberculosis, Marc's father, who used to take Marc caving and also was interested in artifacts, has grown distant and abstracted, an attitude Marc resents. Contributing to Marc's desire for secrecy is the town bully, Mooney (Howard) Moon, who is determined to keep tabs on the boys and follow them in order to cash in on whatever they find. Uneasy also because it seems as if they have violated a special place, Marc persuades the boys not to tell about their find. They return later to explore further, get lost in the cave, and are almost despairing when Eddie spots a brown moccasin ahead and then Marc sights an Indian youth wearing the medallion they had seen in the grave. Marc leads the boys in the direction the Indian youth goes, and the three boys soon find themselves outside. They agree to cover the grave and never reveal its existence. Marc never tells the boys about the shadowy figure that he alone had seen. The story ends with Marc's father informing Marc that his mother will probably be released from the sanitarium in the fall, and since his father suspects what Marc has been up to, Marc decides to own up about his find. His father also agrees to keep the secret. The book is mostly dialogue, with short and uncomplicated sentences that move fast. Most characters are superficially developed, one-faceted, and conventional—Eddie tends to be contentious, Hermie is chubby and studious, Mooney is troublesome and snoopy, and Marc's father is worried and preoccupied—except for Marc, who is better developed but in typical terms. He knows something about spelunking, enjoys collecting and is knowledgeable about Indian relics, worries about his mother, and chafes under his father's abstraction, all conventional attitudes. The personal problem part of the plot ends predictably, but the boys' decision not to tell about their find seems more compatible with late twentieth-century views than those of their time about such discoveries. Roy Clearwater, an old Osage Indian at Marc's mother's sanitarium, is a stock figure not worked well into the plot. The sense of the period's small-town closeness and freedom, the reality of the physical terrain, the emphasis on following rules for spelunking, and respect for the past and Indian culture are worthy features. Poe Nominee.

THE GIVER (Lowry*, Lois, Houghton Mifflin, 1993), futuristic novel of a society in which sameness and lack of pain and conflict have been valued so highly that all color and love have been bleached from life. In this contented but highly regimented society, Jonas approaches his Ceremony of Twelve with some apprehension, since at this celebration the future occupation of each twelve year old is announced, having been carefully decided by the Committee of Elders after long observation and discussion. He is astonished and confused when he is selected to be the next Receiver of Memory, a mysterious position about which he knows little. The living quarters of the present Receiver, now self-designated as the Giver, is the first place Jonas has seen many books and the only place the ubiquitous two-way wall speakers that transmit and record all that is said in the community can be turned off. There the Giver, now an old and very tired man, begins through touch and telepathy to transfuse the memories that he holds for the whole society to Jonas; some of those memories are exciting and delightful, like color and sunshine, and some painful, like grief and war. Gradually Jonas realizes that as he takes these on, the Giver loses them, thereby gaining back some of his strength. He also learns that the last Receiver in training, ten years earlier, found the process too harrowing and chose to be

Released, a choice generally reserved for the very old or the babies not wanted in the community. He has always imagined that this meant they went Elsewhere, to some happy existence, but when the Giver shows him an example of Releasing, performed by his own father, a Nurturer who cares for children during their first year, he is horrified to discover that it is a lethal injection, after which the body is deposited in the trash chute. He protests that it might be good for the community to suffer some memory and is surprised that the Giver agrees and has been waiting for him to come to that conclusion. The Giver points out that if anything happens to Jonas, if he should die or go Elsewhere, the memories he has been given will come back to the community, to people unused to them and unprepared to cope with them. Together they make a plan that Jonas will leave on his bicycle in an effort to get Elsewhere, but the Giver refuses to accompany him, knowing that he can help the people survive the shock and that they will perish without him. Before the next annual Ceremony, the time they have chosen for leaving, Jonas learns that little Gabe, the new child his father has brought home each night for extra care because he has not progressed to peaceful sleeping in the Nurturing Center and to whom Jonas has secretly been transmitting peaceful memories, is to be Released. Appalled, he sneaks out at night and steals food, both forbidden and almost unheard-of practices, and sets out with Gabe to escape. Although they must hide from the search planes and suffer terribly from cold and hunger, they finally reach a place where everything feels different and where with hope they approach houses that seem to be full of color, warmth, and love. Tightly written, the story catches the imagination early and holds interest. Jonas is a well-rounded character, and others are developed sufficiently to be convincing in their roles. The strength of the book is the picture of the community life, which at first seems merely highly organized and grows more bleak and ominous as the story progresses. ALA; Boston Globe Honor; Fanfare; Newbery Winner; SLJ.

GOEWIN (*The Winter Prince**), twin to Lleu*, daughter of Artos (Arthur) by his wife, Ginevra. Always more robust than her brother, she is fiercely protective of him, in spite of recognizing his weaknesses. Intelligent and competent, Goewin would actually be a far better ruler than Lleu, and she knows it, but she is not jealous of him or covetous of his position, only desperately desirous of keeping her own freedom. Because she has often waked Medraut* when Lleu needs medical help, she has heard him cry out in his dreams of his mother, Morgause, and she knows more about his secret thoughts than anyone else. Her attraction to him seems innocent and sisterly to her until, to counter her scorn of his relationship with Morgause, he kisses her in an unbrotherly way and she realizes the possibilities that could lead to incest.

GORDY SMITH (*Stepping on the Cracks**), third son in the large "white trash" Smith family who live not far from Margaret* Baker and Elizabeth* Crawford. Gordy is well known as the neighborhood bully. He regularly picks on the two girls, his sixth-grade classmates, whom he ridicules as Magpie and Lizard, respectively. His antisocial behavior is presented as stemming in part from the abuse he receives from his alcoholic father and also from the desire to hide his older brother, Stuart*, who has deserted from the army. Although they help him with Stuart, the girls are never completely comfortable with Gordy, who is not stable in temperament. Gordy is not a completely credible character, since he seems tailor-made to make a statement about child abuse.

GRAB HANDS AND RUN (Temple*, Frances, Orchard, 1993), realistic novel of contemporary Salvadoran political refugees to the United States and Canada. After the motorcycle belonging to his popular, politically active, architect father, Jacinto, is found abandoned under mysterious circumstances, Felipe Ramirez, 12, the narrator, his mother, Paloma, and sister, Romy*, 8, take Jacinto's advice and "grab hands and run" for safety in Canada. Although for their own sensibilities and safety, the children have been told little of the atrocities committed by government thugs, Felipe knows he is old enough to be impressed into the army, and his suspicions about political repression are aroused when his dog finds a man's arm and hand in the vacant lot where he and his buddy play soccer. With only the barest essentials and the different currencies Jacinto saved up for possible flight, Paloma and the children leave in early fall and travel by bus, foot, boat, and truck, however they can, overland through the mountains into Guatemala and Mexico. They remember to stay calm and pretend to be simple travelers on the way to visit relatives. They occasionally receive help from church people, whose names Paloma has memorized from a list that their local priest gave her. They encounter various hazards. For example, when they are sleeping in a wrecked car, they are captured by soldiers whose captain has designs on Paloma; they must constantly be on guard against helicopters; and they lose a great deal of money to an avaricious boatman who blackmails them into paying double for his service. They must use their wits to get by, and they are not always comfortable with their actions—for instance, when they cheat out of full pay the man who helps them cross the Rio Grande. In Texas, just when they are beginning to feel safe, they are given a lift in a Cadillac by a cigar-smoking American, who to their dismay deposits them at a military guardhouse. A Red Cross van takes them to a detention center, where they face deportation to El Salvador unless they can prove they are political refugees and will be killed if they go home. Felipe, who longs for his father and thinks he might be able to locate him, seriously considers going back, until the local priest, jeans-clad Padre Jim, receives a letter saying that Jacinto is dead. The family decide to continue to Canada. After an interview with representatives of Project Canada and help from Americans, they are temporarily located on a Wisconsin farm, where in the spring about six months later they receive papers admitting them to Canada. Although tight spots along the route hold the reader's interest, the family meet with amazing good fortune and seldom seem as weary, dirty, hungry, or discouraged as might be expected of such fugitives. The political realities are not explored, only alluded to or reported briefly, except for a couple of instances, among them, views of a little girl who has become deranged by her experiences en route. Thus the journey seems more of a trip than a flight. Spunky Romy saves the day several times; Paloma's courage, planning, and wit keep them going; and the problems peculiar to women on such journeys are not overlooked. Most characters are types—some, like the Cadillac-driving American, being highly clichéd—but advance the action as needed. The book is mainly plot and serves to introduce middle graders to a growing international problem. Felipe's use of present tense contributes a sense of immediacy. An interesting aspect concerns attitudes toward Indians, which comes out particularly with reference to the people of Chiapas in southern Mexico. Fanfare; SLJ.

GRAM MCGRADY (*Silent Witness**), Helen McGrady, Jennie McGrady's paternal grandmother. A full-time writer of some fame, Gram is an ex–police officer and FBI undercover agent, who still occasionally carries out tasks for the bureau and maintains contact with other agents. Jennie confides to Gram that she wishes to search for her dad, an FBI agent who disappeared on assignment and is presumed dead. Jennie hopes to find him before her mother remarries. Gram also deeply misses her son. She is a very religious woman who often speaks of God, but never in a pious fashion, and encourages Jennie to pray. She is kind but not gullible, orderly but not rigid, warm but not sentimental, discerning but not judgmental, the best-developed figure in the novel. She and Jennie go over the possible suspects and evidence periodically in an effort to help the amnesiac Sarah Stanford by figuring out what is behind the peculiar happenings in her life.

GRAMS, HER BOYFRIEND, MY FAMILY, AND ME (Derby*, Pat, Farrar, 1994), contemporary realistic family novel set one school year in San Francisco. When Ma (Liz) Halliday announces that she intends to work outside the home and informs her older children that they must now help about the house and with the six-year-old twins, Alice and Anne, Dennie*, 17, is mostly supportive, but Molly*, 13, and Andy, the narrator, 15, have misgivings that are soon borne out by increased chores and mixups over babysitting schedules. Even more disturbing is the unexpected addition to the household of bossy, opinionated Grams*, Pop's (Chris's) mother, after she injures her wrist in a house fire and cannot stay alone. She alienates Liz right away by taking charge of the house, but the children find advantages in having her around. When Grams becomes friends with Harold Wagner, a resident of Cherry Garden Convalescent Hospital, and then announces that she and Harold plan to marry, Pop strenuously opposes the match; he refers to Harold as "that man," and calls the relationship "indecent." The children and Liz are thrilled, but all efforts to placate Pop fail. Sarah Carlson, Harold's married daughter, also objects to the marriage, and a humorous scene ensues when Sarah invites the Hallidays to dinner to plan strategy, and the two families fail to hit it off. Grams confides unhappily to Andy that she and Harold feel that they should call off the wedding and just be friends. Andy passes this information along to Dennie, who suggests that Grams and Harold elope. The children, Grams, and Harold plan the getaway to Reno for late Easter Sunday night. Dennie is to be maid of honor, Molly will be the bridesmaid, Andy is to give the bride away, their local priest will secure a Reno priest for them, and Dennie's boyfriend, Bruce, will drive them in his father's car. The wedding takes place, as it happens, in the chapel of a hospital, because Harold falls and breaks his ankle. Afterward, Grams calls home to inform her son of the marriage. When the children return, Pop seems no more receptive to his mother's marriage than before. Since the Hallidays are sensible people, however, and Pop is a good man at heart, the reader is left with the feeling that eventually Pop and his mother and stepfather will make peace. This is a pleasant, consistently interesting novel about decent, sensible people, who might be found next door in almost any middle-class neighborhood. The various Hallidays are well fleshed and individualized and not the stereotypes they at first threaten to be, except for the twins who are choral figures and play only a small role. Liz's resentments toward take-over Grams seem reasonable, and Chris's are also understandable for a grown son who has come to expect certain behaviors from his mother. Andy is a bland figure, less strongly delineated than his sisters, who run the show. He serves as the reader's eyes into the household, but he changes reasonably in that he learns to pay attention to details of family life and certain interpersonal niceties that "oil the machinery." He is forced to be more aware of the twins and his sisters because of his mother's job. When he forgets to order flowers for a date and his double-date counterpart does, Andy is relieved and later remembers to order some for Grams. He realizes that he is acquiring a sensitive side, a facet of character that Dennie had complained that he lacked. He shows signs of growing into a caring, thoughtful man, though mostly in the book he is on the fringes, too inwardly oriented to influence the action much. Some incidents bother—for example, Harold's broken ankle seems an unnecessary complication, and the Carlsons are phony. Carefully drawn Halliday family relationships set the main problem of what to do about Grams in relief and expose tactfully and nonjudgmentally common assumptions about the elderly and the attitudes of their children when the older generation does not act as expected. School scenes and conversations indicate that, perhaps too coincidentally, the high schoolers are studying intergenerational problems in their social studies classes. The family relationships avoid the nastiness of many teenaged stories, dialogue is extensive and appropriate, the many scenes keep the book moving, and humor is generous and kind. Another point in the book's favor is that the author avoids putting long, tedious ruminations of teenaged angst in Andy's head. SLJ.

GRAN BENEDICT (*Western Wind**), Cora Ruth Benedict, 74, an accomplished painter, self-sufficient woman, and Elizabeth Benedict's grandmother. Gran is sharp, observant, unpredictable, brusquely forthright, and never stuffy and has a good sense of humor. With honesty, she asserts that only people who are reasonably well off, as she is, can enjoy living under the spartan conditions that the simply furnished, dark little Pring Island cottage presents. Gran tells Elizabeth stories about her childhood and life with her husband, Will, and Elizabeth's father, because, as Elizabeth later learns, she has heart disease and is dying. Gran's father was a failed actor. After he divorced Gran's mother, who had no desire for a child, he managed a clothing store. Will Benedict, her husband, tall and thin like Elizabeth, served in World War II and wanted to be a poet but became a lawyer. He inspired Gran's love of poetry, and she has enjoyed painting him, in one picture as a kind of desperado. Not a fussy woman except with language, whose inexact usage she deplores, Gran easily substitutes crackers for bread, makes do without milk, and never yearns for such creature comforts as indoor plumbing. She spends a lot of time painting and sketching yet always seems to know what is going on. She is the most interesting figure in the novel, drawn with depths not explored in the book.

GRANDFATHER (*Journey**), Marcus, Journey's maternal grandfather, Liddie's father, Grandma's* husband. He is a tall, blunt man, a farmer, whose decision to give Journey a sense of family and belonging is evidently sparked when Cat*, Journey's sister, gives him the camera she has become bored with. Grandfather once describes himself as a photographer-farmer. He takes pictures with single-minded zeal, snapping people, actions, objects, animals, even the chickens. In a scene that does not jibe with Journey's age of eleven, Grandfather insists, over Journey's objections, that the boy drive the car so he can snap pictures as they go along. Through his actions and the pictures, Journey eventually sees that his grandfather has always been his most loving protector and thus he moves closer to accepting Mama's (Liddie's) abandonment.

GRANDFATHER LOTT (*The Borning Room**), Abram Lott, freethinking father of Georgina Lott's father, who came to Ohio from New Hampshire in 1820 and cleared land for the family farm, leaving a sugar maple to remind him of his New England home. Although most of the family attend church regularly, each Sunday he chooses one grandchild to walk in the woods and fields and worship silently, as he does. In the pre–Civil War years he is an abolitionist and a devoted reader of the *Liberator*. After he suffers a stroke and lies dying in the Borning Room, neighbors and church people from the community come and harangue him to accept formal religion, warning him of the fires of hell and pleading with him to repent so he can go to heaven. Although he can no longer speak, he motions to show that he cannot agree with them and retains his integrity to the end, as the artist who is painting his death portrait observes and tells Georgiana. As a child of five Grandfather had shaken the hand of Benjamin Franklin, for whom he retains a lifetime admiration, which he passes on to Georgiana, who in old age takes the hand of the artist painting her own death portrait to pass on the tradition of free thought.

GRANDMA (*Journey**), Lottie, grandmother of Journey and Cat*, wife of Grandfather*, mother of Liddie. Quiet, "secretive," Journey says, she early demonstrates the continuity of the generations when she puts on Liddie's sweatshirt and stands in the light with her hair tumbled, looking like Mama (Liddie) in the pictures. Journey notes the resemblance, as he does the likeness between her 1930 picture and that of Mama years later, both also similar in appearance to Cat. Like Cat, Grandma solves problems by staying busy, and hence she has a garden this year that is twice the size of last year's. Although she does not like Bloom the cat, she sees that the animal is important to Journey and allows her to stay.

GRANDMA (*Others See Us**), eccentric matriarch of the vacation compound where the extended family gathers each summer. Outspoken and irreverent, she usually complains at length about not having enough money to keep the big house in repair and about the neighbors, the Winstons, whom she despises. She has a telescope mounted on the widow's walk of her house, from which she keeps track of what is going on in the family and surrounding area, even being able to read lips and learn what people are saying at a distance. This year, to Jared's surprise, she says nothing about money and has had the house fixed up; moreover, she gloatingly announces that the Winstons have put their house up for sale at a price far lower than its value. Jared realizes that she can now read minds, and she has thus been able to break into any house in the area by learning the security code and that she also can read the ATM account numbers and must be responsible for the rash of baffling robberies from the ATM machine in town recently. He suspects that she found something embarrassing or incriminating in the Winstons' house and has blackmailed them into leaving the area. Whether she knew the true character of Annelise* before she fell in the swamp and began to read minds is not clear. While her motive for destroying Annelise is to keep the girl from doing more harm, she also seems to enjoy the contest and get pleasure from the distress she has caused the young people.

THE GRANDMOTHER (*The Cookcamp**), Anita Halvorson, the cook at the construction camp to which the boy comes, who is always referred to as the grandmother. She is a small, warm, sweet-smelling woman, strong, dependable, and very hard working, much respected by the men, who are always polite to her and considerate of her. The grandmother has a strong moral sense and appears outraged that her daughter, the boy's mother, is living with "Uncle Casey." She appears to blame the war for taking her daughter away to the city and the husband to Europe, thus creating this undesirable situation. She is also shown as the only medical help the men have. The last chapter, a kind of epilogue, gives the details of her life and whets the reader's interest about her, although in context it seems an unnecessary and sentimental addition to the book. The dedication to the book, "To the memory of My Grandmother," suggests that the grandmother of the book is based on the author's own grandmother.

GRANT, CYNTHIA D. (1950–), born in Brockton, Massachusetts; author of novels for children and young adults. Her dozen books include two for younger readers—her first novels, *Joshua Fortune* (Atheneum, 1980), about a boy who regrets his hippy mother, and *Summer Home* (Atheneum, 1981), concerning vacation crises—but most are problem novels for the young adult audience, for whom she wrote next. They include *Hard Love* (Atheneum, 1983), about a seventeen-year-old boy's relationship with an older woman; *Kumquat May, I'll Always Love You* (Atheneum, 1986), concerning a girl who decides she can make it on her own after her mother abandons her; *Big Time* (Atheneum, 1992), in which a young girl learns about the realities of becoming a movie star; and *Shadow Man,* which concerns alcoholism. Her *Phoenix Rising Or How to Survive Your Life** (Atheneum, 1989), a *School Library Journal* selection, is a psychological problem novel about a family's difficulties in accepting the death of their older daughter from cancer. Some humor keeps the books from becoming too serious or maudlin. With her husband and sons, Grant lives in the mountains outside Cloverdale, California.

GRAYSON, EARL (*Maniac Magee**), kind, generous, old equipment keeper at Elmwood Park near the zoo in the West End of Two Mills. An ex–minor league pitcher, he gives Maniac Magee his cherished baseball glove as a Christmas gift, tells him stories about his days on the diamond, including when he struck out Willie Mays, and shows him his unbeatable "stopball," a clever pitch that "nearly drove Maniac goofy" because he cannot hit it out of the infield. Grayson makes a home for the boy in the band shell and becomes a surrogate father to him. Grayson is an endearing, although sometimes pathetic, figure.

GREGOR SAMSA (*Shoebag**), tall, mysterious schoolmate of Shoebag. Like Shoebag, Gregor is a cockroach turned human. His real name, that is, his cockroach name, is In Bed. Right away he recognizes Shoebag for the roach that he really is. The only student who dares to stand up to Tuffy* Buck, the school bully, Gregor wears dark reflecting glasses that show the real nature of whoever is reflected in them. In them, Shoebag always appears as a roach, although to all people he appears human. Gregor attends school sporadically, preferring to watch soap operas on the Sony Watchman that he always carries. His ambition is to become a television actor. Gregor helps Pretty* Soft Biddle become a more real person by pointing out how selfish she is, squashes the horrible, seven-legged, black jumping spider that terrorizes Shoebag's family, and ends up doing commercials on television that advertise a brand of chewing gum called Chew Great Breath. Like all the other main figures, he is a caricature through whom the author comments on contemporary human life.

GRIFFIN, PENI R(AE) (1961–), born in Harlingin, Texas; author of fantasy and mystery novels for middle grade and junior high readers. After attending Trinity University and the University of Texas at San Antonio, she worked for City Public Service and Manpower Services in San Antonio for several years, then turned to full-time writing. She won several awards for short stories before publishing her first novel, *Otto from Otherwhere* (McElderry, 1990), about a boy from another dimension who enters the lives of some fifth graders. More time fantasies followed: *A Dig in Time* (McElderry, 1991), in which two children literally dig up the past, and *Switching Well** (McElderry, 1993), a *School Library Journal* Best Book for Children, which combines time travel and historical fiction in having two girls one hundred years apart trade places. Among her mysteries are *The Treasure Bird** (McElderry, 1992), a nominee for the Edgar Allan Poe Award about how a talking parrot helps uncover a lost cache of money, and *The Brick House Burglars* (McElderry, 1994), in which children foil a plot involving insurance fraud. Griffin's novels are well plotted and fast paced, convey a convincing sense of family life, and feature interesting and likable protagonists. Other novels for young readers include *Hobkin* (McElderry, 1992), which mingles fantasy, sexual abuse, and survival, and *Vikki Vanishes* (McElderry, 1995), about kidnapping and child abuse. Griffin has frequently contributed short stories to such magazines as *Isaac Asimov's Science Fiction Magazine, Space and Time,* and *Twilight Zone.* She lives in San Antonio, Texas.

GROM DAVENPORT (*Unlived Affections**), Willie Ramsey's grandmother, who raises him, Kate* Davenport's mother, and Bill* Ramsey's ex–mother-in-law. A retired school nurse, Grom not only runs the house meticulously and rigidly but also controls information about her family. She has spoken to Willie only about his mother as a child; has never mentioned his grandfather Davenport except to say that he is dead; and has told him only that his father was unfit, had run off before he was born, and is dead. To be his own person, Willie has often lied to her, for example, going swimming instead of out with friends as he said he was. Willie learns that Grom's need to control is a defense mechanism to protect herself from feeling abandoned. When her husband left her for another woman, she divorced him. She held Bill in high esteem, until Kate revealed he was homosexual, having at first told her that Bill had run off with another woman. Then Kate, killed in an auto accident, leaves Grom. As Willie learns from Bill's letters about Grom's unhappy life, he begins to understand and appreciate Grom more. He is very angry, however, when he finds out that his father had made the rocking chair for Willie's mother but that Grom had never told him it was his father's work and a gift to his mother. Although Grom never appears in the novel, she is a well-delineated figure, as are Bill and Kate.

GUILT TRIP (Schwandt*, Stephen, Atheneum, 1990), mystery-detective novel set in Minneapolis at the time of publication, in which a high school junior under suspicion of murder gains greater self-esteem and new directions in life.

Rebellious, angry Eddie (Edrich) Lymurek, diagnosed by a school psychologist as suffering from "hyperactivity and unfocused identity" and abandoned once again by his irresponsible father, comes to live, he expects temporarily, with his maternal aunt: unmarried, self-assured, strict Cyn Edrich. At mixed-ethnic Nicollet High, he soon becomes acquainted with beautiful, sophisticated, wealthy Angela Favor, who seems to go out of her way to attract him. But he is warned to stay away from her by basketball-playing friends, especially African-American Alex, whose brother, Adrian, dated Angela and suffered brain damage after he was beaten by her ex-boyfriend—at her provocation, Alex is sure. Angela is a star performer in NETT, the New Energy Theater Troupe for talented teens, whose director, Corey Howe-Browne, has recently been found dead in a Cadillac submerged in Lake Minnetonka under conditions that suggest suicide. He was really murdered, in the opinion of smart, determined black detective Robert Crenshaw. Suspicion falls variously, but chiefly on the angry fathers of young male actors whom Howe-Browne had been convicted of sexually molesting, and then upon Eddie, who was once humiliated publicly by Howe-Browne while trying out for a role in NETT. Through Crenshaw's sleuthing and Eddie's mature decision to face the music when he realizes he has been entrapped, it comes out that Angela has cleverly planned the killing and made Eddie the fall guy. Her motives are several: to demonstrate her power and control over those around her; to strike back at Howe-Browne, whom she feels abandoned her in favor of the boys; and to get back at her father, toward whom she has long harbored intense hostility. Book's end finds Angela in the medical center psychiatric ward and Eddie deciding to live permanently with his aunt, who has stood by him in spite of his erratic behavior throughout the book. The story opens with the gripping scene of Howe-Browne's death, with events unfolding from his point of view. Then it mostly follows Eddie but also sometimes sees matters from Angela's or Crenshaw's perspective. Characters and events are stock for the genre, to some extent brought over from adult whodunits: the femme fatale, the not-so-plodding police detective, the psychiatric adviser, the carefully orchestrated culmination scene in which the principals are gathered and the culprit enticed into exhibiting guilt—while others are typical of teenaged mysteries—the troubled youths, the all-too-fallible parents, the hotshot black sport stars. School scenes show a skilled, provocative social studies instructor, whose carefully planned lessons about authority figures and abuse of power point up the behavior of the fathers, the director, and also, highly ironically, Angela. Social comment on contemporary parenting cannot be missed, teenaged conversation includes topical slang and swear words, and puns add obvious humor. This is lively, consistently engrossing, albeit one-time-only, reading entertainment. Poe Nominee.

GUSTAF (*The Cookcamp**), the driver of the Caterpillar at the construction camp, who befriends the boy. Gustaf has a "face of two colors (part heavily tanned, part lighter where shaded) and a scar on one cheek that made his eye droop and was almost bald.'' Smelling of snoose (snuff), trees, and oily smoke, he holds the boy while he plays cards and puts him gently to bed when the boy falls asleep, saying that he is ''light as a goose down pillow.'' In the Caterpillar, Gustaf takes the boy to the very top of the gravel piles, where the boy thinks he will faint from height and then compares the experience to the pleasure of being on the roller coaster at the fair. Gustaf insists that, after helping with the work in the Cat, the boy eat at the table with the men, saying that ''good men are hard to find.'' Gustaf helps to build the boy's confidence and self-esteem and represents the warmth and goodness of these uncouth outdoorsmen.

H

HAHN, MARY DOWNING (1937–), born in Washington, D.C.; teacher, artist, librarian, and writer best known for a dozen contemporary problem and mystery novels for later elementary and adolescent readers, including *December Stillness* (Houghton Mifflin, 1988), about a girl who tries to help a homeless Vietnam War veteran, which received the Child Study Award. In another vein is the historical novel based on her own childhood memories of World War II, *Stepping on the Cracks** (Clarion, 1991). A winner of the Scott O'Dell Award and a best book of the American Library Association and *School Library Journal*, it concerns an American girl in World War II who becomes involved with a U.S. Amy deserter. Hahn lives in Columbia, Maryland, not far from College Park, the prototype for the town in *Stepping on the Cracks*. For earlier biographical information and title entries, see *Dictionary, 1985–1989* [*December Stillness; Following the Mystery Man*].

HALL, BARBARA (1960–), born in Danville, Virginia; writer and producer for television, editor, and author of novels for young adults. While working on such shows as *Newhart* (CBS) and *Fly Away* (NBC), she was also writing for children and young people such books as the nonfiction *Playing It Safe: Summer Smart Activities for Children* (Methuen, 1986), later expanded as *Playing It Safe: Home, Summer and Winter Street Smart Activities for Children* (Firefly, 1991), and the teenaged novels *Skeeball and the Secret of the Universe* (Orchard, 1987), about a boy who takes refuge from his problems by playing an old arcade game, and the acclaimed *Dixie Storms** (Harcourt, 1990). The latter makes effective use of the familiar conventions of the southern regional novel in telling how a visiting relative from the city brings new perspectives to a southern farm family, in particular, the teenaged girl protagonist. It won a *Booklist* citation and was named to both the *School Library Journal* and American Library Association lists of best books. Hall was graduated from James Madison University, married Nick Harding, a writer, and lives in Los Angeles.

HALL, LYNN (1937–   ), born in Lombard, Illinois; novelist whose books almost all involve farm life or animals, many of them dogs. Her mystery, *The Tormentors** (Harcourt, 1991), concerns a ring that steals dogs and trains them, by brutal means, to be sold as guard animals. It was a nominee for the Edgar Allan Poe Award. Her earlier novel, *The Whispered Horse* (Follet, 1979), a haunting story set in nineteenth-century Scotland, won the Poe Award. Also highly commended was her novel of a dysfunctional farm family in Iowa, *The Leaving* (Scribner's, 1980), winner of the *Boston Globe–Horn Book* Award. Hall attended schools in Iowa and worked in Texas and Iowa until she turned to full-time writing in 1968. She has lived near Garnaville, Iowa, breeding collies for show. For earlier biographical information and title entries, see *Dictionary, 1960–1984* [*The Leaving; The Whispered Horse*].

HAMILTON, VIRGINIA (ESTHER) (1936–   ), born in Yellow Springs, Ohio; author for more than twenty-five years of prominent novels for young people with African-American protagonists. She attended Antioch College, Ohio State University, and the New School for Social Research in New York. Probably her best-known novel is the Newbery Award winner, *M. C. Higgins, the Great* (Macmillan, 1974), set in southern Ohio, as is her novelette, *The Bells of Christmas** (Harcourt, 1989), a highly illustrated period story of a nineteenth-century Christmas. Less clearly located but still set in the American South are *Cousins** (Philomel, 1990), a novel of how the accidental death of one child affects her extended family, and *Plain City** (Scholastic, 1993), about a girl's efforts to find her father and come to terms with his mental illness. All three were named to the American Library Association list of Notable Books for Children; *Cousins* was also on *Horn Book*'s Fanfare List; and *Plain City* was cited by the *School Library Journal* as a Best Book for Children. Among Hamilton's many personal honors are the Hans Christian Andersen Author Award and the Laura Ingalls Wilder Award for total contribution to children's literature. For earlier biographical information and title entries, see *Dictionary, 1960–1984* [*Arilla Sun Down; The House of Dies Drear; M. C. Higgins, the Great; The Planet of Junior Brown; Sweet Whispers, Brother Rush; Zeely*] and *Dictionary, 1985–1989* [*Junius Over Far; A Little Love*].

HAMM, DIANE JOHNSTON (1949–   ), born in Portland, Oregon; teacher, counselor, freelance writer. She grew up in western Montana, attended Beloit College in Wisconsin, and received her B.A. degree from Montana State University and her M.Ed. degree from the University of Washington. During the 1970s she was a teacher and community extension worker in Barranquilla, Colombia, and has also taught in Mexico and Spain. In the early 1980s she was a workshop counselor at Community School in Seattle. Married with three children, she makes her home in Washington State. Her *Bunkhouse Journal** (Scribner's, 1990), inspired by the letters of a pioneer woman, won the Western Heritage Wrangler Award and was named a Reluctant Reader Choice by the

American Library Association. Also for young adults is *Second Family* (Scribner's, 1992), a novel with a contemporary setting. She has written a number of picture books, including *Grandma Drives a Motor Bed,* illustrated by Charles Robinson (A. Whitman, 1987); *How Many Feet in a Bed,* illustrated by Kate Salley Palmer (Simon & Schuster, 1991); *Laney's Lost Momma,* illustrated by Sally G. Ward (A. Whitman, 1991); and *Rockabye Farm,* illustrated by Rick Brown (Simon & Schuster, 1992), which was an alternate Book of the Month selection.

HANK WEBSTER (*Rachel Chance**), bright classmate of Rachel Chance, who works on Grandpa Abel* Chance's farm. From an abusive family, Hank is more comfortable with the unconventional Chances than at home, and although he and Rachel bicker and verbally spar, he is clearly attracted to her long before she realizes it. After a fight with his father, presumably because the man was beating Hank's mother, he runs away, intending to go east, get a job, and finish high school, but he first joins Abel and Rachel on their quest to find Rider, Rachel's little half brother, who has been kidnapped. Because he can drive and help Abel repair the decrepit truck, he is indispensable until they find Rider's father, and Hank then leaves the group and again heads east. A brief scene in the future shows that after five years and World War II, he returns to Rachel.

THE HARMONY ARMS (Koertge*, Ron, Little, Brown, 1992), contemporary novel of a boy's improving relationship with his father set for about a month in the summer mostly in the film community of Burbank, California. Gabriel* McKay, 14, feels self-conscious and embarrassed around his overweight, gregarious father, Sumner*, a second-grade teacher and writer, who loves to entertain on the spur of the moment with his puppet, Timmy the Otter, which he carries with him wherever he goes. Since Sumner has received a movie contract for the book he wrote about Timmy's adventures and since his divorced wife (Gabriel's mother) is leaving on a bicycle trip with her latest boyfriend, Gabriel sulkily agrees to accompany his father west from Missouri to California. Oxley Studio has taken a condominium for them at the run-down, partially renovated Harmony Arms Apartments, a place whose name foreshadows Gabriel's new attitude at the end of the book. Mona* Miller, the manager, a gentle, warm, faded starlet who affects slick tights and similar faddish attire, welcomes them graciously and introduces them to the other eccentric, lovable inhabitants. Mr.* Palmer is a nonagenarian and nudist, who is still deeply in love with his deceased wife, is in tune with such contemporary issues as animal rights and physical fitness, and spends hours doing laps in the pool every day, sans clothes. Obese, alcoholic Cassandra*, once a psychic to the stars, swooshes about on roller blades, dressed in a garish muumuu and Dodgers baseball cap with a breakfast-cereal ruby affixed to it. Intelligent, alert, inquisitive Tess* Miller, Mona's daughter about Gabriel's age, carries her camcorder with her wherever she goes, recording snippets of action and character for possible use in the life story of herself she intends to do some day. Most of the book's interest comes from the interactions among the colorful characters rather than from action. As in a motion picture, the book focuses on only significant episodes in Gabriel's life and presents them largely in dialogue. These include a visit to a studio by bus, with Tess in charge; a dinner of all the residents at Mona's; attending a Montgomery Clift movie, after which Gabriel and Tess kiss passionately on the garage couch and, when Mona finds out, are grounded for a week; participating in an animal rights protest march in downtown Los Angeles, an activity promoted by Mr. Palmer; and an eventful party at Venice Beach during which Gabriel stands up for Sumner against some street thugs who harass Sumner over Timmy, for the first time not attempting to distance himself from his father and launching them into a better relationship. Sumner decides to return to Missouri, having terminated his tenure with the studio because he is unwilling to compromise on how the further adventures of Timmy should be presented. By the time they leave, Gabriel has come to see that the Harmony Arms people, and his father as well, are decent, kind, loving, and accepting, unlike the people back home in Bradleyville, Missouri, whose judgmental attitude and emphasis on conformity he had previously taken as the norm. Gabriel's growing appreciation of his father and of himself, the sympathetic handling of the eccentric residents, and the extensive, accurate, often humorous, occasionally hilarious, and sometimes poignant dialogue make this book about the necessity of not being misled by superficialities consistently engaging. ALA.

HARPER & MOON (Ross*, Ramon Royal, Atheneum, 1993), boy's growing-up novel in a mystery context, set for about a year in a fruit farming area of the Blue Mountains of Oregon south of Walla Walla, Washington. Through his friendship with an older outsider youth, a farm boy learns that interpersonal relationships can be satisfying and also very complicated. In 1937, Harper McDowell, 8, has an on-and-off friendship with Moon* (James Patrick McCarty), the fourteen-year-old son of a ne'er-do-well sign painter. Harper is impressed by Moon's ability to fashion beautiful objects, like toy sailboats, out of found materials. He is also struck by Moon's parents: his father, Paddie*, whose joshing Harper enjoys and artistic talent he admires but whose way of speaking disparagingly of Moon as dumb and foolish gives him pause, and Moon's alcoholic, foul-mouthed mother, Tessie, whom a terror-stricken Harper one day sees fly into a rage, beat Moon, and attack Harper's mother. The narrative then leaps ahead four years to the summer after Pearl Harbor when Harper is twelve. Moon has been orphaned and is regarded as footloose and likable, if unreliable—now disappearing, now turning up for a few days, living no one knows where. In late summer Harper spends a happy ten days in the mountains with Olinger*, an old World War I veteran, who has a little cabin and store there and who is also friends with Moon. One day Olinger takes Harper trout fishing. On the way back to the cabin, Olinger, pistol in hand, forces two rednecks, who vow revenge, to release a bobcat they have trapped and are beating to death for the fun of it. In November, the McDowells hear that Olinger has disappeared. Deeply worried about the old fellow he so much admires, Harper plays hooky and bikes part of the twenty-five miles, then trudges the rest of the way through deepening snow to the empty cabin, pokes around, and finds Olinger dead in the snow, under what appear to be suspicious circumstances. Exhausted by the cold and snow and the trauma of the experience, Harper is rescued by Moon, who turns up at Olinger's, unexpectedly as is his wont, and after seeing Harper safely home, leaves for the army. The sheriff, a slick-talking politician type, suspects the "Moon character" of the murder. Some days pass, during which Harper prowls the abandoned barns and sheds in the community, looking for the place where Moon had lived and hoping to find clues to prove his benefactor innocent. In May, Moon turns up, in uniform but minus one eye from a fall, he says, but with a medal he presents to Harper. The sheriff, having caught Moon in Olinger's cabin with Olinger's missing watch in his pocket, arrests and jails the young man. Quite inexplicably, Moon escapes, taking an old .22 rifle with him. Extremely apprehensive and almost heartbroken, Harper searches through the community haunts again and finds his friend in a small root cellar room Moon has outfitted as a dwelling in the part of the valley called No Man's Land. Moon lies unconscious from a self-inflicted but not fatal gunshot wound. He is soon exonerated of the charge of murder by the coroner's report that Olinger died of a heart attack. In August, Harper and Moon, who is now living in Olinger's cabin, visit Far Point, a beautiful spot in the mountains that the old man loved. There they observe masses of black, gray, and silvery butterflies explode across the rise. Moon remarks that they are Olinger saying goodbye, a sentimental but still satisfying conclusion to the story. The plot moves unevenly and sometimes unconvincingly. Even allowing for events unfolding from Harper's naive and loyal perspective (although he does not tell the story), the few child abuse portions seem deliberately tailored for effect. It seems incredible that the men who discover Olinger is gone do not search the area and find his body and that the coroner's report was so slow in arriving. Moon's attempt at suicide is not sufficiently motivated, since he is never shown as unhappy about not having a family of his own, has lots of friends like the McDowells in the region, and has never seemed depressed. In fact, Moon's impassiveness lessens his credibility as a character. Thus the reader never learns how scarred he may be from his early years of abuse. Also troubling is his almost complete lack of schooling, but the pidgin English he employs seems strained and unnecessary. Scenes are vividly drawn, the McDowells are a winning family, and the section where Harper finds Olinger is beautifully detailed, carefully accelerated in tension, and filled with appeal to various senses, clearly the best part of the book. The descriptions of the out-of-doors reveal a warm appreciation for the natural beauty and resources of the area. ALA; SLJ.

HELP WANTED (Cusick*, Richie Tankersley, Archway, 1993), contemporary realistic thriller, set for a few days one cold October in an unnamed American city. Serious, bright Robin Bailey, a high school senior whose mother is divorced, needs money for a Thanksgiving trip to Florida with schoolmates. With enthusiasm and high hopes, she answers a help-wanted ad on the school bulletin board and to her surprise interviews with the wealthy, eccentric, elderly owner of Manorwood, the heavily wooded estate not far from her house. Manorwood is also the home of Parker Swanson, the handsome, blond "hunk" who is new to school and sought by almost every girl there. Parker's grandfather, Hercules Diffenbach Swanson, or, as he prefers, Herk, hires Robin at $100 a week to catalog for donation to the local library the books in the collection of his son's late wife, Lillith, Parker's stepmother. Also associated with the household are Winifred, the longtime maid; Roy Skaggs, the crude, often besotted handyman, who is also a school janitor; and Claudia, Parker's stepsister, who has been unwell and is grieving for her deceased mother. On the first day Claudia comes to school, she falls precipitously down a stairway. Afterward she insists to Robin that "she" pushed her but refuses to explain to Robin what she means. Later Parker tells Robin that Claudia is his "crazy sister," terribly paranoid and unpredictable. After a series of spooky and terrifying experiences at the mansion and more contact with Claudia, Robin is convinced that the girl needs her protection against some mysterious person who is trying to hurt her. Suspicion falls variously, but especially on Parker, who Robin feels is far too bossy, patronizing, arrogant, and johnny-on-the-spot and may resent the possibility that Claudia will inherit from his family's estate, a circumstance that Herk also resents. Claudia, however, is convinced that her mother, a painter and medium who cut her wrists and threw herself into the ocean, is trying to harm her, because Claudia did not respond in time when Lillith called for help, apparently having changed her mind about suicide. As these events are occurring, another high school girl, Vicki Hastings, disappears without a trace. While Robin is working at the mansion one night, a series of dramatic events occurs. Robin and Claudia see a horrible, decaying hand and hear a threatening, mysterious voice. Claudia flees from the building, Robin hard in pursuit. Robin stumbles over an object, and to her horror finds it is Vicki's decaying body. She is grabbed and dragged to a storage shed and almost raped by Skaggs, the assault being interrupted in the nick of time by Claudia, who buries a pair of scissors in the man's back. Terrified by what has happened, the two girls drag Skaggs's body to a precipice on the edge of the estate, but when Robin objects to disposing of it this way, Claudia turns on her with a gun. Robin learns that Claudia was in cahoots with Skaggs, who killed Vicki. The plan was to hurt Robin and thus to get back at Parker and his family, whom she hates because they dislike her mother. Again in the nick of time, help comes, this time from Parker and Walt, another school friend. It comes out that Parker had been behind Robin's being offered the job of cataloging, as a way of smoking out Claudia as the murderer of his mother, his father's first wife. Winifred confesses that she killed Claudia's mother because she felt that Lillith was plotting to destroy the family. The book overflows with typed characters, gothic conventions, melodrama, sensationalism, cliffhangers, and coincidence. Some plot details are left unaccounted for, motivations do not always hold water, buildup is heavy-handed, and diction is heavily cliché. Since the level of language is easy, events move fast, and teenaged scenes, especially those involving "girl talk" about boys, clothes, and parties, are frequent and have an authentic flavor, the book seems aimed at reluctant or less able readers. Poe Nominee.

HENKES, KEVIN (1960–   ), born in Racine, Wisconsin; prolific and popular writer and illustrator of lighthearted, sensitive picture-story books and realistic novels of family life and domestic adventures. Since his first work, *All Alone* (Greenwillow), a self-illustrated, picture-story book, came out in 1981, he has published about twenty popular books of events children experience in their everyday lives. They explore such matters as imaginary playmates, poking through the house while parents sleep, adjusting to a new baby, starting school, hanging on to security blankets, and adolescent tension with parents. Most of his publications have been picture-story books, among them *A Weekend with Wendell* (Greenwillow, 1987), cited by the International Reading Association; *Chester's Way* (Greenwillow, 1988), an American Library Association Notable Book; *Julius, the Baby of the World* (Greenwillow, 1990); and *Owen* (Greenwillow, 1993). Among his longer fiction are such novels as *Margaret and Taylor* (Greenwillow, 1983), an episodic book of sibling rivalry; *Return to Sender* (Greenwillow, 1984), the amusing story of a boy who writes to his favorite television hero with surprising results; *Two under Par* (Greenwillow, 1987), a problem story of a boy's dislike for his new stepfather; *The Zebra Wall* (Greenwillow, 1988), in which a girl must cope with a new baby in the house and also an eccentric aunt who has come to help; and the highly acclaimed *Words of Stone** (Greenwillow, 1992), a contemporary boy's growing-up story in which two troubled youths attempt to make sense out of their chaotic home lives; it was selected by the editors of *The Horn Book Magazine* for the Fanfare list. Henkes attended the University of Wisconsin and has made his home in Madison.

HERMES, PATRICIA (1936–   ), born in Brooklyn, New York; teacher and author of some dozen and a half books for children and young people about home and school life and nonfiction for adults. After receiving her B.A. degree from St. John's University, New York, she taught junior high English and social studies in Takoma Park, Maryland; became a teacher of the home-bound in Delcastle, Delaware; was writer in residence for the Norfolk, Virginia, Public Schools; and taught English and writing for Sacred Heart Seminary in Fairfield, Connecticut, where she lives. She married Matthew Hermes, research director for a chemical company, from whom she was later divorced, and had five children. The ideas for her books come largely from her own background. The protagonist in her first book, *What If They Knew* (Harcourt, 1980), has epilepsy, a disease she herself had as a child; its sequel is *A Place for Jeremy* (Harcourt,

1987). The feelings about death in *Nobody's Fault* (Harcourt, 1981) reflect her own after she lost a child. Among her other novels are *Be Still, My Heart* (Putnam, 1989), about a girl who thinks she is plain, ordinary, and unattractive; *I Hate Being Gifted* (Putnam, 1990), in which a girl's placement in a gifted and talented program threatens her friendships; and *Nothing But Trouble, Trouble* (Scholastic, 1994), about a girl's attempts to persuade her parents to allow her to babysit. *School Library Journal* cited her *Mama, Let's Dance** (Little, Brown, 1991), about three half-orphaned children who try to take care of one another after their mother abandons them.

HERZIG, ALISON CRAGIN, writer with Jane Lawrence Mali* of nearly a dozen books of fiction and nonfiction for children, including *Mystery on October Road** (Viking, 1991), a short, lighthearted mystery involving three schoolchildren with overactive imaginations, which was nominated for the Edgar Allan Poe Award. With Mali, she has published the novels *A Season of Secrets* (Little, Brown, 1982); *Thaddeus* (Little, Brown, 1984), a Junior Literary Guild selection; *The Ten-Speed Babysitter* (Dutton, 1987); *Sam and the Moonqueen* (Little, Brown, 1990); and *The Wimp of the World* (Viking, 1994). Individually she has written for middle graders the novels *Shadows on the Pond* (Little, Brown, 1985), in which dangerous intruders threaten a beaver pond; *The Boonsville Bombers* (Viking, 1991), a baseball story; and *The Big Deal* (Viking, 1992), about a boy who has problems with the dog he longed to have. With Mali, she also published the photo-essay, nonfiction book, *Oh, Boy! Babies!* (Little, Brown, 1980), a Junior Literary Guild selection. She has made her home in New York City.

HESSE, KAREN (1952–   ), born in Baltimore, Maryland; a writer who in the past has been a teacher, librarian, advertising secretary, typesetter, proofreader, and benefits coordinator at the University of Maryland. Her first novel, *Wish on a Unicorn* (Holt, 1991), concerns a girl who struggles with the problem of a brain-damaged younger sister. Her most highly commended book is *Letters from Rifka** (Holt, 1992), a novel of a Russian Jewish immigrant family based on the memories of one of her older relatives. It won the Christopher Medal and the International Reading Association Award and was named to lists of the American Library Association Notable Books and Best Books for Young Adults, the *School Library Journal* Best Books for Children, and *Horn Book*'s Fanfare. *Phoenix Rising** (Holt, 1994), a novel of the aftermath of a nuclear power plant accident, was also cited by the *School Library Journal* as a Best Book. Hesse has written picture books, among them *Poppy's Chair,* illustrated by Kay Life (Macmillan, 1993), and *Lester's Dog,* illustrated by Nancy Carpenter (Holt, 1993), and an early chapter book, *Lavender,* illustrated by Andrew Glass (Holt, 1993). Another brief book is her sensitive dog story, *Sable**, illustrated by Marcia Sewall (Holt, 1994), which was also cited by the *School Library Journal.*

HOLDER (*Mote**), abusive drafting teacher at Chris Miller's high school and member of the white supremacist group ERWA (Equal Rights for White Americans). When Holder persists in pinching Chris's tennis arm, Chris gives him a bloody nose and must answer to the principal for his conduct. Because Chris is a friend of Mote*, the Vietnam War veteran and drifter who camps down by the river, and Mote's knife was the murder weapon in Holder's death, the authorities assume Mote killed Holder in retaliation for the way Holder treated Chris. Holder also tries to get an African-American schoolgirl, Willa, to perform oral sex in return for dropping his attempt to have her mentally disabled brother committed. She resists him, and, having borrowed Mote's knife for protection, runs off, leaving it behind. Another teacher, Mr. Douglas, also a member of ERWA, killed Holder with Mote's knife, apparently in a dispute over group matters, and possibly over Douglas's relationship with Holder's wife.

HOLMAN, FELICE (1919–   ), born in New York City; poet and author of a variety of books for children. She grew up on Long Island and is a graduate of Syracuse University. Many critics consider her novel, *The Murderer* (Scribner's, 1978), about a Jewish boy growing up in a Polish-dominated Pennsylvania mining town, her strongest book, but probably better known is *Slake's Limbo* (Scribner's, 1974), a story of a boy who lives in the New York subway. With a similar appeal of a living place hidden from adults, *Secret City, U.S.A.** (Scribner's, 1990) is about a group of children who find and rehabilitate a house in an abandoned part of a city. The book won the Child Study Award. Holman has also published picture books and books of poems. For earlier biographical information and title entries, see *Dictionary, 1960–1984* [*The Murderer; Slake's Limbo*].

HOWARD, ELLEN (1943–   ), born in New Bern, North Carolina; author mostly of problem novels and stories for children and young adults, some of which are based on the lives of her own female ancestors. One of these is *Sister** (Atheneum, 1990), an American Library Association selection and companion novel to *Edith Herself* (Atheneum, 1987). *Sister* is an emotionally moving and detailed account of an Illinois farm girl in the 1880s, who is forced to give up her dreams of an education because she must help out at home. For earlier biographical information and a title entry, see *Dictionary, 1985–1989* [*Edith Herself*].

I

INDIA INK TIEDELBAUM (*Buffalo Brenda**), sidekick and shadow of the highly assertive, opinionated, idea-driven Brenda* Tuna and astute observer and reporter of Brenda's activities. India is the middle of the three children of parents who were latter-day hippies and are now almost stodgy, conventional middle class. India's siblings often tease her about her friendship with Brenda, whom the family have dubbed the Philosopher for her pronouncements about life. India received her name because, when she was born, her mother was living in a teepee in a state park attempting to find her "center" and paint the cosmos. During the melee at the school after football players step in the droppings from Flo, the school's buffalo mascot, while practicing for the big game and the coach and principal blow their tops, India gets up enough courage to confront them on Brenda's behalf and persuade them to look ahead to the game the following day and consider the positive effect that having the buffalo mascot will have on team and spectators.

ISABELLA HARRIS (*Learning by Heart**), pleasant, very nice, young African-American woman of twenty-three, whom Mama engages as housekeeper just before baby Jesse is born. Isabella wears a tiny white cap over her extremely short hair and a green uniform with a white apron, modest attire dictated, she says, by her Mennonite faith. She is extremely capable around the house, and always busy, Rachel, the protagonist, says, like Mama. She is patient and practical and helps Rachel to reach out to other people. She insists, for example, that Rachel learn the names of the unruly, fractious Tucker children, so that Rachel can tell them as individuals why she does not like what they are doing when they misbehave or destroy property. Isabella insists that Rachel respect adults and children alike. Very forgiving, Isabella refuses to be unkind in return for racial slurs, of which Rachel describes several. Through Isabella, Rachel also learns that "pure wanting to" can accomplish a lot. Isabella lives with her brother, the Reverend Mr. Harris, a stern, disapproving man of whom she is a little afraid. He does not like her to work for a white family. Isabella is a distinctively drawn character but a little too perfect for complete credibility.

J

JACKIE RAMSDALE (*A Share of Freedom**), half-brother of Freedom Jo Avery. Disturbed by his father's departure from the family and his mother's heavy drinking, Jackie is at first afraid of the dark and strongly dependent on Freedom, but during their trip to Truman Lake he proves his sturdiness. After they are placed in the Quincy home, he develops a strong admiration for Theodore, two years his senior, and their friendship presumably will make Freedom's role in both families easier for her.

JAMES, MARY (1927–   ), pseudonym of the author best known as M. E. Kerr*. As Mary James, Kerr has written *Shoebag** (Scholastic, 1990), an amusing, often exciting, highly ironic, talking-animal fantasy about a cockroach that becomes a human being. *Shoebag* was cited as a best book by *School Library Journal*. Other books published under this name are *The Shuteyes* (Scholastic, 1993), a humorous novel about a boy who is carried off by a parrot to a planet where sleeping is a crime, and *Frankenlouse* (Scholastic, 1994), an offbeat, growing-up story of a boy in conflict with his father.

JANAAN KASHAD (*Show Me the Evidence**), small, beautiful daughter of an American woman and an Arabic man. Although always at odds with her father, who greatly favors his sons and imposes unrealistic restrictions on Janaan, she is especially upset when her baby brother, Adam, dies of crib death while she is caring for him. Surprisingly, her father blames not Janaan but her mother, and they are on the point of divorcing when Janaan is detained as a suspect in the death of Adam and two other infants. The incident brings Janaan and her father closer, and she comes to understand that he thinks she and her mother have no respect for him because they insist on acting like Americans instead of Arabic women. Their misunderstanding is compounded by her father's activity in a radical Arab group, which he finally sees as a destructive force. Political suspicions enter also because the child Lauren is babysitting, Rachael Bloom, who dies when Janaan is in the house, is Jewish. Although Janaan always seems in control of her emotions, actually she envies her friend, Lauren Taylor, for her normal American family. When she is especially disturbed by her father, she slashes a picture of Lauren, evidence to the police that she is capable of violence.

JANE (*When the Road Ends**), foster child of perhaps seven or eight, given the name of Jane Doe after she was pushed from a car on the freeway, scarred by cigarette burns, beaten, evidently with a chain, and so emotionally damaged that she never speaks and hides under the bed, sucking her thumb. Mary Jack Jordan, fellow foster child of the Percys, wants a sister so much that she has virtually taken over Jane's care and has won her trust enough to bathe her, read to her, and keep her from annoying Jill Percy. Although considered mentally disabled by social workers, Jane is intelligent, drawing pictures that reveal her understanding of what is happening around her but never including herself in the pictures. After several weeks at the cabin with Aunt Cecile* Bradshaw, Adam* Correy, and Mary Jack, Jane has improved in many ways, stopped wetting her pants, and shown compassion and love of animals by her concern for Goldy, the stray dog. Remarking on her dark eyes and very fair hair, Aunt Cecile says she looks like a black-eyed Susan. Jane responds by drawing a daisy and smiling, a very rare occurrence, and then drawing her blue pants on the flower. When Mary Jack and Cecile guess that she is trying to tell them her name, she says her first word, "Daisy." At the end, she has also said, "Hi," to Adam, and there is hope that with kindness she may recover, at least partially.

JEREMY SIMMS (*Let the Circle Be Unbroken**; *Mississippi Bridge**; *The Road to Memphis**), white youth, longtime acquaintance of the Logan children—Stacey*, Cassie, Christopher-John, and Little Man—who is caught between his liking for them and his knowledge of what is morally right and the racist attitudes of the whites in his family and the community. Stacey's age of thirteen, Jeremy appears seldom but significantly in *Let the Circle Be Unbroken.* In telling scenes, he inadvertently causes trouble for Cassie and Stacey by giving them photographs of himself as an indication of his respect and liking for them. When Uncle Hammer learns that Jeremy gave Cassie his picture, he angrily lectures both Cassie and Stacey on how, as he sees it, white men abuse black women and about the dangers of cultivating friendship with whites, then burns Jeremy's picture. In *Mississippi Bridge,* Jeremy tells how, after several blacks are evicted from a bus to make room for a family of whites, the vehicle plunges into a river, killing everyone on board. *The Road to Memphis* takes place some ten years later, when Jeremy is about twenty-one. After Moe* Turner hops into the Simmses' truck and hides under a tarpaulin, Jeremy does not reveal his presence and later transports Moe to Jackson, where Stacey and the others hide him. Later, when Harris Mitchum is blamed for helping Moe get away, Sissy, Harris's twin sister, informs on Jeremy to save Harris from being punished for an act he did not commit. When Jeremy tells the truth, he is disowned by his family and must leave the community. He represents whites who are sympathetic to the plight of the blacks and want to see them treated justly.

JERRAM POTTER (*The Christmas Killer**), twin brother of Rose. Although the two were very close when younger, often sharing thoughts and communicating mentally, they have grown apart as teenagers. Jerram now has many interests and activities that Rose does not share, including friendships with old Mackey, the former police chief, and with Carla Fentesso, the third girl missing and found murdered this Christmas season in or near Bethboro, Connecticut. When this connection becomes known to the police, Jerram is questioned but released for lack of evidence. Each twin feels some jealousy of the other. Jerram treats Rose's attraction to a classmate, Daniel, with scorn, and Rose resents his efforts to get her to contact dead Nancy for news of Carla. Their record, kept secretly of their childhood shared dreams that Rose started and Jerram finished, reveals that she was the one seemingly contacted by spirits and he, by ending the dream happily, protected her. Many of the red herrings in the novel seem to point to Jerram as the murderer, and briefly even Rose entertains that possibility.

JESSUP VOLNIK (*The Boggart**), a lively but unusually tidy ten-year-old boy enamored with computers, considered a genius, and inclined to be abstracted. As compared to his older sister, Emily* Volnik, he is the more intellectual and comes up with the solution to the problem of what to do about getting the magical little man they call Boggart* home to Scotland again. Jessup belongs to a group of young computer fans, the oldest one of whom, a dropout named Barry, is not liked by Jessup's mother mainly because he does not go to school. Jessup is also very involved with hockey. In a funny episode, the Boggart accompanies Jessup to practice, is struck by the puck, which he then vaporizes with Old Magic, becomes the puck, is hit by a superzealous boy with a hockey stick, flies in circles around and then outside the stadium, and returns at a critical moment to trip up one of Jessup's opponents in an effort to help Jessup, but he does it in such a way that Jessup is accused of vicious, foul play.

JIM UGLY (Fleischman*, Sid, illus. Joseph A. Smith, Greenwillow, 1992), fast-moving, melodramatic adventure novel set in June, 1894, in the desert of northern Nevada and in California. The story starts and ends in the town of Blowfly, Nevada, where the twelve-year-old narrator, Jake Bannock, has been living with his cousin, termagent chicken grower Aurora Hopper, and her pleasant, poker-faced husband, Axie, since his father, Sam, an actor, died a week ago. Because Aurora threatens to kill Jim Ugly, Sam's part-elkhound, part-wolf dog, insisting he is a sheep killer, and because he is convinced Sam is not dead since Jim Ugly shows no interest in his master's grave, Jake runs away with the dog. He hopes that Jim Ugly's sharp nose will lead him to his father. Before his departure and a factor in his decision is the arrival of two puzzling characters who also seek Sam: Wilhelmina Marlybone-Jenkins, a beautiful actress who says Sam left her practically a widow, and her manager, C. W. Cornelius, who seems interested in whether or not Sam had diamonds. About the same time, D. D. Skeats also turns up. He is a bounty hunter and ex-soldier, whom Jake thinks of as yellowleg because he wears army pants with broad yellow stripes down the outside of the legs. Jake gets from the local doctor the bullet removed from Sam's shoulder after yellowleg shot him some days ago, shows it to Jim Ugly for his father's scent, and follows where the dog leads. The meanderings that ensue take the boy and his dog on the train through various adventures in little towns in northern Nevada and into California and San Francisco. At the Magnolia Theater just over the California line in Truckee, Jake is impressed into the troupe to play William Tell's son (after which he conceives an ambition for the theater), the celebrated marksmanship being displayed by Mrs. Tell, acted by Jenny, a pleasant, outgoing sharpshooter friend of Wilhelmina and Cornelius, who also turn up there. The troupe reaches San Francisco, where Jim Ugly's nose leads Jake about the hills and to a chance sighting of Sam just as he boards a trolley. That night Sam appears at the theater where he plays an Austrian soldier. At play's end, he boldly announces to Cornelius, who is in the audience, that the diamonds that Cornelius and Wilhelmina have been seeking are his, and he accuses Cornelius of hiring yellowleg to pursue him. The slam-bang conclusion quickly enlightens Jake and the reader. Back in Blowfly, Sam takes all the principals to a remote area, the place where, he says, he was led by Jim Ugly and where he discovered Cornelius and yellowleg "salting a mine" with "trash" diamonds that Cornelius had purchased with money stolen from Wilhelmina. With Axie's help, Sam collected the gems and put them into a cheap coffin, which, to keep them from Cornelius, Axie buried, pretending Sam's body was in the box but, without Sam's or Aurora's knowledge, first feeding the gems for safe keeping to Aurora's chickens. Aurora, however, has grown tired of living in the desert and raising and caring for chickens and has just opened the barn door and chased them all out. When she learns what Axie did, Aurora faints dead away at having shooed off a small fortune, Axie groans with pain at her deed, and Cornelius cries out that he is ruined and heads for the train station, with Skeats tight on his heels loudly demanding bounty money. Jake and his father leave for San Francisco. Jake feels good about the prospect of his dad and Wilhelmina's getting married. Although not as outrageous as some of Fleischman's other books, the novel similarly involves fast action, happenstance, and a head-spinning, incident-filled plot; features one-dimensional, flamboyant characters; employs loquacious, theatrical-sounding dialogue and a peppery style; and gives a small sense of what the area and times were like for upbeat, lightweight entertainment. ALA.

JOANNA LOCKRIDGE (*Bunkhouse Journal**), sturdy twelve-year-old who manages a small sheep ranch with her aging Great-Aunt Bea in southwestern Wyoming in 1910. An orphan since shortly after her birth, she has become very competent at the work with the sheep and helping her half-blind aunt run the house, though she welcomes what help her scattered neighbors can give her by supplying wood for the winter, giving her their orphaned lambs, and sometimes haying or doing other ranch jobs on shares. Although she has not been to school, she is an avid reader, proud of her small shelf of books, and has learned to play an old violin. Her friendship with Sandy Mannix is open and frank, and while she is hurt by his interest in Christine at the dance and Karen* Hamilton worries that Sandy may encourage her to expect more affection than he can give, she seems able to cope with disappointment as she does with hardship, inadequate clothes, and isolation. The open ending of the novel leaves room for a possible future for her as Sandy's wife.

JOHNSON, ANGELA (1961–), born in Tuskegee, Alabama; writer mainly known for sensitive picture books with African-American protagonists. She attended Kent State University and was employed in the early 1980s by VISTA as a child development worker in Ravenna, Ohio; since 1989 she has been a freelance writer. Her most highly commended picture book is *When I Am Old with You,* illustrated by David Soman (Orchard, 1990), which won the Coretta Scott King Book Award and the Ezra Jack Keats Award. Among her other picture books, several of which have received commendations, are *Tell Me a Story, Mama* (Orchard, 1989), *One of Three* (Orchard, 1991), and *The Leaving Morning* (Orchard, 1992), all illustrated by David Soman; and *Do Like Kyla* (Orchard, 1990), illustrated by James Ransome. Her first novel, *Toning the Sweep** (Orchard, 1993), shows her ability with the longer form. It is a growing-up story of a girl who visits the California desert to help her dying grandmother move and learns about her grandfather's racist murder, a piece of her heritage her family has kept from her. It was winner of a Coretta Scott King Award and was cited on annual lists by both the American Library Association and the *School Library Journal.* Johnson makes her home in Kent, Ohio.

JOLLY (*Make Lemonade**), the teenaged, single mother for whom LaVaughn babysits. Desperate for a sitter because her previous one left for better pay, Jolly tells LaVaughn three times during the employment interview that she "can't do it alone," a plea that engages the girl's heart. Jolly was a Box Girl, a homeless child who lived on the streets quite literally in a box, along with other Box Girls and Box Boys. For a short period, she lived with Gram, a good foster mother, but after Gram died, Jolly had no one to show her how to do things, like run a home. When LaVaughn chides her about her "just-okay" attitude and "partway-done" way of doing things and asks her if that is how she got pregnant—that is, by having only "partway" birth control—Jolly describes the difficulty of controlling aroused young men. Although LaVaughn recognizes Jolly's response as an excuse, she realizes that in posing the question she herself is arrogant and judgmental. Although Jolly is irresponsible at times and uses LaVaughn, she truly loves her children and has a delightful sense of humor about tough situations that LaVaughn admires. Jolly's descriptions of her problems with sexual harassment at work and her inability to get redress enlist LaVaughn's and the reader's sympathies. Jolly is a well-rounded character.

JONATHAN MCKINNON (*Children of the River**), handsome, big, blond, star football player at Sundara's high school, whom all the girls ogle and the boys envy and who becomes attracted to Sundara. He admires the poem she wrote for English, which alerts him to her feelings about being a refugee, and when he is assigned a research paper on a world trouble spot, he chooses Cambodia and asks to interview her for information for it. Although he enjoys playing football, he refuses to let the game run his life. His friendship with Sundara leads to the breakup of his relationship with the pretty, popular cheerleader, Cathy Gates. Jonathan resents what he feels is the hypocrisy of his parents in advocating social causes but not actively supporting them. He is pleased when Dr. McKinnon decides to volunteer among the Khmer in a camp in Thailand.

JOSELLE STARK (*Words of Stone**), bossy, impulsive, willful friend of Blaze* Werla. Out of a perverse need to strike out at her irresponsible mother, who has dumped her on her grandmother, Joselle fashions words out of stones she finds on the hillside that separates her grandmother's house from Blaze's. Her intention is to "complicate" Blaze's life. She has come to live with her grandmother, kind, gentle, stable Floy Stark, because her mother wants to be alone with her latest live-in boyfriend but tells Joselle she and he are going on a trip west. Joselle, who refers to her mother as The Beautiful Vicki, longs for the father she never knew, resents sharing her mother with what seems to be an endless succession of boyfriends, has problems at school, and sorely tries her grandmother's patience. (Floy tells Blaze that Joselle is a "handful. But a sweetheart, despite all her troubles.") When Joselle accidentally discovers that her mother is at home and not on a trip, Floy packs the girl home in the middle of the night. Floy and Joselle leave without telling Blaze, who has all along been ignorant of Joselle's situation. Joselle seems a type, representative of children from unstable homes, and occasionally is too eccentric for credibility. For example, she taps out songs on her overly large teeth.

JOURNEY (MacLachlan*, Patricia, Delacorte, 1991), realistic novelette of family life set on what sounds like a farm in New England beginning in early spring and covering several months in the late twentieth century and telling of a boy's coming to terms with his mother's abandonment of him and his older sister. Hurt and angry because Mama (Liddie) has simply walked out, leaving him and Cat* with the grandparents with whom they and their mother have been living, and because Grandfather* says she will not be back, Journey, the eleven-year-old narrator, reacts with a sudden burst of fury and smacks the old man. The more independent and pragmatic Cat puts her mind on other matters. She clears her room of things no longer needed or wanted, giving her camera to

Grandfather and her sweatshirt with "Liddie" on it to Grandma*. Right away Grandfather takes a picture of the three of them, all smiling except for Journey, whose face reveals his inner fury. When Mama sends money, as she promised, but no address, Cat gives her money to Journey, who says he will save it to pay for traveling to visit their mother. While Grandfather becomes engrossed in photography, because he has to, says quiet, undemonstrative Grandma, she, Journey, and Cat peruse her picture album, searching for family resemblances and pondering past events. In pictures, Mama looks distant and detached. Grandma says Liddie always did want to be somewhere else. Then Journey remembers walked outside with Mama when he was very young and falling into a brook. Mama walked on, unheeding, but Grandfather picked him up. When Grandfather dandles on his knee little Emmett, Journey's friend Cooper's baby brother, to the rhyme "Trot, trot to Boston," Journey begins to wonder about his father and whether it was he who dandled him to the same rhyme. He worries that maybe Mama left because he was not good enough, but Grandfather responds emphatically that her leaving was not Journey's fault. When Journey asks to see pictures of his father, he is told that Liddie tore up all her photos before she left. He is so disappointed at hearing this that he takes to his bed, claiming a sore throat and being crabby. When Bloom the cat (named by Grandfather after a peony blossom) finds the picture box in Mama's room, Journey tries pasting the pieces together, until he realizes the job is impossible. That realization drives home the certainty that Mama will never return, and he cries. Mrs. MacDougal, Cooper's mother, says truth is sometimes behind pictures rather than in them, a statement that gives Journey some comfort and something else to think about. When Bloom has kittens in the box, Journey photographs them and his family, using the timer and at the very last moment throwing himself across Grandfather's lap. Still bitter when Mama telephones, he announces to her that Bloom the cat is taking care of her babies and is a very good mother. Looking at the pictures Grandfather has strung up along the back wall inside the barn, Journey says maybe he will visit Mama if she sends "words" instead of just money. Cat says Grandfather is taking all these pictures to give Journey a family, things to look back on, evidently meaning they can in some way make up for Mama and the torn-up pictures. Very early one morning, Journey awakens and goes out to the barn where Grandfather has fixed up an office and finds the old man developing and printing negatives of the torn pictures, one being of Mama, Papa, and a baby. Journey suddenly realizes he does not really know what his father's face looked like. Finally he understands (Grandfather says it really happened when Journey saw the print he had taken of himself across his Grandfather's lap) that the knees he jogged on were Grandfather's, not Papa's. Although now he knows that Grandfather's is the face he has remembered as the person who cared for and comforted him, as Grandfather still does, he also has a sense that his parents once loved him, too. Because the story is set up like a series of snapshots of current happenings and of remembered scenes often triggered by them, because some episodes result in or are built around photos Grandfather takes, and because the style is severely understated, the plot seems disjointed and unfocused. Journey (whose name is undoubtedly symbolic) is less interesting as a character than Cat and, especially, Grandfather. While the opening scene grabs the emotions, questions soon arise that are left unanswered. Why, for instance, if Mama has always been abstracted from her family though living with them, does Journey become so disturbed by her departure? Are his problems the result of unsatisfactory family relationships to which Cat has become reconciled? Besides, his behavior seems more typical of a child much younger than eleven. The reader also could benefit from more information about Liddie and Papa. As it stands, the story is less an exploration of the emotional problems of a troubled child than it is a tribute to the power of photographs as a means of cementing family relationships, and the ending, if it is to be taken as conclusive of acceptance and resolution, is abrupt. Striking turns of phrase and clever, ironic insights into human nature typical of MacLachlan's writing add distinctiveness and some humor to this essentially serious, introspective narrative. ALA; SLJ.

JOURNEY OF THE SPARROWS (Buss*, Fran Leeper, with Daisy Cubias*, Lodestar/Dutton, 1991), escape and survival novel of a Salvadoran illegal refugee family, set mostly in Chicago in the 1980s. Sore and bruised after hours, perhaps days, nailed in a cramped crate in freezing weather, Maria Acosta, 15, is dumped by the *coyotes,* who for a price smuggle aliens into the United States, in a warehouse in Chicago, along with her pregnant older sister, Julia* Cordoba, her little brother, Oscar, 4 or 5, and a stranger to them, a Mexican boy named Tomas, 15, whose foot is frozen. Marta, Tomas's aunt, takes them all to her room to rest and later finds them another place to stay in the apartment of Alicia, where they have a mattress on the floor of a small room they share with one of several illegal men. Little Oscar is ill, terribly thin, and so shocked from the trip that he can no longer talk. Lying about her age, Alicia gets Maria a job in the sweatshop where she sews; when the foreman tries to abuse her sexually, Maria fights him off and runs away. Tomas helps out by teaching her English, taking her and Oscar to a church that serves food to the needy, and sometimes finding or making toys for the little boy, who gradually gets stronger. Later, when the foreman leaves and Maria returns to work, immigration officers raid the factory, and Alicia is arrested. At another church, where Maria stands in line for a long time for groceries, the food runs out, and she is turned away, but an old street woman they call the Quetzal* Lady shows her where she can scale a fence and climb through a kitchen window. A priest named Father Jonathan finds her with half a loaf of bread, questions her, gives her more food, and arranges that she will be paid a little for cleaning the church daily. After a difficult labor, Julia has a healthy baby, a girl they name Ramona. Maria sells a couple of her paintings, and they hope to send money to their mother, who stayed in Mexico when their infant sister, Teresa, was too sick to travel. A letter from the woman with whom their mother stayed, however, says that she was arrested by immigration police and returned to El Salvador and that they must arrange to get Teresa. Maria makes the long trip to Mexico and the dangerous crossing back into the United States with the baby, during which she narrowly escapes rape, drowning, and apprehension. The book ends as they ride the bus back to Chicago with hope, having received news that their mother has escaped to Honduras. Although the novel does not attempt to explain why it is American policy to deport Salvadorans to certain death, their fear of the *Guardia,* the repressive political police who killed their father and Julia's husband, is a major emotional factor in their lives. The efforts of a few like Father Jonathan to change refugee policy, the kindness of total strangers, and Maria's sweet and very proper romance with Tomas alleviate the grimness of their precarious survival. The understated style gives this story of courage increased effect. Addams.

JULIA (*Baby**), Sophie's mother, who leaves her baby with Larkin's family because she feels they, more than anyone else on the island, have strong family ties and will love and care well for the child. Julia appears only briefly at the beginning of the novel, where she is twice mentioned, in one short sentence each time, as a silent, solitary young woman holding a baby. She writes regularly to Sophie, and when a year later she returns to the island to claim her child, she explains that she needed Larkin's family's help because her husband was very ill and her own people were not the right sort to care for Sophie. Ten years later, she and Sophie return to the island for Grandma Byrd's* funeral.

JULIA CORDOBA (*Journey of the Sparrows**), older sister of Maria Acosta, who is transported from Mexico to Chicago nailed in a crate with her, their little brother, Oscar, and a Mexican illegal, Tomas. At their home in El Salvador, the *Guardia,* the dreaded political police, killed their father and Julia's husband, raped Julia, and later returned to kill the rest of the family but could not find them as they hid in a ditch. With their mother and baby sister, Teresa, they have made their way through Guatamala and Mexico, but because Teresa is too ill to travel farther, their mother stays in Mexico and sends them on with the *coyotes,* who import illegals for money, often brutally disregarding their health and safety. Julia is pregnant, she hopes by her husband and not by one of the *Guardia,* and she has a very difficult delivery of her baby, Ramona. Not as bright or forceful as Maria and raised in a very proper religious way, Julia nevertheless decides to become a prostitute to provide money to bring Teresa to Chicago after their mother is arrested, but she is saved when a friend sells her treasured figure of San Isidro to finance the trip.

K

KAREN HAMILTON (*Bunkhouse Journal**), married cousin of Sandy Mannix, living on an isolated sheep ranch in southwestern Wyoming in 1910. Cheerful, optimistic, and fun loving, she understands her serious, moody husband,
John, and tries to lighten Sandy's hurt at his seeming disapproval of the boy by
explaining that Sandy's difficult relationship with his father reminds John too
much of his problems with his own rancher father, who threw him out when he
was young, arrived many years later trying to mend their misunderstandings,
and died of tick fever acquired when he was helping with the sheep. Karen has
suffered three miscarriages and is again pregnant during the winter. After her
labor starts early and she must remain lying down for weeks, she makes good-
natured fun of the housekeeping attempts by Sandy and John and converts the
threatening situation into one of warmth and occasional merriment. A city girl,
she has adapted to ranch life with energy and good humor and taught herself
to cope with the months of cold and loneliness. At the novel's end, it is still
not certain that she can keep her baby to term, but as the weeks pass it is more
and more hopeful that this child will be born big enough to survive.

KATE DAVENPORT (*Unlived Affections**), Willie Ramsey's mother, who divorced his father, Bill* Ramsey, after he told her that he was gay. At first, Kate
told Grom* Davenport, her mother, that Bill ran away with another woman,
possibly because she did not want Grom to know Bill was gay or possibly
because she wanted to keep Grom from pursuing Bill to get him to help pay
for the coming baby. At any rate, she decided to keep Bill out of her life. Later
she told Grom the truth about Bill's homosexuality. Kate also lied to Bill about
having a boyfriend, apparently to try to get him back, and also when she denied
that she was going to have a baby, apparently to keep him away. Willie has
mixed feelings about her throughout most of the book but realizes at the end
that he loves her very much in spite of her lies.

KATHRYN ROSE FORREST (*A Little Bit Dead**), the beautiful, eighteen-
year-old prostitute with whom Reece* falls in love and who testifies at his trial

that Sam told her that he and Colby were hunting the Indians' gold and were about to lynch Shanti* when Reece came along, thus corroborating Reece's story. Kathryn first declines Reese's offer of marriage, because, she says, he will always remember she was a whore and hold it against her. Later she changes her mind and agrees to marry him, perhaps because he tells her that he also has a bad past (killing the gold seekers) to live down, perhaps because he tells her publicly that he loves her, or perhaps because he tells her that he is now a rich man. At any rate, it is after the last that she accepts his second proposal. The daughter of a St. Louis judge, Kathryn ran away from home and came west. She is spirited, goodhearted, and smart.

KERR, M. E. (MARIJANE MEAKER) (1927–   ), born in Auburn, New York; graduate of Columbia University; freelance writer and author known mainly for her many contemporary problem novels for early adolescents and teenagers, including *Deliver Us From Evie** (HarperCollins, 1994), about how a family and community in rural Missouri attempt to cope with lesbians in their midst. The book was selected as a best book by *School Library Journal.* Kerr is also the author of the popular mystery-detective series about John Fell, which take place in an exclusive boy's prep school, among them *Fell Back** (Harper, 1989), which was nominated for the Edgar Allan Poe Award. She has written under several other pseudonyms as well, including M. J. Meaker, Ann Aldrich, Vin Packer, and Mary James*. For earlier biographical information and title entries, see *Dictionary, 1960–1984* [*Dinky Hocker Shoots Smack; Gentlehands*].

KIM AXELROD (*Finding Buck McHenry**), eleven-year-old daughter of a well-known sportscaster who has just moved to Arborville. Besides being a skilled fielder in baseball, Kim is clever at directing her father's excessive enthusiasm. She is also compassionate, understanding that Aaron Henry needs to talk about the death of his parents and brother, a subject Jason Ross, the Little Leaguer protagonist, has avoided. She explains frankly that she has moved from Birmingham because her parents have been divorced and her mother got the house and furniture, while her father got her. When Aaron quietly says, "Your dad got the better deal," she shows her vulnerability by blushing and muttering, "Thanks." She saves the day by warning her father in time for him to change the slant of his sportscast and avoid embarrassment all around.

KINDL, PATRICE, author of a strange but widely praised fantasy for young people. Her first novel, *Owl in Love** (Houghton Mifflin, 1993), is about a girl in a contemporary high school who changes at night into an owl, a concept unusual but well evoked in memorable scenes of night flight and hunting. It was named a Notable Book by the American Library Association. Kindl lives in upstate New York with her husband and son. She has worked as an aide to quadraplegics in the Helping Hand Program.

KINSEY-WARNOCK, NATALIE (1956–), born in Newport, Vermont; author of fiction mostly for younger readers. She received her B.A. from Johnson State College in Vermont in art and athletic training in 1978 and subsequently worked as an energy auditor, elderhostel director, and cross-country ski instructor at Craftsbury Sports Center in Vermont. Her first and best-known book, *The Canada Geese Quilt** (Cobblehill, 1989), grew out of her love for her grandmother and a special quilt they made together. This short novel received several distinctions, among them being named as an American Library Association Notable Book. *The Night the Bells Rang* (Cobblehill, 1991), a short novel of events during the last year of World War I for a Vermont farm boy, was a Bank Street College Book of the Year and an American Booksellers Pick. Most of Kinsey-Warnock's publications have been stories for picture books: *The Wild Horses of Sweetbriar* (Cobblehill, 1990), another Bank Street College choice; *The Bear That Heard Crying* (Cobblehill, 1993), a collaboration with her sister, Helen, of the true story of their great-great-great-great aunt, who, when lost in the woods in 1783 at the age of three, was found and protected by a bear; *Wilderness Cat* (Cobblehill, 1992); *When Spring Comes* (Dutton, 1993); *On a Starry Night* (Orchard, 1994); and *The Fiddler of the Northern Lights* (Cobblehill, 1994). She lives near Barton, Vermont, in a frame house she and her husband built in the hills that were once part of the farm she grew up on.

KLASS, DAVID, teacher, author of middle school and young adult sports novels. He graduated from Yale University and lives in Los Angeles, where he has studied filmmaking. For two years he taught English at Atami High School in Japan, the setting for *The Atami Dragons* (Scribner's, 1984), which focuses on high school baseball, and *Breakaway Run* (Dutton, 1987), about soccer, both with American protagonists trying to adjust to the different social patterns of a foreign country. In *A Different Season* (Dutton, 1988) he returned to baseball, this time taking up the question of girls playing on the same team as boys, from the point of view of a boy team member. In *Wrestling with Honor* (Dutton, 1989), a book chosen for the American Library Association Best Books for Young Adults list, he departs further from a straight sports story, with a protagonist who refuses on principle to take a required drug test and suffers damaging consequences. An even further expansion of the genre occurs in *California Blue** (Scholastic, 1994), in which a high school track runner discovers a new species of butterfly on property belonging to the local logging company and finds himself in the middle of a controversy between lumbermen, who make up most of the town's population, including his own father, and environmentalists. It was cited by the *School Library Journal* for the Best Books for Children list.

KLAUSE, ANNETTE CURTIS, born in Bristol, England; librarian and writer of science-fiction and horror novels for teenaged readers. *The Silver Kiss** (Delacorte, 1990), her first book and a vampire novel with a clever twist, and *Alien Secrets** (Delacorte, 1993), a mystery-adventure of murder and intrigue on a

ship going from earth to a planet in space, were both selected as best books by
School Library Journal. Alien Secrets was also cited by the American Library
Association. Both books are well plotted for maximum thrills. Head of child
services at Aspen Hill Community Library in Maryland, Klause lives in Hy-
attsville, Maryland. She received her B.A. in English literature and her M.L.S.
from the University of Maryland, College Park.

KNIGHTS OF THE KITCHEN TABLE (Scieszka*, Jon, illus. Lane Smith,
Viking, 1991), time fantasy for early readers, starring the Time Warp Trio, three
preteenaged friends, Fred, Sam, and Joseph Arthur, the narrator. While celebrating Joe's birthday, Fred, the most impulsive of the trio, opens a strange book
sent by Joe's uncle, a stage magician known as Joe the Magnificent, and simultaneously wishes "to see knights and all that stuff for real." A pale green
mist begins to swirl around the boys, and, with a strange falling feeling, they
find themselves in a clearing being challenged by a knight all in black armor
riding a black horse. When Joe's polite explanations fail to impress the knight,
Fred works out a plan for the boys to wait until he charges and jump aside
when he is almost upon them, repeating the ploy until the knight and his horse
are exhausted and Fred can knock him off with a heavy stick. Before they have
time to rejoice, three other knights bear down on them, introducing themselves
as Sir Lancelot, Sir Percival, and Sir Gawain and thanking the three "wizards"
for ridding them of the Black Knight. Joe introduces himself as Sir Joe the
Magnificent, and his companions as Sir Fred the Awesome and Sir Sam the
Unusual. Immediately, as powerful enchanters, they are pressed into service to
rid Camelot of the twin perils: Smaug the Dragon from the West and Bleob the
Giant from the East. At King Arthur's court, they arouse the enmity of Merlin,
but Joe is able to impress Guenevere with a card trick he learned from his uncle.
Joe beguiles the slow-witted Bleob into fighting the dragon, and both fearful
creatures are destroyed when the giant's stomach gas is ignited by the dragon's
breath and they are blown to smithereens. Now welcome guests at court, the
boys try to teach the stableboys baseball and hit a ball through a window of
Merlin's tower. Just after the three have been knighted by Arthur, Merlin appears
with the ball and a book just like the gift from Uncle Joe, and he shows them
a picture of three boys, dressed in twentieth-century clothes, sitting at a kitchen
table looking at a baseball. Again a mist swirls around them, and the boys are
back in Joe's kitchen, the only proof of their adventure being Guenevere's card,
which Joe finds in his pocket. Although the language is not especially simple,
the novel's brevity, the illustrations, and the humor, centering on burps, nasal
discharge, and body odors, indicate that the audience aimed for is about fourth-
grade level. Older readers will want more development of characters and situations and more sophisticated humor. SLJ.

KOERTGE, RON(ALD) (1940–   ), born in Olney, Illinois; teacher of English
and author of prose and poetry for adults and novels of contemporary and grow-

ing-up problems for young adults. He received his B.A. from the University of Illinois and his M.A. from the University of Arizona and since 1965 has been on the faculty of Pasadena, California, City College. His *The Harmony Arms** (Little, Brown, 1992) was an American Library Association Best Book for Children. It describes how a boy gains greater understanding of his writer father through associating with the eccentric but loving residents of their apartment house complex. Most of Koertge's publications have been poetry, including *The Father-Poems* (Sumac, 1973), *Life on the Edge: Selected Poems of Ronald Koertge* (University of Arizona, 1982), and *High School Dirty Poems* (Red Wind, 1991). For young adults, he has also written *Where the Kissing Never Stops* (Atlantic Monthly, 1987), about a high school boy who has problems with his father's death, his mother's job as a stripper, and his own sexuality; *The Arizona Kid* (Little, Brown, 1988), in which a boy spends the summer with his gay uncle; *The Boy in the Moon* (Joy Street, 1990), about a boy who has trouble coping with changing peer relationships; and *Mariposa Blues* (Joy Street, 1991), in which a boy finds his relationship with his father changing as he moves through his teens. For adults Koertge has written *The Boogeyman* (Norton, 1980), a novel.

KONIGSBURG, E(LAINE) L(OBL) (1930–   ), born in New York City; popular author of humorous novels about contemporary life in family or neighborhood situations and several lively fantasies. She gained prominence in the world of children's literature when her amusing, realistic novel, *From the Mixed-up Files of Mrs. Basil E. Frankweiler* (Atheneum, 1967), won the Newbery Award, and her *Jennifer, Hecate, Macbeth, William McKinley, and Me, Elizabeth* (Atheneum, 1967), was named a Newbery Honor Book, both in the same year. Among her other honored novels is *A Proud Taste for Scarlet and Miniver** (Atheneum, 1973), a clever biographical fantasy about Eleanor of Aquitaine, which was a finalist for the National Book Award and a Phoenix Award Honor Book. *T-Backs, T-Shirts, COAT, and Suit** (Atheneum, 1993) is a *School Library Journal* Best Book about a girl who learns the importance of independence of thought during a community conflict over T-back bathing suits. Konigsburg has almost always illustrated her own books, including several picture books for which she wrote the stories. Among these are *Samuel Todd's Book of Great Colors* (Atheneum, 1990) and *Samuel Todd's Book of Great Inventions* (Atheneum, 1991). She is a frequent speaker for professional groups and has published a selection of her speeches in *TalkTalk: A Children's Book Author Speaks to Grown-ups* (Atheneum, 1995). She lives in Ponte Vedra Beach, Florida. For earlier biographical information and title entries, see *Dictionary, 1960–1984* [*About the B'Nai Bagels; From the Mixed-up Files of Mrs. Basil E. Frankweiler; Jennifer, Hecate, Macbeth, William McKinley, and Me, Elizabeth; A Proud Taste for Scarlet and Miniver; The Second Mrs. Giaconda*] and *Dictionary, 1985–1989* [*Up from Jericho Tel*].

L

LALO BALDELLI (*Baby**), close friend and schoolmate of Larkin, the protagonist. The son of the island innkeeper, he is a kind of second self to Larkin, like a shadow, a facet that is picked up and extended in the tune to which Papa* dances, ''Me and My Shadow,'' and to which at the end of the book, in a symbolic scene of healing and acceptance, Larkin finally dances the soft shoe Papa had been trying to teach her for years. Lalo is protective of Larkin, aware of her unspoken grief about her dead baby brother, and also of Mama's* similarly unspoken grief about the loss of the child who lived only a day. Like Papa, Lalo is afraid of the effect taking in the foundling Sophie might have, especially on Mama. At school, he enjoys Ms.* Minifred's ''wondrous words'' and thinks that she looks ''wondrous'' after she starts keeping company openly with Rebel, the school janitor. Lalo holds Larkin's hand to soften the blow when Julia*, Sophie's mother, arrives to claim her child.

THE LAMPFISH OF TWILL (Lisle*, Janet Taylor, illus. Wendy Anderson Halperin, Orchard, 1991), fantasy of a sea adventure that leads to another world and expands the horizons for a young fisherman. The people of Twill have a hard life, which has made them bitter and fearful. The country is barren and the coast treacherous, and although almost all the families have lost someone to the sea, they must exist as fisherfolk, casting their nets from the cliffs or navigating the swirling waters in their slim boats. Since Eric's parents were drowned, he has lived with his aunt Opal, sharing equally in the fishing and the housework. Eric's only friend is his seagull, Sir Gullstone, which he rescued from the waves when it was small, and whose freedom he tries nervously to restrict, lest the bird come to harm. In the waters off Cantrip's Point, a dangerous promontory near the large whirlpool called Cantrip's Spout, Eric has seen one of the rare and beautiful lampfish. These large, mysterious fish glow as if with an interior light that illuminates their skeletons and are much prized by the people of Twill for their bones, from which they make fishhooks. Although landing a lampfish is usually a community project, Eric hopes to do it by himself, a rare deed considered heroic in the country. Just as he has spotted the fish, however, he is interrupted by a strange man dressed in old-fashioned clothes who predicts bad weather despite the clear sky and makes various incomprehensible statements. Sure enough, the morning darkens and a violent wind starts that lasts several days and takes the life of one of the local men. It is the kind of out-of-season storm usually credited to the Old Blaster, a malicious, vengeful power that the people of Twill fear and try to propitiate. Eric returns to Cantrip's Point repeatedly, where he often meets the old man, whose strange conversation and sudden fits of laughter eventually persuade the boy that this is Zeke Cantrip, the only man who was ever sucked down the whirlpool and shot back up in the spout, although Aunt Opal says Cantrip died a long time ago. Eric visits the old man in his Strangle Point hut, marvels at his strange collection of sea relics, and is amazed to find that in a large tank he has an injured lampfish, which he is treating. Mr. Cantrip tells Eric that his crew of gulls carried the fish to him in a net. When the whole community joins in a lampfish kill, Eric is at first excited and then sickened. Instead of taking part in the revelry afterward, he goes to Mr. Cantrip's hut and agrees, doubtfully, to venture out with him in his boat to see the lampfish at night. In the rosy light of dozens of glowing fish, they steer toward the whirlpool, and the old man deliberately leaps into the sea and pulls Eric after him. They are swirled around and around, Sir Gullstone with them, until gradually they are sucked down into the spinning center. Eric awakens to find himself in what Mr. Cantrip calls Underwhirl*, bedraggled and sleepy but relieved that his gull and the old man have survived with him. Although there is no wind, the sky is filled with what seem to be large, pink clouds gently floating about. Eric realizes that they are lampfish. They set off across the fields of flowers and soft grass. Despite the mild weather and the beauty of the landscape, Eric finds it difficult to walk; the gull is unable to fly but flaps along wearily beside him, as Mr. Cantrip prods and urges them on. At last they come to what looks like a grove of trees but is actually people resembling trees, with some rooted into the ground. They greet Mr. Cantrip and welcome Eric, and speaking slowly with long pauses between their words, give their names and the dates and circumstances of their being washed down the whirlpool. The temptation to join them is great, but the gull flaps off and Eric plunges after him. Just as he is giving up, many lampfish start to move in a circular pattern, faster and faster, so that Eric is caught up in the swirl of what he realizes is the spout. As he revolves ever faster, he nears Mr. Cantrip holding Sir Gullstone. The old man, urgent and serious for once, tells him to let the gull go on his own and when he reaches the top to rage and howl at the sky. Too nearly drowned to make much noise, Eric is trying to swim when the large flock of seagulls spot him, drop a net, and carry him to land. He wakes at Aunt Opal's house. She can make nothing of his explanations and soon refuses to listen. At the beach, Eric finds Mr. Gullstone, too battered to survive but alive long enough for him to say goodbye. He buries the bird, gravely attended by the other seagulls. Eric moves into Mr. Cantrip's hut on Strangle Point and never sees the old man again, but he receives two tokens from the sea, which might have been sent by his old friend: his boots, hurled by a wave onto the beach, and a young seagull, nearly drowned, washed up nearby. The fantasy is inventive but not entirely convincing. The lampfish are too amorphous to be believable and the crew of gulls hard to visualize doing the work described. There is a suggestion that Mr. Cantrip is actually the Old Blaster, an idea that is not fully explored. The picture of Twill, however, with its rugged coastline, rocky soil, treacherous waters, and suspicious people, is well developed, and Eric's happiness, living with the seagulls though now ostracized by the people, is in sharp contrast to the misery of the other inhabitants and points up the theme that openness of mind and willingness to adventure are more important than narrow safety. SLJ.

LASKY, KATHRYN (1944–), born in Indianapolis, Indiana; graduate of the University of Michigan; writer of both fiction and nonfiction for young people. Some of the nonfiction has been illustrated by her husband, Christopher Knight. She has written historical fiction and also a lighthearted mystery-detective fantasy, in which two children become involved with characters from Sherlock Holmes books, *Double Trouble Squared* * (Harcourt, 1991), which was nominated for the Edgar Allan Poe Award. For earlier biographical information and a title entry, see *Dictionary, 1985–1989* [*The Bone Wars*].

LEARNING BY HEART (Young*, Ronder Thomas, Houghton Mifflin, 1993), realistic episodic novel of family life in a small South Carolina town in the early 1960s. The year that Rachel turns ten starts with a disappointment: Daddy has bought a house because the apartment behind his grocery store will be too small for the family of four after the new baby arrives. Although Rachel has loved the excitement of the store, she finds Miss Isabella* Harris, the slender, young African-American maid Mama has hired, warm, comforting, and wise in helping Rachel make sensible decisions and maintain proper attitudes during the year. Included among the trying times are when bossy Grandma Graham, Mama's mama, lives with the family briefly; Great-Uncle Hewitt dies; the unruly Tucker children next door cause trouble in the neighborhood; Rachel comes down with mumps and vomits all over Grandma Graham's heirloom rug on the day of Uncle* Carter's wedding; and Daddy's store goes up in flames, creating financial problems for the family. Mostly, however, Rachel's year is upbeat. She gets new clothes for school, sewn for her by a black seamstress. She visits the library regularly with Isabella and baby Jesse, and Isabella takes out books, too. Daddy buys Rachel a piano, on which she takes lessons and through which she becomes best friends with Pamela* Tucker. She visits back and forth and plays Barbie dolls with classmates Caroline and Cynthia. She follows the progress of Uncle Carter's romance with Miss Macy Mitchell, of whom Grandma Graham heartily disapproves, because, as the family realize, she is simply jealous of Macy. Rachel joins Girl Scouts and attends Girl Scout camp the summer she turns eleven where she solidifies her friendship with African-American Callie* Thompson, the smartest girl in her class and the only black in school. The book concludes with two significant events: Rachel visits Isabella at her house for the first time, because she misses Isabella so much (Mama was forced for reasons of money to cut the maid back to one day a week), and Daddy decides to take a position as manager of a restaurant, which he hopes eventually to purchase. Episodes are consistently interesting but insufficiently developed, being more like sketches than actual scenes. Perhaps this is a fault of the author's choice of the first-person mode. Rachel has been a protected only child. She does not make friends easily and does not talk readily about her feelings and reactions to situations; hence the episodes are limited in scope and also in impact. The book excels in details of day-to-day home and school life from the young girl's standpoint. Characters are firmly drawn, even less important ones, like patient, encouraging Miss Love, Rachel's piano teacher, and the stern Reverend Mr. Harris, Isabella's brother, and Caroline and Cynthia, the typical snippy schoolgirls who form expedient friendships with ease and play such ties against one another. ALA.

LEGUIN, URSULA K(ROEBER) (1929–   ), born in Berkeley, California; science-fiction writer and author of the widely acclaimed Earthsea fantasies for young people. *A Wizard of Earthsea* (Parnassus, 1968), the first book of the trilogy, was a *Boston Globe–Horn Book* Award winner, but the second, *The Tombs of Atuan** (Atheneum, 1971), did not receive a major award at the time of its publication. In 1991, however, it was named an honor book for the Phoenix Award given by The Children's Literature Association for a book published twenty years earlier that has stood the test of time. The third book, *The Farthest Shore* (Atheneum, 1972), seemed to complete the series, but in 1990 LeGuin published *Tehanu: The Last Book of Earthsea** (Atheneum, 1990). This novel treats the leading characters of the first two books in their middle age and sees the world of Earthsea from a more feminist perspective. It was named to the *Horn Book* Fanfare list. For earlier biographical information and title entries, see *Dictionary, 1960–1984 [The Farthest Shore; The Tombs of Atuan; Very Far Away from Anywhere Else; A Wizard of Earthsea]*.

LEMRY (*Staying Fat for Sarah Byrnes**), Cynthia Lemry, Eric Calhoune's swimming coach and Contemporary American Thought (CAT) teacher. Lemry is tough, warmhearted, rigidly fair, smart, knowledgeable, ''a thinking man's coach,'' who runs her CAT class in much the same way as she runs her swim team, with dispatch and substance. Her comments during class sessions are lucid, organized, humane, and always fair, considering the explosive nature of such topics as the reality of God, abortion, and suicide and her obviously liberal tendencies. She provides a safe haven for Sarah Byrnes when Eric tells her about Sarah's abusive father, although she knows it is dangerous to cross the man. Eventually she and her husband adopt Sarah.

LETTERS FROM A SLAVE GIRL: THE STORY OF HARRIET JACOBS

(Lyons*, Mary E., Scribner's, 1992), biographical novel written as letters from Harriet in Edenton, North Carolina, to her dead mother and then other relatives, starting in 1825 when she is twelve and continuing until she escapes to the North in 1842. When her mistress, who has treated her well and taught her to read, dies, Harriet is willed to the woman's three-year-old niece, daughter of Doctor Norcom and his stingy wife. Most of the rest of Harriet's family live nearby, owned by members of the same family and often rented out to various local people. Within the year her father, always a slave rebellious in his heart, dies, as does the old woman who owns Gran and Harriet's uncle and younger brother, John. Although her mistress had promised that she would go free, Doctor Norcom claims Gran, but she is purchased, set free by the aging sister of her former mistress, and moves to a small cottage. Doctor Norcom buys John and starts making sexual advances to young Harriet, hindered only by living in town, where an obvious rape would damage his reputation. At a dance she meets a young free black whom she refers to as R, a man who wants to buy her, but when the doctor refuses to sell, R leaves the area. Soon Harriet, seeking some protection from Norcom, succumbs to the attentions of Samuel Sawyer, a white man who has quarreled with the doctor. She has a boy, Joseph, and a girl, Louisa, by Sawyer, and lives with Gran after Norcom's wife throws her out. In letters to R (like her other letters, not meant to be sent but only to be a release for her emotions) Harriet describes the white reaction to the Nat Turner massacres for which many slaves suffer. Eventually Norcom gives Auburn, his plantation, to his son, James, and Harriet works there as his slave, leaving her children with Gran. In 1835, nearly ten years after her first letters, the threat that they will be brought to the plantation and "broken in" as slaves causes Harriet to run away, hiding at first with friends, and then for a while with a white widow who was a friend of Gran's mistress. John and the children are kept in the local jail for two months in Norcom's effort to force Harriet out of hiding. When Norcom, hearing that Harriet is in New York, goes north, Sawyer buys John and the children, but he does not set them free as he has promised. Her hiding place having become unsafe, Harriet dresses as a sailor, is rowed by an uncle to the swamp where she stays until she comes down with fever, then is smuggled back to Gran's house. For the next seven years, she hides under the roof of Gran's cottage in a space less than three feet high and only seven feet long, unbearably hot in the summer and wet by rain blown in, where she can hear her children playing and sometimes glimpse them through the cracks. Sawyer, going north to marry a white woman, takes John with him as a body servant, and John runs away. After Sawyer's wife learns that Harriet's children are her husband's, she arranges for Louisa to be sent to New York, ostensibly to live with cousins and go to school but actually to be a waiting maid in the family. When a relative arranges voyage with a captain of a sailing vessel, Harriet decides to try to escape to the North. Although hating to leave her son, Joseph, and Gran and terrified that the captain may turn them in for a reward, she hides with another runaway in a tiny cabin until they have been at sea several days, and eventually arrives in Philadelphia. A last narrative section summarizes Harriet's life from 1842 until her death in 1897, telling how she gets help from abolitionists, finds her brother and her daughter and has her son sent north, how she trembles with fear of the Fugitive Slave Act, which could have sent her back to the Norcoms, and how, just before the Civil War, she publishes a book under the pseudonym of Linda Brent, *Linda: Incidents in the Life of a Slave Girl, Written by Herself*. The narrative is followed by photographs of some of the places and characters, family trees, and an author's note explaining that although the letters are fictitious, the incidents recorded are factual. The epistolary style works fairly well, using Harriet's uneducated diction and spelling and showing her development from a naive little girl to a determined and desperate woman. Her story is unusual not only in her ability to read but also in that most of her family stay in the area, providing both moral and practical support, and some of the white people of Edenton as well as the northern abolitionists are helpful. Harriet is credited for bringing the problem of sexual abuse of female slaves into the open for the first time. ALA; Fanfare.

LETTERS FROM RIFKA (Hesse*, Karen, Holt, 1992), epistolary novel of the immigration to America of the Russian Jewish Nebrot family in 1919 and 1920, told in letters to her cousin Tovah by Rifka, 12. They are written secretly in the margins of a book of Pushkin's poetry given her by Tovah and not mailed separately; eventually the book is returned to Tovah from America. Rifka's brother, Nathan, whom she adores, has deserted from the army to warn his younger brother, Saul, that he, too, is about to be impressed, a fate always meaning abuse and often death for a Jewish boy. Their father, Beryl, seizes the moment for the whole family to leave and join the three eldest sons who emigrated to America before Rifka was born. Because she has blond hair and blue eyes and can speak Russian with no accent, Rifka is detailed to act as a peasant girl and distract the guards who search for Nathan on the freight train where they hide, and thereby they are able to leave their village of Berdichev. Their entire trip is beset by nearly fatal problems. In Poland Rifka and then all the others except Saul come down with typhus; at first they hide in a shed and keep the illness secret so they will not be sent back. After they have recovered and gone on to Warsaw, Rifka is discovered to have ringworm, contracted from a Polish peasant girl whom she befriended on the train. The steamship company will not even sell a ticket for her, and with the help of the Hebrew Immigration Aid Society she is sent to Belgium while the rest of the family goes on to New York. In Antwerp, Rifka is taken in by a kind couple and sent for treatment to a hospital where understanding Sister Katrina teaches her Flemish. Very clever at languages, Rifka has also picked up Polish, and the lady from the aid society starts her on English. After a lonely period, she makes friends with the children who play in a nearby park and explores Antwerp, especially enjoying the strange and wonderful foods—bananas, ice cream, and chocolate. More than a year after their departure from Russia, Rifka sails from Antwerp, her ringworm cured but her lovely, curly blond hair all gone as a result of the illness. On the small ship, she befriends a young sailor, Pieter. During a terrible storm, he saves her but later is himself washed overboard and lost. The disabled ship is towed to New York, where Rifka is detained at the Ellis Island hospital for contagious diseases. The ringworm is cured, but because she is bald, the American authorities fear that she is unmarriageable and will become a social responsibility. For nearly a month, she is held at the hospital, where she soon makes herself useful nursing a Polish baby with typhus, learning English, and persuading a Russian peasant boy, Ilya, 7, to eat. Ilya, who is being sent to an uncle he fears, refuses to speak, and the doctors think he must be mentally disabled, but Rifka reads to him from her Pushkin, which he soon learns by heart. At the final examinations before they are both to be deported, Rifka sees that Ilya's uncle is a good man who wants the boy, and she proves to the doctors that Ilya is intelligent by getting him to read the Pushkin. When her own turn comes, she persuades the authorities to let her stay by assertively pointing out that she has been useful and a hard worker and is unlikely to become a responsibility for the state. Her head is beginning to itch, and she is afraid the ringworm has returned, but when her kerchief is pulled off, it is revealed that her hair has begun to grow again. Based on the experiences of the author's great aunt, the book has a wealth of telling detail, the sort of incident, small and large, that a bright girl in her early teens would notice. Since she is writing as much to record her experiences and comfort herself as to enlighten her cousin, the epistolary style seems natural, although some of the information is more to enlighten the reader than for Tovah, especially about the difficulties of life for Jews in Russia. Rifka is a lively, spunky character who develops during her long journey into a self-confident young woman. ALA; Christopher; Fanfare; IRA; SLJ.

LET THE CIRCLE BE UNBROKEN (Taylor*, Mildred D., Dial, 1981), substantial historical novel set in a cotton-growing part of Mississippi in 1934 to 1935, about the Logans, the enterprising and courageous black farm family of *Roll of Thunder, Hear My Cry**, and their sharecropping neighbors. Although several story strands unify the various episodes, early scenes provide a socially revealing and emotionally gripping conclusion to the previous book. Black youth T. J. Avery is tried for the murder of a white merchant of which he is accused at the end of *Roll of Thunder, Hear My Cry*. The narrator, Cassie Logan, now eleven, and her brothers, Stacey*, 13, Christopher-John, and Little Man, both younger, skip school and hitch a ride with local youths going into Strawberry, where they anxiously watch the trial through the courthouse window. In spite of the fine job T.J.'s white lawyer, Mr. Jamison, does of casting doubt on the testimony against innocent T.J., the boy is convicted of the capital crime by an all-white jury in one day. The main problem of the rest of the book also carries over from the previous novel: the Logans' need for money to pay the taxes on their land so that it does not fall into the covetous hands of Harlan Granger, the area's major white landowner, who has already cheated Papa out of government crop money. The Great Depression has hit hard, and since local sharecroppers are being increasingly evicted by their landlords, interest in unionizing builds. Papa even allows the local organizers to hold a meeting in his barn, but eventually he is forced to return to his old job on the railroad to earn money for taxes. Cassie continues to grow in her understanding of the harsh realities of racism, having thus far been protected by Mama, Big Ma, and Papa as best they could. She discovers, for example, that the courthouse bathroom and water fountain are out of bounds for her. She notices that young white men seem unduly interested in teenaged black girls and that the way they behave around the girls worries black adults. Of immediate concern in this regard is that pretty, black Jacey Peters, a girl Stacey has been interested in, is found to be pregnant by the son of a local white landowner. An additional matter is that elderly Mrs. Lee Annie Lees, their sharecropping neighbor, decides she is going to register to vote. Cassie and Mama help her study the Constitution for the test, although everyone knows that the possibility that the white officials will admit her is remote and that the Logans will probably be accused of putting her up to it. Still another complication in the Logans' life is the arrival of cousin Suzella*, whose mother is white. A pretty, pleasant girl of fifteen, she attracts the attention of men of both races, an irritation generally to race relations. Family and community issues unite when, although his hours on the railroad are cut back, Papa cannot come home for the annual church revival in August. Stacey is so determined to help with family finances that he drops out of school and takes off without permission for the sugar cane plantations with his good friend, Moe* Turner. Although the Logans and the black community search diligently for them, neither youth is found until January, when the book reaches a tense and rapid-action climax. Local sharecroppers, angry at being evicted by further cutbacks in production mandated by the federal government, organize a wagontrain protest at the country courthouse in Strawberry, coincidentally at the very time Mrs. Lee Annie unsuccessfully attempts to register to vote. Some violence occurs, and by cleverly pitting the races and pro- and anti-unionists against one another, Mr. Granger breaks the protest, leaving the blacks worse off than before, and later even puts Mrs. Lee Annie Lees out of her house as an example of what will happen to blacks who attempt to rise above their station as the whites see it. On the good side, Mr. Jamison has word that two youths have been found in a Louisiana jail, held on theft charges. The boys are indeed Stacey and Moe. Cleared, they are brought home, and the Logan circle is once more intact. In large part the novel depends on its predecessor for impact and understanding and lacks the emotional pull of the earlier book. The large cast of characters is hard to keep track of, even if one knows the previous book. The economic difficulties, however, the seething racism of the whites, the undercurrent of anger of the blacks, and the strong sense of black cohesion in school, church, and community come through strongly. Cassie tells the story after it has happened. She is still the inquisitive, willful, stubborn, sometimes disobedient, opinionated, bright, hard-working, loyal, and thoroughly likable girl that she was in the earlier book. In general her maturation is convincing, although the situations in which she learns about conditions for blacks seem deliberately fabricated for instructing the reader. The third novel about the Logans, *The Road to Memphis**, takes place a few years later and involves several of the same characters, and *Mississippi Bridge** is a single-incident story about discrimination told by Jeremy* Simms, in which the Logans appear briefly. For a long entry on *Roll of Thunder, Hear My Cry,* see *Dictionary, 1960–1984.* Stone.

LIBBY ON WEDNESDAY (Snyder*, Zilpha Keatley, Delacorte, 1990), realistic problem novel with girl's growing-up and school story aspects set in the very late twentieth century in the town of Morrison, California. Presented mostly in linear narrative but also in remembered scenes and notebook entries, the story tells how an intellectually advanced, socially maladjusted girl learns to relate to her peers. Libby (Elizabeth Portia) McCall, 11, granddaughter of famous writer Graham McCall, lives in the big, old, neglected mansion that the eccentric novelist had built, along with her usually abstracted father, Christopher, a poet; Graham's widow, Gillian; Gillian's sister, Cordelia Wembley; and Elliott Garner, a former teacher who runs a bookstore and likes to cook. Although Libby has been perfectly content with this assorted set of lively, opinionated intellectuals who have overseen her education at home, her mother, Mercedes O'Brien, a stage actress who makes her home in New York City, insists that Libby enroll in public school for the socialization that Mercedes feels the girl needs. Because she is much smaller than the other eighth graders at Morrison Middle School and recites eagerly and well, Libby is jeered, scorned, ostracized, and made the target of such jibes as McBrain, Mighty Mouse, and Little Frankenstein. Libby hides her problems from her family, hoping that by pretending all is well to convince them to allow her to drop out and resume her lessons at home. Ironically, her scheme is doomed when she wins a school creative writing contest, and the visiting author, Arnold Axminster, suggests that she and the four finalists form a writing workshop. Although Libby begs to be allowed to drop out, the family stands firm, and Libby becomes a member of FFW, the Famous Future Writers, as they call themselves, a group that meets every Wednesday afternoon in the reading lab with teacher Ms. Ostrowski, soon known as Mizzo. The workshop includes popular, pretty school leader Wendy* Davis; tall, ungainly Tierney* Laurent, who affects a pink punk hairdo; thin, jittery, stuttering Alex* Lockwood; and husky, muscular, mean Gary Greene, called Gary the Ghoul or G.G.* Although no one is keen about the project at first and Libby dreads the occasions, they all gradually learn to apply Mizzo's suggestions for constructive criticism, grow as writers, and eventually become friends. Ironically, the relationship flowers because of Libby's unusual house, which the others are curious about and yearn to visit. For many Wednesdays, Libby resists inviting them home because she fears they will not only ridicule the place but also make fun of her family. Then, after the group meets one day, Alex drops in unexpectedly;

he is charmed by the rooms full of items from different periods and cultures and, in particular, by Libby's collection of thirties' memorabilia. Libby, who has admired his quick wit, learns that his physical problems, which have also provoked teasing, are caused by cerebral palsy. Encouraged by his visit, she invites Wendy and Tierney to visit and even feels comfortable enough to show them her special retreat, the elaborate treehouse Graham had built for Christopher. Soon the girls are visiting back and forth, with Libby and Tierney comparing their thirties' stuff and Wendy starting a collection of twenties' materials. Gradually Libby learns to hold her own against teasing and sneers elsewhere in school, too, and even to give back as good as she gets. Her courage wins friends for her outside the FFW. When Mizzo is hospitalized after a car accident, Alex suggests the workshop continue meeting, and Wendy suggests using the McCall House. When G.G. turns up and becomes disruptive and Libby asserts herself, the others elect her as chair. The reasons for G.G.'s often bizarre, usually antisocial behavior come clear when one afternoon he fails to show up. He phones Libby, obviously in distress. She hears yelling in the background, and the telephone goes dead. The children rush to G.G.'s and find him unconscious, having been assaulted by his drunken father. Very disturbed by the incident, Libby finally summons the courage to describe her feelings about what happened in her notebook and then writes to Mercedes, saying that she really wants to continue at Morrison Middle in the fall. Although she is still often tense and jittery around people, she realizes she has found some students at Morrison she really likes and who really like her. For a while G.G. lives with relatives, then one day turns up at the workshop. The group has mixed feelings about accepting him back because he is still overbearing and rude, but they recall a tense, suspenseful story he was writing that intrigued them and realize that he was probably fictionalizing his own unsatisfactory home situation. They decide to let him stay and collaborate on a story titled ''The Return of G.G.'' In spite of the abrupt and almost sentimental ending, this is a substantial book filled with many convincingly detailed incidents and a large and interesting cast. The youngsters are too calculated a mixture of types but serve the story well and present strong contrasts to the more retiring, less confident socially but never prissy or superior-acting Libby. Characterizations—Libby's believable maturation, and the warm and affectionate if somewhat genteel tone—are the book's strong points, in addition to the writing episodes, which offer nondidactically many tips (e.g., making character charts) that are certain to appeal to aspiring authors. These episodes are entertaining and have enough story material and character revelation to appeal to readers other than those interested in the writing process. The adults are shown as likable eccentrics, not just from Libby's biased point of view but also increasingly in the eyes of the other children, who find them attractive and winning. SLJ.

LIFE'S A FUNNY PROPOSITION, HORATIO (Polikoff*, Barbara Garland, Holt, 1992), realistic novel of family life set in the town of Spring Creek, Wisconsin, for a couple of weeks late one spring in the early 1990s. The worst thing about life for Horatio Tuckerman, 12, is not having a dad as the other boys do. He loves and is proud of his mother, Evie* Berg, a dentist, although he is uncomfortable with her dating and thinks derisively of her most recent boyfriend as Pink Gums Paul. He admires and is comfortable with his grandfather, the Shakespeare-quoting Old Professor, Benjamin Tuckerman, called O.P.* He has good times with Silver Chief, the husky he got after the family moved from Chicago, and he gets along well with his school chum, Erik, who shares his love for chess. But he often aches for his father, Joshua, a university professor of literature, who also wrote plays and who died of lung cancer caused by smoking. The action starts one cold spring evening when O.P.'s beloved dog, Mollie, fails to return from her accustomed walk. The next morning they post a notice on the community bulletin board, and after school, Horatio and Erik search Thatcher Woods, where on the shore of Arrowhead Lake they find Mollie's body, dead by drowning after she apparently tried to walk on the thin ice. Horatio covers her gently and tearfully with his sweatshirt and leaves her there. At first he cannot bring himself to tell O.P., but when he does, the old man insists on fetching Mollie, and later, after she is cremated, they scatter her ashes in the woods, O.P. quoting from Shakespeare. On the way home, O.P. also quotes from a George M. Cohan song that Joshua liked, "Life's a funny proposition, after all." When Erik falls ill with what eventually turns into acute laryngitis, Horatio hangs out with Erik's younger sister, lively, horse-crazy Angie, with whom he chitchats about fathers, mothers, and life ambitions. They agree that it would be good for O.P. to get another dog, and Horatio persuades the old man to go to the shelter, just to look around. They enjoy visiting the animals, but Horatio thinks he could never work in such a place because he could not stand seeing the dogs' disappointment when the visitors leave them behind. That evening, the second anniversary of Joshua's death, O.P. lights a candle and suggests that they read some poems together. Horatio cannot bear the idea, runs to the woods, experiencing a confusing mixture of emotions, then returns to find his mother and grandfather sitting peacefully together. They are reading aloud poems that Joshua and they had loved. O.P. gives Horatio a photograph album containing pictures of Joshua at camp one summer, and Horatio feels good at seeing that as a boy his father enjoyed doing things that he himself likes to do. He takes O.P.'s burning candle to his room, where he reflects that he and his dad probably spent more time together in the ten years they had than most boys and their dads do in a lifetime. The next day, O.P. changes his mind and returns to the shelter to adopt a reddish female terrier mix with only three legs. He says that he feels an affinity for her because she has had to fight to survive, as he has had to fight to get over his son's death. Sky the terrier settles in with Silver Chief and the family, and Horatio feels, at least for the time being, the peace that comes from being grateful for what one has. Although the subject is serious, the tone of the narrative is positive and upbeat, and the atmosphere is often humorous. The book's strengths lie in its firm characterizations and emotional accuracy, especially the seesaw, roller-coaster range of feelings experienced by a sensitive, family-oriented, well-brought-up boy, who gradually sees that coming to terms with the death of a loved one is no simple task. ALA.

LINDIE (*Others See Us**), slightly overweight but attractive cousin about a year older than Jared, a decent, intelligent girl who has already figured out that Annelise* is not the Miss Perfection the rest of the family believes her to be. Unfortunately, Lindie has bought a copy of the SAT math test in order to rank high and get into Harvard, a secret that nags at her conscience and makes her vulnerable to Annelise's blackmail.

LIPSYTE, ROBERT (1918–   ), born in New York City; newspaperman, writer of sports novels. He is a graduate of Columbia University with B.A. and M.S. degrees and has been a reporter and columnist for the *New York Times.* His novel for young adults, *The Contender* (Harper, 1967), which won the Child Study Award, gives a vivid picture of the world of prizefighting as experienced by the young African-American protagonist. *The Brave** (HarperCollins, 1991), set about twenty-five years later, also occurs partly in the same Donatelli's Gym and several of the earlier characters appear in supporting roles, but the main character is a young half-Indian, waylaid on his way to join the army by a drug dealer and, after a period in a juvenile correction agency, sent to train at the gym. It was named to the *Horn Book* Fanfare list. Both it and a sequel, *The Chief* (HarperCollins, 1993), have memorable scenes of the intense training and fights. Lipsyte's writing is tight, fast paced, and compelling, with good character development and strong sensory descriptions. For young people he has also written *Michael Jordan: A Life above the Rim* (HarperCollins, 1994) and biographies of Jim Thorpe, Joe Louis, and Arnold Schwarzenegger. For earlier biographical information and a title entry, see *Dictionary, 1960–1984* [*The Contender*].

LISLE, JANET TAYLOR (1947–   ), born in Englewood, New Jersey; journalist, novelist. She received her B.A. degree from Smith College and has also attended Georgia State University. Her *Afternoon of the Elves** (Orchard, 1989), a novel about the friendship between a very protected, solidly middle-class child and an imaginative, unkempt, slightly older girl who persuades her that elves live in the back yard, has been much acclaimed. It was named a Newbery Honor book and to the *Horn Book* Fanfare list, as well as the American Library Association Notable Books list and the *School Library Journal* list of Best Books for Children. Also cited by *School Library Journal* are two unusual fantasies by Lisle: *Forest** (Orchard, 1993), about a conflict between the squirrels who occupy Upper Forest and the people of Lower Forest, and *The Lampfish of Twill** (Orchard, 1991), about a strange world under the ocean where change and struggle have ceased. These books, together with her earlier *Sirens and*

Spies (Bradbury, 1985), illustrate her wide range of subject and type, all written with precision and skill. For earlier biographical information and a title entry, see *Dictionary, 1985–1989* [*Sirens and Spies*].

LISTEN FOR THE FIG TREE (Mathis*, Sharon Bell, Viking, 1974), socio-logical problem novel about a blind African-American girl and her growth in understanding of the true meaning of Kwanza, set at about the time of its pub-lication, evidently in New York City. For Muffin (Marvina) Johnson, 16, her blindness is the least of her worries. Since the death of her beloved father a year previously, her mother, Leola, has begun drinking heavily, especially as the Christmas Eve anniversary of the street attack that killed him approaches. She has taken to screaming and insulting neighbors and the police, whom she blames because they were slow to call the ambulance. Muffin has support from three men: Mr. Willie Williams, a preacher who was her father's boyhood friend; Mr. Dale, a well-to-do bar owner with expensive and artistic tastes who lives in an apartment on the floor above theirs; and her boyfriend, Ernie Braithwaite, a steady, responsible worker in a Black Muslim grocery, who plans to become a lawyer. Most of the burden of keeping house, figuring out finances, and mon-itoring her mother, who needs medication for unspecified physical or mental conditions, falls to Muffin, and she mostly manages calmly, only occasionally falling into despair and shouting at patient Ernie. Her own interest is caught up in plans for the Kwanza celebration, a revival of an African festival sponsored by the Black Museum for the six days after Christmas. For this she makes herself a beautiful dress of lemon-colored velvet given to her by Mr. Dale, who has taught her to sew. When she tries on the finished garment and climbs the stairs to show Mr. Dale, she is attacked and almost raped in the hallway, escaping only because Mr. Thomas, a mute, reclusive neighbor, beats off the man with a belt. He is badly injured and cut up by the thug. After a trip to the hospital, she shuts herself in her room, emerging only to cook Christmas dinner and eat it with a couple of neighbors and her mother, who is drinking again. Badly shaken by the experience and her yellow dress ruined, she rejects the idea of going to the Kwanza dance, especially because her attacker was a black man and the idea of racial unity now seems ironic. Then Mr. Dale arrives with a new gown made from the lovely pink suede he has been saving and with Ernie, dressed for the party. At the Kwanza celebration, Muffin comes to understand the true meaning behind the event and gains strength to cope with her fear and anger and her mother's problems. Like all the other Phoenix Award books, this novel was published twenty years before the award, and in this case the time lapse is more apparent than with most others. Written in the period when Black Is Beautiful was a newly popular slogan and pride in heritage was being pushed, it belabors the idea, and the Kwanza celebration is described at action-stopping length. Muffin is a well-drawn character, although her sewing skill strains cred-ibility, but Ernie is unbelievably long-suffering, Mr. Dale is not convincing, and Leola is so self-pitying and irresponsible that a reader's patience is strained.

The suggestion that Mr. Dale is in love with her seems implausible. Phoenix Honor.

A LITTLE BIT DEAD (Reaver*, Chap, Delacorte, 1992), historical adventure novel set among the Yahi Native Americans of the northern California mountains in March, 1876. On his way back to the town of Macland from collecting the furs from his traps, orphaned Reece* (Herbert Reece), 18, rescues a young Indian named Shanti* from three white men—one short, one fat, and one minus an ear. Having already whipped Shanti brutally, they are about to lynch him because, they say, he is just a worthless Indian. Although Shanti speaks no English and Reece no Yahi, the two pledge friendship and exchange gifts, Reece giving his kerchief to Shanti and Shanti an arrowhead necklace to Reece. In town, Reece renews his acquaintance with Mr. Fitzsimmons*, the storekeeper, over poker. He is much taken with Kathryn* Rose Forrest, the pretty new prostitute at Miss Lizzy's place, and he visits her, his first time ever with a woman. When two of the lynchers, one-eared Colby and Little Sam (the short one), show up with a posse and insist that Reece murdered the third man, a U.S. marshal, Fitzsimmons and Kathryn help Reece escape. He reaches his home in spite of a terrible snowstorm, his faithful horse, Packy, leading; then he heads out for Shanti's country, hoping to persuade his Indian friend to testify for him in Macland, the arrowhead necklace pointing the direction. He is overtaken by Sheriff Ames, a decent sort, but on the way back to Macland, they are ambushed by Shanti's group, and Reece is taken by Shanti to his Indian village tucked away in a hidden valley. Shanti shows Reece what the three men were after: a cave with an extremely rich vein of gold. Shanti agrees to go to Macland, where in an almost comic-opera trial, Reece is judged innocent. Finding Reece's cabin burned by Colby and Sam, Reece and Shanti return to the valley, where they discover that Colby, Sam, and some army cohorts have massacred the entire band. Reece and Shanti trail them to the cave, where in a lengthy shoot-out Reece and Shanti trick the men and kill them all. Reece returns to Macland a rich man, but his face has been severely wounded, and he has a broken jaw. He persuades Kathryn to marry him, and Shanti joins the partisans of an Indian who says he is Crazy Horse, intending to devote his life to killing as many whites as he can. An epilogue set thirty years later sees Reece, now some sort of government official, visit Shanti, who has signed an agreement that he will no longer fight against the whites and is apparently living on a reservation. Reece persuades Shanti to return to the Yahi valley, which Reece used the gold to buy for the Indians thirty years earlier. The setting is vague, and events and characters are conventional for the genre, from the noble red men, the good-hearted whores, and the thoroughly crude, vicious, Indian-hating villains to the ambushes, sensationalized gunfights, the hero saved by his horse, gold maps, and dream-vision sequences. The occasional humor suggests the book may be intended as satire, or partly so. The short chapters, sentences, and paragraphs and liberal use of dialogue heighten the pace and sense of action. The interjection of Crazy Horse strains belief and also history, but white attitudes toward the Indians and the laws that prevented Indians from owning land and kept them on the run give the book a historicity beyond the usual gold-fever, Indians-vs.-whites western. If Reece's commitment to doing what is right, as his father had repeatedly instructed him to do, did not bias the reader toward the Indian side, the picture of life in the Indian village would do so. Although the sex scenes stop just short of being explicit, there is plenty of innuendo and leering. Poe Winner.

LITTLE DOG (*The Beggars' Ride**), one of the younger members of Cowboy's* group of homeless street kids. Cowboy found Dog, as the kids sometimes call him, almost dead of starvation, took him in, and, evidently realizing that the boy needed something to give him a sense of purpose and self-worth, provided him with a notebook and made him the group's accountant and recording secretary. Little Dog is the one who suggests that, as her initiation feat, Clare* Caldwell lead the kids in robbing Atlantic Jack's, old A.J.* Morgan's hot dog joint.

LLEU (*The Winter Prince**), with his twin sister, Goewin*, the only legitimate children of Artos (Arthur). A slightly built, frail boy, he suffers from asthma and has frequently been near death, but he becomes an accomplished gymnast and swordsman. Because he hates the idea of killing, he deliberately shoots wide when he hunts until Medraut*, on order from Artos, forces him to face the logic of meat consumption and to kill a stag. His squeamishness, however, does not make him kind and perceptive about the feelings of others, and as a result he arrogantly commands and contradicts Medraut, thereby aggravating his older half-brother's sense of frustration. The last straw is when he taunts Medraut about his parentage in front of Morgause's sons by King Lot, who have not previously known that their mother is also his but know, or at least suspect, that she and Medraut have had a sexual relationship. Lleu is often called "Bright One" or "The Shining One," in reference partly to his name, from the sun god, Lleu Lau Gyffs, and partly to his personal beauty.

L.O.D. (*Cousins**), Elodie Odie, unfortunate girl who claims to be part of Cammy's family, although she is actually a third cousin, adopted by a second cousin who is now a migrant worker in the summers. In desperate need of a friend, she lets Cammy treat her scornfully and is careful not to say anything that might cause a rift, although when Patty Ann deigns to notice her, she drops Cammy for the more popular girl, only to be discarded after a few minutes. Her loss of a sneaker in the river is treated by the other day campers as a joke, but since she has very few clothes, she makes a great effort to reach it and is almost drowned as a consequence. When Patty Ann drowns while saving her, the other children shun her, an attitude encouraged and kept alive by Aunt* Effie until

L.O.D. goes to the migrant camp to live. Although she lords it over L.O.D., Cammy actually likes her much better than she likes Patty Ann.

LOOKING OUT (Boutis*, Victoria, Four Winds, 1988), historical novel set in the steel town of Fairmore Hills, Pennsylvania, during the anticommunist hysteria of 1953. For Ellen Gerson, 12, life has revolved around the political activities of her parents, Jess and Mollie Gerson, who are American communists. Since Jess is an organizer of workers, whom he strongly believes should have more rights, he is often forced out of jobs. The family has moved from apartment to apartment, but now for the first time the Gersons have taken a house, a new one that Ellen likes very much although it is a tract place and like every other one around. Money is scarce, almost every penny going for causes, and Ellen often must babysit her little brother, Mikey, 2, while her parents are at meetings or on marches. The book opens with all four Gersons on their way to New York City to take part in a march protesting the conviction of Julius and Ethel Rosenberg for passing the secrets of the atomic bomb to Russia, a crime of which the Gerson parents maintain the Rosenbergs are absolutely innocent. Ellen finds the anger of the crowds and cries of "kill the reds" frightening. Because the Gersons have arrived in Fairmore Hills at the beginning of spring vacation, Ellen has time before classes start again to get to know Judy Dean, the lively, talkative, popular girl her age who lives across the street. Ellen longs to have an ordinary family, too, and be an ordinary American girl. Like Judy, she wants to learn about makeup and styles of dress and hair. She does not want to worry that her parents' political leanings will become known and thus lose her friends. Ellen sometimes resents her parents' dedication and considers communism a kind of rival for their affections. After a shopping trip with Judy one day, she arrives home to discover her mother in conversation with a Mr. Green, who she knows instinctively is another communist friend who has gone underground and will hide out overnight with the Gersons. She fears Judy will find out who he is. Later, old family friends, the Bakers, arrive, with the news that Mr. Baker has been discharged from his position at a university because he refuses to take the loyalty oath. Ellen's apprehensions increase when she overhears her mother ask Mrs. Baker to "take the kids" if something happens to her and Jess. At school, air raid drills confuse her, since they are, according to the administration, to protect the students against Russia. Ellen has been taught, however, that good things come from Russia. Her own brother's middle name (Leon) comes from some important Russian leader. At school Ellen pairs up with Sue Kitchner on a social studies project involving housing, in which the two girls make a model of the Fairmore Hills tract houses and give an oral report about it. The project provokes a political argument in class about distribution of wealth, and when Sue is called a "pinko," Ellen is afraid to back her up and then is ashamed because she did not. She participates in an act in the school variety show, although she is disappointed when her parents do not attend because they are called away unexpectedly in another effort to help the Rosenbergs, and she is nominated to run for Miss Fairmore Hills Junior High, a distinction of which she is proud. Judy invites her to an end-of-the-year party, and life seem to be going well. On the night of the party, however, word comes that Justice Douglas's stay of execution has been overturned, and the Rosenbergs are put to death early that evening. Ellen listens numbly to the broadcast, becomes sick to her stomach, and goes to bed ill. The next day, Judy reports the events of the party with little sense of the meaning of the Rosenberg case. Ellen realizes that although she likes Judy, she no longer wants to be like her, with shallow values and no broader social convictions. At the next air raid drill, convinced that such activity only heightens international tension, Ellen refuses to participate, although she knows she will be reported to the principal. Hitherto she has tried to be a model student, but her convictions are more important to her now than conformity. Characters are obvious and lack depth, and Ellen's fears, although normal, seem too numerous and tailored for effect. The school scenes are natural, and Ellen's desire to have nice clothes, use makeup, look like the other girls, and be popular seem convincing. Small details, like the songs and singers of the day, give the texture of the period. The Red Menace hysteria is evident but without contextual background to orient the reader. The demonstration march and the Rosenberg execution as reported on the radio are powerful episodes, and Ellen's coming to terms with her parents' convictions and sorting out her own are believable, if perhaps too sudden. Addams.

LOWRY, LOIS (HAMMERSBERG) (1937–   ), born in Honolulu, Hawaii; prolific novelist, twice winner of the Newbery Award. Daughter of an army dentist, she lived in many parts of the world, then attended Brown University and was graduated from the University of Southern Maine. *Number the Stars** (Houghton Mifflin, 1989), a novel about the smuggling of a Jewish family from Denmark to Sweden during World War II, in addition to the Newbery won the Jane Addams Award, was a Fanfare book, an American Library Association Notable Book, and a *School Library Journal* Best Book. Her other Newbery winner, *The Giver** (Houghton Mifflin, 1993), is a very different story—a futuristic fantasy of a highly regimented society in which all painful and disturbing memories have been wiped out. It also was a Notable Book, an SLJ Best Book, and a Fanfare book, and in addition was an Honor Book for the *Boston Globe–Horn Book* Award. Also on the Fanfare list and winner of an International Reading Association Award was her earlier novel, *A Summer to Die* (Houghton Mifflin, 1977), about the death of a sister. Another highly commended novel is *Rabble Starkey* (Houghton Mifflin, 1987), a story of a courageous and successful single mother. It won the *Boston Globe–Horn Book* Award and the Child Study Award and was a Fanfare book. Perhaps better known to young readers is her Anastasia Krupnik series, lighter stories dealing with ordinary concerns of early adolescents. For earlier biographical information and title entries, see *Dictionary, 1960–1984* [*A Summer to Die*] and *Dictionary, 1985–1989* [*All about Sam; Rabble Starkey*].

LUCAS CASTLE (*Phoenix Rising Or How to Survive Your Life**), 20, older brother of Helen and Jessie Castle. Although he seems naturally quiet, after Helen's death he talks even less and separates himself from his family, eating and sleeping elsewhere occasionally and often arguing with his father. A college dropout, a matter that is the source of some of the tension with his father, he is a talented guitarist and composer and works in a music store between gigs. He loved Helen very much and is sorry he did not tell her so. He tries to make up for being delinquent with Helen by paying extra attention to Jessie, especially when he sees how drastically her denial is affecting her life. One of the book's best scenes occurs when he takes her to a B. B. King concert and then afterward to a blues club, where he is recognized for his talent and is invited to join the group for the evening as lead guitar. Jessie is very proud of him and the musical compositions he makes in the story. Lucas seems closer to the sixties than the eighties in his attitudes toward music, disdaining that done "to make money," a point of view his father has trouble understanding. Lucas is a well-drawn figure, charming in an earnest way.

LUCIE BABBIDGE'S HOUSE (Cassedy*, Sylvia, Crowell, 1989), fantasy school novel set at the time of publication in Norwood Hall, a home for orphaned girls. Lucie Babbidge, 11, is despised by her classmates, who regularly refer to her as Goosey-Loosey and Swine, and derided by her teacher, Miss* Pimm, as plain and ignorant. Every day as soon as school is out, Lucie retreats to a storeroom "down a dark hidden stair . . . where no one went." There she secretly plays with an old dollhouse she has discovered and fixed up. Four china dolls become her Babbidge family—Mumma, Dada, Emmett*, 5, and herself— and two clothespin dolls she makes become Olive, the maid, and Mr. Broome, the piano teacher and lodger. Alternating chapters show how Lucie transforms classroom failures and disappointments for which teacher and students scorn her into triumphs for which her family praises her. For example, the Wordsworth poem, "Come into the Garden, Maud," that she cannot bring herself to say in class for even one verse she recites fluently in its entirety in her head to please her pretend family. She also makes up activities for them based on those in *The Adventures of the Pendletons,* a didactic family novel Miss Pimm reads to the class in installments every day. When Miss Pimm decides each girl must write to a "personage" for practice in letter writing, Lucie chooses Delia Hornsby, a name, presumably of the dollhouse designer, that she finds scratched in the paint below the sill on the dining room wall, along with an address in England. She receives a reply from Delia Hornsby Booth, the designer's twelve-year-old great-great-granddaughter, who continues to write letters to Lucie throughout the novel, although Lucie never replies. Before long the activities that Delia reports that her family does are things that the Babbidges have done and seem precipitated by them, though, of course, Delia has no way of knowing this. Matters come to a head when classmates discover the dollhouse and carry off the china dolls. Horror stricken, Lucie comes down with a severe fever and lies ill for three weeks. After she recovers, she continues the game as best she can with the remaining dolls: Olive, Mr. Broome, and the Babbidge baby (a bean) she has named Maud. She tears up her classmates' beds in a vain search for the stolen dolls and is severely lectured by Miss Pimm. Finally, inspired in part by a letter from Delia reporting that Delia and her family have been abducted and imprisoned in a dark room, Lucie deduces where the china dolls are hidden, inside the desk of classmate Rose Beth, and takes them back. The last letter from Delia reports that the Booths are all home and safe, as the Babbidges also now are. In an abrupt conclusion to the book, as Lucie has screwed up her courage and taken charge of things on behalf of the dolls, she also takes control for herself. Reacting to Miss Pimm's hectoring for the first time, she stands straight and tall in class and speaks up pertly and pertinently in a loud, clear voice, astonishing both teacher and students. The book is set up with many short chapters and rapidly changing scenes and is almost all dialogue, either real or imagined. The Babbidge family scenes are cozy, active, and idealized and the most interesting parts of the book. Of the dolls, the most engaging and lively is Emmett, whose quick wit comes out in his almost constant playing with words and repartee. All this, of course, is really Lucie's, since all the doll speeches occur inside her head. These imaginings reveal her to be intelligent, clever, and insightful, indeed the very opposite of Miss Pimm's conception of her. Why events in the Babbidge house should affect the Booths in England is not clear, and stealing back the dolls seems not in Lucie's character as presented to that point. That the recovery of the dolls should result in Lucie's becoming so suddenly assertive also strains believability. Miss Pimm is overly villainized, but the girls' nastiness and meanness seem typical of their age. Left open also is the relationship of the scenes showing Lucie at the seashore with her parents: Are these actual memories of occasions spent with her real parents, or are these scenes also made up? The commentary on teaching methods and discipline in schools cannot be missed. Lucie is obviously emotionally disturbed and certain to be increasingly introverted and withdrawn, in need of help that will probably never come. Her stubborn and sly nature, while in one way her salvation, also contributes to her isolation. Although one wonders just what one is to take away thematically from reading this book, it is consistently fast moving and never dull. Fanfare.

LYDDIE (Paterson*, Katherine, Lodestar/Dutton, 1991), historical novel about the working girls of the Lowell, Massachusetts, textile mills of the 1840s. When a black bear breaks into their Vermont farm cabin, Lyddie Worthen, 13, saves her half-crazed mother, her brother, Charlie*, 10, and her two little sisters, six-year-old Rachel* and four-year-old Agnes. Her mother, however, takes it as a sign that the end of the world is near and insists on going with the two youngest to live with her fanatically religious and mean-spirited sister, Clarissa, and Clarissa's husband, Judah, in Poultney. With hard work, Lyddie and Charlie get through the winter, hoping to keep the farm for the return of their father, who headed west three years earlier and has not been heard from. A letter from their mother saying she has sold the cow and horse, rented the farm to pay debts, and hired Charlie out to the miller and Lyddie to Cutler's tavern shatters their hopes. Their kindly Quaker neighbors, the Stevens family, buy their calf and send their son, Luke, to deliver the stock and the children to their destinations. Mrs. Cutler proves stingy and tyrannical, but Lyddie works hard and makes a friend of the cook, Triphena. When their mistress takes a trip to Boston, Triphena suggests that Lyddie go to see Charlie and check on their farm, the first time in more than a year she has left the tavern. She finds that the miller has sent Charlie to school, and at the farm, to her astonishment, is a black man who introduces himself as Ezekial Abernathy and whom she rightly suspects is an escaped slave, aided by the Quakers. Impulsively, knowing what it is to be virtually a slave herself, she gives him the money from the calf sale, which she had planned to hide there. On her return to the tavern, Mrs. Cutler, who has returned unexpectedly, is furious and dismisses her. Although Triphena urges her to stick around, sure that Mrs. Cutler will change her mind since she has never before had such a good worker, Lyddie heads for Massachusetts where she has heard girls can make good wages in a factory. With the help of money Triphena has pressed on her and a kindly coach driver, she gets to Boarding House Number Five of the Concord Manufacturing Corporation in Lowell, where the landlady, Mrs. Bedlow, the coachman's sister, takes her in hand and sees that she gets decent clothes and a job in the weaving room. At first the incredible noise, the heat, and the bewildering machines almost defeat her, but with the help of a fellow worker, Diana* Goss, she soon masters the necessary skills. Her roommates—proper Amelia, Prudence from Rutland, and Betsy*, who is always reading and making ironic remarks—warn her that Diana is an agitator and dangerous to associate with. Betsy, for all her seeming sarcasm, proves a true friend, reading aloud each night and inspiring Lyddie with a desire to improve her very limited education. In the next two years, she works with fervor, saving every penny to pay off the debts so she and Charlie can return to the farm. She has three visitors. To her astonishment, Luke Stevens comes bringing her a packet containing twice the money she gave to Ezekial with a letter saying he arrived safely in Canada and has purchased his wife and child. Luke is dressed in ordinary clothes, not as a Quaker, and only later does she realize that he is on a mission to transport slaves. A less welcome visitor is Uncle Judah, bringing Rachel, Agnes having died, and saying that he has put her mother in the asylum for the insane and will sell the farm to repay him for their keep. Lyddie writes Charlie, begging him to intervene to keep the farm. Her next visitor is Charlie himself, come to fetch Rachel, since the miller and his wife have taken him for an apprentice and want to raise Rachel as a daughter. He also brings her a letter from Luke, saying that since Uncle Judah was determined to sell the farm, his father has bought it. Luke also is asking her if she will return and live there with him as a wife. Angered at the idea of being bought, she tears it up. Some months later she sees Bridget, an Irish girl she has befriended, being attacked by the weaving room overseer, Mr. Marsden, who has earlier sexually harassed Lyddie. She dumps a bucket of water on the overseer and rescues Bridget but is herself dismissed for "moral turpitude." Luke finds her in the cabin on their old farm. She tells him that she intends to go to the college in Ohio, Oberlin, which Betsy had hoped to enter, but to herself she says that she may come back to Luke if he is still waiting. Scenes of the work in the tavern and the textile mill are graphic and convey a good sense of the unrelenting labor. Lyddie's fierce determination to keep the family together, her dilemma when Charlie points out that the miller and his wife will be like parents to him and Rachel, and her loneliness when she realizes they no longer depend on her are strongly realized elements, but her decision to go to Oberlin does not quite ring true, despite her efforts at self-education in Lowell, and the runaway slave episode seems artificially introduced. ALA; Fanfare; SLJ.

LYDIA KINSEY (*Cat Running**), mother of Cat Kinsey, stepmother of Cliff and Ellen Kinsey, and wife of Charles* Kinsey. According to Ellen, the Brownwood school was Lydia's first teaching position. She was so shy and timid that the children refused to obey her and did very poorly at their lessons. She at first refused to marry Charles Kinsey, whose wife had died just a year before and who was some twenty years her senior, but she finally agreed and took on the responsibility of Cliff, then ten, and Ellen, then thirteen. Lydia is a poor housekeeper and cook, seldom speaks her mind because she is afraid of her husband and stepchildren, and oftens suffers from sick headaches. No one in the family has much respect for her because she never stands up for herself. Because she is so much on the fringes, Cat is able to sneak away frequently and go to the grotto for quiet reflection and play.

LYNCH, CHRIS, author of novels of family relationships for later elementary youngsters and early adolescents. He holds an M.A. from Emerson College in Boston, where he lives and works as a full-time writer and stay-at-home father of two children. His *Shadow Boxer** (HarperCollins, 1993) is a realistic novel with a sports background, which was a choice of *School Library Journal.* It tells of George, 14, left half-orphaned by his father's death, who is determined that his younger brother will not become a fighter like their father, whose life boxing ended. Also set in a sports context is *Iceman* (HarperCollins, 1994), in which a teenaged hockey player's aspirations bring him into conflict with his parents. *Gypsy Davey* (HarperCollins, 1994) concerns a twelve-year-old boy in a single-parent family, who is man of the house for his mother and older sister.

LYONS, MARY E., school librarian, biographer. She has published a guide for teaching literature by women and has received the National Endowment for the Humanities Teacher/Scholar Award for 1991–1992 for the state of Virginia. Her collection of fifteen folktales, *Raw Head, Bloody Bones: African-American Tales of the Supernatural* (Scribner's, 1991), is spooky enough to delight young people but also contains notes, bibliography, and a list of suggested readings to make it a valuable contribution for folklorists. Also scholarly but attractive to children are her biographies of African-American artists and artisans published in a series of small books beautifully illustrated with color photographs and highly acclaimed. Among these are *Sorrow's Kitchen: The Life and Folklore of Zora Neale Hurston* (Scribner's, 1990); *Starting Home: The Story of Horace Pippin, Painter* (Scribner's, 1993); *Stitching Stars: The Story of Quilts of Harriet Powers* (Scribner's, 1993); *Master of Mahogany: Tom Day, Free Black Cabinetmaker* (Scribner's, 1994); and *Deep Blues: Bill Taylor, Self-Taught Artist* (Scribner's, 1994). Also biographical but published as fiction is *Letters from a Slave Girl: The Story of Harriet Jacobs** (Scribner's, 1992), which draws on the autobiography that Jacobs wrote in her older years but presents the material in the form of letters ostensibly written to her relatives living and dead but never sent. It was cited by the American Library Association as a Notable Book and by *Horn Book* on its Fanfare list. Lyons lives with her husband in Charlottesville, Virginia.

M

MACLACHLAN, PATRICIA (1938–   ), born in Cheyenne, Wyoming; graduate of the University of Connecticut; teacher of English and creative writing and critically acclaimed author of picture book stories and novels for middle elementary and early adolescent readers. Although she has written many, often humorous stories that deal with family relationships, she is best known for her Newbery and Scott O'Dell Award-winning book about two motherless children on the western plains, *Sarah Plain and Tall* (Harper, 1985), which was made into a television movie. Cited by the American Library Association are two of her short realistic novels, *Journey** (Delacorte, 1991), about a boy who grapples with the pain of being abandoned by his mother, which was also a *School Library Journal* choice; and *Baby** (Delacorte, 1993), also a Fanfare selection, a poignant story of how a foundling baby helps a family come to grips with the pain of the death of their own child. For earlier biographical information and title entries, see *Dictionary, 1960–1984* [*Unclaimed Treasures*] and *Dictionary, 1985–1989* [*The Facts and Fictions of Minna Pratt; Sarah Plain and Tall; Unclaimed Treasures*].

MAC MACNAMARA (*Revolutions of the Heart**), Cree Indian who comes to Summer, Wisconsin, to stay with relatives and go to high school when his older brother, with whom he has been living and moving around for about six years, goes into a rehabilitation center for his alcoholism. When Mac was about ten, his mother was killed in a car crash, fleeing from an abusive ex-boyfriend. Mac, who has strong self-control and determination to attend college, has promised himself that he will always get good grades, will never take a drink, and will never hit a woman. Although Mac is greatly attracted to Cory Knutson and both of them know that their best friends, Sasha* Hunter and Tony Merrill, are sleeping together, he does not push Cory for sex. After the fishing rights protests, he decides to spend the summer in Canada, visiting the reservations where his parents were born and trying to learn more about his heritage, feeling that if his mother had stayed with her people, she might have had enough stability and self-respect to keep away from abusive men. Whether his relationship with Cory will survive his absence and whether it is doomed anyway by their very different backgrounds are questions left open in the novel.

MAKE LEMONADE (Wolff*, Virginia Euwer, Holt, 1993), contemporary realistic novel set in an unspecified American urban area and revolving around the problems of a teenaged, single-parent mother. The narrator, LaVaughn, 14, is a good and ambitious student. She early decided that the best way to avoid living like her widowed mother, herself a teenaged parent, in an overcrowded apartment complex fraught with social problems, is to get a college education. Naively, she dreams of working in an office, wearing sleek business clothes, and having her own filing cabinet and appointment calendar. Hoping to build up her educational nest egg, LaVaughn answers an ad on her school bulletin board for a babysitter. Her heart is stolen by winsome little Jeremy, 2, and moved by his young mother's obvious desperation, and she agrees to work for Jolly*, 18, never married and also the mother of Jilly, 1, each child by a different, absent, noncontributing father. Jolly's cramped little apartment is filthy with cockroaches and spilled, dried-up, caked-on food and smells of vomit and dirty diapers, but LaVaughn takes control of the children right away and becomes especially close to Jeremy. She gets discouraged, particularly with the filth, which Jolly ignores, and the lack of supplies for the children, and she is afraid Mom will find out that her grade in social studies has slipped, so she takes care to apply herself harder in school. She teaches Jeremy to use the toilet and to make his bed, and she helps him plant lemon seeds, urging him to be patient and wait for the tree to grow, an obvious symbolic parallel to both her own and Jolly's situations. When Jolly is fired from her low-paying job because she resists the sexual advances of her boss, LaVaughn continues to sit for her, although she wonders about the propriety of doing so and evades Jolly's suggestion that she return the money Jolly has paid her—what LaVaughn intends to hang onto and thinks of as her "exit money." She persuades Jolly to attend a session of Steam Class (Self-Esteem Class) with her, and later, by making the contacts herself, enrolls Jolly in the Moms Up Program. Jolly resists for some time before agreeing to participate; she is afraid that if she accepts public assistance, the state will take her children away. She learns her fears are unfounded; eventually the children are also enrolled in day care with the program, and LaVaughn no longer sits for them. Gradually Jolly starts to take hold of her life and even cleans the apartment; with the CPR she learns in class, she saves Jilly's life when the little girl chokes on a plastic tarantula. Book's end finds Jolly well on her way toward achieving her general equivalency diploma and LaVaughn adding to her college fund by other means. LaVaughn tells her story honestly, if garrulously at times, and in spite of the basic seriousness of the subject matter, humor occurs regularly. LaVaughn is a moral child, and she wrestles continually with the dilemma about how she can best help Jolly and still maintain her own objectives. The plot is the book's weakest aspect; it goes as expected, events seeming tailored to show the difficulties young mothers face and the resources provided to help them to better lives if they avail themselves of the possibilities. LaVaughn, Mom, and Jolly are well drawn, and little Jeremy emerges as the sweetheart whom LaVaughn describes. Mom is Jolly caught at a later stage, and LaVaughn epitomizes what education and determination offer. The teachers and social workers speak in classic, textbook voices. LaVaughn's conversational narrative is contemporary in diction, intimate in tone, and arranged on the page in mostly short lines with natural thought breaks. Her descriptions of Jolly's terrible living conditions, poverty, and near-helplessness; the simple, homely details of life with Mom and Jolly; and the interactions between the three leading characters are the book's strong points. ALA; Fanfare; SLJ.

MALCOLM POOLE (*Saturnalia**), 19, indentured manservant of Mr.* Hogwood, wigmaker. Although he is expected to walk two paces behind his master, carrying his packages and springing forward to open doors and drive off offending dogs, Malcolm seizes every opportunity to place himself on an equal footing or, by advising Mr. Hogwood in matters of love, to become his superior. An ambitious, insubordinate rascal, he has his eyes on every pretty girl he encounters and attempts to seduce them with gifts that his master intends for Madam Phipp, recent widow whom Mr. Hogwood pursues with her deceased husband's wealth in mind. Malcolm engineers this courtship to his own advantage, not caring that he makes his master seem a buffoon on every occasion.

MALI, JANE LAWRENCE (1937–), born in New York City; homemaker and writer of fiction and nonfiction for young readers in collaboration with Alison Cragin Herzig*. Their *Mystery on October Road** (Viking, 1991), about three schoolchildren whose overactive imaginations lead them to believe the worst about the new resident in the old house next door to one of them, was nominated for an Edgar Allan Poe Award. With Herzig she has published *A Word to the Wise* (Little, Brown, 1978), a humorous novel about what happens after fifth graders steal their teacher's thesaurus. They also collaborated on the nonfiction *Oh, Boy! Babies!* (Little, Brown, 1980), a photo essay of a class in infant care, which was a Junior Literary Guild selection; and the novels *A Season of Secrets* (Little, Brown, 1982), concerning a girl who worries about her brother with epilepsy; *Thaddeus* (Little, Brown, 1984), in which young Thaddeus's namesake great-great-uncle makes his birthday special, also a Junior Literary Guild selection; *The Ten-Speed Babysitter* (Dutton, 1987), about a fourteen-year-old girl who is left to care for a baby whose father has jetted to the Caribbean; *Sam and the Moonqueen* (Little, Brown, 1990), about homelessness; and *The Wimp of the World* (Viking, 1994), about a family who lives at and runs a motel. She holds a B.S. degree from Columbia University and lives in New York City.

MAMA (*Baby**), Lily, Larkin's mother and Papa's* wife. Mama paints landscapes for island tourists. Larkin can tell Mama's mood by the amount of paint on her clothes (the more paint, the more restless Mama is). Mama is often unconventional in behavior; for example, she lets the children eat all the spice cake batter instead of baking it because it is much better before it is baked. Papa and Larkin are afraid of the effect on Mama if they keep Sophie, the baby who is left at their home by her mother. They are deeply aware of how much Mama longs for the baby boy of whose birth and death she never speaks. Mama is so caught up in her personal grief that she does not realize the hurt Larkin feels because her mother never talks about the dead baby. Papa and Grandma Byrd* help Mama come to terms with her grief and with the eventual loss of Sophie to Julia*, Sophie's mother.

MAMA LEE (*The Star Fisher**), Chinese-born, non-English-speaking mother in the Lee family. Youngest daughter of a patrician Chinese family, she was never taught to cook, and although she has been married for some sixteen years, she still burns many meals. She is proud, stubborn, pessimistic, superstitious, and far more practical than her husband. She often makes her daughter, Joan, do things—for example, shop—that her pride keeps her from doing. Her ambition is to get rich and then return to China to show off. Joan often feels angry toward her, but the girl also realizes that her mother is just an ordinary woman: loving toward her husband, protective toward her children, and caught by circumstances that she cannot control and does not really understand.

MAMA, LET'S DANCE (Hermes*, Patricia, Little, Brown, 1991), realistic family novel set during about five months in a recent year in a rural area at the foot of the North Carolina mountains, involving a runaway mother and the death of a sibling. After their beautiful, lighthearted mother, who loves to dance, abandons them, Mary Belle, 11, the musically gifted narrator, is moved by many often conflicting emotions. She resents having to take care of her little sister, Callie*, 7; feels overburdened with the responsibilities of running the house; knows that she is not really doing a good job of either, although she is trying her best; is puzzled by the note Mama left saying her children mean more to her than anything else; and although the house is free and clear, worries about money, since all their income is from the gas station job of her brother, Ariel*, 16, a serious boy who maintains straight A's. She most fears that the county will find out that they are alone and will send them to foster homes, which happened for a short time not long after the family was abandoned by her father, who was later killed in a mine accident. Out of pride, Mary Belle angrily pulls out all the plants set out in the garden in a generous spirit by their long-time family friend, African-American Amarius* Aikens, about ninety, but relents and allows him to provide them with a sumptuous chicken dinner. She is delighted when Callie is selected queen for the May fair on the last day of school, raids Mama's closet for a dress that can be cut down, and is both pleased and put off when Callie asks her to be a member of her court. Callie has long been thin and pale, and, a week before she is to reign as queen, on the night of the chicken dinner, the little girl comes down with a fever and rash. Mary Belle and Ariel take turns keeping watch over her, and Mary Belle is distressed even more when a letter comes from Mama asking for money. Callie continues to decline, and Mary Belle is both frightened and relieved when Amarius's niece, Miss Dearly Aikens, takes charge. She calls the ambulance to take Callie to the hospital, and for a week and a half Mary Belle remains at the hospital, refusing to leave for any reason, worried and afraid, stealing into Callie's room on occasion with help from Amarius, but Callie never recovers. When she knows Callie is dead, in sharp denial Mary Belle runs into the hills. The next day she is brought home by Amarius and Ariel. Miss Dearly, a minister and social worker, takes over; she plans and conducts the funeral, in which Callie is dressed in the white queen dress Mary Belle had sewed, and then the children become wards of the Aikenses. Miss Dearly persuades Mary Belle that Mama will not return, tells her that she and Amarius have known all along where Mama is, and Mary Belle begins to concentrate on herself for the first time in many months, in particular on playing the piano and writing music. Still, she yearns with all her heart for Callie. Mary Belle and Callie are the only characters developed in some depth, and even they are types: the older sister forced to take charge because of an irresponsible parent, and the sweet, fragile, pretty little sister whom everyone loves and is lost to death. Mary Belle does not hesitate to relay her emotions, and sometimes overindulges in her memories in that respect so that her story becomes melodramatic and sensationalized, as when she says that she howls like an animal when Amarius and Ariel catch her and force her to come home. Although the plot is insufficiently grounded with information about the family prior to Mama's disappearance and overindulges in emotional introspection, it holds the interest. Nevertheless, the book runs a poor second to its better characterized and more skillfully plotted counterpart by Vera and Bill Cleaver, *Where the Lilies Bloom.* The sense of the small-town, rural, mountain setting is pleasingly evoked, both socially and physically. The scenes in the hospital of waiting for news about Callie seem real and genuine, and they increase in tension gradually and sometimes with almost unbearable believability. SLJ.

MANIAC MAGEE (Spinelli*, Jerry, Little, Brown, 1990), humorous sociological problem novel with fantasy aspects, many incidents, and rapid action, set for about a year at the time of publication, mostly in the small Pennsylvania city of Two Mills. Featured is a highly moral, energetic, physically strong, unusually socially conscious white boy, who runs away from home in search of a good home and father and experiences situations that invite the reader to think about such contemporary American concerns as dysfunctional and unconventional families, racism, inadequate schools, the disadvantaged underclass, and urban violence. Jeffrey Lionel Magee, orphaned at three, runs away from psychologically abusive guardian-relatives at eleven, and eventually arrives in Two

Mills, where he lives on the streets during the day and sleeps at night in a deer shed in the local zoo. He soon acquires the nickname of Maniac and over time becomes a legend for his eccentric and heroic behavior. Like a whirlwind out of nowhere he appears suddenly in the white West End, catching football passes one-handed, rescuing a terrified boy from the infamous bully Finsterwald, running railroad rails with ease while reading a book, and mightily belting Giant John McNab's* fastballs for magnificent four-baggers. When McNab organizes his gang, the Cobras, for revenge, Maniac flees into the terrible (in the eyes of the white West Enders) African-American sector known as the East End. There he encounters a gang led by a notorious black youth, Mars* Bar Thompson, but is championed by spunky Amanda* Beale, also black, who takes him home and shares with him her love for books. When Mr. Beale discovers that Maniac is homeless, he takes him in, giving Maniac an address, something he has longed for: 728 Sycamore Street. Maniac appreciates his life with the warm, accepting, and giving Beales (who exemplify the worthy American nuclear family), loves Mrs. Beale like a mother, has ample opportunity to read, and thus keeps up his education. One hot August day, trouble strikes; while enjoying the water from the hydrant, he hears the dreaded words ''Whitey'' and ''move on.'' His fears, not for himself but for the Beales, peak when FISHBELLY GO HOME is painted on the house. Amanda temporarily dissuades him from leaving by enlisting his interest in untying the famous local puzzle, Cable's Knot, which is the ''size and shape of a lopsided volleyball.'' He does so, thus adding tremendously to his legend and earning a year's supply of free pizza. When Amanda's treasured A encyclopedia volume is shredded as an act of harassment, Maniac moves on, jeers and howls of both blacks and whites accompanying him as he walks down Hector Street, which divides West End from East. He spends several happy months with Earl Grayson*, the baseball equipment keeper at Elmwood Park, after Grayson finds him sleeping in the park zoo with the baby buffalo. Grayson helps him fit out an apartment in the band shell and eventually moves in, too, at what Maniac happily calls 101 Band Shell Boulevard, for an unconventional but thoroughly satisfying family existence. Maniac discusses baseball with the old ex–minor leaguer, celebrates Thanksgiving and Christmas with him in style, reads voraciously the old, worn books he buys from library book sales and thus keeps from having to go to school as Grayson wants him to, and teaches the illiterate old man to read. Again without an address when Grayson dies unexpectedly on December 31, Maniac is affronted by the callous behavior of the adults who conduct the funeral and runs again. Days later in dire condition, he finds shelter in a replica-cabin at Valley Forge, where he soon discovers Russell and Piper NcNab, McNab's younger brothers, who have run away. Maniac manages to get them home by sharing his prize pizzas with them, and for some weeks lives a tempestuous life in the McNab house. The place is filthy, the father drinks, the children are left mostly on their own, and antiblack sentiment is rampant. The McNab house is obviously the wrong kind of home. After a variety of episodes and Maniac is still homeless, Amanda stubbornly persuades him to return with her to 728 Sycamore. Maniac now sees this is really his home, since the people here love him and certainly want him. Although Maniac could just as well have ended up with the Pickwells, the white counterparts of the Beals, who also welcome him, the ending seems satisfactory if convenient thematically. The allegorical aspects and social commentary cannot be missed, but the plentiful action and comic, tall-tale atmosphere play down the message and keep it from taking over the book. Characterization is minimal and obvious; the pace is consistently fast; the numerous chapters are very short; the peppery style is highly contemporary in diction and sentence structure and sometimes earthy, explicit, and out for shock appeal; and the tone, in the author's strong storytelling voice, is intimate and informal. The humor is ironic, occasionally slapstick, always topical. ALA; Boston Globe Winner; Fanfare; Newbery Winner.

THE MAN WHO WAS POE (Avi*, Orchard, 1989), mystery-detective novel set in Providence, Rhode Island, for a few days in 1848, in which the historical writer Edgar Allan Poe*, in the role of his fictional detective, Mr. Auguste Dupin, solves a mystery at the same time that Poe writes it. Edmund* Albert George Brimmer, 11, his twin sister, called Sis, and their Aunty Pru, who is their mother's twin sister, have sailed from England to Providence in search of the children's mother. A widow, she had earlier come to America to find, call to account, and divorce her new husband, a Mr. Rachett, who had defrauded her of all her money and fled to America. After about one month of unsuccessful searching for the missing woman, Aunty Pru also mysteriously disappears, having left the children alone in their dingy dockside room with strict instructions not to leave. Two days later (which is when the novel begins), driven by hunger, Edmund goes out to get food, leaving Sis locked in the room. When he returns, he finds the place completely empty and no sign of Sis. Later that night, while frantically scouring the fog-shrouded area, he literally runs into a man carrying a carpet bag, wearing an old army coat, and closely watching a well-fitted house next door to a church. Seeing the boy is dirty, cold, and tear-stained, taking in the bits and pieces of his blurted story about a lost aunty and missing sister and an unkind stepfather (details that parallel Poe's own life), and learning that the boy's name is Edmund, so like his own name, the man takes pity on the child. He engages Edmund to deliver a letter (a suitor's note) to Mrs. Helen Whitman, who lives in the house he has been watching, tells the boy his name is Mr. Auguste Dupin (the name the boy knows him by until the end), and agrees to help him. Henceforth the story follows two interwoven strands, the first and more apprehensible one concerning the boy's missing relatives, the other ostensibly about Mr. Dupin-Poe's courtship of the historical Mrs. Whitman but also about the nature of the man himself. As Avi's novel progresses, Mr. Poe writes Edmund's story as a story within the larger story, while at the same time as Mr. Dupin he solves the mystery of both using the deductive methods of the fictional detective. The complex, convoluted plot becomes increasingly tangled with numerous gothic conventions. The solution comes through careful attention to small details, luck, and help from the boy, who does some important sleuthing on his own. It turns out that Poe's rival for Mrs. Whitman's hand, a Mr. Arnold, is really Rachett, the boy's stepfather. He had taken Edmund's mother prisoner, then mistakenly killed her look-alike, Aunty Pru. With a banker accomplice, he kidnapped Sis through the window of the dingy room and used her to rob a local bank of a shipment of gold from California by lowering her through a narrow air passage from the roof into the bank vault. With the help of the night watch officer named Mr. Throck, Dupin-Poe and the boy apprehend Rachett and his accomplice as they attempt to flee the harbor in a sailboat with the gold and the girl as hostage for a slam-bang climax. Throughout the novel, Edmund and Mr. Dupin offset each other. While Edmund keeps his mind steadfastly on his problem, Dupin-Poe, often in a drunken or near-drunken state, slips from real life into the story he is composing, which ironically also provides the means for him to figure out the real-life case. At the end, also ironically, he is upset because Edmund's Sis is alive, since this is not the way he planned for the story to end. The numerous gothic and mystery-detective conventions are handled with skill and precision and presented in fast-paced, crisp prose. As noted in a postscript, the biographical elements are true to Poe's life and character at this point, including the drinking and slim grip on reality. Atmosphere is especially strong; most of the action occurs during overcast, foggy, or rainy weather or at night, on shrouded docks, and in shadowy graveyards, gloomy, candlelit rooms, and smoky, smelly taverns. Also conventional is the moral commentary arising from the contrast between the barren, dim dockside room from which the girl was kidnapped and where Poe works out most of the puzzle, that is, the place of redemption, and the elegant Powers house (Mrs. Whitman's mother's home), to Poe an inherently evil den, where the villain, thought respectable, does his courting and local elite gather, people whose true, wicked natures Poe's drink-demented mind conjures up as ugly phantasms. Mrs. Whitman appears as good and kind in spite of her surroundings. Mr. Throck, who at first the reader thinks is allied with the evildoers, serves the plot well, since Poe is too cerebral for action and the boy is physically unable to capture the culprits. This is more than a soundly worked-out mystery in which old motifs become fresh. It is also an enthralling picture of one of America's foremost writers near the end of his life. Poe Nominee.

MARGARET BAKER (*Stepping on the Cracks**), eleven-year-old girl who tells the story, daughter of an auto mechanic, and closest friend of Elizabeth* Crawford, daughter of a policeman. Margaret is a plain, shy, dark-haired child, whose mother urges her to think for herself and stick up for herself against Elizabeth, the dominant one in the relationship. More introspective than Elizabeth, Margaret ponders issues. She decides to help Stuart* Smith, the army deserter, out of humanitarian motives rather than self-interest, as does Elizabeth. Although she feels she should tell her father about Stuart because she knows deserting is against the law, she also knows her father always thought highly of Stuart as a paper boy, and she feels that her soldier-brother, Jimmy, who also liked Stuart, would not want her to turn Stuart in. When Margaret informs her mother that Mr. Smith beats his son Gordy*, Mrs. Baker tells Margaret that it is not in their place to interfere, but later she unsuccessfully pleads with Mrs. Smith to take action against her abusive husband. When Mrs. Baker learns that Margaret has been helping Stuart, having lost her son, Jimmy, in action, Mrs. Baker loses her temper, slaps Margaret, but later apologizes. For Mrs. Baker and her husband, Stuart's desertion is a crime punishable by law, but for Margaret, who ironically has done what her mother has been urging her to do—that is, develop independence of thought—the issue is not so simple. The depth of Margaret's thinking on the morality of desertion and war and the conclusions she arrives at are not completely credible for a child presented as being as diffident as she is supposed to be. Margaret and Elizabeth are obvious foils, as are the Bakers and the Smiths.

MARINO, JAN, novelist of problem stories for children and early adolescents. *The Day That Elvis Came to Town** (Little, Brown, 1991), a *School Library Journal* selection, uses an Elvis Presley concert as the catalyst for solving several problems confronting the family of a thirteen-year-old girl, including alcoholism and racial bias. Marino has also written *Eighty-Eight Steps to September* (Little, Brown, 1989), in which a little girl's life changes when she learns her brother is dying. Married, Marino lives in Oyster Bay, New York.

MARIO CALVINO (*"Who Was That Masked Man, Anyway?"**), Frankie Wattleson's pal from next door, whose father was killed in World War II and who is very sensitive to his mother's feelings and wishes. He often says he ought not do something (for example, think about naked girls) because she would not like it. Unlike Frankie, he is a good student. Frankie thinks Mario is a scientific genius and persuades him to rig up the radio apparatus that Frankie found in the basement so that they can wire rooms for sound and listen to Mario's radio in Frankie's house. They call the result their Atomic Radio Remote Relay. Sometimes they combine this setup with the Silver Fox G-Man Walkie-Talkie that Frankie sent for through the mail when it was advertised on a radio show. As Skipper O'Malley, Mario plays sidekick to Frankie as Chet Barker on their world-saving expeditions. All the while Frankie tells Mario what to say and how to behave. Their conversations are hilarious satires, because Mario is practical and literal minded and often questions Frankie about why they are doing what they are doing. Mario is a fine foil for Frankie.

MARK BRITTAIN (*Staying Fat for Sarah Byrnes**), classmate and swim teammate of Eric Calhoune and Steve Ellerby.* Eric describes him as a "pompous turd." Mark is a rigidly fundamentalist Christian, righteous, cocksure, and judgmental. Mark demonstrates against abortion, yet when Jody Mueller was pregnant with his child, he urged her to have an abortion and forced her to go to the clinic alone. His hypocrisy about the sacredness of life exposed, he attempts suicide. Although strenuous advocates of individual responsibility before God, he and his father try to put the blame for his suicide attempt on Ellerby and Eric. The Reverend Mr. Ellerby says that the real problem lies in a philosophy, like that of the Brittains, that expects people to be perfect. After beginning therapy, Mark seems more relaxed and is much less obnoxious. He visits Eric in the hospital and apologizes to the Contemporary American Thought class, both acts of common decency unusual for him.

MARLY (*The Treasure Bird**), stepmother of Jessy, mother of Matt*, and wife of Tad. She is kind, loving, and determined almost to a fault to be a good wife and mother. She urges Jessy to speak instead of using gestures, and although Jessy knows that Marly is right, she sometimes wishes Marly were less conscientious about her mothering. Marly is an interior designer and a native of Texas who does not enjoy her job and life in Wichita, Kansas. After the move to San Antonio, her home town, she is much happier but then begins to fear that the family may have to return to Wichita, where Tad has retained his teaching position, if they cannot find funds to pay the taxes on the big old house she inherited from Great-Uncle Matthew. When one day Jessy overhears Marly and Tad arguing, she is afraid that Marly may divorce Tad in order to stay in San Antonio. Marly assures Jessy that, unlike Jessy's mother, she keeps her promises, and she regards marriage as a promise. She says that she intends to keep the family together. Marly is with the children when they discover the treasure, hoping, sleuthing, and digging right along with them.

MARS BAR THOMPSON (*Maniac Magee**), big, burly African-American youth of about eleven, who carefully nurtures his reputation for ''badness.'' His nickname derives from his habit of eating candy bars. He is also noted for his ''stiff glare . . . [as well as] his super-slow dip-stride slumpshuffle . . . [with which] it was said he could back up traffic all the way to Bridgeport while he took ten minutes to cross the street.'' Maniac accepts and beats his challenges, at one time defeating him handily in a footrace while running backward all the way, a feat Maniac immediately regrets because it humiliates Mars Bar so much. Since Mars Bar is as prejudiced toward whites as the white McNab* family is toward blacks, and equally as ignorant about their way of life, Maniac takes Mars Bar with him to the white Pickwells, a visit that turns out well, and to the McNab house, an encounter that does not, because the McNabs have built a fort as a defense against blacks. Eventually Mars Bar invites Maniac to his house, the two having become friends, and Amanda* Beale starts to call Mars Bar ''Snickers,'' declaring, ''How *bad* can you act if everybody's calling you . . . 'Snickers'?'' Mars Bar is an obvious type who changes predictably.

MARTIN, KATHERINE, born in Memphis, Tennessee. She is a graduate of Mississippi College in Clinton, Mississippi, and lives on a twenty-acre ranch with her husband, Robert. *Night Riding** (Knopf, 1989), her first novel, is notable for sensory evocation, especially in the scenes of riding horseback in the moonlight and of the fear engendered by an abusive neighbor. The novel is dedicated to Martin's mother, who inspired the character of the mother in the novel. It was named to the *School Library Journal* list of Best Books for Children.

MARTIN QUINCY (*A Share of Freedom**), father of Freedom Jo Avery, although neither of them knows of their relationship until the summer of her thirteenth birthday. Fourteen years earlier, Martin had comforted his classmate, Mary Margaret Avery, on the night of their graduation dance when a fire destroyed all the rest of her family. His attraction to Mary Margaret caused a temporary rift between him and his girlfriend, Ona Mae. Later, shortly after he and Ona Mae are married, he learns of Mary Margaret's pregnancy and sends money until she writes him, falsely, that her baby girl died at birth. After he and Ona Mae return to Gabriel, Missouri, to live with his crippled sister and niece, he sees Freedom's picture as winner of the spelling bee and tries, clumsily and arrogantly, to force Mary Margaret to let him share in Freedom's life, threatening that if she does not comply, he will go to court, where her alcoholism will undoubtedly be held against her. While Mary Margaret is in treatment, he gets temporary custody and agrees to take in Jackie, Freedom's half brother, too. Freedom finds him compulsively neat and takes pleasure in repeatedly turning the cookie jar so that only "coo" shows, then watching him move it to show "cookie." Although she agrees with his niece, Laura Nell Gentry, who refers to Martin as the Inspector General and despises him for the way he rides and belittles his son, Theodore, she develops some understanding when his sister, Helen Gentry, tells her how their father, an abusive alcoholic, treated him in the same way. He is developed as such an unpleasant character that Freedom's eventual acceptance is unconvincing.

MARTIN WITHERSPOON (*The Brave**), fat black boy who is assigned to be Sonny Bear's trainer. At first he is bored, having been forced to take the job in Donatelli's Gym by his father, a former fighter. When he meets Jake, Sonny's great-uncle, and realizes that Sonny is truly an Indian, his attitude changes, and he puts his energy into Sonny's training, even coming early to help clean the gym so they will have more time to work. A romantic, he loves the stories of the Running Braves that Jake tells, and he envisions a future with Sonny as the world heavyweight champion. Not at all athletic himself with his weight problem and his owlish glasses, he acknowledges that his skill is with words, and he decides to be publicist for Sonny. When they invade Stick's den, he is extremely afraid that Sonny will kill the young drug dealer, but he is thrilled to be part of the exciting action. He and Sonny are real friends in the end.

MATHILDA OTIS (*Rosemary's Witch**), spiteful, mean, dour witch almost 150 years old, who occupies the cabin near the Morgenthau house and decides to drive the family from the place because it was her childhood home. After Mathilda's mother's death, her father, who suffered from alcoholism, lost the place. Mathilda lived for some time in nearby caves. Her story comes out in bits and pieces through her fragmented, semidemented memories and Rosemary's visions and research in the library. Although the potential is there, Mathilda seems more comic and unfortunate than evil.

MATHIS, SHARON BELL (1937–   ), born in Atlantic City, New Jersey; teacher, writer. She grew up in the Bedford-Stuyvesant district of Brooklyn, is a graduate of Morgan State College in Baltimore, Maryland, and received her master's degree in library science from Catholic University in Washington, D.C. Her brief novel of the love between a little boy and a very old woman, *The Hundred Penny Box* (Viking, 1975), was a Newbery Honor book, and her *Sidewalk Story* (Viking, 1971), about an urban eviction, was cited by *Choice* magazine on its list of children's books for academic libraries. Twenty years after its publication, *Listen for the Fig Tree** (Viking, 1974), a story of a blind girl, was named an honor book for the Phoenix Award of The Children's Literature Association given for books deemed to have lasting literary merit. Like her other writings, it deals with the urban experience of African Americans. For earlier biographical information and title entries, see *Dictionary, 1960–1984* [*The Hundred Penny Box; Sidewalk Story*].

MATT (*The Treasure Bird**), somewhat older stepbrother of Jessy. His mother is Marly*, and his father is a marine who never pays any attention to him, a circumstance that Matt resents. In this, his situation is an obvious and too carefully drawn parallel to Jessy's. Matt is usually kind to Jessy, fondly referring to her as "squirt," but although he realizes that she takes better care of Goldie than he does and very much wants the bird for her own, he refuses to give Goldie up. He does, however, let Jessy care for Goldie, and thus she is able to pick up on the phrases that the parrot repeats. Matt is a moral boy, one who does what he says he will, although on occasion his friend Curtis* tries to get him to do otherwise out of expediency.

MAY (*Missing May**), Summer's* beloved aunt, who dies six months before Summer's narrative begins and is the story's focus. Wife of Ob*, May is a big, heavy, elderly woman, expansive and loving, who keeps a practical garden, has a strong religious faith, and believes in spirits. Summer pays tribute to her by saying, "May was the best person I ever knew. . . . She was a big barrel of nothing but love . . . and she let [people] be whatever way they needed to be." May never appears in the book except in Summer's many recollections and flashbacks. May and Ob loved each other very much and made a loving home for orphaned Summer.

MAYBE YES, MAYBE NO, MAYBE MAYBE (Patron*, Susan, illus. Dorothy Donahue, Orchard, 1993), short, lighthearted realistic novel of family life set in Los Angeles. Serious, meticulous PK, 8, loves her Mama, a single parent who waits tables at The Fancy Restaurant and is concerned about finances, and her two sisters, Megan* and Rabbit*. PK's main concerns revolve around being the middle child, or ''human jam,'' as she calls it, and moving to a larger apartment. As the middle child, she is caught between Megan, who has ''hormones'' and is ''almost-a-teenager,'' is Gifted (*sic*), and often smiles ''secret smiles,'' and Rabbit, a preschooler whom PK bathes every night, to whom she tells stories while the little girl soaks herself clean in the tub, and whose questions she must try to answer. When Rabbit asks PK whether she will behave like Megan when she gets to be Megan's age, PK replies, ''Maybe yes . . . Maybe no . . . Maybe maybe.'' Mama assures PK that her tendency to dramatize matters is her special talent and that she is lucky to have two sisters for support, one on each side of her. Moving to a new apartment means getting rid of some of the many things PK has collected, possibly losing the stories she tells Rabbit because she says she finds them in the built-in clothes hamper in the bathroom, and having to leave behind the big old blue overstuffed chair into which they all like to flop. PK restricts herself to moving just her best collections (the cherry pits and plastic glow-in-the-dark bugs), makes what she feels is her first really independent decision when she suggests that the blue chair will be a fine welcome for the new family, and assures Mama and Rabbit that she can get the stories for Rabbit out of the hamper by ''long-distance.'' Characters are sharply drawn, and the novel has much the same tone of family warmth, love for life, gentle humor, and child's view of the world as the Henry Huggins books but is more deft with language and dialogue. These are people who care genuinely about one another, a family of three girls caught at three different stages, with a wise and loving Mama, who was once like each of them and can help them understand and appreciate one another. ALA; SLJ.

MAZER, ANNE (1953–), born in Schenectady, New York; author of both picture books and novels for young people. She attended the State University of New York at Binghamton, Syracuse University, and the Sorbonne. After working as an executive secretary for a real estate office, she became a freelance writer in 1982. She is married to Andrew Fullerman, a clinical social worker, and has two children. Among her picture books are *Watch Me,* illustrated by Stacey Schuett (Knopf, 1990); *The Yellow Button,* illustrated by Judy Pedersen (Knopf, 1990); and *The Salamander Room,* illustrated by Steve Johnson (Knopf, 1991). *Moose Street* (Knopf, 1992), for middle school readers, is about a young Jewish girl growing up in a predominantly Catholic neighborhood. Her best-known book, *The Oxboy** (Knopf, 1993), is a strange and compelling fantasy set in a world where humans and animals have interbred. It was named to the American Library Association Notable Book List.

MAZZIO, JOANN (BERRY) (1926–   ), born in Clarksburg, West Virginia; engineer, mathematics teacher, novelist for young adults. After attending West Virginia Wesleyan College from 1943 to 1945, she received her B.S. degree from West Virginia University and her M.A. from the University of New Mexico. In the 1940s and early 1950s, she worked as an engineer for what is now NASA in Langley, Virginia, and in Washington, D.C., and at Kirkland Air Force Base, and in the 1960s at Sandia Labs, Albuquerque, New Mexico. Later she taught mathematics at Los Lunas Consolidated Schools, Los Cruces Public Schools, and Cobre Consolidated Schools, all in New Mexico. Her novel for young adults, *The One Who Came Back** (Houghton, 1992), which features two disadvantaged boys living in a trailer court on the outskirts of Albuquerque, was a nominee for the Edgar Allan Poe Award. She has also written a historical novel, *Leaving Eldorado* (Houghton Mifflin, 1993), set in an old gold-mining town like the one she lives in, Pinos Altos, New Mexico.

MCGRAW, ELOISE JARVIS (1915–   ), born in Houston, Texas; artist, novelist. She is a graduate of Principia College in Elsah, Illinois, and studied at the Museum Art School in Portland, Oregon. Much of her early fiction was historical, including *Moccasin Trail* (Coward, 1952), a story of the settlement of Oregon, and *The Golden Goblet* (Coward, 1961), set in ancient Egypt, both Newbery Honor books. Two of her mysteries of the contemporary period, *A Really Weird Summer* (Atheneum, 1977) and *Tangled Web** (McElderry, 1993), have been nominees for the Edgar Allan Poe Award. Her novels are notable for strong characterization and well-handled suspense. She has taught at the college level in both Oklahoma and Oregon and has lived with her husband, author William Corbin, in the Willamette Valley, Oregon. For earlier biographical information and title entries, see *Dictionary, 1859–1959* [*Moccasin Trail*] and *Dictionary, 1960–1984* [*The Golden Goblet; A Really Weird Summer*].

MCNAB, GIANT JOHN (*Maniac Magee**), twelve-year-old white West End pitcher and bully, leader of the street gang called Cobras. He stands five feet eight inches tall and weighs more than 170 pounds, a formidable size that arouses fear among the boys. His fastball is unhittable until Maniac Magee comes along and easily belts his pitches for home runs. Maniac lives with the McNabs for some weeks. Since he has returned to their home the two younger boys, Russell and Piper, who were running away, he feels an obligation to keep them from running away again and in school. The McNab house is ramshackle, filthy with roaches, garbage, and turds, and disorganized. The McNabs are fiercely prejudiced against African Americans and build a pillbox fort of concrete blocks as a defense against the attack they are sure will come from the black East Enders. McNab looks forward to the battle with great relish: ''That's what they are . . . today's Indians.'' Like most of the other characters, he is an obvious type.

MCNAIR, JOSEPH, born in Washington, D.C.; writer of short stories and poems for adults published in such literary magazines as *Cimarron Review* and *Colorado State Review.* His novel for elementary and middle school readers, *Commander Coatrack Returns** (Houghton, 1989), is a witty, often funny novel of family life involving a boy with mental disabilities and his too-protective older sister. It was a *School Library Journal* Best Book. Married, NcNair has made his home in Baltimore, Maryland.

MEDRAUT (*The Winter Prince**), bastard son of Artos (Arthur) and his half-sister, Morgause. Having been displaced in his father's ambitions by his much younger half-brother, Lleu*, he has left Camlan and traveled widely, learning much in Africa and Byzantium, and has spent two tormented years with his mother in the Orkney Islands. All his relationships are ambivalent: he hates his cruel mother but has been sexually seduced by her; he admires and enjoys his half-sister, Goewin*, but frightens her with a nonbrotherly kiss so that their friendship will not turn into sexual love; he both loves and hates Lleu and sometimes torments the boy, even when saving his life; most of all, he loves his father and resents the way Artos prefers Lleu, wanting more than anything for Artos to admit that the sin of incest in his birth is not Medraut's but his own.

MEGAN (*Maybe Yes, Maybe No, Maybe Maybe**), superior-acting older sister of PK. PK thinks it is hard to stay friends with Megan because Megan is very pretty, is almost a teenager and hence has "hormones," is Gifted (*sic*), has many rules and codes, loathes being like anyone else, calls her sisters weenies, and is trying to establish her independence from Mama. Megan's opinion of PK rises when PK artfully arranges her plastic ants on the wall and solves the problem of Rabbit's* stories by telling Rabbit that she can pull tales "long-distance" from the built-in clothes hamper in their old bathroom. Megan also realizes that PK is right about the new people in the apartment needing the old blue chair. One of the funniest scenes in the book is that in which Megan tells PK that at her age a girl learns fascinating things in school about becoming a woman and then makes a pancake in the shape of a uterus. After that, PK no longer wants pancakes.

MERCEDES WASHINGTON (*The Day That Elvis Came to Town**), beautiful pop singer who rents the attic room in the Dohr boarding house. With her "tanned skin, the color of homemade coffee ice cream," her big, green eyes, and curly, black hair, Wanda Dohr thinks Mercedes is the most beautiful woman she has ever seen. Both Wanda and her Momma are much happier after Mercedes arrives because she is always sunny and supportive. After April May Dohr, Poppa's sister, tells Wanda that Mercedes is "a nigger girl," Wanda tells Poppa, who is angry that April May should use such language in his house. Later Wanda mentions April May's remark to Mercedes and learns that Mercedes's mother was white, her father was a black teacher who could only find work as a janitor, and her stepfather was white. She took her stepfather's name of McIver when she enrolled at the high school where she was in the same class as Elvis Presley but attended only briefly because she was soon expelled for being black. Mercedes is bitter about the way she has been treated but is proud that she has made her way in life. She says that no matter what happens, she is still Mercedes Washington. Much about Mercedes seems tailored to inform the reader about race relations.

THE MIDNIGHT HORSE (Fleischman*, Sid, illus. Peter Sis, Greenwillow, 1990), comic fantasy novelette set in the late nineteenth century in the days of stagecoaches and top hats. A skinny little orphan boy, Touch, travels by coach from Portsmouth to Cricklewood, New Hampshire, hoping to contact his great-uncle, Judge Henry Wigglesworth. He is warned by another passenger, kindly Mr. Hobbs, a blacksmith, that the judge is a notorious grouch. At The Red Haven Inn, Touch discovers that the judge is pressuring the owner, young, pretty, sorrowful Miss Sally Hoskins, to sign over ownership of the inn to him. Trade at the inn has fallen drastically since a patron, a barber conspicuous for his gold teeth, disappeared and was thought murdered. Blame attached to Sally's father, who worried himself to death, and gossip started by the judge, according to Mr. Hobbs, has caused the inn to go downhill. Touch finds the judge shifty and arrogant when he applies to him for his inheritance, and the boy prudently refuses to sign papers put to him, especially when the judge assures Touch that all his father, lost at sea, left him was a cash balance of thirty-seven cents and a silver watch, which the boy notes bears the wrong initials. The judge also threatens to put Touch in the local orphan house. Touch hides out with Sally, whose debts Mr. Hobbs has been generously covering, but leaves before the judge holds Sally responsible for his presence. Having heard of the feats of the local ghost, The Great Chaffalo, a magician adept at turning bundles of straw into horses, Touch takes a bundle to Chaffalo's place, where the ghost-magician obliges with a mighty bay, conjured "out of a bit of straw and a touch of midnight," according to Chaffalo. Touch tethers the horse outside Sally's inn while he says goodbye and returns to find the horse gone and only a bunch of moldy straw. He learns from Chaffalo that a thief, Otis Cratt, has stolen the animal. Several adventures and some trickery later, Touch discovers that the judge conspired with Cratt, who has conspicuous gold teeth, to defraud Sally and that the small fortune his father left is a cache of pearls. Cratt tries to flee on the horse, and the judge pursues him, followed by the sheriff. When Cratt attempts to jump the river, Chaffalo turns the horse back to straw. Since no one but Touch has observed Chaffalo, the judge is accused of witchcraft and is shunned by the villagers, who stone his house. Sally retains her inn, which again prospers, and Touch puts the pearls in the bank for future use and becomes the inn's boy-of-all-help. Colorful characters and incidents out of nineteenth-century romance, grandiloquent language, a superabundance of convoluted action, and a slam-bang, it-serves-him-right conclusion produce a raucous novel, which is consistently entertaining although of no great moment. Numerous black-and-white sketches augment the humor. ALA; Poe Nominee; SLJ.

MIKAELSEN, BEN(JAMIN JOHN) (1952–   ), born in La Paz, Bolivia; avid thrill seeker and writer of adventure novels. In the 1970s he attended Concordia College, Moorhead, Minnesota, served in the U.S. Army in Arlington, Virginia, and returned to Minnesota to attend Bemidji State University. Among his other jobs and avocations are parachute jumping, sled-dog racing, polo playing, scuba diving, and piloting both private and commercial planes. He once rode horseback from Minnesota to Oregon and now lives in the mountains near Bozeman, Montana, where he has owned an awards and office supply business and a woodworking business. A 600-pound black bear named Buffy, which he has raised and whom he considers not a pet but a close friend, inspired *Rescue Josh McGuire** (Hyperion, 1991), an adventure story of a boy who runs away with a bear cub rather than give it up for laboratory experimentation. It received an International Reading Association Award and the Spur Award from Western Writers of America. As research for his second novel, *Sparrow Hawk Red* (Hyperion, 1993), he returned to his first language, Spanish, and lived among the homeless in Mexican border towns to get a sense of what his young boy protagonist must suffer to survive. Mikaelsen is much involved with trying to reform Montana hunting laws, particularly to outlaw bear hunting in spring, when cubs are nursing.

MIKE JACOBY (*Tell Me Everything**), Roz Jacoby's kind and patient uncle, the brother of Roz's mother, Ellie* Jacoby. Mike is a big man with a protruding stomach who enjoys the simple things in life. A Vietnam War veteran, he tells Roz that he was a medic during the war and that sometimes he simply could not believe what he heard or even saw until he actually touched the patient. This and the story of Doubting Thomas in the Bible lead Roz to ask Nate Thompson to let her touch the place on his foot where the toes he lost to frostbite had been. Mike runs a small fix-it shop in his living room and likes to go fishing early in the morning. After Roz tells Mike about the ''signs'' that she thought told her that she should seek Nate and includes the nightmares among them, Mike tells her that he, not she, had the nightmares. He was ashamed of them, apparently still about the war, and thus he lied to her about them. He would wake her up, then go fishing, and let her believe the bad dreams were hers. He thinks that going to the family counselor—in fact, having to account to authorities in any way—is ''horseshit,'' but he goes anyway. He is conscientious about being a good parent to Roz.

MISSING ANGEL JUAN (Block*, Francesca Lia, HarperCollins, 1993), fantasy continuing the series started with *Weetzie Bat,* including *Witch Baby**. In the third book, *Cherokee Bat and the Goat Guys,* Angel Juan has returned,

formed a band in which Witch Baby is the drummer, then left to find adventure
and a place for himself in New York City. Now Witch Baby, disconsolate, goes
to New York in search of him, and narrates her strange adventures in the company of the ghost of Charlie Bat, Weetzie's father, who died of a drug overdose
when Cherokee was a baby. Unable to give him up emotionally, Weetzie has
kept his New York apartment in an old brownstone in the meat-packing district,
and Witch Baby goes there, welcomed by an aging gay couple, Mallard and his
blind friend, Meadows, who are writing a book on ghosts. They take her out to
dinner and lend her a carpet, blankets, and food so she can camp out in Charlie's
twelfth-floor apartment, otherwise empty except for an old leather trunk. Then
they leave on a ghost hunt. Witch Baby soon discovers that they have ignored
the real ghost in their building, that of Charlie Bat, who comes out of the trunk
as a dancing light and can be seen as a skinny man in a Fred Astaire top hat
and tails only in mirror reflections or through a camera lens. Together they roam
New York, Witch Baby on her roller skates, carrying her camera, to all the
places mentioned or suggested by her only letter from Angel Juan: a restaurant
in Harlem, where the waitress remembers a Hispanic boy with leaves in his hair;
Central Park, where she finds a tree house Angel Juan has made; Coney Island,
where Charlie starts the Ferris wheel, closed for the winter, and she finds a strip
of pictures from a photo booth with Angel Juan's face on them; the Metropolitan
Museum, where various statues tell her that the solution to her agony over losing
Angel Juan is to let go. Through all their travels she keeps seeing a sinister
figure in white lurking in the background. Although she has a cold and knows
she has developed a fever, Witch Baby sneaks out in the night and sees a
mannequin of Angel Juan in the window of Cake's Shakin' Palace, a diner.
There the figure in white, who says he is Cake, feeds her and leads her through
a hole in the floor down flights of steps and through rooms full of statues of
boys and girls, all in white. Eventually she finds Angel Juan and, because Charlie Bat has followed her, is able to get him out and back to the apartment. In
the end, she sees that she must let Angel Juan go, just as Charlie Bat and Weetzie
must let each other go so that he can finally leave and rest. She returns to Los
Angeles; Angel Juan will stay in the apartment, where Mallard and Meadows
can keep track of him while he plays his songs in the streets and subway. Angel
Juan says that Cake was their fear, his of love and hers of being alone, and that
he is gone now. As in the earlier books, the style is slangy and hip, and the
characters vivid and bizarre—little girls playing hip-hop-hopscotch in Harlem,
a sex-changed couple with their pigtailed child, Charlie Bat's childhood family,
junkies, and pregnant teenagers—all grounded in a very modern realism so that
it is impossible to tell what is fantasy and what is Witch Baby's imagination
and whether the strange underground labyrinth of Cake is really a fevered hal-
lucination. In the present-tense narration, her love and loneliness are strongly
evoked and make her character development believable. SLJ.

MISSING MAY: A NOVEL (Rylant*, Cynthia, Orchard, 1992), short, realistic novel of family life set at the time of publication, in which a young girl and her guardian uncle confront their grief. When she was six and her mother died, the narrator, Summer*, 12, came to live with her buxom Aunt May* and her scarecrow Uncle Ob* in their rusty trailer home near the little hill town of Deep Water, Fayette County, West Virginia. Summer starts her story in February six months after May's death, while she and Ob both still "miss May and hurt" very much. One Sunday while they are making milk-jug bird feeders in the yard, Ob announces that May is present, an idea that disturbs Summer, especially when Ob insists that Cletus* Underwood, a neighbor boy Summer's age whom she thinks a "lunatic," might be able to help him contact May because Cletus once had an afterlife experience. When the effort fails, Ob is so dispirited that for the first time ever, he stays in bed and does not see Summer off to school. Summer is convinced he is "finished." Then Cletus shows up with a newspaper clipping about a spiritualist woman minister in Putnam County, and Ob decides to consult her. They set off in Ob's old Valiant, picking Cletus up at his home, where to Summer's amazement Ob tells the Underwoods the outing is for Summer's sake. Their route takes them past the Capitol in Charleston, a place Cletus expresses a strong desire to visit. Ob's face shows the pain of disappointment when they learn that the Reverend Miriam Young has died, but the reverend's nephew gives them a spiritualist message paper, and they head home. On the turnpike past Charleston, Ob suddenly perks up, turns the car around, and, to Cletus's joy, heads back to the city. The three spend the rest of the day exploring the Capitol, the Science and Culture Center, the gift shop, and the legislators' restaurant, arriving home well after dark. As they walk into the trailer, an owl flies overhead, triggering strong memories in Summer of the time she and May had seen one together and May had said that, like the owl, Summer brought her and Ob good luck. The girl bursts into tears, for the first time able to vent her grief. When she tells Ob that "it has been so hard missing May," he assures her that "people don't ever leave us for good." The trip has been a catharsis for both of them. Now Summer has peace, and the next day Ob brings his cherished, handcrafted whirligigs out to May's garden and reads a few words of blessing from the spiritualist message. As he finishes, "a big wind comes and sets everything free." Summer's loving memories of May and her deep concern for Ob, which ironically blind her to her own deep sorrow and which Cletus and Ob sense, give the book force. They make up for the slender, disjointed plot, which is often lost sight of in the midst of Summer's tender flashbacks and poignant observations, and make the story in effect a memorial to the woman who never appears but is its central character. Humor and hill-country speech and attitudes relieve the sentiment, but some of Summer's comments seem too adult even for an intelligent child raised by older adults, and the symbolism at the end seems forced. Practical Summer, solicitous Ob, loving May, and Cletus of wide-ranging interests are strongly drawn and appealing.

The style often employs sensory and arresting expressions. ALA; Boston Globe Winner; Newbery Winner.

MISSISSIPPI BRIDGE (Taylor*, Mildred D., illus. Max Ginsburg, Dial, 1990), short historical story of racial discrimination in rural Mississippi during the late winter of 1931, companion to *Let the Circle Be Unbroken** and *The Road to Memphis**, which feature the African-American Logan family, first met in *Roll of Thunder, Hear My Cry**. The narrator, white Jeremy* Simms, 10, longs to be friends with the self-possessed Logan children and is bewildered by the attitudes of his elders toward the "coloreds." One foggy, rainy morning while hanging around the country store owned by the redneck Wallaces, he observes Mr. John Wallace urge a white woman to try on a flowered spring hat he has just told a black girl she cannot try unless she purchases it. He also watches as John's father, Mr. Charlie, hassles young black Josias Williams, with whom Jeremy sometimes goes fishing and who has come to catch the bus for a lumbering job on the Natchez Trace. Also arriving for the bus is Big Ma Logan, accompanied by her grandchildren: Stacey*, 10; Cassie, 7; Christopher John, 5; and Little Man, 4. After seeing Big Ma on the bus, the Logans head off to complete an errand, and Jeremy tags along. The children linger at the bridge over the nearby Rosa Lee River, tramping on the creaking, rotting planks and watching the angry, rising waters through the gaps between the boards. Jeremy returns to the store in time to see the blacks evicted from the bus to make room for the late-arriving, large, white Amos family. He sees Josias shoved roughly out the door and down into the mud when he protests. The driver takes off quickly, speeding the bus over the bridge. The machine veers out of control on the wet and weakened planks and plunges through the railing, down into the swollen river. It sinks fast, belly up "like a dead catfish," trapping the white passengers inside fatally. Josias, who observes the incident along with Jeremy, sends the boy to the store to summon the men. Mr. Charlie orders Jeremy to run to church and ring the bell for help, and when the boy returns to the bridge, he sees several white passengers lying dead on the bank where Josias has placed them. Josias's statement that the "Lord He works in mighty mysterious ways," meant to console, causes Jeremy to ponder more seriously the irony of events. The dramatic and poignant ending is overforeshadowed and comes as no surprise, and Jeremy is too obvious an anomaly. Like the bridge, he serves as a metaphor for race relations, as does the episode at the very end, where Jeremy slips into the water to "give [Josias] a hand." The well-drawn scenes are based on the author's father's stories of race relations in his youth, and the extensive dialogue moves the narrative along well. The colloquial, unschooled speech substantiates the setting. Expressive, realistic sketches add details and strengthen the account. For more details about *Roll of Thunder, Hear My Cry,* see *Dictionary, 1960–1984.*

MISS PIMM (*Lucie Babbidge's House**), teacher of Lucie Babbidge's class at Norwood Hall girls' orphanage, who patronizes and derides Lucie frequently.

She has a didactic bent and often draws morals from stories she reads and situations that come up, persists in correcting grammar, lacks humor, and tends to be self-righteous and authoritarian. For some reason, perhaps because Lucie does not toady to her, she picks on the girl. Her efforts to bend Lucie to her will show that she has no appreciation of how to build self-esteem in her students. She has clearly labeled Lucie in her mind as stupid, ugly, and unteachable. Although her methods of conveying subject matter seem adequate, she clearly lacks empathy and compassion. A type figure, she epitomizes what a teacher should not be like.

MOE TURNER (*Let the Circle Be Unbroken**; *The Road to Memphis**), local boy Stacey* Logan's age, whom Cassie Logan has known from early childhood, son of an African-American Mississippi sharecropper. In *Let the Circle Be Unbroken,* Moe is determined to get off the Montier place and sees finishing high school as a way to do it. Later, when times get really tough for the Turners, Moe joins Stacey in running away for a job on a Louisiana sugar cane plantation. Like Stacey, he finds the work excruciatingly punishing and near to slave labor. With Stacey he runs away from the plantation and ends up in jail, accused of theft, but is exonerated and brought home to Strawberry through the help of a lawyer, Mr. Jamison. In *The Road to Memphis,* Cassie thinks of Moe as a sweetheart, and he returns her affection in an undemonstrative way. At the end of the novel, he openly declares his love for her just before he boards the train for Chicago, away from the Mississippi laws that are certain to punish him severely for assaulting a white man. The eldest of seven children, Moe drops out of high school to take a job in a Jackson, Mississippi, box factory and scrupulously saves his wages, hoping to buy a small piece of land to make his family independent. An earnest, dedicated youth, he apologizes often in the novel for inconveniencing his friends, in particular Stacey, who are helping him escape the lawmen. His friends know that Moe was pushed beyond the limits of human endurance by the redneck Aames boys and reacted with a burst of uncharacteristic anger. They are also sure that he will not receive justice in the Mississippi courts. Thus, while the reader, as well as they, realizes that what Moe did was wrong, both legally and ethically, the reader is solidly on Moe's side. Moe represents a certain kind of American black.

MOLLY HALLIDAY (*Grams, Her Boyfriend, My Family, and Me**), third child in the large, close Halliday family, younger sister of Andy, the narrator, and of Dennie*, and older sister of the twins, Alice and Anne. Andy considers Molly a genius because she is a grade ahead of her age in school, being only thirteen but a ninth grader. Molly is pretty, has begun to be interested in boys, and is especially attracted to Martin, Andy's friend, a relationship that is somewhat embarrassing to Andy. Molly, Martin, Andy, and Karen, another school friend, make plans, against Andy's wishes and at the demand of Molly's parents, to double-date for a dance. Andy is relieved when Karen gets chicken pox and he does not have to go. For a school project, Molly visits Cherry Garden Convalescent Hospital, and as a result Grams Halliday meets Harold Wagner (she runs into him with her car while he is jaywalking). Grams and Harold develop a romantic interest in each other, and thus the book's main problem begins. Molly is a credible, likable girl.

MOM (*Make Lemonade**), LaVaughn's mother. She is sturdy and practical, and so tough at times that LaVaughn wonders how someone so soft and loving as she knows her mother can be can also be so hard and unyielding. Mom is skeptical about LaVaughn's accepting the job with Jolly*, fearing that the work will interfere with the girl's study time, but she agrees to let LaVaughn accept the position, at the same time reminding LaVaughn of her ambition to go to college. She often questions LaVaughn about the status of her homework and keeps a close eye on her progress in school, while also allowing the girl a good deal of latitude in making her own decisions. She tells LaVaughn that she will ''make me proud'' by going to college. She herself was a teenaged mother, widowed while LaVaughn was still a baby when her young husband was killed in gang crossfire. Mom is captain of her tenants' council in their large apartment complex and as such is responsible for flyers and similar communications, contacting city officials, and keeping tabs on the building's watchdog committee. Mom sees right away that Jolly must take hold of her life, or things will only get worse for her and her children.

MONA MILLER (*The Harmony Arms**), copper-haired manager of the Harmony Arms Apartments, the place in which Gabriel* and Sumner* McKay stay while they are in Burbank, California. Once a promising starlet, she had her nose altered to make her prettier. According to Tess*, her daughter, the plastic surgery ironically closed her out of better parts as she grew older, and now she only does commercials. Ordinarily Mona dresses in Lycra stretch pants and blouses with ties, but she often appears in whatever garb she is wearing for the commercial she is currently shooting. She is a warm and gentle person, and Gabriel likes her very much. For a while he hopes that she and his father can become more than friends. Mona becomes very upset when she discovers that Gabriel and Tess have been kissing in the garage and grounds Tess. Gabriel is grounded for the same length of time. Mona is separated from her husband, who is also in television and a source of resentment to his daughter.

MONKEY ISLAND (Fox*, Paula, Orchard, 1991), serious contemporary sociological problem novel of homeless persons set in inner New York City for the better part of a year. Clay Garrity, 11, and his pregnant mother have been living in a cramped apartment in a seedy welfare hotel, barely existing on the meager wages of Angela's night computer job. Clay's father, once art director of a thriving magazine, walked out after the magazine folded and he heard the news about the coming baby. After his mother disappears, Clay stays alone in the apartment for five days. Then, afraid of the authorities he knows the neighbor will call, he leaves for the streets, at first sleeping on a porch, finally encountering a "small triangular park" that seems to him "like an island in a stream," cluttered with people sleeping under cardboard boxes and newspapers, black plastic bags scattered around containing their few belongings, and much human debris. Two inhabitants, Buddy* Meadowsweet, a cheerful young black man, and Calvin* Bosker, a bearded, often cynical former teacher, share their wooden crate, few possessions, and little food with him, becoming his guardians and family for over a month. He makes another friend in a compassionate, well-off man named Gerald*, who comes almost every morning and hands out doughnuts and coffee to the park people from a dilapidated, tireless van standing to one side, until one day police and workers cart the van away. Clay keeps watch on the hotel for days; when he sees that other people have moved into the apartment, he realizes that his mother is not coming back. Calvin and Buddy urge him to contact authorities, but he refuses, never having liked his mother's social workers. He becomes aware that his clothes are inadequate for the approaching winter and that he has sores on his feet, ankles, and wrists and lice like other people who live on the streets. He learns the rules of street life, like always wearing all his clothes "in case you have to skedaddle." When he develops a cough that will not stop and shivers constantly, Buddy and Calvin decide to take him to authorities. Before they can, the park is invaded and torn up by a dozen and a half "stump people," hooligans with chains and bats out for a night's sport. In their flight Calvin is lost, and Buddy and Clay spend the night in the basement of a church they break into. Later they find Calvin back in the broken crate, dead drunk, and call an ambulance. Gerald, who continues to bring food, insists that Clay see a doctor and calls a taxi to take the boy to the hospital, where he stays for some days with pneumonia. There a Mrs. Greg from the Child Welfare Association arranges to put him in a foster home. About six weeks after his mother left, Clay goes to live with the Biddles, maternal Edwina and jocular Henry, a post office worker. With them, Clay is almost too model a child, self-contained, reserved, obedient. He likes the Biddles, who are kind and caring and always respectful of him, and he does well in school. But every afternoon he returns to the park looking for his friends, sometimes with Earl Thickens, a school friend whose smile reminds him of Buddy's. In March, he learns his mother has been found in a women's shelter, along with his new sister, little Sophie, and he goes to live with them in another welfare apartment. His mother apologizes for her behavior, saying, "I think I was out of my mind." She says she hopes that he can eventually "get to a place beyond forgiveness," a statement he does not then understand. Just as Clay is giving up hope of ever finding Buddy again, he spies him near the park, working as a bicycle messenger for a Wall Street firm. Through conversation with Buddy, he discovers that making a good life for himself is "going beyond forgiveness," realizes that he is one of the lucky ones who might possibly do it (unlike Calvin who has died), and goes home to share his new understanding of life with his mother. Characters are drawn with clarity and understanding, and there is enough suspense to hold the interest. Since the book is slice-of-real-life fiction, the ending raises at least as many questions as it answers. Conditions in the run-down hotel, on the streets, and in the park are shown as Clay sees them while going from one place to another: the gross graffiti, thievery, crowdedness, terrorism, dope paraphernalia, danger in stairwells and elevators, the constant fear, anger, hopelessness, lack of trust. The simple kindness of Buddy, Calvin, Gerald, and the Biddles shines out like a beacon, offsetting the sordidness, crime, and cruel callousness of some street people and some authorities. The author's restrained, sometimes cryptic style supports the bleakness of the setting but also distances the reader from Clay's "suffering," as his mother calls it, and thus the effect is of an outsider looking in on conditions rather than of seeing and feeling along with Clay. Occasionally speeches voice a sociology textbook attitude, and, since things do improve apparently for Clay when social workers get involved, perhaps the book suggests that the best solution for individuals, at least, is through such established channels. Certainly, although some homeless are shown as cruel and perhaps irredeemable, sympathy is on the side of the street people, and the strong friendship and comforting love of this unconventional family cling to the memory. ALA; Fanfare.

MONTY (*Shadow Boxer**), George's younger brother, the person who is the center of George's life. George says that Monty is a kindhearted boy and tells of his brother's strong attachment to despised Fred* the Head in illustration. Because he is physically ugly, Fred is a social outcast, but he becomes Monty's best friend. Although the two brothers are very close, George and Monty often bicker and sometimes tease each other cruelly. For example, when Monty develops a crush on Linda O'Leary, George advises Monty to go up to her after mass, grab her, and plant a solid kiss on her face as a way of really impressing her. Although he is immediately contrite, George does not stop Monty from doing as he suggested. Linda angrily socks Monty and screams, and the romance ends before it begins. Monty challenges George about the incident, asserting that George is so possessive that he does not want Monty to become friends with anyone else at all. He says that that is why George told him to kiss Linda. After that, Monty starts doing the freaky things that lead to the climax fight in Archie's* gym.

MOON (*Secret City, U.S.A.**), quiet friend of Benno. Moon acts as confidant and counselor to the self-appointed leader of the boys who clean up and occupy an abandoned house. Since both his parents are deaf, Moon uses sign language as much as oral speech and has taught Benno enough signing so they can communicate secretly, even in the presence of other people. Moon has taken the responsibility for his two little cousins, Juan and Paco, whose mother has left a welfare hotel and moved in with the family, trying to teach them the skills necessary to survive on the street, and Benno relies on his judgment before inviting other kids to join their crew. Moon's uncle, Tio Chico, a dwarf-like ex-acrobat who drives a gypsy cab, has taught him to do headstands and other tumbling tricks, by which the boy sometimes earns the family grocery money as a street performer. Tio Chico lends the boys a flashlight and tools without questions, but he also keeps an eye on them and insists that they show him what they are doing, although their secret is exposed on television before he arrives to inspect their house. Despite their excessive crowding, Moon's family seems to have more cohesiveness and genuine concern for each other than Benno's.

MOON MCCARTY (*Harper & Moon**), James Patrick McCarty, the almost feral youth who becomes a friend of Harper McDowell and is accused of murdering Olinger*, the old mountain man. When he is younger, Moon accompanies his parents as they go by truck about the countryside, his father, Paddie*, plying his trade of sign painter, his mother in the truck's back, usually drunk and abusive. Although Moon seldom rides with them, he usually turns up in the area, having gone overland on foot. After the parents die in a truck accident, Moon comes and goes as he pleases, living no one knows where, never attending school, somehow getting by. He speaks in a kind of pidgin English, is very clever with his hands, fashioning interesting objects out of materials he finds, which he bestows on his friends, and he loves animals and birds. His parents have thought him mentally disabled and looked down on him, but Harper knows Moon is intelligent and knowledgeable. Occasionally Moon works as a hired hand for the McDowells but never for money, which seems to mean almost nothing to him. He is described stereotypically as a kind of nature boy. He has a thin, dark face, a ''shock of hair, coarse as a horse's mane,'' ''narrow feet, bare and hard as horn,'' wears ''ragged overalls and faded shirt,'' and has an ''independent walk, catlike, half wild.'' Harper's mother likes him, too, and says that there is ''a fineness in him; a dignity.'' While he is in military service, Moon wins the Soldier's Medal, the highest award for bravery outside of combat, for saving the lives of the men in his company while on maneuvers. After the coroner's report clears Moon of suspicion of murdering Olinger and the sheriff learns how Moon won the medal, the sheriff changes his attitude toward the young man, buys Olinger's cabin for back taxes, and sells it to Moon on long-range terms that Moon can meet, his action reflecting the community's new feeling about Moon. When Harper explores Moon's room in the root cellar, he finds several cleverly fashioned dioramas of scenes important to Moon, among them one that shows him as an abused infant. Apparently Moon was the object of physical and psychological abuse throughout his childhood. It is also revealed that Moon discovered Olinger dead, wrapped him in his quilt as a shroud, and placed a tiny bouquet of blue jay feathers in his hand out of love and respect for the old man who had been one of his few real friends.

MORI, KYOKO (1957–   ), born in Kobe, Japan; poet, author of short stories, teacher of creative writing. In her memoir, *The Dream of Water* (Holt, 1995),

Mori tells of her unhappy girlhood after the suicide of her mother, in scenes juxtaposed against those of her 1990 return visit from the United States after more than a dozen years. Much the same story appeared earlier in fictionalized form in her novel for young people, *Shizuko's Daughter** (Holt, 1993), a *Horn Book* Fanfare choice, although the ending of the novel departs from the facts of her life. Both have been highly praised for their meticulous and sensitive depiction of emotions and their strong sensory elements, especially in realistic and symbolic use of color. Mori has spent most of her adult life in the American Midwest, where she received her Ph.D. degree and now lives with her husband. She teaches creative writing at St. Norbert's College in DePere, Wisconsin, and has published stories and poems in the *Kenyon Review, Beloit Poetry Journal,* and other leading literary magazines.

MORNING GIRL (Dorris*, Michael, Hyperion, 1992), short, quiet novel of family life, more an island idyll than a story in the usual sense. Morning Girl, perhaps eight, and her younger brother, Star Boy, alternate in nine short chapters to describe life with their parents on their unidentified Caribbean island just before the Europeans arrive. Morning Girl, so named because she loves the very early part of the day, begins and ends the narrative. She tells of sibling differences with Star Boy, of her warm relationship with her understanding and supportive parents for whom with deep love she fashions blossom necklaces; of learning that she will have a little sister and of her disappointment when Mother returns from Grandmother's and there is no baby sister; of discussing her appearance with her mother, in an amusing sequence; of sticking up too strongly for Star Boy at an island feast; and of swimming at dawn when curiously garbed strangers arrive in a queer-looking canoe. Star Boy, once called Hungry since he seemed to have an insatiable appetite, tells how his father gives him a new name because the boy loves the night so much. Star Boy enjoys playing tricks on his family by hiding among the rocks, where he pretends he is one, cozy and private, when Morning Girl comes searching for him. He responds to his conscience by speaking up when Morning Girl is blamed for losing a canoe. In the book's only exciting passage, Star Boy describes the hurricane that sweeps across the island, flattening homes and trees but leaving new life in its wake, he himself safe, pressed tightly against the bark of the great tree under which lie the graves of Grandfather and the baby, Little Sister, whom he and Morning Girl never saw. During the village feast celebrating survival and new beginnings after the storm, Star Boy earns reproving glances and reprimands for grabbing food but is delighted when Morning Girl takes his part. In gratitude, he gives her a private name they use only when they are together, The One Who Stands Beside, an action that hints that, as Mother once predicts to Morning Girl, the two will outgrow their childhood difficulties and be good friends some day. A short, italicized epilogue consisting of a portion from Columbus's diary of October 11, 1492, describes how the explorer meets and exchanges gifts with the islanders, how he believes they would make intelligent servants, and how he intends to take six back as presents to the monarchs of Spain. Occasionally the narrative slips, and the tone and diction seem more those of the author than the children. The book's force comes not from action or strong characterization but from the selectively detailed picture of warm family life, typical of any well-functioning home unit, and the reader's knowledge of history—that in just a few years this people, presented probably accurately as close to nature and one another, and their culture will be forever obliterated by the invaders. Style is highly descriptive of nature and often employs figurative language. Fanfare; O'Dell.

MOSE BAKER (*Fish & Bones**), Long Mose, older brother of brain-damaged Fish. A sergeant in the Marine Corps, Mose has just returned to Sun City when the bank is robbed, and gradually Bones Russ comes to believe that Mose did it, mostly for revenge, both for his father's lynching nineteen years earlier and for the townspeople's mistreating Fish. A tall young man with a lightning-quick temper, Mose seldom smiles and has always scared Bones, who is both flattered and disturbed by the attention Mose starts to show him. Bones realizes that Mose deliberately lets his snake get loose at the rattlesnake rodeo and also that he is probably responsible for the snake that terrifies the customers in the Bar & Grill run by Skip Goodweather. Bones also figures out that since Mose's father was lynched for trying to organize voters when he was still a toddler, Fish must have a different father, and he wonders whether this, as well as Fish's mental disability, accounts for the mixture of embarrassment and protectiveness that Mose shows toward his sibling.

MOTE (*Mote**), nickname of Matthew Oliver Thomas, which comes from his initials. A loner and outsider, Mote is a Vietnam War veteran who becomes a friend of Chris Miller. Mote is accused of murdering a local teacher, Mr. Holder*, mainly on the grounds that he is a drifter and his knife was the murder weapon. A father figure to Chris, whose parents are divorced, and of Billy, Chris's pal, whose father is dead, Mote teaches the boys to fish, helps them build a clubhouse and later a small cabin, and prepares them for life by teaching them to think through problems carefully. Mote refuses to turn himself in to the authorities; as a result of the war, he has a strong fear of confinement and dislikes being around people for long periods. Chris helps Mote understand his antisocial tendencies by assisting him in recalling his war experiences. Mote gradually remembers that he had been imprisoned in a bamboo cage and tortured. Although Mote is a central figure in the novel, he appears in few scenes. He is the stereotypical Vietnam War veteran.

MOTE (Reaver*, Chap, Delacorte, 1990), realistic contemporary mystery-detective novel set in a midwestern state, perhaps Ohio or Kentucky, or possibly in Georgia. The narrator, Chris Miller, 17, a talented tennis player and good student, and his long-time buddy and next-door neighbor, Billy, have been close friends during their teenaged years with Mote*, a Vietnam War veteran and drifter. Mote occasionally camps down by the river and has been a surrogate dad for both fatherless boys. When Mr. Holder*, a high school drafting teacher, is found knifed to death, suspicion falls on Mote, because Holder had harassed Chris and Mote's knife was the murder weapon. After Mote flees, Chris, who is completely confident that Mote would not murder, sets out to learn the truth. Numerous complications, tight spots, and fast action ensue, during which Chris develops a friendship with African-American detective Ed Stienert*, a tall, slender, smart, ex–basketball player. Chris and Billy decide to search Holder's house during the funeral, and while hiding in the bushes before entering, see Mrs. Holder and hot-headed Mr. Douglas, the English teacher, leaving together and ponder the ramifications of their relationship. Inside they find hate literature against blacks and pictures, among them one of Holder's wife with a man at a motel, possibly Douglas. They hide while two other youths ransack the house and depart with what the boys later learn is a green ledger. Chris learns from Stienert that Holder was a member of ERWA (Equal Rights for White Americans), a white supremacist group with about a dozen branches, attends a meeting, encounters Douglas there, succeeds in antagonizing him, and is almost knifed by Douglas when Stienert, who has been shadowing Chris, appears and saves him. Then Chris receives threatening telephone calls demanding the ledger from a man he dubs Husky Voice, by whom he is kidnapped and beaten savagely, especially on the legs and feet. He manages to knock out Husky Voice and call Stienert. Stienert discovers that Husky Voice is a ruffian named Bulloch who is involved with the Black Brigade, a black supremacist group hostile to ERWA. The break in the case comes while Chris is in the hospital. The thieves (schoolboys looking for tests) send the ledger to him, having heard about its importance from television newscasts. The ledger is in a code that Chris easily cracks and discovers that Holder was involved in gun running for ERWA. Chris induces Bulloch, who is also hospitalized, to call his boss through a tapped telephone. It comes out eventually through Bulloch that Douglas killed Holder, apparently in a dispute over the gun running and other ERWA activities, and Mote is exonerated. Small details assume great importance, and the reader must take pains to catch them. The author has improvised skillfully on such conventional features as the Holmes-Watson combination, the schoolboy sleuth, and the good-guy cop. The cast of characters is very large but individualized. Chris and Stienert, both sensible and likable if occasionally rash, dominate the book. Bulloch, who speaks in rhymes that are intended to be "cool," seems a phony villain. The schoolteachers are an unsavory lot, although the principal is presented as fair and concerned, the athletic recruiters are downright dishonest, and representatives of the mass media are pushy and callous. Plot aspects are over-foreshadowed, but one notices this only in retrospect. The violence is restrained; some language is earthy, even gross, but typical of youths Chris's age. Racial discrimination drives the plot, but the author avoids explicit statement; and occasional humor, cleverly inserted, provides relief. Chris's personal problems are

worked naturally into the mystery plot: the possibility of getting a tennis scholarship, which may be ruined by the beating; acquiring a girlfriend; his friendship
with Leon, a mentally disabled African-American youth, whom Holder has tried
to get committed and who believes that he must keep a sharp eye on Chris
because Chris reads too many books; his tense relationship with his divorced,
businessman father; and his gradual understanding of hate activities, particularly
in his home town. These aspects and the masterfully concocted plot make this
a top-notch book of its genre. Poe Winner.

THE MOZART SEASON (Wolff*, Virginia Euwer, Holt, 1991), contemporary
realistic novel set in Portland, Oregon, in which a young girl learns that one
touches the lives of others and is touched by others in unexpected ways. Loosely
knit, more a novel of character and introspect than of action, the plot is quickly
summarized. Allegra Leah Shapiro, the twelve-year-old narrator, is a talented
violinist and the daughter of a violinist mother and music professor and cellist
father. In June, just after softball season during which she played shortstop, her
violin teacher, Mr.* Kaplan, informs her that she has been accepted for the
Ernest Block Competition for Young Musicians of Oregon to be held on Labor
Day, the youngest musician selected, that the reward is to play with the symphony, and that the competition piece is Mozart's Fourth Concerto, which he
wishes her to play at least a thousand times during the summer. Although she
practices assiduously, she has her ups and downs learning the piece and fails to
place in the competition; she nevertheless feels good at winning praise from the
judges and from Mr. Kaplan and especially at having kept faith with herself and
done her best. The bulk of the book describes her efforts to define her relation
to her music; tender moments with Heavenly Days, her cat; making a list of
new words for school in the fall; the atmosphere of and mostly small incidents
at concerts, where she often turns pages for adult players for hire; and her
relations with Mr. Kaplan, her parents, her older brother (Bro* David, 16), her
grandmother, and assorted friends. Bro David cautions her against letting the
competition take over her life so that she becomes a ''crazoid'' like their mother's friend, the eccentric soprano, Deirdre* Moreau, whom he calls ''Deeder.''
Mr. Kaplan tells her to say, ''ME: Allegra Shapiro. I'M playing this concerto,''
and then, when it seems she has imposed herself on the piece, that she must try
harder to get to know the nineteen-year-old youth who composed it. Deirdre
tells her to play the piece like the Celtics of the National Basketball Association
play, so that the music is familiar yet always fresh and vibrant. Her parents are
consistently supportive but never pushy, and her best friends, the Asian Jessica,
who wants to be an architect, and Sarah, who studies ballet, go to concerts and
cheer her on. Her Jewish Bubbe (grandmother) Raisa helps, too, when she sends
Allegra, who is Jewish on her father's side, the embroidered purse of Allegra's
Elter Bubbe (great-grandmother), Leah, who hid it in Raisa's suitcase when she
sent Raisa to America from Poland at the beginning of World War II and who
probably died in the Holocaust. Allegra decides that like Leah she must do the

best she can with what she must do, even though it hurts. Allegra also becomes acquainted with her opponents, chubby, dowdy Karen Coleman, who wins the competition and for whom Allegra once substitutes in a local concert when Karen breaks two fingers windsurfing; Christine, her concertmaster; and Steve Landauer, the arrogant, presumed genius who is her new stand partner and who pouts when he comes in second. The other two contestants she meets when they are all interviewed on television the day before the competition. Myra Nakamura also plays the koto and confesses she fights nerves, and Ezra Jones, a rural Oregon youth of a practical mind and sensible bent, at the very end of the book calls a radio station to request they play "Embraceable You" for Allegra. Unifying all this is the mystery about an unkempt, almost toothless, mentally ill old man who dances spontaneously at outdoor concerts, whom Allegra calls Mr.* Trouble, and who is looking for a lost song he calls Waltz Tree. Allegra calls library reference for help, but coincidentally at the first concert after the competition, she realizes what it is, *Valse Triste,* when Mr. Trouble happily informs her that finally they have played his song. The large cast of characters is consistently interesting and memorably drawn. Allegra herself is a charming protagonist, unaffected, modest, satisfied with and gratified with her talent, but never conceited or aloof like her foil, Steve. The dialogue sounds natural, not planned or false, and even the arguments ring accurately. The tone is light and occasionally humorous, as when Deirdre gets very upset about dropping her earring into Mr. Shapiro's instrument, and Bro David puts up cartoons of headless cats around the house after Heavenly Days throws up in his shoe. The style is highly visual and euphonious and filled with details about music and concerts that, because the author is skillful about incorporating them, never overwhelm the slim story but seem integral to Allegra's life. This is a substantial book about a sensitive girl who is very serious about her music but never forgets that the most important thing in life is to be a feeling, caring person. ALA.

MR. BAGGOT (*Saturnalia**), cruel, self-righteous tithingman who gets sadistic pleasure from rapping children on the head with his staff for minor errors in answers to his catechizing. William, the Narraganset Indian printer's apprentice, particularly infuriates him; the boy has a remarkable memory and is able to answer any biblical question, however obscure, in which the tithingman tries to catch him. Because his young grandsons were slain by Indians, Mr. Baggot has a hatred for all "tawnies," as he calls them, and hopes to see William flogged and hanged after being snared in one of the traps he has set, including a plan to pay an Indian girl to entice William into theft and a letter Baggot has forged ostensibly from a Narraganset about a conspiracy to drive the English from the land. When William is defending his great-uncle and cousin from the charge of murdering Mr. Rudd, the eyeglass maker, Mr. Baggot sees his opportunity and accuses William, but he overreaches himself, treading on the jealously held position of Absalom Trulliber, the nightwatchman, who therefore gives an ear to William's evidence and summarily sends Mr. Baggot on his way.

MR. HOGWOOD (*Saturnalia**), wigmaker, whose clumsy courtship of the wealthy widow, Madam Phipp, supplies most of the humor in the novel. A pompous, self-important man, Mr. Hogwood aspires to higher social position than he currently has, although he espouses the philosophy that each person has an assigned station in the world from which he or she should not attempt to rise. This hierarchy is evidenced in the sort of wig that a man wears, the elaborately curled, perfumed and flowing hairpieces like that of Mr. Hogwood being reserved for men of high degree. Blinded by his own inflated self-esteem, he does not see that his manservant, Malcolm* Poole, is cheating him and making him a figure of fun at every turn.

MR. JOSEPH SPEKE (*Saturnalia**), furniture maker and carver of signboards, mantlepieces, and figureheads for ships. Tormented by the death of his own daughter and the memory of a little girl who ran screaming from General Winslow's troops at the massacre of the Narragansets in which he was a participant, he wanders the streets at night, unable to sleep. When he sights Ninnomi, eight-year-old Narraganset cousin of William, through the shed window, he realizes he has found the model he has been seeking for the new figurehead he is to carve. By offering to provide her dinner, he persuades her miserly master, Mr. Rudd, the eyeglass maker, to send her to pose for him. Discovering that she has been nearly starving, Mr. Speke continues to send for her and give her a meal even after he no longer needs her presence for his carving.

MR. KAPLAN (*The Mozart Season**), Allegra Shapiro's kind, astute, elderly violin teacher from the time she was five, who wears sweatshirts with mottoes and whose wife often gives Allegra treats when she comes to the Kaplan house for lessons. Like Allegra's parents, Mr. Kaplan is firm but never domineering. He encourages her to express herself through her music but cautions her against taking over pieces to the detriment of the composer's intent. He not only critiques her technique but prepares her psychologically for concerts and the competition. He is a staunch mentor and friend with whom she sometimes disagrees but whom she trusts completely.

MR. PALMER (*The Harmony Arms**), nonagenarian nudist who lives at the Harmony Arms Apartments, the place in which Sumner* and Gabriel* McKay live while they are in Burbank, California. Bent and thin, he looks like ''a grade of C made by a hurried teacher'' and his skin is thin and droopy. He has a deep voice, very blue eyes, and a kind and gentle manner, which endears him to the other residents. They look after him and are protective of him. He often talks about his deceased wife, Sunny, and is keen on physical fitness and animal rights. He urges the others not to use such products as satchels that are made from animals, and they respect his wishes. After Mr. Palmer dies, Cassandra* enlists the help of Gabriel and Tess* Miller in lifting his body onto a chaise and wheeling him to her old Nash. She intends to take him to the Mojave desert for a few days as he wished, but when she crashes the Nash into a bus stop, she abandons her plans. After he is cremated, his ashes are taken to the desert.

MRS. RACHEL GREINER (*Scooter**), loud, eccentric, elderly woman, who babysits little Petey* Timpkin and becomes Elana Rose Rosen's close friend. At first Elana calls her Mrs. Greiner the Whiner, because the old woman complains a lot about her feet, legs, and various physical and other problems in her life. Elana also notes, however, that Mrs. Greiner has a genuinely affectionate nature and a lively mind and truly loves Petey. Elana also enjoys the stories that Mrs. Greiner tells about her childhood. Mrs. Greiner likes to talk politics, guess riddles, and share recipes, although Elana says she is a poor cook. Something of a craftswoman, she has thousands of beads that she strings in various unusual ways. Mrs. Greiner is a well-drawn, interesting figure.

MRS. VAN GENT (*Nekomah Creek**), the new counselor at Nekomah Creek Elementary School, which Robby Hummer attends and where the Hummers are active in school events. Warned by classmate Amber Hixon that Mrs. Van Gent "comes on real nice, but you better watch what you say," Robby sees the woman as someone intimidating, serious, and austere, although "sort of pretty" with her high heels and hair in a tight bun. He sometimes wavers in his opinion of her but mostly fears she may break up his family, deeming their life too unconventional and inappropriate, since his mother works outside the home and his father runs the house. When Mrs. Van Gent and her dentist husband arrive for the gourmet dinner, to Robby's surprise she wears a thick white sweater and jeans tucked into tall boots and has loosened her hair, which flows down to her waist. She admires the Hummers' house and insists on using first names. Mrs. Van Gent illustrates how wrong stereotypical thinking can be.

MR. SWERDLOW (*"Who Was That Masked Man, Anyway?"**), the serious, long-suffering, young medical student who rents Tom* Wattleson's room while Tom is fighting in World War II. At first because he is curious and later also because he gets caught up in his own melodramatic imaginings, Frankie Wattleson, with Mario* Calvino's help, snoops through Mr. Swerdlow's belongings. Frankie's mother needs Mr. Swerdlow's rent money and tells Frankie to keep out, but Frankie persists, because he would like to see the man move away so that Tom can eventually get his room back. On one occasion, while Frankie and Mario snoop, they knock to pieces Mr. Swerdlow's study skeleton and in their haste put the bones together in odd ways. Later, when they wire the skull for sound, Mr. Swerdlow gets so angry at having his privacy violated once again that he moves out. Frankie, assuming his hero mode, assures his parents that the man was up to no good, but they banish him to the basement anyway.

MR. TROUBLE (*The Mozart Season**), the mentally ill, almost toothless, old man whom Allegra Shapiro becomes curious about because at outdoor concerts he dances on the grass, quite oblivious to other people. She learns that he is searching for a "lost song," what he calls Waltz Tree, or Waltz Three. At the concert after the competition, she discovers that it is *Valse Triste*. Allegra learns from his garbled and confused talk that he apparently had lead poisoning as a child, and in his teens during the Great Depression, he was sent to reform school ("form" school) for setting fires—for being Trouble—although he says he was not responsible. Hence she calls him Mr. Trouble. He lives in a Gospel Mission, makes a little money collecting cans, and attends concerts to find his lost song. Allegra's honest concern for him and her efforts to help him without being intrusive reveal her genuine niceness.

MS. MINIFRED (*Baby**), the librarian at Larkin and Lalo's* school. Ms. Minifred loves words, "wondrous words," and poetry. The children sense her infatuation with the spoken word and also are entranced by her growing romance with Rebel, the school janitor. Rebel takes her riding on his Harley-Davidson and visits her classroom, where he joins in discussions and shows he also has a keen sense of the power and beauty of words. He openly courts Ms. Minifred late in the novel. Ms. Minifred tells the class about the death of her brother, William, a too-obvious foreshadowing scene, and reads Edna St. Vincent Millay's "Dirge Without Music" to the class, a poem that Larkin later finds comfort in reading for herself in Papa's* book. Ms. Minifred's story also gives Larkin the idea that her parents should name her dead brother William.

MS. SAMANSKY (*Buffalo Brenda**), elderly, individualistic, student-oriented music teacher at Florence High School. She is in love with a fish do-nut shop owner named Augie and aids Brenda* Tuna and India* Ink Tiedelbaum in bringing the bison to Florence and making it the school mascot. At the end she marries Augie, who calls her Cookie, and the two move to Maine with Grandpa and Grandma Tuna to become, as Grandpa Tuna puts it, "chartner members of da soon-to-be famnous American Vildlife Rescue Commune and Retirement Refuge and Gourmet Fish Restaurant."

MURIEL WESTA (*The Christmas Killer**), Rose Potter's dance teacher, twin sister to the killer. Both are professional dancers in New York, but Muriel, evidently suspecting her brother's homicidal tendencies, has fled to little Bethboro, Connecticut. Secretly, her brother rents a room in a nearby town, pretending to be a salesman, so that he can keep an eye on his sister and especially on her prize pupil, Rose. The man's addiction to killing during the holiday season is explained by a childhood trauma when, because he peeked at his presents, his mother tied him in a dark cellar and made him hold the body of a dead puppy that was to have been his Christmas present. His mother has died in a fire he started, but because Muriel earlier blamed him, thinking he killed the puppy, his resentment has turned to her. Recently Muriel and her twin have reconciled, and he has agreed to come from New York to her recital to judge whether Rose has potential for professional dance. In the end he kills Muriel, evidently because she realizes he has not reformed. His resemblance to Muriel has confused Wallace Romola, whose damaged brain thinks it is a trick with mirrors, but because Wallace also has been visited by Nancy Emerson's spirit, he hangs around the dance studio and is able to save Rose from the killer.

MY BROTHER SAM IS DEAD (Collier*, James Lincoln, and Christopher Collier*, Four Winds, 1974), historical novel set in the village of Redding, Connecticut, of a family's involvement in the American Revolution, as told by the younger son, Timmy Meeker, about age eleven, and culminating with the tragic execution of the elder son, Sam, an American soldier, by his own forces. Well-drawn characters, a vigorous style, and sound research result in a realistic, stark view of the war. Phoenix Honor. Previously the novel received the following citations: Choice; Fanfare; National Book Finalist; Newbery Honor. For a longer entry, see *Dictionary, 1960–1984*.

MYERS, WALTER DEAN (1937–   ), born in Martinsburg, West Virginia; editor, novelist. He grew up in New York City, attended Empire State College in New York, served in the U.S. Army in the 1950s, and later worked as an editor for Bobbs-Merrill publishers. His novels have ranged from the comparatively lighthearted *Fast Sam, Cool Clyde, and Stuff* (Viking, 1975) and *Me, Mop, and the Moondance Kid* (Delacorte, 1988), as well as its sequel, *Mop, Moondance, and the Nagasaki Knights* (Delacorte, 1992), to far darker pictures of African-American childhood and adolescence, as in *Scorpions* (Harper, 1988), a story about inner-city gang violence, and *Somewhere in the Darkness** (Scholastic, 1992), a sensitive and sometimes nightmarish saga of the travels of a fourteen-year-old boy with his father, who is a recent prison escapee, a man he scarcely knows. Both of these novels were named Newbery Honor books. Many of his other books have received commendations, including three winners of the Coretta Scott King Award: *The Young Landlords* (Viking, 1979), *Motown and Didi* (Viking, 1984), and *Fallen Angels* (Scholastic, 1988), a novel of the Vietnam War. For earlier biographical information and title entries, see *Dictionary, 1960–1984* [*Fast Sam, Cool Clyde, and Stuff; Hoops*] and *Dictionary, 1985–1989* [*Fallen Angels; Me, Mop, and the Moondance Kid; Motown and Didi; Scorpions*].

MY NAME IS SUS5AN SMITH. THE 5 IS SILENT. (Plummer*, Louise, Delacorte, 1991), girl's growing-up novel set in Springville, Utah, and Boston, Massachusetts, about the time of its publication. The narrator, Susan Smith, 17, paints portraits that win local prizes but appall her solid, conventional parents, since the pictures contain surreal elements they do not understand and find offensive. Her family portrait, which wins the all-state high school Master's Award, is especially troublesome. She has painted each member of her extended family, including her long-dead maternal grandparents, as if on pieces of a broken plate, a few connected like a jigsaw puzzle and the deceased looking like mouldering corpses. Worse, she has included Uncle Willy* Gerard, the pilot who deserted both the U.S. Air Force and Susan's Aunt Marianne ten years earlier. When her Aunt* Libby Schroeder from Boston, in Utah for Marianne's second marriage, offers Susan a room for the summer, she jumps at the chance and makes a good start, getting a job in a movie theater and trekking to many galleries, actually getting three of her paintings hung briefly with a show by Thomas Roode, a student at Harvard from a family of artists. All the time she keeps on the lookout for Willy, since Libby has mentioned seeing him twice, she thinks, in Harvard Square, and Susan has never gotten over her childhood crush on him. When she meets him, her infatuation is rekindled, and she sees him frequently, keeping their dates from Libby and even lying that she is seeing the young theater manager, Salvatore Zadcardi, with whom she has a joking friendship. On her eighteenth birthday, after she has cooked lunch for Willy while Libby is at work, he walks her to the theater and she lends him her apartment key to get the jacket he left behind. He does not come to the theater that evening as he has promised, and she arrives back at the apartment to discover that all Libby's valuable antiques have been stolen, as well as her own paintings and even an illustrated letter from Thomas Roode, who is studying for the summer in Italy. Libby's anger at her soon dissipates, but Susan's confidence has been shattered, and she even questions her own decision to stay in Boston and attend the school at the Boston Museum of Fine Arts rather then attending college in Utah. When Libby confides how she struggled to free her own life from her parents' conventional goals, Susan flies back to Utah, tells her mother of her plans, and looks forward to a new start in Boston, probably including Thomas Roode, now back from Italy. A subplot involves Libby's eccentric neighbor, Grace McGregor, and her little dog, Priceless, which does tricks. Sensing the old woman's loneliness, Susan paints an idealized portrait of her son, killed in World War II. When Priceless dies, Grace keeps him in her freezer along with a boneless ham, as she tells David Letterman when she appears on his show with a videotape of Priceless jumping through hoops and singing, which Susan has filmed and sent to the Stupid Pet Tricks segment on the television show. Susan's long-time crush on Willy is plausible, but several elements—she seems sexually naive for an eighteen year old in the late twentieth century, her discoveries of her self are spelled out explicitly, and Libby's relationship with her neighbor, Dan Lavenstein, is unbelievably antiseptic—all make the book seem intended for girls considerably younger than the protagonist. SLJ.

MYSTERY ON OCTOBER ROAD (Herzig*, Alison Cragin, and Jane Lawrence Mali*, Viking, 1991), short, lighthearted, contemporary mystery for younger readers, in which three schoolchildren discover that their imaginations can lead them astray. Only child Casey (Catherine) Cooper, 10, the narrator, has yearned for a big family to move into the dilapidated house next door to hers on October Road, the outskirts of an unnamed American town. Her initial disappointment turns into amazement and puzzlement when a van pulls in and a man wearing a "slouchy hat" and a blue-and-white bandanna over his face unloads a lot of boxes, a large, lumpy thing covered with a blanket, and two huge, hairy four-legged creatures. Although her mother informs her that the creatures are Irish wolfhounds, she immediately calls her best friend, Cats (Catherine) Cooney, whose curiosity is also aroused, and the next day in school not even plans for Halloween the following week divert their attention from the mysterious new-comer. In a humorous episode in which they are motivated by nosiness rather than kindness, they offer to deliver to the newcomer the two loaves of bread that Mrs. Cooper has baked as a welcoming gift but run for their lives when they spot a hairy figure in a window. They conclude that it must be a monster and that the man is a robber. Cats insists on enlisting the aid of classmate Benny Dilmers, who has binoculars, in keeping tabs on the man. Benny over-dramatically maintains that he is a gangster about to take over the town and suggests they dig a tunnel into the basement, since it is probably full of guns. The trio also overreact over such other matters as the newcomer's name (John Smith, which they are certain is an alias) and his gift of apples to the Coopers (they are sure these are poisoned). The break in the case comes when they find a basement window open, enter the room, find that the boxes contain chisels, and under the blanket discover a horse. Cats and Benny flee in terror, but Casey recognizes that the horse is wooden and carved. Left behind by her friends, Casey falls when the stool under the window slips and injures her ankle. The commotion brings the man, whose great dogs turn out to be friendly. He cares gently for her injury, and when she inquires about the bandanna mask, he re-moves it, revealing a face terribly disfigured from burns he says he received in a fire. He reveals that he had once carved animals for carousels. To make amends, Casey places the jack o'lantern she has fashioned by his back door, along with a note apologizing for her behavior and offering to dog-sit. On Halloween, her mother drives her, Cats, and some friends around town for trick-or-treating, and on their return they are pleasantly surprised to see the area around Mr. Smith's house aglow with the lights from many pumpkins carved in a wide variety of interesting shapes. Casey feels good when she spots her pumpkin in the window of his kitchen, and she knows that she and Mr. Smith are now friends. The fast-paced tempo, the humor of misunderstanding and backfire, and the extensive dialogue make for pleasingly diverting reading for those beyond primers and ready for chapter books. Poe Nominee.

THE NAME OF THE GAME WAS MURDER (Nixon*, Joan Lowery, Delacorte, 1993), mystery-detective novel set in the early 1990s. The narrator, Sam
(Samantha) Burns, 15, looks forward eagerly to spending a couple of weeks
with her mother's Aunt Thea Trevor on Catalina Island off the coast of California. An aspiring writer, she hopes for advice from Thea's husband, Augustus
Trevor, a celebrated novelist who hobnobs with the rich and famous. When she
arrives, she is surprised and disappointed to find that Augustus is an ugly, mean-
spirited man, the opposite of gentle, warm Thea. She is also put off by the
remote and isolated 1920s house, finding it dark, cluttered, and unwelcoming,
like a combination of museum and mausoleum. She dislikes having a tiny room
set apart in a high tower at the top of a long, dark stairway. Her disappointment
is lessened somewhat by the news that Augustus is having weekend guests, each
very well known but also, Sam discovers, unappealing in behavior and attitude:
Laura Reed, a wistfully beautiful, throaty-voiced, blond actress; huge, beefy
Buck Thompson, once a professional quarterback and now a prominent sportscaster; arrogant Julia Bryant, a writer of sleazy romantic novels; balding, im-
perious Senator Arthur Maggio, aspiring presidential candidate; and Alex
Chambers, affected designer of expensive clothes. Her wonder at the strange
mixture of guests deepens when she learns that they have been summoned with
threats, not invitations. After dinner on Friday evening, Augustus announces
that he has completed a book of nonfiction about behind-the-scenes behavior of
important people. He says that he has discovered secrets about all his guests
and has incorporated the material into his book. If they solve certain clues ''that
lead to a treasure, he will erase the material from his book.'' Each, including
Thea, is given an envelope containing a clue and told there will be another set
of clues in the morning. When Augustus does not appear for breakfast, Walter
the butler investigates and finds Augustus dead in his office. Since the weather
has turned stormy and the police cannot be summoned because of a dead telephone and high seas, the guests, all of them suspects, scour the house for the
manuscript, hoping to find it before the authorities do. Three more sets of clues

are found but do nothing to brighten the dispositions of the guests, who become tense, argumentative, and hostile toward one another. Sam persuades them to allow her to try to make sense of the clues and succeeds in finding the manuscript in an ancient burial urn but keeps her discovery secret while she reads the manuscript. She learns a dark secret about each person: Laura may have killed her husband; Buck may have thrown a game; Julia may have murdered a writer friend for her unpublished manuscripts; Senator Maggio has ties to organized crime; Alex has connections with a sweatshop; and gentle Aunt Thea killed a man who attempted to assault her. On Sunday morning the weather turns sunny, and Sam lures the suspects, except for Thea, into the wine cellar and locks them up. She divulges her discoveries to Thea, who summons the police. Thus faced with imminent discovery, Thea's longtime companion and housekeeper, Mrs. Engstrom, confesses that she killed Augustus in order to protect Thea. Loose ends, such as how Augustus was killed, do not detract, and numerous conventions will be familiar from the novels of such eminent practitioners of the gothic mystery as Agatha Christie. Best are the snappy style, the quick-step pace, the credible characterization of Sam, who learns to control her impulsive behavior, and the steadily accelerating tension. Poe winner.

NAMIOKA, LENSEY (CHAO) (1929–   ), born in Beijing, China; mathematician and novelist. She attended Radcliffe College and received both her B.A. and M.A. degrees from the University of California at Berkeley. She has taught mathematics at the college level and been a translator for the American Mathematical Society. Namioka is married to a man of Japanese ancestry, and a number of her novels are set in Japan with historical background, notably a series about a pair of samurai, which includes *The Samurai and the Long-Nosed Devils* (McKay, 1976), *White Serpent Castle* (McKay, 1976), *Valley of the Broken Cherry Trees* (Delacorte, 1980), and *Village of the Vampire Cat* (Delacorte, 1981). Among her other titles for older children are *Island of Ogres* (HarperCollins, 1989), *The Coming of the Bear* (HarperCollins, 1992), and *April and the Dragon Lady* (Harcourt, 1994). For middle grade children she has written *Yang the Youngest and His Terrible Ear** (Little, Brown, 1992), a lighter story about a tone-deaf boy in a family of musicians, which was named to the *Horn Book* Fanfare list. It is set in Seattle, where Namioka makes her home with her husband. For earlier biographical information and a title entry, see *Dictionary, 1960–1984* [*Village of the Vampire Cat*].

NARO (*Children of the River**), Tep Naro, the Cambodian refugee husband of Sundara Suvann's mother's younger sister, Kem Soka*. Naro organizes the family's flight from the Khmer Rouge with calm authority. Then and later, he shows good sense and is respected by his family and friends. He represents a good Khmer family head. When the Tep family arrived in Oregon, the only job Naro could find was as a dishwasher. He overworked to provide for his family and for a time was ill. Then he was able to get a job as an accountant, a position for which he was trained. Naro realizes that Sundara is a good girl and only wants to adopt the best of the American ways and thus defends her to his wife.

NAT THE SUPER (*Shadow Boxer**), the scruffy superintendent of the apartment house in which George, Monty*, and Ma live. Chubby, dirty, one-toothed although still young, Nat lives in his office in the basement boiler room. He gives the boys odd jobs so that they can earn a little money. They like him because he is kind, and, being eccentric, he is an interesting person to be around. He takes the boys to help Frank*, the ''elephant man,'' gives them lunch, which looks and smells so bad they cannot eat it, and shows them his girlie calendars. When the tenants have a meeting in which they decide to fire Nat, referring to him as the Pervert in the Cellar, George, who attends in Ma's place, and one other resident vote no. After Nat gives Monty liquor and gets him drunk, however, George realizes Nat is a dangerous person to have around.

NAYLOR, PHYLLIS REYNOLDS (1933–   ), born in Anderson, Indiana; educator, prolific writer. After a career in education, in 1960 she decided to devote her full professional time to writing, producing several different types of novels, perhaps the best known being her series about motherless Alice McKinley, whose humorous middle school and junior high problems introduced in *The Agony of Alice* (Atheneum, 1985) are continued in *Alice in Rapture, Sort Of** (Atheneum, 1989), *Reluctantly Alice** (Atheneum, 1991), and *All But Alice** (Atheneum, 1992). Her sensitive story about a West Virginia boy's love for a dog, *Shiloh** (Atheneum, 1991), was a Newbery Award winner, and a number of her mysteries have been nominees for the Edgar Allan Poe Award, including *The Face in the Bessledorf Funeral Parlor** (Atheneum, 1993), a continuation of the lighthearted Bessledorf series, and *Witch Weed** (Delacorte, 1991), one of a series about the way the supernatural powers of a malevolent neighbor affect a small-town family. For earlier biographical information and title entries, see *Dictionary, 1960–1984* [*The Solomon System*] and *Dictionary, 1985–1989* [*The Agony of Alice; The Keeper; Night Cry*].

NEKOMAH CREEK (Crew*, Linda, illus. Charles Robinson, Delacorte, 1991), warmly amusing realistic contemporary novel of family and school life set in a small Oregon coastal neighborhood, Nekomah Creek, from mid-October through early November. Troubles start for Robby Hummer, the nine-year-old narrator, whose ambition is to become a gallery artist, when his fourth-grade teacher, Mrs. Perkins, who is ''average age for a grown-up'' and a staunch conformist, complains because he spends his recess reading (which he loves) instead of in sports (which he detests). She sends him to Mrs.* Van Gent, the new counselor, who thinks he may have problems at home. His artist mother is back to work with a design firm, his father, a former teacher, is running the house, and the two-year-old twins, Lucy and Russell, have complicated his life. Although Robby maintains he is perfectly happy, later he admits to the reader that he does have mixed feelings about his situation. Usually he is happy and comfortable with the messy house that his parents renovated from an old barn, his rowdy, exuberant siblings, and his casual, fun-loving Dad. But Mom gets tense sometimes with the horseplay and mess, she and Dad bicker, and the twins do get lots of attention. He also feels uncomfortable about his unconventional family, particularly since the father of classmate Orin* Downard is a macho logger who makes Mr. Hummer look like a wimp and another friend, Ben, speaks disparagingly about Mr. Hummer's doing the cooking on a regular basis, calling it "weird." Robby also is embarrassed when his father volunteers to cook a gourmet dinner to auction off at the Nekomah Creek School fall fundraiser and even dresses up like a pig for the annual school Halloween party, where he tends the apple-bobbing booth. Robbie is somewhat relieved about his nontraditional family when he discovers that another classmate, Rose*, who is also a book lover, lives with two "moms" and several "stepsisters." Robbie's troubles escalate when Rose informs him that social workers have decided classmate Amber Hixon is a neglected child and have placed her in a foster home. Now Robbie worries because it seems that teachers, social workers, and government officials have a great deal of power, and he does not want Mrs. Perkins or Mrs. Van Gent, who ironically purchased the gourmet dinner, to decide his home is unsuitable and break the Hummers up. His fears hit a peak when Mrs. Van Gent and her husband mistakenly arrive for dinner at the Hummer house a week early, at a time when things are in complete disarray. Robby's problems with Orin continue over a diorama Robby made for art that is judged best in the school. On the way home, Orin grabs the diorama and tosses it into the creek, ruining it. Although Robby is very angry and considers beating Orin up (although he knows he will get clobbered because Orin is a tough bully), Mom convinces him (in a rare one-to-one talk that he really likes) that beating up Orin will not bring back the diorama and that he should simply make another one for Dad. She also assures him that the mixed feelings he has been experiencing are natural. Unexpectedly, Dad gets a chance to set Robby an example of neighborliness and manliness when Orin's father breaks an arm and a leg in a logging accident. Dad makes a casserole, takes it to the Downards (although he does not like them, but a "man's gotta do what a man's gotta do"), and then even cuts wood for them. Soon Robby gets a chance to show manliness, too. Since he can vouch that Orin was elsewhere when the Thanksgiving charity money was stolen from Mrs. Perkins's desk, he speaks up for Orin and clears his name. The book ends with Dad's "fancy romancey dinner" for the Van Gents, at which, after a stiff beginning, they all, Hummers (sans twins) and Van Gents, settle down to a pleasant, happy, delicious meal with plenty of laughter all around. For the first time in weeks, Robby feels completely safe. Although the author is overly obvious and occasionally intrusive in addressing commonly held stereotypes and such issues as logging in the Northwest and the powers of social workers and Robbie's parents are a shade too perfect, this is a happy, wholesome but not sticky, incident-filled, consistently entertaining story. Robbie's feelings seem completely natural, given his temperament as presented. Scenes at school are lively and credible, if overblown at times to accommodate his melodramatic stance. Episodes at home are also exaggerated for effect: the dinner at which the kids throw spaghetti, the time Lucy flushes underpants down the toilet and causes a flood, the occasion on which the kids gang up and tear Dad's holey undershirt off his back, because it is only going to be thrown away anyway. The book lacks the harshness and spitefulness often found in television sit-com family life or in books of the 1960s and 1970s where parents can do nothing right. ALA.

NELSON, PETER (1953–), born in Minneapolis, Minnesota; freelance journalist and teacher of creative writing at Rhode Island School of Design and St. Lawrence University in Canton, New York; writer of teenaged mysteries. He took a double major, in English and in art, from St. Olaf College in Minnesota and later was graduated from the University of Iowa with an M.F.A. in creative writing. His *Scarface** (Archway, 1991) is a fast-moving mystery-detective novel set in the wilds of northern Minnesota and starring the liberated supersleuth Sylvia Smith-Smith. A nominee for the Edgar Allan Poe Award, it combines efforts to save a rundown resort hotel, ghosts, necromancy, remnants of the Al Capone gangster era, ecology, and romance for well-paced, exciting, if lightweight, entertainment, which hints of parody. Other Sylvia Smith-Smith books include *Night of Fire* (Simon & Schuster, 1992), *Fast Lane West* (Simon & Schuster, 1991), *Deadly Games* (Simon & Schuster, 1992), and *Dangerous Waters* (Simon & Schuster, 1992). The Sylvia Smith-Smith series started with a story for *Seventeen*. Another series of young adult novels revolves around intrepid Mollie Fox, including *Double Dose* (HarperCollins, 1992), *First to Die* (HarperCollins, 1992), and *Third Degree* (HarperCollins, 1992). He also has written screenplays and contributed to such periodicals as *Esquire* and *New England Monthly*.

NELSON, THERESA (1948–), born in Beaumont, Texas; novelist of books mostly for middle grade and young adult readers. Two of her novels have been American Library Association and Fanfare selections, *And One for All** (Orchard, 1989), a historical novel of the protests against the Vietnam War, which was also chosen by *School Library Journal,* and *The Beggars' Ride** (Orchard, 1992), an eloquent account of a group of homeless teenagers on the boardwalk in Atlantic City. The summer that she and her family lived in an Atlantic City basement apartment provided the inspiration and substance for the book. Also named to the *School Library Journal* list of best books is *Earthshine** (Orchard, 1994), about a family whose father is dying of AIDS. Nelson and her family now live in Los Angeles. For earlier biographical information and a title entry, see *Dictionary, 1985–1989* [*The 25¢ Miracle*].

NIGHTJOHN (*Nightjohn**), strong, intelligent young slave who is horribly scarred from whippings and who teaches twelve-year-old Sarny and other slaves to read. Sarny says he is "true black" in color, a skin tone she admires as compared to her own sassafras-tea brown. She often likens his laugh to a low roll like distant thunder. He tells his story to Mammy and Sarny, of how he ran away from a cruel master to freedom in the North but returned to teach reading and writing and was caught. When Mammy asks him what good it is to teach the slaves, since reading and writing will only bring them trouble and punishment, he replies that it is so that they can write about what is being done to them. Nightjohn is an obviously symbolic character, as is Mammy.

NIGHTJOHN (Paulsen*, Gary, Delacorte, 1993), short historical novel of slavery on a pre–Civil War plantation somewhere in the South. Sarny, the twelve-year-old narrator, has been raised to have a slave's fear and lack of respect for the white masters by old Delie, the cook whom she calls Mammy, her own mother having been sold off as a breeder when Sarny was four. Sarny dreads the time when the "troubles" start for her, for then she will also be forced into the breeding shed. The slim, not entirely plausible plot starts when cruel, sadistic master Clel Waller* buys for one thousand dollars Nightjohn*, a young male slave known to be a runner. Sarny says that Waller "brought him in bad," naked, his body scarred from many lashes, shackled to Waller's saddle, forced to run beside Waller, and then immediately sent to work in the sun-drenched fields. The first night, after dark in the sleeping shed, John whispers loudly that he will trade letters for a "lip of chew." Although she knows that reading and writing are forbidden to slaves and punishable by cutting off the thumb, Sarny wants to learn and gives John tobacco she has saved from killing the bugs on the mistress's roses by the white house. Every night thereafter for several weeks, except on those John is too tired from field work, he teaches Sarny her letters. He writes them and she copies them in the dirt with a stick. So delighted that she becomes careless, Sarny writes a word one day where Waller sees it and immediately demands to know who taught her. She lies and evades in spite of blows and shoves, even keeping quiet when he grabs Mammy and first shackles her to the spring house whipping wall, then hitches her up naked to pull his buggy. John speaks up before Mammy is further harmed; he is shackled and the middle toes of both feet chopped off with a hammer and chisel. John lies ill for three nights, Mammy tending him. The second night he resumes teaching Sarny, and on the fifth night he runs, fashioning foot coverings out of rawhide and smearing them with lard and pepper to throw off Waller's vicious, bloodthirsty dogs. Sarny is happy he gets away, although she remarks that "he left me hanging" at the letter J. Fall brings Sarny's "troubles," and she lives in constant fear of discovery. In winter, John turns up late one night and takes her across the fields to a school in a pit roofed over with thick brush. Sarny helps him teach the slaves from the area. In an epilogue entitled "Words," Sarny speaks of John in legendary terms, saying, "Late he came walking," when everyone in the white house is sleeping. The slaves, she says, know he has come because they see his tracks where the drive meets the road: "it be Nightjohn and he bringing us the way to know." Sarny speaks in unschooled, relentlessly stark, serious, understated prose of the inhumane, brutal conditions that encapsulate the worst aspects of American slavery, of horrible beatings, lack of food, clothing, and the simplest of creature needs, animal-like living conditions, and gross inhumanities like forced breeding. Although the plot is underdeveloped, some scenes have power—for example, when John teaches Sarny and when Mammy is hitched to the buggy—but the episode in which poor, addled Alice runs away and is attacked by Waller's dogs and horribly wounded seems excessive, especially since the horrible fates of two other runaways have just been described. An author's note at the beginning of the book says that the events are true. ALA.

NIGHT RIDING (Martin*, Katherine, Knopf, 1989), girl's growing-up novel set near Raleigh Springs, Tennessee, in the late 1950s. Two significant events that greatly affect the life of the narrator, Prin (Elizabeth) Campbell, 11, occur simultaneously: her father enters a hospital with tuberculosis, and the motherless Hammond family moves into the old Thompson place just up the road. Prin's mother, Ada Ruth, pregnant with her third child, is determined to keep their trucking business going and to hang onto the three horses that Prin and her father love. Both Prin and her sister, Jo Lynn, 15, have to give up many expectations, spend a great deal of their vacation helping around the place, and put up with bossy Aunt Map, their mother's sister-in-law, who moves in and tries to direct their lives. For Prin, the Hammond family provides interest in the dreary summer months. Although Jo Lynn scorns Mary Faith Hammond, who has been in her class at school, as cheap and not the kind of person to be friends with, Prin secretly meets and talks with her in a little cave of pine trees between their houses, learning quickly that the older girl is pregnant and realizing, correctly, that from her she can learn things her mother and sister will not tell her, like what *gelded* means. Their acquaintance, at first touchy and antagonistic, deepens into friendship when together they extricate Prin's father's spirited horse, Big Red, from barbed wire, amazing since he usually lets no one but Mr. Campbell touch him. Several times Prin sees Mary Faith's father, Mr. B. Z. Hammond, physically abuse her and once, when she has sneaked out to go night riding on her horse, Flash, she witnesses an argument between Mr. B. Z. and his son, Larry, a high school basketball star, and sees the father throw Mary Faith down the steps. Later she learns that Mary Faith has lost her baby, but it is not until she is in the Hammond house, looking at a beautiful drawing Mary Faith did of Big Red, that she realizes the extent of his abuse. He barges into Mary Faith's room with his pants unzipped, removing his belt, and, seeing Prin, begins to make sexually threatening advances to her. Mary Faith helps her escape. Later, Mose Hardy, a kindly man who is building a house nearby, prevents Mr. B. Z. from molesting Prin when she is out riding. In the meantime, Mr. B. Z.

has been hanging around the Campbell house, ostensibly to help out, but making both Mama and Aunt Map nervous and offering veiled threats when they reject his overtures. The situation comes to a head one night when Prin has sneaked out to ride and Mr. B. Z. intercepts her in the pasture, knocking her off Flash. Before he can pin her down, she hears Mary Faith, who has followed her father, screaming at him to stop. Panicked by the strangers and night noise in his pasture, Big Red charges Mr. B. Z. and kills him. What follows is a conspiracy of silence. Mama helps Prin conceal that she has been out of the house, and Mose Hardy, who has heard the scream and witnessed the killing, gets Mary Faith home so she can pretend she was asleep when the sheriff comes. Big Red is destroyed, Larry Hammond goes into the army and Mary Faith to a foster home, and the incident seems over, but Prin realizes that, even with an understanding mother, she will never be completely confident again and that Mary Faith has been hurt much more severely. The touchy subject of incest is handled well, not as a problem on which to center a novel but as a development from a given situation and group of people. Prin's naive realization that Mary Faith needs a friend battles realistically with Jo Lynn's normal high school snobbishness and their mother's fear that her daughters will be contaminated. Both Prin and Mary Faith are well-developed characters, Mr. B. Z. is frighteningly real, and several of the minor figures—Mama, Aunt Map, and Mose Hardy, especially—are memorable. Prin's voice is believable and does not get tiresome, and descriptions of her night rides on Flash are full of sensory detail. SLJ.

NIXON, JOAN LOWERY (1927–   ), born in Los Angeles; graduate of the University of Southern California in journalism; resident of Houston, Texas; teacher and author of more than eighty mystery and suspense novels for children and adolescents. Four of her books have won the Edgar Allan Poe Award, including *The Name of the Game Was Murder** (Delacorte, 1993), and several others were nominated for the award, including *The Weekend Was* Murder!* (Delacorte, 1992). Both exemplify her mastery at building and maintaining suspense. For earlier biographical information and title entries, see *Dictionary, 1960–1984* [*The Kidnapping of Christina Lattimore; The Mysterious Red Tape Gang; The Seance*] and *Dictionary, 1985–1989* [*The Other Side of Dark; The Ghosts of Now*].

NO KIDDING (Brooks*, Bruce, Harper & Row, 1989), futuristic novel set in Washington, D.C., sometime well into the twenty-first century, after alcoholism has become epidemic and caused sterility in most of the population. Sam*, 14, is one of a new breed of adult-children, self-supporting, self-contained, extremely responsible. He has chosen the Bigelows as foster parents for his brother, Ollie* (Oliver), 10. The couple know almost nothing about alcohol addiction or the intensely systematized government education program called AO for the offspring of alcoholics, and he has closely monitored them during the probation year, after which they will be allowed to adopt the boy. Although Ollie has not been told, Sam committed their mother to an institution known as Soberlife eighteen months earlier and now decides to arrange her release, realizing that since she was never drunk in front of Ollie, she must be capable of controlling her drinking. He has found her a job in a dress shop and a room, both of which she accepts with lack of enthusiasm that does not surprise him, but he is amazed that she has no interest in seeing Ollie again. He arranges, however, to take Ollie to her room the day before his probation period is up, only to find that their mother has wreaked havoc in the dress shop in a drunken rage and waits for them in the chaos of her room, slouched in a chair, a glass of liquor in hand. Ollie's reaction is equally surprising. He takes his saxophone from its case and blows it at her, harsh, condemning sounds that increase in volume and shrillness until he hurls the instrument at her, screams violent fundamentalist religious rhetoric, and runs. Sam suddenly realizes that his mother's drunkenness is a performance, that her glass contains flat cola, and that she has deliberately driven Ollie away so that she can concentrate on Sam, allowing him to be the child he has never been. Back at the Bigelow's, Sam is blamed for Ollie's secret addiction to the intolerant religious attitudes of a group known as the Steemers and for being too controlling. Sam admits to himself that he tried to do too much. Although the book is clearly against alcohol abuse, the theme is strangely ambivalent about responsibility, seeming to condemn Sam for assuming too much, yet describing a society that has forced him into this role. His honesty to himself in the end is to be applauded, but there seems little hope that he can return to childlike dependence and have a happy life with his mother. Similarly, it condemns the Steemers, who think alcohol is the devil's tool to attract weak souls and seems, at least at first, to applaud Prior Marloe, who runs a mission for children forced into adult roles yet has failed miserably with Ollie. Underlying the plot is a tone of increasing horror at the bleak future posited. SLJ.

NORMA PEYTON (*Dixie Storms**), 15, Dutch Peyton's cousin from Richmond, whose visit serves as a catalyst for change in Dutch's life. Norma has a flawless figure that she likes to show off in bikinis and cutoffs; is pretty, charming, and self-assured; knows how to attract men; thinks she is in love with her boyfriend but chases other boys; keeps a journal because she is sure that some day she will be important; says that she and her parents simply "don't communicate" and envies Dutch's warm, supportive family life; is an accomplished gymnast; and has a mercurial temperament, sometimes being very accommodating and at other times moody and even highly sarcastic. She can be disconcertingly outspoken, as when she deplores tobacco growing and hunting and says she does not believe in God, all ideas that go against the Peytons' grain, although they make allowances for her. Through her, among other things, Dutch realizes how fine a family she has. Dutch recognizes that underneath Norma's hardness lies a vulnerability that she comes to pity.

NOTHING BUT THE TRUTH: A DOCUMENTARY NOVEL (Avi*, Orchard, 1991), school novel set for about three weeks at the time of publication in the city of Harrison, New Hampshire. The novel employs an unusual structure, consisting of such passages as diary entries, school memos, letters, recorded discussions, telephone conversations, and news clippings, all reflecting different points of view and expressed in different styles of writing or speaking without connecting narrative. Thus given the "facts," the reader can put the pieces together like a puzzle and determine where truth, or blame, lies for a series of incidents that shake a community. The dearest wish of ninth-grader Philip Malloy is to run with Harrison High's track team, a position for which he has been working out with great diligence. He is much encouraged in this ambition by his parents, especially his father, a former college runner. Philip's grade in English, however, a D from demanding Miss Narwin, disqualifies him, according to Coach Jamison, who urges him to discuss the matter with Miss Narwin ("[but] she's so old-fashioned. Boring.") and always to remember that "one thing sports teaches. A rule is a rule. It isn't always easy." Philip sets about harassing Miss Narwin in homeroom, by, among other disruptive acts, humming when the national anthem is tape-played over the school sound system, although he knows the rules specify standing in respectful silence. The first time he does this, he stops when she tells him to, but the second and third days he persists and is sent to the office. He is suspended by Assistant Principal Palleni for disobeying and not apologizing. When his parents ask for an explanation, he tells them that he was kicked out of class for singing the national anthem. Outraged for what they deem an undermining of traditional American values, they contact neighbor Ted Griffen, who is running for school board. Soon Philip's situation becomes a local *cause célèbre*. The mass media focus on the case, letters pour in, and the values of Harrison High and current education are called into question. All this is a matter of grave concern to school personnel and in particular to Superintendent Seymour because the school budget is soon up for renewal with the voters. Things so fall out that Seymour denigrates Miss Narwin in an attempt to placate Griffen, a blustery sort who uses the matter to make political hay. Seymour suggests that, having taught for twenty-one years, Miss Narwin is out of touch. Soon she is given the rest of the semester off to take a course in teaching literature she had earlier out of noble motives applied for a grant to attend but which had been denied her at that time for lack of funds. Philip is transferred to a former homeroom, whose teacher (a stark contrast to Miss Narwin) he likes, and a little later to another English class. The latter is an especially ironic victory, because now he cannot do as Coach Jamison suggests and go to Miss Narwin to request extra work and thus raise his grade. The coach, all along supportive of the school's teachers, rubs things in to the boy when he says, "Well, look, you did one hell of a number on her" and "I'm always telling you guys—it's what sports is all about—a rule is a rule—to get along you have to play along. Know what I'm saying?" Philip's student friends turn on him, too, complaining that Philip was unfair to a teacher known and respected for her fairness. Book's end finds Philip attending a private school, which, ironically, does not have track and where students are expected to sing the national anthem every morning. This predominantly serious slice of real school life seems sympathetic to the teacher and projects an ironic tone from its beginning (the heading on the standard form for school memos reads: "Where Our Children Are Educated, Not Just Taught") to the equally satirical conclusion, where Philip, whose reputation has preceded him, tearfully laments to his new homeroom teacher that he cannot lead the class in the national anthem because he does not know the words. Though Philip may be taken as typical of self-centered, willful, manipulative, contemporary teens, other students, if on occasion callous and duplicitous, display a higher moral standard. The politics and ethics of the adult culture, parents, school board, and particularly the school administration are laid open for raw scrutiny but without overt judgement or melodrama. Never is Miss Narwin's point of view or position explained to the public, and in effect she is simply abandoned by the administration and left with her career in a shambles. The documentary mode is thoroughly intriguing in itself, since the contrasting styles and juxtaposed points of view and situations have their own peculiar interest and the reader must intuit motivations. It heightens the irony and makes ethical conditions in the school culture even more dark and troubling. ALA; Boston Globe Honor; Fanfare; Newbery Honor; SLJ.

NUMBER THE STARS (Lowry*, Lois, Houghton Mifflin, 1989), historical novel concerning the escape of Jews from Denmark during World War II. After three years of Nazi occupation of Copenhagen, Annemarie Johansen and her Jewish friend, Ellen Rosen, both age ten, are used to seeing German soldiers everywhere. On the night of the Jewish New Year, Ellen comes to stay at the Johansen apartment, since word has been received that all Danish Jews are to be arrested and relocated. Annemarie's father warns them that they are to pretend that Ellen is her sister, Lise, who died in an accident almost three years before. Peter Neilsen, who was going to marry Lise and now comes and goes on mysterious errands, has taken Ellen's parents away. When the German soldiers come in the middle of the night, Annemarie yanks the Star of David that Ellen wears, breaks the chain, and hides it before they are ordered out of the bedroom. When the soldiers are suspicious that one of the daughters has dark hair, Mr. Johansen rips three baby pictures from an album, showing that two of the girls were blond as infants, but Lise had dark hair. They do not admit that later her hair turned blond. The next day Mrs. Johansen takes the girls and Annemarie's little sister, Kirsti, 5, to Gilleleje, on the coast within sight of Sweden, where her brother, Uncle Henrik, is a fisherman. That night a hearse brings the casket of Great-Aunt Birte, for whom they will have a funeral gathering, although Annemarie knows that there was no such aunt. A number of people come quietly, including Peter and Ellen's parents, all ostensibly doing honor to the dead when the German soldiers arrive. Later that night Peter opens the casket, which contains warm clothing and blankets, and leads the first group by dark pathways to Uncle Henrik's boat, the *Ingeborg*. Before leaving, he gives a small package to Mr. Rosen to deliver to Uncle Henrik, emphasizing its importance. After a set interval, Mrs. Johansen, who knows the pathways from her childhood, leads the Rosens to the boat. Annemarie, waking when it is almost morning, is shocked to discover her mother crawling toward the house, having tripped on her dark return and broken her ankle. As Annemarie helps her to the steps, they discover Peter's packet, evidently dropped by Mr. Rosen when he stumbled. Quickly they slip it into a basket and cover it with bread, cheese, and an apple, and Annemarie runs with it toward the harbor, trying to get it to Uncle Henrik before his boat leaves. She is stopped and questioned by German soldiers with dogs. Pretending to be as silly and carefree as her sister Kirsti, Annemarie says it is her uncle's lunch, which he forgot, and she acts annoyed rather than terrified when one of them throws the bread to the dogs, rummages through the basket, and finds the packet. He rips it open and pulls out a neatly hemmed handkerchief, which he scornfully drops and lets the dogs nose before he turns away. Annemarie retrieves it and hastens to the *Ingeborg* to deliver the package. That evening Uncle Henrik tells her that the Rosens and the other people were in a secret compartment built into his boats, as in many other Danish boats, and were delivered to Sweden, still a free country. The handkerchief was impregnated with drugs that attract the dogs but temporarily kill their sense of smell, so that though trained to detect the scent of humans even through rotting fish, the dogs Annemarie met did not sniff out the Jews when the soldiers later came on board. A brief last chapter is set two years later, at the war's end, after Peter has been executed for his Resistance work. Annemarie learns that Lise had also been part of the Resistance and was deliberately run down by a German military car. Annemarie unearths the Star of David hidden among Lise's trousseau items, promising to wear it until she can return it to Ellen. An afterword tells that although Annemarie and the Rosens are fictional, nearly seven thousand Copenhagen Jews were smuggled out of Denmark, and a drug-permeated handkerchief was used by almost every boat captain to thwart German dogs. The story is simply but convincingly told, with Annemarie's heroic part arising naturally from circumstances. Much of the tension comes from Kirsti's babbling, which could easily give away Ellen's identity. Enough historical information is given to orient young readers without burdening the plot. Addams; ALA; Fanfare; Newbery Winner; SLJ.

O

OB (*Missing May**), Summer's* loving, elderly uncle and foster father, husband of May*. Ob very much misses May, his wife who died six months before the book begins. An accepting, kind man, Summer says he "was never embarrassed about being a disabled navy man who fiddled with [the handmade, colorful, unusual] whirligigs all day long," handcrafts that fill their tiny, rusty trailer home. He is thin, has bony fingers, and just the "last bit of hair on his head." Summer's observation that "Ob was a deep thinker [who] was often getting revelations" helps explain his sudden change in attitude on the Charleston trip. Ob uses pungent language and occasionally prevaricates.

O'DELL, SCOTT (1898?/1903?–1989), born in Los Angeles; prolific historical novelist, who donated the annual Scott O'Dell Award for the best historical novel dealing with the Western Hemisphere. Still most popular of his many books is his first, *Island of the Blue Dolphins* (Houghton Mifflin, 1960), a survival story of a Native American girl stranded on an island off the California coast, but others have been highly acclaimed, including three Newbery Honor books: *The King's Fifth* (Houghton Mifflin, 1966), *The Black Pearl* (Houghton Mifflin, 1967), and *Sing Down the Moon** (Houghton Mifflin, 1970). This last book received further recognition twenty years after its publication when it was named an honor book for the Phoenix Award of The Children's Literature Association, which singles out books of lasting literary merit. It is based on the cruel and unmerited relocation of the Navajo Indians in the late nineteenth century. For earlier biographical information and title entries, see *Dictionary, 1960–1984* [*The Black Pearl; Island of the Blue Dolphins; The King's Fifth; Sing Down the Moon*] and *Dictionary, 1985–1989* [*Streams to the River, River to the Sea*].

OF NIGHTINGALES THAT WEEP (Paterson*, Katherine, illus. Haru Wells, Crowell, 1974), historical novel set in late twelfth-century Japan during a power struggle between two rival samurai clans. After her widowed mother is remarried to a deformed potter named Goro, whom she finds revolting, Takiko, beautiful and talented daughter of a noble, welcomes the chance to go to the court of the child emperor. When the ruling Heike forces are defeated and the emperor's grandmother, with the child in her arms and many ladies of the court following her, jumps into the sea, Takiko returns to Goro's farm, where her mother and half-brother have died of fever. Burned and disfigured, she is rejected by her noble lover but finds happiness by marrying Goro and bearing his child. Earlier named to the Fanfare list. For a more detailed entry, see *Dictionary, 1960–1984*. Phoenix Winner.

OLINGER (*Harper & Moon**), the mountain man of about sixty-five with whom Harper McDowell and Moon* McCarty are friends. Olinger lives in the Blue Mountains of Oregon in a cabin that is also part store. He is lean, weathered, tough, mustached, good-humored, and likable, a World War I veteran who won the Bronze Star for bravery in action. Although the old man has been known to go off to Portland "on a toot," the McDowells think his sudden disappearance strange and intend to investigate. When his father delays, Harper goes looking on his own. Olinger is a romanticized figure who suits the plot well.

OLLIE (*No Kidding**), quiet, apparently docile ten-year-old brother of Sam*, who has been for a year the foster child of the Bigelows, without complaint but without enthusiasm. In secret, he has been attending a fanatic religious group called the Steemers, absorbing their hysterical intolerance while pretending to go to soccer or band practices. It is not quite clear whether he has been unaware of his mother's alcoholism, as Sam thinks, or knows about it, as the Bigelows suspect, but he condemns her violently when he sees her drunk. Whether the decent Bigelows, who have been afraid to be assertive for fear of losing their chance at adoption in a society where children are rare, will be able to woo him back to a normal childhood and away from the hate-filled Steemer attitudes is an open question. It is clear, however, that Sam's efforts to control Ollie have been futile and that under the good-mannered, apparently placid facade is a very disturbed boy.

THE ONE WHO CAME BACK (Mazzio*, Joann, Houghton Mifflin, 1992), mystery novel of the disappearance of one of two hikers in the Sandia Mountains near Albuquerque, New Mexico, in the early 1990s. Steady, orderly Alex Grant, red-haired Anglo, and excitable Eddie Chavez, Mexican-American, both fifteen, are friends in the run-down trailer court where they live and have skipped school to hike and pan for gold in the mountains. Together they fantasize about what they will do with their riches: Alex will buy a new car for his mother, Boots*, with whom he has recently come to live, and move Mom and Pop, his grandparents, out of the retirement center to some place where he can again live with them; Eddie will buy a house for his large family so that his mother can kick out Paco Rodriguez, his drunken and abusive stepfather, and hire a good lawyer to get his older brother, Johnny, out of prison. Bruised from Paco's fists, Eddie has stolen his handgun, fearing that the man may start shooting in his next rage. As the November afternoon cools, Alex wants to start home, but Eddie announces that he is going to hide, leaps off in a shower of golden leaves, and is gone. Patient Alex searches for a while until, with growing annoyance, he decides Eddie has run ahead and will ambush him on the trail. When he gets to the place where they hid their bikes and Eddie's is gone, he rides home disgusted; when he finds that Eddie has not come home, he becomes afraid and packs a sleeping bag and some supplies and heads back toward the mountains in the dark. Picked up by the police, Alex is at first relieved, but they refuse to look for Eddie and are suspicious of his story, suggesting that he is helping his friend run away from home. His nightmare deepens when the police, the school counselor, and the Chavez family appear to think he may have killed Eddie. When a bully taunts him and makes anti-Hispanic slurs, Alex gets in a fight in the cafeteria, then walks out of school and home rather than wait in the counselor's office as directed. The only ones who seem to understand his misery are Candy* Arellano, a crippled boy, and Gwen Martens, a schoolmate who takes his story seriously. On Thanksgiving Day, sure now that Eddie must be dead and feeling the need for some sort of farewell ritual, Alex goes to the mountains and makes a cross. Gwen follows him and reads a poem she has brought, Robert Frost's "Nothing Gold Can Stay." Although she asks him to eat Thanksgiving dinner with her and her mother, Alex insists on staying alone. At first he takes out Paco's gun, methodically loads it, and lays out his sleeping bag neatly so searchers can find his body easily. Then he thinks about his grandfather and about Candy, who wants to live despite a broken body, and impulsively leaps up to throw the gun away. Realizing that it might be found by children at the campsite, he runs along the trail to a scree slide, where he heaves the gun away, then loses his footing on the treacherous stones and slides among the bounding rocks down the steep slope. Bruised but not seriously injured, he sits up and sees a hand, which he recognizes as Eddie's, sticking out of the scree. Although the recovery of the body shows there was no foul play and seems to exonerate him, Alex realizes that he will always live with his grief over Eddie's death. The novel concentrates not on the mystery of what has happened to Eddie but on Alex's problems, his inability to convince the police and the Chavez family, his guilt at not having insisted that Eddie go home with him instead of hiding, his loneliness, and his desire to live away from people in the mountains. The anti-Mexican prejudice of the area is shown but not dwelt on. Poe Nominee.

O.P. (*Life's a Funny Proposition, Horatio**), Benjamin Tuckerman, tall, bony, white-haired, white-bearded, dignified grandfather of Horatio Tuckerman, father of Joshua Tuckerman, Horatio's deceased father, and father-in-law of Evie* Berg, Horatio's mother. Three months before the novel starts, O.P. came to live with Horatio and his mother because he suffered a heart attack, had to have a pacemaker installed, and could no longer live by himself. Once a university teacher of Shakespeare in London, England, he often quotes the bard or some other famous poet. Both Horatio and Evie are protective of him, but he has a strength of body and mind that belie his fragile appearance. O.P. understands the need for facing the loss of Joshua and the importance of sharing their grief by honoring Joshua's memory.

ORIN DOWNARD (*Nekomah Creek**), obnoxious, bully son of a macho logger and Robby Hummer's classmate in Nekomah Creek School, where he gets away repeatedly with antisocial behavior, to such an extent that the kids think he must be the cousin of their teacher, Mrs. Perkins. Orin berates and belittles his class-mates whenever he can and Robby's dad at every turn. When Elvis Downard, Orin's dad, speaks to the class about his job, the children are impressed with his toughness, and Robby feels embarrassed about comparing his dad unfavor-ably with Mr. Downard. Later, when Robby and Mr. Hummer visit Mr. Down-ard after his logging accident, Robby feels sorry for the man, lying there so weak and downspirited. Robby also gets another view of Orin's life, since Mr. Downard is rude to the children and Mrs. Downard. Orin also revises his opinion of Mr. Hummer, when he sees how easily this man he thought wimpish can split wood. The Downards and the Hummers are obvious foils.

OSBORNE, MARY POPE (1949–   ), born in Fort Sill, Oklahoma, the daugh-ter of an army colonel; versatile writer of some twenty books of fiction, biog-raphy, and oral tradition for children and young adults. After taking her B.A. at the University of North Carolina at Chapel Hill, she held jobs as a medical assistant, travel agent, and editor before becoming a professional writer. She married actor and writer Will Osborne and settled in New York City and Penn-sylvania. Her first four books were well-received novels for teenagers, that ad-dress the concerns and conflicts typical of the age, among them the somewhat autobiographical *Run, Run as Fast as You Can* (Dial, 1982), about a girl in a military family who move to the South, and *Best Wishes, Joe Brady* (Dial, 1984), about a North Carolina girl who falls in love with an actor. Following these came easy-to-reads *Mo to the Rescue* (Dial, 1986) and its sequel, about a good-natured sheriff and his friends; several books of retellings, including *Jason and the Argonauts* (Scholastic, 1987) and *The Deadly Power of Medusa* (Scholastic, 1988), both written with her husband, *Favorite Greek Myths* (Scholastic, 1989), a Book-of-the-Month Club selection, *American Tall Tales* (Knopf, 1990), and *Mermaid Tales from Around the World* (Scholastic, 1992); middle grade biog-raphies of such figures as George Washington and Benjamin Franklin; and sto-ries for such picture books as *A Visit to Sleep's House* (Knopf, 1989) and *Moonhorse* (Knopf, 1990), both bedtime books for the very young. She has also published fast-paced, lighthearted, well-plotted, middle grade mysteries set in a community of talking insects and starring ⌐herlock Holmes spider who solves tough cases with aplomb: *Spider Kane and the Mystery Under the May-Apple*

(Knopf, 1992) and its sequel, *Spider Kane and the Mystery at Jumbo Night Crawler's** (Knopf, 1993). The latter, nominated for the Edgar Allan Poe Award, follows the unflappable spider as he solves the mystery of his friends' strange disappearances and cracks a case involving a robbery.

OTHER BELLS FOR US TO RING (Cormier*, Robert, illus. Deborah Kogan Ray, Delacorte, 1990), historical novel set during World War II in Monument, Massachusetts, telling of the friendship of two eleven-year-old girls and involving questions of religion and the possibility of miracles. In the Frenchtown section of the city, Darcy Webster, the narrator, being non-French and a Unitarian, is an outsider, a position she is used to since her father's many moves have prevented her from making friends. Then she meets Kathleen Mary O'Hara, also an outsider, an Irish Catholic among French. Another thing the girls have in common is that their fathers are alcoholics, although Darcy's has not taken a drink since she was born, while Mr. O'Hara goes on wild drunks during which he frequently beats his wife and children. Kathleen Mary's energy and imagination sweep Darcy along into various adventures, and her positive, if not always accurate, information about Catholic doctrines and practices opens a new world of possibility and worry to her. Kathleen Mary leads Darcy through a labyrinth of hedges around St. Jude's convent to spy on ancient Sister Angela, whom people believe is a saint and a healer. Darcy is disappointed that a crippled child, brought by her mother, is not instantly cured. When Kathleen Mary sprinkles her with holy water and announces that she is now a Catholic, Darcy is troubled, not sure whether she is now required to abstain from meat on Fridays and go to confession once a week. Her worries are focused on her father, who has been sent overseas and is reported missing. Then the O'Hara family disappears after a drunken rampage. As Darcy waits in vain for some word from Kathleen Mary or about her father, she witnesses the suicide jump from a third story by a young woman she earlier saw seeking help from Sister Angela, and she loses faith that prayer or belief can save her father. Then she comes upon the child who was crippled and learns that the mother credits her sudden recovery to a miracle from God, caused by the intercession of Sister Angela. Darcy goes back through the hedges, finds Sister Angela alone in the garden, and discusses belief with her, and miracles, about which the aging nun says there are many, every day, if you only look; together they pray for Darcy's father. The old nun dies three days later, but Darcy's father is found, reported safe on the day they prayed for him. Just before Christmas, Kathleen Mary's fifteen-year-old brother, who has lied about his age and is about to be sent overseas, comes to tell Darcy that his sister was killed, hit by a car shortly after they moved away as she was running from their father's abusive rage. Just how much a reader is expected to share Darcy's belief in the miracle of her father's safety and what to make of God's part in Kathleen Mary's untimely death are not clear. Although there are some good scenes of flamboyant, red-haired Kathleen Mary leading cautious Darcy, who has straight dark hair and wears glasses, into impulsive activities and Darcy's naive confusion about religion is amusing, the story as a whole seems unfocused and the point of view of a young girl not as convincing as that of characters in Cormier's novels about teenagers. Fanfare.

OTHERS SEE US (Sleator*, William, Dutton, 1993), science-fiction novel of mind-reading abilities set in a New England coastal vacation area in the late twentieth century. The narrator, Jared, 16, comes with his parents late to the family summer compound where Grandma* has the big house, and the family of each of her offspring has a cottage. He longs to see his cousin Annelise*, 16, from San Diego, with whom he is secretly in love. He hides his journal, in which he records his private thoughts and longings, in a spot he discovered under a loose board in the closet, and then he takes a ritual bike ride around the area, tasting the freedom of the place and anticipating seeing his favorite cousin. This time, however, the brakes on his old bike fail on a hill, and he is catapulted into the toxic swamp that borders the road. After he has cleaned up and joined the family on the beach, he begins to hear strange voices making catty or critical remarks about the relatives quite contrary to the words they are actually saying, and he gradually realizes he is reading the thoughts of the others. That night he discovers that his journal is gone. In the morning he learns from Annelise that her journal is also missing, and from reading her mind, in which she is reviewing what she has written there, that it is filled with her true mean and vindictive feelings and nasty comments about her relatives. By clever deduction and elimination of others, Jared realizes that it must be Grandma who has their journals, since she earlier had fallen into the toxic swamp and seems to be cleverly shielding her mind from his probing. Confronted, Grandma admits to both of them that she has their journals and bargains with them: if they go at night and bring her a half-gallon of water from the swamp, which has just that day been protected by a high security fence, she will return their journals. Realizing that Annelise will be even more dangerous if she can read minds, Jared tries to control their nighttime adventure so that he will take all the risk of touching the water, but Annelise is suspicious, tries to wrestle the jug from him, and on the slippery slope loses her footing and plunges into the swamp. Now admitting to Grandma that he can read minds, Jared tries to find out why she would deliberately give Annelise that advantage, and although she will not tell him directly, he begins to see that his cousin's weakness is her overriding desire for admiration and approval and that if she can really know what people think, she may break under the strain. At the beach, Annelise, supposedly watching the youngest cousin, Amy, allows her to run directly into the water, then jumps in, pulls the child out, gives her mouth-to-mouth resuscitation, "saves" her, and blames another cousin for not watching as she says she has asked him to. In the midst of all the grateful family, Grandma appears, says she has seen the whole thing through her telescope, and that Annelise deliberately watched while Amy ran into the sea. Teaming up with Lindie*, 17, the only relative who is not under Annelise's spell, Jared thinks he has the upper hand, but he has already probed Lindie's mind and discovered that she cheated on the SAT exams to get into Harvard and is terrified that it will be discovered; of course Annelise is able to learn the truth. Having been plied by Grandma with beer laced with swamp water, both Jared and Lindie soon have greater powers than Annelise. In a desperate attempt to control, Annelise tries to tell the assembled family about some shady activities Grandma has been engaged in, but the old lady has an ace in the hole: photocopied entries from Annelise's diary that she hands out to family members. Action is fast and inventive, and the mind probing is convincing, although the family members are so secretly antagonistic that one wonders why they spend vacations together. At the end it is suggested that Annelise will be sent to an institution for disturbed teenagers, but there are a number of questions left unanswered. How long will the effects of the swamp water last? Will other after-effects from the toxic substance develop? If it is toxic, why are they not physically ill? Will Grandma get away with what amounts to grand larceny and blackmail? Will Lindie, who has a guilty conscience about the cheating, simply forget it and go happily to Harvard? In the thriller form, which depends on a neat wrap-up, so many dangling ends leave a reader unsatisfied. Fanfare.

OUR SIXTH-GRADE SUGAR BABIES (Bunting*, Eve, HarperCollins, 1990), amusing novel about a classroom experiment designed to teach responsibility, set in Pasadena, California, evidently about the time of publication. Students in Mrs. Oda's sixth-grade class have varied reactions to the assignment to carry with them, for one week, a five-pound bag of sugar, treating it as if it were a child, but Vicki Charlip, 11, welcomes the opportunity to prove to her mother that she is capable of caring for her four-year-old half-sister, Keiko, as her father has proposed while he and his wife attend an art workshop. Vicki encases her "sugar baby" in plastic covered by an old t-shirt, paints on a face (two, since the first is unsuccessful and is subsequently hidden on the back) and curly red hair, and dresses it in old doll clothes. Her best friend, Ellie, makes hers into a junior superman, since in the lottery she drew a boy as her pretend infant, and Horrible Harry Hogan, who sits behind Vicki, makes his into Dracula. Difficulties arise when a new family moves in across the street and both Ellie and Vicki plan ways to meet and impress the seventh-grade son, Sam Shub, whom they secretly call Thunk, short for *terrific* and *hunk*. After a series of embarrassing blunders, Vicki is delighted when Thunk asks her to show him the way to the public library. She hides her sugar baby behind some bushes and asks old Mr. Ambrose, who stands at his front walk waving and smiling and commenting on the weather but otherwise appears senile, to look after it. When she returns, deflated because Thunk was meeting Cynthia Sanders at the library, the sugar baby is gone. Vicki hunts frantically and berates Mr. Ambrose for not watching her charge. Although she apologizes for her accusations, she knows he is upset. In an attempt to hide her own irresponsibility, she buys another bag of sugar and paints a new face, realizing that both her mother and Ellie will know what she has done if they examine the sugar baby and find the hidden face missing. Later Ophelia, Mr. Ambrose's adult daughter, comes to say she cannot find her father. All the neighbors, including Thunk, join in the search, and the police question Vicki. Consumed by guilt, she finally confesses to her mother and Ophelia, who realizes that her father must be in the big department store where he once lost her when she was a toddler. The three arrive there just as the store is closing, and Vicki discovers the old man in the toy department, evidently where he found young Ophelia years ago. At home they find the original sugar baby snug in her basket on their own patio, where Mr. Ambrose carefully put her for safekeeping. Vicki's mother arranges that Keiko fly to stay with them for the two weeks, so that Vicki can babysit her with some adult backup. At school, Vicki confesses her neglect and planned deception and is praised for her honesty. Horrible Harry asks her to a movie. The contrived plot is lightened by a good deal of humor, although the sixth-grade girls' squealing and agonizing about their hair and ears is tiring, and their decision at the end that seventh-grade boys are out of their league is not convincing. The strongest element is the sympathetic portrait of Mr. Ambrose, whose near memory is gone, but whose remembrance of things long past is clear and whose genial personality has made him a neighborhood favorite. SLJ.

OUT OF NOWHERE (Sebestyen*, Ouida, Orchard, 1994), boy's growing-up and dog novel, about an unconventional family thrown together by circumstances somewhere in the southwestern mountains in contemporary times. When the latest boyfriend of his mother, Vernie*, refuses to take him further, Harley Nunn, 13, grabs his duffle bag and walks off into the Arizona desert campground, observed only by an older woman with a station wagon. Named for a motorcycle and a clerk's error (''none'' became Nunn in the space for his father's name), Harley is used to being part of his mother's con schemes or to being deserted temporarily when she finds a new man or is high on drugs, but this time he is definitely on his own. Before the night, which he spends on the floor of an outhouse, he is joined by an abandoned dog, a part pitbull, whom he names Ish (Ishmael), and in the morning, soon after they start walking along the road, they are picked up by the older woman, May Woods. Her own life has just been devastated by the sudden departure of her husband, a church musical director, to join a woman and children he has kept secret for forty years; left with no home and little money, May is heading across the mountains to a house she lived in as a child. Although she is reluctant to complicate her effort to live independently, May takes Harley and Ish with her. At the house they discover that the tenant, Bill Bascomb, is in the hospital after a fall and has not vacated the premises as directed. In fact, he has never discarded anything; both house and shed are stuffed with a miscellaneous assortment of things. They also discover Singer*, 18, a girl of unfailing cheerfulness who has come to help Bill out. When Bill sneaks home from the hospital, a battle of wills begins. May directs Harley and Singer in an intensive cleanup, starting with the kitchen. Bill stays put. It is Ish who finally brings all four of them together. Partly because Harley has never been responsible for anything, he neglects the dog, and it is hit by Bill's truck and injured. Bill takes it to the animal clinic where they suggest it be put down or have its leg amputated. At first Harley tells Bill to have Ish put down but immediately regrets it and plans to get a job to pay for the amputation. Bill hires him to clean out the house and shed and help sell his vast accumulation of junk, giving half the profits to pay for Ish's operation. To Harley's dismay, Singer decides it is time for her to move on. In the end, Bill is moving to the shed, Harvey is taking over his room, Ish is learning to walk with three legs, and May has acquired a son, a dog, a newly adopted cat, and a hired man living on the property, all full of love for each other. Despite their quirks, Harley, May, and Bill are appealing characters, each with a chip on the shoulder but genuinely capable of love. Singer is less believable, almost a fairy-godmother type, appearing and disappearing conveniently for the story line. The roles played by Ish and Bill's old, lovable mongrel, Coo, are catalysts for the changes in the human relationships. SLJ.

OWL IN LOVE (Kindl*, Patrice, Houghton Mifflin, 1993), strange fantasy set in the late twentieth century in a New York town about a wereowl, a girl who seems a normal, though unusual, human in the daytime but turns into an owl at night. Although her parents are only simple witches, who make a meager living selling love potions, telling fortunes, casting minor spells, and performing herbal healing, Owl Tycho, 14, is a shapeshifter, able to transform, pretty much at will, into a barn owl to hunt for rodents to feed herself and to supplement her parents' mostly vegetarian diet. At school she is a loner, considered odd because she never brings lunch, has a grayish complexion, and seldom speaks, but only her science class lab partner, plump, assertive Dawn* Mitchell, guesses that she has a crush on their teacher, fortyish Mr. Lindstrom. Owl's obsession turns into an almost nightly vigil in the tree outside his suburban house where he lives alone, his wife having left him and their son, Dawn reports, going to some kind of boarding school. In the nearby woods Owl discovers a strange, clumsy barn owl whose inability to catch mice puzzles her, and also a sinister boy who seems to be camping out in the bitter cold with a pup tent and other gear he took from Mr. Lindstrom's house. The behavior of the owl baffles her. When it flies directly at her, she slashes its breast, and it falls into some bushes, where the boy appears almost immediately. Her suspicions aroused, Owl tries dropping mice and voles to him, food he devours ravenously, and she realizes that he too is a wereowl, though a remarkably unskillful one. When Dawn, who lives near Mr. Lindstrom, reports that police are hunting an escaped convict in their neighborhood, Owl persuades her to help move the boy, whom Owl now calls Houle, rhyming the name with hers, and who is feverish from his infected wounds, to the Mitchell garage. She discovers that Dawn is helping her only because, having noted a strong resemblance, she believes that Houle must be Owl's brother. After a few days the complications so add to Owl's stress that she cannot transform from owl back to human. Her parents, who are naively kind and try to be understanding, are worried; her father thinks he may be at fault, having given Dawn, when she came seeking a love potion, a spell to keep kid gloves white, having misunderstood her request. Now viewing Dawn as a possible rival for Mr. Lindstrom's affections and finding her bringing the teacher to see the boy in the garage, Owl flies ahead to warn him. The story culminates in a scene that reveals that Houle is really Mr. Lindstrom's son, sent to a mental institution some years before, that Dawn has no romantic interest in Mr. Lindstrom but is trying to save the boy, and that Owl and Houle, who are very distant cousins, are obviously meant to mate for life, as owls do. Since Houle is only fifteen and Owl, now again in human form, even younger, they agree to live with their own families until they are old enough for marriage, giving Owl plenty of time to teach Houle the skills he needs. Most of the action is told in the first person by Owl, with brief passages of Houle in the mental institution. These are confusing, since they are in the third person and set in the past, although in Owl's narrative he is already in the woods, yet there is nothing to indicate that they are flashbacks. The most convincing part of the story is Owl's description of her life as a bird: the joys of flight, the beauty of the woods at night, the luscious delicacies in her diet of live mice, rats, and grasshoppers. ALA.

THE OXBOY (Mazer*, Anne, Knopf, 1993), brief, legend-like fantasy set in an imaginary world much like preindustrial England except that it has a history of animal-human matings, from which has grown a rabid hatred of mixed-blood offspring who are tracked down and killed by the dreaded blue hunters. For his first five years the unnamed narrator has lived happily with his lovely human mother and his father, a mixed-blood ox, keeping mostly apart from other people and pretending that she is a widow and her husband is a beast of burden. Then, betrayed by a beggar to whom the mother has been kind, they are sought out by the hunters, mostly local men with their faces painted blue. The ox father escapes to the forest. The boy and his mother flee to a distant town where she works as a seamstress and eventually marries again. The only contact with the real father comes when she finds the paper for her son, the silvery document that traces ''pure'' ancestry and is necessary for his enrollment in school, left under the clothes of her laundry basket, with hoof prints nearby. From the document the boy learns that his father's name is Albertus. Although the oxboy is not very good at schoolwork, he is strong and does not look too unlike the other children, so he is tolerated, if not fully accepted. For a short time he even has a friend, who admits that he would like to help the part-animals being destroyed. He falls in love with a pretty schoolmate, Suseen, and takes the blame when she breaks a window in the house of Old Xerry, the carpetmaker. The oxboy works for Old Xerry for a month to pay for the window, but when the other children tease Suseen, she turns against him. Later the oxboy sees the old carpetmaker hide a deer-man under the rugs in his cart, pretending to the hunters that he has seen nothing. Constantly drawn away from people to the peace and freedom of the forest, the oxboy one day saves a mixed-blood otter from a talking eagle, hides when hunters kill the eagle, and takes the otter home, keeping him secretly in his attic room, and occasionally smuggling him out past his stepfather to play in the stream. This is their downfall; one day they are discovered by a group of hunters that includes his stepfather. The otter is shot, and the boy is arrested. After a year in prison he is released to the hostile town. For the sake of his mother, his stepfather lets him stay briefly, then turns him out. His mother packs him a knapsack of food and early in the morning walks with him to the edge of the fields; from the shadows a great brown ox emerges. Recognizing his father, the boy climbs on his back and, as the sun rises, they plunge into the forest. Although simply told and printed in large type with well-leaded lines, the book does not seem intended for very young readers. Parallels to Nazi Germany and other repressive societies dedicated to ethnic purity are obvious, especially in the songs and ritual sayings of the people, always ending in ''Pure blood of the human race.'' The restraint of the telling, however, and the mythlike tone keep it from seeming didactic. Unlike stories from the oral tradition, it uses strong, sensory description, in particular that of the ox father and the otter, and the character development goes beyond types. ALA.

P

PADDIE MCCARTY (*Harper & Moon**), Patrick McCarty, sign painter father of Moon*, the almost feral youth who is friends with Harper McDowell and is accused of murdering Olinger*, the old mountain man. Paddie disparages Moon, telling Harper that his son "can't talk straight. . . . And don't know what he's sayin', either, half the time. He ain't quick, like ye." Paddie apparently thinks his son is mentally disabled. After Paddie and his wife, Tessie, are found dead, their truck having plunged over a cliff, both of them probably drunk, Harper remembers "Paddie's little kindnesses—the candy corn, the sly talk, the clever tricks," and wants to have that Paddie back and to forget the Paddie who was cruel to his son. Later Harper learns that Paddie and Tessie abused Moon from infancy. Paddie is an interesting, deftly drawn figure, a foil for Harper's kind and supportive father.

PALOMA HERNANDEZ RAMIREZ (*Grab Hands and Run**), common-law wife of Jacinto Ramirez, well-known Salvadoran political activist, and mother of Felipe* and Romy*, the children with whom she flees for safety to Canada. She is a courageous, decisive, well-organized woman, who manages to extend their money and find help along the way. Attractive, she sometimes uses her good looks to their advantage, but often she elicits unwanted attention from the soldiers they encounter. At home she worked as a maid, in the detention center she helps in the kitchen, and in Wisconsin, she studies to become a mechanic, at which occupation Felipe says she shows great aptitude.

PAMELA TUCKER (*Learning by Heart**), thirteen-year-old daughter of the "white trash" (Pamela's own term) family that move into and live briefly in the house next door to Rachel's. Isabella* Harris observes that Pamela has a gift for playing the piano. The girl comes regularly to practice on Rachel's instrument, easily picking up the tunes that Rachel's fumbling fingers mutilate and playing them with improvisational skill. It is not until Pamela moves away that Rachel realizes that Pamela has become her closest friend. Pamela is one of the most interesting figures in the book, although she is overdrawn in her melodramatic defensiveness, for example, being described as having "snake eyes" and spitting out her words.

PAPA (*Baby**), John, Larkin's father and Mama's* husband. The editor of the island's only paper, Papa is a complex combination of seriousness and levity, realism and romanticism. He loves to tap dance and finds it relaxing after work, refuses to speak of his infant son's death, and like Mama, has left Larkin to cope with her grief by herself. On the other hand, he fears for the effect Sophie, the child abandoned at their house, may have on Mama if Mama refuses to let go of Sophie as she has refused to let go of their dead baby boy. Papa dances with Sophie and plays the rock, paper, and scissors game with her. It is Papa more than anyone else whom Sophie carries in her memories.

PAPA LEE (*The Star Fisher**), Chinese-born father in the Lee family. In China, Papa studied to pass the government exams in the classics and poetry. When, after the 1911 revolution, the exams were ended, there was no work for him. He and Mama* emigrated to the United States, first to Lima, Ohio, where they started a laundry, and then to Clarksburg, West Virginia, where they set up another laundry. Papa loves to read books of philosophy, writes poetry, and is fun loving, imaginative, and a perpetual optimist. A very hard worker, he organizes the new laundry in a flash, certain that customers will soon be parading through the door. He is very disappointed when they do not come but remains cheerful. He encourages the children to try to understand their fearful, proud mother, and she in turn urges them to understand their impractical, proud father.

PAPA PEYTON (*Dixie Storms**), a widower, father of Dutch and Flood*, grandfather of Bodean*, brother of Aunt Macy, uncle of Norma*. Papa is wise in giving advice to Dutch but is also stubborn, controlling, and hard on people, though apparently less so as the years have gone by. Papa insisted on buying a cheap tractor, instead of the John Deere tractor Flood wanted, but since the tobacco is doing so poorly because of the drought, they cannot make the payments anyway. Papa is determined to hang on to the farm, however, since that has come down in the family and family is extremely important to Peytons. It turns out that Flood's money is the means for doing that. Years ago, Papa and his brother, Eugene, Norma's father, fell out because Eugene, who received a deferment during the Korean War in which Papa served, took off for the city and a good-paying job instead of taking care of the farm. All this time the brothers have barely communicated. In the interests of family, Papa relents and swallows his pride to take Norma in until she can go to live with her mother after the Eugene Peytons are divorced. Like the other main characters, Papa is roundly drawn, with some contradictory facets that give credibility. Dutch loves and respects him very much, and, although he is firm with her, he is also consistently kind and understanding.

PATERSON, KATHERINE (WOMELDORF) (1932–   ), born in Tsing-Tsiang, China; missionary, teacher, novelist, twice winner of the Newbery Award and holder of many other prestigious recognitions. Her first three books are set in ancient Japan: *Sign of the Chrysanthemum* (Crowell, 1973), *Of Nightingales That Weep** (Crowell, 1974), and *The Master Puppeteer* (Crowell, 1976), a National Book Award Winner. *Of Nightingales That Weep* won further acclaim twenty years after its publication when it was named winner of the Phoenix Award of The Children's Literature Association, given for books of lasting literary merit. Her two Newbery Award books, *Bridge to Terebithia* (Crowell, 1977) and *Jacob Have I Loved* (Crowell, 1980), both have twentieth-century settings, as have *Come Sing, Jimmy Jo* (Dutton, 1985), *Park's Quest* (Dutton, 1988), and *Flip-Flop Girl** (Dutton, 1994). She returned to historical fiction, however, in *Lyddie** (Dutton, 1991), about a girl who works in the Lowell textile mills in the early nineteenth century. The daughter of a clergyman, Paterson spent her childhood in both China and the United States, attended King College, received her M.A. degree from Presbyterian School of Christian Education in Richmond, Virginia, and her M.R.E. degree from Union Theological Seminary in New York, and has served as a missionary in Japan. For earlier biographical information and title entries, see *Dictionary, 1960–1984* [*Bridge to Terebithia; The Great Gilly Hopkins; Jacob Have I Loved; The Master Puppeteer; Of Nightingales That Weep*] and *Dictionary, 1985–1989* [*Come Sing, Jimmy Jo; Park's Quest*].

PATRICK (*Alice in Rapture, Sort Of**; *Reluctantly Alice**; *All But Alice**), special friend of Alice McKinley in seventh grade, a category that implies no romantic interest, after having been her boyfriend in sixth grade. To Alice's surprise, he brings her a large box of Whitman's chocolates on Valentine's Day. Although he sits around hinting, Alice does not open it and offer him a piece because she has just eaten two brownies. When Alice's brother, Lester, points out that this was a faux pas, she is appalled, but Lester supplies a solution: the next day she calls Patrick, says the box was so beautiful that she could not bear to open it, but now she plans to do so and wants him to have the first piece. He arrives in record time, samples the sampler, and even takes a handful home. Some days later Patrick vomits on the school bus, and the other boys plan a trick when he returns to school. They prompt all the girls to scream and shrink away when Patrick boards the bus, direct Alice to pretend to barf in the aisle, and even have a bag of fake vomit to spill on the floor. Only Alice refuses to go along with the mean joke, and she saves Patrick from humiliation. In return, he kisses her twice, right there on the bus in front of all the other kids.

PATRON, SUSAN (1948–   ), born in San Gabriel, California; author of light-hearted stories of family life published in picture-book and novel form, for which she draws on her own remembered feelings for inspiration. Her first three books—*Burgoo Stew* (Orchard, 1991), *Five Bad Boys, Billy Que, and the Dust-*

dobbin (Orchard, 1992), and *Bobbin Dustdobbin* (Orchard, 1993)—are picture-story books connected by the same characters: old Billy Que, some stubborn boys, who are his friends, and two "dustdobbins" named Hob and Bobbin, who live in the dust under Billy Que's bed. *Dark Cloud Strong Breeze* (Orchard, 1994), another picture book, is a rhythmic, circular tale for very young children. Recognized by the American Library Association and *School Library Journal, Maybe Yes, Maybe No, Maybe Maybe** (Orchard, 1993) represents a stride in a new direction, being a short, realistic novel about the problems of being the middle of three daughters. The humor and upbeat tone recall the Henry Huggins books by Beverly Cleary. After receiving her B.A. from Pitzer College and her M.L.S. from Immaculate Heart College, School of Library Science, Patron took a position with the Los Angeles Public Library, where she became senior children's librarian. She has served on the Caldecott Committee of the American Library Association, taught children's literature, and served on the board of advisers of public television's *Storytime.* She has contributed to *Expectations,* an anthology in braille for children, and has reviewed for such publications as *School Library Journal* and *Five Owls.* Married, she lives in Los Angeles.

PAULSEN, GARY (1939–   ), born in Minneapolis, Minnesota; educated at Bemidji State University in Minnesota and the University of Colorado at Boulder; prolific author of outdoor nonfiction and of novels with nature settings for adults and children. His contemporary survival novel, *The Voyage of the "Frog"** (Orchard, 1989), which takes place on stormy seas off the California coast, was both an American Library Association and *School Library Journal* choice for their best books lists. *The Winter Room** (Orchard, 1989), an episodic period novel of family and farm life set in northern Minnesota, was both an American Library Association choice and a Newbery Honor Book. *The Cookcamp** (Orchard, 1991), a quiet period story set among the lumbermen of northern Minnesota, was a *School Library Journal* selection. *Nightjohn** (Delacorte, 1993) is a starkly dramatic slave story and an American Library Association pick. For earlier biographical information and title entries, see *Dictionary, 1985–1989* [*Dogsong; Hatchet*].

PECK, RICHARD (1934–   ), born in Decatur, Illinois; educated at Exeter University in England and at DePauw and Southern Illinois universities; popular and much-honored writer of some two dozen books for young adults in several genres. His *Bel-Air Bambi and the Mall Rats** (Delacorte, 1993) is a facetious satire on contemporary relationships between the generations. It was chosen by *School Library Journal* as a best book. Peck, who lives in New York City, has received many awards for his writings, including the 1990 National Council of Teachers of English/ALAN Award. For earlier biographical information and title entries, see *Dictionary, 1960–1984* [*Are You in the House Alone?; Dreamland Lake*] and *Dictionary, 1985–1989* [*Blossom Culp and the Sleep of Death; Princess Ashley; Remembering the Good Times*].

THE PENNYWHISTLE TREE (Smith*, Doris Buchanan, Putnam, 1991), brief, bittersweet novel of friendship, set in Hanover, Georgia, in the period of its publication. Jonathan Douglas, 11, and his friends, Craig, Alex, and Benjy, have long claimed the huge live oak in the Douglas front yard as their own hangout, with a rope on which they can swing to the porch banister and back, and a hiding place where Jonathan keeps his pennywhistle wrapped in plastic. When a new family moves in down the block on the other side of Craig's beautifully kept yard, trouble moves in with them. There seem to be numerous little girls, with an older brother, a sixth grader like Jonathan and his friends, and a little brother, a toddler. The new family, named George, travels in a beat-up old school bus with the top cut off, which the neighbors consider an eyesore, and Mrs. George, clearly pregnant, comes every day to use the Douglas telephone. In the days that follow, the George children take over the neighborhood, playing mainly in the Douglas yard where the older brother, Sanders, is protective to his siblings and belligerent to outsiders. They seem to have no toys of their own but freely use whatever they find in the yard. Jonathan's father, a mild-tempered writer, tries to ignore them, but his mother, who restores Victorian houses professionally, is thoroughly annoyed. Jonathan feels beleaguered, almost a prisoner in his own house, since he does not want to join them or to fight. A musical boy, he is delighted when the flute he has ordered arrives, but the occasion is almost spoiled by the presence of Sanders at the music store and the great longing in his voice when he says he wishes he had one, too. To salve his conscience, Jonathan digs out his old three-wheeler from the storeroom to give the George children. They are delighted but still leave the toy in the Douglas yard and play there. When school starts, Sanders is rude and uncooperative, refusing to pass out schedules and hamming instead of reading when it is his turn to read aloud. Mrs. George loses her baby, and that loss, which mirrors the series of stillbirths Mrs. Douglas had after Jonathan, changes the relationship of the two boys. The truth comes out: the toys that Mrs. Douglas has insisted that the George children take home are sold by their father at the flea market. Sanders confesses that he cannot read and begs Jonathan to teach him. Jonathan gives Sanders his pennywhistle and, despite knowing that his old friends will scorn his new friendship, plans to teach Sanders to read. Early in the morning, he is startled when Sanders appears and announces that they are moving, immediately. Jonathan ruffles through his books, finding some easy, funny ones, and thrusts them at Sanders, insisting that he can learn to read by practicing on them. At first reluctant, Sanders accepts them and scrabbles up the live oak for the pennywhistle, which he hides with the books under his shirt, while his father bellows for him to come help with the move. The story is contrived, with the double coincidences of both Jonathan and Sanders loving music and both having siblings die at birth. Sanders is too adept at the whistle and too solicitous of his siblings to be quite believable, but his toughness moderates the sentimentality of the story, and the upper-middle-class neighborhood's reaction to the poor white family in their midst is on target, particularly the dilemma posed for well-meaning people like the Douglas parents. ALA; SLJ.

PETER NICHOLS (*Remember Me**), good-looking young man, once a class-mate of Shari Cooper, who dies in a motorcycle accident. He appears to Shari in the cemetery after her funeral and helps her adjust to her changed circumstances. Although sweet, kind, and often humorous, he seems unsteady in resolve. At the end, Shari learns that he feels guilty because he committed suicide by driving his motorcycle into a truck. He helps her uncover her murderer, and she helps him overcome his guilt by persuading him to face the dark shadow that pursues him. Because he killed himself, he has not had the opportunity to "go into the light," a particularly blissful afterlife state. He knows that Shari did not kill herself because he once observed her in that condition, although she herself was not aware of it. Hence he agrees to help her find her murderer.

PETEY TIMPKIN (*Scooter**), silent little boy, friend of Elana Rose Rosen. He lives in 2H in the Melon Hill apartment complex in which she lives, brings home her scooter after her accident, and becomes her shadow and adoring follower. Although everyone else thinks he is mute, including Elana's mother, who takes him to a specialist, he talks to Elana occasionally. His first words to her concern his precious sky-blue woolen hat: "This blue hat is magic." His home may be abusive; that situation is not explored because Elana's narrative is necessarily limited. His family life, however, seems dysfunctional. Petey is a favorite with all the children and is dearly loved by Mrs.* Rachel Greiner, his babysitter. Petey is an engaging, mysterious, pathetic little figure.

PHOENIX RISING (Hesse*, Karen, Holt, 1994), novel of the aftermath of a nuclear disaster, set in rural Vermont near North Haversham, presumably in the near future. On a marginal sheep farm, Nyle Sumner, 13, lives with her grandmother (her mother and her grandfather have died). Her father, unwilling to face his wife's death and the responsibility of a child, has left with no further communication. Although they are only a short distance from the nuclear plant at Cookshire where the leak occurred, prevailing winds blowing to the east have kept the contamination away from them, despite having destroyed Boston and much of the rest of New England. Nyle's one friend, Muncie Harris, is a dwarf whose parents, renters of a small house from Gran, are terrified that radiation will somehow damage her further. Nearby lives Ripley Powers, 15, a big redneck whose dog, Tyrus, often kills Gran's sheep. When Gran welcomes two evacuees from Cookshire, Mrs. Trent and her son, Ezra, 15, to live in the house, Nyle is at first annoyed and hesitant to go near the seriously ill boy, especially since they stay in the darkened back bedroom where Nyle's mother and grandfather both died. Reluctantly, she accepts the chore of sitting with Ezra while Mrs. Trent has supper, and since the boy does not speak and seldom moves, she starts reading aloud *Slake's Limbo* to pass the time. Gradually Ezra shows signs of listening and begins to talk, asking questions about sheep farming and the activities in the house, but refusing to have the heavy curtain pulled back from the window for fear of further radiation, which could make his condition much worse. Very slowly, through the fall and winter, he takes step after step toward recovery: standing by his bed, moving with canes, allowing the curtain to be pulled, accepting the puppy that Nyle and Gran give him, and finally going outside with Nyle. A competent farm girl, she teaches him to drive the truck and to load hay, to direct Caleb, their border collie, in moving the sheep from pasture to pasture, and to bring in stove wood. Since many people are afraid of anyone from the contaminated area, they keep the presence of the Trents secret from the neighbors, but the school principal sends home classwork for Ezra with Nyle, and Muncie, deeply hurt, suspects that something has happened to make Nyle too busy for her formerly frequent visits to the Harris home. Toward the end of winter, Ezra is well enough to start school, catching the bus with Nyle and with Muncie, who refuses to speak to them. Although Nyle is nervous, she has begun to love Ezra deeply and is delighted that he still seems to like her, even when other friends are available. As they walk up the hill one afternoon, with Muncie trailing behind, Ripley appears and taunts Ezra as he often has taunted Muncie. Suddenly fed up, Nyle attacks him. As he holds her at arm's length, Ezra rushes in to defend her. Ripley, furious because his dog Tyrus has died from eating contaminated meat, knocks Ezra down and relieves his anger by beating him viciously. Muncie swings her heavy backpack at Ripley's head and knocks him away. Although the girls, with Gran's help, get Ezra into the house, they cannot stop his bleeding, and he is soon in the hospital. It is April before Nyle is allowed to visit Ezra, who is near death. She is holding his hand as he dies. Although Nyle bitterly blames Ripley, Gran explains that Ezra had leukemia, so severe he would have died slowly anyway, and points out that it is up to Nyle to try alert people to the dangers of nuclear plants. Although the book focuses on the few people at the farm, broader ramifications are introduced by a visit to Nyle's aunt and uncle, who raised cattle at the edge of the contaminated zone and have to give up their farm and everything they own when all their stock and fields are radioactive, and the irony that Ezra's father, one of the first to die, was an official at the plant who believed in its safety. Unlike most other postnuclear novels which are set after a bomb attack, this one develops a picture of what actually could happen without war, and, most chilling, how the rest of the country, unaffected by the disaster, seems to forget it as people forgot Three Mile Island and seem to be forgetting Chernobyl. The few characters are all well developed, and life on the farm, essentially returned to early twentieth-century style, is evoked believably. SLJ.

PHOENIX RISING OR HOW TO SURVIVE YOUR LIFE (Grant*, Cynthia D., Atheneum, 1989), psychological problem novel set for about a year in an unnamed contemporary American city that describes a family's problems in accepting the death of the older daughter, Helen, 18. Ever since Helen was diagnosed with cancer when she was fourteen, the Castles have refused to admit that she might die, and when she does, at the end of her senior year, the family remains in varying degrees of denial. Mom turns to drink and feels she has been a failure as a mother (all too realistic reactions), and Dad plays a lot of golf and often argues with Lucas*, 20, a musician. They bicker frequently, and Lucas slams out of the house (also too realistic a situation). The narrator, Jessie, 17, is especially hard hit because she and Helen were very close and shared a room. At school, Jessie is the "resident comedian," but inside she hurts. Bad dreams trouble her, and she feels lonely and isolated and is sure no one can help, especially not Dr. Shubert, the psychiatrist who she feels must have "dated Freud" because she seems so old. Since she can use the money, Jessie takes over Helen's babysitting job but finds associating with Sara Rose and dealing with her naive questions very painful. She develops a distorted image of herself as too fat, although her parents worry about her thinness and coax her to eat. Eventually panic attacks drive her to voluntary seclusion in her room, which she refuses to leave and lets almost no one else enter. Earlier, in clearing out Helen's things, she encountered the diaries Helen assiduously kept and began to read them. Starting with chapter three, the novel alternates Jessie's narrative and excerpts from Helen's diaries from January to June of the year Helen died. The entries support Jessie's view of her sister as warm, affectionate, and talented. Helen is in love with life and with her boyfriend, Bloomfield*, and plans to go to junior college, teach, and write, having placed a poem and an article in school publications and begun a novel, *How to Survive Your Life*. Because she realizes life is short and must be made immediate, Helen forgives Bloomfield for running out when loose-tongued Bambi* Sue Bordtz blabs about the cancer and eagerly accepts his invitation to the graduation party. Near the end of her senior year, knowing that she will die soon but refusing to be cowed, she chooses to write on the phoenix for a paper on mythological creatures, attacking the subject from the bird's point of view and emphasizing the rebirth or ongoing life idea. Although Helen's diary gives Jessie new perspectives on Helen, life in general, herself, and her family, Jessie continues in seclusion, a mixture of conflicting emotions. She upbraids Bloomfield for dumping Helen and even contemplates suicide. Dr. Shubert says that she is punishing herself, idealizing Helen, and simply refusing to face facts. Lucas blows up at her over her attitude, and Bloomfield clowns around, even climbing a ladder to her room to urge her to come out. Jessie blames herself for not telling Helen she loved her, although she does finally admit that she knows that Helen knew, and accuses Lucas of not telling Helen he loved her, when, according to the diary, Helen asked. As if stabbed, he breaks down and weeps uncontrollably, and she weeps, too, venting her grief in such a catharsis that her next dream of Helen leaves her in peace. By March, going on a year after Helen's death, Jessie is still not able to go to school but is beginning to get bored at home. Lucas composes a song to Helen that is an emotional consolation to Jessie, and when Sara Rose asks Jessie (as she has done dozens of times before) to come out and play, this time Jessie responds with a happy yes. Like Helen, she has come to see that the life that one has is to be lived and that Helen will live on in their many memories of her. While some details about the progress of the disease appear in the diaries— for example, Helen's worrying about the effects of the chemotherapy and the frailness of her body as contrasted with her bloating stomach—the emphasis is on the family's grieving and inability to accept the death, and particularly on Jessie's painful coming to terms. By the end there are signs that the other members of the family are also healing. Both Jessie's story and Helen's diary are in present tense, bringing events into the reader's dimension, and giving a psychologically sound sense of the mourning process. The family's typicalness sets events in relief. Fat, obstreperous, promiscuous Bambi provides a good foil to the Castle girls, and Lucas and Bloomfield are convincing in their ways. While the contemporary idiom gives the characterizations credibility, it may soon date the book. Many amusing scenes tone down the seriousness of the subject and prevent sentimentality. SLJ.

PHULAN (*Shabanu**), older sister of Shabanu, betrothed to Hamir, and after his death, married to his younger brother, Murad, who had been Shabanu's intended. Although Shabanu sometimes thinks that Phulan is silly, simply too filled with romantic ideas, and generally lacking resourcefulness, she is also very proud of her beautiful sister. While Shabanu represents the independent woman who must yield to the demands of a patriarchal society, Phulan typifies the girl who accepts society's strictures and looks for ways to use them to her advantage. After Hamir's death, for example, Phulan pressures Shabanu to go along with the decision of their parents to give her to Murad and to marry Shabanu to a wealthy, middle-aged official who has spoken for her, because Phulan sees that the arrangement is beneficial to herself.

PIKE, CHRISTOPHER, born in Brooklyn, New York, and raised in Los Angeles, where he makes his home. He worked at such various jobs as computer programmer and house painter, before becoming a writer of mystery and suspense novels for teenaged readers. Although some critics have complained that his books are too gratuitously violent and graphic with gore, others praise his good characterization and sensitively explored motivations, and his books, published mostly in paperback, remain very popular. *Remember Me** (Archway, 1989), nominated for the Edgar Allan Poe Award, is a gripping mystery-fantasy in which a dead girl tells the story of how she is murdered and her killer tracked down. Altogether since 1985, he has written more than two dozen thrillers, whose titles give a sense of their content, among them, *Last Act* (Archway, 1989), *Witch* (Archway, 1990), *Fall into Darkness* (Archway, 1990), *Bury Me Deep* (Pocket Books, 1991), *Master of Murder* (Pocket Books, 1992), *Road to Nowhere* (Pocket Books, 1993), and *The Last Vampire* (Pocket Books, 1994). He has also written novels for adults in a similar vein.

PINKWATER, JILL, born in the Bronx, New York; author of self-illustrated nonfiction books and light novels for middle school and teenaged readers. Her *Buffalo Brenda** (Macmillan, 1989) is the zany story of a ninth grader and her friend who organize an underground newspaper in school and provide a live buffalo for a football team mascot. It was an American Library Association Notable Book for Children. She also published *The Disappearance of Sister Perfect* (Dutton, 1987), a mystery-detective novel in which a girl gets involved in a dangerous religious cult; *Tails of the Bronx: A Tale of the Bronx* (Macmillan, 1991), a novel of a group of Bronx children who search for missing cats and encounter the problems of homelessness; and *Mister Fred* (Dutton, 1994), in which sixth graders suspect that their teacher is a space alien. Earlier she published a fantasy, *Cloud Horse* (Lothrop, 1983), and the nonfiction books *The Natural Snack Cookbook: 151 Good Things to Eat* (Four Winds, 1975) and *Superpuppy: How to Choose, Raise, and Train the Best Possible Dog for You* (Seabury, 1977). The last was done with her husband, humorist Daniel Pinkwater, who is noted for his funny novels and picture books for children and with whom she lives in the Hudson Valley of New York State.

PINTOFF, ERNEST, motion picture and television director, animator, professor of film at the University of Southern California. He won an Academy Award for *The Critic* and is the author of *The Complete Guide to American Film Schools and Cinema and Television Courses* (Penguin, 1994). His novel for young people, *Zachary** (Eriksson, 1990), a mystery set shortly after World War II involving a Nazi living under an assumed identity, was an Edgar Allan Poe Award nominee. Pintoff has also published an autobiographical account, *Bolt from the Blue: A True Story* (Northwest Publishing, 1992). He makes his home in Hollywood.

THE PLACE WHERE NOBODY STOPPED (Segal*, Jerry, illus. Dav Pilkey, Orchard, 1991), folktale-like novel set in Russia starting about 1890 in a community of woodcutters between Vitebsk and Smolensk, so poor and isolated that no travelers ever stay, although Yosip the baker sends loaves daily to the cities in both directions. One day a scholarly Jew, Mordecai ben Yahbahbai, with his wife, Ginzl, and his little girl, Liebeh, 6, arrive and announce that they are to wait at this remote spot until Shimkeh, their cousin, brings them passports to America, for which they have given him their life's savings. Since there is no inn, they move in with Yosip, who has the only real house in the area. Ginzl immediately becomes a real aid to Yosip in his baking, Liebeh makes friends with the woodcutters' children, particularly Yuri, 10, and Mordecai, though he does no practical work, brings interest and joy to all with his storytelling and music. Yosip's happiness is interrupted annually by the visits of the Cossacks under the leadership of the cruel Sergeant Major, come to impress anyone between the ages of sixteen and forty-five into the army. Because he must hide Mordecai, he cannot cook the soldiers a lavish meal and must endure a vicious beating, losing another of his teeth each year. After ten years, he has no remaining teeth, Mordecai's family has grown by ten more children, and still the passports have not arrived. In the meantime Liebeh has tricked her father into teaching her to read by hiding in a closet and listening while he instructs her younger brother, and she and Yuri have fallen in love. Because his daughter, he thinks, is too good for an uneducated woodcutter, Mordecai will listen to none of their pleas until, with the connivance of Ginzl, whose father also had opposed her marriage, they demonstrate that Yuri, too, has learned to read, instructed by Liebeh. Just as the woodcutters fetch the priest from Smolensk, Cousin Shimkeh, disguised as a woman and accompanied by his beautiful but stupid wife, also approaches the Place Where Nobody Stopped, not to bring the passports but to hide out from the police. He is intercepted by the Cossacks on their annual visit and, terrified, turns the other way. Since this is the Sergeant Major's last trip before retirement, he brings a set of false teeth for Yosip, arriving just in time for the wedding. Mordecai, fortunately, has grown too old for the army and the woodcutters are already servants of the czar, so the soldiers join the wedding celebration, and the local people plan to build a schoolhouse where Mordecai will teach all their children. Scorning the cruel treatment of the Sergeant Major, Yosip throws the teeth into the fire. The storytelling tone carries this unlikely tale along with humor. Mordecai's eternal optimism contrasts neatly with Ginzl's clear-eyed view of life, and Yosip's simple goodness makes him a winner in happiness rather than a dupe of his long-time visitors. ALA.

PLAIN CITY (Hamilton*, Virginia, Scholastic, 1993), girl's growing-up novel set probably in southern Ohio in the early 1990s. Buhlaire Sims, 12, feels that she does not really belong anywhere—not with the other children from the Water House, a series of buildings on stilts near the river owned by her family, or in Plain City itself, where the Water House people are looked down upon and most of the other seventh graders shun her. One problem is her straw-colored hair in Rasta twists, which makes her different from her African-American family; another is the exotic dancing of her mother, Bluezy Sims, an entertainer who travels a good part of the time, leaving her with Aunt Digna, Uncle Sam, and Uncle Buford, her father's siblings, and nearly blind Aunt Babe, her mother's sister, all at the Water House. Buhlaire has always accepted the story that her father is "missing," and has assumed that means missing in Vietnam, until one day Grady Terrell, a teasing classmate, goes too far and she retaliates by pouring chocolate milk down his shirt. The principal, to whom she is sent, points out to her that the Vietnam War ended five years before she was born and that her father, Theodore "Junior" Sims, is not only alive but back in Plain City. That night Uncle Sam takes her and Aunt Digna to hear the first set at the night club where Bluezy is singing, and to Buhlaire's delight her mother calls her up to the stage to sing with her the last number, "Let It Be." As they are closing, Buhlaire sees a hand and a light-colored wrist reaching through the spotlight toward her, and although the bouncer removes the person immediately, she realizes that it was her father. The next day she skips school and walks around town, as she usually does after school, striding through good and bad parts and the outskirts, knowing someone is following her and thinking it is Grady. When she is caught out near the interstate highway in a sudden whiteout, she calls out and is answered by both Grady and a man she recognizes as her father. He gets them to an underpass where he and a number of other people are living. Although he is ragged and smells terrible, she is delighted to see him and begins to remember playing ball with him and other experiences from her early childhood. He gives them soup and, rummaging through a pile of belongings, produces an envelope with pictures from the past, but also more recent pictures of her, evidently given to him by Aunt Babe at times when he sneaked into the Water House while the others were away. Although there are some disquieting elements—Junior is clearly mentally disturbed and a strange woman claims to be his mother—Buhlaire goes home with Grady, determined to get the $400 she has saved and leave the Water House to live with her father. To her surprise, Grady knows him, having grown up in The Shelter From Any Storm, where his father is the manager. Although Mr. Terrell tries to dissuade her from giving Junior money and her own family is appalled that she has gone to see him, she gets half her money from the bank and sets off to find her father again, with Grady insisting on accompanying her. Junior takes the money eagerly but is not much concerned when Buhlaire, having realized that she cannot cope with his mental instability, tells him she will not be living with him now. She also understands that her mother and Uncle Sam are in love and that part of the feeling against her father and against her is black prejudice against light-skinned people, since Junior's mother, stepmother to Digna, Sam, and Buford, was white. In the last scene, in which the river has flooded and she goes in a boat with Uncle Sam to help rescue people, Buhlaire becomes reconciled to the relationships within her family and to the fact that her father will probably not get well. Although the plot resolution is logical, it is not emotionally realized in the novel. Buhlaire's shifts in understanding come too suddenly to be convincing and at times when she is feeling too passionate. Grady transforms abruptly from tormentor to rescuer and seems impervious to Buhlaire's spurning and scornful words, an implausible character. ALA; SLJ.

PLUMMER, LOUISE, author of novels for young adults. She has a master's degree in English from the University of Minnesota and lives in Provo, Utah, where she teaches writing. Her first novel, *The Romantic Obsessions and Humiliations of Annie Schlmeier* (Delacorte, 1987), is about a high school senior whose family has just immigrated from the Netherlands. Both it and *My Name Is Sus5an Smith. The 5 Is Silent** (Delacorte, 1991) capture the bewildering emotions of teenaged girls who become infatuated with men they know are not suitable. The first received Honorable Mention in the Delacorte Press Prize for an Outstanding First Young Adult Novel contest, and the second won the Utah Arts Council Creative Writing Competition for a young adult novel, as well as being cited by *School Library Journal* on its Best Books for Children list. Plummer and her husband have four sons.

POE, EDGAR ALLAN (*The Man Who Was Poe**), the historical writer, who, assuming the persona of his fictional detective, Auguste Dupin, helps Edmund* Brimmer find his lost relatives and apprehend bank robbers. Poe is described as dark, glowering, and intense, often absorbed, and having difficulty separating the reality of Edmund's life from the reality of his own and from the story he is writing. He has come to Providence, Rhode Island, to court Mrs. Sarah Helen Whitman, also a real-life figure. She is reluctant to encourage Poe's suit because her mother opposes him, favoring Mr. Arnold, and because Poe has a reputation as a drinker. In real life, Poe becomes engaged to her, but she soon ends their engagement because Poe resumes drinking in violation of his pledge not to do so. In real life, Poe's wife, Virginia, died in 1847, the year before the time of the novel. Poe's name for her was "Sis." In the novel, Poe apparently intends for Edmund's Sis to be found dead in the story he is writing, and he seems disappointed that she is recovered alive from the robbers. The historical Poe died in 1849.

POLIKOFF, BARBARA G(ARLAND) (1929–), teacher and writer of fiction and nonfiction books for middle grade readers. She was educated at the University of Michigan (B.A.) and the University of Chicago (M.A.) and has taught high school English and been an editor and volunteer teacher of writing workshops in Chicago elementary schools. *Life's a Funny Proposition, Horatio** (Holt, 1992), an American Library Association Best Book, is set in a wooded area of Wisconsin much like that where Polikoff and her family spend weekends. A story of family life and growing up, light on the surface but serious underneath, it employs details similar to those in her own life, including coming to terms with the death of the father and having a husky dog for companionship. *Riding the Wind* (Holt, 1995), a novel, tells of a girl's attempts to use an inheritance to buy an Arabian horse she longs for. *My Parrot Eats Baked Beans* (Whitman, 1987) is a nonfiction book illustrated with photographs, in which children talk about their pets. She has also written biographies. Polikoff married a lawyer, has three children, and has made her home in Chicago.

POPEYE (*Beyond Safe Boundaries**), the dental mechanic (denture maker) who works for Elizabeth Levin's dentist father. Popeye is a highly skilled technician, whose puffy cheeks provoke the nickname used by everyone but his employer, who always addresses him as Mr. Coetzee out of respect. Like many other Colored [*sic*] (half-white, half-black) men, he has an alcohol problem arising from poor self-esteem, and also in his case, from unfortunate personal circumstances. He was educated in England, where he married a white woman. They lived in a mixed-racial neighborhood in the Port Elizabeth area, until the government decreed that the region was for whites only. The Coetzees got a divorce, so that Mrs. Coetzee and their son, Willem*, who can pass for white, could continue to live there. Popeye is very kind to Elizabeth Levin, to whom he tells stories, and extremely proud of his bright, charismatic son. After Willem is murdered by the police, Popeye is found dead in his car, a suicide. His death moves Elizabeth's father to tears. Popeye's experiences show how apartheid severs families and ruins the lives of decent, worthwhile people.

PRATHER, RAY, born in Florida; freelance writer for European television and film industries, author and illustrator of a variety of books for young people. He was educated at Cooper Union in New York City and has lived in Europe and Africa and traveled extensively in Asia. Among his published picture books is *Double Dog Dare* (Macmillan, 1975). He has also written and illustrated books published in Kenya and Tanzania. *Fish & Bones** (HarperCollins, 1992), a mystery with an African-American boy as protagonist that involves the revelation of a lynching some twenty years earlier, was a nominee for the Edgar Allan Poe Award. It is set in Florida, which Prather considers home.

PRETTY SOFT BIDDLE (*Shoebag**), Eunice Biddle, lovely little blond girl of seven, daughter of the Biddles who take in Shoebag the cockroach after he becomes a human boy. She, and they, never know that Shoebag is not really a person but simply take him at face value. Because she is so attractive and makes a good deal of money doing television commercials for Pretty Soft toilet paper, Pretty Soft is nicknamed for her product, pampered, and indulged. She has a private tutor named Madame Glorious Gloria Grande de la Grande, a once-star actress who has lost her looks and now earns her living teaching budding stars. She is supposed to teach Pretty Soft academic subjects but mostly concentrates on such matters as cultivating charm and avoiding wrinkles. When Pretty Soft enters regular school, the child is virtually ignorant of academic subjects. Pretty Soft is never without mirrors about her, looking glasses that match the colors of the rooms in the Biddle house, uses creams lavishly, and avoids other children, whom Madame G. de la G. [*sic*] tells her are just "civilians." After Gregor* accuses Pretty Soft of being selfish and heartless, the girl helps Shoebag rescue his mother from the dreaded spider in an attempt to prove she cares about people other than herself. At the end, ironically, Pretty Soft has become more human in the moral sense, while Shoebag, who has always been so, returns to his roach form, and each child is happier than before. Pretty Soft is a type character, distorted for effect.

A PROUD TASTE FOR SCARLET AND MINIVER (Konigsburg*, E. L., illus. E. L. Konigsburg, Atheneum, 1973), fantasy-biography of Eleanor of Aquitaine. While Eleanor is in heaven awaiting the arrival of her second husband, Henry II of England, the story of her turbulent life is told by several of the historical figures associated with her. Convincing characters, a lively, irreverent style, and sound research combine for an entertaining and enlightening picture of the times and one of history's most fascinating women. Phoenix Honor. Earlier the book was selected by *Choice* and Fanfare. Phoenix Honor. For a longer entry, see *Dictionary, 1960–1984.*

Q

QUALEY, MARSHA (RICHARDSON) (1953–), born in Austin, Minnesota; writer of novels set in the lake country of the upper Midwest. She attended Macalester College in 1971 and 1972 and received her B.A. degree from the University of Minnesota in 1976. She has lived in Montana, Texas, Arkansas, Pennsylvania, and Wisconsin, but now makes her home in St. Paul with her husband and four children. *Revolutions of the Heart** (Houghton Mifflin, 1993), which was cited by the *School Library Journal* as a Best Book of the year, concerns prejudice against Native Americans in a small northern Wisconsin town. Among her other novels are *Everybody's Daughter* (Houghton Mifflin, 1991) and *Come In from the Cold* (Houghton Mifflin, 1994).

A QUESTION OF TRUST (Bauer*, Marion Dane, Scholastic, 1994), animal novel whose real focus is on a family's troubled readjustment when the parents separate, set in an unnamed American town in the contemporary period. Since his mother has left and taken her own apartment, saying she is suffocating in her marriage, Brad, 12, has refused to visit her or speak to her on the telephone and has pressured his little brother, Charlie, 8, to do the same, explaining to him that she will long for them so much that she will come back. Both boys are lonely, especially because their father, an accountant, buries himself with his computer in his basement office and seems to notice little of what they do, unless they break his rigid rules. When a ragged, "thin-fat" cat shows up, they feed her and keep her hidden in their shed, knowing that their inflexible father will not let them keep her, saying they are too irresponsible for pets. Charlie's horrified report that the cat's insides are spilling out at first alarms Brad, but he soon realizes that she is giving birth to two kittens. The first is a handsome black cat with white markings, which Brad names Tuxedo. He tricks Charlie into letting him claim Tuxedo, leaving to the younger boy the second one, a mottled three-color female with a face half light, half dark like her mother. Although Tuxedo seems disinclined to nurse, the boys are not alarmed until they discover his body half eaten by his mother. Assuming that she has killed him, they drive her off and are left with the problem of nurturing the young orphan. After checking in the library, they start a regimen of feedings with an eye dropper every three hours, stroking the kitten's belly to induce elimination, and cleaning up the excrement. Brad has the additional problem of buying canned milk and other supplies, although he has already had an advance on his allowance. He solves this by pilfering change from his father's dresser and, when that is not enough, twenty dollars from his wallet. It becomes harder and harder to keep Charlie from running off to see their mother or talking to her. Relations between the boys grow strained. The situation comes to a head when Brad discovers that the cat has been returning through a broken shed window. Thinking that she will kill the second kitten, Charlie turns the hose on her and, when she retreats up a tree, blasts her out of it and runs off. Desperate, Brad calls on his father. He grimly drives Brad, the cat, and the kitten to a veterinarian, who hears the whole story and explains that the cat probably did not kill Tuxedo but was trying to rid her nest of offspring dead from natural causes. She commends Brad for his responsibility and says the cat seems to be all right but will need to stay overnight for observation and shots. At home his father admits that he has been wrong about some things, but still insists that Brad repay every penny and talks about how trust holds a family together. Brad sees the falseness of that premise, but he begins to understand why his mother left and how, in his own way, he has been acting as inflexibly as his father. Knowing where Charlie will have run to, he rides his bike to his mother's apartment and waits on the step there with his little brother for their mother to come home from work. Although nothing about the future is explicit, there is an assumption that the boys will be allowed to keep the kitten, now named, appropriately, Muddle, and that they will learn to share their time between their father and mother. The strongest element in the novel is the sense of almost unbearable pain both Brad and Charlie suffer from the breakup of their parents and the misery of their misguided efforts to get their mother back. The parallels between their mother and the cat are not too exact or overemphasized but add dimension to their devotion to the kittens. The reasons for their mother's departure are clear from a number of telling details and should be understandable to the middle school audience for which the novel is intended. SLJ.

QUETZAL LADY (*Journey of the Sparrows**), old street woman who takes a shine to Oscar, Maria Acosta's little brother. Eccentric and probably mentally ill, the woman wheels a shopping cart full of newspapers and her other belongings and carries on a question-and-answer conversation with herself. She believes Oscar looks like her younger brother and brings him toys, including a kite and a kitten to play with. Evidently a street person for a long time, she tells Maria that she used to climb into the church kitchen to steal food when she was younger and more agile, and she shows the girl where to get over the fence and into a window. Oscar names her the Quetzal Lady because she wears clothes of many colors, like the beautiful Central American bird they found and released from a trap on their long foot journey.

R

RABBIT (*Maybe Yes, Maybe No, Maybe Maybe**), Rebecca, PK's little sister. Rebecca is a preschooler who attends day care while her single mother, who works at The Fancy Restaurant at night, sleeps. Rabbit has lots of questions, which PK tries to answer, loves stories, which PK tells her every night while Rabbit soaks in the tub and sucks on the washcloth, and tends to be insecure in the face of the impending move to a new apartment. PK confides in her bicycle, called Bike, that she will try to be more attentive to Rabbit. When Rabbit was very young, she could not say her name correctly, pronouncing it Rabba, which became the name PK gave to the main character in the stories that she tells Rabbit. Since Rabbit loves to nibble on carrots, the family adapted the name Rabba into Rabbit. Rabbit is an earnest, charming little girl.

RACER (*The Beggars' Ride**), one of the younger members of Cowboy's* group of homeless street kids. Racer sports a patch over one eye, which he apparently thinks makes him look tough, but he mostly pushes it aside so that he can see better. He likes to tease and is a great talker. His conversations with Clare* Caldwell are the source of most of her information about members of the group. Racer is very close to Shoe*, with whom he ran away from a home for disturbed children, and, though loyal to the gang, he considers Shoe his special buddy and chief concern. He and Shoe work as a team in various scams to get money for the group. Racer is the one who suggests that A. J.* Morgan must have something interesting and important hidden in his basement that the group should investigate.

RACHEL CHANCE (Thesman*, Jean, Houghton Mifflin, 1990), novel of the kidnapping of a young child by a traveling evangelical group and his sister's efforts to retrieve him. In Rider's Dock, north of Seattle, of the 1940s, the unconventional family of the narrator, Rachel Chance, 15, is looked down upon, a family, she says, "of refugees and misfits, well acquainted with untidy predicaments." Grandpa Abel* Chance is a cantankerous old man, a drinker, and a freethinker. Although a Rider by birth, Rachel's mother, Lara, has moved to her father-in-law's farm after the death of her husband in 1933 and two years before the book's opening has given birth to an illegitimate son, Rider, whose father she refuses to name. Also in the household is Jonah, Abel's nephew with mental disabilities. Living nearby are Grandpa's friend, enormously fat Druid Annie, a healer and fortune teller, and Hank* Webster, 16, hired help, a bright boy from a dysfunctional family of jailbirds and wife abusers who wants an education. The revival meeting of Billy Bong and the Anointed Children of Almighty God is locally sponsored by Pastor Woodie, a rigidly self-righteous man who insists that Lara should put little Rider up for adoption. In the fervor worked up by the revival and with Lara out of town to help Chance cousins after a death, Pastor Woodie calls to press his claim that Rider should be given up to "a good Christian home." Abel drives him off with his shotgun. The next morning Rachel wakes to smoke, discovers the field is burning, and shoves Rider into Jonah's arms while she runs to help free the trapped cows and chickens. When she returns, Jonah is hiding under the porch weeping. Finally, they get his disjointed story: some men in black suits came, hit Jonah, and took Rider away. And, Jonah insists, Pastor Woodie was in the car. The police think Jonah has either hurt or neglected to watch Rider and has made up the story. A few people are helpful. One woman drives to Spokane to get Lara; the pharmacist, whose wife once gave their life savings to Billy Bong, forces the police chief to put out inquiries, but the evangelical group denies having the child, and the chief soon has other trouble to deflect his attention as Hank's uncle beats his wife, Betty-Dean* Webster, again; Betty-Dean kills him with his shotgun, breaks out of jail, shoots up the town, and disappears. In the weeks that follow, the Chance family incredibly can interest no one with power in their loss, and the family begins to disintegrate under the strain. Rachel is sure that Billy Bong's sister, Pearl Sweet, whose own infant son died and who looked covetously at Rider, has her brother. She persuades Abel to drive her to Soap Lake, where they have learned Billy Bong's group is performing next, their group swelling to include Annie and Hank before they have gone far. On the way they camp with fruit pickers, and Rachel, who knows that Rider's father follows the crops and remembers seeing and talking with him once, wishes she knew his name so she could ask about him. Because the old truck gives them trouble, they miss the revival in Soap Lake, follow on and have other difficulties and a major breakdown. Determined to try to get Rider, Rachel leaves in the middle of the night and hitchhikes to Yakima, with only worried Hank knowing. At the revival she sees Pearl Sweet with Rider, his blond hair dyed dark, follows them to a house, and hides in a garden next door until Pearl puts Rider into the yard to play. Although Rachel has feared that he might have forgotten her, he runs to her and raises his arms to be lifted over the fence. Rachel faces Pearl down, daring her to call the police and risk going to prison. The only implausible element occurs a little later when she coincidentally finds Rider's father, who is astonished but delighted to discover that he has a son, since Lara has not told him, not wanting to burden a man with no job in the Great Depression. The oddly assorted Chance family is full of memorable characters, with strong-willed Rachel the most competent and clear-thinking. Billy Bong's sleazy revival has enough shady incidents on its record to make the kidnapping believable, especially since the self-righteous local church people are sure they will provide a more "Christian" home than the Chance farm. The deep and accepting love among Grandpa Able, Lara, Rachel, Jonah, Rider, and even the cousins from Spokane, shared also by Annie and Hank, makes a strong case for acceptance of the unconventional family. ALA.

RACHEL WORTHEN (*Lyddie**), little sister of Lyddie, age six when the book starts and eight or nine when she comes to Lowell. Having been underfed and mistreated by her aunt and uncle, she is terribly thin and unable to talk when she first arrives at the Lowell boarding house. Lyddie reads to her and buys a primer and a book of nursery rhymes and tries to teach her, and she improves. When Lyddie comes down with fever, Rachel nurses her devotedly. Since children are not allowed in the boarding houses, she becomes a doffer, even though small, thereby qualifying as a worker. Their brother, Charlie*, who works for the miller and has been taken on as an apprentice, comes to fetch her back to Vermont, since the miller's wife is willing to adopt her and send her to school. Although Lyddie is devastated to lose her, she knows that Rachel's cough will turn into a more serious lung condition if she stays at the mill and that the miller's wife, who has made and sent with Charlie a pretty dress and a frilly bonnet for Rachel, will be a good mother to her.

THE RAIN CATCHERS (Thesman*, Jean, Houghton Mifflin, 1991), novel of a girl's growing up in an unconventional family of women near Seattle at the time of publication. The narrator, Grayling Jordan, 14, lives with her grandmother, Garnet Waverly Templeton; her great-aunt, Minette Waverly Minor; their cousin, Olivia Thorpe, who is dying of cancer; Minette's daughter Yolande, a novelist who has been divorced from her abusive husband; and their friend, Belle Russell, an African-American doctor badly crippled by arthritis. Gray's mother, Norah, a high-powered businesswoman, lives in San Francisco where she fled shortly after her husband was deliberately run down and killed by a man he saw commit a hold-up, leaving Gray as an infant with her grandmother. Gray's friend, Colleen Clement, is the daughter of a doctor, a domineering man now married to a shallow, anorexic woman only a few years older than his daughter, whose custody he had wrested from her mother while she was in a mental institution. The women follow a quiet, accepting but ritualistic life, notably in their afternoon tea, at which they retell family experiences, shaping chaotic real life into a fictional pattern with beginning, middle, and end, so that they can think of it without pain. Gray, Colleen, and Aaron Ripley, 16, who is painting the house, are given their tea on the porch, not in the dining room with the grown women, a distinction symbolically important, although they can listen to the conversation through the curtains of the open window. During the summer several events occur that push Gray toward adulthood. Olivia, who has been a loving, nurturing mother figure, dies; Gray visits her mother in San Francisco; she has her first date and receives her first kiss, from Aaron; and Colleen runs away from her father to live with Gray's grandmother. Olivia's death, Gray suspects, is hastened by Belle and Garnet, who have promised to do what Olivia wants when the time comes. Unfortunately, Colleen's father also has suspicions about Olivia's death and uses them as blackmail to try to force the women to send his daughter home, even though the ex-convict brother of his present wife is staying with him and has attacked Colleen. Grandmother Garnet refuses to be intimidated, and Colleen for once stands up to her father, saying that Gray was alone with Olivia when she died, a falsehood in which all the women concur. The romance with Aaron is sweet and low key, surviving despite Gray's humiliation at discovering that Belle engineered their first date. Gray's mother has planned that she will spend her last three years of high school in San Francisco and insists that Gray come to look over the school. The girl is torn between her reluctance to leave the home she loves and her hope that her mother is sorry to have rejected her and at last really wants her. Her visit is almost a repeat of earlier ones, with her mother far too busy to spend time with her. Instead of waiting in the closely locked apartment, as she did when she was younger, this time Gray explores the city and attracts the attention of a strange, sinister young man who calls himself "the dancer" and says he can get her anything she wants. Impulsively, she suggests a gun and is appalled when he shows up at the apartment and makes threats when she says she does not want it. In her mother's furious reaction when Gray tells her the story, she realizes that Norah lives in fear, and she finally gets the story of why her mother abandoned her suddenly fourteen years earlier: she was being followed by the man who killed Gray's father. Although hurt at being abruptly sent home, Gray is still able to understand that her mother is continually running away, burying herself in work, and refusing to face the fears, defeats, and embarrassments of life as the women at her grandmother's house do, by making them into stories they can cope with. At the end Belle marries her longtime friend, a retired dentist, and moves to Hawaii. Gray and Colleen, now accepted as women, move into the two empty chairs around the tea table, and Gray is able to relate the fiasco of her trip to San Francisco, knowing that by making it a story she can come to terms with it. The theme that something good, a story, can be made out of the bad experiences in life is echoed in the title, which refers to the way the girls, and the women before them, set pots to catch the summer rain that drips through the honeysuckles and use it to rinse their hair, turning the unpleasant weather condition into something useful and sweet. Throughout the novel there is a strong sense of the warmth and supportiveness of the household of women. Gray and Colleen are both believable teenagers and the older women are strongly characterized. SLJ.

REAVER, CHAP (HERBERT R.) (1935–1993), born in Cincinnati, Ohio; chiropractor educated at Palmer College of Chiropractic in the District of Columbia; teacher of creative writing in junior high and author of two well-regarded novels for young adults that deal with racism against African Americans and Native Americans in a mystery-adventure context. After establishing a successful practice in Cincinnati, Reaver moved his practice and family to Marietta in Georgia, the home state of his wife, a real estate agent. He took up writing, contributing many articles and short stories to periodicals and humor magazines. For his first venture into long fiction, *Mote** (Delacorte, 1990), he received the Delacorte Press Prize for an Outstanding First Young Adult Novel and the Edgar Allan Poe Award. *Mote* is the gripping and well-plotted account of a teenaged boy who, in investigating the murder of a teacher, encounters a white supremacist hate group. *A Little Bit Dead** (Delacorte, 1992) is a historical adventure set among the Yahi Indians of northern California in 1876, which also received the Poe Award. Underlying both books are issues of growing up, dealing with conflict and relationships, acquiring a sense of responsibility, and gaining independence of judgment. His novel *Bill** (Delacorte, 1994) was posthumously published. About a southern girl's friendship with her dog, Bill, and her relationship with her alcoholic father, it was a selection of *School Library Journal*.

REECE (*A Little Bit Dead**), Herbert Reece, a youth of eighteen who was orphaned when his father died, probably of pneumonia. Reece and his father had come west from Kentucky south of Cincinnati hoping to earn enough money to buy land and then send for Reece's mother and sister. Reece often recalls his father's moral advice and philosophical ruminations and is sometimes helped by such practical suggestions of his father as always having a fire laid in the stove and waxing his matches to protect them from moisture. Reece is conscience stricken when he realizes that he had actually enjoyed the shoot-out with Colby, Sam, and the soldiers. He tells Kathryn* Forrest that he will never kill again. A clever young man, he tricks Colby into admissions at the trial and also tricks Colby, Sam, and the soldiers into firing at one another in the confrontation at the cave. After the trial, he consults the judge about securing land for the Indians and is advised to buy it and hold it for them, since the law forbids them to own land. Reece buys the valley, but only thirty years later does Shanti*, the Indian Reece rescued, learn that the valley of his youth belongs to him and his few people who are left.

REEDER, CAROLYN, author of *Shades of Gray** (Macmillan, 1989), about the aftermath of the Civil War, one of the most highly honored historical novels of recent years. It won the Scott O'Dell Award, the Jefferson Cup, and the Child Study Award, was named an honor book for the Jane Addams Award, and was listed as a Notable Book by the American Library Association. Her second novel, *Grandpa's Mountain* (Macmillan, 1991), also set in the mountains of

Virginia, is about the establishment of the Shenandoah National Park in the Great Depression years and the opposition from property owners in the area. Her novel of prohibition years, *Moonshiner's Son* (Macmillan, 1993), explores the conflict between the mountain people for whom making liquor is a way of life, their only source of cash to pay taxes, and indeed a matter of pride, and the reformers and revenue agents determined to stamp out the practice. Reeder is a teacher and a history buff who knows the Blue Ridge Mountains well. She lives with her husband in Glen Echo, Maryland. For earlier biographical information and a title entry, see *Dictionary, 1985–1989* [*Shades of Gray*].

RELUCTANTLY ALICE (Naylor*, Phyllis Reynolds, Atheneum, 1991), third in a series narrated by Alice McKinley of Silver Spring, Maryland, following *The Agony of Alice* and *Alice in Rapture, Sort Of**, this book recounting her first semester in junior high. At first, the terrible things about seventh grade—the boys are shorter than the girls, math is too hard, there is no toilet paper in the johns, among other problems—greatly outweigh the good things, but gradually Alice begins to enjoy most of the school life and decides to make it a year when she will be friends with everyone. This goal is almost thwarted by Denise Whitlock, the large eighth-grade girl who sits in front of her in language arts class, teases her for not having a mother, bullies her in physical education, and selects her especially to haze on SGSD, Seventh Grade Sing Day, on which seventh graders are trapped and forced to sing the school song, the penalty for a poor performance being a dousing in the toilet. Since Alice is tone deaf, she confesses to her brother Lester, 19, that she is terrified. When she is surrounded by Denise and her friends in the parking lot, Lester unexpectedly shows up, casually puts his arm around Alice's shoulder, and walks her away, a brotherly rescue not typical of his usual jaundiced attitude toward her. Alice finally solves her conflict with Denise by choosing her to interview for a biography-writing project and finding positive things to say about her. As she matures, Alice's own problems no longer dominate her whole attention, and she worries about the love life of Lester, whose old girlfriend, Marilyn, wants to come back and whose recent girlfriend, Crystal, does not want to give him up, and that of her father, who has been unaware that the assistant manager of his store is in love with him and has asked her to a concert along with a woman he met in Ocean City. After that problem solves itself, Alice impulsively asks her beautiful teacher, Miss Summers, to a sing-along of *The Messiah* with the family, making it seem her father's idea, an incident that almost backfires but turns out well when she confesses and they find it amusing. Alice's two close friends, Pamela and Elizabeth*, and her former boyfriend, Patrick*, figure in most of the episodes but less prominently than in *Alice in Rapture, Sort Of.* The humor, not so totally concentrated on twelve-year-old romance, is more varied. What holds the series together and keeps it interesting is the character of Alice, a girl who, as Denise says in her biography, has guts. SLJ. For details of *The Agony of Alice,* see *Dictionary, 1985–1989.*

THE REMARKABLE JOURNEY OF PRINCE JEN (Alexander*, Lloyd, Dutton, 1991), fantasy novel of magic, miracle, and growing up set in the mythical Oriental kingdom of T'ang. A ragged, old man calling himself Master Wu appears at the Jade Gate of the Celestial Palace in the capital city of Ch'ang-an and tells the king of a realm far to the north of exceptional peace and happiness. Young Prince Jen immediately sees opportunities for adventure and volunteers to travel there to discover for his father the faraway king's secrets of ruling well. Accompanied by his portly, clownish retainer Mafoo (from whom he is soon parted), he embarks on a trip that stretches over many months and is fraught with numerous perils and close encounters. Jen changes, not unexpectedly, from a palace dandy of unrealistic expectations and vain aspirations to a royal personage worthy of assuming the crown. In various happenings, he loses each of the seemingly modest but, as it turns out, powerful objects chosen by Wu as gifts for the faraway king: an iron sword; an old saddle; a wooden flute; a small, bronze bowl; a sandalwood paintbox; and a bird-shaped paper kite. As Jen loses these objects he becomes increasingly reduced in circumstances. At his lowest, he is confined in the dread cangue, or Collar of Punishment, where he almost starves to death, and then lands in the palace dungeon. As Jen travels, he becomes more and more aware of social and economic injustices in his father's realm and of the hatred that the peasants and less affluent harbor for the crown. He rights wrongs as he can along the way, symbolically healing the kingdom on personal levels with acts that hint of social reforms when he becomes king. The people he meets include dishonest, cruel courtiers, who treat him badly because they do not, or refuse to, recognize him as prince, and commoners who have encountered injustice and live on the barest subsistence level. The magical objects provoke adventures for their possessors, often perilous, sometimes mischievous, occasionally benevolent. The sword, which never fails to defeat its foe and lusts for blood, falls into the hands of a villainous thief known as Natha Yellow Scarf, who with it gathers a band of such size that he terrorizes the kingdom and even usurps the throne. Li Kwang, the general who is to protect Jen on the journey, is intrigued by the saddle that appears to him to be golden, rides it, and leads his men into a mountain cavern, where they are turned to stone. Eventually they are revivified when they help to defeat Natha. The bowl, which produces gold coins, is instrumental in the downfall of a cruel, corrupt official. The kite brings out of a coma a little girl whose parents have been slain during Natha's depredations. The paintbox comes into the possession of a painter who uses its implements to paint a landscape from which there comes a tiger who gobbles up Natha. The flute is a major device for unifying the narrative, since it falls to Voyaging Moon, a former, ill-used slave girl with whom Jen falls in love and who becomes famous for the music she makes on it. After the two are parted early in the narrative, Jen searches diligently for her, abandoning his original objective. He finds her, and all the other major characters collide, at the capital city in the rousing, conflict-filled climax, where Natha is defeated and Jen is restored to his rightful position. Voyaging Moon and Jen marry and are virtuous rulers under whom T'ang becomes an ideal realm, with almost no officials and few problems because everyone lives by the golden rule. In the last chapter, somewhat of an epilogue, many years later Jen and Voyaging Moon decide to attempt the journey to the northern kingdom. Not far from the city, they encounter an old man, who to their amazement looks like the old Master Wu of the original journey. They realize that he had popped up during Jen's journey under various names—Shu, Chu, Fu—but is really Master Hu, the beloved teacher of Jen's early years who had mysteriously vanished from the palace. Under the different guises, he inspired Jen's quest in order to instruct the prince in truths about life and, in particular, about being a good king. The novel is typical of Alexander's writing. The plot sweeps across the landscape, with a large, superficially developed array of characters and many action-filled events, which seem confusing until the reader realizes that action is more important than keeping things straight. The theme is obvious: the outcry of the masses and their need for moral rulers. Coincidence, cliffhangers, grandiloquence, colorful characters, sudden reversals of fortune, a breezy, twinkle-eyed tone, and a vigorous, individualized style combine for a story that leaves the reader breathless but also entertained. SLJ.

REMEMBER ME (Pike*, Christopher, Archway, 1989), mystery-fantasy set in contemporary Los Angeles. After her death, pretty, blond Shari Cooper, 18, tells the story of how she dies and tracks down her killer. Before her death, Shari gets on variously with her well-off parents, is extremely fond of her handsome, diabetic brother, Jimmy, runs with a popular crowd in school, and has one very close girlfriend, Jo Foulton, who is highly interested in the psychic. Late on the evening of Beth Palmone's birthday party in Beth's parents' beachfront, fourth-floor condominium, Shari participates in a seance Jo puts on. While Jo uses Shari as a conduit for contacting the deceased brother of another guest, Shari suddenly jumps up from the floor, races to the balcony, and soon is found dead on the pavement below. The five other young people assure Detective Lieutenant Garrett* that Shari jumped, but he remains skeptical, investigates the scene thoroughly, and discovers clues that eventually point to murder. In the cemetery after her funeral, Shari encounters Peter* Nichols, the deceased young man whom they had been trying to contact at the party. She persuades him to help her in the quest for her murderer, since she does not want to be remembered as a suicide. With Peter's help, she spies on her friends and even enters their dreams and the dreams of some of the adults in her life in order to pick up information. Late in the novel, Shari discovers that Amanda* Parish, the daughter of the Coopers' housekeeper, is really the Coopers' child, having been switched at birth with Shari. It comes out that, jealous to the point of derangement, Amanda pushed Shari to her death, and in a harrowing climax scene, Amanda, also a diabetic, tries to kill Jimmy, her sweetheart and Shari's brother, by giving him an overdose of insulin and injecting an air bubble into his bloodstream. As the bubble makes its way toward Jimmy's heart, Shari enters his blood and in a dream sequence persuades Jimmy to pop the air bubble and thus saves his life. Garrett turns up before Amanda gets away and arrests her. Shari and Peter are pleased later to read in the Los Angeles newspapers that Shari's reputation is cleared. The characters are typical of whodunits and teenage novels and are individualized sufficiently for the plot. The young people have shallow values, cut one another down with snide and personal remarks, are preoccupied with sex, and routinely "trash talk," an unlikable lot on the whole. Associating with Peter and her after-death experiences cause Shari to see how superficial she was, and near book's end she does several deeds that raise her in the reader's and her own self-esteem. The dark Shadow that pursues and threatens her repeatedly after the fall (Peter has one, too) represents her undesirable inner self, and when she finally turns and faces it, she begins to be able to control her afterlife existence and turn it to good ends. Although they hold up the story, the lengthy conversations create a solid picture of teenaged life, and the concept of the murdered actively bringing the killer to justice works well. Shari's new-found abilities as an incorporeal being and her ruminations with Peter on the nature of the afterlife engage the intellect as well as the emotions. Poe Nominee.

RESCUE JOSH MCGUIRE (Mikaelsen*, Ben, Hyperion, 1991), animal and survival novel set in western Montana in the 1980s. Although he used to love camping trips with his father, Sam, Josh McGuire, 13, has begun to fear the man, who has been drinking heavily and acting mean since the death of Tye, Josh's older brother. When his father kills a female bear on a spring hunting trip, then denies that she was a nursing mother, Josh sneaks out of their camper at night and retraces their trail to find the cub. Although he hits Josh brutally, Sam lets him put the cub in the camper and take it to their small ranch in the Bridger foothills near Bozeman. Josh consults his friend, Otis Sinclair, a retired university professor who leads a reclusive life caring for sick and wounded birds and animals brought to him by the Fish and Game Department, about feeding the cub, which he calls Pokey, and sleeps with it in the barn. When he learns that he will not be allowed to keep it and that it will probably be sent to the state research lab and killed, he decides to run away. He fits a box for Pokey to the back of Tye's motorcycle, a dirt bike his brother sometimes let him secretly ride, collects some supplies, and sneaks out after his parents are asleep, but the family border collie, Mud Flap, follows and insists on riding on the gas tank, as she used to do with Tye. Josh heads for the most isolated place he knows, the Paradise Valley near the Gardiner entrance to Yellowstone Park. By the time he is high in the mountains, a vicious spring blizzard has struck. In the storm, he loses Mud Flap, but he crawls into a hole with Pokey, and, cuddled with the cub in his sleeping bag, survives, although he suffers some frostbitten fingers. When the sun returns, Mud Flap turns up, and Josh manages to start a fire with the few matches he has brought. Since he needs food, he makes a trip to Gardiner, where he calls Otis, asking him to tell his mother, Libby, that he is safe, since he is afraid to face his father's anger. Although he is not aware of it, an intense search has begun, and the media have been playing up the story of a young boy trying to save a black bear cub. Sam is furious at the publicity, since he will not admit to killing a nursing bear sow, and his attitude worries Deputy Brewster Bingham, who is in charge of the case and is concerned that Libby may be in danger. Because at first no one knows that the motorcycle is gone, the search has centered on the Bridger foothill area, but the long-distance call, discovered by Bingham, changes the picture. Not knowing whether he can trust Otis to report the boy, Bingham puts his place under surveillance, and when Josh calls again, this time from a cabin he has broken into, because Mud Flap has been badly injured by a male bear, an officer follows Otis. The professor meets Josh and picks up Mud Flap to take her to a veterinarian, but when Josh sees a second car follow Otis down the trail, he thinks his friend has betrayed him, revs up the bike, rides madly up the trail in the dark, and flips off into the trees, wrecking the bike, breaking his arm, and badly injuring his leg. With great difficulty he drags himself back to the cave where he has left Pokey, crawls with the bear into the back of the cave, and there the rescue crew finds them. After the first part of the book, the point of view shifts from Josh to Otis to Bingham to Libby, even occasionally to Sam. In the end, with great media attention and the governor, up for reelection, involved, the cub is saved from experimentation and given to Otis to keep with Josh's help, spring hunting of bears is suspended, Sam promises to go to an alcoholic treatment center, and the ending seems upbeat, but an author's note points out that spring bear hunting has been resumed in the Bozeman area. Mostly a straightforward and plausible adventure story, the novel also contains a strong antihunting, pro-environment message. Characters are adequate for their roles, with Josh and Pokey the best developed. IRA.

REVOLUTIONS OF THE HEART (Qualey*, Marsha, Houghton Mifflin, 1993), realistic novel about prejudice against Native Americans set in the small northern Wisconsin town of Summer in the late twentieth century. Popular, lively Cory Knutson, 17, grounded by her mother and stepfather for having taken the pickup without permission and crashing it, works at Mr. Bartleby's motel to pay for the damage. She reluctantly accompanies her mother and her mother's Indian friend to a powwow and meets quiet, intense Harvey Mac-Namara, called Mac*, who is new in high school and living with relatives. In the next months her life concentrates on her mother's increasing heart problems and her own growing attraction to Mac. Neither is easy to cope with. Although she has always lived in Summer, she has never realized before how sharply divided the town is between Indians and whites, with relatively little interaction between the groups. She finds notes in her locker, ''Only whores do it with injuns,'' and other abusive and bigoted messages, and once about fifty condoms spill out when she opens the door. Mature beyond his years, Mac exercises great self-control, and Cory's fury is soon eclipsed by her grief when her mother dies of heart failure. Temporarily living with Cory and her stepfather, Mike, who earlier adopted her, are Cory's older brother, Rob Kranz, and his young wife, Elaine, back in Summer so that Rob can take a job soon to open at a local plant. To Cory's dismay, Rob seems to be turning into a typical Wisconsin redneck. Conflict erupts over the right of Indians to spear spawning fish in Summer Lake, based on a nineteenth-century treaty. Like a majority of the other white men in town, Rob resents this right and plans a protest to make the Indians too uncomfortable to come to Summer. After an argument over this, Mike kicks Rob out of the house and leaves for the weekend. The whole town takes sides. When Cory tears down posters for the protest in all the motel rooms and refuses Bartleby's order to replace them, she quits, taking the motel keys without noticing. At the protest where her best friend, Sasha* Hunter, sides with the Indians, Cory finds Rob, tries to persuade him to leave, and is horrified to see that he is carrying a gun. In the park where they agreed to meet, Cory finds Mac hiding under a picnic table bleeding badly from a head wound inflicted when racists chased and threw bottles at him. Because Mac does not want to go to a doctor, fearing this will inflame passions, and her home is too far away, she takes him to the motel and lets them into the one room unrented because it needs repairs. There she cleans him up, decides he is right that the cut is not serious, and, hearing a bunch of protesters whooping it up in the parking lot, lies down on the bed with him to wait until it is safe to leave. They are awakened by the entrance of garrulous Mr. Bartleby, who likes to talk and soon lets the whole town know that Cory sneaked into the motel to make love to an Indian. Mike returns to bail out Rob, arrested for carrying a concealed weapon. When Rob, furious because an Indian was given the job he expected, makes bigoted remarks, Cory lies and tells him she "did it" with an Indian. He strikes her and cuts her face with his ring, and in her fall she breaks her arm. Cory refuses to press charges but says she never wants to speak to Rob again. Three weeks later he seeks her out, apologizes, and asks her to help with a surprise fiftieth birthday party for Mike. To the party he has asked both Mike's white and his Indian friends. Cory is amazed at how well they get along, but also realizes that the accord may be superficial and that, as with her and Rob, it will take more than words and a party to make a long-term healing. The dynamics of a small town are well evoked, and Cory is an attractive, not-too-perfect protagonist. Mac is admirable, almost too self-possessed and understanding to be believable, while Mike is a strong character, devastated by his wife's death and distraught at the troubles of his stepchildren, but still warmly supportive. The fishing-rights dispute is more a matter of pride on both sides than of economic substance. SLJ.

RICE, BEBE FAAS, author of novels for young adults. Her mystery, *Class Trip** (HarperCollins, 1993), about serial killings on an island in an isolated Vermont lake, was a nominee for the Edgar Allan Poe Award. Set in 1906 on the Canadian prairie, *The Year the Wolves Came* (Dutton, 1994) is a chilling fantasy about a girl who discovers her mother was descended from wolves.

Among her other titles are *Love You to Death* (HarperCollins, 1994) and *My Sister, My Sorrow* (Dell, 1992).

THE ROAD TO MEMPHIS (Taylor*, Mildred D., Dial, 1990), historical novel, third in the series of novels about the Logan family, of community life among African-American farmers and sharecroppers in Mississippi from early October through early December, 1941, several years after the events of the author's Newbery Award-winning *Roll of Thunder, Hear My Cry** and after *Let the Circle Be Unbroken**. Cassie Logan, now seventeen and in high school in Jackson and looking forward to college and possibly studying law, describes the terrible events that occur after her brother Stacey*, now almost twenty-one, and two local friends, Little Willie Wiggins and Moe* Turner, Cassie's sometime sweetheart, return from Jackson where they all work in a box factory, while Cassie is still at home on summer vacation. Several local boys—including Stacey, her brothers Christopher-John and Little Man, and very fat Harris Mitchum, about 350 pounds—go on a coon hunt, Cassie tagging along. They run into Jeremy* Simms, son of local redneck Charlie Simms, and his cousins, the Aames boys. Statler Aames baits Harris, then sets his hounds on the black youth, frightening Harris into climbing a tree from which he falls, sustaining various injuries and breaking his leg in two places, which permanently cripples him. Trouble strikes again the weekend after Thanksgiving when they return home from Jackson for the Reverend Mr. Gabson's funeral, accompanied by Clarence* Hopkins, a local boy who has joined the army. In nearby Strawberry on Saturday, Clarence is harassed by the Aames rednecks when he tries to buy some headache powders, and later the same day the Aames boys also harass Moe. Moe turns on his tormentors, striking them with a tire iron and wounding one of them, perhaps fatally. He quickly takes refuge in the Simmses' truck, and Jeremy drives him away, but local whites assume Harris has helped Moe escape. Knowing there will be no justice in Strawberry, the youths—Stacey, Cassie, Clarence, and Little Willie Wiggins—decide to drive Moe to the train in Memphis and send him off to safety with the Logans' Uncle Hammer in Chicago. Their trouble-filled journey by car through the Mississippi night along Route 51 is obviously metaphorical, like that in the author's *The Gold Cadillac,* of the tribulations of blacks in America in their long, hard quest for justice, freedom, and happiness. Along the way, Stacey's 1938 Ford develops troubles, but the gas station operator slights him in favor of white customers. Cassie is abused verbally and physically when she approaches a ''whites only'' bathroom. They evade harassing rednecks by turning down a lonely side road, where they hide until morning. Two white hunters help them with the needed fan belt for the car, and they continue to a town with a hospital, since Clarence's headaches have become extremely severe, but they are refused help. An old black woman named Ma Dessie takes Clarence in, and the rest push on. They arrive in Memphis on Sunday morning to a buzzing, crowded railroad station, where they learn from an old shoeshine man that the Japanese have bombed Pearl Harbor and there is no space on the Chicago train. They seek help of a friend of their Jackson cousins, Solomon Bradley*, a black lawyer and newspaperman of some eminence. They stay at his place Sunday night while Stacey contacts Uncle Hammer, a ticket is secured for Moe, and the car repaired. Fed and rested, they put Moe on the train in the morning and return to Ma Dessie's for Clarence, only to discover he has died of an attack of some sort. They inform the army of his death and return home, arriving in Strawberry to find Harris about to be hauled to jail and maybe lynched for helping Moe to escape. In the altercation that follows, Jeremy owns up to rescuing Moe and is beaten up and disowned by his father. Despised by his family and local whites, Jeremy joins the army. Cassie returns to school, older and wiser for the few days' terrible events, and Stacey hopes his job in Jackson is still waiting for him. Although ensuring Moe's safety is the book's main problem, other matters also contribute tension and texture: Cassie's relationship with Moe and her crush on the older, well-educated, sophisticated Solomon Bradley; Cassie's growing interest in law and the possibilities for improving life for blacks through reinterpretation of laws; the pregnancy of Cassie's unmarried friend, Sissy Mitchum (Harris's twin), and Sissy's relationship with Clarence, the baby's father; the Logans' relationship with Jeremy Simms; and the beginning of World War II and black attitudes toward it and serving in the army. The elder Logans appear infrequently; the focus is on the younger generation. Cassie is growing to be much like her mother, sensible, cautious, and idealistic, and Stacey mirrors Papa, hard working, responsible, and protective. A few too many untoward incidents happen to the Logans and their friends by way of instructing readers about racism, and the trip is overextended, the Aames brothers are faceless, overdrawn villains, and Cassie, by her own admission, ''smart mouths'' too often and is too often Cassie-on-the-spot; still, this large and substantial story shows Cassie and Stacey to be developing appropriately and consistently holds the attention. For more details about *Roll of Thunder, Hear My Cry,* see *Dictionary, 1960–1984,* and about *The Gold Cadillac,* see *Dictionary, 1985–1989.* C. S. King Winner; Stone.

ROBERTS, WILLO DAVIS (1928–   ), born in Grand Rapids, Michigan; author of more than eighty books, most of them mystery, suspense, medical background, and historical novels for adults. Many of her books for children also are mysteries—some lighthearted, like *The Minden Curse* (Atheneum, 1978) and *More Minden Curses* (Atheneum, 1980); some are full of suspense, like *Megan's Island* (Atheneum, 1988), winner of an Edgar Allan Poe Award, and *To Grandmother's House We Go** (Atheneum, 1990), a nominee for the Poe Award. Among her more recent books are *Jo and the Bandit* (Atheneum, 1992), set in Texas just after the Civil War; *What Are We Going to Do about David?* (Atheneum, 1993), about a boy sent to live with a grandmother he hardly knows; *Caught* (Atheneum, 1994), a tense novel of runaways and the mystery that awaits them at their destination; and *The Absolutely True Story . . . How I Visited Yellowstone Park with the Terrible Rupes* (Atheneum, 1994), about a miserable and threatening trip in a motor home. Roberts gained material for this last novel in her extensive travels with her husband, a writer-photographer, in a motor home equipped with a built-in office. For earlier biographical information and title entries, see *Dictionary, 1960–1984* [*More Minden Curses*] and *Dictionary, 1985–1989* [*Megan's Island*].

RODOWSKY, COLBY (1932–   ), born in Baltimore, Maryland; teacher, prolific writer, mostly of problem novels for older children and young adults. After receiving her B.A. degree from the College of Notre Dame of Maryland, she taught in a Baltimore public school for two years, then moved to a school for special education, an experience that led to several of her novels, including the first two, *What about Me?* (F. Watts, 1976), about a girl whose younger brother has Down syndrome, and *P. S. Write Soon* (Watts, 1978), about a crippled girl writing an idealized version of her life to a pen-pal. Several of her books are connected, as are *Evy-Ivy-Over* (Watts, 1978), its sequel, *Julie's Daughter* (Farrar, 1985), and *H, My Name Is Henley* (Farrar, 1983), which employs some of the same characters with a different protagonist. Among her other novels are fantasies: *The Gathering Room* (Farrar, 1981), which is set in an old Baltimore cemetery where a boy befriends spirits of the dead, and *Keeping Time* (Farrar, 1983), in which a street performer escapes to sixteenth-century London. Typically her novels deal with a world of parental abandonment, poverty, and death, but they mostly have humor and an upbeat ending, like *Sydney, Herself** (Farrar, 1989), about a girl whose father died before she was born and who decides, against all credible evidence, that he was a member of a popular Australian rock band. It was selected as a Best Book by the *School Library Journal,* as were *The Gathering Room* and *Julie's Daughter,* both of which were also cited by the American Library Association on lists of commended books. For younger children, Rodowsky has written *Dog Days,* illustrated by Kathleen Collins Howell (Farrar, 1990), and for even younger ones, *Jenny and the Old Great Aunts,* illustrated by Barbara Roman (Macmillan, 1992). She is married to Lawrence Rodowsky, a judge on the Maryland Court of Appeals, has six children, and lives in Baltimore.

ROLL OF THUNDER, HEAR MY CRY (Taylor*, Mildred D., Dial, 1976), historical novel about the problems an African-American family face in keeping their land and values in racist Mississippi during the Great Depression year of 1933–1934, as seen by spunky, inquisitive Cassie Logan, 9, the second eldest child. Fine characterizations and rich details of family and community life drawn from stories the author's father told result in a tense and vivid novel about physical and spiritual survival against great odds. Also about the Logans are the novels *Let the Circle Be Unbroken** and *The Road to Memphis**. Stone. Previously *Roll of Thunder, Hear My Cry* received the following citations: Books Too Good; Boston Globe Honor; Contemporary Classics; Fanfare; National Book Finalist; Newbery Winner. For a longer entry, see *Dictionary, 1960–1984.*

ROMY RAMIREZ (*Grab Hands and Run**), Romelia Ramirez, 8, little sister of Felipe* and daughter of Paloma* and Jacinto. With her mother and brother she flees for safety from El Salvador to Canada to escape the repressive Salvadoran political regime, after Jacinto, a known political activist, disappears. At home she does poorly in school because she daydreams a lot, according to Felipe, who tells the story, but on the trip she displays wit, perception about people, and a good deal of common sense. For example, she quickly understands that her mother is in danger from the soldiers they encounter and thus sometimes creates minor disruptions and hindrances to put the men off. When one of the Canadian interviewers asks the little family how the Canadians can be sure they will keep the law once they reach Canada, having broken the law to enter the United States, Romy replies by using the rock, fire, or paper game. Her point is that life is stronger than law.

ROSE (*Nekomah Creek**), Robby Hummer's classmate at Nekomah Creek Elementary School. She has long, dark, tangled hair and big, green eyes, wears long flowered skirts and big bulky sweaters, which her mother makes, shares Robby's love of books, and is his source of information about what happens to Amber Hixon and about social workers in general. She and her mother share their home with another single mother who has several daughters, Rose's "stepsisters"—a nontraditional family that contrasts with Robby's. Her report to Robby that Amber has been placed in a foster home raises his fears about what Mrs.* Van Gent and social workers might do because of his unconventional family. Later she tells him that a social worker tracked down her dad, who has been delinquent with support money, a matter that causes Robby to revise his opinion of social workers.

ROSEMARY'S WITCH (Turner*, Ann, HarperCollins, 1991), lighthearted witch fantasy. When the Morgenthaus move into the spacious old house on the hill overlooking the little New England town of Woodhaven in 1991, a dream comes true for all four of them. Dad, a history professor, now can have a room for his book collection on Abraham Lincoln; Mom, a dancer, one for practice; Nicky, 11, one for his rocks and fossils; and shy, inarticulate Rosemary, 9 (from whose perspective most events are seen), a place for dreaming and pondering how she, the only ordinary member of the family, she thinks, can become special, too. Almost immediately, she senses something is wrong; the woods look spooky, and while exploring the barn, she and Nicky hear goosebump-raising noises (although he refuses to admit it). Then the family misses possessions: Dad, his favorite china teacup; Mom, a bag of clothes; and Rosemary, her cherished new bike. Lost objects are also the topic of conversation among the regulars at Mrs. Nan's local restaurant, where someone associates the strange occurrences with the Morgenthaus' arrival. Unknown to them all, Mathilda* Otis, a misanthropic witch, has taken over an abandoned cabin in the woods near the Morgenthaus' house, and in preparation for celebrating her 150th birthday soon, has decided to drive the Morgenthaus from the house, which had been her childhood home. She "calls" the bike to her, swipes other objects, reclaims and refurbishes her old doll, Emily, and summons to her aid the wild black cat of the area and then sends him to the house to give the Morgenthaus fleas. Because he has seen the bike being called—that is, he has seen it move across the landscape seemingly by itself—fat, loquacious Ernie* Smith, a neighbor boy Rosemary's age, drops in. The two children compare observations, conclude a witch is at work, and make a pact to inform each other if more untoward events occur. Mathilda plagues the area with extended fog and rain followed by a superabundance of toads (a plague that provokes some funny scenes). Rosemary has discovered the figure of a young girl drawn in one of the yellow roses on the wallpaper of her room, a child with corkscrew curls and a dour, spiteful expression, guesses she may have been a previous occupant, decides to become a researcher (her specialty now within the family), and with Ernie visits the local library, where her suspicions are confirmed. She concludes that the witch was once that little girl. Fearing that her family may move because they have become so uncomfortable in the house and hoping that, if she can find a home for the witch with a warm home life like her own, the witch may be persuaded to leave the Morgenthaus alone, Rosemary ponders what home means to her and may mean to the witch. She gathers up things that spell home—Maude, her cherished ceramic cat; some chocolate candy; a warm, heavy, white sweater; and her favorite book, *The Long Winter*—and clutching tightly her dearest possession, Freddy her teddy, she visits the cabin, coincidentally on the witch's birthday. In a melodramatic scene in which the witch gradually diminishes in fierceness, Rosemary gives the witch and Emily the various items, last of all, Freddy. She tells the witch that the old house is no longer her home and that with these presents the witch should make another home for herself, and then flees. The weather returns to normal, and the toads disappear. The next day, Rosemary explains to her family what happened, casting the witch's tale into a "ghost story." Later she finds her bike and Freddy by the porch wall. The plot's several conveniences do not detract from the pull of this consistently entertaining fantasy for middle graders about a girl's willingness to sacrifice her dearest possessions in order to help the people she loves and also the being who seems to be the enemy. The Morgenthau family scenes are warm and inviting and foiled with the witch's childhood of deprivation and an alcoholic father. Rosemary's occasional second-sight visions are acceptable because she is presented from the beginning as imaginative, sensitive, and aware of subtle nuances. Scenes range from highly humorous to frightening to melodramatic to heartwarming. Interspersed among the main story's episodes are chapters featuring Mathilda, told from her point of view, and others set in the local restaurant. They place events in perspective and create credibility through providing information as well as contributing humor, although much of the humor in the restaurant passages may be over the heads of many later elementary readers. Characters have distinct personalities, even the minor ones among the restaurant regulars who appear only briefly—for example, Johnny Preston, the truck driver who worries that because his eyesight is failing he will lose his only means of livelihood, and the proprietor, Mrs. Nan, who, always indoors, relies on the television weatherman, Johnny Quill, as the ultimate authority on the elements. As a result, the little town takes on color and presence. The Morgenthaus are typical of a late twentieth-century family, in which the members seek a way of life with more balanced family relationships. Mathilda is a typical witch misanthrope, although why she should have become so because her father drank and lost the house is not clear. Under the lightheartedness, however, the story takes a serious look at what constitutes a family and satisfactory home life. The style makes generous use of attention-getting figures—for example, Woodhaven is described as ''a town like a hat someone had thrown away for being too plain,'' and diction is sensory. SLJ.

ROSS, RAMON ROYAL (1930–   ), born in Walla Walla, Washington, the son of a farmer; college professor and prolific writer of educational materials; author of novels for middle school and early teenaged readers. His first novel, *Prune* (Atheneum, 1984), about the unusual friendship between a prune, a muskrat, and a magpie, was named a Notable Work of Fiction by the Southern California Council of Literature for Children and Young People. *Harper & Moon** (Atheneum, 1993), a boy's growing-up story with mystery, child abuse, and friendship aspects set in the mountains of northeastern Oregon near where Ross himself grew up, was cited by *School Library Journal* and the American Library Association. Ross was graduated from Central Washington University with a B.A., the University of Idaho with an M.Ed., and the University of Oregon with an Ed.D. He has been a professor of education at San Diego State University since 1961 and a visiting lecturer at various universities and colleges in the United States and abroad. Prior to taking the position in San Diego, he lived with his wife and children on a small prune farm near Walla Walla and taught in public school. Currently he teaches classes in children's literature and storytelling and trains teachers and clinicians to work with children with reading and learning difficulties. He lives in the foothills of the mountains east of San Diego.

RUSHFORD, PATRICIA H(ELEN) (1943–   ), born in Rugby, North Dakota, daughter of a farmer; raised in Longview and Vancouver, Washington; was graduated from Clark College in Vancouver with an A.A.S. and Western Evangelical Seminary in Portland, Oregon, with an M.A. in Christian counseling; nurse, teacher, and speaker and writer for adults of helping articles and books on such topics as parenting, women's issues, money management, aging, mental health, and marriage relationships; author of novels for young adults. She conducts workshops and retreats across the United States and has appeared on radio and television talk shows, including *Prime Time America* and *Focus on the Family*. Her first novel for teenagers and preteenagers was *Kristen's Choice*

(Augsburg, 1986), about an injured girl gymnast who falls in with a dubious crowd. Her *Silent Witness** (Bethany House, 1993) was nominated for the Edgar Allan Poe Award. It is one of a series of fast-paced mysteries starring intelligent, sensible, alert, sixteen-year-old Jennie McGrady, including *Too Many Secrets* (Bethany House, 1993), *Deceived* (Bethany House, 1994), and *Pursued* (Bethany House, 1994). Rushford is director of the Oregon Association of Christian Writers Conference. She and her husband, Ron, an investment counselor, live in Vancouver.

RYLANT, CYNTHIA (1954–), born in Hopewell, Virginia; writer of short stories, some published in picture-book form, poetry, and novels for elementary and middle school children. She is a critically respected author, who has won awards and citations for her work, including the prestigious John Newbery Medal and the *Boston Globe–Horn Book* Award for *Missing May** (Orchard, 1992), a short, realistic, often poignant, sometimes funny novel, in which a young girl and her uncle attempt to adjust to the death of his wife and her aunt. *Missing May* was also named to the American Library Association list of best books. For earlier biographical information and title entries, see *Dictionary, 1985–1989* [*A Blue-Eyed Daisy; A Fine White Dust; A Kindness*].

S

SABLE (Hesse*, Karen, illus. Marcia Sewall, Holt, 1944), dog novel set in Vermont in the late twentieth century. When an emaciated, dark brown stray dog wanders into their rural yard, the narrator, Tate Marshall, 10, gives her water, instantly falls in love with her, and names her Sable. Tate's mother, who as a child was injured by a dog, wants nothing to do with Sable, but her father, who makes furniture in his backyard shop, lets Tate make her a bed out of an old packing box half filled with sawdust covered by an old quilt. Cleaned up, brushed, and fed, Sable becomes a handsome and lively dog—unfortunately, too lively. She roams the neighborhood and brings home trophies: an old rubber boot, a wedge of frozen chocolate cake, a door mat. Neighbors complain. Pap chains her, but she soon learns to free herself. Two weeks later, Pap takes Tate and Sable when he delivers cabinets in Concord, New Hampshire, to a doctor who has a big, fenced property. Pap manipulates the doctor into offering to keep Sable, and Tate realizes that her father has planned it all along. Furious, Tate decides to fence a run big enough for Sable, a project she finances herself and determinedly completes despite splinters, blisters, a smashed thumbnail, and various setbacks. With old Mr. Elton Cobb, their slow, kindly neighbor, she rides to Concord, planning to retrieve the dog, only to learn that Sable has taken off weeks ago. At home, the storm through which they have been driving has wrecked their shed and torn branches from their trees, but Tate's fence is almost undamaged. On the strength of her demonstrated drive and ability, Pap starts teaching her his trade, which she has always preferred to housework but which he previously has said is not for girls. Some weeks later, Mr. Cobb stops and carries from his car a weak, bony brown dog he has found limping down the road, still wearing the braided collar Tate made her. This time even Mam welcomes Sable, and when she is fed and her bleeding paws are healed, she no longer wanders. The story is simple, to be read by children Tate's age or younger, but Tate's character is well developed, and both Mam and Pap are rounded figures. Tate's tight-lipped anger at losing her dog helps the book avoid sentimentality. SLJ.

SACKS, MARGARET, raised in Port Elizabeth, South Africa; resident of Memphis, Tennessee, with her husband and two children; writer. Her book for young people, *Beyond Safe Boundaries** (Dutton, 1989), cited by *School Library Journal,* is a revealing historical novel set in South Africa in the late 1950s and early 1960s. It tells of a white girl's growing up amid increasingly tense race relations. A strength of the book comes from its ironic depiction of the effects of apartheid on young people of all races. In addition, she has published *Themba* (Lodestar, 1992), a picture book also set in South Africa.

SAM (*No Kidding**), intelligent boy of fourteen who has taken on the responsibility for his drunken mother and his younger brother, Ollie*. Sam works in a printing shop, the only employee not a recovering alcoholic. He insists that the Bigelows, whom he has chosen as foster parents for Ollie, send the boy to a school that does not have an AO (Alcoholic Offspring) program, since, in a perverse way, he blames his own interest in the AO program with starting his mother's drinking. His father has earlier become entranced with the intolerant Steemer religious doctrine and left the family to bring salvation to the Eskimos. Sam is almost unbelievably capable and respected in a society that now has very few children.

SAM DAILY (*And One for All**), 17, best friend of Wing* Brennan and idol of Geraldine* Brennan. Sam retains the love but incurs the displeasure of the Brennan family for his protest activities during the Vietnam War, the conflict in which Wing is killed. Sam tries to keep Wing from enlisting, and when Wing comes home on leave before departing for Asia, Sam attempts to persuade him to defect to Canada. Sam opposes the war for several reasons, among them that it is an internal civil conflict in which others should not intervene and that the war benefits mainly such wealthy interests as munitions manufacturers. Sam also lost his father in the Korean War. Geraldine has always held Sam in high regard, loving his gentle ways and the imaginative anecdotes he makes up for the younger children about neighborhood landmarks. For a while after Wing's death, Geraldine resents Sam's political activism against the war, until she realizes that in his way he also is fighting the foe, which he sees as not the Vietnamese but war itself. Although too typical of the antiwar set, Sam is an interesting and likable figure.

SAM DAVIDSON (*The Broccoli Tapes**), quiet, self-contained older brother of Sara, the narrator. Always a loner, Sam does not suffer from lack of friends in Hawaii as his sister does, but he becomes equally obsessive about caring for Broccoli, the wild cat they rescue, and he is more successful than she is in dealing with Eddie* Nutt, the prickly boy they meet in the lava field. Extremely sensitive, Sam cannot bear to watch sad, embarrassing, or violent events on television and will not fight even when provoked. His father says that Sam protects himself too much, and both his mother and his grandmother worry that he is afraid of making emotional commitments for fear of getting hurt. Their common interest in Broccoli brings Sam closer to Sara, and his concern for both the cat and Eddie begins to break down his self-imposed emotional barriers.

SAM THE CAT DETECTIVE (Stewart*, Linda, Scholastic, 1993), humorous talking-animal fantasy, a take-off on the private eye novel. Sam, a cat detective, shares the Manhattan office of Hunnicker, a bookstore owner, and does his sleuthing after Hunnicker closes up his shop for the night. One evening, Sugary, a pretty black-and-yellow, blue-eyed, year-and-a-half-old puss, consults Sam about a robbery at her apartment. A valuable jade necklace has been stolen from her ''roommate,'' Mr. Crandle, a jeweler, who, she insists, will be ruined unless it is recovered. Sam swings into action in expert private eye fashion with the help of various feline friends: Spike, observant but otherwise none too bright; several neighborhood cats; a stylish redhead named Sue, who lives at the grooming shop called Kitten Kaboodle and thus picks up all the gossip; and Stretch, who ''rooms'' with Cheater Rivera, a human fence, who operates out of a back room at the Kit Kat Klub. Sam discovers that Sugary's robbery was only one of three burglaries in the same building that night. Other thefts have occurred in a particular sequence; in each case the burglar left behind a peculiar odor later identified as turpentine; and each apartment had recently been repainted. Sam deduces when and where the next break-in will probably occur, and with a cadre of cat allies stakes out the apartment. When the thief strikes, the cats attack him and create such a ruckus that the police are summoned and soon apprehend the culprit. Sam plays the Sam Spade role to the hilt, and he and his feline cohorts are well-known cat and human types. Sugary, for example, is both a decorative apartment house pussycat and Sam's sometimes petulant, occasionally assertive girlfriend, who displays a typical amount of jealousy, possessiveness, and acumen. Except for understanding and using human speech among themselves and employing reasoning powers beyond those normally attributed to cats, the animals do nothing that is out of line for such clever, discerning creatures as these are represented as being. They travel from floor to floor by dumbwaiter, for instance, and have learned from observation how to operate the microwave, computer, and telephone. They know human speech but never converse with humans. Sam acquired his detecting prowess from having once been the mascot of the local police precinct. The cats' dialogue is an ongoing source of amusement, at least for the reader acquainted with the form, being filled with witty quips, punny fun, and mildly satirical jibes. Purposefully of no great consequence, the story is faithful to the cats' point of view, consistently amusing, and heavy on fast action. It shows that the author is well acquainted with the ways of indulged pet cats. Poe Nominee.

SASHA HUNTER (*Revolutions of the Heart**), daughter of one of the executives of the local plant, a more cosmopolitan girl than most others in Summer High School, which she entered the previous year. She also stands out as being the most liberal, the first to suggest a series of meetings to try to improve understanding between the white and Native American students. Ironically, her boyfriend is Tony Merrill, son of one of the most confirmed bigots of the town. To please her, Tony tones down his racism and accepts Cree Mac* MacNamara as a good friend. Sasha and Tony also come from opposite sides of the economic and educational barriers in the small town. She admits to Cory Knutson that she and Tony have sex, saying that it is the only time when their differences do not matter. Sasha helps Cory get even with the boy who has been putting scurrilous notes and condoms into Cory's locker by finding out who is responsible and helping her fill the forty-odd condoms he left with water, molasses, and catsup, then distracting his attention after baseball practice so that Cory can dump them all on his head. As a result, both girls are barred from the senior prom, but Sasha, who lives with a young and unsympathetic stepmother, has Tony and thinks the escapade worth it.

SATURNALIA (Fleischman*, Paul, HarperCollins, 1990), historical novel set in wintry Boston in 1681, giving a slice of life in the religiously repressive Puritan community and centering on a young printer's apprentice. William, 14, whose real name is Weetasket, is a Narraganset Indian, captured in the infamous Great Swamp fight of December 19, 1675, in which many of the then-neutral Narragansets were massacred and others captured and sold as slaves. William has been fortunate to be apprenticed to Charles Currie, a kindly and learned printer, who has taken William into his large family and, finding him highly intelligent, educated him in English, Latin, and Greek. Still, William slips out at night, although it is forbidden to be on the streets after curfew, and he wanders the town, playing a song from his childhood on his bone flute, hoping to make contact with his twin brother, Cancasset, from whom he was separated after their capture. William's brilliance is especially goading to Mr.* Baggot, the tithingman, who drops in unexpectedly to catechize the children, hoping to catch the apprentice in some error so that he may be punished and bring a sense of justice to the zealot whose grandsons were killed by Indians. Mr. Baggot also suspects William of trying to contact other Narraganset slaves and hopes to snare him in this or other wrongdoing. One night William's flute melody is answered by a light in a dilapidated shed, and he discovers his great-uncle Michamauk, who, with his little cousin Ninnomi, has been bought by Mr. Rudd, the cruel and miserly eyeglass maker, a man notorious for abusing his servants and apprentices. Michamauk tells him that Cancasset was sent as a slave to Barbados and killed trying to escape. Because they are nearly starving, William brings food on subsequent nights and in turn is instructed by Michamauk in Narraganset lore, which he has nearly forgotten or was too young to learn before the massacre. On the evening of Saturnalia, which only Mr. Currie's family celebrates with the traditional reversal of roles between servants and masters, William finds a crowd gathering outside the eyeglass shop and sees the body of murdered Mr. Rudd, with an apprentice's contract clamped between his teeth,

Mr. Rudd's name written in as the apprentice and the master's name given as Satan. At first Michamauk and Ninnomi are suspected, but William points out that neither of them can write. Mr. Baggot turns the accusation against William, who is able to convince the crowd that the murderer was a former Rudd apprentice, misused and returned for vengeance. Michamauk and Ninnomi seize the opportunity to escape across the frozen swamp. Faced with the possibility of joining them, William opts to fulfill his apprenticeship with Mr. Currie, but to return when he is free to his own people and use his remarkable memory to preserve their culture. Intertwined with William's story are those of Mr.* Joseph Speke, furniture maker, and the more amusing stories of the Widow Phipp, Mr.* Hogwood, the wigmaker who courts her, and his rascally manservant, Malcolm* Poole, as well as a number of other Boston personages. Although the novel is short, it is compelling, the style economical and deft, with both humor and tense drama. Little sympathy is shown for the self-righteous Puritans or the pompous bewigged wealthy. The snow, freezing puddles, and filthy streets form a memorable sensory setting for the story. ALA; Boston Globe Honor; Fanfare; SLJ.

SCARFACE (Nelson*, Peter, Archway, 1991), realistic mystery-detective novel set one recent summer on Rainy Lake near International Falls, Minnesota. Because her divorced mother is spending the summer in Europe, Sylvia Smith-Smith, 17, decides to take a job as handygirl with her father's Uncle Elliot, who owns a run-down fishing resort hotel called Mesopotamia-Neanderthal on Rainy Lake. The major problem—saving the resort, which is in danger of going under—is supported by two subplots: Sylvia's romance with Baxter Hall, the handsome, athletic, clean-cut son of wealthy Kenneth Hall, owner of a lavish estate nearby, and discovering who owns the Mystery Woods, a heavily wooded tract of some six thousand acres. Because certain property restrictions have been violated, this wooded parcel will soon be auctioned off, and a good deal of discussion and tension over its possible development have resulted. Sylvia soon makes friends with the other help, among them Kari, also a maid, a tall, beautiful blond her age curiously lacking in self-assurance; and Gordie, a lifeguard, handyman, and jokester, who seems naive and slow but who Sylvia soon detects is really quite clever. Uncle Elliot's need for money occupies her mind. When Gordie's Uncle Dug spins stories about the resort's history as a whorehouse and playground for unsavory types like Baby Face Nelson and Scarface Al Capone and remarks that a trunkful of Capone's money is still somewhere in the area, Sylvia decides, with Kari's help, to stage a sighting of Capone's ghost pleading for his money. She then submits an article about this happening to the sensationalistic tabloid, *National Interrogator,* reporting it as a true experience. Requests for hotel reservations rise immediately. Among the guests are Madame Tedescu, a mysterious old woman dressed in black, and her assistant, an elderly man named George. Madame Tedescu soon holds a seance in Capone's old room, during which a ghostly voice suggests that the money might be in the basement. A search reveals a secret cellar, in which, to their surprise, Madame

Tedescu imprisons Sylvia, Kari, and Gordie, but not Baxter, who suddenly defects. Using a plastic card, Sylvia opens the lock, and after harrowing experiences they arrive at Uncle Dug's place. To their surprise, he reveals that all along he has had the trunk, under his table, and that it contains about $800,000. After they get back to the hotel, Gordie fires off a July 4 rocket to distract Madame Tedescu and George, and Uncle Elliot and his friends capture them. Madame Tedescu is unmasked as Capone's moll and George as her son. Sylvia learns that Baxter's defection was faked in an effort to help her group get away, and their romance resumes. In a community meeting about the Mystery Woods, several community groups and wealthy individuals bid on the land, but suddenly Gordie reveals that he is the owner by right of inheritance through his father. The Capone money is distributed variously to help the economy of the area without disturbing its ecological balance. Sylvia returns to New York City, feeling that the summer has been worthwhile and puts her romance with Baxter on hold. Plot motivations are often strained, and coincidence abounds. The very large cast of characters, some historical like Uncle Elliot's friend Bronko Nagurski, the football player, are mostly obvious types, the liberated Sylvia and the All-American Baxter, for example, the claims of the Native Americans to their previous land are not omitted, and the romance seems patterned on the usual girl-meets-boy novel for teenaged girls. Occasionally the story parodies the mystery form, and some purple prose passages support that attitude, but the plentiful action, staunch, smart heroine, well-paced tension, and interwoven plots sustain the interest. *Scarface* is one of a series of mysteries starring Sylvia Smith-Smith. Poe Nominee.

SCHWANDT, STEPHEN (WILLIAM) (1947–   ), born in Chippewa Falls, Wisconsin; educator and author mostly of mystery novels for teenaged readers. He was graduated from Valparaiso University with a B.A. and from St. Cloud State University with a B.S. and received his M.A. from the University of Minnesota–Twin Cities. He has taught high school English and American literature in Minnesota schools and been a part-time instructor at Concordia College in St. Paul and at Normandale Community College in Bloomington, Minnesota. His first novel, *The Last Goodie* (Holt, 1985), in which a high school senior investigates the death of his childhood babysitter, was named a best book by both the New York Public Library and the Philadelphia Public Library, was a Child Study Association Best Book of the Year, and was nominated for the Edgar Allan Poe Award. Since then he has published *A Risky Game* (Holt, 1986), a psychodrama; *Holding Steady* (Holt, 1988), in which a boy tries to deal with the accidental death of his father; *Guilt Trip** (Atheneum, 1990), an Edgar Allan Poe Nominee, in which a high school youth becomes involved with a theater group and murder; and *Funnybone* (Atheneum, 1992), a mystery involving drugs.

SCIESZKA, JON (1954–   ), born in Flint, Michigan; elementary school teacher, author of books for children in primary and middle school. After receiving his B.A. degree from Albion College, Michigan, and his M.F.A. degree from Columbia University, he became a teacher at the Day School in Manhattan, where he lives with his wife and two children. His first publications were unorthodox picture books retelling folktales with a new twist, the first being *The True Story of the Three Little Pigs, by A. Wolf, As Told to Jon Scieszka,* illustrated by Lane Smith (Viking, 1989), which was named an American Library Association Notable Book. It was followed by *The Frog Prince, Continued,* illustrated by Steve Johnson (Viking, 1991). For his best-known book, *The Stinky Cheeseman and Other Fairly Stupid Tales* (Viking, 1992), he again teamed up with Smith, and the result was named a Caldecott Honor book. For children who can read chapter books, he has published a series known as the Time Warp Trio series, featuring three boys who travel in time: *Knights of the Kitchen Table** (Viking, 1991), set mostly in the period of King Arthur and his knights; *The Not-So-Jolly Roger* (Viking, 1991), an adventure with pirates; *The Good, the Bad and the Goofy* (Viking, 1992), about the Wild West; and *Your Mother Was a Neanderthal** (Viking, 1993), in which the boys go back to the stone age. Although adults and older children may enjoy his twisted folktales and the unconventional illustrations, Scieszka says he writes specifically for the early elementary children he teaches, who love silliness and find gross details of bodily functions and nauseous food highly entertaining. A more recent picture book is *The Book That Jack Wrote,* illustrated by Daniel Adel (Viking, 1994), retelling the nursery rhyme with new material.

SCOOTER (Williams*, Vera B., illus. Vera B. Williams, Greenwillow, 1993), contemporary realistic episodic novel in which a young girl describes domestic adventures the summer she and her mother move into a large apartment complex at 514 Melon Hill Avenue in New York City. Elana Rose Rosen, 9, feels unhappy and alienated, until her mother, a single parent who works in the morning and attends school in the afternoon, pushes her out the door of 8E on her blue-and-silver-wheeled scooter. As Elana is practicing jumps and tricks, the wheels catch on a crack in the sidewalk, and Elana falls, bangs her head, and is whisked off to the emergency room. That experience and the huge bandage she comes home with gain her notoriety in the mixed-ethnic complex and several friends, among them Asian Adrienne Thieu, whose parents own the local variety store and who helps Elana get a screen to put around her living room sofabed; African-American Eduard, a skateboard enthusiast; Asian Vinh; and several Caucasians, Siobhan and her bossy older sister, Beryl, who tries to look sexy, and loudmouth, bullying Jimmy Beck, with whom Elana is never really friends but to whom she accommodates. (The children's races are revealed through the illustrations.) Chief among her friends are little Petey* Timpkin, 4, a strange, silent child, and his elderly babysitter, Mrs.* Rachel Greiner, whom Elana helps babysit Petey. When Petey's mother is in the hospital, the two children make soup. In the process, they mess up Mrs. Rosen's kitchen to such an extent that she becomes quite irritable. Then Elana throws a temper tantrum because she feels unappreciated, but most of the time she and her mother get along well. Elana's account, however, reveals that she misses her father and that her father and mother are at odds. Mrs. Greiner, whom at first Elana thinks of as a whiner but whom she later comes to enjoy, takes Petey to the store for a red baseball cap to cheer him up while his mother is in the hospital for an operation. He chooses a sky-blue woolen one instead, which henceforth he always has with him. The summer's main events are the visit from Toronto of Nanette, Elana's cousin her age, and the Borough Field Day at the end of the season. Elana and Nanette have cozy conversations, shop at Thieus' store and downtown, go to the beach, make fruit punch, and pinch-hit for Mrs. Greiner with Petey. In preparation for Borough Field Day, the apartment complex orders special rose-red t-shirts for the children, who fill out entry slips for various individual and group events and publicize the competition with signs made cooperatively. Even Petey, who is too young for the regular competitions, enrolls and practices diligently for what everyone is sure is a legitimate somersault contest. To his and the other children's great disappointment, no such event has been scheduled; they have misread the advertising flyer. After all the other children compete creditably and win ribbons or acclaim of some sort, Petey begins somersaulting across the park. The other children gradually join in, until the entire lawn is filled with tumbling and rolling young bodies. Elana declares Petey the winner, and the book concludes with everyone going home happy. Elana supplements her account with exuberant sketches of the children scattered around the margins of the pages and with numerous acrostics that head chapters. They hint at what will happen, and summarize or amplify events. For example, Elana's feelings about what each child is like are given in acrostics based on the initials of their names. Elana's story is simply told in engaging, sometimes elaborate, concrete detail. Humor of situation and character is gentle and often ironic, and minor characters are briefly but distinctively sketched. The result is a charming, upbeat, and convincing, if unevenly plotted, account of two months in the life of an average young city girl, whose parent and neighbors are trying hard to make good lives for themselves. The book strongly recalls Ruth Sawyer's *Roller Skates,* which is set in an earlier era and like *Scooter* is somewhat autobiographical. ALA; Boston Globe Winner; Fanfare.

SCOTT CHAMBERS (*Silent Witness**), handsome young man Jennie Mc-Grady and Gram* McGrady meet while on their trip to Florida. At first he appears to be a surly, hostile sort, allied with a disagreeable, possibly unprincipled group of environmental protesters, presumably determined to protect dolphins. After he is fired from his job at Key West, Gram and Jennie learn that he has a record of minor police offenses, but Gram has faith in him and gets him another job. Throughout most of the book, he appears on the edge of the law, the chief suspect, but later he is proved innocent. By that time, Jennie has also resolved her crush on him, and they remain just friends. Scott decides to continue his schooling to become a marine biologist, an ambition he conceived from watching a Jacques Cousteau film when he was a child.

SEARCHING FOR DRAGONS (Wrede*, Patricia C., Harcourt, 1991), second in a series of fantasy novels known as the Enchanted Forest Chronicles, which gently parody the conventions of folk literature. In the first novel, *Dealing with Dragons,* the Princess Cimorene, bored with palace life, has run away, become servant to the dragon Kazul, and has involved herself in an ongoing struggle between the dragons and the wizards who are trying to usurp their territory. *Searching for Dragons* is told from the point of view of Mendanbar, young king of the Enchanted Forest, whose main effort since assuming the crown has been to avoid formal state occasions and the princesses who are setting their caps for him. When he discovers a portion of the forest has been burned away, leaving only bare stumps and ash and destroying the magic that protects it, he asks advice of the witch Morwen, who sends him to consult Kazul, now female king of the dragons. Cimorene greets him with the news that Kazul has disappeared. Although they are leery of each other, since Mendanbar is afraid of silly princesses and Cimorene resists being rescued by any hero, they realize that the wizards must be responsible for both problems and that the interests of both of them lie in finding Kazul, so they set off together. Their quest involves them with many strange acquaintances and magic elements, including a dwarf who spins straw into gold and keeps being paid with children he does not want; a giant who is persuaded to give up pillaging and ravaging and become a consultant; a defective magic carpet that lurches and dips and lands them only halfway to their destination; a pedantic magician so concerned with method and theory that he has difficulty with practical spells; and an uncle attempting to prove his wickedness by abandoning his brattish nephew, a crown prince, in the Enchanted Forest. They eventually discover Kazul being held in a cave by wizards, whom they are able to melt with soapy water laced with lemon juice, a formula that ironically does not work on witches as in traditional story but is effective, temporarily, on wizards. During the adventures, Cimorene and Mendanbar, who have no patience with the princesses and heroes of tale, realize that they are each attracted by the unconventional outlook of the other. They are married at a huge party attended by dragons, elves, witches, magicians, and many other inhabitants of the forest and surrounding country, but no wizards. Since the novel is mostly poking fun at the conventional patterns of fairy tale, the dangers and threats are never very serious, and the interest is in the cleverness with which the expected is turned on its head. Sometimes it seems a bit precious but on the whole is good, lighthearted entertainment. ALA; SLJ.

SEBESTYEN, OUIDA (1924–   ), born in Vernon, Texas, author of historical and contemporary novels for young people. Her *Words by Heart* (Atlantic/Little, Brown, 1979), a novel of an African-American family in Texas in 1910, won the International Reading Association Award. It was followed by *On Fire* (Atlantic, 1985), which follows the fortunes of Tater Haney, the boy who shot Ben Sills in *Words by Heart.* With a contemporary Southwest setting, *Out of Nowhere** (Orchard, 1994), a *School Library Journal* Best Book for Children, explores the formation and mutual value of a nontraditional family. Among Sebestyen's other titles are *Far from Home* (Little, Brown, 1980) and *IOUs* (Little, Brown, 1982). She lives in Boulder, Colorado, is divorced, and has one son. For earlier biographical information and a title entry, see *Dictionary, 1960–1984* [*Words by Heart*].

SECRET CITY, U.S.A. (Holman*, Felice, Scribner's, 1990), sociological problem story of a group of boys, most of them homeless, who discover and rehabilitate an abandoned house in some large, northern U.S. city, probably New York, set in the period of its publication. After the death of Jojo, his beloved grandfather, Benno, 12, feels stifled in the tenement apartment of his family. With his friend Moon*, he wanders far from their barrio and discovers an abandoned section of the city, mostly the rubble of wrecked buildings but with a few substantial houses still standing. Struck by the irony of empty buildings when the alleys and doorways where he lives are full of homeless people, Benno is fired with a desire to explore and fix up one of the houses. He and Moon find a way into one basement, and, with a flashlight borrowed from Moon's uncle, they check out the house and are amazed at the space. They recruit Moon's young cousins, Juan and Paco, who with their mother have recently moved into the family's already crowded apartment, and Willie, a homeless boy living in an alley, and taking discarded brooms, mops, buckets, and chips of soap, they start to clean the place. At night they carefully cover with trash the basement window through which they enter, leaving Willie, who finds the house cleaner, safer, and even less lonely than his alley, as their "night watchman." Later they add to their group Alfonzo, from Haiti; Louie, a large boy about their age; and Louie's little brother, Ozzie, 5, who have lived in the alley near Willie. In the house they get water from a leaky pipe in the basement, use a bucket under the sink drain, and make the toilet work by pouring water into the tank. Each boy has his own specialty: Benno is the acknowledged leader; Louie provides the prime muscle to clear the yard and build a barricade of junk around it; Paco and Juan dig and plant a vegetable garden; Alfonzo cooks the pigeons Louie kills and makes stews and corn cakes from the food the others bring. They have two main problems: a pack of wild dogs lives in the area, which they refer to as "the Space," and a gang known as the Poisons controls streets they must cross between their home territory and the Space. Eventually they discover other residents of the area, or Secret City, as they privately think of it: an old man they call McWhat and his tamed wild dog named Ironsides, living in the basement of a wrecked house. When they hear Ironsides howling dismally, they investigate and find that the old man has broken his leg. He bullies them into setting it for him, but despite their efforts to keep him clean and feed him and the dog, the leg becomes infected and McWhat delirious. With great effort and threatened by the dogs, the boys carry him on a makeshift stretcher to a hospital, where the social counselor, Marie Lorry, grills them but obtains very little information. Nevertheless, when they return to inquire about the old man, she woos them by buying them breakfast and turning a blind eye as they scavenge food from the tables to take to their house, and they gradually begin to trust her. Events come to a head for two reasons: Marie and her friend, Pete Powell, a newsman, come to see the house, and one of the Poisons follows Louie home. Pete writes a series of laudatory articles, but the Poison leader, chased by police, implicates all the boys to get a reduced charge, and the police lay siege to the building. Pete and a television crew show up, videotape the whole scene, and with the publicity force the mayor to change plans from upscale apartments for the area to good-quality, low-cost housing. In the end, Marie and Pete have set up a private commission to monitor progress, Marie has found places for all the homeless kids, and Benno and Moon have renamed their house Jojo's Space. Despite a number of implausibilities, it is easy to get caught up in the earnestness of the boys, their pioneering spirit, and their hard work and ingenuity. The television-publicity-to-the-rescue ending is a cliché, but the need depicted and the indifference or inability of the bureaucracy to provide a solution are real enough. Except for Benno and Moon, who seem to be Hispanic, and Alfonzo, from Haiti, the ethnic origins of the characters are not specified. Child Study.

THE SECRET KEEPER (Whelan*, Gloria, Knopf, 1990), mystery novel set shortly before the time of publication in a private club on Lake Michigan in the northwestern part of Michigan's Lower Peninsula. Three years later, Anne Lewis, a college student, describes the summer she serves as keeper (companion sitter) for Matt Stevens, 10, at the Beaches, the exclusive lakeshore club where Matt's maternal grandparents, the Larimers, and about a dozen other families, all long-time friends, own well-appointed summer homes. During the employment interview, Mrs. Larimer informs Anne that Matt is not to have any contact with his father, Bryce*, who, she says, is an unsavory sort. She warns Anne about the rumors that are rife about Bryce and about the death of his wife, Jess, the Larimers' only child, by car accident. Although at first both she and Matt feel strange, because it is also his first summer with the Larimers, Anne undertakes her job with enthusiasm, pleased at having the chance to vacation in so much luxury. She notices how the other residents seem protective of Matt and attributes it to his newness. Ed* Lindner, a local youth who acts as naturalist for the children and also as keeper for another boy, fills Anne in on details about the region and the Larimers. He says Jess's parents and the other residents never accepted Bryce, a local boy and son of a Beaches groundskeeper now dead, and that the Stevenses' marriage was rocky. While Anne and Matt are taking a walk at the edge of the estate one day, Bryce appears, and, after conversation, Anne, who admits to being impressionable, can see no reason for their disliking the handsome, muscular, blond man. She agrees to communicate with him by notes left in a particular place and enable him and Matt to get together occasionally. At another meeting, however, she is taken aback at the intense anger he shows toward the Larimers and the residents, regarding them as arrogant, callous interlopers who are training Matt to be as insensitive to the environment and other people and as materialistic as they themselves are. An argument Anne overhears between Dr. and Mrs. Bradford, relatives of the Larimers, increases her apprehension that there is more behind Jess's death and the Larimers' dislike for Bryce than she has been told. Events rise to a climax when Bryce wins the canoe race held annually by the Beaches for the area, and Matt, proud of his father's success and happy to see him again, runs to the man and is carried away by truck. A hunt ensues with no success, and, after Thomas*, the Ottawa Indian maintenance man, says that Bryce's father had a remote hunting cabin near Newberry in the Upper Peninsula of Michigan, the residents decide in a meeting to send Mr. Larimer and Dr. Bradford there to recover Matt and deal with Bryce. The men return with Matt, and, although the news gets out that Bryce has gone to California, Anne is sure that they killed him. She has also learned that Bryce had assaulted and killed Jess, but that in return for his agreeing to let the Larimers have Matt and to leave the area, the Larimers faked her death in a car accident. Realizing she knows too much, Anne worries when the Larimers invite her to accompany them on a boat cruise to Georgian Bay, fears for her own safety, and leaves for home hastily. Much later she learns that the club land has been deeded to the state and is being allowed to return to its former wild condition. The author builds tension gradually and relentlessly. She skillfully mingles Anne's growing understanding of the determination of the residents to protect the Larimers and to deceive the authorities—to do whatever is necessary to protect their reputations and have their way—with the girl's personal problems of her divorcing parents and her attraction to Bryce and Ed's attraction to her. The upshot is that she becomes increasingly isolated, with no one in whom she can confide. Characters are drawn with more dimension and subtlety than is usual for the genre, and the plot lacks the normal array of red herrings, the emphasis being on the revelations about Bryce and the characterization of the residents as a whole. Especially strong is the natural appearance of the region—dunes, beach, shoreline, boardwalk, bogs, small towns, thronging tourists—and the ethos of the residents, exclusive, ingrown, patronizing, arrogant, a people certain that they are right and that their wealth guarantees them special privileges. Poe Nominee.

SEGAL, JERRY, for many years a writer of movies. His amusing, legend-like novel for children, *The Place Where Nobody Stopped** (Orchard, 1991), is set in czarist Russia. An American Library Association Notable Book, it is the opening novel of a planned trilogy, From Vilebsk to Texas, which he wrote to tell his children and grandchild about the hardships and setbacks their immigrant great-grandparents suffered to come to America. Segal and his wife live in Los Angeles.

SEIDLER, TOR (1952–   ), born in Littleton, New Hampshire; writer of text materials for children and of novels for children and young adults. After graduating from Stanford University, he became a freelance contributor to the Harcourt Brace Jovanovich Language Arts program, work that turned his attention to books for children. His first published book, *The Dulcimer Boy,* illustrated by David Hockney (Viking, 1979), received a fiction award from *Washington State Writer's Day.* Among his novels for children are *Terpin* (Farrar, 1982), a *New York Times* Outstanding Children's Book of the Year; *A Rat's Tale,* illustrated by Fred Marcellino (Farrar, 1985); and *The Tar Pit* (Farrar, 1987). His fantasy, *The Wainscott Weasel**, also illustrated by Marcellino (HarperCollins, 1993), about an unlikely romance between a weasel and a fish, was named an American Library Association Notable Book. Seidler has also published a novel for adults, *Take a Good Look* (Farrar, 1990).

SEVENTEEN AGAINST THE DEALER (Voigt*, Cynthia, Atheneum, 1989), realistic girl's growing-up novel set during January and February in recent years in the small Chesapeake Bay town of Crisfield, Maryland, the last in the Tillerman family cycle, of which *Dicey's Song* received the Newbery Medal. Human interest takes precedence over plot, which offers few digressions and proceeds much as expected. Events are strongly focused from the perspective of (but not told by) Dicey, the eldest of Gram Tillerman's grandchildren, now twenty-one and still proudly and fiercely independent. Dicey has dropped out of college, having found classes irrelevant to her ambition, and is determined to make a go of her own boat-building business. Other story aspects involve her romance with Jeff Greene (of *A Solitary Blue*), who is in his last year of college, and her relationships with her high school-aged siblings—beautiful Maybeth, who still struggles with her classes, and lively Sammy, who hopes for a tennis scholarship—and their Gram, with whom the three children live on the family farm. Her other brother, brilliant James, is away at Yale University on a scholarship and appears briefly at the beginning while on Christmas vacation. After working at boat shops for experience and at McDonald's for start-up money, Dicey opens her business in rented quarters in Crisfield. Business is slack and money very tight. She agrees to sand and paint thirty sloppily constructed small boats for her landlord, Claude Shorter, and takes an order for a sailboat from wealthy Tad Hobart, who gives her an earnest check of $500. Her disappointment is great when her shop is broken into and her much-prized tools are stolen. She is told that she should have purchased insurance, and when Hobart cancels his order and she feels duty-bound to return his check, she also realizes she should have put their agreement in writing. She sees that although she may know simple boat building, she does not know basic business practices. A drifter, who says his name is Cisco Kidd, asks for a job, and when refused, continues to hang around her shop, occasionally helping and talking a lot. Graying, sophisticated, articulate, he insinuates himself into her confidence, and since he seems in need and because she feels somewhat obligated to him, she allows him to sleep in the shop while she takes a few days off to nurse Gram, who has pneumonia. Cisco absconds with a large check she has received from Shorter and has asked Cisco to deposit but has been too ignorant to endorse "For deposit only." From this painful experience, Dicey learns that work and determination are not all that she needs to succeed. She also needs knowledge. She agrees to marry Jeff, who urges her to study boat building and whom she realizes she needs for comfort and moral and intellectual support. She realizes that she also needs to give more of herself to him and to her family, since she has sorely neglected them all in her intense desire to succeed. While events hold the reader's attention throughout, this portion of the total Tillerman story seems less successful than its predecessors. Cisco is a phony figure, too obviously shallow and devious and a person whom the reader has trouble believing that Dicey, who has been fairly astute about human nature, would not see through right away. It is hard to understand why she lets him hang around as long as she does. Characterization, however, is the book's strong point, as it is in the other novels. Some have criticized Dicey's decision to marry Jeff as a too convenient way out of the plot, but it appears accurate to her development at this stage. Gram, Maybeth, Sammy, and Jeff remain as portrayed in the earlier books, still strongly individualized and very likable. Dicey's long-time friend, African-American Mina Smiths, of *Come A Stranger,* now aspiring to study law, appears long enough for her romantic problems to contrast with Dicey's relationship with Jeff. Scenes of family members with one another and with their friends have power. Much of the book is devoted to Dicey's internal ruminations and reflections on her own and life in general; these also have power. The family musical sessions, as in the previous books, counterpoint events and contribute their usual charm. Another good aspect is the presentation of Dicey and Jeff's romance as solid and satisfying although minus the panting-passion episodes that often appear in teenaged novels. For details about other Tillerman novels, see *Dictionary, 1960–1984* and *Dictionary, 1985–1989.* SLJ.

SHABANU: DAUGHTER OF THE WIND (Staples*, Suzanne Fisher, Knopf, 1989), episodic contemporary realistic girl's growing-up novel, set among the nomadic "people of the wind" of the Cholistan Desert of Pakistan. The intelligent, resourceful, strong-minded narrator, Shabanu, 12, loves her desert life with her closely knit family: kind, practical Dadi*; warm, gentle Mama; her beautiful sister, Phulan*, 13; vague Grandfather, once a soldier for the area nawab; and grumpy, fat Auntie, wife of Dadi's brother, and her two small sons. Shabanu also loves their camels, which, although the basis of their existence, she appreciates for themselves alone, especially gentle, reliable Guluband, a lively dancer. Life in their rude hut is often demanding and austere but satisfying in its human intimacy and closeness to the earth. Almost two-thirds of the book is given to establishing the general setting in which these people live and also to the particulars of getting ready for Phulan's wedding to Hamir, a youth in an oasis some distance away. In preparation for the wedding, Shabanu accompanies

Dadi on the exciting journey across the desert and over the mountains to the northwest to the Sibi Fair, where they sell their camels, which are noted for their high quality, including, to Shabanu's sorrow, Guluband. The camels bring such a good price that the family will be able to provide a handsome dowry for Phulan, with money to spare for luxuries for the family and even some for Shabanu's dowry. While Dadi bargains and socializes, Shabanu keeps house in their lean-to, but Dadi takes some time out to take her to the carnival with its excitement of merry-go-round, Ferris wheel, and assorted acts and vendors. On their return, Shabanu and the other women travel to Channar Pir, the shrine at which the annual women's festival is held. Shabanu enjoys the company of her favorite aunt, Sharma*, her mother's cousin, who is notorious for having violated custom by leaving an abusive husband. Later, when they are home again, a violent sandstorm hits. Mithoo, a baby camel whom Shabanu birthed, and Grandfather wander off. Mithoo is found safe, but the old man is discovered near death, and after he dies they take his body to Derwar to be buried according to his wishes in the cemetery of the nawab. They then travel to the oasis of the family of Phulan's fiancé, and while the two girls are getting water from the canal, they are accosted by Nazir Mohammad, the wealthy landlord of the area, who is hunting with several of his men. When he offers to give Phulan to whichever man bags the most quails, Shabanu creates a diversion, and the girls escape. The upshot of this incident is the murder of Phulan's fiancé and political and social repercussions that result in Phulan's being wed to Murad, Hamir's brother and Shabanu's intended, and in Shabanu's being betrothed to become the fourth wife of Rahim-*sahib,* Nazir Mohammad's older brother, also wealthy and a member of the area's ruling council. After Phulan's wedding, they return to their desert hut, Shabanu chafing at what she feels is an irrevocable injustice done to her but knowing also that political exigencies and family safety were at stake in her parents' decision. After her periods start and she knows that her wedding is not far off and Dadi informs her that she can no longer work with the animals but must learn household arts, she decides to run away to Aunt Sharma. When Mithoo, who has followed her, breaks a leg and she cannot go on for his sake, she simply waits for Dadi to find her. She endures without a cry the hard beating he gives her, her solace Aunt Sharma's words to always keep ''your innermost beauty, the secrets of your soul, locked in your heart . . . so that he [Rahim-*sahib*] must always reach out to you'' and thus be able to endure what may be a difficult marriage. The plot is discursive, serving as a line on which the author can hang information about these little-known desert dwellers. A clear problem, which becomes dramatic, is introduced fewer than 100 pages before the end of the 240-page book, the reader's interest being held in the earlier portions by the vivid delineation of desert life. The main characters, if mostly types, are clearly drawn, and some minor ones are memorable, like fuzzy-headed Grandfather and unhappy Auntie, both victims in their ways. Even Mithoo, the baby camel, exhibits a charming kind of jester personality. Strongest, however, is the local color. Details of nomadic life—the camel economy, interclan strife, class consciousness and tension, festivals, everyday life from mostly the woman's point of view, customs, the demands of patriarchy—make the story of an independent girl caught in her culture's restrictions compelling and mitigate the author's tendency to tell rather than show. A sequel, *Haveli,* continues Shabanu's story with her marriage to the wealthy official. ALA; Fanfare; Newbery Honor.

SHADES OF GRAY (Reeder*, Carolyn, Macmillan, 1989), historical novel set in the Virginia Piedmont just after the Civil War, when Will Page, 11, whose Confederate family has been wiped out by the war, goes to stay with his aunt, whose husband, being philosophically pacifist, fought for neither side. The difficulties of postwar rural life, the prejudice of neighbors, and Will's gradual understanding of his uncle's position combine to show the results of the conflict in a way different from most other Civil War stories. The novel earlier won the Child Study Award. ALA; Jefferson; O'Dell. For a more detailed entry, see *Dictionary, 1985–1989.*

SHADOW BOXER (Lynch*, Chris, HarperCollins, 1993), realistic novel of family life set in Boston in the early 1990s. Ever since the death of his father, Tommy, a professional boxer, of fight-incurred injuries five years before the story starts, George, 14, by his own admission, has tried to live up to his mother's request that he be the man of the family. Serious and conscientious, schooled by nuns, he takes it upon himself to watch over and bring up his younger brother, Monty*, correctly. While in general he demands and encourages good behavior, his greatest wish is that Monty not follow their father into the fight game—what Ma calls ''Satan's sport''—a problem that unifies the otherwise loosely connected episodes. In the process of ''raising'' his brother, George reveals himself to be an overly earnest boy, one who has not only Monty's good in mind but also subconsciously acts out of excessive pride. He has a need, recognized only late in the book, to maintain control. Some episodes are poignant, as when George takes Monty to visit their father's grave and when Monty furiously throws a rock through the window of the apartment where his best friend, Fred* the Head, had lived with his abusive, drunken father. Some scenes are light—for example, when George makes fun of Monty's ''air guitaring'' and Monty teases George when George takes a dislike to the Big Brother, Chaz*, whom Ma selects for them. The boys have paper routes and earn extra money doing chores and errands, on one occasion for Frank*, an ''elephant man.'' They assist Nat*, the superintendent of their building, called Nat the super, until he is fired as a ''pervert.'' Both boys greatly admired their father, but George, being older and having been instructed in boxing by Tommy, knows better what fighting did to their father's physical and mental health and has a greater understanding of Ma's hatred for the game and fear of their being drawn into it. Occasionally the two boys spar, so that Monty will be able to defend himself, but George keeps a sharp eye on the younger boy, particularly after Uncle Archie*, Tommy's brother and trainer and absolute persona non grata to Ma, opens a gym near by. When Monty spends more and more time away from George, skips school, and has abrasions and bruises he cannot hide, George rightly suspects the reason and confronts Archie, who persuades George to let him handle Monty in his way. Archie continues to instruct the younger boy, who is talented in the ring, and, after Monty knocks down a bigger boy one day, shows him a video of his father being horribly mauled in the ring, which devastates the boy emotionally. Later the two brothers have one last match in the makeshift ring behind their apartment house, during which Monty knocks down George and then bursts into tears. George gets up and hugs Monty. The two walk together into the house, gloves left unheeded on the pavement behind them. The reader must attend carefully to George's narrative for important background details and connections, since after a prologue of George's last instruction-match with Tommy, the episodes occur *in medias res*. Only gradually does the reader become aware that Monty and Ma's advice to George to lighten up is appropriate. Although contemporary terms, allusions, and trash talk will tie the book to the early 1990s, strong characterizations, even of minor figures; the well-depicted single-parent, working-class family; the strong bond between the brothers; just enough sports jargon and scenes; a breezy, intimate style with a good blend of humor and seriousness; and extensive dialogue make this different kind of sports and boys' story compelling. SLJ.

SHANNON, GEORGE (WILLIAM BONES) (1952–   ), born in Caldwell, Kansas; librarian, storyteller, critic, author of stories for picture books, reteller of stories from oral tradition, and novelist for young adults. After receiving his B.S. from Western Kentucky University and his M.S.L.S. from the University of Kentucky, he served as librarian in public schools in Bremen, Muhlenberg County, and Lexington, Kentucky. He has lectured on children's literature and published many articles on the subject in such periodicals as *The Horn Book Magazine, Catholic Library World,* and *Wilson Library Bulletin.* Among his several scholarly works are *Humpty Dumpty: A Pictorial History* (Green Tiger, 1981), *Storytelling: A Selected Annotated Bibliography* (Garland, 1986, with Ellin Greene), and *A Knock at the Door* (Oryx, 1992), a volume in the Oryx Multicultural Folktale Series. His picture books include *The Piney Woods Peddler* (Greenwillow, 1981), *Bean Boy* (Greenwillow, 1984), *Dancing on the Breeze* (Bradbury, 1991), *Climbing Kansas Mountains* (Bradbury, 1993), and *April Showers* (Greenwillow, 1995), by various illustrators. He has also published the well-received books of retellings, *Stories to Solve: Folktales from around the World* (Greenwillow, 1985) and its sequels. His first novel for young adults, *Unlived Affections** (Harper, 1989), a sensitive sociological problem novel revolving around homosexuality and family relationships gone awry, was cited by *School Library Journal.* Shannon lives in Eau Claire, Wisconsin.

SHANTI (*A Little Bit Dead**), the Yahi Indian youth whom Reece* rescues from the white lynchers; who befriends Reece in return by taking him into his family, showing him the gold cave, and helping him defeat Colby, Sam, and the soldiers; and who joins Crazy Horse against the whites. Shanti and two friends had taken gold from the Indians' cave and traveled to the soldiers' fort hoping to trade the location of the cave for land for the Yahi. Colby, Sam, and the U.S. marshal who was later murdered by Colby and Sam followed Shanti on his way home, shot his companions, and captured him. They whipped him and threatened to lynch him in an effort to make him reveal the location of the mine. Shanti later joined Crazy Horse and fought against the whites for many years, finally signing an agreement not to resist them any longer and living far from his old home in the hidden valley. Thirty years after rescuing him from the lynchers, Reece finds Shanti and persuades him to return to the valley, which Reece has purchased for the Indians with the gold from the cave.

A SHARE OF FREEDOM (Wood*, June Rae, Putnam, 1994), girl's growing-up novel set in contemporary times in Gabriel, Missouri. Although Freedom Jo Avery, 13, wins the spelling bee at the Fourth of July celebration, the day is spoiled for her and her half-brother, Jackie* Ramsdale, because their mother, Mary Margaret Avery Ramsdale, has been drinking, as she has been doing with increasing frequency since her husband left and she returned with the children to the town of her youth, and she has been evicted from the fairgrounds. This time even Effie Waisner, the older woman who shares their duplex and usually can talk sense into Mary Margaret, is not able to stop her binge, and she ends up in the hospital. Freedom's great fear is that she and Jackie will be sent to separate foster homes as Miss Harbaugh, the social worker, has suggested, while their mother goes to a treatment center, since Effie has heart trouble and is not considered a fit guardian. Leaving an enigmatic note for Effie and clues to make Miss Harbaugh think they have gone to St. Louis, Freedom takes her babysitting money and a child's wagon full of supplies, and in the middle of the night she heads off with Jackie for Truman Lake, where they have camped with Jackie's father. Despite a plethora of obstacles and bad luck, they manage to get to the lake, escape detection, and survive until a tornado hits the campground and destroys their tent and supplies. Admitting defeat, Freedom telephones Miss Harbaugh, who picks them up and says that a couple new in town have generously agreed to take in both of them. To her horror, Freedom discovers that this is Martin* and Ona Mae Quincy, high school classmates of her mother, who have moved back to Gabriel to live with Martin's crippled sister, Helen Gentry, and her daughter, Laura Nell, a girl who has always taunted and made snide cracks at Freedom. Although Helen is kind to Freedom and interests her in quilting, Laura Nell remains nasty, Ona Mae is clearly hostile, and Martin is a puzzle: smarmy and too inclined to touch and even hug Freedom, but a neatness fanatic and psychologically abusive to his own son, Theodore, 10. Jackie soon worships Theodore, and gradually Freedom and Laura Nell forge an understanding in their support of the boy and their dislike of Martin, whom they refer to as the Inspector General. Freedom is shocked and horrified when she overhears an argument between the Quincys revealing that Martin is her father, about whom her mother has never been willing to tell her. After considerable trauma, Freedom learns that Martin gave her mother emotional support after her family all died in a fire, that he was married to Ona Mae before he knew of Mary Margaret's pregnancy, and that she lied to him that her baby was born dead. Freedom realizes that there is fault and merit on both sides and that they can all be more whole if she can share her time and love with both families. While Freedom's humiliation at her mother's drinking, her resourcefulness when she and Jackie run away, and her increasing need to learn the identity of her own father are psychologically sound, the difficulties of their stay at Truman Lake are piled on too heavily and her acceptance of Martin at the end is too sudden to be convincing, especially when he has been pictured as such an un-likable person. SLJ.

SHARMA (*Shabanu**), cousin of Shabanu's Mama, called Aunt Sharma by Shabanu and Phulan*. Sharma illustrates what can happen to an independent woman in the male-dominated Cholistan Desert society. When her husband abused her and their daughter, Fatima, Sharma slowly built up her own herd of goats and sheep and left him, taking Fatima with her and existing on her own. Gray-haired and wrinkled from the desert weather, the thirty-year-old woman is bold and outspoken enough in her independence to frighten most of the men. Shabanu's father, Dadi*, however, enjoys her company and listens to what she says, although he will not go against the patriarchy to make it possible for Shabanu to have a different way of life. Although an outcast, Sharma participates in the women's festivals, like *mahendi,* the part of the marriage ceremony in which the bride is instructed how to behave toward her husband and is painted for the wedding. Sharma's words to Shabanu about how to retain her dignity and self-respect after she is married to the middle-aged, wealthy politician, Ra-him-*sahib,* give the girl some consolation.

SHILOH (Naylor*, Phyllis Reynolds, Atheneum, 1991), dog novel set near Friendly, in northwest West Virginia, presumably in the 1980s. Wandering the hills near his rural home, the narrator, Marty Preston, 11, is followed by a scrawny beagle, too scared to come near and cringing away from an outstretched hand but responding eagerly to a friendly whistle. Knowing that his family has little enough food for themselves and no money for veterinary bills, Marty tries to send the dog home, while secretly hoping it will stay and in his own mind calling it Shiloh, after the old schoolhouse where he first saw it. Marty's father, Ray Preston, a rural mail carrier, says that their brutal, redneck neighbor, Judd Travers, has spoken of buying a new hunting dog and insists on driving Marty and Shiloh to Judd's trailer. There the dog is greeted by Judd's vicious kick and a promise of a whipping if it runs off again. With a vague hope of buying the dog from Judd, Marty collects cans along the road edge, although he knows it would take him years to make enough that way. When the dog shows up again,

Marty takes it up the hill and builds a pen and a crude shelter for it. Then begins a struggle to save enough food from his own meals to feed Shiloh and to come to terms with the lies and evasions necessary to keep the dog a secret from his parents and his two little sisters, Dara Lynn and Becky. Judd drives by to tell them to be on the lookout for the beagle, and Marty evades a direct promise. After about a week, Marty's mother follows him one evening and discovers Shiloh but promises to give Marty one day to figure out a solution before telling his father. That night Marty is waked by a dog yelping, dashes in the dark up the hill, and discovers that a German shepherd has jumped into the pen and savaged the beagle. His father carries Shiloh to the Jeep and drives the dog and Marty to Doc Murphy, who sews up a big leg wound and cleans its chewed-up ear. Reluctantly Marty's father agrees to keep the dog until it gets well, but he insists that they then take it back to Judd. The incident has caused tension between Marty's parents, since his father resents his mother's keeping the secret from him, and confuses his little sisters. When Judd, having learned where the dog is, comes by, Marty's mother suggests that they buy Shiloh, but Judd will not sell and demands that the dog be returned by Sunday. After sleepless nights, Marty decides to face Judd directly. Sunday morning, very early, he sets off alone toward Judd's trailer and sees him shoot a deer out of season, and a doe at that. Seizing the chance, Marty bargains with Judd: he will not tell the game warden if Judd will give him Shiloh. At first astonished, Judd makes his own bargain: he will sell Shiloh to Marty for forty dollars, paid with twenty hours of work of Judd's choosing. Marty makes him write out and sign the agreement. For two weeks Marty works harder than he ever has before, with Judd sometimes thinking up extra jobs while he sits drinking beer and watching. After the first week Judd laughs at Marty and says their agreement has no legal value because there was no witness, and continues to taunt the boy as dumb. Stubbornly, Marty sticks to his side of the bargain even when Judd finds fault with everything he does. Gradually they begin to talk a bit, about dogs and about Judd's father who beat him from the time he was four but did take him hunting a couple of times. On the last day, Judd gives Marty an old collar for Shiloh and says nothing about taking the dog back. The simple animal story is moving because the Prestons are so well drawn, with their pride despite poverty, their firm sense of right, and their love for each other. The Appalachian setting is well evoked, in both its beauty and its code of ethics that Marty must defy to save the dog. ALA; Newbery Winner.

SHIZUKO'S DAUGHTER (Mori*, Kyoko, Holt, 1993), growing-up novel of a Japanese girl in the late twentieth century whose mother's suicide when she is twelve mars the rest of her childhood and nearly destroys her own possibility for happiness. Yuki Okuda and her mother, Shizuko, have been very close, brought together even more by the coldness of Yuki's father and his frequent absence. When Yuki arrives home from her piano lesson and finds her mother slumped in front of the open oven door with the unlit gas turned on, she knows without being told that the suicide was caused by her father's indifference and long-term affair with a woman in his office. Although Yuki, a skilled artist, a champion runner, and an A student, is complimented on her maturity and her control, she is hiding the pain and sense of disorientation that her mother's death brings. After a year in Tokyo with an aunt, she is summoned home to Kobe for her father's wedding, where she cannot bring herself to be more than barely polite to the woman he is finally marrying. Her home life from that time on, until she is through high school and leaves for an art school in Nagasaki, is miserable, with her vindictive stepmother, who resents Yuki's achievements and any reference to her mother, and her father, who shows her no affection and always sides with his new wife in any dispute. She is also prevented by her father from keeping in touch with or visiting her maternal grandparents and her aunt, although he makes an exception on the third anniversary of her mother's death, when special prayers are offered, and three years later on the occasion of her aunt's wedding to a man who at one time was in love with her mother. Both times, her grandmother finds her cold and stubborn and believes that the girl has forgotten Shizuko; in reality Yuki, although she realizes that she seems unfeeling, is making a great effort to keep from breaking down in front of her relatives. In Nagasaki, which she has deliberately chosen because she can support herself there and it is a long distance from her father and stepmother, she becomes close friends with Isamu, a fellow student, but shies away from any romantic overtures, being afraid to love anyone when so many relationships end in bitterness or sadness. Then she gets a package from her father, the first communication since she has left; in it is her mother's sketchbook, the only thing he has saved from the fire to which his present wife has consigned everything that belonged to Yuki and her mother. There is no note, and she cannot bring herself to thank him, but looking through the pictures, some of her father before their marriage and many of Yuki as a child, she realizes that her mother's love was strong and that she herself need not turn away in fear from love. Although the novel covers the years from 1969 to 1976, the events of those years are not as memorable as the mood, which captures Yuki's sense of abandonment and isolation, as well as her anger. Many small elements are telling: she makes drawings of all the clothes her mother made for her and her stepmother discarded; she cannot bring herself to eat any creature that has been alive; her horror of death is so great that she secretly throws out all the preserved frogs her science class is scheduled to dissect. Many of the incidents are peculiar to the Japanese culture. Her mother chooses suicide rather than divorce because a child, especially if there is only one, remains with the father after divorce in Japan. Her father's compulsion to placate his second wife at whatever cost to him or his daughter is an effort to save face; if one wife commits suicide and a second leaves a man, he would be suspect and not considered fit for the managerial position he holds. In evocative prose, the author draws scenes that recur in the mind like Asian paintings, but the most memorable element is the characterization of Yuki, a girl with inner strength that emerges despite unhappy circumstances. Fanfare.

SHOE (*The Beggars' Ride**), undersized, undernourished, bad-complexioned member of Cowboy's* gang of homeless street kids, who take in Clare* Caldwell. Shoe never talks, just giggles frequently, and is very close to and dependent on Racer*, who protects and cherishes him. The two work together on various scams. Racer tells Clare that Shoe's family apparently all died in a fire. The two boys met in a home for disturbed children and ran away from it together.

SHOEBAG (James*, Mary, Scholastic, 1990), amusing, ironic, talking-animal fantasy set in Boston in recent years. Shoebag, a resilient young cockroach, lives happily with his father, Under the Toaster, and mother, Drainboard, in the Biddle apartment, having acquired his name, as did his parents, from the spot he occupies in the house. One day he awakens from a dream to find himself changed into a small human boy with red hair and blue eyes. The Biddles assume that he is a victim of amnesia, take him in, call him Stuart Bagg, enroll him in school, and accept him as their son and brother to their beautiful, narcissistic, seven-year-old daughter, Eunice, better known as Pretty* Soft from the television toilet paper commercials in which she appears. Although his real parents think that he is dirty and loud, as most humans are in their cockroach opinion, they hope that now, having a human form, he will be able to squash to death the horrible, seven-legged, black jumping spider that terrorizes the Under the Toaster family, an act that ironically Shoebag can never bring himself to carry out. At school, Shoebag is pushed around by bully Tuffy* Buck, a big bruiser who threatens all the pupils who are different in some way. Shoebag's other problems include, in addition to wanting to be a roach again (though mirrors always show him as a roach even when he appears human to others), worries about whether or not his real family will be exterminated by the Zap man the Biddles summon regularly. Moreover, the Persian cat belonging to the family on the third floor poses a constant threat to his parents, in particular to his mother, who hides, among other places, in the front hall lily plant where she can be near Shoebag to give him moral support. At school he forms the outsiders into a group in defense against Tuffy, replete with theme song, and is befriended by an older, tall, strange youth named Gregor* Samsa, who always wears dark reflecting glasses and who turns out to be the catalyst for solving the book's main problems. After Gregor taxes Pretty Soft with being selfish, she helps rescue Shoebag's mother, whom the horrible spider has captured in his silk dragline and imprisoned on top of the electric clock in the kitchen. Pretty Soft tumbles from the ladder in the process and suffers facial contusions, thus losing her position making commercials and being forced to assume the more normal life of schoolgirl. Gregor, who reveals that he is also a roach, decides to become a television star and gives Shoebag the spell that will return him to his family.

Despondent at having lost Shoebag's younger brother, Coffee Cup, to the dreaded spider, Under the Toaster decides the family will hitch a ride when the Universal Parcel man next comes, and they all end up in a huge store in a shopping center just outside the city, where to their delight there is an excellent deli. Most characters, and in particular the children, are caricatures, and the plot relies heavily on coincidence and is less tense than anticipated, the main thrust being to comment on matters of contemporary society, most of which are probably of more interest to young people or adults than the book's intended audience of middle graders. A wide range of ideas is touched on, like school life; the ways of school administrators (the principal, whose name is Mr. Doormatee, keeps reminding the pupils that "the word principal ends in *p a l,* and that's what I am, too, your pal," but Shoebag never finds him especially helpful); support groups; emphasis on appearance and charm; earning money for college; parenting (the roach and human families are foils); child labor; excessive killing during animal hunts; the importance of respecting the right of everything to exist; perseverance; and the great significance of cooperation and forbearance ("The world is very strange . . . [thinks Shoebag]. All we can do, it seems, is stick up for each other, and for ourselves"). Information about insects and arachnids is worked in without didacticism, in a manner reminiscent of *Charlotte's Web.* Most of the novel's force comes from the conversations, which often patter on, are lively, and ironic in particular in the differences they pose between the way humans and roaches look, act, and feel. Humor comes mostly from such dialogue and from social comment, but also from inversions of common expressions and wordplay (Drainboard remarks, "Worms have no backbone . . . [and therefore] I have no use for them"). Most ironic of all, the book succeeds in rendering coackroaches attractive, especially through Shoebag's tenacious ability to make the best of things and through the depiction of his parents as thoroughly understandable, solicitous, and responsible. SLJ.

SHOW ME THE EVIDENCE (Ferguson*, Alane, Bradbury, 1989), mystery novel set in an unnamed American town, presumably in the 1980s, involving the crib death of three babies and the suspicion of murder that falls on an innocent teenager. Tall, blonde Lauren Taylor and petite, dark Janaan* Kashad, both seventeen, have been best friends for years, but since the sudden infant death of Janaan's six-month-old brother, Adam, while Janaan was babysitting him, Lauren has seen sudden depression and tension in her friend and is sometimes rejected, but Janaan agrees to come with her to babysit Rachael Bloom, a pretty, golden-haired infant. While Lauren is playing with Rachael on the lawn, a woman pushing a baby carriage stops to talk, picks up Rachael, then refuses to give her back and shows Lauren her own "baby," a rag doll, in the carriage. Frantically, Lauren tries to grab screaming Rachael back and is shouting for Janaan, who is inside, when a workman sitting in a truck across the street comes up, talks calmly to the woman, patting and stroking Rachael, until a man, obviously the woman's husband, appears, lifts the baby from her grasp, gives her back to Lauren, and leads his demented wife away. Lauren puts the exhausted baby down for her nap, but a few minutes later, Janaan goes to check on her and finds her dead. Because Lauren is despondent and refuses to go to school, Janaan arranges a meeting for her with a group of sudden infant death (SID) volunteers, who help her somewhat. The next day Janaan is arrested, since one of the SID volunteers has told police that Janaan picked up her baby in the supermarket the same day it died, also at about six months old. Lauren is questioned by detectives who obviously have made up their minds that Janaan is somehow guilty, but for lack of evidence, both girls are released. The graves of the three babies are opened and all three coffins are empty. When Lauren and Janaan later realize that neither of them has mentioned the woman with the rag doll, they tell the police and find them so unwilling to consider anyone but Janaan as a suspect that the girls decide they themselves must investigate. Looking for similarities in the three deaths, besides their age and blondness, they realize that each baby was buried the day of its death without being embalmed, in accordance with their families' religious customs (Adam's father is Arabic, Rachael's Jewish, and the other baby is a Baha'i). Lauren has a sudden, wonderful hope that the babies may still be alive, and Janaan insists on a late-night visit to the cemetery to look for clues. At a house on the edge of the graveyard they spot a truck like that of the workman they saw the day Rachael died, and they are peeking through the window when the same workman grabs them from behind and holds a knife to Janaan's throat, but not before she has spotted the little suit Adam was buried in among a pile of clothes on the floor. The man makes them take off their outer clothes and ties them back to back, admitting that he managed to touch each of the babies with a deadly poison he has perfected, one that in minor doses will turn people into zombies and in larger doses kill them instantly, but with just a tiny touch will make them temporarily seem dead. He has been able to dig the infants up, revive them, and sell them to childless couples. He proposes to give each of the girls a touch that will make them helpless, then throw their bodies into a pond so it will look as if they went for a midnight swim and drowned. As he prepares his powder, Lauren manages to kick him, knocking the poison in his hand all over him, and killing him instantly. The girls are rescued, and since the man has kept meticulous records in order to blackmail the adoptive parents later, the babies are retrieved. Although the solution is bizarre, it is so well worked out that it is acceptable, and a number of the scenes are gripping, especially those in the police station and the cemetery. Lauren, the protagonist, is the typical attractive, privileged high school senior; Janaan is a more interesting and complex character. Poe Winner.

SILENT WITNESS (Rushford*, Patricia, Bethany House, 1993), realistic, contemporary, mystery-detective novel, set mostly on an island off Florida's Gulf Coast, which follows *Too Many Secrets,* the first in a series about Jennie McGrady. Jennie, 16, happily accepts Gram* (Helen) McGrady's gift of a birthday flight to Florida, where Gram, a writer, expects to gather information for a

series of articles on dolphins. A bomb scare delays their take-off from the Portland, Oregon, airport, and while they await clearance, Jennie overhears a puzzling exchange between a man called Tim and a woman addressed as Maggie,
which indicates that he thinks that the girl with them, who looks completely
oblivious of her surroundings, may have been the target of the bomb. In a rented
car, Gram and Jennie motor through central Florida to Key Largo, where protesters from the Dolphin Protection Agency picket Dolphin Playland. One of
them, Scott* Chambers, a surly, handsome, green-eyed youth with curly brown
hair, they later also encounter at Key West, where he is fired from his job with
a cruise line for reprimanding a passenger for harming coral. Gram secures him
a job with the marine biologists at Dolphin Island near Fort Myers, where she
plans to do the bulk of her work. Jennie and Gram arrive there to discover that
the girl, woman, and man from the Oregon airport are also guests. Sarah Stanford, 14, has been in a semi-catatonic state for two years from having observed
the murder of her father and is enrolled in a therapy program with a particularly
sensitive dolphin named Delilah. Although her uncle, Tim Hudson, resists the
therapy, her mother, Maggie, and Maggie's husband, Dr. Carl Layton (Sarah's
father's former partner in their psychiatric clinic), are hopeful that the program
will restore Sarah's memory and ability to speak, although they know that that
will be dangerous for her, since she may be able to identify her father's murderer. Untoward events occur: Delilah is poisoned with "speed"; Gram and
Jennie's car is forced off a bridge into the bay, from which they are rescued in
the nick of time; and the abandoned cabin in which Jennie and Sarah spend
time together is set afire, almost killing them. Suspicion points to Scott, who is
taken into custody. Sarah has confided in Jennie that she has regained her memory to a large extent and has been pretending to be an amnesiac because she
fears the murderer. While she is in the hospital after the fire, the murderer
strikes—Dr. Layton—but is foiled by Jennie's quick action in a stairwell from
which he falls to the concrete below. To cover gambling losses, he had killed
Sarah's father in order to marry Sarah's wealthy mother. Characters are types
but suit the plot, which is fast and carefully paced. Motivations are not entirely
clear, details are not completely accounted for, and the reader is led to believe
that Sarah was much younger than twelve when the murder occurred, but the
book holds the attention throughout. Although a stereotype, Gram is drawn with
depth, and, unusual for a teenaged novel, Jennie shows good sense in her relations with boys, likes to use her head, respects adults, and talks to herself
without self-righteousness or sensationalism. She also prays (following Gram's
example) in her head and without sentimentality. Her need to find out what
happened to her presumed-dead father is left unresolved, and so the door is open
for another book about her. Poe Nominee.

THE SILVER KISS (Klause*, Annette Curtis, Delacorte, 1990), contemporary
horror fantasy set in the middle-class American suburb of Oakwood. The action
proceeds in chapters alternating between the two main characters: attractive Zoe

Sutcliff, 16, a schoolgirl, and Simon* Bristol, a beautiful, silver-haired youth doomed to roam the earth as a vampire or undead. The two meet by chance one night in the park, where Zoe, almost oblivious to the news that a woman has been found murdered nearby, has gone for refuge to mull over her troubles: the impending death of her mother to cancer; her feelings of anger, sorrow, abandonment, and resentment that her grief-stricken, financially overburdened father has no time for her; and the imminent move to Oregon of her best friend, Lorraine, who buys her a crucifix necklace as a parting remembrance. Zoe sees Simon again and is much struck by his beauty and air of loneliness and sorrow. At the same time, he yearns for her warmth and understanding and the taste of her blood. Then a second murder occurs in the neighborhood, a woman in an alley, also with her throat slashed, and Zoe realizes that it could easily have been Lorraine, since when the two of them recently walked by the alley, a little boy asked Lorraine to go that way with him. While Zoe is mostly wrapped up in her family tragedy, Simon works on his own personal problems, keeping under surveillance an adopted boy of about six named Christopher, a strange child who slips out at night to prowl the neighborhood. Zoe and Simon's uneasy friendship progresses, and on Halloween he visits her at her house after the trick-or-treaters have left. They talk long and intimately, she sharing her fears about her mother and deteriorating family relationships and he telling her his troubling story of becoming a vampire three hundred years earlier. He says he deplores the way he must live, has murdered only seldom, and is searching for a way to kill Christopher, who is his older brother and the murderer of the women. Zoe believes him, feels comforted by him, and is able to comfort him; before she is even aware of what is happening, he gives her the vampire silver kiss, puncturing her throat to drink her blood but not killing her, the wound almost immediately healing. Eventually Zoe agrees to help Simon kill Christopher, which they do in the park in a highly suspenseful struggle. Zoe is protected from Christopher by Lorraine's crucifix and uses it to plunge the boy into a pit, where he is impaled on sticks and dies. Zoe considers asking Simon to make her mother one of the undead in order to keep her, but, since she knows that Simon is so very unhappy, she discards that idea and decides to accept her mother's death as a release from physical pain and to help Simon end his existence and thus give him release from his psychological torment. When they meet in the park at midnight, he gives her his most cherished possession, a painting of his family, and she helps him scatter to the wind the soil of his native England that he has kept in a special case. They sit with arms entwined until dawn, when they kiss and he fades from sight as the sun rises, free now to die because he is going to his death willingly. Although in the manner of its genre, the book emphasizes action, grotesquerie, and melodrama, these gothic elements are held in check. The author sets up the mystery of Simon and Christopher well and keeps Zoe in danger in the reader's mind to the very end. Although Simon is sympathetically presented, the reader is also kept constantly aware of his real nature. Giving the book substance beyond romantic thrills is its telling portrayal of the feelings of a bright, sensitive, only child, about to lose the artist mother whom she loves and also admires deeply as a person and creative influence. Zoe's struggle to accept what she comes to realize she must is handled without didacticism. SLJ.

SIMON BRISTOL (*The Silver Kiss**), very handsome, silver-haired youth, a vampire, with whom Zoe Sutcliff becomes friends and who gives her the silver kiss of the vampire. According to Simon, who tells his story to Zoe, he lived originally in England in the mid-1600s, the son of a prosperous wool grower and merchant, who forms a business relationship with a mysterious man from the continent named Wulfram von Grab. Von Grab kidnaps Simon's older brother, Christopher, and turns him into a vampire. Christopher kills their mother, slashing her throat and sucking her blood; lures victims for von Grab; and when Simon falls into a dissolute life in London, lures him for von Grab. Tired of working for von Grab, Christopher tricks Simon into allowing him to turn Simon into a vampire and into killing von Grab, thus releasing Christopher from bondage but making Simon an undead also. Henceforth, Simon searches the world for Christopher, hoping to kill him for killing their mother and for turning him into a vampire. As Simon tells his story, it is easy to like him and sympathize with him, but his manner of life, also by his own account—skulking, drinking animals' blood, occasionally killing humans for their blood—items judiciously planted to keep the reader aware of his undead nature and vampire inclinations, make him a tensely ambivalent and dangerous character. Simon's manner of speaking, which is slightly archaic, adds to the credibility of his story.

SING DOWN THE MOON (O'Dell*, Scott, Houghton Mifflin, 1970), historical novel about the evacuation of the Navajo people from their land in the 1860s, their death march to Fort Sumner, and their confinement at Bosque Redondo. The narrator, Bright Morning, having survived kidnapping, enslavement, and escape from Spaniards, must not only endure these additional terrible events but must also rouse her husband, Tall Boy, from his apathy so he can escape imprisonment and together they can flee back to their own country, where their child will be born free. The novel earlier was cited on Choice and Fanfare lists and named a Newbery Honor book. Phoenix Honor. For a longer entry, see *Dictionary, 1960–1984.*

SINGER (*Out of Nowhere**), recent high school graduate who moves in and helps out wherever there is need in the community. Competent at housework, painting, repairing roofs, and every other job that comes to hand, she is also unfailingly optimistic and good humored, so that May Woods calls her, with some asperity, Miss Positive Thinking. Although her mother is dead, Singer claims that she is still around, spreading love and good spirits. Her father, she says, is in a hospital, but she is vague about where. In the end, she takes a bus to be close to him, she says, but it is not clear whether this is literally true. She is the voice for most of the understanding among the other characters and is the first person whose love Harley Nunn is able to accept. While she is convenient to the plot, she is not a very convincing character.

SISTER (Howard*, Ellen, Atheneum, 1990), realistic period novel of family life and a girl's growing up set in the 1880s in a farming area of Illinois. Alena Ostermann, 12, is big sister to five younger siblings, soon to be increased to six. She yearns to continue her schooling and is happy when she overhears Father promise Mother that she can get her elementary diploma. Previously Father has maintained that, being a girl, Alena should give up school and help at home. Alena is delighted with the new young teacher, John Malcolm, whose educated speech she savors and whose golden-haired good looks thrill her, even though he crossly disciplines her wiggly little sister, Faith, 5. Alena is extremely pleased when he praises her essay, asks permission to save others she writes, and suggests she may be able to win a four-year scholarship to normal school. One fall night, however, her life suddenly changes direction. She is awakened by Mother, whose water has broken, and ordered to send Fritz, 8, to summon absent Father, a neighbor woman, and relatives to come and help. During the night, Alena, frightened, puzzled, shocked, and worried, since she knows almost nothing about how babies come, mostly watches and sometimes helps as her mother gives birth prematurely to a very small yet seemingly perfect baby girl. Alena is deeply moved by the wonder of the tiny child, and when Mother asks her to name the baby, chooses the most beautiful name she can think of: Matilda Jane. Matilda Jane does not thrive, however; she cries and wheezes a lot, refuses to eat in spite of the efforts of Mother, Aunt Louisa, and the neighbor woman, and on the third day dies. Aunt Louisa stays on for about a month while Alena continues in school. When Louisa goes home and Mother grows thinner and grayer every day and shows no interest in anything but little Samuel, Father sadly asks Alena to give up school and help. Although Mr. Malcolm gets angry when Alena tells him she is quitting, she feels duty to family comes first. Months of unrelenting household toil follow. She is pleased with Father's gratitude and the praise of relatives, but sometimes she gets so weary that she becomes sharp with the children and even slaps often fractious Faith. Inwardly she longs for school, but outwardly she tries to remain cheerful and obedient to her responsibility. In December she turns thirteen, and in early spring has her first period, a very frightening experience. She has received no instruction about her sexuality, and she worries that she may be having a baby. She yearns to talk to Mother about what is happening. Having cleaned herself up, she encounters Mother coming from her room, her usual vacant stare on her face. When Mother calls out for her baby, Alena loses control, screams that the baby is dead, strikes Mother, and then sinks to the floor in tears, overcome with shame. The shock of the blow brings Mother back from whatever world she has been in, and she drops to the floor to comfort her daughter. When school starts in the fall, Alena chooses not to return. She feels out of place, since her friends have graduated, and knows that she is still needed at home, because Mother will soon have another baby. When she informs Mr. Malcolm, he at first reacts with anger but then offers to prepare lessons for her to do at home. She acknowledges his kindness and looks forward to living "each day as best she could, loving and helping those who needed her, and still [having] something for herself. . . . It would not harm anyone if she dreamed." The author creates the moment well. Especially well-realized scenes include the dramatic birth and first period episodes and the humorous yet poignant one in which Faith insists that the surprise that she has been told will come in the fall and that begins with "b" is a flock of butterflies. Farm life in a big family is well evoked from the woman's vantage, as are attitudes toward women's roles—for example, the idea that women do not need schooling and must put family before all else. Father protests in one instance that William, 10, should not miss classes but assumes that Alena will withdraw completely. Equally true to the times is Alena's and the other girls' lack of sex education. The scene at school where the girls gather around Alena and question her about the events surrounding Matilda Jane's birth reveals their appalling ignorance and misconceptions. *Sister* and the other books in which Alena appears, the novel *Edith Herself* and the story *The Chickenhouse House,* are based on pioneer family history the author learned from her grandmother and great-aunt. For details about *Edith Herself,* see *Dictionary, 1985–1989.* ALA.

SLEATOR, WILLIAM (WARNER, III) (1945–   ), born in Havre de Grace, Maryland; pianist, author of picture books and novels of science fiction and fantasy. A graduate of Harvard University, he has served as accompanist at the Royal Ballet School in London and the Boston Ballet Company. His picture books have been illustrated by Blair Lent, Trina Schart Hyman, Ruth Sanderson, and Steven Kellogg. He has written a number of ingenious science-fiction novels and fantasies, including *Others See Us** (Dutton, 1993), based on the premise that water contaminated by a chemical plant gives those who drink or fall into it the ability to read minds, a power that proves more a curse than a gift at a family reunion. It was named to the *Horn Book* Fanfare list. For earlier biographical information and title entries see *Dictionary, 1985–1989* [*The Boy Who Reversed Himself; The Duplicate; Interstellar Pig*].

SLEPIAN, JAN (1921–   ), born in New York City; speech pathologist and author. Her best-known novel is *The Alfred Summer* (Macmillan, 1980), a story about a boy with cerebral palsy, which won the *Boston Globe–Horn Book* Award; its sequel is *Lester's Turn* (Macmillan, 1981). *The Broccoli Tapes** (Philomel, 1989), usually listed as an animal novel, is really about family relationships brought out by the adoption of a stray cat. It was named an American Library Association Notable Book and a *School Library Journal* Best Book for Children. Among Slepian's other novels are *The Night of the Bozos* (Dutton, 1983), with a carnival setting, and *Risk N'Roses* (Philomel, 1990), about a girl who has a beautiful older sister with mental disabilities and a magnetic but wild friend in the crowded city. Slepian attended Brooklyn College and the University of Washington, and received her M. A. degree from New York University. For earlier biographical information and a title entry, see *Dictionary, 1960–1984* [*The Alfred Summer*].

SLOTE, ALFRED (1926–), born in Brooklyn, New York; television producer, author best known for his sports novels for middle grade readers. He has B. A. and M. A. degrees from the University of Michigan and studied at the University of Grenoble on a Fulbright scholarship. He is now retired from his long-time position as producer, writer, and director at the University of Michigan Television Center. Most of Slote's books are baseball stories, as are *Jake* (Lippincott, 1971) and *Finding Buck McHenry** (HarperCollins, 1991), a novel that incorporates much information about the old Negro Leagues as well as vivid descriptions of games and convincing pictures of the emotions of eleven year olds. Both it and *Clone Catcher* (Lippincott, 1982), a futuristic fantasy, were nominees for the Edgar Allan Poe Award. For earlier biographical information and title entries, see *Dictionary, 1960–1984* [*Clone Catcher; Jake*].

SMITH, DORIS BUCHANAN (1934–), born in Washington, D.C.; author of books for children and young adults on contemporary problems. She has lived in Georgia most of her life, attended South Georgia College in Douglas, and has been a freelance writer since 1971. Her novel for middle grade children, *A Taste of Blackberries* (Crowell, 1973), probably still her best-known book, was one of the early modern books to deal with the death of a child. In *The Pennywhistle Tree** (Putnam, 1991) she writes for the same audience a story of a "trashy" family that moves into a conventional and house-proud neighborhood, told from the point of view of a boy who has always lived there. It was cited on both the American Library Association Notable Book list and the *School Library Journal* list of Best Books for Children. For somewhat older children, *Return to Bitter Creek* (Viking, 1986) has stronger characterization and evocative use of the Appalachian setting. For earlier biographical information and title entries, see *Dictionary, 1960–1984* [*A Taste of Blackberries; Tough Chauncey*] and *Dictionary, 1985–1989* [*Return to Bitter Creek*].

SNIPER (Taylor*, Theodore, Harcourt, 1989), novel of mystery and suspense set on a game preserve in Orange County, California, in the period of its publication. After an automobile accident puts the chief handler, Alfredo Garcia, in the hospital, Benjamin Jepson, 15, finds himself in charge of Los Coyotes Preserve while his father, director of the big cat research park, and his mother, a professional photographer, are in Africa. The only adults on the preserve are two inexperienced Hispanic handlers who know little English, a crippled handyman, and a Kenyan who has been living at Los Coyotes while he waits to take the state veterinary exams. Ben's mother has always considered her son disappointingly mediocre because he lacks her driving ambition and determination and prefers playing the guitar with Alfredo to studying, a view of him his father does not share. Ben's nightmarish test of resolve begins one night when, awakened by the peacocks' screaming, he discovers the gates to two of the compounds are open and several of the lions loose within the perimeter fence, including Rocky, a huge cat Ben raised from a cub, now become his single-minded and jealous protector. With some difficulty, he and the handlers get the lions back into their compounds except for two gentle, harmless females that have been shot. Repeated calls to Africa fail to contact his parents, who are investigating poachers in the Serengeti and are no longer in radio contact with the park headquarters. Left to his own devices, Ben buys padlocks for all the compound gates, shifts cats from the outer compounds where they are exposed to the road, and at the suggestion of Deputy Metcalf of the local substation puts up bamboo screening along the front fences to hide the animals. Nevertheless, in the nights that follow they find Rocky and Rachel, a cheetah that has been a house pet, shot by a high-powered rifle with a nightscope, and Ben himself is shot at. A fire, clearly arson, threatens their area and requires the temporary evacuation of all the big cats. Ben and his friends, Jilly Coombes and Sandy Gilmore, puzzle over whether any of the neighbors, who have feared and resented having the preserve in the area, might be responsible, and conclude that the most likely is Richie Lewis, a beer-drinking, bullying redneck several years older than Ben. Then they learn that Richie died in an automobile accident before the fire could have been started. Eventually it is determined that the killer of the animals is a recently paroled convict against whom Ben's father was an expert witness in a trial years before. With the help of Ben and Sandy, Deputy Metcalf apprehends and arrests the man. Ben's mother calls from Nairobi, in a rush to catch a plane, with just time enough to say she and his father have had a "wild" adventure and with no interest in any report he might have on the preserve. Through his experience, Ben has gained enough self-respect to realize that her approval is no longer necessary to him. This boy's growing-up story aspect is the weakest part of the novel, plausible but not nearly as interesting as the gripping action and the information about the various animals. Except for Ben, the human characters are just functional, adequate to their parts. Several of the big cats—Rocky, Rachel, the aging Nellie, who is dying of bone cancer, and Dmitri, the thirteen-foot-long Siberian tiger, in particular—are more developed and intriguing, and the problems of caring for and moving the often dangerous and unpredictable animals are fascinating. Some consideration is given to questions of whether wild animals should be kept prisoner, even for research or in an effort to preserve a species. Poe Nominee.

SNYDER, ZILPHA KEATLEY (1927–), born in Lemoore, California; teacher and author of many popular, critically cited, realistic novels of family life for middle grade and teenaged readers. Among these are *Libby on Wednesday** (Delacorte, 1990), in which a writing workshop helps an odds-out girl learn to relate to her age group, and *Cat Running** (Delacorte, 1994), about a gifted athlete who overcomes her negative feelings toward Okies during the Great Depression. Both books were cited by *School Library Journal.* For earlier biographical information and title entries, see *Dictionary, 1960–1984* [*The Changeling; The Egypt Game; The Headless Cupid; The Velvet Room; The Witches of Worm*].

SOKA (*Children of the River**), Kem Soka, wife of Tep Naro* and aunt of Sundara Suvann. Although she frequently berates Sundara for not staying strictly to Khmer ways, it comes out that she is afraid that she is not keeping her promise to Sundara's mother to bring the girl up properly. Sundara usually defers to her aunt, except that she continues to see Jonathan* McKinnon even though she has been forbidden to do so. Soka softens toward Jonathan and his family when she learns that Jonathan's father was the doctor who restored her son Pon to health. For many years, Sundara thinks that Soka hates her because Soka's newborn baby died on shipboard, the baby Sundara's mother had told the girl to take good care of, but Soka assures Sundara that she knows the girl did everything she could and that the baby's death was not Sundara's fault. The two women have thus for a large part of the book been on the outs through simple misunderstanding and lack of communication, much of which resulted from the cultural separation of generations.

SOLOMON BRADLEY (*The Road to Memphis**), well-educated, well-dressed, sophisticated, older African-American man. A lawyer, newspaperman, and entrepreneur, he assists Stacey*, Cassie, and their friends in getting Moe* Turner to the Memphis railroad station and on his way to Chicago. Bradley is Harvard educated, well off, and involved in many activities to advance the cause of blacks. Cassie develops a crush on him, which he notes but does not exploit. Through him, she sees new possibilities in life for herself. He is the black counterpart of the white lawyer, Mr. Jamison, who often advises and helps the Logans.

SOMEWHERE IN THE DARKNESS (Myers*, Walter Dean, Scholastic, 1992), boy's growing-up novel set in African-American sections of New York City and other communities, including Cleveland, Chicago, Memphis, and Marion, Arkansas, presumably in the 1990s. When Jimmy Little, 14, who makes his home with Mama Jean, a close friend of his long-dead mother, encounters a tall, dark man in the hall, he does not recognize him as Crab, his father who has been in prison for several years. He is appalled when Crab tells Mama Jean that he has come to take Jimmy with him to Chicago, where he has a job, and they have to leave immediately. Secretly, Mama Jean gives Jimmy fifty dollars and warns him not to tell his father that he has it. On the trip in a gray Dodge, Jimmy learns disturbing things about his father: Crab is seriously ill with kidney trouble; he has escaped from the hospital and is wanted by the police; he may have robbed a gas station on their route. There is no job waiting in Chicago, and actually they are headed for Arkansas, where Crab grew up, to confront Rydell, the man who probably engaged in the holdup and shot the armored car guard, the crime for which Crab was wrongly convicted. In Chicago, Crab looks up Mavis, a friend whom he expects will accompany them to Arkansas, along with her son, Frank, a young boxer a little older than Jimmy and definitely hostile to him. Leaving Jimmy to find his way alone in the strange city, Crab goes to play the saxophone with a band he used to be part of. When a telephone call to their rooming house summons Jimmy to come and get him, the boy finds him ill and depressed, realizing he is no longer able to play well enough. When Mavis refuses to go with them, Crab rents a car, using someone else's credit card, and they start south. Before they reach Marion they fix a flat tire in the rain, are hassled by a suspicious policeman in a drive-in restaurant, and then followed by the policeman for some time before they can shake him. At Marion they visit High John, a conjure man, who lets Crab know in his own way that he has not long to live. The next day they encounter Rydell, who is not willing to tell the truth. Giving up, Crab takes Jimmy down to the creek where he used to fish and tries to talk to him. Warned that police have been looking for him, he decides to catch a freight train heading west, but police intercept him, and as he runs away he collapses. Jimmy sits by him in the hospital until he dies, stays for the funeral, and then gets back to New York with money Mama Jean has sent. The strongest element in the book is the vacillation of emotion in the two main characters. Crab, knowing that he is dying, still keeps trying to plan ahead, to think of some way out of his predicament, and to persuade Jimmy that although he has done many illegal things, he did not kill the guards. Jimmy is scared, wary of any commitment to the man he does not know, and homesick for Mama Jean, but gradually he gains compassion for his parent and ends up hoping that Crab's last grimace is a smile of understanding for him. His own rumination about how he will treat a son when he has one shows that the experience has not been wasted on him. Fanfare.

SPIDER KANE AND THE MYSTERY AT JUMBO NIGHTCRAWLER'S (Osborne*, Mary Pope, illus. Victoria Chess, Knopf, 1993), lighthearted detective fantasy set in recent years among a community of talking insects, sequel to *Spider Kane and the Mystery Under the May-Apple*. Earnest young butterfly Leon Leafwing; his beautiful, gossamer-winged butterfly sweetheart, Mimi; "Hawk" Hawkins, a well-known actor moth; and two ladybugs, Rosie and Little Pickles, caterers to their insect neighbors, are all lieutenants in detective Spider Kane's Order of the MOTH (Mission: Only To Help). While Spider is away on a case, all the lieutenants except Leon (to his great chagrin) receive invitations in Spider's handwriting on blue notepaper and signed with his secret initials to meet him at a certain time at Jumbo Nightcrawler's Supper Club. All but Little Pickles, who is unexpectedly detained by a fire, go to the club, but no one comes home. Then La Mere Leafwing, Leon's peremptory mother, also receives an invitation, one intended for him, Leon is sure, but which she insists on honoring. She also disappears, as it happens on the very night Spider returns. More suspicious events follow, including break-ins by robber hornets at Hawk's house and Little Pickles's place, and a visit to Little Pickles by Saratoga D'Bee, the blowsy, bewigged chanteuse from Jumbo's. She begs Little Pickles to help her find some gold that a certain "creep" wants so that he will not hurt her children. Spider is sure that the "creep" is responsible for the disappearances of his friends and deduces that he is one Raymond Johnson, who, Spider says, is the "most wicked robber-fly on earth." Also known as the Bald Buzzer, Johnson was once a legend on the Mississippi for his singing. He became involved with the Hornet Underworld and turned river pirate. To smoke out Johnson, Spider organizes an act involving Leon, Little Pickles, and himself for amateur night at the club. Spider wows everyone with his hot clarinet, and persuaded to sing along, Saratoga becomes so enthralled by the music and sings so enthusiastically that she throws off her wig and thus is unmasked as Raymond Johnson. It is also soon discovered that Johnson sent the invitations in hopes of securing gold stolen from some mining ants, the very theft that Spider had been investigating. Events speed along with some tension, much coincidence, and more good humor than taut suspense. Extensive dialogue and wordplay add to the fun. Characters are human types, and the all-wise Spider, modeled on Sherlock Holmes, solves the mystery in the tradition of his predecessor by close observation and clever deduction, in Spider's case, from fairly obvious clues. A list of characters with descriptions helps to keep the large cast straight, and numerous black-and-white drawings showing the anthropomorphized creatures in various activities add considerably to the humor. This is one of a series intended as fun reading for later elementary and middle school readers about the arachnid sleuth, who always unravels the mystery that baffles everyone else. Poe Nominee.

SPINELLI, JERRY (1941–   ), born and raised in Norristown, Pennsylvania; magazine editor and writer of novels of adolescent life, which, while funny on the surface, address serious concerns sensitively and accurately, if hyperbolically. He received his A.B. from Gettysburg College and his M.A. from Johns Hopkins University and studied further at Temple University. He was an editor with the Chilton Company in Radnor, Pennsylvania, until he became a professional writer in 1989. In his mid-thirties, he married Eileen Mesi, a writer and mother of six children. Events with this ready-made family precipitated his first novel, *Space Station Seventh Grade* (Little, Brown, 1982), about an impulsive and troublesome junior high boy who contends with his parents' divorce and acquiring a stepfather. It was praised as convincingly funny. Its sequel is *Jason and Marceline* (Little, Brown, 1986). Among his other books for later elementary and early adolescent readers is *Who Put That Hair in My Toothbrush?* (Little, Brown, 1984), which makes humorous use of sibling rivalry; *There's a Girl in My Hammerlock* (Simon & Schuster, 1991), in which a girl goes out for wrestling; and *Fourth Grade Rats* (Scholastic, 1991), which deals with peer pressure. His most highly acclaimed book is *Maniac Magee** (Little, Brown, 1990), which won the Newbery Award, was named to the Fanfare and the American Library Association Best Books lists, and received the *Boston Globe–Horn Book* Award. It is the fast-paced, incident-filled, often poignant, frequently amusing story of an orphaned boy who runs away from his foster home in search of a family to love him and finds one in the racially divided town of Two Mills, Pennsylvania. Although some critics find Spinelli's books overloaded with meanings, too filled with crude humor, and strained for effect, others find them refreshing, witty, true to adolescence in broad outlines, credible in dialogue, and hilariously entertaining. His other titles include *School Daze: Report to the Principal* (Scholastic, 1991), *Who Ran My Underwear Up the Flagpole?* (Scholastic, 1992), and *Picklemania* (Scholastic, 1993). A contributor to anthologies for adults, he lives in Norristown, Pennsylvania.

STACEY LOGAN (*Let the Circle Be Unbroken**; *Mississippi Bridge**; *The Road to Memphis**), African-American youth, brother of Cassie, Christopher-John, and Little Man Logan, and about the same age as the Logan children's white acquaintance, Jeremy* Simms, and their black sharecropping neighbor, Moe* Turner. In *Let the Circle Be Unbroken,* Stacey shows that he is beginning to feel himself a man. He asserts his opinions more in family matters, even sassing Mama sometimes, begins paying attention to girls, worries about the Logan finances, and runs off to cut sugar cane in Louisiana to earn money for taxes, Moe with him. The Louisiana experience is a terrible, harrowing one of brutality, excruciatingly hard labor, and dishonest bosses who withhold wages for trifles and keep the workers in virtual bondage. Stacey and Jeremy are ten in *Mississippi Bridge,* where Big Ma, Stacey's grandmother, is evicted from a bus because she is black and thus is spared from death when the bus plunges from a bridge into a swollen river. On the periphery of events in this book, Stacey plays a major role in *The Road to Memphis,* where he is the principal means by which Moe Turner gets to Memphis. At the book's opening, Cassie and the boys are awaiting Moe's return from Jackson by bus. To their surprise, Stacey arrives driving a wine-colored, 1938 Ford, which he has purchased from Mr. Jamison, the sympathetic white lawyer in Strawberry, who has often befriended the Logans. Stacey is extremely proud of the car and takes excellent care of it, even paying it off within a few months of purchase. It is with this car that the youths strike out for Memphis and Moe's freedom from unjust prosecution. They have troubles with the car along the way but eventually succeed. While they stop at a gas station for help, some redneck whites taunt them, and they later discover that one of them has raked a long gash in the side of the car, ruining the finish. Although it is a devastating blow to Stacey, he takes this humiliation in stride, recognizing that it is more important to get Moe away safely than to lament or attempt to square this act of vandalism and racism.

STAPLES, SUZANNE FISHER (1945–   ), born in Philadelphia, Pennsylvania; journalist and author of novels for young adults. Raised in northeastern Pennsylvania, she was graduated from Cedar Crest College with a degree in literature and political science and became a correspondent for United Press International, working for many years in Asia, including Hong Kong, Pakistan, Afghanistan, and India. She also worked on foreign news for the *Washington Post*. Her first novel was *Shabanu** (Knopf, 1989), about a spirited and independent Pakistani girl growing up among the nomads of the Cholistan Desert, who comes into conflict with her people's traditions for girls. Filled with telling detail about a culture little known in the West, it was an American Library Association Notable Book and a Newbery Honor Book and was named to Fanfare. Its sequel is *Haveli* (Knopf, 1993). Staples has also lived in New York City and central Florida.

THE STAR FISHER (Yep*, Laurence, Morrow, 1991), biographical novel about one week in the life of a Chinese-American family in the hills of West Virginia in 1927. American-born, resilient, capable Joan Lee, 15, describes what happens when she, her brother, lively Bobby, 10, her sister, Emily, 8, and their immigrant parents, scholarly Papa* and proud, shy Mama*, arrive by train from Lima, Ohio, at the small town of Clarksburg, the first Chinese to take up residence there. On the way from the train station, they experience the first of several acts of discrimination. A scruffy, snuff-taking, red-haired man jeers, "Darn monkeys," and swears at them and later paints scurrilous slogans on their fence. Papa sets up his laundry and Mama starts housekeeping in the old schoolhouse they have rented from the retired mistress, elderly Miss Lucy, who is also their next-door neighbor and becomes their staunchest friend. Miss Lucy invites the children to tea and cookies, a delightful occasion brought to an abrupt close when they smell smoke and the children realize that Mama, a miserable cook, has burned their meal. Miss Lucy offers supper, but the proud parents refuse. That night in bed together, to quiet Emily's fears, Joan tells her the Chinese legend of the star fisher, in which a farmer marries a bird-woman, holding her against her will, and of how their daughter is rejected by area children because she is different. The Lees have very little money, and Joan is humiliated at having to do the shopping, which is her responsibility because Mama's English is poor and she is too proud to show their poverty. At school, the principal, Miss Blake, patronizes Joan, and classmates look down on and pick on her, but she makes the acquaintance of another outcast, Bernice*, who is disliked because her family are on the stage, and later the two girls become friends. Discouraged when customers fail to arrive, Papa retreats into reading his philosophy books, and Mama becomes increasingly prickly and brooding. When Miss Lucy brings leftovers, insisting that they will only be thrown out, Mama proudly rejects them, and Joan, as often happens, feels caught in the middle between love and loyalty to her Mama and respect and liking for her new, well-meaning friend. Joan solves the problem by pointing out to Mama that Miss Lucy is the last of her line. Mama, thinking it is terrible that Miss Lucy has no family, is able to accept Miss Lucy's offer to help by regarding her as family. Miss Lucy begins by teaching Mama to bake apple pies. Although every effort results in terrible failure, Mama finally makes a fine one for the pie auction at the church social. Mama's skill becomes known, and customers flock to the laundry, with some help from Miss Lucy who telephones her former students to urge them to patronize the Lee laundry. The Lees celebrate their new prosperity and sense of belonging with Miss Lucy at a picnic on a hillside overlooking the valley on Sunday afternoon. Although episodes and the basic story line come from the experiences of the author's own family, the author creates the moment well, and the main characters seem real, much of the plot lacks conviction in context. The several episodes of discrimination seem fabricated to make their point, and the rednecks are too obviously so, being, for instance, former pupils of Miss Lucy who were poor students. As presented, the pie scenes seem borrowed from television sit-coms, and that Mama's one fine pie should so change the community's attitude toward the Lees is hard to accept. Although Joan sometimes feels like the daughter in the legend, she also comes to see that Mama is like the bird-woman, out of her element. For the most part, however, the star fisher legend seems obtrusive and worked laboriously into the plot. Overall, the book lacks the freshness and conviction of the author's earlier *Dragonwings* and *Child of the Owl,* but projects well the family's values, hopes, and willingness to work for good lives in this new and often hostile land. For details about *Dragonwings* and *Child of the Owl,* see *Dictionary, 1960–1984.* Christopher.

STAYING FAT FOR SARAH BYRNES (Crutcher*, Chris, Greenwillow, 1993), realistic contemporary novel of family and school life set in Spokane, Washington, and revolving around a physically disabled victim of child abuse. Two intersecting story strands drive the narrative of intelligent, perceptive, thoughtful Eric Calhoune, 17, so fat by his own admission that he thinks he deserves his nickname of Moby (from *Moby Dick*): his friendship since childhood with Sarah Byrnes, a classmate, and his relationship with Mark* Brittain, a strongly fundamentalist Christian and also a classmate. Both Eric and Sarah feel marginalized from their peers—he by his girth, she by the disfiguring scars (her name is a terrible pun, Eric thinks) on her face and hands that she says she got when she was three and pulled boiling spaghetti onto herself. She says that her father refused to have the scars repaired in order to teach her a lesson. Eric feels so strongly about his relationship with Sarah that when he started swimming and began to lose weight, he gorged himself in order not to be more "normal" than she. When the book opens, Sarah, who has built up a reputation for intense verbal and physical hostility toward anyone who crosses her, is in the Child and Adolescent Psychiatric Unit at the local hospital, having suffered some sort of breakdown that renders her unable to speak. Eric visits her faithfully every day, following the staff's instructions to speak conversationally to her about things the two did together and current school happenings, although she does not respond. Thus, much of the first half of the book consists of flashbacks. The reader learns how bully Dale* Thornton, once the arch-rival of both children, became their ally in producing the underground paper, *Crispy Pork Rinds,* to get back at their common enemy, Vice Principal Mautz. Eric and his chum, Steve Ellerby*, iconoclastic son of a controversial Episcopal priest, join in ragging Mark, their swim teammate, and also lock horns with him in Contemporary American Thought (CAT). Both are under the direction of well-liked if tough teacher-coach, Ms. Cynthia Lemry*. In CAT, Eric's favorite class, the assignments produce lively discussions on such weighty matters as the nature of humans, the nature of God, the existence of God, and abortion, to the last of which Mark is vehemently opposed. Tension rises when Eric dates, at her instigation, Jody Mueller, the "classiest-looking" girl in school but the one whom Mark considers his. Jody confides to Eric that she had an abortion of Mark's child. Confronted about this by Eric, Mark says Jody lies. At the hospital, Sarah, who has pretended to be mute to get away from her abusive father, acknowledges that she lied about her burns, when confronted by the information given to Eric by Dale that her father had deliberately maimed her to get back at her mother in a domestic dispute. When Mr. Byrnes, convinced that Sarah is faking, frequents the hospital hoping to catch her out, Sarah bolts, hides in Lemry's garage, and reenters school. During an explosive discussion in CAT over the sacredness of life, Sarah accuses Mark of hypocrisy in his attitude toward her because of her scars, and Jody tells of her abortion. His duplicity exposed, Mark attempts suicide, prompting his father to persuade Mautz to bring pressure on Eric and Ellerby to admit that his son's effort to end his life was their fault and on Lemry to alter her class. Lemry takes a leave, and the two boys refuse to admit blame in a dramatic, tense scene in which Ellerby's minister father effectively silences both Mautz and Mr. Brittain. Lemry is convinced that only Sarah's mother can put Mr. Byrnes in jail and out of Sarah's life, since she alone can testify to the abuse she and Sarah suffered before she walked out fifteen years earlier, thus substantiating Sarah's story of long-term abuse. Lemry and Sarah drive to Reno, where Mrs. Byrnes is thought to be working, but, once located, the woman refuses to testify. Convinced that Eric knows where his daughter is, Mr. Byrnes kidnaps Eric in Eric's car, knifes him for information about Sarah, ending Eric's career in competitive swimming for the year, and then disappears. Carver* Middleton, Eric's mother's boyfriend, deduces that the man is hiding out in the Byrnes house, finds him, and beats him up. Carver does some time, Sarah is adopted by the Lemrys just before her eighteenth birthday, Mr. Byrnes is sent to prison for assault, Mark seeks therapy, and Ellerby and Eric leave for college. Abundant humor of character, situation, and language lighten the substance of this basically very serious book, which addresses a number of important current issues, more than one two-hundred-page novel for young people should have to support. Although the class discussions about these problems slow the plot, they grab the intellect. Not only timely but also well reasoned and easy to grasp, they are fascinating in themselves. Most characters are overdrawn, almost caricatures, but Eric, who is deeply concerned about his friends, especially Sarah, so often feels "scorched on the desert of humiliation," and is sincerely determined to follow the right course when confronted by dilemmas, is a worthy protagonist, and Sarah is too tough and enduring to provoke pity. The diction has the earthiness of contemporary teenaged talk as well as a wealth of well-turned phrases. Descriptions of swim practices ring true, and Eric's flight from Mr. Byrnes rivets the attention. This capably written, consistently entertaining novel boldly takes on important controversies and examines the problems of the physically disabled and abused without sentiment or sensation. SLJ.

STEAL AWAY (Armstrong*, Jennifer, Orchard, 1992), slave-escape novel set mostly in 1855, in which two girls, a white orphan and an African-American slave, make their way from Virginia to the North. After the death of her parents in Vermont, Susannah McKnight, 13, is taken by her Uncle Reid, a minister, to his farm at Front Royal, Virginia, where she is horrified that he owns slaves and dismayed when she is given one, Bethlehem, a girl about her own age. Extremely lonely in the household that consists of her relentlessly stern uncle, her hypochondriacal aunt, her cousins—spoiled and mean-spirited Fidelia, 14, and handsome, vain Byron, 17—Susannah starts a secret project of teaching Bethlehem to read, naively unaware of the danger in which it puts a slave. Offered what she understands is a key to a better life, Bethlehem is both attracted and afraid, but she learns quickly. When spring comes, Susannah decides to run away to Vermont and enlists Bethlehem's aid, again not realizing how dangerous this is for the black girl. Because Byron has been making sexual threats to her, Bethlehem decides to go along. Dressed as boys, they start off, with Susannah naturally assuming the lead, but her overconfidence causes them to lose their horse, and the sight of a coffle of stolen slaves, which they watch from hiding, makes her begin to understand the vast difference between the risks they take. Susannah has shown Bethlehem a map, but neither of them has much idea of the great distance of the journey they are undertaking. Both, however, are stubborn, and they persist with few mishaps until they reach Emmitsburg, Maryland, where they see a poster advertising for their return. After that they stay off the roads and no longer beg for food. Susannah steals eggs from chicken coops, but in the dark she trips, falls on her knife, and badly cuts her arm. As they stumble on, Susannah's arm gets worse and in the rainy weather she becomes feverish. Although she urges Bethlehem to go on alone, the black girl approaches a farmer in a field, asking for help. Fortunately he is a Quaker, and his family take the girls in, nurse Susannah through her illness, which has become pneumonia, and secretly send the girls on their way. Susannah still expects Bethlehem to come with her to Vermont, but Bethlehem and the Friends who secretly transport them know that runaway slaves are not safe in any state, and somewhere in New York State they part, Bethlehem going on to Canada and Susannah to the farm of neighbors in Vermont. The story is told with a complicated series of frames, the most extensive being set in 1896, when Mary Emmons, 13, goes with her grandmother, Susannah, to Toronto to see Bethlehem, who is dying of consumption, and to set the story down before it is too late. With Bethlehem, who has been a teacher, is an orphan named Free, 13, who lives with her and cares for her. Initially hostile, Free gradually accepts Mary and her grandmother and helps write out the story of their escape, as it is told alternately by Susannah and Bethlehem. The novel starts with a letter, dated 1928, from Mary, now a nurse in Manila, to Free, enclosing the manuscript with her own comments, hoping that the black girl, now a teacher herself, will understand the love that took her grandmother to Toronto and will no longer resent what she clearly thought an intrusion on Bethlehem's last days. It ends with a letter from Free to her granddaughter, Julia, dated 1960, saying that she has never had courage to reread the manuscript, but she wants the girl to know what happened. Central to the novel is the relationship between the girls: Bethlehem and Susannah in the 1850s and that between Mary and Free, which parallels it in the 1890s. In both the white girls are full of goodwill but obtuse, unaware of the terrible experiences that create a gulf between them and the African Americans. Besides being an exciting adventure story, the novel is strong in exploring these often unspoken differences and in not simplifying a complex situation. ALA.

STEINER, BARBARA A(NNETTE) (1934–   ), born in Dardanelle, Arkansas; teacher and prolific, versatile writer of some four dozen fiction and nonfiction books for children and young people, mostly in series, under her own name or the pseudonyms Alix Ainsley, Anne Daniel, Kate D'Andrea, and Annette Cole. After being graduated with bachelor's and master's degrees, respectively, from Henderson State College in Arkansas and the University of Kansas, she taught in elementary schools in Missouri, Kansas, and Colorado for fifteen years. She has published science books for children, for example, *Biography of a Polar Bear* (Putnam, 1972); poetry, including *Hat Full of Love* (Tempo, 1983); and a set of lighthearted books for younger readers about animal-loving Oliver Dibbs, among them *Oliver Dibbs and the Dinosaur Cause* (Macmillan, 1986) and *Oliver Dibbs to the Rescue* (Macmillan, 1986). She has written novels for young adults, including *Secret Love* (Scholastic, 1982), *Searching Heart* (Scholastic, 1982), and others whose titles reveal their direction. *Ghost Cave** (Harcourt, 1990), an Edgar Allan Poe Award nominee, draws on her childhood, when her father collected and sold Indian relics. A mystery-adventure, it tells how three schoolboys in 1954 find the skeleton of an Indian boy in a cave in the hills of northern Arkansas and strive to keep their discovery secret from the town bully. In addition, she has published *The Phantom* (Scholastic, 1993), a ghost story; *The Dreamstalker* (Avon, 1992) and *Night Cries* (Avon, 1993), both horror novels; and mystery-detective novels, including *Foghorn Flattery and the Vanishing Rhinos* (Avon, 1991). Steiner has been a frequent contributor of stories, plays, and poems to children's and teenagers' magazines and religious publications, among them *Humpty Dumpty, Ranger Rick,* and *Childlife.* Steiner has made her home in Boulder, Colorado.

STEPPING ON THE CRACKS (Hahn*, Mary Downing, Clarion, 1991), historical novel set in the middle-class town of College Hill, Maryland, against the background of World War II from late 1944 to March 1945, in which a young girl is caught between the dictates of patriotism and the demands of compassion. The narrator, shy, plain, dark-haired Margaret* Baker and her sixth-grade classmate, pretty, blond, bold Elizabeth* Crawford, are next-door neighbors and best friends. Both have brothers in the war and are somewhat aware of its effects and progress through shortages, news reports, and letters. The book's main plot revolves around the major problem in their everyday lives: their bullying classmate Gordy* Smith, who with two pals terrorizes them at every turn. One October morning on the way to school, Gordy shoves Elizabeth down, bloodying her leg, dumps out her school supplies, rips up her homework, and swears to "get" the girls if they tell. Elizabeth plans revenge by wrecking the boys' play hut in the woods, which lies just over the railroad tracks. Undaunted by Margaret's protests about the "crazy man" who Gordy assures her roams there and Margaret insists she once saw, Elizabeth persuades Margaret to help her trash the place, but the girls are puzzled by signs of occupation. In December, Elizabeth gets the idea that the crazy man is a Nazi spy and decides they should investigate. They discover that Stuart* Smith, Gordy's older brother and an army deserter, is living in the hut. Margaret wants to inform on him and is increasingly bothered by the morality of remaining silent, but also, after conversations with Stu, who says he is a conscientious objector, she wonders about war as a means of problem solving. Pragmatic Elizabeth, however, takes advantage of the situation to blackmail Gordy. When the winter cold intensifies, Stu falls ill, and the girls smuggle aspirin, cold medicine, warm clothes, and food to him, and like Gordy, even play hooky to sit with the ill man. When it becomes obvious he needs medical help, they enlist the aid of Barbara, a young war widow and ex–school friend of Stu, who takes him to a doctor and then to her parents' house for nursing. A subplot revolves around the reasons for Gordy's antisocial behavior and frequent black eyes and facial bruises. Mr. Smith drinks and abuses his large family both verbally and physically. When Stu is well enough to try to do something about the increasingly intolerable situation in his house and confronts his father, the man goes berserk. Police come, and Stuart is arrested and taken to a military hospital. Eventually the mother and children move in with relatives in North Carolina. Later the girls learn that charges against Stuart will probably be dropped because of his family's problems and the broken eardrum he suffered from the beating his father gave him. They also learn that Stuart and Barbara have fallen in love and plan to marry. The girls look forward to the end of the war, but Margaret and her family have come to no resolution about the emotional dilemma into which Stuart's desertion has plunged them, especially since Margaret's brother, Jimmy, is killed in battle. Action is plentiful, and the dialogue and girls' attitudes and activities are credible. The characters, however, are commonplace and too carefully foiled, and hiding the brother so near residences for so long strains belief, especially since the smoke from the fires Stuart and the children build for warmth and cooking would surely attract attention and the boys come and go frequently. The family abuse seems an unnecessary element, since having an older son in the service and family pride would be enough to justify a father's being hostile to a deserting son. In recent years also, it seems abuse has become a handy rationalization for a child's antisocial behavior and a trite story motivation. Best are the details that bring the times to life—about radio programs, movies, clothing, blue and gold window stars for servicemen, shortages, and especially the homefront views about battles, the progress of the war, the enemy, patriotism, and army service. ALA; O'Dell; SLJ.

STEWART, LINDA, born in New York City; writer of crime novels, television movies, series shows, and documentaries, and author of books for middle grade readers, under her own name and the pseudonyms Kerry Stewart and Sam Stewart. After taking her B.A. from Brandeis University, she held various positions in advertising firms in New York City and did freelance advertising for such agencies as Citizens for Clean Air and the Urban League and was editor and writer for *Consumer Action Now.* Her lighthearted, fast-moving, cleverly worked out *Sam the Cat Detective** (Scholastic, 1993), about an unflappable tomcat who enlists the aid of neighborhood cats to solve the mystery of a local apartment house robbery and catch the culprit, was nominated for the Edgar Allan Poe Award. The prototype of Sam the cat is Stewart's own cat, while that of Sam the detective is the fictional Sam Spade.

STIENERT (*Mote**), Ed Stienert, the tall, slender, athletic, African-American detective with whom Chris Miller becomes close friends while they work on uncovering the murderer of a local teacher, Mr. Holder*. Stienert is in his late twenties, was a college basketball player, and works well with big, tough, older Frank Baker, his white superior. They often trade the roles of good cop–tough cop while interviewing people. Stienert sometimes adopts a black dialect that he calls soul talk but can speak educated English equally as well. His and Chris's conversations about language provide some humor, and their discussions about discrimination give insights into the feelings of blacks in contemporary society. Stienert is a ''cop's cop'' in that he never stops working (he is always on the lookout for a certain rapist, for example) and is tough but humane. His girlfriend, Kate, is pursuing a doctorate and would like him to go into teaching because she fears for his safety. Stienert has a crescent-shaped scar under one eye and is nicknamed Moon. Since Chris has a similar scar, Stienert calls Chris Little Moon. Stienert is a well-developed, likable character.

STONEWORDS: A GHOST STORY (Conrad*, Pam, Harper, 1990), gothic
ghost and time-travel fantasy set in a large old country house on an isolated
island somewhere in the United States in the late 1900s. A friendship between
a contemporary girl and a ghost girl from 1870 clarifies the modern girl's relationship with her grandparents and especially her mother. Jessie, Zoe's hippie-
type, "maybe even a little crazy" mother, who has named her from a stoneword,
or inscription, on a local tombstone, leaves her with Zoe's maternal grandparents, without the slightest sign of regret or loss. Zoe feels abandoned but also
comfortable and secure with kind and loving Grandma and PopPop, but she
nevertheless envies the attention Oscar, their fat old pug dog, gets from Jessie
on her brief, infrequent visits. When PopPop decides to refurbish the child-sized
playhouse he had built for Jessie, a "pretty girl" of about eleven appears to
Zoe and claims it is hers. Although Zoe* Louise is bossy and pushy, the two
girls become fast friends and often play together. Since Zoe speaks out loud her
conversations with Zoe Louise but they cannot hear any answers, Grandma and
PopPop think Zoe has an imaginary playmate. Months pass and turn into years
as the two girls continue to play in the yard, playhouse, and Zoe's room. Zoe
learns that Zoe Louise has parents and a younger brother named Oliver and that
the entrance to their time frame is the old stone staircase off the kitchen where
Grandma stores her vacuum cleaner and that is forbidden to Zoe because it is
considered unsafe. Eventually Zoe learns the secret of the stairs that enables her
to enter Zoe Louise's dimension. There, she, Zoe, becomes the ghost—bodiless,
unseen, and unheard. When the girls are together, Zoe Louise often remarks that
the day is her birthday, that her Papa is bringing her a pony, and that she wants
Zoe to come to her party. On one of Jessie's visits, Zoe accompanies her mother
to the woods out in back to pick honeysuckle vines. Jessie says that some thorny
bushes Zoe finds there are pink roses planted when "that little girl died" in an
accident some one hundred years earlier—the little girl whose name was "Zoe
something." As Zoe Louise becomes increasingly insistent that Zoe come to
her party, Zoe grows more and more curious about how the girl died. On the
birthday, Zoe and Zoe Louise pick raspberries from the thorny bushes Zoe's
mother told her were memory roses, and Zoe learns that Zoe Louise's last name
is LaBarge. Then Zoe discovers in old newspapers in the basement a story about
the tragic death of eleven-year-old Zoe Louise LaBarge in a mysterious kitchen
fire. Zoe reenters Zoe Louise's time and discovers Zoe Louise and Oliver trying
to light the candles on the birthday cake. The fire gets out of hand and spreads
through the kitchen. Oliver escapes, and Zoe manages to pull Zoe Louise to
safety on the stone staircase. Back in her own time, Zoe learns from her mother
that the thorny bushes are not memory roses at all, indeed never have been, her
mother tells her, but raspberries. Zoe assumes that there has been no death and
that her action enabled Zoe Louise to survive and grow up. Now an early adolescent, Zoe feels closer to her mother than before, and for the first time she
even "waved wildly" when Jessie leaves and she watches her mother's departing car pass through the trees. Since the reader only knows what Zoe chooses

to tell in this first-person narrative, it is hard to judge whether or not Zoe Louise is a figment of Zoe's imagination, created out of loneliness and loss and scraps of conversation she may have overheard. Zoe even calls the ghost girl Zoe Louise at the beginning of their relationship without being told the name by Zoe Louise herself. Moreover, it does seem strange that the grandparents, who are apparently long-time residents, are unaware of the LaBarge story whereas Jessie seems to have some idea of it. Zoe Louise is a strongly developed figure, however, an aspect that strengthens the credibility of the fantasy, and certain events, such as the trashing of the playhouse, seem attributable only to her action. Characterization varies. Jessie is a strange, lost figure, one the reader both blames for her callousness toward her daughter and at the same time feels sorry for. The grandparents are the almost perfect senior generation. Zoe and Zoe Louise are foils, with Zoe apparently gaining from the more assertive Zoe Louise the courage, independence, and understanding that help her come to terms with her mother. Tension increases steadily and holds well. The gothic elements are less obtrusive and the style more skillful and figurative than in most other novels of this type, but how much of the story is real and how much Zoe makes up remain in question. Boston Globe Honor; Poe Winner.

STRIDER (Cleary*, Beverly, illus. Paul O. Zelinsky, Morrow, 1991), contemporary animal novel of a dog that helps a boy straighten out his troubled relationship with his father and achieve self-esteem; sequel to *Dear Mr. Henshaw*. In diary entries, Leigh Botts, now fourteen and going into high school, tells how he and his friend Barry Brinkerhoff find a dog abandoned on the beach, bravely trying to obey commands to sit and stay even after several days. The boys take him food and water, persuade him to come with them, and decide to share joint custody. The dog, which they call Strider, is recognized by Leigh's mother as a Queensland heeler, a cross between a dingo and a shepherd. Much of Leigh's time during the rest of the summer is spent in running with Strider on the beach and keeping him out of the sight of Mrs. Smerling, landlady for their "garden apartment," a little one-bedroom house in Pacific Grove, California, that Leigh calls "the shack." Because Strider whines and cowers miserably when told to sit or stay, the boys train him to respond to the commands written on cards and so have the only dog around that can read. Before school starts, Leigh buys a shirt in a thrift shop, brand new but outrageously colored with stripes and dots differing on each section and sleeve. On the first day a wealthy boy, Kevin Knight, challenges him, saying that the shirt is his, given by his mother to the thrift shop before he had a chance to wear it. When Kevin tries to grab the shirt, Leigh dodges away, and a chase ensues, one that is repeated each morning until the whole school knows both boys and the rivalry over the shirt is forgotten. Because the Brinkerhoffs have a big, fenced yard, Leigh leaves Strider there during school, but he spends far more time with the dog than does Barry, who is going out for football. During the fall, Leigh's father shows up several times, at first trying to pump Leigh about men in his mother's life, then revealing that he was unable to pay for a new transmission and has lost his big tractor-trailer rig and taken a job in a nearby gas station. When Leigh is very ill during Christmas vacation, his father sits with him and fixes him supper. In January, Leigh and Barry quarrel about their joint custody, but eventually agree that since Strider clearly shows a preference for Leigh, he can own the dog, with Barry as friend to both. In the spring Leigh goes out for track and gets to know a red-haired girl he admires, Geneva Weston, who runs the hurdles. When Mrs. Smerling, who has known about Strider all along, suggests that he build a fence, Leigh asks his father for help, and they spend a happy day working together, during which his father's new girlfriend shows up and is introduced. Later, he and his father have their first real conversation. By May, nearly a year after the diary starts, Leigh has three good friends, Barry, Geneva, and Kevin, an accepted place on the track team, continued good rapport with his mother, an improved relationship with his father, and, the catalyst for everything else, a "noble" dog. Although the novel lacks the focus and emotional force of its predecessor, it is a pleasant extension of Leigh's story, true to the worries and delights of boys in their early teens and the adjustments necessary after families are broken. The chapters are often too long and explicit to be entirely believable as diary entries, but they stay true to the voice of a boy Leigh's age in the late twentieth century. Fanfare. For details of *Dear Mr. Henshaw,* see *Dictionary of American Children's Fiction, 1960–1984.*

STUART SMITH (*Stepping on the Cracks**), the army deserter hidden by his younger brother, Gordy*, and aided by Margaret* Baker and Elizabeth* Crawford. Stuart is ashamed of having deserted yet maintains war is immoral and justifies his behavior on that ground. He is presented as having been a skinny youth, often teased, a respected paper boy, and a reader. He shares poems he likes, especially ones against war, with the girls, whom he calls his "angels of the battlefield." He is very fond of and grateful to Gordy, since he cannot go home because of his abusive, alcoholic father. Stuart is the stereotypical conscientious objector.

SUMMER (*Missing May**), the twelve-year-old narrator and foster daughter of Uncle Ob* and Aunt May*. Summer loves both of them dearly, knows they cherish her, and misses May far more than she realizes, since she is so greatly concerned with Ob's reaction to his wife's death. Cletus*, her character foil whom she resents, tells her to strike out and use her imagination, and Ob tells her she is too serious and to lighten up. She looks down on Cletus, not realizing that with his catholic tastes and spirited ways he is more normal for the age than she. When she and Ob visit the Underwoods, she sees how proud his parents are of him and realizes that he has never invited her home because of her attitude. Although they are poor, her family has been happy and secure, and Summer does not realize that she is thought disadvantaged until a classmate's composition describing her shows her as a "sad welfare case." Her grief and loneliness come out gradually in her narrative.

SUMNER MCKAY (*The Harmony Arms**), Gabriel* McKay's father, a second-grade teacher. He made up Timmy the Otter, a puppet, to entertain Gabriel when the boy was very little. Later Sumner used Timmy to interest his students in learning to read and then wrote down Timmy's adventures in a book, which was published and picked up by a major West Coast movie studio. Sumner carries Timmy wherever he goes, embarrassing Gabriel and causing the people in Bradleyville, Missouri, to make fun of him behind his back. Although gregarious and seemingly self-assured, Sumner has a shy streak. His ego improves when he finds the courage to stand up to the studio and refuse to continue with adventures for Timmy that he considers inappropriate. After he has a talk about sex with Gabriel and Gabriel stands up for him against the street thugs at the beach who are harassing Sumner about Timmy, Sumner and Gabriel are closer than they have ever been.

SUSANNAH AND THE PURPLE MONGOOSE MYSTERY (Elmore*, Patricia, illus. Bob Marstall, Dutton, 1992), realistic contemporary detective novel set in a neighborhood of old and run-down houses in Oakland, California, one in a series about the supersleuth sixth grader, African-American Susannah Higgins. Lucy, also eleven and by her own admission not as smart as Susannah, who is nevertheless her best friend, plays Watson to Susannah's Sherlock. Lucy tells how, with her help and that of willing and energetic if none-too-bright Knievel Jones, Susannah directs the enterprise to bring to justice the arsonist who has been setting fires in their neighborhood. After the garage and then the back porch of their good friend, elderly Quiggy (Miss Quigley), go up in flames, Lucy is certain the arsonist is Theresa, a dark, unpleasant girl her age who has just been placed as a foster child with Quiggy. Lucy remembers Theresa as the girl who, years before, had been accused of setting on fire the shed containing school playground equipment. Then suspicion falls on a Mr. Peterson, who keeps turning up to press Quiggy to sell her house to him; on Mr. Reid, Quiggy's grouchy, hostile next-door neighbor, in whose trash pile the children discover an empty lighter-fluid can; and on irritable Ruth, Quiggy's younger cousin who now lives with Quiggy, dislikes Theresa, and urges Quiggy to accept Peterson's offer. Complicating matters is the testimony of Mrs. Weinberger, another neighbor, which involves a boy named Harry who wears a purple t-shirt and rides a purple Mongoose mountain bike. Led by Susannah, the children pursue clues that take them across the city to the library, where they learn that a certain Leviathan Corporation has been constructing condominiums in areas where homes had been leveled by fire; a nature preserve, where they find Harry and learn that he was a decoy for the arsonist; and an office building, where they check out the Leviathan company and add to Susannah's store of information and suspicious figures. Things come together at the end after a dramatic fire at

Quiggy's house. The children, trapped in Theresa's room in the attic, make a harrowing escape out of the attic and onto the roof via sheets tied into ropes. They are rescued by Toby, Quiggy's handsome nephew and handyman, whom Susannah exposes by a process of elimination as the arsonist. He has been in the pay of Leviathan and responsible for several fires that enabled the company to buy up the land for a song after the dwellings were destroyed. The mystery moves rapidly with plenty of action, extensive dialogue, and cliffhangers, and it makes good use of conventional mystery-detective characters and situations. Susannah is invariably right in her deductions, and Lucy and Knievel are satisfactory foils to her and to each other. This is a pleasant, consistently entertaining example of the genre for middle readers. Poe Nominee.

SUZELLA RANKIN (*Let the Circle Be Unbroken**), half-white daughter of Mama Logan's nephew, Bud Rankin, a man Mama's age, whom Mama loves like a brother. Suzella is pretty, with creamy skin, good in school, pleasant, and hard working. Everyone likes her but Cassie Logan, who stays jealous of Suzella for most of the book. Although Suzella is nice to everyone, she informs Cassie that she hopes to marry white and that her mother urges her to ''pass.'' Suzella is an irritant in the household, especially to Uncle Hammer, because of her biracial heritage, and since the men of both races are attracted to her, she is also an irritant in the community. The white boys at first think she is white, and she lets them think it, attitudes that the Logans realize are dangerous for everyone in their racist times. Suzella's parents eventually get a divorce and she goes to live with her mother.

SWITCHING WELL (Griffin*, Peni R., McElderry, 1993), time-travel fantasy with strong period elements. In late April of 1891, Ada* Bauer, almost thirteen, is fed up with caring for her many siblings and yearns for the future, when, her mother assures her, women will have the vote and more control over their lives. Ada visits the old well in the Haunted Lot near her house in San Antonio, Texas, tosses some brown sugar candy into the water, and wishes herself one hundred years into the future. On the same day of the month in San Antonio in 1991, Amber* Burak, Ada's counterpart in age and social status, is angry and apprehensive when she discovers that her parents are separating. She goes to the same well, tosses in a cinnamon fireball candy, and wishes herself back one hundred years to the days when families remained intact. Both girls find some familiar city landmarks, and both have trouble with such matters as money, clothes, and terminology. Found by Mr. Bauer, a druggist, Amber is taken to the orphanage of whose board Mrs. Bauer is a member. The monotonous diet consists mainly of potatoes and cornbread, and the children must work hard about the place when they are not in class, which is dreary in itself, and are often switched on the legs or struck about the face, the matron demanding obedience and submission. Amber's best friend is Ethel, a girl her age, who is troubled about her younger brother, Grof. Since he cannot talk and has difficulty following instructions, the matron is convinced that he is feebleminded and plans to send him to a mental institution. Amber suspects that his problems stem from deafness, proves it to Ethel and the other children, and when the orphanage directors inspect the place, defies rules to inform them, wins Mrs. Bauer to her cause, and saves the boy. She becomes a hired girl for Mrs. Bauer, who needs one desperately now that Ada is gone, and eventually figures out that in order to return to her own dimension she must do so on a significant holiday, like the Fourth of July, since she arrived on a celebration associated with the Alamo. She writes her plans in a diary, and on the Fourth she tosses into the well her last cinnamon piece and immediately finds herself back in 1991. Soon after Ada arrives in 1991 San Antonio, she is rescued from a child molester by an alert policeman, who takes her to the station to which Mr. and Mrs. Burak have come for help in finding Amber. Mrs. Burak, a social worker, takes Ada to a homeless shelter, where an assertive, bright, African-American girl named Violet* Little becomes Ada's adviser and protector. Homeless personnel think that Ada's story is too wild to be believed and fear she is mentally disabled. During her psychiatric evaluation, Ada simply refuses to give details about her life, telling the psychiatrist that she has promised someone never to tell. Her ruse works, and she becomes the ward of Mrs. Burak. Ada is happy with the otherwise childless Buraks, though she misses the excitement of her own people-filled house, and locates and visits the Haunted Lot. She discovers that Violet is now living in the Streicher Children's Home near by, a place that was once a large residence next door to the Bauer house. In Violet's room, they find Amber's diary, hidden there by the mischievous son of the house, Billy. From the diary they get the idea of returning Ada on July Fourth. Ada tosses some chocolate candy into the water and lands back in the nineteenth century. Not long after Amber's return to the twentieth century, Mr. Burak discovers that a box had been deposited thirty years earlier in his name at his firm. It was intended for a Violet Little. Inside are a letter dated 1961 and stamps and coins from Ada Bauer Streicher, the wealthy lady who also donated her house for homeless children. Her gift, a sign of her gratitude to the twentieth-century girl who had been kind to her, substantiates the time travel, as does Amber's diary. Just how the well works its switching magic is never completely clear, but evidently a mischievous fairy is involved. The cast of characters in both dimensions is large and hard to keep straight. The girls' adventures appear in alternating chapters, and for a while the action is confusing, a situation that is complicated by the similarity of their names. The girls' several unsuccessful attempts to get back home keep the main plot problem forceful, but interest comes largely from the generously detailed social contrasts. Scenes have power—for example, that in which the Civil War veteran husband of the Bauers' cook, having become addicted to opium for his war wounds, exacts a supply of the drug from Mr. Bauer. Amber realizes that Mr. Bauer is a counterpart of sorts to the pushers of her day. Both girls learn that every era has its concerns, injustices, and celebrations, that times impinge on one another, that some problems, like family pressures, are timeless, and that everyone must do one's best with whatever life brings. SLJ.

SYDNEY, HERSELF (Rodowsky*, Colby, Farrar, 1989), girl's growing-up novel set in an unnamed American town in the late 1980s. Although her mother has told her that her father, an Australian graduate student she met during an exchange year at a university in Sydney, died a year after her birth, the narrator, Sydney Downie, 15, is convinced that her father is really one of the Boomerangs, a famous Australian rock group. At the progressive alternative girl's school she attends and at which her mother teaches history, Sydney is in the writing class of Sam Klemkoski, a sculptor specializing in fine wood carvings. Spurred on by his sometimes bizarre assignments and the obvious disbelief of a new student, Natalie Gatling, Sydney expands this fantasy until she is convinced that her father is Jamie Ward, the quietest of the Boomerangs, and she sticks to her belief despite her mother's exasperation and Sam's suggestions that she drop it. Other problems in her life include her living arrangements. She and her mother share a house with Mrs. Hubbard, who pretends she is not renting to them because zoning codes forbid apartments in their area but who is as domineering as the most undesirable landlady. Also troublesome is the family on the other side of their back hedge, the Martins, who have plenty of money but emotionally neglect their younger son, Porter, for whom Sydney babysits. Other complications include a budding romance between her mother and Sam and the way her two best friends turn against her to become followers of Natalie. When Sam assigns a personal letter for the writing class, Sydney does not write to Jamie, as she has told the other girls she will, or to his mother, who she discovers is dead, but to Wally Martin, Porter's fifteen-year-old brother, bawling him out for staying at his boarding school or camp instead of spending some time with his little brother who, she tells him, is a neat kid. To her surprise, he comes home for spring vacation, and they end by being friends with a shared passion for Boomerang records. A quarrel between her mother and Sam, caused by Mrs. Hubbard's priggish nosiness about their relationship, finally spurs her mother to look for a new apartment, and Sydney's intervention gets them back together. In their move she finds a picture of her father, realizes that she looks like him, and drops her fantasy of Boomerang blood, since reality is now looking better to her. Written as a class project in self-awareness, the book is full of Sydney's essays and sketches in response to Sam's writing class assignments and her perceptive asides about her school (not as progressive or laid back as it pretends to be), her friends (typically snide but still necessary to her happiness), her mother (so accommodating that she is continually being put upon), Sam (having the usual problems of a first-year teacher), and Mrs. Hubbard (a landlady to be avoided at all costs). Although predictable, the novel draws a good picture of a bright high school sophomore and makes both amusing and touching reading. SLJ.

T

TANGLED WEB (McGraw*, Eloise, McElderry, 1993), mystery concerned with a young stepmother and her child, set in Portland, Oregon, in the early 1990s. In the form of a journal written in her blank book, Juniper Webb, 12, tells about the first summer of her father's second marriage, four years after the death of her mother, Margo, to a much younger woman, Kelsey Morgan Blockman, 25. Juniper likes Kelsey and adores her two-year-old son, Preston, but as she starts her journal, she thinks "there's something funny about Daddy's new wife." In the middle of a casual, friendly conversation Kelsey will "shut the door," somehow closing the subject abruptly. When Juniper and her best friend, African-American Alison Fisher, ask Kelsey where she grew up, she answers vaguely, seemingly unable to think of a town name to give them. Encouraged by the visit to their school of a writer for young people, the girls decide to write their own mystery, with lively Alison giving most of the suggestions and prodding Juniper to snoop and discover that Kelsey dyes her hair, that all the labels are cut out of her clothes, and that she carries nothing in her wallet except her driver's license and her social security card. While to Alison it is an exciting game, Juniper worries that Kelsey is in some sort of danger. Her father, obviously thinking that she is jealous, is annoyed at her nosiness, makes light of her evidence, and credits any odd behavior on Kelsey's part to the fact that she is pregnant. Juniper does not tell him about two disturbing happenings: a tall, blond man has been following her and Alison, appearing at the swimming pool and the mall and other places they are together, but leaving abruptly when they look at him. Also, as they come down the escalator in the mall one day, with Preston in his stroller, a woman going up the other side shouts at them, "Robbers!" or perhaps "Robert." The girls haunt the mall, hoping to see the woman again, but Juniper only runs into the blond man. Close up, she sees that he is just a boy, confronts him, and learns that he is Pete Eliot, a friend from second grade who has just moved back to town and wants to renew their acquaintance. When Alison goes off to Minneapolis to visit, Juniper and Pete continue their detective work, concentrating on finding the woman who shouted at the girls. By investigating the only places on the fourth floor, where her escalator was headed, they discover that she is Blanche Mitchell, a representative for a beauty-supply business. When Juniper calls her, giving an assumed name, she is clearly annoyed, but she does admit that she thought for a moment that the child was her nephew, Robert. While babysitting Preston, Juniper sees a tiny rim of reddish gold under his black hair and realizes that, like his mother's, it is dyed. Then Kelsey starts campaigning to move to the country. Upset at the idea of leaving her friends and the house she loves, Juniper asks whether she knows a Blanche Mitchell. Kelsey's reaction is so extreme that even Juniper's father sees that something is wrong, and the whole story comes out. Preston is not Kelsey's son but her little brother; she is not twenty-five but nineteen; her real name is Sharonlee Shelby; she stole Preston from her mother, an alcoholic who was mistreating him, took the identity of a friend who moved to Australia, used her expertise from working in a beauty shop to disguise their looks, and now is terrified that her Aunt Blanche will trace her and that Preston will be returned to their mother. Although shaken by the deception, especially about her age, Juniper's father stands by his wife and wants to go to the authorities. Kelsey, having been given to her mother as a child when her father tried to get custody, is sure her mother would be awarded Preston and balks. To break the impasse, which is making them all miserable, Juniper again contacts Blanche, meets her in the mall, tells her the whole story, and takes her home to meet her father and talk to Kelsey. With her aid, they are able to adopt Preston. The gradual revelation of clues is skillfully handled, as is the red herring of Pete, but the strongest element is the picture of Juniper, who is uncomfortable to be prying, worried that she may be acting out of unwitting jealousy, yet afraid that Kelsey and especially Preston may be in real trouble. While the entries are too sophisticated for a twelve year old, she is described as good at writing and her voice rings true. There is no reason in the plot for Alison to be black, and her race makes no difference at any point. Poe Nominee.

TASTE OF SALT (Temple*, Frances, Orchard, 1992), historical novel set in Haiti and the Dominican Republic beginning about ten years before the February, 1991, inauguration of the people's priest, Jean-Bertrand Aristide, as president of Haiti. The narrative is divided into three sections, the first and last told by Djo, 17, a street boy, and the middle part by Jeremie, a schoolgirl the same age, who falls in love with him. Djo lies on the brink of death in his bed in the clinic for the poor in Port-au-Prince founded by Titid, as Aristide is affectionately called. Djo has been been horribly burned in the firebombing of Titid's shelter for homeless boys, the Lafanmi Selavi, by government thugs called Macoutes. Djo tells his story at Titid's request to Jeremie, who sits by his bedside with her tape recorder. Sometimes Djo speaks coherently and forcefully; at other times his narrative is interrupted by lapses into unconsciousness. His story starts with his childhood in a large family of Cité Soleil, the biggest and poorest slum in Port-au-Prince. Abandoned by both parents, he and his cousin (and foster brother) Lally live by shining shoes and cars and using their wits, until, beaten savagely by a man on the street, Djo is restored to health by Titid and the two boys join Titid's group of homeless youths. His task is to help teach the boys to read. Djo turns rebellious, goes out on his own, and is kidnapped and transported by truck to the Dominican Republic, where he spends several years in virtual slavery as a laborer cutting cane on a *central,* or sugar plantation. The work is brutally hard and the bosses cruel, but an old Haitian laborer named Donay* helps him rise in spirit above the pain and degradation and keep the hope of home alive. When Donay dies of exhaustion and perhaps tuberculosis, Djo goes into great debt to buy his dear friend a coffin, abandons their carefully laid plans to escape, and labors for three years to pay off the debt. When he attends another man's funeral and recognizes the coffin as the one he is buying for Donay, he realizes he has been cheated and runs off with another Haitian laborer, the boy Roro. They follow the irrigation ditch westward up into and over the mountains, traveling by night. Home again, Djo aids Aristide's election campaign, working in the north, and three nights before Aristide's inauguration is wounded in the terrorist attack. Exhausted by the strain of telling his story, he falls into a coma, and for some three days of the eight or so that Jeremie is in the clinic with him, she tells him her story, because the clinic orderly suggests that her voice might restore Djo to consciousness. From another local slum, the fatherless Jeremie is early recognized as bright by nuns; encouraged by her mother to get an education in order to get out of the country, she earns her school fees by working as a cleaning girl at the convent. Although the nuns adhere to the church directive outlawing Artistide's antigovernment activities, his passionate and compassionate sermons and idealism win her to his cause. She notices that after the dictator Duvalier leaves the country and a general becomes president, one who it is hoped will usher in a new era, the same repressive conditions continue. During the next election, one promoted by the United States, thugs invade the polling place, and to escape them, Jeremie crawls over a wall covered with broken glass, severely lacerating and scarring her hands. On her fifteenth birthday, she attends vespers at Artistide's church. During the service, the church is attacked by thugs, who pelt it with stones and scream obscenities all night long. On another occasion, the girl learns thugs are on their way to attack Titid's church and tries to warn him. The church is burned to the ground, but Aristide escapes. While she sits at Djo's bedside, one of the nuns visits to urge Jeremie to accept a scholarship to the University of Paris, but the girl refuses. Their voices awaken Djo, and he finishes his story beginning with the escape from the Dominican Republic and ending with the firebombing and Lally's death. Although many have died and the struggle will be hard, Djo and Jeremie agree that hope lives on and feel they can best help themselves by continuing to help Haiti. Although he never appears directly, only in the children's stories, Aristide dominates the book, his idealism and compassion arousing tremendous loyalty and admiration in his young followers. The people's sordid lives contrasted with the hopes held out by the collective resistance advocated by Aristide, government terrorism and barbarism shown against the compassion and kindness of the young priest, the tremendous odds against reform since even the church opposes his efforts—these give the book its great power. The style employs local dialect and speech rhythms judiciously. The title comes from the folk cure for zombies: a taste of salt will restore them to life. Addams; Fanfare.

TAYLOR, MILDRED D., born in Jackson, Mississippi; teacher and author of realistic stories for children, most noted for her several novels about Cassie Logan and her relatives, the African-American family in Great Depression Mississippi about whom her first book, the Newbery Award–winning *Roll of Thunder, Hear My Cry** (Dial, 1976), revolves. One of the most critically acclaimed novels for young people by a black writer, *Roll of Thunder, Hear My Cry* was also a *Boston Globe–Horn Book* Honor Book and a finalist for the National Book Award, listed in *Children's Books Too Good to Miss,* named a Contemporary Classic and to the Fanfare list by the editors of *Horn Book,* and given the Recognition of Merit Award by the George G. Stone Center for Children's Books. Continuing the Logans' story is *Let the Circle Be Unbroken** (Dial, 1981), also a George G. Stone Book, and *The Road to Memphis** (Dial, 1990), a George G. Stone Book and winner of the Coretta Scott King Award. *Mississippi Bridge** (Dial, 1990), a short, graphic account of racial discrimination, is a companion novel and winner of the Christopher Award. For earlier biographical information and title entries, see *Dictionary, 1960–1984* [*Roll of Thunder, Hear My Cry*] and *Dictionary, 1985–1989* [*The Gold Cadillac*; *The Friendship*].

TAYLOR, THEODORE (1921?/1924?–), born in Statesville, North Carolina; journalist, film producer, and writer. He attended Fork Union Military Academy in Virginia, worked on newspapers in Virginia, Washington, D.C., and New York, and served in both the merchant marine and the U.S. Navy. He has also been a Hollywood press agent and has produced and directed documentary films. His best-known book, *The Cay* (Doubleday, 1969), a novel of a blind boy and an old African-American man stranded on an island in the Caribbean, was followed nearly twenty-five years later by *Timothy of the Cay* (Harcourt, 1993), which he calls a "prequel-sequel," the story of the old man in his youth and of the boy's rescue, the operation that restores his sight, and his return to the island to do homage to the old man's memory. Taylor has also received commendation for his Cape Hatteras trilogy about Teetoncey and Ben O'Neal. Two quite different novels of suspense are *Sniper** (Harcourt, 1989), about the unexplained and threatening shootings of some of the tigers and other big cats at a California game reserve, and *The Weirdo** (Harcourt, 1991), about poaching and murder in the Powhatan Swamp of North Carolina. Both have appeared on lists for the Edgar Allan Poe Award, the first as a nominee and the second as a winner. Taylor and his wife live in Laguna Beach, California. For earlier biographical information and title entries, see *Dictionary, 1960–1984* [*The Cay; The Odyssey of Ben O'Neal; Teetoncey; Teetoncey and Ben O'Neal*].

T-BACKS, T-SHIRTS, COAT, AND SUIT (Konigsburg*, E. L., Atheneum, 1993), lighthearted realistic novel of family and community life set at the time of publication, in which a twelve-year-old girl learns the importance of maintaining an independent mind against the pressure of conformity. To get away from her two best girlfriends, who demand that she sign a contract specifying total immersion in the pool if any one of them has a "bad hair day," diffident Chloe Pollack flies from Ridgeway, New Jersey, to spend the summer with her stepfather's sister, Bernadette*, in Peco, Florida. She promises her stepfather to help Bernadette and "to give the unexpected a chance." The unexpected soon confronts her at every turn, from the rugged independence of the tall, taciturn, forty-something Bernadette, to her vegetarian diet of greens and mushrooms gleaned from her back yard, to her big, black labrador, an ironically gentle, ex-drug-sniffing police dog named Daisy. Chloe becomes Bernadette's helper as she drives a van early every morning for Zack's Meals-on-Wheels commissary carrying food to seniors, workmen, and tourists. For seven years, Bernadette has topped Zack's sales list, her main area being the highly coveted Talleyrand shipyards and docks. Disaster strikes when Wanda, Zack's girlfriend, and her sister, Velma, both generously endowed physically, don T-back bikinis and move their vans into Talleyrand and adjoining sites, pulling almost all Bernadette's trade away. Their attire also arouses the ire of a group called COAT (Citizens Opposing All T-backs), led by the church of the Reverend Mr. Butler. A media circus and plenty of plot entanglements ensue as Zack hires Bayard* McKnight, who wears a suit, to bring a lawsuit against Bernadette to force her to wear a T-back, too. Bernadette simply refuses to do so and also refuses to tell why she will not. When COAT prints up t-shirts saying "T-shirts Not T-backs," Wanda, Velma, and the others wear t-shirts, wet, with nothing underneath, which exacerbates the controversy and provides more sensationalism for the media to exploit. While this is going on, Chloe engages in a little, she thinks harmless, entertainment by dropping hints to Tyler, Velma's snide son, that suggest that Bernadette is a witch. Since Tyler is going to summer school at Butler's church and Butler finds out that Velma is Tyler's mother and may expel the boy for her behavior, Tyler tells the church people that Bernadette is a witch to divert attention from his mother. Chloe learns quite by chance that Bernadette has had a mastectomy, a matter that explains her aunt's reluctance to wear a T-back or a swimsuit and also her refusal to explain why she will not. Chloe tries to get Bernadette to offer medical records as proof that she is not a witch. When rebuffed, she apologizes for her actions and gets the hugs that make her feel really good at last about her relationship with her aunt. Because he says there is no way a person can prove she is not a witch, Bayard persuades Bernadette to quit Zack and become a legal secretary. COAT gets the city council to pass a law against T-backs, driving Zack's business to another city, where he tries the same T-back tactic for garnering trade. The detailed style and snappy, contemporary conversation make scenes lively and vivid and support well the serious themes that underlie the surface humor. Best are the main characters—Chloe, who learns to appreciate hard work, look beyond the obvious, think ahead, and stick up for what she knows is right—and especially Bernadette—strong yet pathetic, a victim of circumstances over which she has no control and to which she refuses to yield but who turns out to be a powerful role model for the once narrow-minded, judgmental, introverted girl. A poignant figure is old Grady Oates, an amputee who befriends Bernadette and Chloe but who gives under pressure because he needs the money. The villain is Zack, whose greed nearly destroys several lives. Inserted stories about historical dissidents like Galileo and Savonarola remind the reader that the difficulties of standing up for one's beliefs against public opinion have not only occurred in the twentieth century. SLJ.

TEHANU (LeGuin*, Ursula K., Atheneum, 1990), fantasy subtitled "The Last Book of Earthsea," completing the story of the enchanted archipelago and the archmage, Ged or Sparrowhawk, of *A Wizard of Earthsea.* The protagonist is Tenar, of *The Tombs of Atuan,* now the widow Flint, mother of two grown children, living at Oak Farm on Gont. The action starts at about the time of the climax of *The Farthest Shore,* with Lebannen (Arren) a minor character. Tenar, or Goha, as the local people call her, takes in a young girl, about age six, who has been abused sexually and physically, pushed into a fire and left for dead, her right hand and the right side of her face charred to the bone. Tenar calls her Therru, and although she lives despite all predictions, she never smiles and seldom speaks. When word comes from Ogion, mage of Re Albi, who was once Tenar's guardian, she takes the little girl to his isolated stone house and is with him when he dies, having first given her his true name, Aihal, assured her with joy that change has come, and told her to wait. She waits in his house with Therru, not knowing for what until a dragon, Kalessin, arrives on the cliff edge, bearing Ged, terribly weakened and ill. Tenar and the local witch, Aunty* Moss, nurse him until his body revives, but his spirit remains despairing, since he has lost his powers of wizardry. When representatives of the king come from Havnor, seeking the archmage to come to the coronation, Ged panics and hides in Aunty Moss's house until Tenar sends him directions to go to her farm in Middle Valley where they will not look for him. When Aspen, wizard of the wicked lord of Re Albi, puts a curse on Tenar, she flees with the child to Gont Port and the ship just arrived from Havnor, pursued by Handy, one of the men who abused Therru. Lebannen takes her aboard the ship and to Valmouth, explaining that the Wizard Masters of Roke have been unable to choose a new archmage and have followed their only clue, which the Master Patterner proclaimed in a vision, "A woman on Gont." Tenar can think only of an old woman Ogion told her of once, descended from the time when dragons and people were one, who somehow retained her dragon nature, but knows the woman would have died long ago. Home again, Tenar finds that Ged has taken a job as a goatherd high in the mountains. She works very hard at the neglected farm through the late summer and autumn. The night of the first hard freeze, Handy and two other men try to break into her house to have their way with her and finish torturing Therru. Ged, bringing the goats down from the high pasture, follows the men and almost kills one with a pitchfork, while the others flee but are caught by the villagers and charged with murder, the woman, Therru's mother, having been beaten to death. Since Ged has lost his powers and with them a wizard's prohibition against sex, he and Tenar make love, his first experience, with Tenar guiding him. They live together as man and wife until her son, Spark, returns from the sea and claims the farm, as is his right. Receiving news that Aunty Moss is ill, Tenar, with Ged and Therru, returns to Re Albi and is intercepted by Aspen, who reinstates the curse on Tenar while Therru slips away. After a night of humiliations, Aspen and other men take Tenar and Ged to the edge of the cliff, intending to have him push her over and then fall himself, but the dragon, Kalessin, summoned by Therru, arrives, destroys the evil men, calls the child by her true name, Tehanu, and promises to come back for her at the right time. The idea that the abused child is also a dragon like the woman in the story is a difficult concept, though it is well planted numerous times in the narrative. Just what will be Therru's power in the future is also unclear, so that despite the subtitle, another book seems necessary to complete the series. Unlike the earlier novels, this one explores the meaning of women's lives and power, how it contrasts with that of men, and whether their secondary status is innate or a result of their training and lack of trust in themselves. Although as a story it is not as strong and compelling as either of the first two in the series, the characters of the abused child, Tenar as a middle-aged woman, and Ged as an aging man are memorable, and the style is skillful. Fanfare. For details of the earlier books in the series, see *Dictionary, 1960–1984.*

TELL ME EVERYTHING (Coman*, Carolyn, Farrar, 1993), realistic psychological and sociological problem novel set in recent years in which a girl grapples with her mother's sudden death. Since her mother died a hero's death the previous autumn in a fall from a mountain while trying to rescue a lost teenaged boy, Roz (Rosalind) Jacoby, 12, has been living in a ramshackle house in Newburyport, Massachusetts, with her maternal uncle, Mike* Jacoby. Roz often flashes back to life with Ellie* Jacoby, to such activities as baking bread, camping, and sharing Bible stories like those of Doubting Thomas and Abraham and Isaac. Ellie often prays and refers to the Bible since she finds solace in religion from the rape that resulted in Roz's birth. Thinking about her mother has become almost an obsession with Roz, and sometimes she mixes fact and fantasy. In school, she is put on in-house suspension after she strikes with her fist as hard as she can a classmate who derisively questions her report on the *Challenger,* in which she says that her mother died in the explosion. When her suspension teacher, Ms. Givens, tells her students to write an essay on why they are in suspension, words fail Roz, and she draws pictures of her mother instead. After school she decides to call Nate Thompson, the Montclair, New Jersey, boy her mother died rescuing, as she does regularly, just to hear his voice so that she knows he exists (she never speaks to him). This time she is disturbed to discover that the number has been discontinued and that the new number is unlisted. Still another blow falls when Mike tells her that the school has referred them for family counseling. In the counseling session, she again, as is her custom in uncomfortable situations, withdraws inside her head. She has also begun to have nightmares, from which Mike awakens her but which she never remembers afterward, and starts her periods. Taking these various occurrences as divinely ordained signs, she decides to go to Montclair and look up Nate. She wants to ask him what really happened up there on the mountain. To earn bus fare she takes a paper route, which she enjoys, buys the tickets, and sets out in May, leaving an obscure but, she hopes, reassuring note for Mike. She camps in a Montclair public park and finds the school and Nate easily, but in conversation with the troubled youth she learns nothing except that her mother appeared on the ridge above him like an "angel" and then suddenly disappeared. Roz asks to touch the place on his foot where he lost three toes to frostbite in the experience, so that, like Thomas, she can believe the incident really happened. A policeman finds her in her tent, and Mike retrieves her. Some weeks later, Roz decides it is time to bury Ellie's ashes. She plans the simple service, in every part of which Mike concurs, reassuring her that he had loved Ellie, too. The three of them—Roz, Mike, and Joan, Ellie's part-wolfhound, part-greyhound dog—are Ellie's mourners. Roz has come to see that in her painful life Ellie, who often talked to God, was also "answerable to God" in more than one sense, and Roz asks that that phrase be inscribed on the simple gravestone. She also thinks that, like Isaac in the story of Abraham and Isaac, Roz herself has been a kind of sacrifice. What Roz wants now is a settled life with Mike and Joan, her paper route, and some friends her age. Although she never appears, the maladjusted Ellie dominates the book, her pain and outrage driving her daughter's life and affecting her brother's months after her death, the details of which are never made clear. Mike is a winning figure, Roz's teachers are uniformly supportive but helpless, and Nate is a sad figure, caught between what he feels he should do—make some sort of amends for Ellie's death—and the orders of his parents and their lawyer to keep clear for fear of a lawsuit. Since Roz is so obsessed with the loss of her mother in the first chapters, it is hard to believe she could acquire and execute a paper route and plan her trip so efficiently. (Also, paper circulation managers customarily require adult consent, and Mike learns only later that she has a route.) The conclusion seems overly optimistic, and most likely Roz's and Mike's problems are not over. Best are the depiction of Ellie and Roz's life together as seen in the girl's recollections and the funeral scenes, which are presented in heartrending detail. ALA; SLJ.

TEMPLE, FRANCES (NOLTING) (?–1995), elementary teacher and writer mostly of novels for middle schoolers and teenagers; raised in Virginia, France, and Vietnam. Her first novel, *Taste of Salt** (Orchard, 1992), grabbed the attention of critics. It graphically describes the repressive conditions and political terrorism in Haiti under the dictatorship against which Jean-Bertrand Aristide leads collective resistance, as seen from the vantage of a teenaged boy and girl. It won the Jane Addams Award and was named to Fanfare by the editors of *The Horn Book Magazine.* Temple said that the book came about after she saw pictures of demonstrations and read some of Aristide's speeches and "wondered what it would be like to be one of them, called to be a mover and shaker in a country trying to make a new start, pitted against the giants of political terrorism and our global economy." *Grab Hands and Run** (Orchard, 1993), also about the downtrodden, describes the difficult flight of a family of Salvadoran political refugees to the United States. It developed from stories told to her by a particular group who lived with her own family while awaiting Canadian citizenship and was named to both the *School Library Journal* and Fanfare lists. *The Ramsay Scallop* (Orchard, 1994) is a historical novel set in the Middle Ages; *Tonight, by Sea* (Orchard, 1995) tells of Haitians planning to escape to the United States by boat; and *Tiger Soup* (Orchard, 1994) retells an Anansi story from Jamaica. Temple lived in Geneva, New York, with her husband and three children.

TESS MILLER (*The Harmony Arms**), daughter of Mona* Miller and friend of Gabriel* McKay, about his age. She is intelligent, knowledgeable about many things, and streetwise. While on the bus to the movie studio, she shows him how to behave so that street people will not accost him. At first the two children do not get along well, but later they not only become friends but also develop a romantic interest in each other. Each is surprised at how quickly passion consumes them, and because of the experience, both are more aware of their sexuality. By the end of the story, they find touching comfortable rather than only erotic. Tess carries a camcorder wherever she goes and plans to make two movies. One, called *The Big Nap,* will concern Elvis Myata and star Gabriel, while the other will be about her own life and be called *Mundo Tess.* Tess is an always interesting figure.

THESMAN, JEAN, author of both mass-market series novels and more highly commended young adult novels, many of them concerning family relationships. The Whitney Cousins series and the Birthday Girls series were both published by Avon in the early 1990s. Also published by Avon were *Who Said Life Is Fair?* (1987), which has been described as a "better than average teen romance," and *Running Scared* (1987), a suspense novel involving militant terrorists, which was named to the American Library Association Best Books for Young Adults list. Both of these books were also on the ALA Recommended Books for Reluctant Young Adult Readers lists, as was *The Last April Dancers*

(Houghton Mifflin, 1987), a novel concerned with a father's suicide, which was also an ALA Best Book for Young Adults. One of her most intensely compelling novels is *Rachel Chance** (Houghton Mifflin, 1990), a novel of a teenaged girl in an unconventional family whose little half-brother is kidnapped by an evangelical religious group and her determined efforts to get him back. The American Library Association named it to both its Notable Books for Children list and its list of Best Books for Young Adults. A quieter novel, *The Rain Catchers** (Houghton Mifflin, 1991), about a girl in a household entirely of women, is also an ALA Best Book for Young Adults and, in addition, a *School Library Journal* Best Book and winner of a Golden Kite Award. *When the Road Ends** (Houghton Mifflin, 1992) deals with a different sort of family, three foster children and an adult with disabilities who are spending the summer in an isolated cabin. It was named an ALA Notable Book for Children. Among her other titles are *Molly Donnelly* (Houghton Mifflin, 1993) and *Cattail Moon* (Houghton Mifflin, 1994). Most of Thesman's novels are set in Washington State, where she makes her home.

THIMBLE (*The Beggars' Ride**), big, fierce, often cross member of Cowboy's* gang of homeless street kids, the only girl before Clare* Caldwell arrives. Racer* tells Clare that Thimble is prickly because she considers Cowboy hers: "She's crazy, that's all. Chased off I don't know how many other girls before you came along. Trouble with Thimble, she thinks everybody and her sister is out to take Cowboy away. Shoot, sometimes she kinda looks at *me* crooked. How weird is that?'' Cowboy found Thimble on the street, beaten and bruised, and took her into his group. Clare learns that Thimble had also been molested by Griffey. For a long while, Thimble is hostile to Clare, but she helps Clare when Cowboy insists, for example, when the two girls steal a pair of running shoes for Clare because she needs shoes. At the end, Thimble and Clare have formed a friendship of sorts through adversity.

THOMAS (*The Secret Keeper**), the Ottawa Indian maintenance man at the Beaches, the exclusive club at which Anne Lewis acts as keeper (companion-sitter) for Matt Stevens. With a steady, well-paying job, Thomas is better off than most of the other residents of Eagletown, the village of Indians not far from the club. Having worked for the Beaches for many years, Thomas knows the residents well and has become privy to most of their secrets, including how Jess Larimer died. Thomas keeps his own counsel, and when Anne consults him about whether or not she should report the disappearance of Bryce* Stevens to the police, he replies that the Beaches is "not my tribe." He means that she should mind her own business, as he has been doing. Thomas teaches young Matt to fish, a sore point with Bryce, who feels that he should be doing this for his son.

TIERNEY LAURENT (*Libby on Wednesday**), tall, chunky girl with a pink punk hairdo. She dresses in expensive, deliberately sloppy clothes and affects an attitude of disdain and perpetual anger. Tierney is a member of the FFW (Famous Future Writers) workshop at Morrison Middle School, along with Libby McCall, Wendy* Davis, Alex* Lockwood, and G.G.* When Libby visits Tierney at home, she gains insights into Tierney's behavior. Tierney feels inferior to her stunningly beautiful mother and gorgeous older sisters. Tierney and Libby share an interest in memorabilia from the thirties, a hobby that spurs Wendy to collect materials from the twenties. Tierney gradually becomes more confident of her own worth and less hypercritical. Her stories for the writing group tend to be composed of bits and pieces culled from conventional detective novels. Mizzo tactfully says they are "derivative," and Alex thinks they might work as parody.

A TIME OF TROUBLES (van Raven*, Pieter, Scribner's, 1990), historical novel of displaced persons one summer during the Great Depression in the United States. For more than four years, Roy Purdy, now almost fifteen, has conscientiously traveled by bus every Sunday from his home on the eastern shore of Maryland to visit his father, Harlow, at the Maryland state prison, where Harlow is serving time for burning down his employer's canning shed. Roy has dropped out of school to support his stepmother, Ruth Ann, and baby half-sister, by working for a local boat builder. After Harlow is released and Ruth Ann takes off for her parents' house with the baby, Harlow decides to leave for California, where he has been promised a job as a security guard. He and Roy take the bus to Chicago, then to Wichita, where their money runs out; failing to find work, they hop a freight and ride until they are put off in a few miles somewhere in the countryside. Along with a young couple, Ted and Emily Wheeler, and their baby son, they join up with Walt and Martha Landon and their polio-disabled daughter, Mary, who is Roy's age. The bank has foreclosed on the Landons' farm, and they are heading west in their old Reo truck. The little group travels the long, hard, dusty route, and although they have problems with the truck and California authorities, they reach Riverside safely, mostly due to Walt's generosity and Ted's mechanical ability. Harlow proves unhelpful, having, Roy thinks, lost moral integrity in prison and being overly fond of the bottle in spite of repeated assertions that he will never drink again. In California, the novel picks up speed with tension between orange growers and pickers. The Landons, Purdys, and Wheelers are but a handful of the hundreds of out-of-work persons who vie for jobs and are at the mercy of the growers. The group uses the truck for shelter as they squat on land the growers allow the pickers to use. Walt, Ted, and Roy are chosen sporadically to pick, as are other men, but picking jobs and pay are uncertain. Harlow, who has learned that his promised position is with the Growers' Association, will not associate with the pickers, and when Roy refuses to accompany him into Riverside and the apartment provided for them because his sympathies lie with the pickers, Harlow turns nasty. He allies himself with the "goons" who harass the pickers. When strike talk spreads, the growers evict more than a thousand pickers from the squatting grounds. Roy and Mary assist Kevin Olsen, a young social worker, in relocating the pickers onto the state-owned fairgrounds. Roy, Walt, and Mary collect left-over food and day-old bread from local merchants for the strikers until the growers intimidate the merchants into refusing to help and a big, heavy truck runs the Reo off the road, breaking an axle. One day, Harlow, drunk, and a couple of other goons run over with their truck and kill Walt as he is guarding the fairgrounds gate, and they set fire to the fairgrounds barn. They are arrested for arson and murder, and the novel stops abruptly with Roy sensing that the struggle for survival will be long and hard but that they eventually will be all right. Characters are one-dimensional, functional types. Roy, who becomes more mature and faces important decisions, and the selfless, capable Walt are the best developed. Style is for the most part bland, at times even plodding. The scenes of the displaced persons along the route and of the poverty and hardships of the California pickers are clear and vivid and the best part of the book. The kindness of those who help the travelers on the way and after they arrive is in stark contrast to their reception from the growers: the black man who shows them how to ride the rails; the generous boarding-house woman from whom Harlow ironically plans to steal until Roy stops him; the waitress in the cafe in Cordelia; the earnest social worker; and the bold young lawyer, Peter Barlow, who en-courages the pickers to organize and strike, although he is reviled in the area as a red, because he sees collective action as the only way for the workers to get fair treatment from the growers. A little romance between Roy and Mary adds interest and some dimension to their characters. O'Dell.

TO GRANDMOTHER'S HOUSE WE GO (Roberts*, Willo Davis, Atheneum, 1990), mystery of family secrets ferreted out, set mostly in Nettleford, Missouri, in the period of its publication. The fatherless Gilbert children, Rosie, 10; Na-than, 8; and Kevin, 11½, learn that their mother, who has had a stroke, is going to be hospitalized for some months. Since neither Mrs. Kovacs, their landlady with whom they have been staying, nor their Aunt Marge will be able to keep them, they will be sent to three different foster homes. They decide to run away to their grandmother, whom they have never met and about whom they know very little. They stow away in a horse trailer being delivered by Mrs. Kovac's friend, Hank, to a town not far from Nettleford, and walk through the night until they find Woodruff Road and, at the end of a cul-de-sac, what must be their Grandmother Woodruff's house, a huge brick building, derelict, partially burned, evidently abandoned. As they begin to explore, they are startled to be intercepted by a grim-looking woman with a walker and appalled when she admits that she is their grandmother but says firmly that they cannot stay. They are received in a friendlier manner by Great-Uncle George, their grandfather's brother, who gets around better than their grandmother but still walks with a cane. He agrees, however, that they cannot stay and points out that in four days, when their social security checks arrive, there will be money for bus tickets back to their home in Illinois. He rustles up food for them and helps them make up beds in two dusty rooms on the second floor but warns them not to wander around into the other wings because the floors are unsafe. The children know that he is concealing something; Rosie has twice seen a face at a second-story window when both their grandmother and Uncle George are in the kitchen. Their grandmother has called Aunt Marge to say she is sending them back in a few days, the first time she has spoken to either of her daughters since she gave them away to her sister, Aunt Maude, when their mother, Lila, was about Rosie's age. There are other mysteries: a small flower garden is well tended, although the vegetable garden, which they really need, has gone to weeds; there are three rocking chairs with worn cushions on the porch; Uncle George has made a frosted carrot cake and gives them fresh marshmallows in their hot chocolate, although neither he nor their grandmother likes sweets; he is generous with the food but carefully locks the pantry door; several times, when they are all together downstairs, they hear someone moving on the second floor. Their chance to investigate comes the next day when their grandmother develops chest pains and Uncle George rushes her to the doctor. Exploring the part of the house where they have been forbidden to go, they run into their grandmother's sister, theatrical Ellen Waxwell, who has been thought to have died in a fire years before and been buried in the family plot. When their grandmother and Uncle George return and discover that Kevin forgot to lock the pantry and matches are missing, the truth comes out: Ellen, an actress, is also a pyromaniac. Since she was terribly unhappy in a mental hospital and managed to escape and set the house on fire, their grandmother had sent her children to Aunt Maude and lived a life of deception, caring for and guarding her mentally ill sister while the body of a hired girl killed in the fire lies under Ellen Waxwell's tombstone. After a desperate search, they find evidence that Ellen was hiding in a cave on the property and has been buried in a cave-in. Although the plot is reminiscent of various well-known novels, among them *Jane Eyre* and Cynthia Voigt's *Homecoming,* the pace and tone keep the novel pleasantly creepy and the children are convincing. Most of the action is seen through the perceptions of Rosie, who is more sensible than Kevin and protective of Nathan. The author resists the temptation to make everything turn out perfectly. At the end, their grandmother and Uncle George still plan to send them home on the bus. They will probably be able to stay with Mrs. Kovacs, but their mother's condition is uncertain. Poe Nominee.

THE TOMBS OF ATUAN (LeGuin*, Ursula K., illus. Gail Garraty, Atheneum, 1971), second fantasy of the islands of Earthsea, this one set in the Kargad land of Atuan, east of the main archipelago. Having been chosen as a young child to be the present incarnation of the continually reborn priestess of the Nameless Ones, Tenar, now renamed Arha, learns the rituals of her office and how to traverse in complete darkness the labyrinth beneath the ancient temples. When she discovers Ged, the great mage from western islands, with a light in the sacred place, she at first traps him and, to punish him for desecration, watches through peepholes as he weakens. Then she finds excuses to talk to him and prolong his life. Eventually she renounces the dark gods of her training and escapes with him to Havnor. The novel earlier was cited by Choice and Fanfare, was a National Book Finalist and a Newbery Honor book. Phoenix Honor. For a longer entry, see *Dictionary, 1960–1984.*

TOM WATTLESON (*"Who Was That Masked Man, Anyway?"**), Frankie Wattleson's older brother, a returned World War II veteran. Frankie is sure that Tom is a war hero and pressures Tom to tell about his adventures, always to be rebuffed. Frankie persists, informing Tom that everybody knows that Tom's exploits in the war were great and that, since he, Frankie, listens to the radio so much, he knows that everybody is right about Tom. After Tom describes in a long, detailed speech the assault on the beach in the Pacific in which he was wounded, Mario notices that Frankie looks sick.

TONING THE SWEEP (Johnson*, Angela, Orchard, 1993), girl's growing-up story set in the California desert near Little Rock, a town east of Los Angeles, occurring about the time of its publication. The narrator, Emily, 14, goes with her mother, Diane, to the desert home of her unconventional grandmother, Ola Werren, who has inoperable cancer, to help Ola sort her belongings and move to Cleveland to live with them. Although Diane does not get along well with her mother and hates California, Emily, who has spent part of every summer there, loves the freedom of the dry, sparsely populated country and adores her grandmother. Ola sails along the straight roads in her red convertible, her hair in dreadlocks, her scarf blowing behind her, and is friends with everyone in the area. Knowing that she will not be coming back for a long time and that her grandmother will never return, Emily borrows a video camera and makes a record of Ola's life and friends to preserve the place for them both. Among those important are Martha Jackson, a neighbor who always has a house full of foster children, including David Two Starr, 16, who has been Emily's close friend since they were toddlers; Roland, the artist, and his dog, Jake; the "aunts"—Margaret, Rachel, Ruth, and Sara Title—whose irrepressible laughter fills Emily's summer memories; and Miss Sally Hirt, who runs the highway store. As she cruises from one friend to another on the back of David's motorcycle, Emily comes to understand more about her grandmother and her mother and why her own mother has always resented their move to California. When Diane was fourteen, her father, after working and saving for a long time, bought the red convertible, a symbol to him of the freedom and power that blacks were denied in Alabama. Ironically, it led to his death. Diane found him by the car, shot by someone who had scrawled "Uppity Nigger" on its side. Ola fled with her daughter in the red convertible to California, pulling Diane from her friends and relatives and settling in an unfamiliar environment, without giving the girl time to grieve for her father. Emily has heard about the southern custom of "toning the sweep," repeatedly striking the sweep, a type of farm machinery, with a hammer, thereby announcing the death to the neighborhood and helping to send the spirit on its way. The night of a big picnic in honor of her grandmother, Emily swipes the red car and drives to an abandoned water tower, the nearest thing she can find to a sweep. There she is joined by Diane, who has guessed her purpose, and together they strike the metal tower in honor of the long-dead man and also in anticipation of Ola's death. The novel is brief but moving, with strong characterization of even minor figures. Although Ola, Diane, and Emily are obviously African Americans and David, one assumes from his name, is a Native American, the other desert dwellers are not identified by race or ethnic background. Despite Emily's discovery of the racially motivated murder of her grandfather, the book is refreshingly free of polemic or even overt discussion of prejudice and bigotry, thereby increasing its impact. ALA; C. S. King Winner; SLJ.

TONNIE (*When She Hollers**), Tish's sadistic, sexually abusive stepfather, who has violated her since she was a child. Tish feels Tonnie knows her inside and out, and hence is very adept at manipulating her feelings and behavior. He can speak in a ''Daddy voice'' and pretend deep love and concern, is jealous of her boyfriend, humiliates her with rude comments about her ''not-so-little butt'' and her ''zits,'' and calls her a ''lying, pregnant slut'' when, knife in hand, she demands that he no longer molest her. He defends himself by saying that she ''asks for it.'' He also calls her a ''piece of shit,'' pointing out that shit is an acronym of her name. On the rare occasions that he is nice to her, she fears him most of all. His wife, Barbie, Tish's mother, has borne him three children and is pregnant with his fourth. She accepts and seems to enjoy his sexual attentions and is aware that he visits Tish but refuses to admit it. Tonnie spends most of his nonworking time at home and is well regarded by neighbors and friends. Since his reputation in the community is good, Tish is sure that no one would believe her story of repeated rape if she summoned the courage to tell it. Mr. Battle, the lawyer, wants her written story in case she attacks Tonnie and wounds or kills him or Tonnie assaults and wounds her.

THE TORMENTORS (Hall*, Lynn, Harcourt, 1990), mystery about a dog theft and resale ring in Albuquerque, New Mexico, set about the time of its publication. Youngest of five siblings, the narrator, Sox (Cesare) Newmann, 14, gets along fine with his brothers and sister, his Hispanic mother and his German father, but his real love is Heidi, his black German shepherd that he bought as a puppy four years earlier. After he and his brother Hans leave Heidi in the back of the pickup while they play video games at the Bronco Mart and she is missing when they return, Sox is devastated. His whole family help him hunt for her, but she seems to have disappeared completely. Sure she would not have run off on her own, Sox questions Jesse White Crow, manager of the Bronco, who dredges from his memory a picture of a red truck with a white topper on the back, driven by a white man with a mustache or a beard, which came in for gas while the boys were playing the video game. With this slim thread of evidence, Sox starts his persistent search, even persuading his mother to call the police, although she is afraid of authority figures, and riding his bike in a widening circle through the streets around the Bronco. Four days later he sees the truck and gets a good look at the driver, but he cannot read the license or follow it far in the traffic. Since the policeman he talked to said there had been a number of dog thefts in his part of the city, all of watchdog-type breeds and therefore probably for resale as guard dogs, he writes to newspapers in twenty cities asking if they have run any ads for watchdogs for sale from Albuquerque. Two answers come, both enclosing a classified ad for guard dogs from Angel Kennels, with a post office box number. The post office refuses to give him the name of the box renter, but the sympathetic employee admits that the box would be at the south branch. Sox haunts the South Albuquerque Post Office, and after long waits sees the truck more than once, finally tracing it to an old warehouse at an abandoned airport. His brothers Hans and Ric agree to pose as potential buyers, but they report that Heidi is not among the dogs for sale. Still determined to follow every lead, Sox rides his bike to the warehouse, asks for a job, and, after being refused, uses all his charm to get the man in the office, P. J. Valarian, to show him the cramped dog pens. When Monte, the man with the red truck, comes in, he is suspicious, but Sox feeds him a story about being fascinated by the idea of vicious killer dogs and flatters him until Monte shows him the cruel methods of converting ordinary, large dogs into guard animals. For days Sox returns, buttering up Monte and helping him, although the treatment of the dogs makes him sick. Then Monte lets him ride along as he collects blue slips, registration forms from the American Kennel Club, which unscrupulous breeders get by inflating the size of litters and then sell to the Angel Kennel so their guard dogs appear to be AKC registered. While they are out, Monte spots and steals a white German shepherd. When they get it back, Valarian is angry because the dog is tattooed, and the antagonism between the two kennel owners flares up. Sox tries to get away, and Monte locks both him and Valarian into one of the pens, then starts to give the white shepherd a fatal shot. Sox climbs the side of the pen and jumps down on Monte, who bangs his head on the floor, throws him in the back of the red pickup with the dog, and heads for Mexico. The boy pries open the tailgate, pushes the dog out, and rolls after him. When Sox awakens, he is in a hospital with his family surrounding him. Going on tips and the license number he has earlier given them, the police have responded to the report of the theft of the white shepherd by investigating Angel Kennels, finding Valarian in the dog pen, sending the highway patrol to look for Monte, and picking up Sox and the dog. Although the thieves have kept no records, the police trace a complaint letter from a purchaser who says the black shepherd they sent is too gentle to be a guard dog, and they are able to return Heidi to Sox. A rather brief, simple story with no complications, the mystery gets its power from the intensity of Sox's love for Heidi and his determination to get her back. Descriptions of the training methods are sure to anger any animal lover. Poe Nominee.

THE TREASURE BIRD (Griffin*, Peni R., McElderry, 1992), contemporary mystery-detective novel in a family life context. Shy, fearful Jessy, 10, a Wichita, Kansas, schoolgirl who is small for her age and stutters, is bitterly disappointed and resentful when her mother writes, once again, that it will be impossible for Jessy to spend her summer vacation with her at the commune with which she is currently affiliated. Jessy's fears and discomfort increase when her stepmother, Marly*, an interior designer, learns that she has inherited her Great-Uncle Matthew's big old house and substantial acreage on the outskirts of San Antonio, Texas, and Marly and Dad decide to relocate there with Matt*, Jessy's older stepbrother. Although taxes and repairs pose major challenges, the family look forward to having more space, and Marly is delighted to be back in home territory again. Jessy is disappointed that Great-Uncle Matthew left her several heirloom samplers instead of Goldie, the talking parrot, which he left to Matt. Rumor, supported by conversations with Great-Aunt Lucy, Matthew's sister, and Curtis*, a local African-American youth with whom Matt makes friends, suggests that a treasure in gold is buried somewhere on the property. After unsuccessful attempts to find the cache, Jessy suspects that such phrases as "Goldie is a treasure bird" and "Talk is gold," which Goldie repeats, may be clues and carefully writes them down. Eventually she shares her suspicions with Matt and Curtis, and all three search diligently, making use also of the samplers, but to no avail. The break comes when phrases Goldie says, which they thought were "ghost bank" and "gay tank," are really "post bank" and "gate yank." They find a large mason jar containing gold coins and two envelopes under the gatepost near the creek. The letters are in Great-Uncle Matthew's hand and explain that, to save the property from foreclosure years before, Matthew's father had stolen the coins from his miserly brother, Lamar, and had hidden the remainder to be handed down. Since Matthew had promised his father never to tell, he chose Goldie as the medium for informing his descendants. Matthew taught Goldie clues, which, coupled with the samplers, would disclose the location of the gold to those clever and persistent enough to detect and follow them. Marly and Tad pay their bills, Curtis buys a house for his family with his share, Dad lands a job substitute teaching, and Marly starts her own decorating business. Jessy develops in confidence as expected, and, except for Marly, who has depth, the other characters are definitively if one-dimensionally drawn. The treasure bird concept is inventive and carefully worked out, but Great-Uncle Matthew, who never appears, seems too devious for credibility and that he also stuttered is too coincidental. This is a pleasing, warm story of traditional family values in a blended family context and of positive relationships in spite of difficult times. The tone and general pattern are reminiscent of the novels of home life written by Elizabeth Enright and Madeleine L'Engle. Poe Nominee.

THE TRUE CONFESSIONS OF CHARLOTTE DOYLE (Avi*, illus. Ruth E. Murray, Orchard, 1990), action-filled, quick-tempoed adventure novel with Victorian and gothic elements set on the high seas for about two months beginning in June of 1832, in which a naive, genteel young woman learns not to trust in appearances. When her father, a well-off businessman stationed in England, takes his family back to Providence, Rhode Island, prim, proper, obedient Charlotte Doyle, 13, is scheduled to follow on a ship of his choosing as soon as her school lets out. Although several incidents that take place before and just after she embarks on the *Seahawk* hint of trouble, Charlotte tells how she boards at Liverpool as directed, sailing under the care of Captain* Andrew Jaggery. She describes how she is warned not to come by a member of the decrepit crew, and how over her protests the elderly black cook, Zachariah*, gives her a knife for protection. She calls the men "as sorry a group . . . as I had ever seen: glum . . . defeated" and sullen, and the ship appears old and sea-worn. She soon warms to the captain, whose elegant manner toward her (though murderous toward the crew) and fashionable quarters reassure her that he is a gentleman like her father and "a man to be trusted." She takes it to be a "slanderous tale" when Zachariah informs her that Captain Jaggery has been unspeakably cruel to the crew. He says that since they failed in seeking justice in the courts against him, they have signed on again to seek revenge. Thus when the captain admonishes her to be on the lookout for a "round robin," a written pact to mutiny, she is solidly on his side and spies for him. She finds her way about the ship, becomes a kind of "ship's boy" at running errands and doing odd jobs, and even reads aloud from the Bible to the men, an act they much appreciate. The captain becomes more and more verbally and physically abusive and keeps the men at their tasks almost constantly. One afternoon eighteen days into the voyage, Charlotte ventures into the forecastle to fetch a needle for a sailor, overhears a disgruntled conversation among some crew, spies a pistol in the sailor's duffle, and catches a glimpse of a round robin. She reports her findings to the captain, who summons the crew. When he admonishes them, he is told point-blank that he is unfit to command by a Mr. Crannick, whose arm he had amputated on a previous voyage in punishment. The captain retaliates by shooting Crannick in cold blood, and when Zachariah refuses to shove the body overboard without a burial service, he has Zachariah flogged mercilessly. After the men push Zachariah's hammock overboard in burial, the captain becomes even more harsh, evidently to reassert his dominance, since Charlotte, a mere girl, had had the temerity to protest his actions against Zachariah. Realizing now that she has misjudged the captain and the men, Charlotte asks to join the crew to atone for the two deaths she believes she has caused. The second half of the novel follows her exploits as Mr. Doyle, a man before the mast. She is accepted by the crew when she proves her bravery and worth by climbing to the top of the royal yard, 130 feet up, a feat she accomplishes in the book's most suspenseful scenes. She sleeps in the forecastle with the men and toils alongside them. Her skin becomes dark and weathered, and her hands tough like leather.

During a terrible hurricane she is sent aloft and is saved from plunging to her death by Zachariah, an angel or an apparition, she does not know which. During the same storm, Mr. Hollybrass, the first mate, is found slain, with Charlotte's knife in his back. In the brig awaiting trial for murder, she learns that Zachariah is alive and has been hiding in the hold. Convicted, the captain acting as judge and jury and none of the men speaking on her behalf lest the captain find out about Zachariah, Charlotte is sentenced to be hanged from the yardarm. While in the brig awaiting execution, she and Zachariah determine, by a process of elimination, that the captain killed the mate. They hatch a plot to get at his weapons cache, but the captain is tipped off by a turncoat, pursues Charlotte onto the bowsprit, loses his footing, and falls into the sea. The men make Charlotte captain in his stead. Once in Providence, Charlotte soon finds the requirements of being a lady too constraining, is chagrined that her father disbelieves her diary of the trip, and runs off to join Zachariah on the *Seahawk,* which sails by morning tide, one of the more capable crewmen now serving as master. The accent is on fast-action adventure, of which the book provides a full measure. The conventions of melodrama abound, with hardly a sensationalistic technique left out: faces in the gloom, whispers in the dark, inscrutable leers and smirks, too-gracious smiles, treachery, intrigue, improbable feats, face-offs, obvious symbols (Charlotte cuts her hair), impossible tasks, the villainous captain, stowaways, cliffhangers. Most characters are types, and Charlotte herself matures predictably, losing her naiveté and snobbery as she gains a more wholesome set of values based on honesty and hard work. Curiously, the milieu she joins and eventually subdues is male. Her triumph is that of a woman over a man's world, but, ironically, her heroism is male. Descriptions are highly colorful, sea language is used frequently but judiciously, and the numerous plot twists and turns rivet the interest. For the young, less initiated reader, most of the book's pull will probably come from identifying with Charlotte. For those whose reading experience has been broader, pleasure will also come from seeing how Avi manipulates the numerous conventions and moves Charlotte through them—in short, how he makes this masterful concoction of unreal realism credible and keeps it constantly at the boil. ALA; Boston Globe Winner; Fanfare; Newbery Honor; SLJ.

TUFFY BUCK (*Shoebag**), tall, husky, mean schoolmate of Shoebag, the cockroach turned human. Tuffy has black hair and a squashed-in nose from fighting so much and is the self-declared ''boss'' of the entire school. He has viciously cowed almost all the students, who either follow him slavishly or carefully avoid him. He writes verses about the terrible acts he intends to do to Shoebag and leaves them in Shoebag's jacket pocket. At assembly the principal reads a page Tuffy wrote about how his father had gone to Florida and killed four alligators. The principal urges the children to tell Tuffy to congratulate his father on this great feat. Most of the students do, in order to stay in Tuffy's good graces. Shoebag does not, thinking it ironic that the principal is also encouraging the students to contribute to the Save the Seals campaign. At the end, Tuffy still has it in for Shoebag but is much taken with Pretty* Soft Biddle, who butters him up shamelessly with flattery.

TURNER, ANN W(ARREN) (1945–   ), born in Northampton, Massachusetts; prolific and versatile author of nonfiction, novels, picture books, and poems for children. She received her B.A. from Bates College and her M.A.T. from the University of Massachusetts; married Richard Turner, a teacher; and taught high school English in Great Barrington, Massachusetts. She has also been an assistant house manager at a home for young women with drug problems and an operator for a Northampton intervention center crisis hot-line. Her first books were the nonfiction *Vultures* (McKay, 1973) and *Houses for the Dead* (McKay, 1976), a book about mourning rites and burial customs. She then turned to novels, publishing, among others, *A Hunter Comes Home* (Crown, 1980), set among Eskimos, and picture books, including *Dakota Dugout* (Macmillan, 1985), about living in a prairie sod house, both American Library Association Best Books. Others followed, including books of poems, among them *Street Talk* (Houghton Mifflin, 1986) and *A Moon for Seasons* (Macmillan, 1994), and picture books like *Heron Street* (Harper, 1989), the story of a marsh, and *Through Moon and Stars and Night Skies* (Harper, 1990), about cross-cultural adoption. *Rosemary's Witch** (HarperCollins, 1991), a *School Library Journal* Best Book, is a lighthearted fantasy-thriller about a misanthropic witch who tries to drive a family from their house. Her other novels include *Third Girl from the Left* (Macmillan, 1986), about a mail-order bride who goes from Maine to Montana; *Grasshopper Summer* (Macmillan, 1989), a novel set in 1874 in which a Kentucky family move to Dakota Territory and experience grasshopper plagues; and *One Brave Summer* (HarperCollins, 1995), in which a girl learns about friendship and mother-daughter relationships.

THE TWIN IN THE TAVERN (Wallace*, Barbara Brooks, Atheneum, 1993), deliciously Dickensian mystery set in Alexandria, Virginia, presumably in the early nineteenth century. The orphan Taddy, 10, has lived with his Uncle and Aunt Buntz, but as they are dying of a plague brought by a ship, his uncle tells him, "Nothing is what you think," and, after advising him to find his twin, adds, "Be careful, lad. Trust . . . no one!" When two men, coming at night to steal the furniture, discover him hiding, the leader, Neezer, suggests that a fatal accident to the boy might solve their problem, but the other, Lucky, fears the hangman's noose. As a compromise, Neezer offers "a warm place to sleep, good meals served regular, and no questions asked" as an alternative to the workhouse. They take the boy, renamed Toady, to an inn called the Dog's Tail on the waterfront, where he finds that the meals are scraps left on plates by the rough diners and the warm place to sleep is under a kitchen table, a space he must share with their slavey, a waif called Beetle*. His life is almost unrelieved misery: drudgery in the kitchen and tavern, cold and painful rounds with Lucky, who delivers ice, and continual hunger, with Beetle lording it over him and Neezer quick to knock him about and even lock him in the ice house for punishment. A few incidents bring a slight relief. The cook, Mrs. Scrat, Neezer's timid wife, saves him scraps; Mrs. Diggles, who runs the bakery on the ice route, slips him a few cookies; Beetle reminds Neezer that "a puny subjec' " like Toady will not last long in the ice house; and Neezer lets him out to protect his investment. His life is dramatically changed when Mrs. Mainyard, a beautiful widow who owns a mansion on the ice route, rents his services from Neezer as a pantry boy. Since he has seen the present pantry boy, Jeremy, who looks enough like him to be his twin, Taddy is excited, but when he starts working at the big house dressed in clothes just like Jeremy's, the other boy seems to be gone. Taddy tries very hard to give satisfaction, since Mrs. Mainyard's house is at least warm and he is able to smuggle some leftovers back to the tavern for Beetle. A large number of other characters enter his life: Professor Greevey, who lives at the Dog's Tail, tutor to mean Madelina and sweet Dora, Mrs. Mainyard's daughters; John Graves, the handsome man who appears to be courting Mrs. Mainyard and whom Taddy fears; and old Simon, the strange, possibly demented furnace man, who lives in the cellar, among others. The convoluted plot solution reveals that truly nothing is what it seems. Mrs. Mainyard, second wife of the deceased Mr. Mainyard, is really still the wife of Professor Greevey, both involved in a scheme of smuggling diamonds frozen in the ice Lucky delivers, and Madelina is their daughter; John Graves is really the brother of the deceased Mr. Mainyard, secretly trying to trace what happened to his nephew; Jeremy is not Taddy's twin but a boy who left the Mainyard house for unrelated reasons; Simon is a faithful servant who, after Mr. Mainyard's death, rescued his infant son and took him to the Buntzes, servants dismissed by the second Mrs. Mainyard; and Dora is the twin Taddy has been seeking. The tone and style are reminiscent of the novels by Leon Garfield and Joan Aiken, though not as ironic as Garfield's or as exaggerated as Aiken's. The Dog's Tail is a grimy and menacing setting, Neezer is a brutal villain, and through all his terror and dreadful experiences, Taddy is a stalwart protagonist, but Beetle captures center stage as the most interesting character. Poe Winner.

U

UNCLE CARTER GRAHAM (*Learning by Heart**), brother of Rachel's Mama, who at thirty-six is still under his mother's thumb. Grandma Graham opposes his plans to marry Miss Macy Mitchell, a divorcee whom he met while visiting Great-Uncle Hewitt at the nursing home where Macy works. Uncle Carter has devoted his life to taking care of the homeplace, where he and Grandma Graham live. Once he makes up his mind to marry Macy, however, he quietly carries out his plans, although occasionally they go awry. For example, he sells off some acreage for money to buy a double-wide mobile home, intending that Grandma Graham occupy it. After the house is delivered and put in place, Grandma Graham promptly announces that although the house is hard to get into, Carter does not need to put in an extra step for her, because she will not be visiting them much. The Graham children clearly get her point: Grandma Graham will continue to live in the family residence. Carter and Macy will have to occupy the smaller mobile home. The incident is a good example of how Grandma Graham gets her way and dominates her family.

UNDERWHIRL (*The Lampfish of Twill**), land to which Eric is sucked down the whirlpool, along with his pet seagull and Mr. Cantrip, who has been there before. According to the old man, it is the most ancient and most beautiful world of earth, the core from which the present world evolved. Over time, it was enveloped by oceans and submerged, until all signs of it vanished, but it remains connected to the upper world by a series of whirlpools. Underwhirl is lit by lampfish, which float overhead, giving off a rosy light. When a lampfish is killed in the upper world, one from Underwhirl spins up the spout, seizing the opportunity to have a chance at life, although it will eventually be killed, too. It is a place of beauty, with soft green grass and flowers, a contrast to barren Twill, but it is also timeless, like death. Since there is no change in Underwhirl, the people who have landed there become rooted like trees and gradually are so slowed down that they cannot communicate with newcomers since the space between their words is too long.

UNLIVED AFFECTIONS (Shannon*, George, Harper, 1989), sociological problem novel set in 1983 in the town of Ottawa, Kansas, in which a boy discovers information about his family that changes his views of his relatives and of himself. Willie Ramsey, 18, has been raised by Grom* Davenport, his maternal grandmother. According to Grom, his mother, Kate*, and her boyfriend died in a car accident when he was two and Willie's father ran off and died before he was born. Now that Grom is dead of a stroke, Willie feels cheated; he had looked forward to college and walking out on cold, distant, controlling Grom. While getting the house ready for the auction of furniture and personal effects, Willie enters his mother's room, which Grom had kept locked, and discovers wedged in the back of a desk drawer a shoebox full of letters from his father to his mother starting in August of 1964, about a year before his birth. He learns from the detailed letters that he was named after his father, Bill Ramsey, and that Bill left Ottawa to hone his craft of woodworking with a noted master named Whitehead* in Berea, Kentucky. In Berea, Bill meets a young college student named Larry with whom he falls in love. He writes to Kate of their growing affection and says he still loves Kate but in a different way. Grom, who had apparently thought a good deal of Bill up to then, writes to Bill to inform him about the coming baby, but Kate denies to Bill that she is pregnant and divorces him. The correspondence nevertheless continues, with Kate writing about a couple of romances but never, evidently, about Willie. When Willie is two, Kate is killed, and the letters stop. Willie thinks that his father is probably still alive and living in Berea with his friend, Evan, a pharmacist whom he met after Larry left him, and running Whitehead's business. One of Willie's few cherished possessions is a hearts-and-ivy carved rocking chair that is referred to in the letters and that Willie has clung to in spite of Grom's orders to throw it out. He learns that Bill made it for Willie's mother. Although Willie has always associated the chair with his childhood, he never before understood Grom's antipathy to it. In addition to sorting out information and his feelings about his parents and Grom, Willie must also deal with his relationship with Libby, a new girl in school to whom he is attracted. Reluctantly, bit by bit, near the end of the book, he tells her about his father, and in answer to her question about whether or not he will go to visit Bill, he says that his father is, after all, the only one who can tell him about his mother. He takes two boxes of mementoes, his mother's letters and Grom's crochets, to the cemetery. Kneeling at their graves, he cries "for all they'd lost. Cried for his father and cried for himself." In sadness but at peace, he buries the boxes by their graves "as dearly and deliberately as only one in love can do." Although not an epistolary novel in the strict sense, Bill's letters make up a large portion of the book. They are lively and detailed and reveal Bill to be a likable person and an unusually articulate letter writer—perhaps too much so for complete credibility. As Willie becomes engrossed in learning about his father, mother, and grandmother from the letters, the book becomes a gripping mystery, but what happened to Bill is never completely explained. Willie also discovers that the mother he had idealized was less than perfect and that the grandmother he had despised had been molded by the school of hard knocks. Willie's mood swings—anger, pity, fear, determination, sorrow, shame, and more—seem appropriate and are understatedly caught. Although homosexuality is important to the story, the book is mainly about family relationships gone awry. SLJ.

V

VAN RAVEN, PIETER (1923–   ), college professor and author of novels for young adults. His most highly acclaimed book is the historical novel *A Time of Troubles** (Scribner's, 1990), which traces a group of displaced, down-on-their-luck people during the Great Depression as they make a slow and difficult way west across the United States to California in the hope of finding work and a good life. It won the Scott O'Dell Award for Historical Fiction. Van Raven has also published *The Great Man's Secret* (Scribner's, 1989), an American Library Best Book for Young Adults about a fourteen-year-old boy's relationship with a legless, reclusive writer; *Harpoon Island* (Scribner's, 1989), about the efforts of a schoolteacher of German descent to make a new life on a sparsely populated island in World War I; and *Pickle and Price* (Scribner's, 1990), about the friendship between a boy and an African-American ex-convict. Van Raven was formerly with the U.S. State Department cultural office.

VERNIE (*Out of Nowhere**), LaVerne, irresponsible young mother of Harley Nunn. An exotic dancer when she is employed and something of a scam artist all the time, she has never been a devoted mother, having left Harley or forgotten him briefly a number of times when a new man came into her life or she was on drugs. Since she did not know which of three men might be Harley's father, she said "none" when asked, hence the boy's last name. Her scheme at the book's opening is to get her current man to let Harley ride with them to Houston by pretending that he is going to visit an older man he called Daddy, a surrogate father who died two years previously. At an Arizona desert campground, she pretends to discover that Daddy has just died of a heart attack and his motor home has been hauled away, a story the man refuses to buy. He offers, with bad grace, to buy the boy a bus ticket, but Harley has no home to go back to and is fed up with being part of Vernie's cons. When he asserts his independence, she flares up and tells him she is sick of the burden he has been to her life, and the car pulls away in a cloud of dust. Later, when his dog Ish is injured, Harley gets in touch with her, hoping to get some money for the vet. Vernie, who has a new man friend, offers to steal and sell things belonging to an old one, and the boy realizes that she is not going to change and that he cannot lean on her.

VIOLET LITTLE (*Switching Well**), assertive, smart, African-American girl who befriends Ada* Bauer, when Ada comes into the twentieth century and is sent to a shelter for homeless children. Violet, herself a runaway, helps Ada with clothing, introducing her to bras, for example, and explains rock music and words like *teenage, ninja,* and *mutant* to her. She accepts Ada's story about coming from the nineteenth century and serves as her protector. When Ada is afraid she will be sent to a madhouse, Violet coaches her on how to make up an acceptable story (''Keep it [your untrue story] simple''). Violet is good at figuring out how to bend rules to her benefit and make the system work for her but otherwise is highly moral. She says ''the Man'' keeps her from her parents, whom she loves dearly. Ada learns that Violet's father left the family so that her mother can get the welfare money that she needs to care for Violet's mentally disabled little sister and ill grandmother at home instead of putting them in institutions. Violet ran away to keep expenses down, so that her mother's relief checks will go further. Her friend, Grandad Burak, says that the stamps and coins Ada left to Violet should ''add up to a tidy sum'' and help her family financially. Violet is a strongly drawn character, one of the best in the novel.

VOIGT, CYNTHIA (1942–   ), born in Boston, Massachusetts; teacher and highly regarded writer of contemporary novels for children and young adults. The most praised of these are her several strongly characterized books about the Tillerman family and their friends, including the Newbery Award–winning *Dicey's Song* (Atheneum, 1982). The last book in the series, *Seventeen Against the Dealer** (Atheneum, 1989), in which Dicey, now a college dropout, tries to start her own boat-building business, was selected as a best book by *School Library Journal. When She Hollers** (Scholastic, 1994), also a *School Library Journal* choice, concerns a girl who is sexually abused by her stepfather. For earlier biographical information and title entries, see *Dictionary, 1960–1984* [*The Callendar Papers; Dicey's Song; A Solitary Blue*] and *Dictionary, 1985– 1989* [*Building Blocks; Come A Stranger; Izzy, Willy-Nilly; Sons from Afar*].

THE VOYAGE OF THE "FROG" (Paulsen*, Gary, Orchard, 1989), contemporary realistic sea adventure and boy's growing-up novel set on the ocean southwest of California and west of Baja California. After fourteen-year-old David Alspeth's ''own sweet uncle,'' Owen, dies, leaving David his cherished fiberglass sailboat, the *Frog,* and requesting that the boy scatter his ashes at sea, David sets out from the Ventura harbor at sunset, Owen's favorite time to sail. David leaves on impulse, without checking supplies or telling his parents of his intention, a ''night sail for Owen.'' At nine the next morning, after fifteen hours of sailing without event except vibrantly beautiful blue lights over the waters, he scatters the ashes lovingly over the "huge slate-blue saucer or dish," then dumps the container in, angry at this remaining evidence of his great loss. Almost immediately he is challenged by a rough, rogue storm wind from the northwest and while lowering the sails is caught by a sail rail in the head and dumped unconscious through the cabin hatch. This is the first in a series of misfortunes David survives before he is seen at the end of the book heading home after about a week and a half at sea. David awakens some twenty hours and 300 miles after the terrible wind storm to a very sore head, a badly bruised and lacerated body, and a cabin in shambles, his location unknown. Recalling Owen's instructions about boatsmanship, he pumps and pumps for hours to clear the hull, takes stock of his meager supplies (about twenty gallons of water, seven cans of food) and equipment (wristwatch and radio useless) and sleeps soundly from weariness that night in his bunk, only to be jolted awake by bumping and a horrible scraping sound, which he later identifies as a shark attack and which repeats during the night as the creatures strike the reflection of the moon on the boat. The weather becalmed, David dries clothes, ropes, and cushions on deck, cleans up, and bags and saves even the trash for possible use. He comes upon Owen's log from a shoreline sail, "The Voyage of the *Frog*," reads bits that give him some insights into his uncle, and later adds a few words of his own. Only quick thinking and rapid reflexes save him from being run down by a tanker another night, an incident that provokes feelings of extreme hatred and anger before he gets himself under control. Concerned about his dwindling food supply, he is relieved when a strong night wind awakens him and he sets an eastward course, sure that he will hit the California coast. Other incidents involve encountering a pod of sporting killer whales on the high seas and almost crashing on a beach. When he takes stock, he realizes the shoreline is completely unfamiliar and concludes that he must be off Baja California. He anchors in a small bay to get some much-needed rest and near dusk is awakened by a horrible stench—a large pod of whales playing in the quiet waters around him—weighs anchor, and heads north. Another storm finds him more able to cope, and soon he encounters a small coastal freighter, which stops. When the captain assures David that there is no way they can tow the *Frog,* David decides to sail his boat home, and, after receiving supplies of food and fuel and assurance that the ship will contact his parents, he embarks on the remaining 350 miles by coastal waters to Ventura. The details of the trip convey the conviction of actual experience, and nautical language, although used extensively, never overwhelms or obscures. The single-character, third-person narrative remains enthralling from start to finish. Particularly exciting scenes involve the sharks and whales and the approaching tanker, the latter being a terrific fingernail-biter episode. David changes not unexpectedly but appropriately in his ability to cope at sea but also somewhat in attitude toward life. He reflects, for example, on the futility and self-destructiveness of anger and hate and on how he now knows what being truly poor and hungry really is. The style, in typical Paulsen fashion, is highly sensory, so that not only David's feelings become palpable but also the ocean winds, waters, and sun. This top-notch tale of adventure is assisted by a clear diagram of the boat at the beginning and a map of David's journey at the end. ALA; SLJ.

W

THE WAINSCOTT WEASEL (Seidler*, Tor, illus. Fred Marcellino, HarperCollins, 1993), animal fantasy set in modern times in the Wainscott woods on the South Fork of Long Island, New York. In Wainscott, the weasels, whose counterparts in other places spend most of their time hunting food, are here blessed with free time to dance and enjoy a rich social life because a brilliant weasel, Bagley Brown, figured out a way to steal eggs from the McGee Farm chicken coop by way of a tunnel that he persuaded moles to dig. Only his son, Bagley Brown, Jr., knows what happened to the revered Wainscott Weasel: just as the tunnel neared its goal, an owl swooped down and carried away Bagley, who was stamping on the ground to direct the moles. Bagley, Jr., who had sneaked out to watch the tunnel completion, foresaw the disaster and tried to warn his father, losing an eye to the owl's claws. Since then he has shied away from weasel frolics and always wears a black eye patch, which the others think is a sign of mourning and consider an affectation. In reality he has fallen in love with a beautiful striped bass named Bridget, whom he watches from a hollow log on the edge of the pond and to whom he brings an offering of insects each evening. In the weasel community the arrival of beautiful Wendy Blackish from North Fork creates a stir and attracts the attentions of Zeke, eldest of the five tough Whitebelly brothers. Although her aunt and uncle, with whom she is living, look down upon these swaggering young weasels, Zeke soon becomes her favorite partner at the frequent dances in the woods. Unexpectedly she encounters Bagley, Jr., who takes her to see the pond and for whom she has a brief yearning, but she soon settles on Zeke, who asks Bagley to be best weasel at their wedding. Through the increasingly dry summer, Bagley, Jr., has been bravely staying away from the pond on the request of Bridget, who points out that it is not seemly for a weasel to love a fish, and when the bullfrog, Paddy, hunts him up and tells him that the pond is in trouble, he is surprised to see how it has shrunk. All the pond life forms are being harassed by a greedy osprey with a nest on a platform atop a telephone pole. On the day of the wedding, Bagley, Jr., sees that he must do something to save Bridget and the other remaining fish, who are too easily spotted in the shallow water. Spurred on by Paddy's confidence in his superior brain, he devises a plan to lower the nest and transport it to a dead tree by another, larger pond. With great courage and difficulty, he steals a reel from a careless fisherman, climbs the telephone pole, makes a basket of fishing line around the nest, persuades a flock of sparrows to push it off the platform, lowers it, and gets a turtle to drag it into hiding. Then, exhausted and dehydrated, he almost expires by the side of the road, only to be saved by the weasels from the wedding, who have been alerted to his predicament by Paddy. During his week-long illness, the weasels move the nest, and the rains start again. He is visited by Bridget, who makes her way up the brook to tell him that it is time for her to go out to sea and to give him a precious, moist kiss before she leaves. Although his love is gone forever, he finds that his reputation has grown and, like his famous father, he is now known as the Wainscott Weasel. The story is told with a rather formal seriousness, and details of the dance floor made of slippery pine needles and the smells and sounds of the woods are attractively sensory. Although not as compelling as *The Wind in the Willows* or *Watership Down,* to which the novel is inevitably compared, and the concept of a romance between a weasel and a fish is bizarre, Bagley's heroic moving of the osprey nest is gripping and the bittersweet ending appropriately captures a reader's emotions. ALA.

WALLACE, BARBARA BROOKS, born in Soochow, China, author of a large number of books for young people in the past twenty-five years. She attended schools in Hankow, Tientsin, and Shanghai, China, in Claremont, California, and Pomona College and the University of California at Los Angeles. A number of her books have developed into series, including her first, *Claudia* (Follett, 1969), which was followed by *Hello, Claudia!* (Follett, 1982) and *Claudia and Duffy* (Follett, 1982), all for middle grade readers. Other series include *Hawkins* (Follett, 1977), *The Contest Kid Strikes Again* (Abingdon, 1980), and *Hawkins and the Soccer Solution* (Abingdon, 1981), and the Miss Switch fantasies, starting with *The Trouble with Miss Switch* (Abingdon, 1971) and *Miss Switch to the Rescue* (Abingdon, 1981). Her early novel, *Can Do, Missy Charlie* (Follett, 1974), is based on incidents from her life in China, and *Victoria* (Follett, 1972) was inspired by a boarding school she attended in the Philippines. Two of her better-known novels are exciting Victorian melodramas: *Peppermints in the Parlor* (Atheneum, 1980) and *The Twin in the Tavern** (Atheneum, 1993), which won an Edgar Allan Poe Award. Wallace has also written several picture books, and she has worked at a variety of clerical and secretarial jobs and taught in a secretarial school. She married James Wallace, Jr., in 1954, has one child, and lives in Alexandria, Virginia.

WALLER (*Nightjohn**), Clel Waller, the cruel master of the ante–Civil War plantation on which Sarny, Mammy, and *Nightjohn** live. From Sarny's descriptions of him, he appears to enjoy having unlimited power over other people, and although it is not clear why he buys John, a slave known to run away, perhaps it is because he thinks he can break him. From the conversation that Sarny reports having heard in the white house, it seems that Waller's wife feels that he spent too much money on John when the plantation is not financially comfortable. Sarny describes Waller as "pale white maggot ugly" and as smelling of "bad sweat and whiskey and smoke and fat food." On one occasion she says he walks from the house, spitting, making gas, and bellowing like a bull. She says the slaves call him "dog droppings and pig slop and worse things" behind his back. Waller is intended to be the epitome of the worst type of slaveholder but even so seems overdrawn.

WANTED . . . MUD BLOSSOM (Byars*, Betsy, illus. Jacqueline Rogers, Delacorte, 1991), light, realistic novel of family life and domestic adventures, the fifth in the series about the Blossom family and some close friends, set in a rural area with hills and caves somewhere in the United States, probably South Carolina, from Thursday through Sunday in October. Although related subplots also involve the other Blossoms, the focus is again on Junior, who sparks the story when, with the best of intentions, he digs a complicated tunnel in the yard under the pines for Scooty, the school hamster that is Junior's responsibility for the weekend. When Scooty disappears shortly after being introduced to the tunnel and Mud, the golden dog with the red bandanna collar belonging to Pap (grandfather) Blossom, has dirt on his paws and pine needles in his coat, Junior assumes Mud devoured the hamster and insists the dog is a murderer. Maggie (his older sister) suggests they put Mud on trial. Maggie becomes the prosecutor, Pap acts as judge, Ralphie (a neighbor boy) serves as the defense attorney, and Michael (a friend), Vern (Junior's older brother), and Dump (Junior's nondescript dog) form the jury. The proceedings are held in absentia, because the defendant refuses to come out from under the porch, where the trial is being held. From various clues, Ralphie deduces that the hamster is not dead but was stolen by Vern and Michael and so announces at a dramatic moment, hoping unsuccessfully to make a grand impression on Maggie. For some time Maggie and Ralphie (erstwhile sweethearts) have been on the outs, because Ralphie, in an unguarded moment, accused Maggie of using him. Their relationship hits bottom when Ralphie "wins" Mud's case, but when Ralphie calls Maggie by telephone and inadvertently blurts out to Vicki Blossom (the mother) that he loves her thinking he is talking to Maggie, Maggie arranges for Ralphie to regain face. She helps him "find" the lost cane of Mad Mary Cantrell, the neighborhood eccentric who lives in a cave nearby. Other story strands feature Vicki, who buys a ravishing new pantsuit to go out with her new beau; Vern and Michael, who left their backpacks in Mad Mary's cave and are afraid to return for them; and, especially, Mad Mary herself. After Ralphie and Maggie find Mary's food bag containing a dead possum in the ditch by the side of the road, Pap realizes she has been missing for some time. He investigates her cave and finds the backpacks but no Maggie. Later she is discovered in the hospital, having been found unconscious of malnutrition and worms. Home again and clean for the first time in Blossom memory, Mad Mary shares Junior's room for the night. Next week Junior returns Scooty to school, and now "wise beyond his years in responsibility and hamsters" cautions a classmate about caring for Scooty. The book is almost all dialogue, with short, convincing, conversational sentences. Shifts in point of view and scene occur frequently, so the several stories appear to occur almost simultaneously, much like television or movie switches. The tone is light, occasionally comic, and always upbeat. Although much of the reading pleasure comes from seeing the same likable characters tackling still more family problems, the book is strong enough to stand on its own. Pap is laid back as usual, and Mud is winning, although the reader is kept guessing about his guilt. Ralphie is a sympathetically smitten swain, and Junior remains an impulsive and naively imaginative little boy. Best, as in the other Blossom books, is the picture of a loving, warm, cooperative family, forgiving, nurturing, supportive, a wholesome television home sit-com cast within the pages of a book. For details about another book in the series, *The Blossoms and the Green Phantom,* see *Dictionary, 1985–1989.* ALA; Fanfare; Poe Winner; SLJ.

WE ALL FALL DOWN (Cormier*, Robert, Delacorte, 1991), novel of suspense set in Burnside, Massachusetts, about the time of its publication. Four middle-class high school boys from nearby Wickburg, led by Harry Flowers, enter and trash a house in Burnside owned by the Jerome family, ripping furniture, smearing walls with feces and urine, vomiting on the carpet, all in a senseless binge of vandalism. When Karen Jerome, 14, comes home and interrupts them, Harry and two of the other boys hold her and prepare to rape her. She breaks away and runs to the basement door, where Harry grabs her, then pushes her down the stairs. This is witnessed by Buddy Walker, the fourth boy, who is drunk and has been trashing the room of Karen's sister, Jane, 16. It is also witnessed by an observer hiding in bushes outside, a character who calls himself The Avenger and says he is eleven years old. Karen is hospitalized in a coma, and the rest of the Jerome family get the house repaired and try to pull themselves together. Buddy, who is deeply disturbed because his father has left the family to live with a younger woman, is shocked and revolted by what he has done, but he is manipulated through his dependence on gin by Harry, whom he both loathes and fears. He finally calls Jane anonymously and says he is sorry, then begins to trail her in the Wickburg Mall, until, when he stumbles and falls at the foot of the escalator, she speaks sympathetically to him and they become acquainted and start going together. In the meantime, a neighbor who has been out of town returns, learns about the Jerome house, and gives the police the license number of Harry's car, which he had noted down as suspicious the night of the trashing. To Buddy's surprise, Harry says that he was a lone vandal and gets his father to pay the damages, but he also says that Jane gave him the house key, implying that she was his partner in the trashing. Although Jane eventually persuades her parents that she lost the key and that Harry is lying, their initial distrust shakes her. Karen gradually comes out of the coma and relearns to talk, but she cannot remember anything after the moment she opened the house door. Buddy's love for Jane has given him strength to stop drinking, but he worries about what Karen might remember, and he has never been able to make himself enter the Jerome house again, even to pick Jane up. The Avenger, seeing Buddy and Jane together and kissing, is incensed that she is seeing one of the trashers, and his rage turns against her. He lures her into a shed, knocks her out with ether long enough to tie and gag her, then tells her he is going to cut her up. She recognizes him as a middle-aged handyman named Mickey Stallings, whom the neighbors call Mickey Looney. Since she has always been nice to him, he removes her gag, and she is able to stall and convince him that he is not eleven, therefore not The Avenger who shot a school bully and later killed his own suspicious grandfather years ago. Returning to reality, he sobs and cuts both his wrists. Jane is rescued physically unharmed but hurt badly by her secret knowledge that Buddy was one of the trashers. The title is appropriate; none of the characters comes out unscathed, except possibly Harry Flowers, who was already evil and may be planning to stalk Jane, with his phony concern for Buddy as an excuse. Buddy, dropped completely by Jane, is drinking heavily again. Jane, devastated after her first real love has proved deceptive, is emotionally badly damaged. Although Buddy is the main character and potentially the most sympathetic, his inability to stand up to Harry and his dependence on drink keep him from being an attractive protagonist, and Jane, although not as flawed, never really engages the reader's empathy. Despite his writing style, which is crisp and sometimes vivid, Cormier's cynical middle-class sociopaths have become a cliché and the downbeat endings predictable. Poe Nominee.

WEASEL (*Weasel**), infamous renegade who terrorizes the region in southern Ohio where Nathan Fowler and his family live and who killed Ezra* Ketcham's Shawnee wife and unborn child and cut out Ezra's tongue. An Indian fighter sent out by the U.S. government to make the territory safe for settlement by removing the Indians, he became so cruel and wanton in killing them that the Shawnees called him Weasel. Once the Shawnees were killed, driven off, or removed to Kansas, Weasel, now a psychopathic killer, turned on the settlers, raiding and stalking, so that his very name strikes terror among the whites. Nathan finds him alone and dead in his cabin, apparently the victim of an infection brought on by a wound to his foot.

WEASEL (DeFelice*, Cynthia, Macmillan, 1990), realistic period novel located for a few weeks in 1839 in southern Ohio in what was once Shawnee Native American Indian territory, in which a boy learns that forgiveness is ultimately more satisfying than revenge. Nathan Fowler, the eleven-year-old narrator, his sister, Molly, 9, and their widower father, a farmer, live in a small, remote cabin near the Ohio River. Their father having gone hunting six days earlier and not yet returned, the anxious children are alone in the cabin when late one night a bearded stranger, dressed in tattered animal skins and wearing a tall hat, whom they learn is Ezra* Ketcham, knocks at the door, silently hands them their dead mother's gold locket, and beckons to them to follow him. Assuming their father must have suffered some mishap, they take their dogs, their mother's medicine bag, and some supplies and follow the stranger through the night. At dawn, the sight of a shadowy figure slipping through the woods near the river turns the man's face "murderous," and with a stick, he writes the word WEEZL in the dirt. The children recognize that he refers to Weasel*, a legendary Indian fighter turned notorious renegade. To their horror, he shows them his tongueless mouth, indicating that the atrocity was Weasel's doing. He leads them to his home, a structure made of poles and bark similar to a Shawnee *we-gi-wa*. Inside they find Pa burning with fever from a leg badly infected with jagged wounds from a bear trap, evidently set by Weasel. With Ezra's help they treat Pa with herbs, and he slowly recovers. Two days after arrival, Nathan bravely returns alone to the cabin to feed the animals. He finds that Weasel has shot Miz Tizz, the sow, killed the chickens, and stolen the piglets, Job the horse, and Crabapple the mule. On the way back to Ezra's, Nathan is stalked and then captured by Weasel. The boy manages to get loose while Weasel lies in a drunken sleep on the cabin floor and rides to Ezra's on Job. In spite of his father's praise for his courage and restraint and his assertion that somehow Weasel will get what he deserves, Nathan castigates himself for not having taken revenge and rid the world of the killer, who, he has learned, also killed Ezra's Shawnee wife and unborn child. His guilt grows into anger, hatred, and determination for vengeance. Kind-hearted, sensible Molly leaves a letter for Ezra in the stone wall near the cabin, urging him to follow his wife's people who have been removed to Kansas. One night carrying Pa's gun, Nathan sneaks out to Weasel's cabin and bursts in at dawn, intending to shoot the man, only to find Weasel lying dead from apparently a slow, lingering death from a leg wound. Horrified, Nathan informs Ezra, and the two bury Weasel. On the first day of April, the Fowlers drive to town in the wagon for the annual spring celebration and fiddlers' contest, and, although he still feels anger and guilt, Nathan enjoys himself and thinks he would like to take up fiddling. In mid-May, Molly finds in the wall a note from Ezra telling them that he is going to Kansas and that "Weezl is small now." With the note are Ezra's stovepipe hat for Nathan and a carved locket with some of Ezra's hair for Molly. Nathan realizes that Ezra is right about Weasel. What happened with Weasel has become small compared to the greatness of life that went on while Weasel was around and still goes on. The understated, laconic style supports well the horror of Weasel's misdeeds and the boy's moral dilemma, emotional trauma, and rites of passage into manhood. The treatment of the Indians and white attitudes toward them and intermarriage between whites and Indians are dramatized on a microcosmic scale, as is the irony of an Indian fighter, once regarded as a hero, who has gone bad and turned on his own people. Also evident are the early maturation of pioneer children and the self-sufficiency of the settlers, while the sense of forest isolation is very strong. Although it is unlikely that Weasel should not have harassed this family earlier and the characters are types known from westerns and Indian novels, the plot is gripping and moves to a credible conclusion. Sentiment toward Indians, presented sympathetically through the father's speeches to the children and in reverse through Weasel's boasts, seems late twentieth century. Information about Daniel Boone and white settlement is interesting but obtrusive. ALA; SLJ.

THE WEEKEND WAS **MURDER!** (Nixon*, Joan Lowery, Delacorte, 1992), murder-mystery with ghost fantasy aspects set in present-day Houston, Texas. Tall, clumsy, redhaired Liz (Mary Elizabeth) Rafferty, the sixteen-year-old narrator, grows in self-esteem as she unmasks a murderer. Liz has a summer job in the health club at the Ridley Hotel. Registered as guests are Roberta Kingston Duffy, a famous mystery writer much like Nixon herself, and Eileen Duffy, Roberta's beautiful red-haired daughter, an actress. They, along with a troupe of professional actors, are putting on a murder-mystery for the weekend guests to solve. Some hotel employees have bit parts, Liz among them. She is to "discover" the body, which will be in room 1927, a lavish suite reputed to be haunted, where Liz and her good friend, Tina Martinez, 19, an aspiring psychologist, hear a ghostly voice just before the pretend mystery begins. On Friday evening, Eileen, actress-director, plays the detective in charge and releases the information that gets events going, masterfully playing her part then and also as the weekend progresses. About the same time, Liz and her boyfriend, Francis Liverpool the Third, called Fran, also an employee, observe a dumpy, middle-aged woman being escorted by a tall policewoman. Liz recognizes the woman as Stephanie Harmon, a witness for a stolen securities and money laundering trial, and later learns that Harmon is sequestered in room 1929, next door to 1927. When Liz goes to room 1927, as instructed, she discovers the body, not of an actor as intended but of Frank Devane, owner of a failed savings and loan. Matters get very convoluted with mistaken and assumed identities, red herrings, and fingers of suspicion variously pointed and discredited. Liz has a strong feeling that the ghost of room 1927 can help unravel the real mystery. On one sighting, the ghost makes an issue of calling her attention to the telephone, and on another he directs her view toward the balcony window. She eventually deduces that the murderer is the sequestered witness, and it is learned that Harmon was once a business associate of Devane. Harmon overheard telephone conversations that enabled her to seize the moment and gained access to Devane via the balcony, cleverly later relocking the room. A wide assortment of characters appears as the two mysteries, the pretend and the real, play themselves out in interlocking fashion. Some characters are paired, for example, real Detective Jarvis (who appeared in *The Dark and Deadly Pool,* an earlier mystery involving Liz at the Ridley) and Eileen Duffy, who develop a romantic attraction for each other. Tension builds in fine fashion, with a full measure of gothic devices and some humor, especially involving a couple of health club regulars, elderly women who bumble in and out of events with more energy than sense. No information is withheld, and readers can work out the mystery along with Liz. The novel was written for middle school and junior high students of Houston to act out and solve and is almost all dialogue. Poe Nominee.

WEIN, ELIZABETH E., folklorist, author. As a child she lived in England and Jamaica before her family settled in Pennsylvania. She received her B.A. degree in English from Yale University and her M.A. in folklore from the University of Pennsylvania, where she has been a Javits Fellow working on a Ph.D. degree. Her novel, *The Winter Prince** (Atheneum, 1993), is an unusual and compelling retelling of the King Arthur story from the point of view of his son by incest, called Medraut in the novel. It was named to the *Horn Book* Fanfare list. Wein is a member of the North American Guild of Change Ringers, ringers of church bells, and is a writer for the guild newsletter.

THE WEIRDO (Taylor*, Theodore, Harcourt, 1991), mystery set in the Powhatan Swamp of North Carolina, near the Virginia border, in the 1980s. Sam (Samantha) Sanders, 16, who lives on a farm at the northern edge of the Powhatan, has always hated the swamp, especially since, seven years before, she discovered the body of Alvin Howell dumped in the bushes just across from their house. When Buck, the valuable Weimaraner her aunt and uncle have left in her care, takes off into the swamp after a bear and will not respond to her calls, she puts on her waders and follows his yapping for several miles. Realizing that it will be dark long before she can retrace her trail, she gives up the chase, finds a fire-hollowed stump, and climbs in to spend the night. At the first gray light she hears the plusht-plusht of boots tramping past and sees a very large man carrying something slung over his shoulder, and she thinks she sees a foot sticking out from the wrapping. A few minutes later he splashes back without his burden. Badly shaken, she figures that the man dumped what he was carrying in the sand suck, a notorious quicksand bog, and she remembers two shots she heard at twilight, unusual since hunting has been banned in the Powhatan for five years. From the sound of his vehicle engine starting and her knowledge of the sand suck's position on maps, she is able to orient herself and decides that the best plan is to head for Lake Nansemond and follow the shoreline to the house of the spillwayman, John Clewt, from which she can call home. Despite her badly blistered and bleeding feet, she reaches Clewt's house, only to be chased by two dogs onto the porch roof. After several hours' wait, Chip* Clewt, 17, whom she has heard referred to as a weirdo but has never met, arrives in his boat, lifts her down from the roof, and when she has called her mother, carefully tends to her badly injured feet. Sam is shocked by his appearance, one side of his face handsomely normal and the other side and one hand slick and almond colored, the result of burns in a plane crash ten years earlier. Thus begins their friendship, unusual because Sam's father, a Coast Guard bo'sun, is a rabid hunter and Chip, who has been working for a year and a half with graduate student Tom Telford to track and count bears in the Powhatan, is dedicated to persuading the Wildlife Service to continue the hunting ban for another five years. When Tom does not arrive in Raleigh, where he was headed when Chip last left him in the swamp, finding what happened to him becomes a second preoccupation. At the same time, Sam, who has long been tormented by dreams of Alvin Howell and now worries about the early morning swamp walker, wonders if Tom's disappearance is tied to the earlier murder. Together they follow the nebulous clues while Chip continues to document the bear population and enlist the National Wildlife Conservancy in preserving the hunting ban. At a local meeting of hunters, Chip speaks and is jeered, and Sam openly defies her father, who has previously intimidated her. In a compromise decision, the Wildlife Service allows deer hunting to restart but extends the ban on bears for another five years. With the help of Sam and Chip, the local deputy, Ed Truesdale, eventually proves that both Tom and Howell were murdered by a redneck poacher, the man Sam saw in the early morning in the swamp. Throughout, the narration is interrupted by passages from a paper about the Powhatan written by Chip for English class, presumably in the following year, at The Ohio State University. These pieces, together with descriptions of Chip's work with Tom and his trips into the swamp later with Sam, give a vivid picture of the beauty of the strange place and the fascinating bears he tracks. The low-key romance is tactfully introduced, with Sam, unused to dating, and Chip, self-conscious about his appearance, both lonely but awkward with the opposite sex. The local hunters, with their rusty pickups, billed caps, and coarse jokes, are convincingly intolerant of outsiders and college boys. Poe Winner.

WENDELL PADGETT (*Forest**), younger brother of the protagonist, Amber*. Wendell, a lively, almost hyperactive eight year old, admires his sister extravagantly and is delighted to be included in her adventures. Although she continually has to remind him to keep his voice down and walk carefully on their night adventures and is very angry when he reveals that the squirrels have attacked them, she mostly is encouraging to him. He is excited at the idea of studying the squirrel civilization and enthusiastically enters her scheme to consult Professor Sparks, an expert on animal life. His biggest contribution is financial: when the bus tickets cost twice what Amber expects, leaving her no money for their food, he reveals that he has his entire life savings, $65.68, much of it in small change, in his pockets. This makes it difficult to keep his pants from slipping down over his hips. He joins his father's squirrel hunt reluctantly, insists that he admit that he smacked Amber, an incident his father would like to forget, and frequently defends his sister to him, demanding, ''Don't you know anything about her by now?''

WENDY DAVIS (*Libby on Wednesday**), beautiful, popular student leader at Morrison Middle School and member of the FFW (Famous Future Writers) club to which Libby McCall also belongs. Wendy streaks her golden hair and blues her eyelids in the latest fashion and dresses in baggy, acid-washed jeans and Reeboks. Libby notes that Wendy "always looked . . . the way you were supposed to . . . with the right kind of hair and clothes, not to mention size and shape." Wendy has a dazzling smile, which she has learned to use to her advantage, and sprinkles her speech generously with "like" and other current modes of expression. Her early stories for the writing workshop deal with clothes and romances temporarily on the rocks that proceed to predictable conclusions. When Libby visits Wendy's home, she discovers nothing particularly distinctive about the Davises. The best adjective she can come up with to describe them is *nice,* though earlier she wrote in her notebook that Wendy "is a phony." Wendy is a kind of chameleon, taking on the color of whatever attracts her at the moment. Her writing becomes less juvenile and improves under the criticism she receives in the group, as Wendy herself seems to become more genuinely herself as the weeks pass.

WESTERN WIND (Fox*, Paula, Orchard, 1993), realistic contemporary novel of a girl's growing up and family life set mostly on a tiny, rocky island in Penobscot Bay off Maine. The uncomplicated plot is quickly summarized. Bright, articulate, and mature beyond her years, Elizabeth Benedict, 11, resents having to spend the summer with Gran* Benedict, 74, because her parents want exclusive time with her newborn brother. Gran, a painter, has rented for July and August a spartan cottage on Pring Island, a place that Elizabeth at first finds forbidding and uncomfortable, just as she finds her grandmother. Gradually she comes to appreciate the area's natural beauty and isolation, as well as Gran's stories, pictures, and self-possession. Elizabeth also spends time with Aaron*, perhaps eight, the small, lively, willful son of the strange family who are the only other occupants of the island, Helen and John Herkimer, the parents, and their rude, bold daughter, Deirdre, 14. When Aaron runs away on the Herkimers' sailboat on a foggy evening, Gran and Elizabeth help hunt for him. The excitement and exertion of the search are too much for Gran, who falls ill and must be hospitalized. Elizabeth learns that Gran has been suffering from heart disease and understands what Gran meant when earlier she told Elizabeth that her parents had not sent her *away* from home but *to* Gran. Gran suffers a stroke and dies a few weeks later, after Elizabeth has returned to school. After the funeral, Elizabeth and Aaron savor the drawings Gran made of Elizabeth at various tasks during the summer. Although there are lively conversations and physical action, the book has an air of suspended animation, of waiting for something to happen, as though the reader is viewing events from a vast distance or perhaps through a window. The visual aspect is strong: the dark, ramshackle little cottage that lacks such amenities as electricity and a bathroom appears before the reader's eyes, as do the rocks, gullies, and shore of the island. The natural beauty and isolation of the area come through strongly. The stories Gran tells about her youth and life with her deceased husband and Elizabeth's father add to the static feeling. The socially inept Herkimers, however, contribute liveliness aplenty; their quirkiness contrasts with Gran's ordered existence, and they foil Elizabeth's own family, Aaron being the Benedict baby a half dozen years in the future, if the Benedicts persist in overprotecting him, and Elizabeth, if she continues to feel sorry for herself, may become rude, disagreeable, and argumentative with everyone like Deirdre Herkimer, of whom Gran remarks, "She's fighting a war. . . . To show there is nothing in the world that pleases her." The thinking reader early assumes that Gran's health may be the reason for Elizabeth's trip, because Gran tires easily, a conclusion amply supported by the Herkimers' efforts to prevent Gran from searching, and when Aaron becomes friends with Elizabeth, the reader rightly assumes that he will be the catalyst for a change in Elizabeth's attitude. Gran steals the book; Mrs. Herkimer is too disdainful and pretentious to convince; Deirdre is too obviously at odds with everyone; and Elizabeth grows in understanding believably. The style is uniformly crisp and polished, and the theme that change and adjustment are axiomatic in life is interestingly ironic. The title comes from one of the poems from which Gran quotes, an anonymous one four hundred years old called "Absence," which speaks of love and loss and also makes Elizabeth uncomfortable at first. Boston Globe Honor; SLJ.

WHAT HEARTS (Brooks*, Bruce, HarperCollins, 1992), contemporary boy's growing-up novel in four parts, the first when Asa has just completed first grade, the fourth during his seventh-grade year. An unusually intelligent and imaginative child, Asa comes home with his perfect report card, various awards, and, best of all, a bunch of bright red radishes he has grown in the first-grade project, brimming with things to tell his mother, only to find her preoccupied, sitting on a suitcase waiting for a taxi that will take them forever away from Washington, D.C., and his father, to live with Dave, who will become his stepfather. In the second segment, entitled "Not Blue," Asa at nine has honed his skills in entering and fitting into new schools, six since he left Washington. The third is set when he is eleven, living partly in a fantasy of a baseball game, partly in his real-life effort to learn baseball from his bullying stepfather. The fourth, the title story, occurs near Raleigh, North Carolina, when he is twelve and encounters his first love, only to learn that he and his mother are leaving town and Dave. All are skillfully written, developing Asa as an unusual, bright, slightly calculating character, consciously determined not to appear arrogant. The most moving example is in the second piece, where he gives up his plan to recite "The Highwayman" jointly with sweet, feckless Joel, substituting instead "Little Boy Blue," which he recognizes as an inferior poem but which Joel is able to memorize. In the third and by far the longest segment and in part of the fourth, the resemblance in character, situation, and major problem posed for the reader is disturbingly similar to that in *The Moves Make the Man* by Brooks: the antagonistic stepfather, the contest of wills played out in a sports competition, the emotionally unstable mother in and out of mental hospitals, the question of the morality of the manipulative boy. Moreover, the tone is almost identical to that of much of the earlier book. ALA; Fanfare; Newberry Honor. For details of *The Moves Make the Man* see *Dictionary, 1985–1989.*

WHELAN, GLORIA (ANN) (1923–), born in Detroit, Michigan; best known as an author of novels for middle grade and young adult readers and of short stories and poetry for adults. After receiving her B.A. and M.S.W. from the University of Michigan, she served as a social worker in Minneapolis and Detroit and later taught American literature at Spring Arbor College in Michigan. She lives in northern Michigan, the area that furnished the setting and material for several of her novels. Her murder-mystery, *The Secret Keeper** (Knopf, 1990), which was nominated for the Edgar Allan Poe Award, is set in an exclusive resort on the shore of Lake Michigan. *The Pathless Woods* (Lippincott, 1981) is a biographical novel of Ernest Hemingway's sixteenth summer, which was spent at the Hemingway cottage on Walloon Lake. Other Michigan-set novels include the historical fictions *Next Spring an Oriole* (Random House, 1987), *Night of the Full Moon* (Knopf, 1993), both about pioneer involvement with Indians in the mid-1800s, and *Hannah* (Knopf, 1991), about a blind girl's efforts to get an education in Michigan in 1887. Contemporary novels set in Michigan include *A Clearing in the Forest* (Putnam, 1978), in which an old woman fights to save the forest from big business, and *That Wild Berries Should Grow* (Eerdmans, 1994), in which a girl discovers the excitement of nature and the out-of-doors while spending the summer with her grandparents on Lake Huron. Whelan has also written stories published as picture books, including *A Week of Raccoons* (Knopf, 1988) and *Bringing the Farmhouse Home* (Simon & Schuster, 1992); a Stepping-Stone Book for beginning readers, *Silver* (Random House, 1988); and a historical novel of Vietnamese refugees, *Goodbye, Vietnam* (Knopf, 1992). Whelan's writings for adults have appeared in such literary magazines as *Kansas Quarterly, Michigan Quarterly, Ontario Review,* and *Literary Review.*

WHEN SHE HOLLERS (Voigt*, Cynthia, Scholastic, 1994), contemporary novel of sexual abuse set one school day in an unnamed, present-day American city. The book opens dramatically at breakfast as high school senior Tish confronts with a survival knife Tonnie*, the stepfather who has abused her sexually since childhood. Terror stricken but determined, the knife a precarious defense, she orders him never to enter her bedroom and bathroom again. Counterpointing the horror of this ugly domestic scene is the apparent oblivion to her action of Tish's younger half-siblings and especially of her mother, Barbie. Tish knows that Barbie pretends to be unaware of her husband's nocturnal visits to Tish. Although she is now pregnant with her fourth child by Tonnie, she has been steadily replenishing the supply of birth control pills into which, she must know, Tish dips. Tonnie berates Tish, belittles her, pretends hurt feelings, and accuses her of adolescent hysteria when her voice rises to a scream. He attempts repeatedly to intimidate her, and after Tish throws milk in his face, he storms out in anger, vowing retribution that evening. Tish leaves for school pondering her situation and that of classmate Miranda, whose suicide sets in relief the turbulence and fear of the scene with Tonnie. Miranda was found naked, hanging from the tree outside her house, six months pregnant, Tish knows, by Miranda's father. As the day wears on, the reader follows the progressive deterioration of Tish's personality. Her confusion, shame, pain, terror, loneliness, sense of futility, self-disgust, determination to live, desire to kill herself, attempts to shed her skin, her mystical (but frighteningly convincing) out-of-body experiences: these feelings war with one another, escalate, compete for dominance, and culminate in a curious combination of abject despair and firm resolve. Having hid for safekeeping the survival knife in her right shoe, Tish gets into trouble with her gym teacher because she refuses to put on sneakers, screams out her defiance and fear, and is sent to the principal. Since she is unable to communicate the reason for her belligerence to the female teachers and then to the male principal, the man telephones her stepfather (who is her legal father) to come and get her. Realizing that dire consequences will follow when Tonnie picks her up, Tish flees from the school. She manages to find her way to the law office of a classmate's father, who handles causes and hardship cases. Mr. Battle's calm sympathy and capable demeanor elicit her tortured, ''He fucks me,'' and her fear of returning home. Mr. Battle engages her as his client for one dollar, instructs her to put her story down on paper, leave it with him in a sealed envelope, and call him at 8:00 every morning and 10:00 every night. The book's open ending is emotionally riveting. That evening as Tish arrives home, ''The door started to open, and terror reached out for her, reached up from her belly to grab on to her heart.'' The image ''of how much world stretched out around the few square feet of house that Tonnie owned'' offers a slim hope, and ''she wrapped her hand around the idea and held it out in front of her, like a knife.'' The reader is left to imagine what follows. Psychologists report that Tish's behavior is typical of girls who have suffered long-term, regular abuse. Tonnie is depicted with enough dimension to make him no faceless villain but an all-too-human sadist, a monster who is outwardly a stalwart and devoted family man whose transgressions his middle-class neighbors would never suspect. Tish's mother is a sad, forlorn figure, imprisoned by her husband's demands and her own dependency, and knows it, and the adults in school are also painfully ineffectual for other reasons, and know it. That Tish's schoolmates should regard Miranda as a whore is also all too hurtfully credible. The short, often fragmentary sentences convey with terrible effectiveness the relentless and steady fracturing of Tish's mind and spirit. SLJ.

WHEN THE ROAD ENDS (Thesman*, Jean, Houghton Mifflin, 1992), novel of life in an unconventional family of foster children and an adult with disabilities, set in the country north of Seattle at about the time of its publication. The narrator, Mary Jack Jordan, 12, has been in foster homes for as long as she can remember and wants desperately to stay with the Percys, Father* Matt, an Episcopal priest, and his nervous, disagreeable wife, Jill. Mostly Mary Jack is afraid that any move will separate her from Jane*, the child of about seven or eight who has been badly abused and never speaks. Jane is terrified of most people, hides under the bed, and wets her pants, but she has gradually come to trust Mary Jack. Their fragile situation is made more precarious by the arrival of a new foster child, Adam* Correy, 14, a tough, hostile boy who has never before been in foster care and is determined not to like it. When Father Matt's sister, Cecile* Bradshaw, is badly injured in an automobile accident that kills her husband, he brings her to the house. Jill erupts in anger, threatening to leave. As a result, it is arranged that Mrs. Bradshaw, who suffers from memory loss, aphasia, and one injured arm, will go with the three children to spend the summer in a cabin on the Monarch River, with fat, lazy, mean Gerry hired to drive and take care of them. Gerry, however, leaves in the night, taking all the food money but not the car, since Adam has swiped the keys from her purse. For the next weeks the other four cope, concealing Gerry's absence from Father Matt on his weekly visits. With Adam's help, Mrs. Bradshaw, now Aunt Cecile to the children, learns to sign her name again, and Mary Jack writes the rest of the checks for groceries, pretending her "mother" is teaching her how. They have some difficult times, but the only real threat comes from Don Snyder, a renter in a nearby cabin, who suspects that something is wrong and seems to enjoy causing trouble. After an ugly scene with him, Adam disappears, having smashed all the windows in Snyder's car. Mary Jack, trying to chop kindling, badly cuts her leg. Aunt Cecile, even with double vision and one bad arm, drives her to the hospital, but on the way back detours to the horse farm of Al Stewart, whom Aunt Cecile knew in high school. Al helps them home, pries their whole story out of Mary Jack, and continues to aid them. He suspects that Adam is spending nights in his barn where earlier they took a stray dog having puppies. In the end, Snyder has left the area, Adam returns, and Jane says her first words. Although nothing is certain, it appears that Aunt Cecile may winterize her cabin and keep the three children there with her permanently. The rather simple survival story is made memorable by the characterization, especially of Mary Jack, with her clear-sighted honesty, her burning desire to belong to a family, and her devotion to Jane. She sees the foster system for what it is—a safety net that provides no real security—and she knows that she has to rely on her own spunk and intelligence to survive. Although she is unusually competent for a twelve year old, she occasionally comes close to despair as she tries to provide stability for her little group, each one damaged in his own way. ALA.

WHITEHEAD (*Unlived Affections**), the elderly master woodworker in Berea, Kentucky, who teaches Bill* Ramsey woodworking, with whom Bill lives during part of the time he is in Kentucky and is writing letters to Kate* Davenport, and whose business Bill eventually takes over, having become almost like a son to the Whiteheads. Mr. Whitehead is as meticulous and tightlipped about woodworking as Grom* Davenport is about her house and affairs, but he lightens up with Bill as time passes and Bill becomes more skillful with wood. A reverent and loving artisan for whom wood is more than just a material to be used, Whitehead resists Bill's carving hearts and ivy on the rocking chair Bill makes for Kate, thinking such decoration not needed on fine wood, but Bill carves the design anyway. After Mrs. Whitehead has a stroke, Whitehead is as careful and loving about taking care of her as he is about approaching a new piece of wood, Bill notes. After she dies, he and Bill work nonstop for two days to make her coffin, and when they are finished, he tells Bill to use the rest of the wood for Whitehead's own coffin, so that he and his wife can be buried ''in one tree together.'' In a letter to Kate, Bill says that he hopes that Kate and her boyfriend can have the kind of marriage that the Whiteheads have had. When Bill tells Whitehead that he is gay, the old man says that it does not matter as long as Bill does his work, an answer that does not entirely satisfy Bill.

"WHO WAS THAT MASKED MAN, ANYWAY?" (Avi*, Orchard, 1992), comic realistic novel told entirely in dialogue and set in a middle-class neighborhood in Brooklyn, New York, in 1945. The cleverly worked out plot can be summarized simply. A mischievous, recalcitrant schoolboy, addicted to radio adventure shows and determined to regain his room and his radio, succeeds by promoting a romance between his war veteran brother and his sixth-grade teacher. At the same time he learns that real-world heroism may exact a price that radio shows ignore. Frankie (Franklin Delano) Wattleson, 11, is so hooked on radio shows that he routinely neglects his homework, thinks and speaks like his radio heroes, imagines malefactors around every corner, and fancies himself as the mighty hero who will make the universe safe. Since his behavior has become irresponsible and even boorish, his parents have confiscated his radio. Kept after school yet again, this time for reading *Radio Digest* instead of the assigned textbook, he learns that Miss Gomez's sweetheart has died of war wounds in Europe. Then a letter comes to the Wattlesons informing them that their son, Tom*, who was wounded fighting against Japan, is coming home. Since Tom's room is now rented to Mr.* Swerdlow, a medical student, and she needs the rent money, Ma decides that Frankie will move to the basement so that Tom can have Frankie's room, a decision that rubs even more salt in Frankie's wounds. Complications pile up as the episodes (as the chapters are called) proceed, and Frankie attempts to get rid of the boarder and recover his radio. Frankie and his bosom buddy, Mario* Calvino, snoop in Mr. Swerdlow's room and shadow him, convinced he is a racketeer, Frankie pretending to be the world-saving hero, Chet Barker, and Mario playing his sidekick, Skipper O'Malley. Once Frankie even shadows Miss Gomez, disguised in a long dark coat and a mask. When he sees her weeping on a park bench, he approaches her and in a disguised voice assures her that he will take care of her. The conclusion is highly ironic, because, unlike almost everything else the two boys attempt, this time Frankie's plans succeed. After another snooping incident, Mr. Swerdlow angrily moves out. Frankie persuades his mother to attend a bogus meeting at school at the very time Miss Gomez has arranged through Frankie to make a home visit. She meets Tom instead, and although Frankie tearfully owns up to manifold acts of chicanery, the last episode, set six months later, indicates that he has achieved his objective of recovering his room and his radio. His shenanigans continue, however; he and Mario wire Tom and the new Mrs. Wattleson's bedroom for sound (as they once did when Mr. Swerdlow lived in it) and listen in on the newlyweds' conversations. The theme—that heroism can be more complicated and difficult than popular fiction implies—appears naturally in the fast-moving plot, and the inclusion of excerpts from such actual radio shows as "The Lone Ranger," "Captain Midnight," and "The Shadow" supports the boys' characterizations and increases the plausibility of their actions, as well as enhances the ironic nature of the entertainment appreciated by the nation then at war. Frankie's parents are typically overworked, preoccupied, and concerned about their sons. The school scenes have the ring of truth, and the boys' melodramatic activities and overreactions, tied in with the radio shows Frankie has been listening to, become a kind of hilarious comedy-of-errors hero show in themselves. Some well-worn dunce material appears (the board stretched between the boys' upper-story windows so that they can slip from one house to the other and which eventually breaks down) and some poignancy (Tom's story of his fear under fire and his wounding) undergirds the comedy and points up the theme. The subplot about Uncle Charley, who was sent to jail for running a numbers racket, ironically the relative whom Frankie thought he would love to meet, shows the man as a real, if repentant, cad, the antithesis of a hero as Frankie thinks of one. The dialogue Frankie makes up and the boys' affectations when they are on their Chet Barker–Skip O'Malley escapades are wonderfully hilarious. Never dull, skillfully concocted light reading with some thought-provoking undergirding ideas, the book has the added bonus of giving a limited but vivid, nondidactic sense of the times. ALA.

WILLEM COETZEE (*Beyond Safe Boundaries**), sweetheart of Evie* Levin and her mentor and ally in the anti-apartheid effort and friend of Elizabeth Levin, Evie's much younger sister. The son of a white woman and Popeye*, Mr. Levin's Colored (*sic*) (half-white, half-black) dental mechanic (denture maker), Willem passes for white but identifies with nonwhites. He helps Elizabeth win her first tennis trophy by insisting that she can do anything she wants to if she tries hard enough and verbally pushing her to excel. He is charismatic also in his leadership role in the African Movement, and Elizabeth admiringly watches him run an important planning meeting at the university. He cleverly insists on alibis for all the movement leaders but is caught by police anyway and imprisoned in solitary confinement. The group knows that he will not emerge from jail alive, because the pattern for such political detentions has been for the police to murder the prisoners and to inform the public that the prisoners committed suicide in some way. At the end of the book, Elizabeth's father says that the government is terrified of such liberal-minded, inspired, and inspiring leaders as Willem and that Willem knew that it was just a matter of time before he fell victim to the establishment. He says that Willem "was prepared to be a martyr."

WILLIAMS, VERA B. (1927–   ), born in Hollywood, California; educator, political activist, and highly regarded author and illustrator of picture-story books. She was graduated with a B.F.A. in graphic art from Black Mountain School in North Carolina in 1949. She taught in two schools, which she also helped to found, in New York State, Gate Hill Cooperative Community and Collaberg School, both in Stony Point; taught in Everdale School in Ontario; and was an instructor at Goddard College in Vermont. She has also been active in antiwar pursuits. All self-illustrated, her picture books have been honored with many awards, in particular, *A Chair for My Mother* (Greenwillow, 1982), which was a Caldecott Honor Book and received both the *Boston Globe–Horn Book* Award for Illustration and the Other Award. It remains her most acclaimed and popular book. Its sequels are *Something Special for Me* (Greenwillow, 1983), a Caldecott Honor Book and a *Boston Globe–Horn Book* Winner for Illustration, and *Music, Music, for Everyone* (Greenwillow, 1984), a Jane Addams Honor Book. Also highly regarded, her other picture books include *Three Days on a River in a Red Canoe* (Greenwillow, 1981); *Cherries and Cherry Pits* (Greenwillow, 1986); *Stringbean's Trip to the Shining Sea* (Greenwillow, 1988), with daughter Jennifer; and *"More More More" Said the Baby* (Greenwillow, 1990). Several of her books have been issued in large-print editions, on tape, and in Spanish. They have been praised for the freshness and vigor of the color and design in their illustrations, the warm family spirit of their texts, and their celebration of the working-class family unit. *Scooter** (Greenwillow, 1993), her first novel, won the *Boston Globe–Horn Book* Award for text, was named an American Library Association Best Book for Children, and was listed in Fanfare by the editors of *The Horn Book Magazine*. It tells how a girl's silver-blue scooter helps her adjust to a new home. As in her picture books, the illustrations and text not only work with each other to convey the story but are also, taken together, skillfully executed graphic art.

WILLY GERARD (*My Name is Sus5an Smith. The 5 is Silent.**), ex-husband of Aunt Marianne, with whom Susan becomes reacquainted in Boston. An attractive scoundrel, he charmed Susan when she was seven by looking seriously at her paintings and "flying" her (swinging her by her ankle and wrist in the yard), and he charms her again when she starts seeing him in Boston. She ignores the fact that he stole all Marianne's wedding gifts when he disappeared and does not let the way he insists she get him a free pass at the theater where she works warn her that he is still a moocher. After he has stolen all her Aunt* Libby's antiques, carpets, and cameras, Susan is personally most upset because he also stole all her own paintings, an illustrated letter from her artist friend, Thomas Roode, and the armadillo necklace that he gave her ten years earlier and that she has worn ever since. In the end she admits that he was just what her mother called him—irresponsible, untrustworthy, and shiftless—and she agrees with her friend Salvatore that he "definitely was a slime."

WINDSOR, PATRICIA (1938–   ), born in New York City; editor, educator, novelist. She attended Bennington College and Westchester Community College, has taught at the college level, and has been a senior editor at Harper & Row. Her best-known books are mysteries, including *Killing Time* (Harper, 1980), about modern-day Druids in New York State, descendants of ancient Celtic settlers, and *The Sandman's Eyes* (Delacorte, 1985), which won the Edgar Allan Poe Award. Also considered for the Poe Award was *The Christmas Killer** (Scholastic, 1991), a novel of suspense about a serial murderer who strikes in the holiday season. Windsor has also written contemporary problem novels, short stories, articles, and song lyrics. For earlier biographical information and a title entry, see *Dictionary, 1985–1989* [*The Sandman's Eyes*].

WING BRENNAN (*And One for All**), older brother of Geraldine* Brennan and dear friend of Sam* Daily. He is presented as fun-loving, mischievous, and rebellious, though respectful to his family, a decent, all-American boy. He often teases Geraldine, for example, by turning off the basement lights when she is down there, because he knows she is afraid of the preserved snakes stored there. A poor student, he has some sort of undiagnosed learning disability and has no desire for college, although his parents push him to go so that he can avoid the draft. They often argue with Wing about his school performance and college. Wing loves the tin lizzie car that he calls Old Red and his fat, old dog named Kizzy and has a job after school. He buys a toy train for Christmas for Dub, the Brennans' youngest child, using money his parents wanted him to save for college. In spite of their opposing views about the involvement of the United States in the Vietnam War, Wing and Sam remain close friends. An additional irony in the book is that Wing got good grades on his school report the January he enlists. Wing is killed in Vietnam.

THE WINTER PRINCE (Wein*, Elizabeth E., Atheneum, 1993), highly untraditional retelling of the story of King Arthur (here Artos) and his illegitimate son, Modred (here Medraut*) by his half-sister Morgause. Told in the first person by Medraut and directed to his mother (called his godmother), it explores the strained love-hate relationship with his father and his father's legitimate twins, Lleu* and Goewin*, by Guenevere (here called Ginevra). After being away for six years—the first four in Europe, Africa, and Byzantium, the last two with his mother in the Northern Islands, the Orcades—Medraut returns to Camlan in midwinter to find Lleu, now fourteen, who has always been frail and now evidently is dying. Having acquired healing skill in his travels, Medraut nurses Lleu, and gradually, as he recounts the story of that winter, the horrors of his earlier two years with Morgause come out—how she tormented and tortured him, deliberately set his broken hand to be crippled, and, though it is not said directly, seduced him to incest. Artos, who recognizes Lleu's weakness and arrogance, asks Medraut to teach the boy and guide him, with the promise that when Lleu is sixteen and named prince of Britain, Medraut will be regent. Although Lleu so hates killing that he will not hunt, he is lithe and agile and becomes a skilled swordsman. At Medraut's suggestion, Artos sends for Morgause's four sons by King Lot to be fostered at court, but everyone is appalled when they are accompanied by their mother. As a guest, Lot's wife, and the high king's sister, she cannot be turned away without cause, but Lleu sickens, and gradually Medraut realizes that she is subtly poisoning the boy. Finally, he accuses her before Artos, who sends her away. Instead of going north to King Lot, however, she goes to see Igraine, her mother, and returns in a blizzard so severe that even Artos cannot refuse her entrance. There she plots and extracts a promise from Medraut, driven to fury when Lleu reveals his true parentage to her four sons, to kidnap Lleu, so she might hold him for ransom in exchange for greater power in the realm. With Agravain, the most disaffected of Lot's sons, as co-conspirator, Medraut takes Lleu on what is ostensibly a hunting trip, with Goewin along, included unwittingly to serve as messenger back to Artos. The remainder of the novel is the terrible journey, during which power shifts from Medraut, who is suffering from fever, to Lleu and back, until the two alone, both close to death, reach an accord and recognize their true love for each other. The melodramatic plot is not as important as the tone of the novel, a sense of foreboding that grows almost unbearable before the end. The only characters well developed are Medraut, Lleu, and Goewin, although Morgause's devious evil pervades the action and Ginevra's practical common sense helps provide balance. Morgause's four sons by Lot, closer to Lleu's age than Medraut's, have no illusions about their mother but more than anything still desire her love or her notice, so that they are jealous even of her tormenting of Medraut and Lleu. The title comes from the part Medraut plays in the annual rhymers' pageant. This is a strange and disturbing novel. Fanfare.

THE WINTER ROOM (Paulsen*, Gary, Orchard, 1989), realistic episodic novel of family and farm life set in northern Minnesota in possibly the 1930s, since tractors still have lugs and threshing machines are used. In narrative almost completely without dialogue, Eldon looks back to when he was about eleven and describes major events of each season, dividing his story into four distinct sections. In ''Spring,'' he tells in especially pungent, richly sensory language of the messiness and smells on the eighty-seven acres of cleared land at the edge of the forest that make up the family farm. Living with him are his hardworking father and mother; disparaging, teasing older brother, Wayne; and Uncle David, a kind of great-uncle, and David's friend, Nels, both very old immigrants from Norway. Eldon describes the interior of the house and barn and the family living and sleeping quarters. He relates with great relish and subtle humor how Wayne leaps from a hayloft, expecting to hit the back of their massive plow horse, Slacker, misses, and lands in a manure pile, unsuccessfully trying to emulate the hero in a Zane Grey novel. "Summer" brings plowing, huge threshing meals, and "hard, hard work," made lighter and more pleasant by helpful neighbors. Going to Jenny's Lake for a picnic always marks the beginning of fall. Then comes Eldon's least favorite activity, butchering the steer, pig, chickens, and geese, scenes graphically summed up with: "they stink and there is blood and blood and blood and more blood and I hate fall." Eldon notes that only Rex the dog likes the killing. In "Winter," after preparations for cold weather like draining the tractor radiators are done and snow starts, the family gathers after supper in the living room, called the winter room because it is used only during that season. While the others range themselves about the old wood stove and Mother knits, Uncle David tells stories (which, if interesting, seem intrusive, added, and not integral to the narrative), beginning always with that of Alida, his beautiful young wife in the old country who died in childbirth. Other stories concern a terrible Viking named Orud who kidnaps a witch woman and is said to live with her under the sea at the mouth of a fjord; an eccentric lumberman called Crazy Alen who immigrated from the old country and played extraordinary practical jokes; and a magnificent woodcutter who "was such a wonder with an ax that they [other cutters] would stop" to watch him. This last tale arouses Wayne's ire when Father says the story is really about Uncle David when he was young. Although Eldon recognizes the metaphorical and universal aspects of stories, the more literal-minded Wayne angrily complains that Uncle David is bragging and that this and all his other tales are lies. Broken in spirit, Uncle David does not storytell for several nights, and Eldon is so angry he wants to punish Wayne. After a vigorous fistfight over the matter in the hayloft, the boys observe Uncle David below standing at the woodpile. They watch as a strange and miraculous power seems to emanate from the earth and pervade his body so that just once more he can hoist two double-bitted axes and split a large log as deftly and cleanly as he once did. That night, Uncle David resumes his stories, to the family's joy and relief. "I knew," concludes Eldon, "we would listen for always." The book has no single problem to bind events together, the pace is leisurely for the most part, tension is almost completely lacking, and characterization is minimal. The story's strength comes from Paulsen's ability to appeal strongly to all the senses, employ engaging turns of phrase, and in nostalgic but never sentimental style project the tone of memoir, thereby evoking the timeless power and basic goodness of life close to the soil and the natural world. The introduction, called "Tuning" and signed "G.P.," is so overwritten as almost to keep one from reading further, but the body of the book is an eloquent and controlled panegyric to farm life. ALA; Newbery Honor.

WITCH BABY (Block*, Francesca Lia, HarperCollins, 1991), unconventional girl's growing-up story, sequel to *Weetzie Bat* set in the Los Angeles area about the time of its publication, in which Witch Baby finds answers to her questions, "What time are we upon and where do I belong?" In a sort of modern-day commune of aging hippy-type movie makers live Weetzie Bat and her lover, My Secret Agent Lover Man; a gay couple, Dirk McDonald and Duck Drake; Weetzie's alcoholic mother, Brandy-Lynn; Weetzie's daughter, Cherokee; and a friend, Coyote. In another bungalow on the place live Ping and Valentine and their Chinese-African-American son, Raphael, with whom Witch Baby is secretly in love but who has a serious crush on Cherokee. Various others are at least occasionally in residence, mostly fitting together amicably, except for Witch Baby, now probably an early adolescent, who does not fit in at all. Although the others are fond of her, she is a loner, snarling and biting and taking pictures of the others in unflattering moments, and each night she cuts three stories of disasters or mayhem from the newspaper and posts them on the wall of the room she shares with beautiful, blond Cherokee. When Dirk and Duck go to Santa Cruz to visit Duck's family, she stows away in the trunk, and, feeling just as lonely among Duck's many younger siblings, she tells Duck's mother, Darlene, that he and Dirk are lovers. Darlene is stunned, and Duck's stepfather makes crude jokes. Hurt and insulted, Duck and Dirk leave and camp for several days on the way home, taking Witch Baby along but ignoring her. When they get home, Darlene and all the siblings are there, to make peace with Duck. All the residents are making a movie, *Los Diablos,* about South American Indians who find a glowing blue ball and use it to decorate themselves and their walls, only to die because it is the radioactive part of an old x-ray machine. My Secret Agent thinks it is his idea, but it really comes from a clipping Witch Baby planted where he would find it. On the set of *Los Diablos* Witch Baby meets Angel Juan Perez from Mexico, and they become very close. She even plays for him her drums, which she abandoned when Raphael went off with Cherokee after she taught him to play. Then Angel Juan disappears, and she learns that his family are illegal aliens, running from immigration officers. Inconsolable, she demands to know who she really is, and My Secret Agent Lover Man tells her the truth: that when Weetzie wanted a baby and he did not, she went ahead and got pregnant by Dirk or Duck, and being angry, he left and fell under the spell of a woman named Vixanne Wigg but eventually returned to Weetzie. Nearly a year later, they found a baby in a basket on their doorstep, Vixanne's baby that he knew was his and that he and Weetzie took in and called Witch Baby. Witch Baby straps on her skates and goes off to Hollywood, where she finds Vixanne at a Jayne Mansfield Fan Club Meeting, which seems to be dedicated to denying pain and evil. Fed up with denial, Witch Baby returns to her family, who have been terribly worried and are delighted to see her again, and they take a timed-exposure picture of all of them, the only picture in which Witch Baby has been included, to post on the clock where she has a snapshot for each hour except twelve, since at last she knows what time she is upon and where she belongs. Stylistically, the book is very unusual, written almost as if in code; figuring out what is actually happening and what is in Witch Baby's mind is a challenge. The language, particularly the dialogue, is slangy. Gradually the motley assortment of people in the ''family'' emerge as distinct, even memorable characters, and the glimpses of action fit into a narrative. The book's strength is in its revelation of Witch Baby's pain, which makes her seek out articles about horrors, shave off all her hair, snap and scratch and destroy things, and which she can only drive away by playing her drums. After she returns and Weetzie admits that they all need to learn to face pain as she does, Witch Baby feels she has a place in the family and can express her own love for them. SLJ.

WITCH WEED (Naylor*, Phyllis Reynolds, illus. Joe Burleson, Delacorte, 1991), present-day mystery fantasy, fifth in a series concerned with how the extraordinary powers of old Mrs. Tuggle affect a family in a small Indiana town, even after her death. In the immediately preceding novel, *The Witch's Eye,* Mrs. Tuggle has died in a fire that has destroyed her house, but her green glass eye has been picked up by Stevie, the little brother of the protagonist, Lynn Morley, 11, and after creating much trouble and nearly causing Lynn to be drowned, has been thrown into the flooded creek by her friend, Mouse (Marjorie) Beasley and its spell broken. In a conference with the school psychologist, Dr. Long, Lynn tells the whole story and assures him that now she is fine and does not need his services. Although he does not believe her, he says he has an open mind and gets her to promise that she will come to him if she is troubled again. She looks forward to a lazy, pleasant summer. Before long, however, she begins to smell a sweetish odor coming from the direction of the creek and finds strange, purple flowers that seem to turn toward her and hum growing near the banks. While Mouse is visiting her mother, who now lives in Ohio, Lynn tries to renew her old friendship with Betty, Kirsten, and Charlotte Ann, girls from her class, and is snubbed. After Mouse returns, they try again, with no success, and disturbing things start happening. Dead seagulls, their necks broken, are thrown against the doors of both the Morley and the Beasley houses. Lynn and Mouse find that their three classmates, with two other girls, are meeting down by the creek and chanting the same words Mrs. Tuggle used to repeat. From a rare book, *Spells and Potions,* in Mr. Beasley's bookshop, where Lynn and Mouse work on Saturdays, they learn that the words are the names of the nine Great Subordinate demons, and they are horrified that Betty and the other girls have looked at the book and tried to buy it. When the girls discover Lynn and Mouse spying on them, they threaten harm to Mouse's mother if she does not join their coven and suggest that by witchcraft she may be able to get her mother to return. They knock Lynn unconscious by pressing one of the purple flowers on her face. Lynn appeals to Dr. Long again, and he takes one of the flowers to a horticultural department, where the botanists identify it as a variety of a plant called witchweed. Lynn tries to kill all the flowers by the creek with weedkiller but does not have enough poison, and the flowers remaining seem to be spreading. On the night of August 1, the date of a witch's sabbat, Mouse calls her, terrified, saying that the girls are coming to take her to her initiation down among the purple flowers. Lynn seizes a can of gas from her father's shed, pours it in a circle around the flowers, and sets it on fire. Although the flames burn the whole meadow and threaten the Morleys' house, the spell is broken. A strange light glowing briefly from the house built where Mrs. Tuggle's used to be, however, promises material for further books in the series. While the plot does not hold up under close scrutiny, the story is sufficiently spooky to keep a middle school audience breathless. Lynn is well drawn as a practical, no-nonsense girl, thereby making the eerie happenings seem plausible. Poe Nominee.

WOLFF, VIRGINIA EUWER (1937–), born in Portland, Oregon; graduate of Smith College; novelist; teacher of English. *The Mozart Season** (Holt, 1991), a lighthearted, perceptive story about a talented girl violinist, was selected by the American Library Association as a Notable Book. *Make Lemonade** (Holt, 1993), cited by both the American Library Association and *School Library Journal* and named to the Fanfare list by the editors of *Horn Book,* is a sensitive and detailed novel of the problems of a teenaged, single-parent mother. For earlier biographical information and a title entry, see *Dictionary, 1985–1989* [*Probably Still Nick Swansen*].

WOOD, JUNE RAE (1946–), born in Sedalia, Missouri; journalist, author of novels, short stories, and articles. She attended Central Missouri State University and married William A. Wood; they have one daughter. A staff writer for the *Sedalia Democrat,* Sedalia, Missouri, she has also published articles and short stories in *Family Circle, Reader's Digest, Home Life,* the *Lookout, New Ways,* and *School and Community.* Her novel for young people, *A Share of Freedom** (Putnam, 1994), which was cited by *School Library Journal* as a Best Book, concerns a girl's efforts to cope with the problems of an alcoholic mother and her discovery of the identity of her real father, a book notable for its well-developed characters. Her earlier novel, *The Man Who Loved Clowns* (Putnam, 1992), about a man afflicted with Down syndrome, was inspired by a mentally disabled member of her own family.

WORDS OF STONE (Henkes*, Kevin, Greenwillow, 1992), contemporary boy's growing-up novel set during the summer in a rural area near Madison, Wisconsin. For five years, small, shy, red-haired Blaze* Werla, 10, has consoled himself for the death from cancer of his beautiful mother, Reena, by making up imaginary friends, each of whom he ''buries'' every July near the anniversary of her death. Each has a small stone that serves as a headstone under the big black locust tree on the hill behind the house that he and his painter father, Glenn, share with Nova, his maternal grandmother. One morning just after burying his latest pretend companion, Ortman, he is horrified to see the name REENA spelled out in large letters with stones on the hillside. A couple of days later in the same place he reads FIRE! YOU'RE ON FIRE, words that are a horrible reminder of the fire at the fairgrounds in which he received terrible, scarring burns on his legs. Although Blaze is unaware of her existence, the words have been constructed by an angry and impulsive girl his age, Joselle* Stark, who is staying over the hill with her grandmother, Floy, while her mother is off on a trip to the Pacific Ocean with her latest boyfriend. Having learned about Blaze's history from Floy, Joselle has fashioned the words deliberately—as she says, to "complicate" Blaze's life—and has also inscribed them in marking-pen tattoos high up on her thighs. After they meet and form a friendship mostly dominated by Joselle, who has lied about the time of her arrival at Floy's and her family situation, Blaze thinks that Claire, his father's sweetheart, may have been responsible for the stone words. One rainy day, Joselle arrives at Blaze's house and invites him to play in the rain with her. Through her sodden t-shirt, he reads the "tattoos," realizes she has deceived him, and reacts with violence, pushing her down and tearing a button from her new sweater. Shortly after, Joselle and Floy discover that Joselle's mother has been at home all along, and Floy takes Joselle there. Blaze holds within himself his pain over what has happened, equivocates when asked about Joselle, becomes gradually friendlier to Claire, starts to paint the canvas his father has stretched for him, and finally visits Floy, from whom he learns the truth about Joselle and her mother. Early one morning just before school starts, he spots stones on the hillside spelling I'M SORRY, wakes his father, an indication that he finally is opening up psychologically, and heads off for Joselle's. After an attention-getting opening in which Blaze is seen "burying" Ortman, the plot proves weak; characterization is the novel's strong point. The sensible, stable grandmothers are paired, and patient, understanding Glenn and pretty, lively Claire are sparingly but tellingly drawn. The two children are complex and probably irreparably scarred by circumstances, but Blaze changes too rapidly, and Joselle's story is left unfinished. For example, Blaze goes off to Floy's house after the fight with Joselle because "he knew he would have to face Joselle sooner or later," an action that moves the story along but is not appropriate to Blaze's character as presented or logical within the framework of the plot. Moreover, fourteen of the book's twenty-four short chapters are told from Blaze's perspective (though not by him), and the remaining ten from Joselle's, a convenient mechanism for presenting information to the reader about Blaze's stone problem. The effect, however, is to engage the reader also in Joselle's life. As a result, the conclusion, which focuses on Blaze, is unsatisfying, and Joselle's return and her subsequent behavior are left unexplained. Occasionally the language does not seem accurate, as when, for example, in a Joselle chapter, the girl realizes that "Blaze had been the perfect candidate for deceit, and Joselle had gladly taken advantage of his innocence," a statement that sounds like the writer's voice instead of the way Joselle would think it. In spite of such shortcomings and the overly obvious symbolism, the novel sympathetically relates the efforts of two troubled youngsters to make sense out of chaotic lives—in the one case from a tragic death and accident and the probable remarriage of his father, in the other from the irresponsible behavior of a selfish, uncaring mother. Fanfare.

WREDE, PATRICIA C(OLLINS) (1953–   ), born in Chicago; financial analyst and accountant, author of books of fantasy for adults and young people. She received her A.B. degree from Carleton College in Minnesota and her M.B.A. from the University of Minnesota, was married to a financial consultant, divorced, and lives in Edina, Minnesota. She has served as a rate review analyst for the Minnesota Hospital Association and as a financial analyst and senior accountant for B. Dalton Bookseller. Since 1985 she has been a full-time writer. Her best-known novels for young people are called the Enchanted Forest Chronicles, starting with *Dealing with Dragons* (Harcourt, 1990), followed by *Searching for Dragons** (Harcourt, 1991), *Calling on Dragons* (Harcourt, 1993), and *Talking to Dragons,* originally published by Tempo in 1985 but rewritten as part of the series (Harcourt, 1993). All take the conventions of the fairy tale and turn them upside down, with a runaway princess who does not want to be rescued by a hero and a young king reluctant to assume the pomp of his position. Among Wrede's other novels are *Shadow Magic* (Ace, 1982), *Daughter of Witches* (Ace, 1983), *The Seven Towers* (Ace, 1984), *The Harp of Imach Thyssel* (Ace, 1985), and *Caught in Crystal* (Ace, 1987). She has also contributed to several anthologies of fantasy and science fiction.

Y

YANG THE YOUNGEST AND HIS TERRIBLE EAR (Namioka*, Lensey, illus. Kees De Kiefte, Little Brown, 1992), humorous novel for middle grade readers about how nine-year-old Yingtao Yang, youngest in a family of musicians, copes with the problem of being tone deaf. Since the family has moved from Shanghai to Seattle, presumably about 1990, where his father is an alternate violinist in the symphony, the family has had inadequate income, and the father tries to supplement it by giving music lessons. Hoping to acquire new students by showing how well his pupils perform, he trains his four children as a string quartet—Eldest Brother on first violin, Second Sister on viola, Third Sister on cello, and Yang the Youngest on second violin—to climax his recital. The first three are proficient and enthusiastic musicians. Only Yingtao is unable to do his part adequately, his failure credited by his parents and his first two siblings to laziness and lack of practice. Third Sister, his favorite, realizes that her little brother actually cannot hear the difference between the true tones and the squawks his violin produces. Afraid that he will ruin the recital, he and Third Sister cook up a scheme to have Yingtao's friend, Matthew Conner, a boy with a real love of music and talent for the violin, sit behind a screen and play the second violin part while Yingtao moves his bow. Because Matthew has been sitting in for Yingtao during the quartet practices, much to the relief of the Yang siblings, he knows the part better than Yingtao does. The trouble is that Matthew's father, who was once a professional baseball player, thinks that music is making his son into a wimp and forbids him to go to the Yang house until his baseball improves. Yingtao's father, upset that his son has skipped a quartet practice to go to a Mariners' game with the Conners, announces that he may play no more ball until his violin playing improves. The day of the recital, the Conners, who have been especially invited by Yingtao's pianist mother, arrive without Matthew, who has told them he is sick. With some minor glitches, the quartet goes off well until the four Yang children stand at the end and Third Sister knocks over the screen, revealing Matthew with his violin. Clever Third Sister apologizes to the audience for "this little trick on you" to show what a talented musician Matthew is. Mr. Conner, amazed by his son's ability, suggests that he should begin lessons and persuades Mr. Yang that Yingtao has real talent for baseball. All the Yangs compliment Yingtao on his generosity and nobility in giving up his quartet part to his friend. Mr. Conner persuades the Yang family to attend a neighborhood game in which Yingtao performs very well, and at last he is accepted for his real talent. Beyond the rather implausible bow-sync plot, the book gets lots of fun out of cultural and language misunderstandings. Yingtao cannot understand how Mr. Conner, who is out of work and too poor to pay for music lessons, can own a car and live in a house with nice furniture and separate rooms for his two sons. Matthew cannot understand how the Yangs can all have valuable musical instruments yet use orange crates for bureaus. Yingtao is embarrassed when Matthew asks to go to the bathroom, since he thinks his friend wants a bath and the tub contains the live carp for dinner. Matthew is continually having to explain American terms like what it means to be laid off or to babysit. The Yang children's aspirations to fit into American life—Third Sister's adoption of ''Mary'' for her school name, Second Sister's desire to earn money caring for children, Yingtao's love of being a shortstop— are treated gently as natural adaptations to a new environment, not rebellious tendencies. Even Yang the Youngest's inability to hear music is not a great disability once the family pressure is relaxed. He is a little wistful at being left out, but mostly he is relieved. Fanfare.

YEAR OF IMPOSSIBLE GOODBYES (Choi*, Sook Nyul, Houghton Mifflin, 1991), autobiographical novel set in North Korea, starting in 1945 during the Japanese occupation and continuing during occupation by the Russians until the protagonist and most of her family finally escape to the South. Under the oppressive Japanese domination in Kirimni in Pyongyang, the mother of Sookan, nearly ten, runs a sock factory, with young women workers toiling to meet the almost impossible quotas set by implacable Captain Narita. Because Sookan's father and three older brothers have disappeared in the North and her older sister is in a convent, the family consists only of Mother; Grandfather, a gentle scholar; Sookan's little brother, Inchun, 7; Aunt Tiger; and her son, Kisa. Soon Grandfather dies, having stood up earlier to Japanese torture but being now disheartened by their gratuitous acts of cruelty. One day they round up all the sock girls and take them off to be forced prostitutes for the troops. Sookan suffers at a school run by the Japanese where instruction is mostly an attempt to make the children hate the ''White Devils.'' Suddenly the war is over, and the Russians are in charge. At first the food and relative kindness of the Russians make all seem better, but soon it is apparent that they are coercing the people more cleverly but just as cruelly. All the Koreans are organized into work gangs. Sookan and Inchun go to the Little Proletariat school, where children are fed propaganda and encouraged to inform on their families. Finally, Cousin Kisa one day rushes in to say he has seen Sookan's father, who has been driving a truck delivering raw materials from the North to trade for rice from the South and has been secretly arranging escapes, having already rescued his three older sons. It is arranged that Sookan and Inchun, with their mother, will set off at night with a guide, but Kisa and Aunt Tiger insist on staying behind to provide cover for them. At a checkpoint along the way, their mother is pulled from the line and the children follow after the guide, as they have been told to do, but the next morning they learn that he was a double agent, informing, for a fee, on those he has been paid to help. For several days they hang around the area, scrounging what food they can and hoping their mother will reappear. They even take the desperate step of going to the guardhouse and asking for their mother. They are questioned but released and told to go home. An old man sweeping the station gives them directions to a friendly conductor who will help them get across the tracks, which run near the thirty-eighth parallel, the boundary to South Korea. The old conductor, pretending to be brusque, directs them to the end of the train; then, when no one is looking, he tells them to crawl under it. On the other side they run down the hill, squat against the embankment, and remain motionless as the searchlight sweeps over the cornfield they must cross. In the rain they can hear guard dogs barking. To make less noise, they remove their shoes, and the cornstalks cut their feet. They climb over a small hill and come to a river, crossed only by a railroad bridge, the ties spaced widely apart. With great difficulty, they crawl across the bridge, run to a barbed-wire fence, and, unable to lift the wires enough, burrow under it, and race for the lights of Red Cross tents in the distance. An epilogue briefly finishes the story of their escape: the Red Cross workers bandage their feet, locate their father's address, and put them on a bus to Seoul. Their shocked father and brothers greet them with the news that their mother has not arrived. Six months later, she also appears, having been a maid and prisoner in the household of a Russian colonel and at last run away and made her way alone to the south. Eventually Sookan's older sister and the other nuns arrive, bringing the news that Aunt Tiger and Kisa have been shot as traitors. The Korean War starts, but the narrative does not continue into the new period. The tale of great humiliation and hardship is relieved by the strong love and sense of responsibility Sookan feels for her little brother, who vacillates between being almost unbelievably mature and whining and crying like a baby. Their final escape at night to the fence marking the boundary of the South is memorable. Although there are no kindly Japanese, several of the Russian soldiers are pictured as sympathetic. ALA.

YEP, LAURENCE (MICHAEL) (1948–   ), born in San Francisco; editor of story collections, reteller of stories from oral tradition; author of novels for young people, mostly about the Chinese-American experience. His *Dragonwings* (Harper, 1975), about a young Chinese boy's experiences on emigrating to California at the beginning of the twentieth century, was a Newbery Honor Book and the 1995 Phoenix Award Winner of The Children's Literature Association. *The Star Fisher** (Morrow, 1991) follows an immigrant Chinese family who encounter discrimination when they try to establish a laundry business in West

Virginia in 1927. A Christopher Award Winner, the book is based on experiences of Yep's relatives. His Serpent's Trilogy, which starts with the revolt against the Manchus in China, culminates with the Newberry Honor book, *Dragon's Gate**, about the building of the Union Pacific Railroad through the Sierra Nevada Mountains. For earlier biographical information and title entries, see *Dictionary, 1960–1984* [*Child of the Owl; Dragonwings*].

YOUNG, RONDER THOMAS, born in Anderson, South Carolina; writer of essays and short stories for adults and of *Learning by Heart** (Houghton Mifflin, 1993), an episodic novel of family life in a small South Carolina town in the early 1960s as seen from the vantage of the ten-year-old daughter. A first novel that excels in details of day-to-day life, it was an American Library Association Notable Book for Children. Young was graduated from the University of South Carolina and lives in Norcross, Georgia, with her husband and three sons.

YOUR MOTHER WAS A NEANDERTHAL (Scieszka*, Jon, illus. Lane Smith, Viking, 1993), fourth in a fantasy series about the present-day Time Warp Trio—Joe, the narrator, Fred, and Sam—who time-travel with the aid of a book of magic given Joe by his uncle, a stage magician. (See *Knights of the Kitchen Table**.) Now somewhat accustomed to the problems of landing in a different time period, the boys plan carefully, deciding to head for 40,000 B.C., when ordinary modern skills will seem like powerful magic and they can easily impress the people they land among. Each gathers what seems most important to him: Fred brings a slingshot, a Swiss army knife, and other potential weapons; Sam has tools and gadgets; Joe holds tightly to *The Book* and carries as much other magic paraphernalia as he can. When the green mist that accompanies their time travel settles, they find themselves in a forest of giant ferns, naked, with none of their equipment. They are terrified by what seems to be a dinosaur scaring away a group of cavemen, but they soon discover that the beast is really a false head carried by three girls who introduce themselves as Nat-Li, Lin-Say, and Jos-Feen. The girls take them to a cave peopled entirely by females led by Ma, a woman who reminds them strangely of Joe's mother. Although the women shut them into a small cave within the larger one, the boys escape and fall into a pit, where they are found by the cavemen, a group considerably less savvy than the women. Though warned through signs by their leader, Duh, not to, the boys leave the pit and encounter a saber-toothed tiger, which they manage to scare off. Figuring that they must get to the cave, where there may be a painting that will return them to the twentieth century, they start back but first encounter an earthquake and a woolly mammoth. At the cave entrance, they discover that the quake has dislodged a huge stone that blocks the entrance and trapped Nat-Li inside. When they cannot push it aside, even with the help of the cavemen, Sam tries using a fulcrum and lever, and the stone is rolled away. After a cheerful party in which both men and women join, Ma leads them through the small cave to a further recess, where they see a cave painting of three figures resembling the three boys, and they find themselves back in Joe's room at home, still holding all the equipment they collected. Seeing them, Joe's mother makes comments that indicate she has known about their magic traveling all the time. Although ingenious, the book makes no attempt to be convincing fantasy and gets its humor from elements like the Boog, the half-rotted food of the cavemen, and the wisecracking dialogue of the boys. While not in simple vocabulary or syntax, it is brief, almost all action, and not developed more than is necessary for a quick, amusing read for elementary schoolchildren. SLJ.

Z

ZACHARIAH (*The True Confessions of Charlotte Doyle**), kind, wise black man of perhaps fifty who befriends Charlotte Doyle on her transatlantic voyage from Liverpool to Providence, Rhode Island, in 1832. He is the eldest man in the crew and a sailor from his youth in Africa. He is illiterate, and his knowledge, Charlotte says, is limited to the sea. He has a strong sense of justice, however, and faith in the judicial system. Thus he and the crew have decided that once at Providence, he shall contact authorities to expose Captain* Andrew Jaggery's brutal treatment of the men. Charlotte has reservations about the potential for success of this scheme (a foretelling of her own lack of success with her father). Zachariah makes sailors' garments for Charlotte so she can be more active while on the ship. These later become her sailor's uniform, and she wears them when she returns to the *Seahawk*. Zachariah is a type; a reader knowledgeable in this kind of story knows right off that he is a faithful "good guy." There are shadings of character, however, that individualize him.

ZACHARY (Pintoff*, Ernest, Paul S. Eriksson, 1990), mystery and suspense novel set in Oakville, Connecticut, in the period immediately following World War II. One of the few Jews in Oakville, Zachary Silver, 12, is preparing for his bar mitzvah, but his mind is more on basketball, drawing, and his beautiful new art and music teacher, Mary Beth Porter. After school he and his friend, Buddy Goodson, sneak off to Black Rock by the lake for an illicit smoke and, hiding in the bushes, see their history teacher, a war hero named Greg Bondi, and Miss Porter making love on a picnic table. Then, just as he starts to remove her black panties, Coach Ryan, Mrs. Bondi's brother, appears and knocks Bondi out. Buddy takes off in panic, but Zachary stays on to see Big Lew Heinz, the brutal and corrupt local cop, chase Ryan off, return to send Miss Porter away, then jab Bondi repeatedly with a knife. Ryan is arrested for the murder, and Zachary, as the secret and only witness, suffers from fear and guilt. Since Ryan accuses Heinz of being the killer, Lieutenant Harry Roth is sent from Waterbury to investigate, and he seeks out Zachary repeatedly, even allowing the boy to work as a "partner" and eventually getting the whole story from him. To Zachary's surprise, Roth does not rush out and arrest Heinz but explains that he is after bigger game, a Nazi war criminal who may be hiding out in town. Complications abound. Buddy is struck by a hit-and-run car and hospitalized in a coma. Zachary's father dies suddenly, apparently from a heart attack. Zachary, still enamored of Miss Porter, cannot understand how she can go out with Heinz, especially as she seems afraid of him. Finally, it becomes apparent that Roth is an FBI agent, that Heinz has been extorting protection money from Zachary's father and other businesspeople and blackmailing Miss Porter, and that the new chemical engineer in the local plastics factory, Carl Frederick, is really Karl Friedrich Heinzmann, notorious Nazi and Heinz's older brother. In a culminating scene, Zachary sneaks into the factory at night and is followed by Heinz, who chases him with a heavy chain. Zachary escapes across the thinly frozen factory pond, the ice cracks, and Heinz, who is following the boy, plunges into the polluted water. Roth appears, jumps in after him, and pulls him out, afterward explaining to Zachary that even Heinz is a human deserving justice. The adventures go on and on, with some tense scenes, good in themselves but too numerous and often implausible. Far stronger is the setting in the mid-1940s, with the radio shows, comic strips, clothes, even the Brill-creamed hair styles of the period. Zachary's brother, Lenny, is a typically derogatory older sibling, and his mother and father are concerned but overworked and often distracted parents not really aware of what is happening with their sons. Poe Nominee.

ZANE PERKINS (*Cat Running**), eldest child in an Okie family, temporarily staying in Okietown near Brownwood, California, who becomes friends with Cat Kinsey and is her classmate in school. Cat dislikes him immediately, when she first sees him. He is sitting on the fringes and is barefoot and dressed in ragged overalls. She thinks he looks disgusting and has a smart-alecky mouth because he chides her about her running, remarking that she is "purty fast for a gal, but I could whup you. Real easy." When he wins the footrace running barefoot, she feels guilty about refusing to run unless she can wear slacks. Zane is a proud boy and protective of his younger brothers and little sister, watching over them and trying to keep tabs on them. Later, after Cat becomes friends after a fashion with Sammy, his little sister, he becomes protective of Cat, too. He is a good student and has a positive attitude toward life, in spite of his family's many problems.

ZOE LOUISE LABARGE (*Stonewords**), the young ghost girl whom Zoe first sees when PopPop decides to fix up the playhouse and with whom she is friends for about seven years. When first seen, Zoe Louise wears a lavender cotton dress with tiny pink buttons and heavy brown shoes and has long hair bound in two thick braids. Although Zoe notices right away that Zoe Louise is translucent, like a block of ice, she thinks she is the prettiest girl she has ever seen. Impatient and willful, Zoe Louise brings about the book's climax when she insists on having her own way about her birthday celebration. She decides to light her cake early in order to get her present, a pony, sooner than her father plans to give it to her. She starts the fire that apparently caused her death back in 1870, a death prevented more than one hundred years later by Zoe's quick action.

LIST OF BOOKS BY AWARDS

The following novels have been cited for the awards indicated and appear in this dictionary. Nonfiction books and collections of short stories are not included.

JANE ADDAMS PEACE ASSOCIATION CHILDREN'S BOOK AWARD

Journey of the Sparrows

Looking Out

Number the Stars

Taste of Salt

AMERICAN LIBRARY ASSOCIATION NOTABLE BOOKS FOR CHILDREN

Afternoon of the Elves

Alien Secrets

All But Alice

And One for All

Baby

The Beggars' Ride

The Bells of Christmas

Bingo Brown, Gypsy Lover

The Boggart

The Borning Room

The Broccoli Tapes

Buffalo Brenda

Bull Run

The Canada Geese Quilt

Cousins

Crazy Lady

Dixie Storms

Dragon's Gate

Everywhere

The Giver

The Harmony Arms

Harper & Moon

Jim Ugly

Journey

Learning by Heart

Letters from a Slave Girl

Letters from Rifka

Life's a Funny Proposition, Horatio

Lyddie

Make Lemonade

Maniac Magee

Maybe Yes, Maybe No, Maybe Maybe

The Midnight Horse

Missing May

Monkey Island

The Mozart Season

Nekomah Creek

Nightjohn

Nothing But the Truth

Number the Stars

Owl in Love

The Oxboy

The Pennywhistle Tree

The Place Where Nobody Stopped

Plain City

Rachel Chance

Saturnalia

Scooter

Searching for Dragons

Shabanu

Shades of Gray

Shiloh

Sister

Somewhere in the Darkness

Steal Away

Stepping on the Cracks

Tell Me Everything

Toning the Sweep

The True Confessions of Charlotte Doyle

The Voyage of the ''Frog''

The Wainscott Weasel

Wanted . . . Mud Blossom

Weasel

What Hearts

When the Road Ends

''Who Was That Masked Man, Anyway?''

The Winter Room

Year of Impossible Goodbyes

BOSTON GLOBE–HORN BOOK AWARD HONOR BOOKS

The Giver

Nothing But the Truth

Saturnalia

Stonewords

Western Wind

BOSTON GLOBE–HORN BOOK AWARD WINNERS

The Giver

Maniac Magee

Missing May

Scooter

The True Confessions of Charlotte Doyle

CHILD STUDY CHILDREN'S BOOK COMMITTEE AT BANK STREET COLLEGE AWARD

Secret City, U.S.A.

CHRISTOPHER AWARD

Letters from Rifka
Mississippi Bridge
The Star Fisher

CORETTA SCOTT KING AWARD WINNERS

The Road to Memphis
Toning the Sweep

THE HORN BOOK MAGAZINE FANFARE LIST

Afternoon of the Elves
And One for All
Baby
The Beggars' Ride
Bingo Brown and the Language of Love
The Borning Room
The Brave
Bull Run
Celine
Cousins
The Giver
Grab Hands and Run
Letters from a Slave Girl
Letters from Rifka
Lucie Babbidge's House
Lyddie
Make Lemonade
Maniac Magee
Monkey Island
Morning Girl
Nothing But the Truth
Number the Stars
Other Bells for Us to Ring
Others See Us
Saturnalia
Scooter
Shabanu

Shizuko's Daughter
Somewhere in the Darkness
Strider
Taste of Salt
Tehanu
The True Confessions of Charlotte Doyle
Wanted . . . Mud Blossom
What Hearts
The Winter Prince
Words of Stone
Yang the Youngest and His Terrible Ear

INTERNATIONAL READING ASSOCIATION CHILDREN'S BOOK AWARD

Children of the River
Letters from Rifka
Rescue Josh McGuire

JEFFERSON CUP AWARD FOR HISTORICAL FICTION

Shades of Gray

JOHN NEWBERY MEDAL HONOR BOOKS

Afternoon of the Elves
Catherine, Called Birdy
Crazy Lady
Dragon's Gate
Nothing But the Truth
Shabanu
Somewhere in the Darkness
The True Confessions of Charlotte Doyle
What Hearts
The Winter Room

JOHN NEWBERY MEDAL WINNERS

The Giver
Maniac Magee

Missing May
Number the Stars
Shiloh

SCOTT O'DELL AWARD FOR HISTORICAL FICTION

Bull Run
Morning Girl
Shades of Gray
Stepping on the Cracks
A Time of Troubles

THE CHILDREN'S LITERATURE ASSOCIATION PHOENIX AWARD HONOR BOOKS

Listen for the Fig Tree
My Brother Sam Is Dead
A Proud Taste for Scarlet and Miniver
Sing Down the Moon
The Tombs of Atuan

THE CHILDREN'S LITERATURE ASSOCIATION PHOENIX AWARD WINNERS

Enchantress from the Stars
Of Nightingales That Weep

NOMINEES FOR THE EDGAR ALLAN POE AWARD BEST JUVENILE MYSTERY

Breaking the Fall
Calling Home
The Christmas Killer
Class Trip
Coffin on a Case
Double Trouble Squared
The Face in the Bessledorf Funeral Parlor
Fell Back
Finding Buck McHenry
Fish & Bones

Ghost Cave

Guilt Trip

Help Wanted

The Man Who Was Poe

The Midnight Horse

Mystery on October Road

The One Who Came Back

Remember Me

Sam the Cat Detective

Scarface

The Secret Keeper

Silent Witness

Sniper

Spider Kane and the Mystery at Jumbo Nightcrawler's

Susannah and the Purple Mongoose Mystery

Tangled Web

To Grandmother's House We Go

The Tormentors

The Treasure Bird

We All Fall Down

The Weekend Was *Murder*!

Witch Weed

Zachary

WINNERS OF THE EDGAR ALLAN POE AWARD BEST JUVENILE MYSTERY

Coffin in a Case

A Little Bit Dead

Mote

The Name of the Game Was Murder

Show Me the Evidence

Stonewords

The Twin in the Tavern

Wanted . . . Mud Blossom

The Weirdo

SCHOOL LIBRARY JOURNAL BEST BOOKS FOR CHILDREN

Afternoon of the Elves

Alice in Rapture, Sort Of

Alien Secrets

And One for All

Bel-Air Bambi and the Mall Rats

Beyond Safe Boundaries

Bill

Bingo Brown and the Language of Love

Bingo Brown, Gypsy Lover

The Borning Room

The Broccoli Tapes

Bull Run

California Blue

Cat Running

Catherine, Called Birdy

Celine

Checking on the Moon

Commander Coatrack Returns

The Cookcamp

The Day That Elvis Came to Town

Deliver Us from Evie

Dixie Storms

Earthshine

Everywhere

Flip-Flop Girl

Forest

The Giver

Grab Hands and Run

Grams, Her Boyfriend, My Family, and Me

Harper & Moon

Journey

Knights of the Kitchen Table

The Lampfish of Twill

Letters from Rifka

Libby on Wednesday

Lyddie

Make Lemonade

Mama, Let's Dance

Maybe Yes, Maybe No, Maybe Maybe

The Midnight Horse

Missing Angel Juan

My Name Is Sus5an Smith. The 5 Is Silent.

Night Riding

No Kidding

Nothing But the Truth

Number the Stars

Our Sixth-Grade Sugar Babies

Out of Nowhere

The Pennywhistle Tree

Phoenix Rising

Phoenix Rising Or How to Survive Your Life

Plain City

A Question of Trust

The Rain Catchers

Reluctantly Alice

The Remarkable Journey of Prince Jen

Revolutions of the Heart

Rosemary's Witch

Sable

Saturnalia

Searching for Dragons

Seventeen Against the Dealer

Shadow Boxer

A Share of Freedom

Shoebag

The Silver Kiss

Staying Fat for Sarah Byrnes

Stepping on the Cracks

Switching Well

Sydney, Herself

T-Backs, T-Shirts, COAT, and Suit

Tell Me Everything

Toning the Sweep

The True Confessions of Charlotte Doyle

Unlived Affections

The Voyage of the ''Frog''

Wanted . . . Mud Blossom

Weasel

Western Wind

When She Hollers

Witch Baby

Your Mother Was a Neanderthal

GEORGE G. STONE CENTER FOR CHILDREN'S BOOKS RECOGNITION OF MERIT AWARD

Let the Circle Be Unbroken

The Road to Memphis

Roll of Thunder, Hear My Cry

WESTERN HERITAGE AWARD

Bunkhouse Journal

INDEX

Names and titles in ALL CAPITAL LETTERS refer to the actual entries of the dictionary, and page numbers in *italics* refer to the location of the actual entries in the dictionary.

for environmental sympathies, 48; on bully by girl, 239; on girl by girlfriend, 5; on girl by squirrels, 107; on girl by stepuncle, 256; rapes, 58; street, 163. *See also* assaults; battles; conflicts; fights; rivalry; wars; war novels
attic, children trapped in, 317
attorneys. *See* lawyers
Atuan, 333
Auburn plantation, 155
auctions, pie, at church social, 307
Augustus Trevor, 209
Aunt Babe, 243
Aunt Bea, 43, 138
Aunt Buntz, 340
Aunt Cecile Bradshaw, 55, 136, 364
Aunt Digna Sims, 243
AUNT EFFIE, *14*, 71, 165
Aunt Erna, 35
AUNT LIBBY SCHROEDER, *15*, 207, 376
Aunt Macy, 83, 234
Aunt Map, 215
Aunt Marge, 332
Aunt Marianne Gerard, 207, 367
Aunt Opal, 151
aunts: assumed dead in fire, 333; beloved, dies, 184, 191, 315; buxom, loving, 191; Cambodian refugee, 59, 210; fanatically religious, 169; fat, grumpy, 284; foster parent, 120; four, 334; great, half-blind, 43, 138; has had mastectomy, 325; houseproud, 14; hypochondriacal, 309; independent, 289; independent, good role model for judgmental, introverted niece, 326; invented, 219; irascible, conscientious, 59, 302; maiden, strict, 120; nearly blind, 243; nurse, African-American, 94; perfectionist, 71; sister of stepfather, ruggedly independent, 325; sophisticated, 15; step, of strong convictions, 24; superb salesperson, 325; tart-tongued, bossy, 78; vegetarian, 325; violates Pakistani custom by leaving abusive husband, 285; warm, gentle, 209; wife of pacifist, 286
Aunt Sally, 7
Aunt Thea Trevor, 209
Aunt Tiger, 378
AUNTY MOSS, *15*, 326
Aunty Pru, 91, 179
Aurora, planet in space, 8
Aurora Hopper, 137
Austin family, 87
Australians, graduate student, 319
authors: of book on ghosts, 190; visiting, suggests contest winners start a writing workshop, 159
autobiographical novels, 277, 378. *See also* biographical novels

automobiles: 1938 Ford, 265; red, sporty, 105
avalanches, 88
The Avenger, 354
Avery, Freedom Jo, 135, 183, 288
AVI (AVI WORTIS), *15*, 179, 338, 365
A volume encyclopedia, cherished, 10, 178
award books. *See Appendix*
awards. *See* rewards
Axelrod family, 101, 146
axes, uncle raises high two double-bitted, 370
Axie Hopper, 137

Babbidge family, 93, 168, 192
babbling, of young sister, dangerous, 220
Babcock family, 21
babies: aborted, 308; all blond, 294; apparently dead, revived and sold, 294; birth of brother, 30, 51, 133, 153; birth of sister, 13, 298; born dead, 237; boy premature, 79; dead, suddenly, 294; death of Cambodian refugee, 302; doll made of a bean, 169; doll named Maud after Wordsworth, 169; foundling girl, 17, 45, 143; girls switched at birth, 10, 260; mother unmarried, 63; rag doll, 293
BABY, *17*, 173
baby carrier, used for stolen statue, 65
Baby Face Nelson, 275
babysitters: arranged for half-sister, 228; elderly, kind, loving woman, 204, 238, 277; girl of 12, 7; teenaged boy, 91; teenaged girl, 56, 139, 174, 194, 281, 293, 319. *See also* nannies; nurses
backpacks, left in eccentric woman's cave, 353
Baer Machines, baseball team, 101
BAGGOT, MR., *202*, 274
Bagley Brown, Jr., the weasel, 351
Bagley Brown the weasel, 351
Bailey family, 128
Baja California, coastal ocean, late 20th century, 348
Baker family (*Fish & Bones*), 102, 199
Baker family (*Stepping on the Cracks*), 91, 112, 180, 311, 315
bakeries, 20, 341
bakers, Yosip, 242
Baker Street Irregular, 86
balcony, girl thought to have committed suicide by jumping from, 260
Bald Buzzer, robber fly, 304
ballet, girl studies, 201
Baltimore, Maryland, late 20th century, 72
Bambi Babcock, 22
BAMBI SUE BORDTZ, *18*, 32, 240
bandanna, man wears over face, 208
bands: army, boy of 11 member of, 42; Slick and the Boys, 41; the Goat Guys, 190
bankers, in farming area, 81
bankruptcy, of resort, imminent, 275

keep family together, 171; to keep freedom, 112; to live away from people, 223; to move to country, 322; to read better, 24; to succeed at hotel management, 97. *See also* ambitions
desk, Boggart falls asleep in, 33
destinations: Chicago, 264; Memphis railroad station, 63, 264, 302, 305
Detective Jarvis, 357
detective novels: African-American detective, 119, 199; cat detective, 273; children detectives, 86, 207; Edgar Allan Poe, 179; girl detective, 316; lost treasure, 275, 337; murder, 199, 260, 209, 294, 357; mystery, 63, 321; prep school, 99; space, 8; spider detective, 303
detectives: African-American, 120, 200, 312, 316; boy and police, 127, 200; cat, 273; college basketball player, 312; fictional, writer assumes persona of, 179, 245; girl, 8, 316; girl who was murdered seeks own killer, 260; horse, mother's boyfriend, 353; Mr. Auguste Dupin, 179; nicknamed Moon from scar, 312; police, 109, 260; question teenaged babysitter, 294; spider, 303; youthful, 65, 99, 100, 275, 321
"The Deuce," (42nd Street in New York City), 36
deviants, sexual, social worker, 63
devil, dead boy pretends to be, 109
Devil's Bridge, 80
Devonshire Place, London, late 20th century, 86
diabetics, 10, 260
dialects. *See* style, use of language
dialogue. *See* style, use of language
diamonds: chickens eat, 138; smuggled in ice, 19, 341
DIANA GOSS, *82*, 170
Diane, 334
diaries: girl keeps, lost, found, 11, 318; of Columbus, portion, 198; of dead sister, 240; helps girl regain her dimension, 11; portion of novel, 218. *See also* style, structure
diary entries, xeroxed and distributed, 227
Dibbs family, 72
Dicey's Song, 283, 348
Dicey Tillerman, 283
dictators, in Haiti, 323
didactic novels: *The Adventures of the Pendletons*, teacher reads to class, 168; ecology and environment, 47, 358; reflects various attitudes toward homosexuality, 82. *See also* problem novels
Dietrich Herz, 41
A Different Season, 147
Diggles family, 20, 341
A Dig in Time, 119

Dignity: Lower Income Women Tell of Their Lives and Struggles, 44
diners, sinister, 190
Dinky Hocker Shoots Smack, 146
dinners: "fancy romancey," 212; fiasco, 82, 114; gourmet, 204; kids throw spaghetti, 213
dinosaurs, fake, 380
diphtheria, 35. *See also* illnesses
directors, theater: father, 33; murdered, 120
"Dirge Without Music," poem by Millay, 18, 205
Dirk McDonald, 371
The Disappearance of Sister Perfect, 242
disappearances: bear counters, 359; caretaker with money, 364; dragon, 279; foster boy after smashing car windows, 364; friend hiker, 223; hamster, 353; illegal immigrants, 371; robbery suspect and mother, 103; sister from locked room, 179; spider detective's cohorts, 303; toddler, 254; vice president and pension funds, 97
disasters: girl fascinated by, 371; near, baby choking, 7; nuclear, aftermath, 238. *See also* accidents
discoveries: boy of Native-American Indian artifacts, 110; girl and Native-American Indian boyfriend, in motel room, 263; grandmother's sister living secretly in house, 333; mentally ill neighbor by mother, 6; mother's suicide, 290; new type of butterfly, 47
discrimination. *See* ageism; apartheid; classism; prejudice; social classes, distinctions between
diseases. *See* illnesses
disfigurement, burned face, 307, 326
disguises: boy dresses up as radio sleuth, 365; dyed hair on toddler, 254; obvious, of hotel owner, 97. *See also* impersonations
displaced persons, Great Depression, 53, 331
District of Columbia, Washington, late 20th century, 86
divorces: contemplated, 135; gives girl to father, house to mother, 146; brother and wife, 19, 83; parents getting, 56; white woman and Colored South African man, 245
DIXIE STORMS, 83, 123
Djo, 85, 322
Dmitri the Siberian tiger, 301
Doc Murphy, 290
Doctor Norcom, 155
doctors: African-American woman, 255; agrees to keep dog, 271; Civil War, 42; helps Cambodians in Thai camp, 59, 60, 140; inexperienced, 35; new, 83; psychiatrists, 240; rural, 290. *See also* healers; psychiatrists; psychologists; *under individual names*

GORDY SMITH, 91, *112*, 181, 311, 315
Goro, 222
Goss, Diana, 82, 170
Gothic elements. *See* style, narrative conventions
governments, repressive, Haiti, 322
governors, of Montana, 262
GRAB HANDS AND RUN, 113, 329
Grace, 61
Grace McGregor, 207
grades, English, too low for track, 218
graduation, dances, 183
Grady Oates, 326
Grady Terrell, 243
graffiti, racial slurs, 178, 306
Graham family, 343
Grakk, 8
GRAM MCGRADY, *114*, 278, 294
GRAMS, HER BOYFRIEND, MY FAMILY, AND ME, 82, *114*
Grams Halliday, 82, 114, 194
Gram Tillerman, 283
Gram Tut, 7
Gran (*Letters from a Slave Girl*), 155
Gran (*Phoenix Rising Or How to Survive Your Life*), 238
GRAN BENEDICT, 3, *115*, 360
grandchildren, approve grandmother's marrying again, 114
granddaughters, great-great, of dollhouse designer, 168
GRANDFATHER (*Journey*), 53, *116*, 117, 140
Grandfather (*Shabanu*), 284
Grandfather (*Year of Impossible Goodbyes*), 378
grandfather-grandson, novel of, 160
GRANDFATHER LOTT, 35, *116*
grandfathers: cantankerous, 253; crotchety, 3; dead, 280; dying, 94; famous writer, 159; gentle scholar, 378; Holocaust survivor, 4; jostles friend's baby brother, 141; laid back, owns dog named Mud, 353, 354; quotes Shakespeare, 161; resourceful, 41; Rumanian immigrant, 37; takes pictures of family, 141. *See also* grandmothers; grandparents; old persons
GRANDMA (*Journey*), 116, *117*, 141
GRANDMA (*Others See Us*), *117*, 162, 226
Grandma Babcock, 22
Grandma Byrd, 17
Grandma Drives a Motor Bed, 125
Grandma Graham, 343
Grandma Tuna, 205
Grandmother, 59
THE GRANDMOTHER, 69, *117*
grandmothers: activist, 29; bossy, opinionated, 114; boy close to, 29, 31; controlling, 119;

cooks for road builders in Minnesota forest, 69; custodial parent, 255; death of, 143; disagreeable, 24; eccentric, 17, 44, 176; evicted from bus because is African American, 305; ex-police officer and FBI agent, 114; foster-parent, 344; girl resents living with, 140, 374; grim-faced with walker, 332; her son and his son live with, 373; hospitalized, 360; ill, 38, 348; independent, forthright, 115; in nursing home, 71; Jewish, 210; of African-American girl, white, 244; painter, 3, 115, 360; quilter, 50; raises grandson, 119; religious, 114, 295; resented by daughter-in-law, 114; restaurant manager, 58; senile, 56; sheep farmer, 238; spoils son's marriage, 43; step, eccentric, 105; storyteller, 50; strongly moral, 117; unconventional, 334; unknown by children, 332; writer on dolphins, 114, 294. *See also* grandfathers; grandparents; old persons
Grandmother Woodruff, 332
Grandpa Chance, 253
grandparents: act as parents, 34, 222; foster girl, 313; wealthy members of exclusive Lake Michigan club, 281. *See also* grandfathers; grandmothers; old persons
Grandpa's Mountain, 257
Grandpa Tuna, 37, 41, 205
grandsons, slain by Native-American Indians, 202, 274
The Grandstand, 101
Granger, Harlan, 157
GRANT, CYNTHIA D., *118*, 239
Grant family, 34, 51, 222
Grasshopper Summer, 340
Graven Images: Three Stories, 104
graves: brothers visit father's, 286; dug secretly on farm, 25; family, 198; Native-American Indian mound, 110; reopened, 294
gravestones: examined by girl and boy, 3; simple, for mother, 328
graveyards. *See* cemeteries
Grayling Jordan, 255
GRAYSON, EARL, *118*, 178
Great-aunt Birte, 219
The Great Chaffalo, 188
Great Danes, 65, 97
Great Depression: California, 53, 57; homeless people, 331; Mississippi, 157, 192, 264, 266
The Great Gilly Hopkins, 235
great-grandmothers, 70
The Great Man's Secret, 347
Great Swamp fights, 274
Great-Uncle George Woodruff, 332
Great-Uncle Matthew, 182, 337
great-uncles, slaves, 274
Great Work, fight against Manchu rulers, 88
Greene, Ellin, 287

Greevey, Professor, 341
Greg Bondi, 383
GREGOR SAMSA, *118*, 246, 292
The Grey King, 70
grief: Boggart's over death of friend, intense,
32; coming to terms with, 176, 191; family
shares, 224; need for grieving denied, 334;
over aunt's death, 316; vented with tears,
32, 240
Griffey, accordion player, 18
Griffey, sexually exploitive social worker, 20,
63, 72, 330
GRIFFIN, PENI (RAE), 119, 317, 337
Grof, 11, 317
GROM DAVENPORT, *119*, 145, 344, 364
grottoes, secluded, becomes girl's refuge, 53
group homes. *See* homes, foster
groups: support for children of AIDS parents,
89; writers', meets Wednesday afternoons,
159, 110
Growers' Association, California, 331
growing-up novels
—boy's: Arizona desert, 228; Boston, boxing,
286; California game preserve, 300; Burbank, California, pre-teen, 125; intelligent
and imaginative, pre-teen, Washington,
D.C., 361; imaginative, artistic, 373; Maryland pre-teen, 72; Ohio pioneer, mid-19th
century, 355; Oregon farm, 126; prince,
259; surviving alone on sailboat trip, 348;
traveling with ex-convict father, 302, 331;
United States town, 28, 29
—girl's: African American, California, 334;
California overprotected singleton, 159;
Cambodian refugee, 59; Chesapeake Boy
sailboat builder, 283; Chicago independent,
55; Communist-sympathizing parents, 166;
England, 13th century, 54; Great Depression, California, 53; high school sophomore
in search of father, 319; hippy-types, Los
Angeles, 370; Illinois farm, late 19th century, 298; in family of women, 255; Japanese, 290; Jewish immigrant, 156; Maryland
pre-teen, 7, 9, 258; Pakistani nomad, 284;
Penobscot Bay, Maine, 360; Pittsburgh with
grandmother, 58; Salvadoran refugees, 142;
South Africa, 25; southern hills, moonshiner
father, 27; southern Ohio, 243; Tennessee,
215; talented painter, 206; Virginia farm,
83; Wisconsin among prejudice against
Native-American Indians, 262; with alcoholic mother, 288
guard dogs, stolen dogs resold as, 336
guardhouses, mother sought at, 379
Guardia, political police, 143
guardians: African-American adults of abandoned white children, 177; street people of
homeless boy, 195

Guatemala, 113, 143
Guenevere, 148
Guenivere, 368
guests: at resort, various, 275; weekend, assorted unsavory figures, 209
Guests, 85
guide, betrayer, 379
guilt: over unintentional betrayal, 6; parents
feel over mentally handicapped son, 67
GUILT TRIP, *119*, 276
guitar players: 168, 240, 301. *See also* musicians
Gulf Coast, Florida, late 20th century, 294
gulls, carry wounded lampfish, 152
gunfights, 164
gun running, 200
guns. *See* weapons
GUSTAF, 52, 69, *120*
Gwen Martens, 51, 223
gyms, boxing, 13, 36, 196
Gypsy Davey, 171
Gypsy Lover, 30

habitat, endangered, 47
HAHN, MARY DOWNING, *123*, 311
hair: African-American girl has straw-colored,
243; destroyed by ringworm, 157; girl dyes
hair orange, 62; in dreadlocks, 334; pink
punk, 159, 330; stepfather's dyed, 322; step-
mother's dyed, 321
hairy figures, in window next door, 207
Haiti, late 20th century, 322
Haitians, in America, 280
half-breeds, 35
HALL, BARBARA, 83, *123*
HALL, LYNN, *124*, 335
Hall family, 275
Halliday family, 82, 114, 193
Halloween: 208, 212, 296; Boggart causes
misadventures on, 33
hallucinations, 71, 190
Halmoni to the Picnic, 61
Halvorson, Anita, 69, 117
HAMILTON, VIRGINIA (ESTHER), 23, 71,
124, 243
Hamilton family, 42, 139, 145
HAMM, DIANE JOHNSTON, 42, *124*
Hammond Eggleson, 47
Hammond family, 215
hamper, bathroom clothes, contains stories,
185
hamster named Scooty, 353
handicapped persons: amputee, 326, 338; auto
accident victim, 98, 363; blind gay man,
190; blind girl, 163; blind, nearly, aunt, 243;
boy minus three toes, 189, 328; boy of five
unable to talk, 105; boy thought mute, 238;
brain-damaged boy, 102, 199; brain-

286; emotional breakdown, 63; emotionally
disturbed girl, 327; emotionally disturbed
mother since rape, 92; fever, 168, 222, 255,
356, 368; fever, rash, 177; headaches, severe, 63, 264; heart attack, 94, 223, 384;
heart disease, 3, 116, 288, 360; heart failure,
262; hiccups, 78; infected wounds, 229,
280; intestinal, 63; Karposi's sarcoma, 89;
kidney trouble, 302; laryngitis, 161; leukemia, 47, 239; lung problems, 25, 255; malnutrition and worms, 354; memory loss, 55,
364; mental, from lead poisoning, 205;
mental, of girl, 295; mental and physical,
from witnessing drowning, 14, 71; miscar-
riage, 215; mumps, 153; of mother, 262; of
World War II army deserter, 311; panic attacks, 240; paranoia, 128; plague, 340;
pneumonia, 54, 195, 284, 309; radiation
sickness, 238; result of childbirth, 55; ringworm, 156; spirit, despairing, 326; stroke, 3,
50, 116, 332, 360; tuberculosis, 110, 215,
310; typhus, 156; unspecified, 163. *See also*
accidents; injuries; wounds
illustrators: Anderson, Wendy, 151; Bobak,
Cathy, 28; Bowman, Leslie W., 50; Burleson, Joe, 372; Chess, Victoria, 303; Davis,
Lambert, 23; De Kiefte, Kees, 377; Donahue, Dorothy, 185; Frampton, David, 41;
Garraty, Gail, 333; Ginsburg, Max, 192;
Konigsburg, E. L., 246; Marcellino, Fred,
351; Marstall, Bob, 316; newspaper, 41;
Pilkey, Dav, 242; Prather, Ray, 246; Ray,
Doborah Kogan, 225; Robinson, Charles,
211; Rogers, Jacqueline, 353; Sewall, Marcia, 271; Sis, Peter, 188; Smith, Joseph A.,
137; Smith, Lane, 148, 380; Wells, Haru,
221; Williams, Vera B., 277
Ilya, 157
imaginary worlds, like pre-industrial England,
230
immigrants: Chinese, 87, 176, 234, 377;
German, 41; Norwegian, 369; Rumanian,
37; Russian, 156; Salvadoran, illegal, 113,
142. *See also particular nationalities*
Imperialists, 93
impersonations: angel and devil, 109; boy of
star football player, 23; brother as son, 322;
brothers as potential dog buyers, 336; children, of well-known personalities, 67; detective as school chocolates seller, 65;
disturbed, hate-filled boy as placid, good-
mannered, 222; escapees as funeral atten-
dees, 219; ex-baseball star as school janitor,
101; girl, serious, as silly child, 220; girl as
friend in Australia, 322; girls as boys, 309;
Jewish girl as Russian peasant, 156; Jewish
girl as sister, 219; killer of salesman, 205;
male cousin as woman, 243; ox-man as

beast of burden, 230; refugees as travelers,
113; robber-fly as female singer, 304; several, 260; slave girl as sailor, 155; smuggler
as tutor, 341; smuggler as wealthy widow,
341; sociopath as Miss Perfection, 13, 117,
162, 226; student as nun, 26; teen boy of
boy he murdered, 49; wife of ox-man as
widow, 230; writer as detective, 179. *See
also* disguises
imprisonment, Navajo at Bosque Redondo, 297
I'M SORRY, spelled out in stones on hillside,
374
In Bed the cockroach, 118
incest: brother-sister, 187, 368; father-daughter,
216, 363; mother-son, 187, 369; possible,
112; suspected, 165
Inchun, 378
independence: boy of mother, 347; of thought,
girl gains, 325, 338; woman seeks, 228
INDIA INK TIEDELBAUM, 40, *133*, 205
Indiana: late 20th century, Middleburg, 97;
small town, 372
Indian fighters, sent out by United States government, 96, 257, 355, 356
Indians: novels of, 164. *See also* Native-
American Indians; *particular group*
India the dog, 107
infatuations: hired hand boy, girl classmate,
125; recorded in journal, 13; with beautiful
cousin, 226; with science teacher, 229; with
uncle, 207. *See also* crushes; romances
informants, guide, double agent, 379
Ingeborg (fishing boat), 220
inheritances: big old house and land, 182, 337;
castle with boggart, 32, 33; judge greedy for
boy's, 188; Mystery Woods, 276; old
stamps and coins, 348; pearls, 188; sailboat
from uncle, 348; sampler, talking parrot,
337; thirty-seven cents and a silver watch,
188.
initials: left on vandalized car, 105; secret, 303
initiations: into teenaged gang in mall, 20; into
teenaged gang involve "hits," 22; into
witchcraft, 372
injuries: ankle, 88; arm, 69; blinding, 88; boy
hit by sail rail, 349; broken arm, injured leg,
262; broken fingers windsurfing, 202; broken leg, 88; broken leg and various other
wounds, 264; broken leg, camel's, 285;
burned face, 308, 358; burned face and arm,
60; burns in firebombing, Haiti, 322; by
dog, 271; cat's, in fall, 250; concussion, 55;
crippled arm, 55; crippling of hand, deliber-
ate, 368; cut arm, 309; dog by male bear,
262; dog's leg, amputated, 229; facial
contusions, 292; fall, 228; feet blistered and
bleeding, 358; feet cut by cornstalks, 379;
foot, results in renegade's death, 355; from

schoolhouse, home and laundry in, 306
school life: commentary on, 219; junior high, 258
school novels: boys' school, 99; California, 159; handicapped child, Spokane, Washington, 307; humorous, Ohio city, 67; misfit girl, 168; New Hampshire, 218; Oregon coast, 211; zany, 40
school projects, biography writing, 258
schools: activities with parents, 204, 212; administrators put down, 41; art, Nagasaki, 291; boarding, 81, 99, 168; convent, in Haiti, 323; exclusive boys' prep, 99, 100; expulsion feared, 67; for educable mentally disabled, 67; GED program, 174; high school, 262; high school, Elvis Presley's, 79, 188; inadequate, 177; in Belgium, 58; in outdoor pit, for slaves, 214; in San Francisco, planned, 256; junior high, 258; lively discussions of current issues, 308; new, sixth for boy, 361; paper on phoenix, 240; political indoctrination, 378; private, 219; progressive alternate girls', 319; project, visit nursing home, 194; skipping, 157, 222, 244, 287; storeroom, refuge, 168; suspensions, 218; suspensions, girl for striking classmate, 327
school scenes, 18, 22, 29, 30, 40–41, 51, 53, 56, 67–68, 78, 105, 115, 120, 151, 154, 159, 166, 168, 205, 208, 211, 218, 223, 224, 227, 229, 237, 243, 258, 262, 274, 292, 306, 319, 327, 363, 365, 372. *See also* school life; school novels
SCHWANDT, STEPHEN (WILLIAM), 119, *276*
science fiction, novels of: space, 8, 93; mind reading, 226
scientists, girl wishes to become, 28
SCIESZKA, JON, 148, *276*, 380
scoldings, letter from brother's baby sitter, 319
SCOOTER, 277, 367
scooters: blue-and-white-wheeled, 277; boy recovers from girl, 238
Scooty the school hamster, 353
Scorpions, 206
Scotland, late 20th century, 33
SCOTT CHAMBERS, *278*, 295
scoundrels, attractive, 367
scratches, on car, with barrette, 105
sculptors, wood carver, 319
sea adventures, 151, 338
sea captains: cruel villain, 383; *Seahawk*, 51. *See also* sailors
seacoasts, treacherous, 151
seagulls: dead, thrown at doors, 372; pet, 343
Seahawk (ship), 51, 338
seamstress shops, 83
The Seance, 216

seances: at birthday party, 260; in Capone's room, 275
Sean Kilroy, 87
sea novels: Atlantic, 338; Pacific, 348
search-and-destroy missions, against squirrels, 107
searches: for a home, 177; for book manuscript, 209; for boy's living place, 127; for Capone's treasure, 275; for father, 137, 177; for lost song, 202, 205; for older vampire brother, 296; for runaway boy, intense, 262, 360; for secret of ruling well, 259; for stolen dog, 335; for stolen dolls, 169; murdered girl for murderer, 260; prince for slave girl, 259; vampire for vampire brother, 297. *See also* quests
SEARCHING FOR DRAGONS, 279, 375
Searching Heart, 310
A Season of Secrets, 130, 175
seasons, book follows year, 369
Seattle, Washington, late 20th century, 255, 363, 377
SEBESTYEN, OUIDA, 228, *279*
Second Family, 125
The Second Mrs. Giaconda, 149
second sight, girl has, 268. *See also* mind reading; telepathy, mental
Second Sister, 377
Secret City, 280
SECRET CITY, U.S.A., 131, *280*
THE SECRET KEEPER, *281*, 362
Secret Love, 310
secrets: caretaker's absence, 364; cat and kitten in shed, 249; dark, about guests, 210; evacuees on farm, 239; family, 332; incorporated into book, 209; Indian caves, 110; presence of dog, 290
security guard, job promised, 331
seductions, son by mother, 187, 369. *See also* molestations, sexual; rapes; sexual assaults
seeds, lemon, planted, 174
SEGAL, JERRY, 242, *282*
segregation: school, South Carolina, 1960s, 49; South Africa, 26
SEIDLER, TOR, *283*, 351
Self Awareness, class project in, 319
self-esteem: elevated, 29, 41, 121, 165, 268, 301, 337, 357; gained, 169; low, 36, 56, 67, 126, 363; raised, 119, 160, 314, 316
Self-Esteem Class, 174
self-righteous persons, pastor, small town, 254
senators, balding demagogue, 209
Seoul, South Korea, 379
Sergeant Alfred Brooks, 36
Sergeant Major, cruel, 242
series books
—Alice McKinley, *ALICE IN RAPTURE,*

skipping school. *See* school, skipping
skull, wired for sound, 204
Skurzynski, Gloria, 100
Sky Tagaloa, 36
Sky the terrier, 161
Slacker the plow horse, 369
slacks, father refuses to let daughter wear, 57
Slake's Limbo, 131, 238
slaughterhouse, bison to go to, 41
The Slave Dancer, 107
slavery: American, brutal aspects of, 215; novel of, pre-American Civil War, 214; virtual, of Chinese workers, 88
slave escape novels, 155, 309
slaves: African-American, pre-Civil War South, 214, 309; conditions for extremely inhumane, 215; escaping, 42, 309; girl marries prince, 259; known runner purchased, 214, 353; Narraganset Indians, 274; Navaho girl of Spaniards, 297; North Carolina, 155; on Dominican sugar plantation, 85, 323; runaway, 35, 170; teaches slaves reading and writing, 214; woman hitched to buggy, 214
slaveys, in tavern, 340
SLEATOR, WILLIAM (WARNER, III), 226, *299*
sleeping places: outhouse floor, 228; under kitchen table, 340
SLEPIAN, JAN, 38, *299*
Slick and the Boys, music combo, 41
Slim McGranahan, 13, 89
slings, to carry baby, 65
SLOTE, ALFRED, 101, *300*
slums, Port-au-Prince, 322
"slum stew," 69
small-town life, Georgia, 78
Smaug the Dragon, 148
SMITH, DORIS BUCHANAN, 237, *300*
Smith, Joseph A., 137
Smith, Lane, 148, 380
Smith family (*My Name Is Sus5an Smith. The 5 Is Silent*), 15, 206, 367
Smith family (*Stepping on the Cracks*), 91, 112, 180, 311, 315
Smiths, Mina, 284
Smith-Smith family, 275
smugglers: of alien artifacts, 8; of diamonds in ice, 341; of illegal immigrants, 142, 143
snake catchers, 103
snakes, loose in crowd, 103, 199
snares, set for apprentice, 202
sneakers: gift from teacher, 105; girl refuses to wear to gym, 363; lost in river, 71, 165
Snickers, nickname for "bad" black youth, 182
SNIPER, *300*, 324
snoose, road builders spit, 69

Snuglis, 65
Snyder, Don, 364
SNYDER, ZILPHA KEATLEY, 53, 159, *301*
Soap Lake, Washington, 254
Soberlife, 217
social classes: distinctions between, 39, 282, 339; evidenced by types of wigs, 203. *See also* apartheid; classism; discrimination; prejudice
social comment: book teaches several current issues, 308; king's rule, 259; on contemporary family life, 57; on corporation morality, 316–17; on parenting, 23, 68, 120, 219; on teachers, 168, 192; plentiful, 293; teens without high moral values, 37, 50; war as means of problem solving, 311; welfare families, 348
social life, of weasels, rich, 351
socials, church pie auction, 307
social supports, for single mothers, 174
social workers: African-American woman, 10, 177; becomes foster parent of girl from another dimension, 318; exploits charges for sex, 20, 72; feared, 288; helps homeless boy, 195; helps homeless orange pickers, 332; places girl in foster home, 212, 267; takes homeless girl to shelter, 318; sexually deviant, 63
societies: patriarchal, Pakistani, 289; secret, student, 99; The Sevens, 99
sociopaths: beautiful cousin, 13; high school boy, 355
sock girls, Korea, forced to be prostitutes, 378
softball, girls', 201
SOKA, 59, 210, *302*
soldiers: African-American, 63; African-American, dies of undisclosed physical malady, 265; American Revolutionary War, 206; dead of massive unspecified attack, 63; ex, wears army pants with yellow stripes down outside of legs, 138; German, World War II, 219; killed accidentally, 87; tells story of wounding, 334; Vietnam War, 272; wins Soldier's Medal, 197; World War II, 127, 197, 204, 264, 365
A Solitary Blue, 283, 348
SOLOMON BRADLEY, 265, *302*
The Solomon System, 211
Someday I'll Laugh about This, 73
somersault, contest, boy practices for, 278
Something Special for Me, 367
Something Upstairs, 16
SOMEWHERE IN THE DARKNESS, 206, *302*
songs: George M. Cohan, 161; lost, Waltz Tree, 202, 205
Sonny Bear, 35, 84, 183
sons: father embarrasses, 316; opposes moth-

lantic, Liverpool to Providence, 51, 338, 383. *See also* journeys; quests; searches; trips

Voyaging Moon, 259

Vultures, 340

waifs: drudge in tavern, 19; girl, neighbor, 6; orphaned boy, 126; slavey in tavern, 340. *See also* boys, waifs; children, waifs; girls, waifs

THE WAINSCOTT WEASEL, 283, *351*

Wainscott Woods, Long Island, 351

Waisner, Effie, 288

waitresses: cocktail, mother, 34; mother, 185

walk, super-slow dip-stride slump shuffle, 182

Walker family, 354

WALLACE, BARBARA BROOKS, 340, *352*

Wallace family, 192

Wallace Romola, 61, 206

WALLER, Clel, 214, *352*

wallets, stolen, 37

Wally Martin, 319

Waltz Tree, 202, 205

Wanda Sue Dohr, 78, 187

WANTED . . . MUD BLOSSOM, 44, *353*

Ward, Jamie, 319

warehouse, kennel for stolen dogs, 336

warnings: "nothing is what you think," 340; not to board ship, 338; not to wander in derelict house, 333; trust no one, 340

war novels: American Civil, 41; American Revolution, 206; World War II, 219

wars: American Civil, 41, 286; American Revolution, 206; averted, 107; considered immoral, 315; effectiveness as means of problem solving, 311; experiences recalled, 199; morality of Vietnam War questioned, 12; Pacific sector, brother wounded in, 334; squirrels on humans, 107; World War II, 219. *See also* battles; conflicts; fights; Vietnam War; war novels; World War I; World War II

Washco, 58

Washington, D.C
—late 20th century, 86, 105, 361
—mid-21st century, 216

Washington, Mercedes, 78, 187

Washington Monument, site of march against Vietnam War, 12

Washington State
—mid-20th century: Rider's Dock, 253
—late 20th century: Seattle, 377; Seattle, near, 255, 363; Spokane, 307

Watchdog Committee, in apartment complex, 194

watchdog-type dogs, stolen, 336

Watch Me, 185

water: fountains, forbidden to blacks, 158; supply low on sailboat, 349

Water House, 243

Watership Down, 352; rewritten with gophers, 7

waterspouts, 152

watertowers, substitute for sweep, 335

Watson, girl plays to friend's Sherlock, 316

Watterson family, 181, 204, 334, 365

Waxwell, Ellen, 333

Wayne, 369

WE ALL FALL DOWN, 70, *354*

weapons: back pack, 239; brother carries, 263; dustpan full of plaster dust, 65; murder, knife, 131, 199, 200; pitchfork, 327; rifle with nightscope, 301; slingshot, 380; stepfather's handgun, 223; Swiss army knife, 380. *See also* shotguns

Weasel (*The Face in the Bessledorf Funeral Parlor*), 97

Weasel (*Weasel*), 96, 355, 356

WEASEL, 80, *355*

weasels: killed by owl, 351; novels of, 351; partying, 351

weather: bad, sent by witch, 268; bitterly cold, 87; foggy, 3, 360; hot, dry, 234; intense fog, 179; rainy, foggy, 192; sandstorms, violent, 285; stifling hot, 84; stormy, 209

weaving room, textile mill, 82, 170

Webb family, 321

Webster, Darcy, 225

Webster family, 25, 125, 254

wedding band, clue to buried treasure, 27

wedding gifts, stolen, 367

weddings: actor father and actress, 138; army deserter and war widow, 311; aunt and long-time boyfriend, 79; father's, 291; granddaughter plans, 82; high school sweethearts, 284; in Enchanted Forest, 279; older sister to younger sister's betrothed, 241; planned, 114, 284; rushed, 103; Russian, 243; Uncle Carter's, 153; youth and prostitute, 164

Wednesdays, writers' group meets on, 159

weed killer, ineffective on witchweed, 372

THE WEEKEND WAS MURDER!, 216, *357*

A Weekend with Wendell, 129

A Week of Raccoons, 362

weeping, of father after he beats daughter, 77

Weetasket, 274

Weetzie Bat, 190, 371

Weetzie Bat, 31, 189, 370

WEEZUL, 356

Weimaraners, 358

WEIN, ELIZABETH E., *358*, 368

THE WEIRDO, 324, *358*

welfare: checks, 72; family depends on, 348; for homeless, 195. *See also* social workers; volunteers

Wells, Haru, 221

witches: attempts to drive family from home, 184, 268; Enchanted Forest, 279; Halloween, 33; ignorant, filthy, 15; "laid" with girl's dearest possession, 268; local, 326; mean, spiteful, 184; misanthropic, 267; more comic than evil, 184; Norwegian, 370; parents, 229; village, 15; was disadvantaged child, 268; woods power "laid," 94; woman reputed to be, 24, 325. *See also* enchanters; enchantresses; mages; magicians; wizards
The Witches of Worm, 302
The Witch's Eye, 372
WITCH WEED, 211, *372*
witchweed, 372
Witherspoon family, 36, 84, 183
witnesses; sequestered, 357; to murder, 383
wives: beautiful but stupid, 243; dies in childbirth, 370; disagreeable, 98; fearful, poor homemaker, 171; Pakistani, leaves abusive husband, 285; Poe's, called "Sis", 245; timid, 341. *See also* abuse, wife
Wizard Masters of Roke, 326
A Wizard of Earthsea, 154, 326
wizards: melted with soapy water, 279; Merlin, 148; wicked, 326; without power, 326. *See also* enchanters; mages
Woe, funeral director, 97
WOLFF, VIRGINIA EUWER, 174, 201, *373*
womanizers, manservant, 175
women: alcoholic, 52; annual festival of Pakistan, 285; a bird, in Chinese legend, 307; car mechanic, 24; Chinese-American, patrician, 176; dead, contact with sought, 191; independent, must yield to patriarchal society, 241, 289; inferior status of in Pakistani society, 285, 289; Pakistani, leaves abusive husband, 289; rights of, 67; serves brother as best man, 24; spiritualist and minister, 191; wears muumuu and Dodgers' baseball cap, 52, 125. *See also* girls
WOOD, JUNE RAE, 288, *373*
Woodbine the squirrel, 106
wood carvers, teacher of writing, 319
woodcutters: magnificent, 370; poor community of, 242
Woodhaven, New England, 267
Woodie, Pastor, 3, 25, 254
Woodruff Road, 332
Woods, May, 228, 297
woodworkers: elderly Master, Kentucky, 344, 364; father, 28; gay, 365; master, in Kentucky, 28, 344, 365
words: fashioned of stones on hillside, 31, 140, 373; healing power of, 18; list for school, 201; librarian loves, 18, 205
Words by Heart, 279
WORDS OF STONE, 129, *373*
Wordsworth, poem of, girl recites, 168

A Word to the Wise, 175
workers: Chinese, gambler, 87; Chinese, hypochondriac, 87; Chinese, pessimist, 87; Chinese, quarrelsome, 87; Chinese, thief, 87; man calms demented woman who grabbed baby, 293
workers' rights, 83, 166, 170
work gangs, Koreans forced into, 378
workhouse, alternative offered, 340
workshops: author suggests student writers start, 159; student, creative writing, 110, 331, 360
World War I, veteran of, 126. *See also* war novels; wars
World War II: College Hill, Maryland, 311; Denmark, 219; homefront, 365; period, Minnesota forest, 69. *See also* war novels; wars
Worm Brain, 28, 30
Wormer family, 67
Wormer the Wondrous, 68
Worthen family, 169
Wortis, Avi. *See* AVI
wounds, Indian hurt by racists, 263. *See also* accidents; illnesses; injuries
WREDE, PATRICIA C(OLLINS), 279, *375*
Wrestling with Honor, 147
writers: E. A. Poe, 179, 245; father, 29, 125; girl aspires tobe, 209; good with parody, 7; grandfather famous, 159; grandmother, 114; mean-spirited, ugly man, 209; mystery, 357; of sleazy novels, 209; on dolphins, 294; sports, 183; student group, 7, 110, 159, 331; uncle, celebrated novelist, 209; youthful, 160, 240
writing: classes, 319; creative, contest, 159; forbidden to slaves, 214; taught to slave by slave, 214, 214; tips, worked into story, 160
Wrong Man, 27
Wyoming, early 20th century, southwestern ranch, 42, 138, 145

Xerry, 230

Yahi Indians, 257
Yakima, Washington, 254
Yang family, 377
YANG THE YOUNGEST AND HIS TERRIBLE EAR, 210,
yards: junk-filled, 5; manicured, 5
Yard sale, boys help "elephant man" with, 108
YEAR OF IMPOSSIBLE GOODBYES, 61, *378*
The Year the Wolves Came, 263
The Yellow Button, 185
the yellowleg man, 138
A Yellow Raft in Blue Water, 85
Yellowstone Park, late 20th century, 261
YEP, LAURENCE, 87, *379*, 306

About the Author

ALETHEA K. HELBIG is Professor of English Language and Literature at Eastern Michigan University. A former president of the Children's Literature Association, she has published more than one hundred articles in professional journals such as *Children's Literature*, and *The Children's Literature Association Quarterly*, and reference books such as *American Women Writers, Writers for Children*, and *Masterplots*.

AGNES REGAN PERKINS is Professor Emeritus of English Language and Literature at Eastern Michigan University. She has published numerous articles in journals and reference books, including *A Tolkien Compass, Unicorn, Children's Literature, The Children's Literature Association Quarterly, Writers for Children*, and *Masterplots*. She is co-compiler of the poetry anthologies *Newcoats and Strange Harbors* (with Helen Hill), *Straight on Till Morning*, and *Dusk to Dawn* (both with Hill and Alethea Helbig).